PENGUIN BOOKS

THE PENGUIN BOOK OF HEBREW VERSE

T. Carmi was born in New York City in 1925, to a Hebrew-speaking family, and settled in Israel in 1947, serving with the Israel Defence Forces for two years and then attending the Hebrew University. He was Ziskind Visiting Professor of Humanities at Brandeis University in 1970, Visiting Fellow of the Oxford Centre for Postgraduate Hebrew Studies between 1974 and 1976 and poet-in-residence at the Hebrew University of Jerusalem in 1977. Subsequently, T. Carmi became Visiting Professor of Hebrew Literature at the Hebrew Union College, Jewish Institute of Religion in Jerusalem, from which post he took a leave of absence in 1979 to be Visiting Professor at Stanford University in the Department of English. In 1986, he was Visiting Professor at Yale University in the Department of Near Eastern Studies and Literature and the Department of Comparative Literature, and at New York University in the Departments of English and Hebrew and Judaic Studies.

Over the years, T. Carmi lectured and gave poetry readings at many universities and at the Poetry Center in New York. He took part in the International Poetry Festival in London in 1971 and 1976, in the Poetry International in Rotterdam in 1975, and in the Jerusalem International Poets' Festival in 1990 and 1993. In Israel, he was awarded the Shlonsky Prize for Poetry, the Brenner Prize for Literature, the Prime Minister's Award for Creative Writing, and the Bialik Prize for Literature. Between 1987 and 1988, he held the Guggenheim Fellowship for Poetry and Translation. During his lifetime, he published thirteen volumes of poetry, and a fourteenth volume was published posthumously. Four collections of his work have appeared in English translation: *The Brass Serpent*, *Somebody Like You*, *T. Carmi and Dan Pagis: Selected Poems*, and *At the Stone of Losses*. His work has also been translated into other languages, among them French and German. He also translated several well-known plays into Hebrew, including *A Midsummer Night's Dream*, *Measure for Measure*, *Hamlet*, *Othello*, and *Cyrano de Bergerac*.

T. Carmi died in Jerusalem in 1994.

THE PENGUIN BOOK OF

HEBREW VERSE

EDITED BY T. CARMI

PENGUIN BOOKS

PENGUIN BOOKS
Published by the Penguin Group
Penguin Books USA Inc., 375 Hudson Street,
New York, New York 10014, U.S.A.
Penguin Books Ltd, 27 Wrights Lane, London W8 5TZ, England
Penguin Books Australia Ltd, Ringwood, Victoria, Australia
Penguin Books Canada Ltd, 10 Alcorn Avenue,
Toronto, Ontario, Canada M4V 3B2
Penguin Books (N.Z.) Ltd, 182–190 Wairau Road, Auckland 10, New Zealand

Penguin Books Ltd, Registered Offices: Harmondsworth, Middlesex, England

First published in the United States of America in simultaneous hardcover and paperback editions by The Viking Press and Penguin Books 1981
First published in Great Britain in simultaneous hardcover and paperback editions by Allen Lane and Penguin Books 1981

7 9 10 8 6

ISBN 0 14 04.2197 1
(CIP data available)

Printed in the United States of America
Set in Monophoto Ehrhardt

CONTENTS

PREFACE

THIS anthology spans the full range of Hebrew poetry, from the Bible to contemporary Israeli writing. To the best of my knowledge, it is the first such collection in English. More surprisingly, it is also the first comprehensive selection in Hebrew. This strange state of affairs is partially explained by the fact that the texts representing the first thousand years of post-biblical poetry came to light only at the turn of the century. Many of the major poets are not yet available in collected or critical editions. Scholars are still engaged in the arduous task of processing thousands of manuscripts from the hoard of the Cairo Genizah. No one can predict how much of this will prove to be of literary interest or how it will affect our overall view of the development of Hebrew poetry. Unknown poems, and even poets, are constantly being retrieved from the vast storehouse of undeciphered manuscripts. A comprehensive anthology of Hebrew poetry is, therefore, in the nature of a draft which should be revised periodically as new material is presented to the reader.

There are, to be sure, Hebrew editions of individual authors, especially from the Andalusian period onwards, and collections which encompass a specific age or geographical area. No student of Hebrew poetry can fail to be indebted to the monumental compilations of J. Schirmann: *Hebrew Poetry in Spain and Provence* (Jerusalem–Tel Aviv, 1956) and *Anthology of Hebrew Poetry in Italy* (Berlin, 1934). The innovative publications of H. Brody, M. Zulay and E. Fleischer have radically changed the picture of medieval Hebrew poetry. The collections of D. Yellin, A. M. Habermann, S. Mirsky, D. Yarden and others have acquainted us with a large variety of previously unknown texts.

In compiling this selection I have, of course, drawn on these, and many other, standard sources. However, the desire to present a comprehensive anthology obliged me to track down a multitude of scholarly publications in out-of-the-way journals and *Festschriften*, rare editions that have not been reprinted for centuries, and liturgical collections from all over the world which have never been ransacked for their poetic gems. As a result, this volume includes many poems which have never been previously anthologized or even published in critical editions; poems which have never been dislodged from their original setting in a local liturgical rite; and even poems (e.g., some of the *Hekhalot* hymns on pp. 195–201) which have never been printed as poetry but, strange as it may seem, are printed as prose in the few editions in which they are to be found. Early in the work of compilation – I should add that, except in rare cases, I have limited myself to printed sources – I realized that I must give chance a chance to proffer its unexpected gifts. Such a moment of delight was the 'discovery' of the unusual 'Death of Moses Sequence' (pp. 266–74) in an Italian rite (Bologne, 1538). The poems were clearly lying in wait for me and testing my patience and persistence.

Although I have attempted a systematic review of the corpus of Hebrew poetry, I am fully aware of the extent to which such an endeavour exceeds the capabilities of a single person. Suffice it to mention that I. Davidson's classic *Thesaurus of Mediaeval Hebrew Poetry* (New York, 1924–33) lists about thirty-five thousand poems from printed sources, and since the index was printed, thousands of additional poems have been published. Ideally, the preparation of a comprehensive anthology should be undertaken by a team of experts. Professor Schirmann has pointed out that

> the study of Hebrew poetry demands a knowledge of many subsidiary subjects, such as history, bibliography, palaeography, linguistics and liturgy. The full comprehension of Hebrew texts occasionally necessitates their comparison with texts written in other languages . . . The research into their origins entails a knowledge of several languages (e.g., Aramaic, Syriac, Byzantine Greek, Latin, Arabic, Spanish, Italian and Provençal) and the closer we approach our own time, the more languages are required.[1]

It goes without saying that I do not even faintly resemble this renaissance figure. My main justification for rushing in where scholars fear to tread is that I have read all this material as a poet, in search of the most rewarding literary prizes.

Obviously, poems culled from such a wide variety of sources have presented serious textual problems. Many of the editions are corrupt, the readings are often suspect and the meanings obscure. I would not have been able to cope with these problems without the help of the many scholars I consulted over the years. I am especially indebted to Professor Gershom G.

1. J. Schirmann, 'Problems in the Study of Post-Biblical Hebrew Poetry', *Proceedings of the Israel Academy of Sciences and Humanities*, Vol. II, 1968, pp. 228–36.

Scholem for having placed his unpublished version of the *Hekhalot* hymns at my disposal; and to Professor Ezra Fleischer for his elucidations of many textual difficulties. Professor M. Greenberg, Dr J. Licht, Professor Y. Ben-Shlomo, Professor H. Blanc, Dr I. Gruenwald and Professor Y. Ratzaby all gave me valuable advice in their respective fields. Other acknowledgements are noted in the Table of Poems; but even a partial list of my benefactors would turn this preface into a 'Scroll of Thanksgiving'. I am, of course, solely responsible for all sins of omission and commission. 'Who can be aware of errors? Cleanse me from my unknown faults . . .' (Psalms 19.13).

While writing the Introduction, I was fortunate in being able to consult two pioneering works, recently published in Hebrew: E. Fleischer's *Hebrew Liturgical Poetry in the Middle Ages* (1975), and D. Pagis's *Change and Tradition: Hebrew Secular Poetry in Spain and Italy* (1976). Both these books are the first comprehensive surveys in their respective fields (secular poetry was especially neglected by Hebrew scholarship), and this is yet another indication of the state of research. My indebtedness to these books is very great, and were I to cite every instance of it, the Introduction would suffer from a serious case of footnote disease.

The biblical selection, as the reader will readily observe, is no more than a sampling of different genres of biblical poetry. Small as the selection is, I was surprised to notice how often it is echoed in the subsequent poems. Originally, I had planned to use one of the recent translations of the Bible. However, upon closer reading, some of them struck me as too 'poetic' for a volume of prose translations, while others were marred by idiosyncratic conjectures or a disregard for recent Hebrew research. I therefore felt duty bound to prepare my own eclectic versions, which would be consonant with the general tone of the volume. I have followed the translation of the Jewish Publication Society (*The Torah*, Philadelphia, 1962) in rendering the second person singular by 'You' or 'you' when referring to the Deity, rather than by 'Thou'. 'The biblical writers,' as Professor Orlinsky has pointed out, 'made no distinction between God on the one hand and man or animal on the other so far as the pronoun (*'attáh*, "Y/you") or verbal form (e.g., *nishbá'ta*, "Y/you vowed") was concerned. God and the serpent and Pharaoh – all are addressed directly by *'attáh*.'[1] The notes to the biblical translations in this anthology

1. H. M. Orlinsky, 'The Rage to Translate', *Genesis, the N.J.V. Translation*, Harper & Row, New York, 1966, p. xx.

are far from exhaustive. They are meant to indicate to the reader the surprising range of plausible interpretations advanced by authoritative biblical studies. My brief foray into the enchanting maze of biblical scholarship has convinced me of the truth of Professor Greenberg's conclusion: 'The beginning of wisdom in biblical study is the realization that the Bible is an exotic book about which modern readers understand very little.'[1]

The broad scope of the anthology has imposed severe limits on the modern section. Modern Hebrew poetry deserves a far more generous representation and I can only apologize for this discriminatory practice. Many poets whom I admire, and who would figure in any anthology of twentieth-century Hebrew verse, have of necessity been omitted. Nonetheless, the modern section does include poets born in the thirties, thus affording the reader a glimpse of contemporary Israeli poets against the background of a long and varied tradition. In translating the modern poems, I have consulted the verse translations listed in the Select Bibliography.

In choosing the poems, my main criterion has been literary merit. But this aesthetic bias had to be tempered throughout by a consideration of what would remain of the poem in an English prose translation. Many fine Hebrew poems have been omitted because their most admirable effects – a rich texture of sound or an intricate web of allusion and reference – would be totally lost in translation or would require a forbidding apparatus of notes and comments. The final selection was also affected by considerations of variety in genre, form, subject matter and geographical area. I have not included any poems in order to 'represent' a specific school of poetry, although I have attempted to offer as varied a selection as possible and to draw attention to lesser known centres, such as the Yemen, Turkey and North Africa. I realize that the most controversial omission is that of nineteenth-century Haskalah ('Enlightenment') poetry. Though this is an intriguing and crucial chapter of cultural history, the poems themselves are, to my taste, lacking in literary merit.

The monumental scope of many of the medieval poems has led me to excerpt and, sometimes, to abridge more than I had originally intended. Again, I am conscious of the fact that this procedure is open to question. As witnesses for the defence, I could summon some of the poets themselves. In the Spanish school, it was not uncommon for poets to move sections or

1. In *Ariel, A Quarterly Review of Arts and Letters in Israel*, No. 32, Jerusalem, 1973, p. 207.

verses from one poem to another, in keeping with the conventions of the particular genre. Thus Samuel Hanagid's poem (p. 295) appears both as an independent composition and as the introductory section to a long panegyric. Where the poems consist of independent, loosely linked sections, the presentation of judicious extracts can, I think, be defended. I have, however, also taken the liberty of excerpting long poems that are not constructed in this way. The length of these poems is often due to an extensive acrostic pattern which, in turn, dictates an accumulation of verses, a series of repetitions and variations, rather than the sequential development of a theme. Given the static nature of such poems, I felt that abridgement would not do too much violence to the original. At worst, the part would seem stronger than the whole, for the intensity of the short passage is not always maintained throughout the long work. Faced by the choice of total exclusion or partial presentation, I decided to make these poems available to the reader in an abridged form.

Although the translations are in prose, they are not word for word. I have tried to render the poems idiomatically and to capture something of their tone and movement, without 'betraying' their literal level. Occasionally, where I have felt that a more literal translation would prove too cumbersome, I have resorted to paraphrase. Doubtless, in the process, I have become one of Translation's thieves, as Marvell has it:

> He is Translation's thief that addeth more,
> As much as he that taketh from the store
> Of the first author.

I have aimed to keep the notes to the translations to a minimum and to supply the reader with essential background information in the Table of Poems.

Mr Stephen Mitchell reviewed the entire English manuscript with 'a cold eye'; I could not wish for a finer blend of critical severity and warm sympathy. Mr Dom Moraes edited some of my earliest drafts and, in fact, initiated the project by suggesting it to Penguin Books in 1963. Mr Hans Schmoller and Mr Nikos Stangos, formerly of Penguin, and Mr William Sulkin, the present poetry editor, have been unfailingly helpful and encouraging. To Dr Moshe Spitzer I am indebted for invaluable typographical, as well as scholarly, guidance. My deepest thanks are due to the Librarian and staff of the Schocken Institute, Jerusalem, and of the Oriental Reading Room of the Bodleian Library, Oxford, for their cooperation.

I should like to record my gratitude to the foundations and institutions that have generously assisted me over the years: in Israel, the President's Fund, the Office of the Prime Minister, the Ministry of Education and Culture and the America-Israel Foundation; in the United States, the National Translation Center, the Lucius N. Littauer Foundation, the Memorial Foundation for Jewish Culture and the Israel Matz Foundation; in England, the Arts Council of Great Britain. A two-year Visiting Fellowship at the Oxford Centre for Postgraduate Hebrew Studies enabled me to complete the project. It is a pleasure to acknowledge my thanks to the Principal and staff of the Centre. I am also grateful to Professor M. L. Rosenthal, Professor John Wain, Dr Harry Shukman, Mr Leon Wieseltier and Mr Jonathan Wilson for instructive comments concerning the English text; to Mr Stanley Burnshaw, Mrs Mollie Oren and Professor Ezra Spicehandler for their advice and help; to Professor Benjamin Hrushovski for kindly agreeing to write a special 'Note on the Systems of Hebrew Versification' for this volume; to Mr Curtis Arnson for editorial research and the preparation of the Glossary; and to Mr Y. Ben-David for vocalizing and proofing the Hebrew text. Although I would be happy to fulfil the dictum of the *Tractate of the Fathers* 6.6: '. . . whoever reports a thing in the name of the person who said it brings deliverance into the world', I fear I have overlooked the names of friends whose insights have been incorporated in the book.

Finally, I should like to dedicate this book to Dan Pagis. Though he is in no way responsible for my errors of judgement or fact, I must hold him accountable for his unflagging encouragement and active help at every stage of the work.

T. CARMI

INTRODUCTION

THE selection in this volume extends from the Song of Deborah, written some 3,000 years ago, to poems written in Israel by authors born in the 1930s. The reader is probably more aware of the point of departure and the modern scene than of the intervening periods of Hebrew poetry, with the possible exception of the medieval Spanish school. The first thousand years of post-biblical poetry are relatively unknown, even to the Israeli reader. Some of the later periods have also passed into oblivion. It is generally, and erroneously, believed that Hebrew poetry developed sporadically, that it was mostly liturgical and, moreover, written in a dead language. The main reason for these misconceptions lies in the peculiar fate and nature of Hebrew poetry.

Its distinctive historical features are its chronological span and geographical distribution. It has been written virtually without interruption from biblical times to the present day. Over the centuries its main centres were in Palestine and Spain, Babylonia and Italy and Germany and Eastern Europe. But it also had important branches in North Africa, the Balkans, Yemen and Holland.

This longevity and mobility involved several fresh and, sometimes, false starts. Centuries of continuity were followed by bouts of amnesia, and then a rediscovery of neglected treasures. This meant that Hebrew poetry could be at very different stages of its development, during the same period, in different geographical areas. The time-tables are far from synchronized: the classical period of liturgical poetry in Palestine extended from the sixth to the eighth century; the classical period of secular and liturgical poetry in Spain began in the eleventh century. In Germany and northern France, the Ashkenazi style emerged in the twelfth century; the characteristic Hebrew-Italian style took shape in the sixteenth century.

As it moved from one centre to another, Hebrew poetry assimilated the thematic and prosodic conventions of the surrounding culture. It borrowed the cutlery, and sometimes even the furniture, of the host country. Sonnets, for example, were being written in Hebrew at the beginning of the fourteenth century, a generation before Petrarch and some two hundred years before their appearance in English and in French. The sonnet fared well in

Hebrew; it enjoyed a long and varied history. Occasionally, however, the itinerant guest borrowed patterns that did not suit the climate and customs of the next location.

Yet despite dispersion in time and place, Hebrew poetry maintained its own internal tradition, which both absorbed and transformed the external influences. Once a centre is established, it begins to lead a life of its own and to interact with other centres of Hebrew creativity. Its development is then determined by a complex network of relationships and tensions: between its original matrix and the impact of the dominant literature; between the resultant fusion and the attraction of other Hebrew centres; between the prestige of a revered tradition and the need for innovation; between its inherited prosody and the local pronunciation of Hebrew. Radical techniques, which aroused fierce polemics in one centre, may be taken for granted in a different climate as conventional components of the 'tradition'. The nature of the poetry may also be drastically affected by a change in the social status of the poet and in the make-up of his public.

Post-biblical poetry developed in Palestine, under late Roman and Byzantine rule, in the centuries preceding the Muslim conquest (636). This is the period that witnessed the remarkable flowering of the *piyut*, that is, liturgical poetry, which made Palestine the centre of Hebrew letters until the late eighth century.

The *paytanim*,[1] liturgical poets, were generally cantors. On every Sabbath and festival, they surprised their congregations with new compositions which elaborated on the subjects of the biblical lection or the specific theme of the holy day. Many communities boasted their own 'house poets' and, consequently, their own anthologies of prayers in verse and rhythmical prose. The difference in the make-up of the congregations – some were more scholarly than others – may partially account for the varying levels of complexity in the *piyut* and even in the works of a particular *paytan*.

On the basis of the available material, Professor Ezra Fleischer has divided the long history of the Eastern *piyut* into three loosely-defined periods: the pre-classical *piyut*, covering the fifth and sixth centuries, and culminating with Yose ben Yose; the classical period, from the mid-sixth to the late

1. *Paytan* is a Hebrew form of the Greek *poiētes*, 'maker'. It appears in Hebrew sources of the second century C.E.

eighth century, which began with Yannai and was dominated by Eleazar ben Kallir; and the late Eastern period, *c.* 750–1050, when Palestine ceased to be the dominant centre and the majority of poets lived in Babylonia (Iraq) and North Africa.

Little is known of the origin of the *piyut*. The first four or five centuries of post-biblical poetry are sparsely represented by the poems in the Talmud, the ecstatic hymns of the *Hekhalot* mystics, several alphabetic prayers of great antiquity, and fragments on parchment or papyrus from Dura Europus in Syria (early third century) and Oxyrynchus in Egypt (? third or fourth century). These are practically the only survivors. There is little doubt, however, that poetry was being written throughout this period, and that it had succeeded in evolving a new style no longer subservient to the biblical model. The extent of the change can easily be appreciated by comparing a hymn from the Thanksgiving Scroll with a stylized lament or a simple devotional poem from the Talmud. The fact that the vast corpus of the Talmud, which spans almost five centuries, contains so little poetry, testifies, at most, to the absence of a bond between the poetic creation of the period and standardized religious practice.[1]

Though the pre-classical *piyut* appears fully formed in the monumental *avodot* of Yose ben Yose, there are several links to the poetry that preceded it, such as the use of alphabetic acrostics and the prevalence of the 'quadripartite rhythm' (a line of verse composed of four units, each of which contains two heavily accented words). There are also apparent connections to early poetic *targumim*, the Aramaic paraphrases of the Bible that were improvised in the synagogue up to the end of the second century C.E.; to techniques of the *derasha*, the synagogue homily that replaced the Aramaic paraphrases; and to rhetorical devices employed in the Midrash.

In full or partial form, most of the major genres[2] are already encountered in the pre-classical period. They were, with very rare exceptions, unrhymed. The alphabetic acrostic set the limit of the line of verse. Word-metre was often the organizing rhythmic principle. The vocabulary was mainly biblical, though the *paytan* enlarged the semantic field of many words, and did not

1. E. Fleischer, *Hebrew Liturgical Poetry in the Middle Ages* (in Hebrew), Keter Publishing House, Jerusalem, 1975, pp. 41 ff.

2. A detailed description of some of these genres, such as the *avoda*, the *kerova* (*kedushta*) and the *yotser*, is given on pp. 51–5.

THE DISTRIBUTION OF HEBREW POETRY

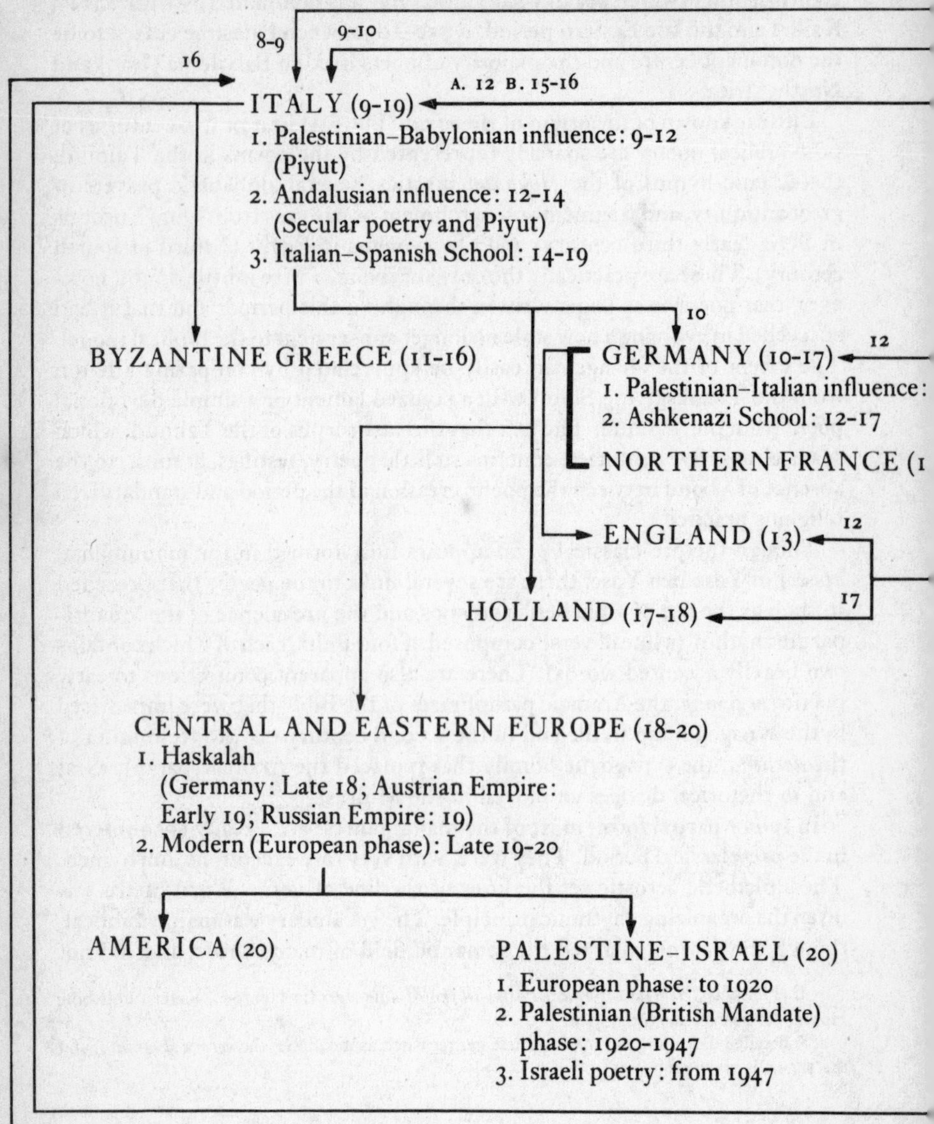

8-9
9-10
16
A. 12 B. 15-16
ITALY (9-19)
1. Palestinian–Babylonian influence: 9-12 (Piyut)
2. Andalusian influence: 12-14 (Secular poetry and Piyut)
3. Italian–Spanish School: 14-19
10
BYZANTINE GREECE (11-16)
GERMANY (10-17)
12
1. Palestinian–Italian influence:
2. Ashkenazi School: 12-17
NORTHERN FRANCE (1
ENGLAND (13)
12
17
HOLLAND (17-18)
CENTRAL AND EASTERN EUROPE (18-20)
1. Haskalah (Germany: Late 18; Austrian Empire: Early 19; Russian Empire: 19)
2. Modern (European phase): Late 19-20
AMERICA (20)
PALESTINE–ISRAEL (20)
1. European phase: to 1920
2. Palestinian (British Mandate) phase: 1920-1947
3. Israeli poetry: from 1947

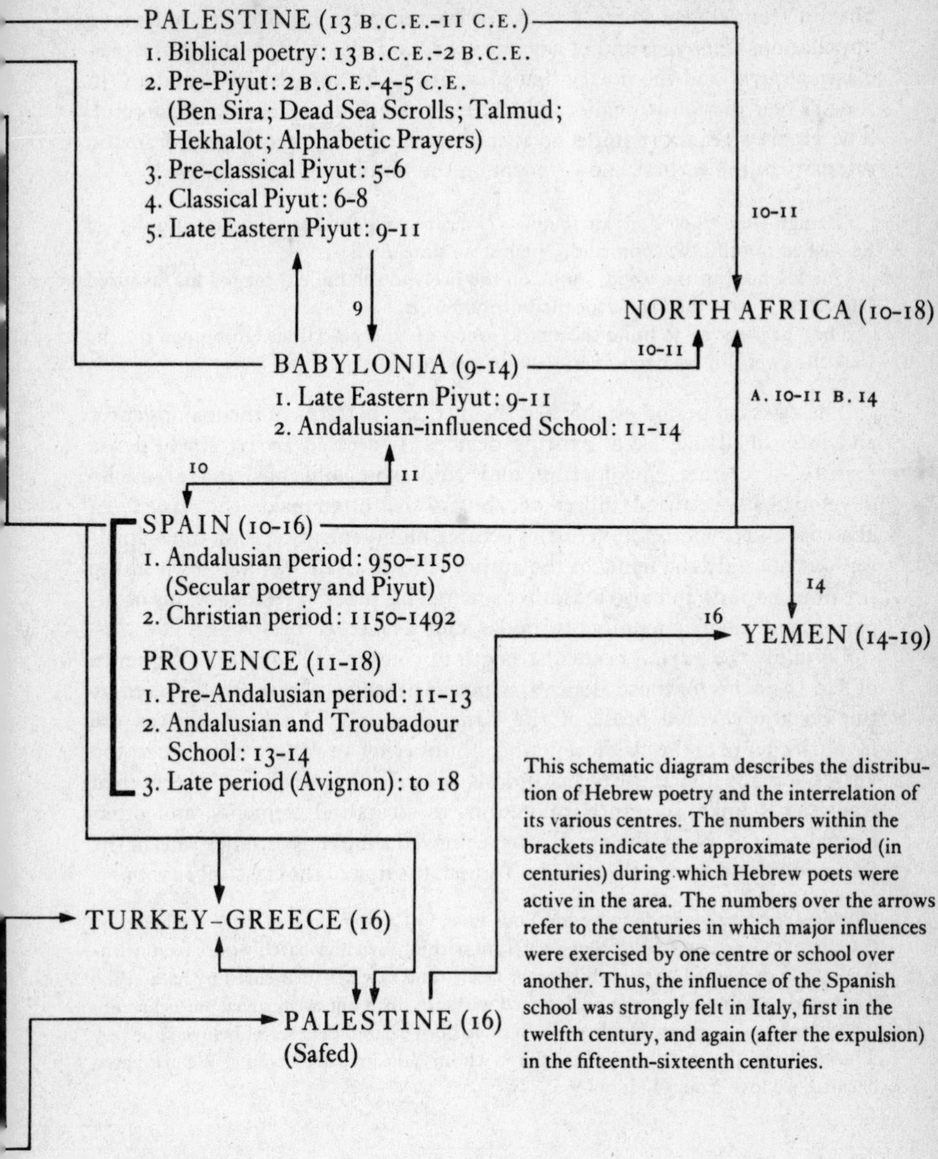

This schematic diagram describes the distribution of Hebrew poetry and the interrelation of its various centres. The numbers within the brackets indicate the approximate period (in centuries) during which Hebrew poets were active in the area. The numbers over the arrows refer to the centuries in which major influences were exercised by one centre or school over another. Thus, the influence of the Spanish school was strongly felt in Italy, first in the twelfth century, and again (after the expulsion) in the fifteenth-sixteenth centuries.

abstain from coinages. He was as yet restrained in his use of emblematic appellations (*kinuyim*) and of aggadic sources. Generally speaking, the pre-classical *piyut* and the poetry that preceded it are surprisingly 'modern' in tone. Their diction is unadorned and their rhythms are clear and forceful. The Hebrew reader requires no special training to appreciate the dramatic intensity of the earliest known poem on the binding of Isaac (p. 201):

... Benign One, when You said to him: / 'I desire your child as a fragrant offering' – / he rushed to fulfil the command, / he lost no time at all.

Quickly he split the wood, / took up the fire and the knife, / loaded his favoured one, Isaac, / with the faggot for the burnt offering.

Then he went on to build the altar, / stood up and placed his lamb upon it; / he took the sword in his hand / and took no pity at all ...

The classical period established the intricate patterns of the major genres and intensified the use of existing devices. It created an extremely dense texture of epithets, neologisms and Midrashic allusions and gradually developed a specialized, inbred vocabulary that often makes the *piyut* seem abstruse and cryptic. The acrostics became highly intricate, sometimes spelling out not only the name of the author (this in itself was unknown in the previous period), but also his father's name, his place of residence, his occupation, and even concluding formulas such as *ḥazak*, 'be strong!'

Certainly the *paytan* needed strength to compose a *kedushta*, a sequence of 8 to 15 poems (or more, depending on the liturgical occasion), climaxed by the ecstatic rhymed prose of the 'sanctification'. The *kedushta* was the favourite genre of the classical period. Numbering anywhere from 150 to 300 verses, it made liberal use of anadiplosis, long alliterative chains, stereotyped transitional links, scriptural quotations as structural elements, and other formal devices. Nevertheless, it often achieved a moving simplicity, as in the following poem from a *kedushta* by Yannai, the first of the classical *paytanim*:

Our eyes are weak with longing for Your love, O Loving One, / for we are hated by the enemy. / Look how afflicted we are from within, / see how hated we are from without – / as You looked on the affliction of Leah / and saw her tormented by hate. / She was hated within the house / and detested without. / But not every loved one is loved, / nor every hated one hated: / there are some who are hated below, yet beloved above. / Those whom You hate are hated; those whom You love are loved. / We are hated because we love You, O Holy One!

The outstanding innovation of the classical period was the introduction of rhyme as a standard feature of liturgical poetry. Rhyme now set the boundary of the line of verse and of the strophe. There was only one rhyme to a strophe (e.g., aaaa, bbbb), and all the strophes of the same poem were, as a rule, identical in the number of lines, the metre, and the rhetorical pattern. The gain in resonance was, however, offset by a loss of rhythmical tautness.

The development of the *piyut* and the changes it underwent in the late Eastern period can be understood only in the context of its relationship to public prayer. During the pre-classical and classical periods, the obligatory benedictions which the congregation recited had assumed a fixed form. However, the overall pattern of the liturgy had not yet been standardized, and so the *paytanim* enjoyed a great deal of latitude. In fact, their monumental sequences, which were recited by the cantor or prayer-leader, could replace entire prose passages of the liturgy. The design of the poetic sequence was determined by the 'liturgical stations' – the obligatory benedictions or biblical verses – in the particular prayer to which the *piyut* was joined. In other words, each poem or group of poems in the sequence led up to a prescribed station or destination in the liturgy. The progression of poems within the sequence was governed by a clear pattern of strophic structure and acrostic development, but in certain sections the poet was given licence to expand *ad libitum*. The sequence, then, had a threefold obligation: to the subject of the biblical reading or holy day; to the liturgical stations of the prayer which it inhabited; and to the fixed pattern of the constituent poems.

The *piyut* forfeited its status as 'versified prayer' when the entire text of the liturgy became sanctified and the first prayer books were edited in ninth-century Babylonia. Henceforth, it could no longer serve as an alternative to passages of the codified rite; it had to content itself with being an ornamental insertion, an embellishment to a rigidly formulated text. The tension between the *piyut* and the established liturgy found expression in the antagonistic attitude of several Babylonian authorities. They viewed the *piyut* as a foreign body that was invading the precincts of a sacred territory and undermining the dominion of prayer.

This crucial change in status was partly responsible for the decomposition of the monumental forms. Where the classical *yotser*, for example, had consisted of seven or eight poems, each of which led to its liturgical station, the late Eastern *yotser* shrank considerably; and later generations of liturgical poets in Spain, Italy and Germany, no longer conscious of the architectonic nature of the genre, singled out some of its components and treated them as autonomous units.

Another major factor that contributed to the disintegration of the *piyut*'s compositional nature was the changeover from the Palestinian triennial cycle of biblical lections to the Babylonian annual cycle. In Palestine, the Pentateuch was divided into 154 or 167 sections and the entire cycle of readings was completed in about three and a half years. Yannai, for example, wrote *kerovot* for every section of the Palestinian cycle. In Babylonia, the weekly pericopes were enlarged (each one averaging approximately three Palestinian sections), their number was reduced to 54, and the full cycle was completed in one year.

Obviously, the Babylonian synagogue, even when it wished to preserve Palestinian customs, could not accommodate the three classical *kerovot* which now corresponded to its enlarged pericope. This would have been impossible for formal reasons: each *kerova* was a self-contained sequence; and undesirable for practical reasons: it would have taxed the patience of the congregation and of the heavenly hosts. It was at this point that local cantors began to edit and abridge classical compositions, creating their own collages which catered to popular taste. Since choirs played an increasingly important role in the synagogue, the cantors also enlivened the insertions with choral refrains. The most famous choral composer was surely a ninth-century *paytan*, known as 'The Anonymous', who wrote over five hundred *pizmonim* ('choruses'), which he grafted onto the *kerovot* of an earlier colleague (Simeon ben Megas, *c.* sixth century). The outcome of such editorial licence was that the overall structure, the logic of internal development, the relationship to the liturgy, and, of course, the authorship of the original composition, were often blurred beyond recognition. Scholars have, to their dismay, come across late Eastern *kedushta*-sequences which slowly reveal themselves to be the product of a dozen different pens.

Almost all of Hebrew poetry up to the tenth century is liturgical. This, however, does not mean that it is all 'religious' in the limited sense of the word, requiring the reader's consent to a system of belief or dogma. Since the *piyut* is generally linked to the biblical portion of the week, to the appropriate passages from the Prophetic books and, on special occasions, to the theme of the day, the range of subjects is almost unlimited. As long as the *paytan* observes the formal links, at the prescribed points, to the liturgical framework, he can, and does, digress at will. He can move, within the confines of the same sequence, from the lyrical to the dramatic, from narrative to supplication, from meditative poetry to mystical hymns. Thus a *kerova* sequence by Yannai can contain an invective against the oppressive Byzantine rule and Christian theology; or a detailed description of the mysterious growth of the human foetus; or a lethal condemnation of Woman:

> Her sin is as bitter as death / . . . she dominates like death . . . / there is death in her eyes, death in her feet, and the angel of death dances before her.

A poet by the name of Samuel, using a verse from Habakkuk as his springboard, can describe the earthquake that shook Tiberias in 748 (though, admittedly, it is not often that one can glean such precise information from Eastern *piyutim*), and Kallir can write a blow-by-blow account of the terrible battle at the end of days between the mythical monsters Behemoth and Leviathan (p. 227).

Though the late Eastern period presided over the disintegration of classical genres and, in general, favoured a less rhythmical line and less demanding norms of rhyming, it also witnessed a classical revival in the works of its finest poets, Sa'adiah Gaon and Samuel Hashelishi. Samuel (fl. late tenth century) was a master of the taut and melodious Hebrew line. Sa'adiah (882–942), the most original poet and thinker of his time, was the major link between the Eastern and Spanish schools.

In several important respects, Sa'adiah prefigured the radical innovations of the Andalusian school, the most famous school in medieval Hebrew poetry. He was among the first to write secular verse on public issues, such as his fierce polemics against the Karaites. He introduced new rhyme-patterns: alternating rhyme (abab), and the four-unit line rhyming aaab, cccb, which later evolved into the characteristic Hebrew-Spanish quatrain. He paved the way for the introduction of philosophical themes into sacred poetry. But above all, it was his philological approach that left a lasting imprint on the Spanish school. Though the Spanish poets rejected his highly idiosyncratic system of analogical word-formation, they accepted his doctrine of the return to biblical Hebrew.

This doctrine was set forth in Sa'adiah's *Egron*, which he composed in Egypt in 902, some twenty-five years before he settled in Babylonia. The

Egron was the first Hebrew dictionary, the first rhyming dictionary and the first essay on Hebrew poetics. It was also the first formulation of the concept of *tsaḥot*, stylistic 'purity', which became one of the basic ideals of the Spanish school, from its earliest period in Muslim Andalusia to its last days in Christian Spain.

The enormous jigsaw puzzle of the *piyut* began to reveal its contours only with the discovery of the Cairo Genizah ('hiding place'). This momentous event – momentous for almost every branch of Hebrew scholarship – has been aptly described as a cluster of miracles. It was a miracle that the community in Fostat (Old Cairo), which is known to have bought its synagogue in the ninth century, perpetuated the customs and liturgy of the Palestinian rite. It was a miracle that they, and subsequent generations, held the written word in such esteem that any piece of writing in Hebrew could not simply be thrown away, but had to be stored in a special lumber-room. It was a miracle that hundreds of thousands of fragments were deposited in this windowless room in the synagogue's attic from the eleventh to the nineteenth century. And it was nothing less than a miracle that they were preserved from decay and were not discovered prematurely.

In 1896 two ladies from Cambridge, on a visit to Cairo, bought some Hebrew manuscripts as a memento. On their return, they showed them to Solomon Schechter, then Reader in Rabbinics at Cambridge University. He realized, to his amazement, that he was looking at a fragment of the Hebrew original of Ecclesiasticus.

Schechter immediately travelled to Cairo and, with the permission of the keepers, crated some 100,000 fragments and shipped them to England. In his account to the London *Times* in 1897 he recorded his lively impressions:

> It is a battlefield of books, and the literary productions of many centuries had their share in the battle, and their *disjecta membra* are now strewn over its area. Some of the belligerents have perished outright, and are literally ground to dust in the terrible struggle for space, whilst others, as if overtaken by a general crush, are squeezed into big, unshapely lumps, which even with the aid of chemical appliances can no longer be separated without serious damage to their constituents. In their present condition these lumps sometimes afford curiously suggestive combinations; as, for instance, when you find a piece of some rationalistic work, in which the very existence of either

angels or devils is denied, clinging for its very life to an amulet in which these same beings (mostly the latter) are bound over to be on good behaviour and not to interfere with Miss Jair's love for somebody. The development of the romance is obscured by the fact that the last lines of the amulet are mounted on some I.O.U., or lease, and this in turn is squeezed between the sheets of an old moralist, who treats all attention to money affairs with scorn and indignation. Again, all these contradictory matters cleave tightly to some sheets from a very old Bible . . .

When Genizah material began to be published, scholars were able to identify the provenance of other manuscripts, in both private and public collections, which had somehow stolen out of Cairo before Schechter's arrival. Today Genizah manuscripts are to be found in Budapest, Leningrad, Paris, London, Oxford, Manchester, New York, Philadelphia and other cities. The capital of the Genizah is, of course, Cambridge. Schechter's metaphor of a 'battlefield of books' is, unfortunately, still relevant. It is not uncommon for a researcher to discover that the fragment he is deciphering is part of a composition that is dispersed over three continents.

About forty per cent of the Genizah material consists of poetry, and the bulk of the poetry dates from the late Eastern period. It was among these manuscripts that Yannai was discovered (see p. 87), as were hundreds of other *paytanim*, and tens of thousands of unknown creations, some of monumental scope and unusual beauty. It was the Genizah that revealed the extent of Sa'adiah's achievement and 'resurrected' major poets of the Andalusian period, such as Ibn Khalfun. A great many questions remain unanswered and a vast quantity of material still awaits processing, not only in the boxes of the Genizah, but also in countless Hebrew manuscripts and early printed books stored away in libraries throughout the world.

The state of research and the magnitude of the task can be illustrated by two noteworthy examples. Samuel Hanagid and Solomon ibn Gabirol are among the greatest Hebrew poets of all time: yet the bulk of Hanagid's poems was published for the first time (by D. S. Sassoon) as late as 1934; and over forty unknown secular poems by Ibn Gabirol were first published only three years ago (edited by H. Brody and J. Schirmann). There can be little doubt that the Genizah and other manuscript collections hold many more revelations in their undeciphered leaves.

Up to the tenth century, the lineage of Hebrew poetry is fairly clear. All the *paytanim* of the classical period flourished in Palestine. From the middle of the ninth century, Babylonia, with its network of Talmudic academies and its highly organized Jewish community, superseded Palestine as the dominant centre of Jewish scholarship, setting the tone for the late Eastern period. Meanwhile, branches had sprung up in Egypt, North Africa and Syria, which, like Palestine, acknowledged the authority of Babylonia and its liturgical customs.

At the end of the ninth century Hebrew poetry made its first appearance on European soil, in southern Italy. The early Italian school was an offshoot of Palestine, and produced a distinctive synthesis of Palestinian (classical) and late Eastern elements. Germany, under the direct influence of Italy, produced its first major poet, Simeon the Great, in the tenth century. Here again, the Palestinian-Babylonian blend is clearly discernible.

The complexion of Hebrew poetry – one is tempted to say its physiognomy – was dramatically transformed in the tenth century with the emergence of the Andalusian school (Andalusia, at the time, encompassed most of the Iberian Peninsula) and the appearance of secular poetry. When Dunash ben Labrat of Cordoba – he was born in Fez and studied under Sa'adiah in Baghdad – first adapted the quantitative metres of Arabic to Hebrew; when he awkwardly imitated Arabic genres, forms and images; when he wrote the first, almost apologetic, secular poems and the first *piyutim* in the new style – he performed one of the most drastic operations in the history of Hebrew poetry. His opponents were quick to point out, in vicious polemical verse, that the quantitative metres of Arabic did violence to the nature of the holy tongue. But within decades Hebrew submitted to, and then quickly mastered, the techniques of the Andalusian school.

Hebrew poetry spans some five hundred years in Spain, which are divided into two major periods: the Muslim period (*c.* 950–1150) and the Christian period (*c.* 1150–1492). By the beginning of the eleventh century, the first of the giants of the 'golden age' (*c.* 1020–1150) had arisen: Samuel Hanagid – Samuel the Prince, who for twenty years commanded the Muslim armies of Granada, and whose epic and lyrical accounts of military campaigns trace a sudden arc to the Song of Deborah. He was followed by three outstanding figures: Solomon ibn Gabirol, a passionate, introspective poet and major philosopher; Moses ibn Ezra, virtuoso technician and theoretician; and

Judah Halevi, 'the sweet singer of Zion', perhaps the finest poet of this school.

Secular Hebrew poetry was born at the courts of Jewish grandees who served as courtiers to Muslim rulers, at first in the caliphate of Cordoba (927–1013) and later, after the dissolution of the caliphate, in the smaller Muslim principalities. This aristocratic birth set its mark not only on the subjects of the poetry, but also on its style and character. Its main genres were panegyrics, laments on the death of the patron or his relatives, songs of self-praise, invectives aimed at the patron's rivals, the poet's rivals or, when the need arose, against the hard-fisted patron himself; aphoristic verse; stylized wine songs and love songs which, to the accompaniment of instrumental music, regaled the company gathered for a drinking session in the palace garden in springtime or the palace courtyard in winter. There were also genres of a more personal nature, such as complaints and meditative poems. The courtly milieu and the financial dependency of the poet (who was often well aware of the power of his pen) account for the rhetorical and epistolary nature of this poetry. It was urban and elegant, and it delighted in ornate metaphors.

There were other shaping forces as well, namely, the powerful attraction of Arabic verse, and the highly motivated desire to revive biblical Hebrew.

The unusual symbiosis of Hebrew and Arabic culture had begun in Babylonia and in other Muslim lands, where Jews wrote their Talmudic, philosophical and linguistic treatises in Arabic (though almost always in Hebrew script). It also had a preparatory stage of over two hundred years in Spain, beginning with the Muslim conquest and the ascendancy of the Umayyad dynasty (756).

Inspired by the model of Arabic poetry, especially that of the Abassid period (750–1258), secular Hebrew poetry was essentially limited to two forms: the non-strophic *qasida* (or *qit'a*, if it was less than ten verses long) and the strophic *muwashshaḥ*. The *qasida* was the most common, or 'official', form. It employed a quantitative metre and a single rhyme throughout the poem; its line of verse consisted of two symmetrical hemistichs. 'In secular poetry . . . there is no trace of the paytanic strophic system, the Arabic forms reign supreme.'[1] The *muwashshaḥ* (see p. 30), a varied and complex form,

1. S. M. Stern, *Hispano-Arabic Strophic Poetry*, Oxford University Press, 1974, p. 77.

relieved the monotony of the classical pattern and gave the poets scope to exhibit their structural inventiveness.

The revival of biblical vocabulary and images was stimulated by strong national sentiments and reflected a current of rivalry with the host culture. For the Arabs, the stylistic excellence of the Koran was proof of its veracity and divine inspiration. The Jews countered this by championing the Hebrew of the older Book of Books. Again and again poets expressly state that their intention is to glorify the ancient tongue, to demonstrate that it is equal, if not superior, to the reigning language. Judah Al-Ḥarizi (fl. early thirteenth century) announces this with great candour in his rhymed introduction to *Tahkemoni*:

When I saw the work of Al-Hariri the heavens of my joy were rolled together and the rivulets of my mourning flowed, because every nation is concerned for its speech and avoids sinning against its tongue, whereas our tongue which was a delight to every eye is considered a brother of Cain [i.e. Abel, *Hevel*, meaning 'vanity'] . . . Like a sick person who suffers from an eye-infection and is unable to see the sun and believes the sun to be at fault, not realizing the defect in himself, so most of our fellow-Jews scorn the sacred tongue because its virtues are beyond them, and cannot see the light even if they have eyes . . . Therefore I compiled this book in order to display the force of the sacred tongue to the holy people.[1]

Earlier in the introduction, Al-Ḥarizi describes a beautiful maiden who, like Rebecca, comes to the well and offers him 'the liquid of her thoughts' and 'the milk and honey that are under her tongue'. When he asks who she is, she replies: 'I am your mistress, the holy tongue, and if I find favour in your eyes, I shall be your companion. Provided that . . . you sanctify my great name . . .' And, in fact, the poets were faithful to their mistress. Though they continued to write their theology, grammar and poetics in Arabic, well into the Christian period, they wrote their poetry almost exclusively in Hebrew.

Biblical purism was an ideal; it was never completely realized. It found its fullest expression in the secular poetry of Moses ibn Ezra, at the zenith of the 'golden age', then gave way to a more synthetic Hebrew in the Christian period. In actual practice, purism did not mean slavish imitation of biblical style, but rather an imposed limitation on the vocabulary and grammatical

1. Quoted by A. S. Halkin, in 'The Medieval Jewish Attitude Toward Hebrew', in A. Altmann (ed.), *Biblical and Other Studies*, Harvard University Press, 1963, pp. 235, 240.

forms in order to achieve maximum clarity. Secular poetry, which was stricter than the *piyut* in the observance of purism, did however enlarge the vocabulary of Hebrew by extending the semantic range of biblical words (a stratagem previously employed by the pre-classical *paytanim*), and by a widespread use of loan-translation. It was also considerably influenced by Arabic syntax and idiomatic usages.

The reinstatement of biblical Hebrew would not have been possible without the extensive philological research begun by Sa'adiah in his *Egron*. The quantitative metres of the Andalusian school demanded a thorough knowledge of the finer points of Hebrew grammar. Though all grammarians were not poets, all poets were, of necessity, accomplished philologists. Dunash ben Labrat, the founder of the Spanish school, and his bitter rival, Menahem ibn Saruk, were both 'court grammarians' in the service of Ḥisdai ibn Shaprut. Ibn Gabirol completed a long didactic poem on Hebrew grammar at the age of nineteen. Abraham ibn Ezra, the precursor of the Christian period, occupies a place of honour in the history of Hebrew linguistics.

Of the many ornamental techniques developed by the Andalusian school, one deserves special mention: the art of scriptural insertions. This consisted of an adroit and fluent weaving together of biblical quotations, from a short phrase to an entire verse. The quotation could be verbatim, slightly altered, or elliptical; it could create a broad spectrum of effects by assuming an altogether different, and even contradictory, meaning in its new setting. At times, an entire poem is chequered with quotations from a specific and relevant biblical passage. In such cases, the strands of quotations and allusions cease to be an ornamental device and become the very fabric of the poem, a sustained metaphorical texture.

The technique was used to great effect in humorous texts. Here, for example, are some of the biblical verses from which Al-Ḥarizi weaves a descriptive passage:

Song of Songs 1.4	'Lead me! – We will follow you eagerly!'
Genesis 39.12	'He got away from her and fled outside'
Proverbs 23.4–5	'Do not toil to acquire wealth . . . When your eyes light upon it, it is gone, for suddenly it grows wings and soars like an eagle towards heaven'
Judges 5.30	'A wealth of dyed embroideries for the victors' necks'

Genesis 32.3	'And he called that place Mahanaim [i.e. Two Companies]'
Deuteronomy 22.28	'When a man chances upon a virgin who is not betrothed and forces her to lie with him'
Deuteronomy 22.27	'For the man came upon her in the open fields and, though the girl cried for help, there was no one to save her'
1 Samuel 1.8	'Why do you weep'
Genesis 39.17	'The Hebrew slave . . . came to me to dally with me'
Song of Songs 1.13	'My lover is for me a bag of myrrh as he lies on my breast'
Numbers 23.24	'He will not rest till he devours his prey and drinks the blood of the slain.'

These verses provide the materials for a rapid (and, in the original, brilliantly rhymed) catalogue of the exploits of a flea:

. . . And should you say: I will follow him eagerly, / he gets away and flees outside. / And even if you catch him once or twice, / he slips out of your hands, / suddenly grows wings / and soars like an eagle toward heaven. / Often he hides by the maidens beneath their embroidered cloth, / going from their loins to their thighs. / He conceals himself between their breasts / and calls that place the Two Companies. / When he chances upon a virgin who is not betrothed, / or upon a married woman, / he clings to her and lies with her / until his misdeeds make her scream; / and though the maiden cries for help, no one comes to save her. / And should you ask her: 'Why do you weep, why do you clamour?' / She replies: 'The pitch-black slave came to dally with me / and bedded in my bosom. / My lover is for me a bag of myrrh as he lies on my breast. / . . . All night long he fans the flames of battle / and will not rest till / he devours his prey and drinks the blood of the slain . . .'

Secular Hebrew poetry's aristocratic upbringing did not confine it within the palace walls; it quickly gained a wide and appreciative public in Spain and in distant lands. Its triumph was complete when it infiltrated the *piyut* and thus reached the masses in the synagogue. For the first time in Jewish history the *paytan* was not only a 'deputy' or 'delegate' of the congregation (*sheli'aḥ tsibur*), but a professional poet who was bound by the same conventions and judged by the same aesthetic criteria as the secular poet. The first two generations of *paytanim* after Dunash ben Labrat (d. *c.* 990) hesitated to accept his innovations, but from the time of Ibn Gabirol (b. 1021/22) onwards, the greatest *paytanim* were also the greatest secular poets.

These poets, as Professor Dan Pagis has observed, 'actually related to society in two different ways. In their secular poetry they were attached to a reading or listening public, not to mention individual patrons. In their sacred poetry they were attached to the congregation and the synagogue. In the works of a particular poet and *paytan* there were stylistic affinities between the two domains, but each domain was even more strongly related to the corresponding domain in the works of fellow-practitioners. For example, the secular poems of Moses ibn Ezra bear less resemblance to his own *piyutim* than to the secular meditative poems of Samuel Hanagid, his predecessor in the Andalusian school.'[1]

In point of fact, the *piyut* led a double life in Spain. On the one hand, it continued to evolve within the framework of its own long tradition, assimilating new strophic patterns and thematic material. It also invented new metrical schemes and even produced a specific syllabic system of its own. It was far more varied and experimental than secular poetry. On the other hand, it acceded to the conventions of secular poetry, in whole or in part. Its diction tended to vary, depending on the tradition within which it was written. Only those *piyutim* which accepted the secular modes without reservation tried to observe the rigorous precepts of biblical purism.

A striking example of the marriage of the sacred and the profane is afforded by a famous poem by Judah Halevi:

Ever since you were my home-of-love,
my love has camped where you have camped.
For your sake, I have delighted in the reproaches of my admonishers;
let them be, let them torment the one whom you tormented.
It was from you that they learned their wrath, and I love them
for they hound the wounded one whom you struck down.
From the day you despised me, I have despised myself,
for I will not honour what you have despised . . .

The poem is written in the classical monorhymed form (the hemistichs are here printed as separate lines). Its vocabulary and imagery are typical of the

1. D. Pagis, *Change and Tradition: Hebrew Secular Poetry in Spain and Italy* (in Hebrew), Keter Publishing House, Jerusalem, 1976, p. 4.

secular genre. The 'admonisher', for instance, is one of the stereotyped characters of love poetry; his function is to intensify the suffering of the languishing lover by abusing him. It is only with its last line –

> until Your anger has passed and again You will redeem
> Your own possession, which You once redeemed.

– that the poem reveals itself as a *piyut*. And it is even more surprising to learn that, except for the last line, this *piyut* is an adaptation of an eighth-century Arabic love poem.[1]

This is an extreme, though far from unique, instance of the infiltration of secular love imagery into sacred poetry. A more common and widespread example of the interaction can be seen in the enthusiastic adoption of the *muwashshaḥ* form by the *paytanim*.

The *muwashshaḥ*, or 'girdle poem', is an Arabic strophic poem (possibly for choral recital), which regularly alternates sections with separate rhymes and others with common rhymes (e.g., aa bbbaa cccaa, etc.). According to some scholars, its form was inherited from ancient Spanish folk poetry. Its themes were frankly hedonistic: celebrations of drink and love. It entered secular Hebrew poetry in the generation of Samuel Hanagid, shortly after its appearance in Arabic in Andalusia at the beginning of the eleventh century. Secular Hebrew girdle poems often conclude with a couplet in vulgar Arabic or Romance dialect, some of which were probably taken over in their entirety from Arabic or Romance folk songs. But despite its dubious ancestry and its suspect character (it was condemned by Maimonides for 'arousing the spirit of harlotry') it became one of the favourite vehicles of the *piyut* in Spain. Some of the most beautiful and moving medieval liturgical poems, not infrequently in the form of a dialogue between the lovers, God and Israel, were written as girdle poems. Moreover, the *piyut* outstripped secular poetry in the invention of novel and complex girdle patterns. The alacrity and ease with which the *paytanim* took to the *muwashshaḥ* is partly due to the fact that the repertoire of the *piyut* already included a great variety of 'girdle-like' patterns.

The speed with which the Andalusian school imposed itself upon the centres of Hebrew poetry throughout the world is one of the most striking phenomena in the annals of Hebrew poetry. By the beginning of the eleventh

1. As pointed out by I. Levin, in *Hasifrut*, Vol. III, Tel Aviv University, 1971, pp. 118–19.

century, poets in Babylonia, Egypt, North Africa and Palestine were already writing in the Spanish style. From the middle of the twelfth century Provence became an adjunct of the Andalusian poetic empire. At the same time, poets in Italy abandoned the Palestinian paytanic style, and began to write secular and sacred poetry in the Hispano-Arabic manner. Greece, Turkey and Yemen followed suit. The conventions of the Spanish school became so pervasive that one is often hard put to identify the geographical provenance of a poem in the Andalusian style.

The only centre that did not pay total homage to the Andalusian school was the German-French, or Ashkenazi, centre. Some of its greatest poets, such as Ephraim of Regensburg and Ephraim of Bonn (twelfth century), did experiment with a limited range of quantitative metres, but little secular poetry was written in Ashkenaz (Germany) and the theory of ornamentation hardly influenced its poetry. From its very inception, as an offshoot of Italy, the Ashkenazi school jealously guarded its received tradition, which was predominantly Kallirian. An index of its veneration can be seen in the fact that it was the first centre to produce exegetical commentaries on the *piyutim* that figured in its rite. Though it produced great poetry in its classical period (tenth century) and during its typically Ashkenazi phase (twelfth and thirteenth centuries), it was probably the most 'provincial' centre of Hebrew poetry. Historical circumstances – the ravages of successive Crusades and the brutal pogroms during the year of the Black Death (1348–9) – partly account for this. The poetic efforts of the Ashkenazi school concentrated on passionate penitential verse (*seliḥot*) and dirges (*kinot*), many of which recorded the harrowing experiences of the Rhineland communities.

The golden age in Spain was brought to an abrupt end in 1140 with the invasion of the Almohads, a fanatical Berber sect from North Africa. After the destruction of the Jewish centres of Andalusia, the communities moved north, to Christian Spain. By the end of the thirteenth century, the Reconquest had spread southwards, leaving only the small kingdom of Granada under Muslim domination. New centres of Hebrew poetry now arose in Toledo, Saragossa and Barcelona, as well as in northern areas, such as Navarre, which had never been under Muslim rule. Meanwhile, an important centre of learning and poetry developed in Provence (which then designated the entire area of southern France between Spain and Italy).

The patronage of Hebrew poetry did not disappear in Christian Spain. There were Jewish princes, courtiers and administrators in the service of Christian kings, who, like their Andalusian predecessors, spread a protective wing over poets and scholars. However, the extent of patronage and the centrality of the court were considerably diminished. The poetry tended to become more personal, more realistic, reflecting larger areas of individual life and public experience. The language became more catholic, incorporating elements from rabbinic Hebrew and from the terminology introduced by the translators of Jewish Arabic classics. The tensions between the Jewish aristocracy and the masses found expression in social satire, intended for a large, popular audience.

Yet despite the radical change in social context – the poets were now living among Christians, and the vernacular was Spanish – the Andalusian school continued to exert a powerful influence. The assimilation of thematic and formal elements from Spanish and Troubadour poetry was very gradual and rarely resulted in extreme departures. This can be observed in the works of the greatest poets of the Christian period. Both Meshullam da Piera (d. after 1260) and Todros Abulafia (1247–after 1295) show signs of Troubadour influence. In the case of Da Piera, the changes are mainly stylistic. Abulafia, though he succeeded Da Piera, is far more traditional and occasionally shows the Troubadour imprint mainly in his choice of subject. To a certain extent this is also true of his contemporary Isaac Hagorni, the most original poet in Provence and one of the most intriguing figures of the Christian period.

The major innovation of the Christian period was the introduction of narratives in rhymed prose, interspersed with metrical poems. Of these works, the best known genre was the *maqama*. Although the first Hebrew *maqama* (by Solomon ibn Tsakbel) was apparently written shortly before the destruction of Andalusia, the genre reached its full stature in the work of Judah Al-Ḥarizi (*c.* 1170–after 1235).

The flowering of the *maqama* provides yet another example of the prestige enjoyed by the Andalusian school. The model was Arabic: it had been fashioned by two celebrated poets in the East, Al-Hamadani (967–1008) of Hamadan in Persia and Al-Ḥariri (1054–1122) of Basra in Iraq. Al-Ḥarizi first translated the classical *maqamat* of Al-Ḥariri and then proceeded to write his own *maqama* sequence, the *Taḥkemoni*. The majority of rhymed narratives deviated from the Arabic pattern. Many of them drew upon

European Christian sources and, in their use of structure and plot, resembled European stories of the time.

However, all the poems in the *maqamat* and in the related genres of rhymed narrative strictly adhered to the classical *qasida* form (quantitative metre and uniform rhyme). Though traditional, they had a far-reaching effect on the subject matter, tone and *dramatis personae* of secular poetry. The narrative and dramatic framework gave the poets licence to put poetic monologues in the mouths of lovelorn women, impotent greybeards, hospitable yokels, lecherous adulterers and even pathetic roosters fleeing the butcher's knife. The *maqama* framework also enabled the author to stage poetic duels; to appear in the double guise of counsel for the defence and the prosecution, alternately praising and condemning women or wine; and to record autobiographical experiences.

The intense persecutions of 1391 and the oppressive edicts and mass conversions that followed upon the Disputation of Tortosa (1413–14) gradually destroyed the fabric of Jewish life and letters in Spain. The Christian period of Hebrew poetry came to an end with the expulsion of the Jews from Spain in 1492 and from Portugal in 1497.

The expulsion signals the beginning of a new era in Hebrew poetry. The exiles and refugees flooded the shores of the Mediterranean and initiated a resurgence of poetic creativity in North Africa, Turkey, and Palestine. In Safed, the school of mystics which gathered around Isaac Luria in the sixteenth century provided Hebrew poetry with the inspiration of the Kabbalah, and this new source of energy quickly radiated out to Yemen, Holland and Italy.

While Hebrew poetry was being expelled from Spain – it had previously been expelled from England (1290) and France (1306, 1322 and 1394) – it was refining the *ottava rima* in Italy, in some of the most delicate lyrics ever written in Hebrew.

Italy, it will be recalled, was the first European host of Hebrew poetry. It was also, in many ways, the most hospitable. The history of Hebrew poetry in Italy extends from the ninth to the nineteenth century. It is of particular interest because in the course of this millennium, it mirrored all the existing schools, tried out all the Hebrew metrical systems, until finally achieving its distinctive style. This Italian style played an important role in shaping the poetry of seventeenth-century Turkey, Holland and Palestine, and, as we shall see, was bequeathed to the poets of nineteenth-century Austria, Germany and eastern Europe.

The first three centuries in Italy produced some major works, such as Amittai ben Shephatiah's *yotser* (p. 235), in the Palestinian-Babylonian manner. The Jewish community in Italy, the oldest in Europe, had had strong links with Palestine during the classical period of the *piyut*. In fact, some of the early Palestinian *piyutim* survived only because of their inclusion in the Italian rite. Subsequently, like all the Jewish communities of Europe, Italy accepted the spiritual leadership of Babylonia. As a result, it was never aware of the clash that had taken place in Babylonia between the sanctified obligatory ritual and the *piyut*. It treated both with almost equal reverence, and its *paytanim* proceeded to embellish those areas of the standardized liturgy that were less encumbered with poetic insertions. It was also oblivious to the linguistic tension that had existed between paytanic and rabbinic Hebrew in the late Eastern *piyut*. Loyal to both strata of the language, it produced a hybrid diction, peculiar to itself.

In the latter part of the twelfth century Hebrew poetry in Italy succumbed to the lures of the Andalusian school. In this case, the name of the missionary is known: Abraham ibn Ezra, the renowned poet, exegete, grammarian and astrologer from Tudela. He embarked on a voyage in 1140 and systematically introduced the Andalusian norms into Italy, Provence, France and England. It was during his stay in Italy that he wrote a scathing critique of the dominant paytanic style. His sarcastic polemic (inserted in his commentary to Ecclesiastes) reflected the classicistic, rationalistic ideals of the Andalusian school. He took the Kallir style to task for being hermetic and affected; for using imprecise metaphorical language; for ignoring the biblical context from which it derived its stereotyped emblematic appellations; for sacrificing clarity and grammatical decorum on the altar of rhyme; and, finally, for using Talmudic and Midrashic language as well as the specialized and, in his view, corrupt paytanic forms.

Ibn Ezra's critique and the chapter on Andalusian versification which he included in his 'Book of *Tsaḥot*' (Mantua, 1145) had a lasting effect on Hebrew poetry in Italy. It led to the banishment of the paytanic style and the disappearance of word-metre. It imposed the Andalusian conventions which, despite the subsequent emergence of rival systems, enjoyed official recognition almost until modern times.

A hundred years after Ibn Ezra's fateful visit, Italian elements began to assert themselves in Hebrew poetry, at first surreptitiously, and then in open defiance of the hallowed tradition. Immanuel of Rome (*c.* 1261–*c.* 1332), one of the wittiest and bawdiest of poets, introduced the sonnet into Hebrew around 1300. The thirty-eight sonnets which he interspersed in his famous *maqama* collection (*Maḥberot Imanu'el*) reflect both the *dolce stil nuovo* and the burlesque style then current in Italian letters. They also strike an original compromise between Andalusian and Italian prosody.

His sonnets adhered to a quantitative metre. In this respect, they were not disloyal to the Hispano-Arabic rule-book. But Immanuel chose an eleven-syllable line, corresponding to the standard Italian *endecasillabo*. Though he observed the regular pattern of 'long' and 'short' units, he no longer made a phonetic distinction between them. He was, in fact, writing quantitative-syllabic verse, that did not offend the traditionalists and, at the same time, pleased the Italian-oriented ear. This innovation affected the norms of rhyme and strophic pattern; it also introduced new notions of caesura and stress, borrowed from Italian prosody. By originating quantitative-syllabic metrics and by introducing the Italian sonnet into the Andalusian *maqama*, Immanuel sparked the fusion of Spanish and Italian elements.

From the fourteenth century onwards, Hebrew poetry increasingly assimilated Italian themes and strophic forms. Moses da Rieti (1388–after 1460) introduced the *terza rima* into Hebrew and was the first to use an overtly syllabic metre which disregarded the distinction between 'long' and 'short' and accorded with the Italian pronunciation of Hebrew. Joseph Tsarfati (d. 1527) reflected the high point of the Renaissance in his consummate love poems in *ottava rima*. The remarkable Frances brothers, Jacob and Immanuel (seventeenth century), were Baroque poets in their rhyme patterns, genres and subjects. Moses Ḥayim Luzzato (1707–47), the noted mystic and moralist from Padua, wrote dramatic poems in the Arcadian manner. His allegorical *Tower of Strength* was openly modelled on Guarini's popular pastoral drama *Il Pastor fido*. Luzzato's verse-plays (which are not represented in this selection) were far superior to his occasional verse and exercised a profound influence on Hebrew literature in eastern Europe a century after his death.

Throughout these centuries three metrical systems coexisted: the Spanish quantitative metre in monorhymed poems; the quantitative-syllabic metre in most of the strophic forms borrowed from Italian; and the syllabic metre which, despite its correspondence to Italian models, enjoyed only a limited vogue. A great many poets employed both the quantitative and quantitative-syllabic systems; and some did not hesitate to make use of all three systems.

The characteristic Hebrew-Italian style which evolved between the fifteenth and seventeenth centuries testified to an unusually close rapport between the two languages. At its extreme, this took the form of macaronic poems, alternating Hebrew and Italian lines; poems which paired Hebrew and Italian rhyme-words; echo-poems, in which the echo of the Hebrew word yields an Italian word (e.g. *yekara* ['dear one'] . . . *cara*); and even poems which could be read as both Hebrew and Italian. Needless to say, such *tours de force* were, as a rule, quite forced. But they illustrate the degree to which Hebrew poets felt at ease in both cultures.

Hebrew enjoyed a high status among the Humanists, some of whom studied under Jewish scholars and poets. Hebrew presses were founded in Italy as early as the fifteenth century, in the period of the incunabula. Unlike his predecessor in Spain, the Hebrew poet in Italy was not competing with the dominant culture; he saw himself as a collaborator in a joint venture. This collaboration was sorely tried, but not disrupted, by the severe oppressions that accompanied the Counter-Reformation in the latter part of the sixteenth century. Despite the harassing restrictions of the Roman Church, this was the period that witnessed the appearance of bi-lingual editions of original devotional poetry as well as translations of *piyutim*.

Hebrew poets often played an active role in Italian letters. Immanuel of Rome had no misgivings that he was betraying his 'Hebrew mistress' when he exchanged sonnets in Italian with Cino da Pistoia and Bosone da Gubbio. Judah Abrabanel (*c.* 1460–1530), who fled his native Portugal in 1483, was the celebrated author of *Dialoghi di Amore*, a classic of Italian philosophic prose. Judah Sommo (1527–92), author of the first known Hebrew drama, *The Comedy of Marriage*, was a renowned Italian playwright and producer at the Gonzaga court in Mantua, and author of a pioneering treatise on Renaissance stagecraft. His fame was such that he was exempted in 1580 from wearing the yellow badge required of the Jews. He was also admitted as a *scrittore*, though not as a full member, to the 'Academy of the Lovesick' (*Accademia degl' Invaghiti*), which was not open to Jews.

Similar Jewish academies, for the propagation of Hebrew poetry, music and drama, arose in Italy towards the end of the sixteenth and throughout the seventeenth century. Leon da Modena (1571–1648), a Rabbi and Italian playwright, was one of the moving spirits of the musical academy founded in the Venice ghetto in 1628. It bore a facetious Italian name, 'Academy of Boors' (*Accademia degli Imperiti*) and a resounding Hebrew name, 'When We Remembered Zion'. In Florence, the society known as the *Anelanti* ('Aspirants') commissioned Immanuel Frances to write a Hebrew text for an opera (1670) and a cantata which was performed in two synagogues. The eruption of messianic currents in Italy in the seventeenth century also gave rise to religious and mystical societies. *Shomrim Laboker* ('Association for Vigils') and *Me'irey Shaḥar* ('Those Who Arouse the Dawn') had branches in several cities and encouraged the composition of religious poetry which was sung to instrumental accompaniment. Such societies functioned until the nineteenth century and played an important role in the development of Hebrew poetry.

The devotional poetry inspired by these societies is not, strictly speaking, classed as *piyut*. The distinction that had once been clear-cut between poetry having a defined function in the liturgy and non-liturgical poetry had already begun to be obscured in the latter part of the Spanish period. In addition to secular poems on religious themes, there were a great many devotional poems that lacked any fixed liturgical 'address'. The same holds true for the enormous output of religious poetry, in later centuries, in North Africa, Greece, Turkey and Yemen. These works were in the margin of the ritual. They were often composed as occasional pieces to celebrate events in the private or public domain: weddings, circumcisions, or synagogue inaugurations. Few of them entered the prayer book or, to be more precise, the rites of the various Jewish communities throughout the world. These rites had assumed their final shape during the fourteenth and fifteenth centuries, and after the invention of printing, the 'editing' of the prayer books was essentially completed.

Given its enormous diversity, chronological range and geographical dispersion, what are the factors that give Hebrew poetry its cohesion and justify the use of that much abused word 'tradition'? First and foremost, the cement of biblical Hebrew. Though Hebrew poetry cultivated different stylistic prejudices at different periods – sometimes preferring the rabbinic idiom, or the specialized allusive usages of the classical *piyut* – biblical Hebrew remained, and continues to be, the base of the language. This is one of the reasons why Hebrew, despite its multi-layered formation, did not develop the schism that characterizes classical and modern Greek, or literary and vernacular Arabic. It is also the crucial factor that enables a Hebrew reader to choose a poem written in fifth-century Palestine, tenth-century Spain or fifteenth-century Italy, and to read it with pleasure and ease.

The long, sprawling tradition is held together not only by the infrastructure of biblical Hebrew, but also by the larger cultural frame of reference, the sources studied so intensively, committed to memory, commented upon and reinterpreted in each generation, until they become an almost subconscious layer of the national memory. It is further reinforced by the repetition of central themes and motifs, which are capable of transmitting the traumas of history, whether the martyrdom of entire communities during the Crusades, the *autos-da-fé* of the Inquisition, or the extermination of more than half of the Jewish population in Yemen in the seventeenth century. One could, for example, compile an extensive anthology of poems on the theme of the binding of Isaac (*akedot*), from Talmudic to modern times, that would mirror these and other events in the idiom of the respective periods. Even the limited selection in this volume indicates the recurrence of such themes as the death of Moses or the longing for Zion. It is as though one were walking through a house of mirrors, constantly catching glimpses of familiar scenes from different angles of vision.

A great many *piyutim* are, of course, inaccessible without the help of a critical key. Secular poems in the Spanish manner often require familiarity with their Arabic prototypes. Poems from Italy may exhibit peculiarities of syntax and gender that cannot be understood without reference to Italian. Poems from Yemen often wear a heavy Kabbalistic veil. But in every period of Hebrew poetry one finds poems of extreme complexity as well as of great simplicity – this is also true of the Bible – and much of this poetry, certainly more than is generally supposed, is readily available to the modern reader.

The extreme swings of the stylistic pendulum were possible precisely because Hebrew was not spoken. At a given moment in its history, it could summon up one of the strata of the language, invest it with renewed authority and make it the dominant diction of the period. The tendency towards a more eclectic language seems to manifest itself when the popular base of the poetry is broadened and writers are called upon to mine a more realistic vein.

The rabbinic idiom reasserted itself in the late Eastern period, when Hebrew poetry was no longer centralized in Palestine but was catering to the needs of far-flung communities throughout the East. A similar trend was evident in the poetry of Christian Spain, both secular and sacred, when the poetic scene was no longer as compact as it had been in Andalusia and when a large, popular audience had come into being. In this particular historical context, another important factor contributed to the emergence of a less 'aristocratic' style: the need to translate the Arabic classics of Jewish scholarship for the benefit of Jews in Christian lands. The concerted efforts of the translators in Provence and Christian Spain created a more heterogeneous diction, which became one of the strands of modern Hebrew.

The stylistic pendulum can be observed in action on the threshold of the modern period. Abraham Mapu (1808–67), the first Hebrew novelist and an important figure of the Haskalah ('Enlightenment') movement, cast his biblical romance *The Love of Zion* in archaic biblical Hebrew. But when he came to write a contemporary social satire, *The Hypocrite*, he apologized to his readers for having recourse to the 'black and comely Babylonian maiden', i.e. rabbinic Hebrew.

The Haskalah (1781–1881) was a movement that advocated the secularization of Jewish life and the emancipation of the Jewish people. It began in Prussia as a rationalist, cosmopolitan movement and, by the middle of the nineteenth century, assumed a romantic-nationalist aspect, as its major centres shifted to eastern Europe. The wave of pogroms that struck Russian Jewry in the 1880s tarnished the ideal of emancipation, undermined its feasibility, and initiated the earliest organized Zionist movement, known as *Ḥibat Tsiyon* ('The Love of Zion').

Though one must admire the courage and tenacity of epic poets such as Judah Lev Gordon (1830–93), and the gentle lyricism of poets such as Micah Joseph Lebensohn (1828–52), the poetry of the period is largely devoid of aesthetic interest.

It may be idle, or even suspect, to speculate on the reasons for the literary decline of a given era. Talent and genius are not predictable, and it is only hindsight that enables the literary historian to pigeon-hole his eagles. Still, in the case of the Haskalah, some of the contributing factors may have been the didactic, moralistic and nationalistic bias of its poetry; the relative isolation of the Jewish communities in eastern Europe from their host cultures; the sudden exposure of the Jews to foreign, and often antagonistic, social forces, and the resultant feelings of inferiority; the disregard of centuries of Hebrew poetry, of the enormous storehouse of potential poetic equipment;[1] and, finally, the legacy of the Hebrew-Italian school, which consisted of the syllabic system, a limited repertoire of feminine rhymes and a pseudo-biblical mannerism. The Ashkenazi pronunciation of Hebrew in Russia, Poland and Germany blurred the syllabic patterns and rhymes which had evolved organically within the Italian tonalities. The metrics of the Haskalah poets (their favourite was the eleven-syllable line) no longer had any relation to the actual sound of the language.

It was only with Ḥayim Naḥman Bialik (1873–1934) that Hebrew recovered from its stroke of amnesia, began to rediscover important chapters of its long history, and found its modern voice. In 1890 Odessa was the centre of Hebrew letters. By 1920 it was superseded by Palestine. This critical transition affected the prosody of Hebrew poetry, its musical key and, of course, its themes and locales.

Under the influence of Yiddish, Russian and German, the syllabic system was discarded in favour of the tonic-syllabic or accentual system (the alternation of stressed and unstressed syllables, as in English, German or Russian verse). This change was effected mainly by Bialik, the acknowledged leader of the Odessa circle.

It was a welcome and, in retrospect, natural change, since it renewed the link of Hebrew poetry to the patterns of stress that had marked biblical verse and parts of the early *piyut* in Palestine and Italy. This is not to imply that all these systems are identical. The precise metrical nature of biblical and early classical Hebrew poetry is still a subject of scholarly discussion. But the principle of stress, whether of phrases, words or feet, is common to all of them. Hebrew poetry, after having practised the quantitative metrics of

1. 'For when the poets of the Haskala or the era of Enlightenment set about reviving Hebrew, they found for their endeavours, in Berlin or Vienna, in Zolkiew or Vilna, no usable past. The masters of medieval song had long sunk into oblivion, and even their names faded from memory. "Who is Yannai?" asks in 1829 the best informed scholar of the times [S. J. Rapoport]. The choicest lyrics of Judah Halevi were clean forgotten until his *diwan* was recovered and parts thereof printed in 1840 and 1864 by S. D. Luzzatto.' (S. Spiegel, 'On Medieval Hebrew Poetry', in L. Finkelstein (ed.), *The Jews: Their Religion and Culture*, Schocken Books, New York, 1973, p. 112.)

Arabic in Spain and the syllabic metrics of Italian, was, in a sense, returning to its origins, to a quality inherent in the language, when it reverted to accentual rhythms.

The change in musical key forced upon Hebrew when it moved to Palestine was, however, far more traumatic. This was the changeover from the Ashkenazi pronunciation, then current in Europe, to the Sephardic pronunciation that became standard in Palestine. Thus a line (from a poem by Bialik) that sounded something like

ḥsúl beyséynu óydoy hóyze

('our house-cat, still day-dreaming'), became:

ḥatúl beténu odó hozé.

The fluidity and flexibility of *ashkenázis* was replaced by the harsher, end-stressed beat of *sefaradít*. Many of the older poets, the founding fathers of modern Hebrew poetry in its European phase (1880–1920), were incapable of making the transition. Their ear was too finely attuned to the Ashkenazi musical patterns in which they had been reared. Bialik, who settled in Tel Aviv in 1924, only attempted *sefaradít* in his children's poems. A few of his contemporaries did try to transpose their earlier works into *sefaradít* so that they should make musical sense to younger readers and future generations. The attempt was rarely successful. Not surprisingly, those Ashkenazi poems that were written in free biblical cadences suffered least in transit.

Bialik had the distinction of providing Hebrew poetry with a new idiom which fused together the various strata of the language. These strata, as we have seen, tended to remain disparate, mainly because of the absence of living speech. Moreover, since the cultural sources were clearly demarcated, revered and rehearsed, words had difficulty in arriving unaccompanied; they were usually followed by a host of intrusive relatives. The result in Haskalah poetry was a mosaic technique, a patchwork quilt of involuntary quotations and allusions that stifled the individual voice.[1]

1. This florid, euphuistic style, known as *melitsa*, should not be confused with the deliberate and artful manipulation of biblical verses practised by the Hebrew-Spanish poets in the Middle Ages (see pp. 27–8). Bialik, in describing his younger contemporaries, wrote: 'The reign of *melitsa* [of Haskalah poetry] declined. The biblical verse no longer walked before them like a blind man's cane, but skipped after them playfully.'

History thoughtfully paired Bialik with Saul Tchernikhovsky (1875–1943), the other major figure of the period. Bialik's biography, his *shtetl* (small town) background, religious education and subsequent encounter with secular culture (see p. 132), were typical of the East European Hebrew writer. His poetry, his unerring linguistic instincts, seemed to recapitulate successive stages of Jewish history. He was (at times, reluctantly) the voice of the people at critical moments in their history.

When two walls collapse, they sometimes meet at the moment of falling and form an arch. Bialik's poetry forms such an arch over the ruins of the traditional world into which he was born; and it reflects the collapse of the tradition. The world of faith . . . revealed itself as an absurdity; the certainty of accepted ideas disintegrated into despair. It is the expression of this despair – in more or less old poetic forms reshaped with great freedom – that gives Bialik's world its unique tension.[1]

Tchernikhovsky was far removed from the 'collapsing walls' of the traditional world. His upbringing was untypical: he received a secular Hebrew education and a thorough grounding in Russian literature. The landscapes of his childhood – the fertile fields and vast steppes of the border region between Crimea and the Ukraine – were a powerful presence in his poetry until his dying day. His nature poems have a wealth of detail, a breadth and freedom of expression, that were unique in Hebrew poetry. He was by far the most European Hebrew poet of his generation. His translations, from fifteen languages, of national epics and of Renaissance and Romantic works (see p. 133), reminded Hebrew poetry of the larger cultural frame of reference within which it had flourished in the Spanish and Italian periods. While Bialik devoted endless energy and erudition to the in-gathering (*kinus*) and editing of forgotten Hebrew sources, Tchernikhovsky was engaged in a parallel venture: the in-gathering of European classics, from antiquity to his time, from which Hebrew poetry had been severed in the ghetto-centuries. He was acutely aware of the need to revitalize Hebrew poetry not only by the infusion of new themes, but also by refocusing attention on formal and aesthetic problems, and by cultivating European genres, such as the ballad, the sonnet and the narrative idyll. In an affectionate monograph he paid homage to Immanuel of Rome, the first Hebrew sonneteer, and in the preface

1. Tuvya Rübner, 'Chaim Nachman Bialik', in S. Burnshaw, T. Carmi and E. Spicehandler (eds.), *The Modern Hebrew Poem Itself*, Schocken Books, New York, 1966, p. 18.

to his own sonnets, he bewailed the musical poverty of Hebrew poetry.

Compared to Bialik, Tchernikhovsky was an outsider; he seemed to be more at home in the *Odyssey* and *Kalevala* than in the Talmud and *Zohar*. And though he consistently enlarged the vocabulary of Hebrew – some of his favourite areas were flora, fauna and the female anatomy – his idiom was far less flexible and resonant than Bialik's. The novelty of Tchernikhovsky's interests and the range of his cultural sources sometimes elicited extreme reactions. In retrospect, however, it is clear that he was neither the 'pagan' nor the 'Greek' that some of his critics made him out to be. It would be more accurate to say that Bialik and Tchernikhovsky provided Hebrew poetry with two basic models: the one intensely Jewish, steeped in the Yiddish and Hebrew lore of the East European milieu; the other more aware of European literature. In the works of later poets, each of these attitudes could be carried to extremes; but, on the whole, they complemented each other and contributed to the synthesis effected by Israeli poets.

Bialik's linguistic achievement is all the more remarkable when we remember that, unlike Pushkin, he did not have a nanny from whom he could learn the secrets of popular speech. Nor could he eavesdrop on the women at work in the kitchen, as did J. M. Synge, for the simple reason that the women in Odessa between 1890 and 1910 – when he was writing his greatest works – were not gossiping in Hebrew. He was, of course, aware of the challenge. In 1910 he wrote: 'I am now particularly taken by the folk genre. The Hebrew language has never experienced it, and there is something especially piquant about the situation: folk-songs in a language that is not spoken!'

But although Hebrew was not revived as a spoken language in Palestine until the end of the nineteenth century, it was not, as is commonly thought, 'dead'. It was, of course, the language of study and prayer, but prayer that was generally understood and not recited by rote. And it is important to remember that the prayer book is actually an anthology of the various layers of Hebrew. It was also the language of family observances and communal festivities, of legal and commercial documents, of historical chronicles, municipal records, tombstone inscriptions, and irreverent parodies of sacred texts; as well as the *lingua franca* of Jews from various countries.

Aharon Megged, the Israeli novelist, has admirably summed this up:

The revival of the Hebrew language is not like Lazarus arising miraculously from the dead. It is more like the Sleeping Beauty awakened by the Prince. She was not dead, she had only been dormant for a long time; and she was not rotten bones but a real beauty. Now when you betroth her and bring her into your house, your problem is how to make this noble, aristocratic princess, adorned with jewels and clad in purple, do all the domestic work, soil her hands, break her back cooking, washing and tending the garden in the back yard. Contrary to Eliza Doolittle of *Pygmalion*, she is quite all right at fancy parties, but she misbehaves in the market place . . .[1]

The 'market place' was Palestine. There Hebrew poetry faced one of its harshest trials: the need to adjust to a new geography, to a Mediterranean texture of light and seasons and sounds. The fact that this landscape was also 'familiar', that these hills and rivers had been sung before by poets who inhabited them in real life or in the life of the imagination, was both an advantage and an impediment. The literary memory had to make way for fresh, immediate vision; the individual memory had to contend with a new biography. Though Hebrew poetry had returned home and would gradually begin to recall its older, forgotten strata, the initial stages of the return were far from idyllic.

Some poets frankly admitted failure: 'A blossoming winter contrived to entice me / but I dreamed of the deserts of snow,' wrote David Shimoni, who first came to Palestine in 1909. There were poets who took refuge in childhood memories, writing from behind closed shutters in Tel Aviv or Jerusalem, just as the early painters in the bare Judean or Galilee hills continued to inhabit an imaginary, cloud-filled École de Paris. Others, and one can hardly blame them, latched on to the exotic, postcard aspects of the country: camel, desert and palm tree, snatching at mementos in the strange Oriental country, ransacking the Bible for glittering analogies.

Broadly speaking, it was the poets of the Palestinian period (1920–47), such as Karni, Greenberg, Lamdan, Shlonsky, S. Shalom and Alterman, who put the Sleeping Beauty to work in the fields. These were the poets who first introduced the rhythms of the spoken language into Hebrew poetry and brought it, somewhat belatedly, into the twentieth century. And as so often in the history of Hebrew poetry, the new surge of creativity was accompanied and catalysed by an influx of foreign influences; in this case, Russian Futurism and Symbolism, and German Expressionism. This, however, is only a partial list of the imported schools. A glance at the biographies of the poets, even in this limited selection, will give the reader an inkling of the

1. In 'How Did the Bible Put It?', *Encounter*, January, 1971, pp. 39–40.

varied cultural backgrounds, both Jewish and European, that were vying with each other. The Palestinian phase witnessed an unusual compression of poetic techniques and ideologies, and an accelerated, almost abnormal, rate of development and change. Processes that in literatures with a normal 'family life' may extend over many decades were here telescoped within a short, turbulent period.

Hebrew poetry's encounter with its homeland often produced poems of an ecstatic, almost messianic tone, such as Abraham Shlonsky's 'Toil' (p. 534), which was written around 1927, and forms part of a sequence named after Mount Gilboa in the Valley of Jezreel:

Dress me, good mother, in a glorious robe of many colours, / and at dawn lead me to toil.

My land is wrapped in light as in a prayer-shawl. / The houses stand forth like phylacteries . . .

Here the lovely city says the morning prayer to its Creator. / And among the creators / is your son, Abraham, / a road-building bard of Israel.

And in the evening twilight, father will return from his travails / and, like a prayer, will whisper joyfully: / 'My dear son Abraham, / skin, sinews and bones, / Hallelujah! . . .'

Shlonsky (1900–1973) was one of the leading modernists of his time: iconoclastic, aggressively secular, the *enfant terrible* who spearheaded the revolt against Bialik's 'classicism'. He translated the poems of Yesenin, Mayakovsky and Blok; he shocked the traditionalists by making 'Maimonides stare at a portrait of Bakunin'. Yet even he, when he came to celebrate his pioneering days, found himself drawn to sacred imagery. He appropriated the landscape by compounding biblical allusions with spoken rhythms and neologisms. He dressed himself in Joseph's coat of many colours – a very festive outfit for a day's work at tarring roads. And he summoned up a familiar scene from the traditional Jewish home: the blessing that the father bestows upon his children when he returns from the synagogue on the eve of the Sabbath. He does not see himself as an ordinary poet but rather as a 'road-building *paytan*' of Israel. Defiance and piety, innovation and tradition are played off against each other throughout the poem.

The trials of the pioneer, the spiritual and physical possession of the land (the landscape became one of the main protagonists of Hebrew verse and prose), the zeal of the return – these were prominent themes of the

Palestinian period. But the fervour was also counterpoised by a starker account of the realities of everyday life. Lea Goldberg (1911–70) shows us the darker side of the picture in her poem 'Tel Aviv 1935' (p. 553) – the year she emigrated to Palestine:

The masts on the housetops then, / were like the masts of Columbus' ships, / and every raven that perched on their tips / announced a different shore.

And the kit-bags of the travellers walked down the streets / and the language of an alien land / was plunged into the *ḥamsin*-days / like the blade of a cold knife . . .

Like pictures turning black inside a camera / they all turned inside out: pure winter nights, / rainy summer nights of overseas, / and shadowy mornings of great cities.

And the sound of steps behind your back drummed / marching songs of foreign troops, / and – so it seemed – if you but turn your head, there's / your town's church floating in the sea.

This is a far cry from Shlonsky's pioneering ecstasy. It is a violent poem: the earth heaves like a sea; disembodied kit-bags walk on the street; alien languages – those the poet hears and, presumably, those she carries within herself – slash at the parched eastern day; and the entire country is like the obscure interior of a camera, reversing all it sees and hears, turning white into black. In fact, the operative principle of the poem is the reversal of memory and of physical objects. The terror of the last stanza is heightened when one recalls the old Hebrew legend that at the end of days all the synagogues of the world will converge on the Land of Israel. This, too, is reversed: it is not the synagogue, but the town church that will float into view, the moment one dares look back. And for Lea Goldberg, the translator of Petrarch and Dante, the Church represented not only pogrom and persecution; it was also the repository of precious art and music.

By now there are several generations of Israeli poets who have not 'known the pain of hovering between two homelands' – a phrase taken from a poem by Lea Goldberg. Their perception of the desert was not impeded by the memory of soft European mists. They were born in, and into, Hebrew. They took much for granted and, for a time, revelled in their sense of primacy. It is doubtful whether any of them (and they are now in their forties or fifties) would write a hymn to the Hebrew language, as did Ḥayim Lensky from his prison in Leningrad, or Nathan Alterman from his sidewalk café in Tel Aviv.

The language is their birthright; it was not, consciously or unwittingly, competing with foreign models; it was not compensating or over-compensating for something lost or surrendered; it was not struggling to liberate itself from the gravitational pull of a many-layered tradition. The motto of the Israeli period, in the years following the War of Liberation of 1948, could have been a line from a poem by Ayin Hillel: 'I hate rhetoric (*melitsot*) as the forest hates the picnickers'; or a line from Yehuda Amichai: 'I, who use only a small part / of the words in the dictionary . . .'

The entire modern period could be studied in terms of the relationship of spoken Hebrew to written poetry. The rate of change, until some twenty years ago, was both exhilarating and unnerving. Shlonsky, the brilliant innovator, whose coinages fill an entire dictionary, had outrageously compared Bialik in the thirties to a huge bus, blocking a one-way street. But Shlonsky himself turned into a double-decker in his lifetime. Some of the younger poets and critics rediscovered other modernists, such as Avraham Ben Yitsḥak and David Vogel, who had developed a personal poetic idiom, having little to do with the Bialik tradition or with Shlonsky's rhetorical modernism. And the picture was further complicated in the fifties, when the younger poets turned to Anglo-American models.

This created a fairly distinct cleavage between the poetry – and, one might add, the criticism – of the modernizers and of their at first loyal, and then rebellious, progeny.

However, even the rebellious progeny soon discovered that fluency, immediacy and localism, though salutary and refreshing, could not substitute for historical depth; that the poetry would be impoverished if it did not regain its awareness of Jewish history and of Hebrew literature; and that, as Eliot pointed out, 'tradition cannot be inherited and if you want it, you must obtain it by great labour'.

Here again, one of the many wheels of Hebrew poetry came full circle: whereas the older writers attempted to free the language of involuntary associations, to silence – or, at the very least, to control – the background music of an obtrusive tradition, the younger writers in Israel have had to make a deliberate effort to repossess much that their forerunners had tried to repress.

Whether the poet wills it or not, there is often an element of counterpoint in Hebrew poetry. However colloquial the rhythms and even the diction, it is heard by the alert reader against the background of biblical poetry and of an uninterrupted poetic tradition. And some of the finest effects of modern

Hebrew poetry still result from the tension between everyday speech and the undertones and overtones of a shared heritage.

Here, for example, is the opening stanza of a poem by Yehuda Amichai, entitled 'A Sort of Apocalypse':

The man under his fig tree telephoned the man under his vine: / 'Tonight they will surely come. / Armour the leaves, / Lock up the tree, / Call home the dead and be prepared.'

The introduction of the anachronistic telephone into the body of a famous biblical idiom for peace and peace of mind – 'They shall sit every man under his vine and under his fig tree and none shall make them afraid' – is enough to jolt any Hebrew reader. But something is also happening on the physical, visual level. The peace-loving vine and fig tree shed their symbolic roles and are transformed into routine accessories of field camouflage.

Shlonsky, in his celebration of the road-building pioneers, heightened the meaning of the prosaic, investing it with religious significance. Amichai is dragging the familiar rhetoric down to earth. But in both cases, the underground waters of a great body of literature, having its source in the Bible, find their way into the channels that are being cut open by the spoken language.

Amichai's lines are representative of the individualistic, anti-dogmatic, anti-ideological tone of many of the younger poets. In some cases, this becomes a desperate attempt to step out of history. The individualization of Israeli society over the past twenty-five years has often led writers to rebel against the sentiment of collectivity, of being an exposed nerve within a very nervous system. And, needless to say, one often finds both impulses, pulling in opposite directions, within one and the same writer.

But it is still very much a case of conscious acceptance of, or resistance to, a shared history and a common heritage, even though the younger writers have rejected the eastern European view of literature as an agent of the national revival, a sort of audio-visual aid to communal morale.

A poem such as Amir Gilboa's 'Isaac', entirely modern in tone and technique, may serve as a final illustration of the way in which Hebrew, at a given moment, can draw on a wide range of linguistic and historical associations. The fact that this can be done with relative ease, that the memory cells of

Hebrew are constantly on the alert and react to the faintest impulses, imposes a responsibility upon the poet to exercise tact and restraint.

At dawn, the sun strolled in the forest / together with me and father / and my right hand was in his left.

Like lightning a knife flashed among the trees. / And I am so afraid of my eyes' terror, faced by blood on the leaves.

Father, father, quickly save Isaac / so that no one will be missing at the midday meal.

It is I who am being slaughtered, my son, / and already my blood is on the leaves. / And father's voice was smothered and his face was pale.

And I wanted to scream, writhing not to believe, / and tearing open my eyes. / And I woke up.

And my right hand was drained of blood.

The title of the poem alerts the reader to the biblical story, with which he is familiar from childhood. He is prepared to encounter overt or veiled references to the biblical narrative, but the opening stanza frustrates these expectations. A child-like voice tells of an idyllic stroll, together with the sun, through the forest. This scene is superimposed on the familiar biblical tableau. The innocence of the stroll seems to parallel the naiveté of Isaac's question in Genesis: 'Here are the fire and the wood, but where is the sheep for the holocaust?' And a fleeting allusion to the Song of Songs, like the sound of a distant pipe ('His left hand is under my head and his right arm embraces me') strengthens both the idyllic strain and the expectancy of dread.

The second stanza suddenly thrusts the poem back into focus. Two key words from the Isaac episode come out into the open: the 'knife' and the 'trees' (*etsim*). In Genesis 22, *etsim* means 'the wood [for the burnt offering]'; in the poem, as elsewhere in the Bible and in common usage, it refers to the 'trees' of the superimposed scene.

The opening line of the second stanza moves as swiftly as the flash it describes. It is fluent and literary and in marked contrast to the child's comment, which is intentionally awkward in Hebrew. Though the choice of words is not entirely colloquial, the syntax and rhythm are childlike and totally convincing. Such contrasts recur throughout the poem and give the literary usages an unquestioned tone of modernity and immediacy. *Abba*, here translated as 'father', is really the equivalent of the English 'daddy'; but *hatsila*, 'save', is a more stylized usage. These linguistic contrasts take place within an analogous juxtaposition of the traditional context and the intimate details of everyday life.

The intimacy of the child's voice, of *abba* and of the family reunion at lunch, is now grasped in its contemporary setting; it is a poem about the Holocaust, one of the dominant themes of modern Hebrew poetry. The father is both the legendary Patriarch, the Father of the tribe, and the poet's own father, who was murdered in the European forest.

In its language, images and events, the poem shuttles back and forth between the past and the present. The tableau and the real scene dissolve into each other. Personal biography, national memory – all become one in the childlike voice of the nightmare. The biblical motif ceases to be a 'subject', as it would have been even a generation before Gilboa. The identification is so total and, at the same time, so ambiguous, that it can hardly be paraphrased.

The simple, day-to-day history of Israel and of the Jewish people conspires to remind the Hebrew poet that he is a point in time, and that time has a way of exploding unexpectedly.

T. CARMI

NOTE ON MEDIEVAL HEBREW GENRES

THE following note is limited to an account of three of the major *piyut* genres: the *avoda*, the *kerova* and the *yotser*. Other genres which are represented in the anthology are discussed in the Introduction and Table of Poems.

1. THE AVODA

The *avoda* ('service'; pl. *avodot*) is a detailed description of the sacrificial service on the Day of Atonement in the Temple.

It begins with a brief review of the creation of the world, then sketches the history of humanity from Adam through the Patriarchs to the consecration of Aaron as High Priest. This serves as a transition to the second part: a vivid account of the priestly ritual in the Temple, mainly based on a tractate of the Mishnah entitled *Yoma* ('The Day'). Many of the *avodot* end with a rhapsodic picture of the High Priest – as he steps forth from the Sanctuary radiant and unharmed – modelled on Ben Sira's panegyric (p. 183). Yose ben Yose's unrhymed *avodot* (p. 87) established a pattern followed by *paytanim* for many centuries to come. I. Davidson's *Thesaurus of Mediaeval Hebrew Poetry* lists some forty different *avodot*, the last of which was composed (not for synagogal use) in the nineteenth century in Italy.

The *avoda* is the principal feature of the *Musaf* ('additional') prayers on the Day of Atonement.

2. THE KEROVA

The *kerova*[1] (pl. *kerovot*) is a sequence of poems related to, and inserted between, the benedictions of the *Amida* ('standing') prayer in the daily liturgy. The *Amida* (pl. *Amidot*) is the core of each of the prescribed daily services and was therefore also known as *Hatefila*, 'The Prayer' *par excellence*.

1. The origin of the name is uncertain. Some scholars maintain that it is derived from *karova*, the Aramaic designation of the reader who chanted the prayers.

There are various forms of *Amida* for different occasions and, accordingly, various forms of *kerova*. By far the most popular during the classical period was the *kedushta* (pl. *kedushta'ot*) which embellished the *Amidot* of Sabbaths and Holy Days. These *Amidot* enjoyed special prestige since their third benediction included the *Kedusha* (hence the name of the sequence, *kedushta*), the prayer of 'Sanctification', describing the exalted praise of God by the angels (as quoted in Isaiah 6.3 and Ezekiel 3.12).

The classical *kedushta* consists of three major sections which are demarcated by conventional devices and stereotyped liturgical formulas. They are subdivided into eight or more poems. Though the poems are intricately linked to the liturgy, to the readings from the Bible and the Prophets and to each other, they generally form independent, self-contained units.

The first section (poems 1–3) has a defined liturgical function: it corresponds to the first two benedictions of the *Amida* and to the beginning of the third benediction. The second section (poems 4–5) elaborates on the theme of the sequence. The third (poems 6–9) can be expanded at will by creating a chain of (often autonomous) poems: 7^1, 7^2, 7^3, etc. However, poem 8 is bound to introduce the *Kedusha*. Most *kedushta'ot* end at this point. Some of the *paytanim* added a ninth poem, which was inserted between the verses of the *Kedusha*, and was occasionally expanded into a small series: 9^1, 9^2, 9^3, etc.

As developed by Yannai (p. 87), the constituent poems of the *kedushta* adhere to the following pattern:

1. The *magen* ('shield'): three monorhymed quatrains, composing a partial alphabetic acrostic. The last line alludes to the first verse of the relevant portion from the Pentateuch and is then reinforced by several scriptural quotations related to the theme. A concluding stanza – a tercet or a quatrain – begins with the last word of the preceding quotation and closes with a reference to the first benediction, 'Shield of Abraham'.

2. The *meḥaye*: same structure; three quatrains complete the acrostic; they are linked by the second verse of the biblical portion to the concluding stanza, which leads into the second benediction, 'Who revives [*meḥaye*] the dead' (e.g. p. 218).

3. The *meshalesh* (from *shalosh*, 'three'): four couplets containing an acrostic of the author's name. The last couplet alludes to the first verse of the reading from the Prophets recited on this particular occasion and is again followed by several scriptural quotations.

4. This poem has no fixed pattern, though it is often made up of three quatrains. Its distinctive features are the concluding word 'Holy (One)' and the absence of any acrostic (e.g. p. 215).

5. Ten couplets with a partial alphabetic acrostic (e.g. pp. 219–20).

6. Eleven quatrains, complete alphabetic acrostic. The relevant biblical quotation precedes the poem and is sometimes designed as part of the opening line of each quatrain.

7. One to three poems, of varying length and form, in which the author displays his technical virtuosity by means of involved patterns of word-play, alliteration, acrostics and chain verse (e.g. p. 221).

8. The *siluk* ('conclusion') serves to introduce the *Kedusha* and is, therefore, the climactic point of the sequence. Varying in length and form, it is usually written in rhymed rhythmical prose (e.g. pp. 218–19). Its ecstatic account of the celestial domain is often reminiscent of *Hekhalot* hymns (pp. 195–201). The *siluk* always ends with 'As it is written: *And one called to another and said: Holy, holy, holy, is the Lord of Hosts*' (Isaiah 6.3).

9. The *Kedusha*, alternating rhythmical prose and alphabetic poetry (e.g. pp. 215–16). This central hymn, like other parts of the service, had not yet been standardized in Yannai's time and so he was able to compose a different version for each of his hundred and fifty *kerovot*.

Some of the classical *paytanim* after Yannai, and especially Eleazar ben Kallir (p. 89), modified the pattern of various components but did not alter the overall structure. In a typical Kallir *kedushta* the third poem is composed of monorhymed quatrains; the fourth is in cadenced, rhymed prose; the fifth is again composed of quatrains and includes an acrostic of the author's name; the sixth consists of rhymed tercets in some acrostic order, with a choral refrain after every third stanza, ending with the word 'holy' (e.g. pp. 221–3). Many of Kallir's innovations became standard practice in the composition of the *kedushta*.

The *kerova* disintegrated into its components after the classical period (see pp. 19–20) and was replaced by the *yotser* as the dominant genre of the late Eastern *piyut*.

3. THE YOTSER

The *yotser* (pl. *yotserot*) is a sequence of poems inserted in the 'Reading of the *Shema*' of the morning prayers. The 'Reading' consists of benedictions, liturgical verses, prayers and three extended passages from the Pentateuch. Its high point is the affirmation of the unity of God: 'Hear [*Shema*], O Israel, the Lord is our God, the Lord is One' (Deuteronomy 6.4). The sequence derives its name from the opening line of the first benediction before the *Shema*: 'Who creates [*yotser*] light and forms darkness'. In its expanded form, as a sequence for the Sabbath and Holy Days, the classical *yotser* consists of seven poems:

1. *Guf hayotser* ('the body of the *yotser*') is the most important component of the sequence. It often celebrates the wonders of creation or hymns the specific festival or event (e.g. Amittai ben Shephatiah's '*Yotser* for a Bridegroom', p. 235), or takes its theme from the biblical portion. It is usually composed of rhymed tercets in alphabetic sequence, the last line of each stanza being a scriptural quotation. The acrostic is interrupted after every third tercet by a choral stanza (ending with the word 'holy'), which begins with the last word of the preceding tercet. The acrostic of the author's name is embedded in one or more of the choral stanzas. The final tercet or line alludes to the *Kedusha* which immediately follows the first poem.

2. The *ofan* ('wheel'; pl. *ofanim*) is the ecstatic angelogical *piyut*, describing the heavenly host. It serves as a link between the first and the second verses of the *Kedusha*. Lacking a fixed pattern, it initiates a new alphabetic acrostic which may carry over to subsequent poems. (For various types of *ofanim*, see pp. 238–9, 243–4, 320–22 and 365–6; Judah Halevi's *ofan*, pp. 338–9, is in the Andalusian *muwashshaḥ* form.)

3. The *me'ora* ('light'; pl. *me'orot*) precedes the closing formula of the first benediction before the *Shema* '. . . Creator of lights [*me'orot*]'. It generally interprets the 'light' symbolically as the light of the Torah, of Providence, or of the redemption of Zion (e.g. p. 364; for a *me'ora* in the *muwashshaḥ* form, see pp. 420–21).

4. The *ahava* ('love'; pl. *ahavot*) introduces the second benediction before the *Shema*: 'Who has chosen His people with abounding love'. Like the preceding poem, it consists of four (or five) monorhymed verses which either continue an alphabetic acrostic or embody the author's name. The *me'orot* and *ahavot* are often the lyrical climaxes of *yotser* compositions (e.g. 'Resurrection', p. 254; for *ahavot* of the Spanish school, see p. 317 and 'To the Rivals', p. 335).

5. The *zulat* (pl. *zulatot*), the second most important component of the

sequence, is named after the conclusion of the prayer that follows the recitation of the *Shema*: '. . . there is no God besides [*zulat*] You'. Written in monorhymed quatrains, it begins a new alphabetic acrostic. The quatrains often end with scriptural quotations, taken in sequence from the appropriate reading from the Prophets. In the choral *zulat* (e.g. p. 233), each quatrain is followed by a couplet which introduces a second rhyme. (Other *zulat* patterns are found on pp. 255 and 377–9.)

6. The *mi kamokha*: a four-line stanza, containing an acrostic of the poet's name, which serves as a bridge between two liturgical verses from the Song of the Sea (Exodus 15.11 and 18): 'Who [*mi*] is like You [*kamokha*], O Lord, among the mighty?' and 'The Lord shall reign for ever and ever'.

7. The *ge'ula* ('redemption') is inserted before the final benediction of the *Shema* prayers: 'Who has redeemed [*ga'al*] Israel'. In the late Eastern period, this poem (then known as *adonai malkenu*, 'the Lord is our God') was 'doubled' by the addition of an eighth poem (e.g. p. 256) entitled *ve'ad matay* ('and how much longer'; the origin of the name is unknown).

The 'classical' pattern of the *yotser* was formulated during the late Eastern period. It was the preferred genre and many of the leading *paytanim* wrote monumental cycles of *yotserot* for each of the 54 pericopes of the annual Babylonian cycle. Towards the end of the period, apparently after the tenth century, the *yotser* decomposed as a result of the clash between the *piyut* and the standardized prayer. However, some of its components developed into separate and comprehensive *piyutim* in Spain and in Europe.

NOTE ON THE SYSTEMS OF HEBREW VERSIFICATION

by Benjamin Hrushovski

VERSE and rhyme, used in serious poetry as well as in a variety of other kinds of writing (e.g. grammars, historical chronicles, gravestone inscriptions and community annals), were an omnipresent feature of Hebrew culture in all periods and in all centres of the Jewish dispersion. Marked by strong tendencies of formalism and conservatism, the forms of Hebrew verse have nevertheless changed radically as Hebrew culture interacted with Greek rhetoric, Arabic secular literature, Italian Renaissance poetry, German eighteenth-century verse, Russian Romanticism and Futurism, Yiddish folklore, and English modernism. Almost all possible systems of rhythm and rhyme had been active in Hebrew literature in one period or another. Given a language with a stubborn core of vocabulary, morphology, spelling, imagery and basic mythology, the differences in formal systems were largely responsible for the great divergencies in the nature and poetics of Hebrew poetry in its major historical centres.

One must bear in mind that a Hebrew poet – in Rome, in Mainz, in Yemen, in Vilna, in Petersburg, in New York – was always placed at an intersection of at least three traditions: (a) the modes of Hebrew writing perpetuated in his own community; (b) the distinctly different poetic forms developed in his own language, Hebrew, in other cultural centres, either of his own time or in the past; (c) the poetic norms predominant in the language of the country in which he lived, the language which he read and spoke daily. A shift of orientation from one to another of these poetic systems was often responsible for the changes evolving in the forms or in the very nature of Hebrew verse.

Since in most periods the adherence to prevalent poetic norms was a rather strict one, it is possible to outline a number of major 'areas', or systems of genres and forms, which governed certain geographical and historical domains. The following simplified survey will present some typical features of the most important areas in the history of Hebrew poetic forms.

THE BIBLE

Biblical poetry, and perhaps biblical literature as a whole, provides a most flexible system of expressive form. The basic principle is parallelism. A poetic unit consists of two (or more) versets (or 'colas') displaying traits of equivalence in their rhythmical make-up (the number of stresses), their syntax and semantics, as well as in many additional features, such as syllable-numbers in parallel words, sound-repetition, and morphology. In most cases, however, there is neither a permanent nor a fixed parallelism of whole versets. Usually at least two or three kinds of parallelism will be applied, but we never know in advance which exactly, whether it will be complete or partial, word-for-word or verset-for-one-word, whether it will be based on synonymy, equivalence or opposition, in a direct or in a chiastic order. In any given pair of versets there is a mutual reinforcement of the overlapping patterns of parallelism – of meaning, syntax, and stress – all of which are based on the same unit: the major word, which alone carries the phrasal stress and the lexical meaning. Since each verset consists of a small and tightly compressed group of words (three or four), the effect is conspicuous and strong. (In translation these are not words but rather word groups, as in the English Bible.)

The system of this type of rhythm may be described as semantic-syntactic-accentual free parallelism. It is based on a cluster of shifting principles, the most prominent one being the semantic-rhetorical, the most obviously restricted one being the rhythmical. In later periods the rhythm of this poetry was taken to be basically accentual. Indeed, in biblical poetry the number of stresses per verset, though free, is clearly restricted – usually 2, 3, or 4, and quite often equal or similar in both versets of a pair (e.g. 3+2, the so-called 'dirge metre'). The number of syllables between these stresses, though perceived from the point of view of later and more rigorous metres as entirely free, was sometimes very much regulated as well: two adjacent stresses in one clause were precluded, and if a word was too long it had a secondary stress, thus providing usually 1 or 2 unstressed syllables between adjacent stresses. As a result, scholars have often perceived syllabic regularity in biblical versets. No systematic rhyme is to be found in the Bible, but there is a very pervasive usage of alliteration, sporadic end-rhyme, puns, acrostics and formulas, either embellishing or reinforcing the major principles of parallelism.

Here is an example of a poem of a rather ordered type:

הַאֲזִינוּ הַשָּׁמַיִם וַאֲדַבֵּרָה   וְתִשְׁמַע הָאָרֶץ אִמְרֵי־פִי.
יַעֲרֹף כַּמָּטָר לִקְחִי   תִּזַּל כַּטַּל אִמְרָתִי,
כִּשְׂעִירִם עֲלֵי־דֶשֶׁא   וְכִרְבִיבִים עֲלֵי־עֵשֶׂב.

(1) Give ear, O ye heavens, and I will speak;
(2) And hear, O earth, the words of my mouth.
(3) My doctrine shall drop as the rain,
(4) My speech shall distil as the dew,
(5) As the small rain upon the tender herb,
(6) And as the showers upon the grass.
(Deuteronomy 32.1-4; the Authorized Version)

There are 3+3 stresses in each of the first two pairs of versets, and 2+2 stresses in the last pair (though here the first words are long and could have been pronounced as having a secondary stress, making the lines equivalent to the previous ones). The first two versets are almost entirely parallel. But the words הַאֲזִינוּ ('give ear') and וְתִשְׁמַע (literally 'and she will hear') are synonymous in meaning and not in morphology. 'I will speak' and 'the words of my mouth' are neither synonymous nor syntactically equivalent, but their meanings are parallel. The last pair is not an independent sentence, but each of its versets is parallel to the second word of the previous pair and is governed by the previous verb. There is variation in the equivalent words: 'heavens' and 'earth' are parallel by opposition; 'rain' and 'dew' both express fruition by water, but one is strong and the other subtle, rather like two poles of one scale. There is also a concatenation of the three pairs: versets 3 and 4 unfold the theme of the first pair (the unnamed object of the verb in 1 becomes the subject of phrases 3 and 4); versets 5 and 6 parallel the second word in 3 and 4. This almost perfect parallelism (changing in the following parts of the same poem) is variegated here too; thus the connotations of the words referring to water in the last four versets are chiastically ordered: the water is strong (3) – weak (4) – weak (5) – strong (6).

Many poetic texts in the Bible are, however, less symmetrical. The same principles are applied, though with greater freedom and flexibility, as one may observe in the opening of Isaiah 1 (p. 156). There is usually a greater variety in the number of versets in a group, as well as a second level of organization in which several groups of versets are combined in one long sentence. Symmetry, predominant in the previous example, is amply used by the prophets, but is usually engulfed in the wider flow of the argument. Thus, the formulaic opening of Isaiah 1.2, which is rather close to our previous example:

שִׁמְעוּ שָׁמַיִם	וְהַאֲזִינִי אֶרֶץ	כִּי יהוה דִּבֵּר
Hear, O heavens	and give ear, O earth:	for the Lord hath spoken

consists not of two but of three parts, the first two paralleling each other rigorously and the third remaining 'free', with the resultant structure *aab*. A thorough analysis of the whole passage will show a complex network of equivalence relationships in which every word participates in one way or another, and which is reinforced by the pervading imagery and prophetic tone.

THE POST-BIBLICAL PERIOD

During the first centuries after the close of the Bible, various rhythmical forms were developed, with no single established rigorous system. Parallelism of phrases, reinforced by rhetorical figures, is discernible everywhere. It seems, however, that several kinds of more regular rhythms evolved during that period. The basic tendency was to regularize the biblical accentual tradition, primarily into a 4-stress pattern. There were, however, three distinctly different interpretations of this basic rhythm:

(a) A permanent number of words per verset, e.g. four words as in some of the *Hekhalot* hymns (see pp. 195–6) and in a number of short Talmudic epigrams or poetic passages (e.g. גזע ישישים, p. 192); or three words as in the *akeda* איתן למד דעת (p. 201).

(b) A regular number of major stresses, whereby one stress often subordinated two words. Thus the *avoda* by Yose ben Yose (p. 209) lends itself to a reading in a regular pattern, as accepted by most scholars, of 4 + 4 (or 2 + 2/2 + 2) major stresses:

אַזְכִּיר גְּבוּרוֹת אֱלוֹהַּ / נֶאְדָּרִי בַּכֹּחַ // יָחִיד וְאֵין עוֹד, / אֶפֶס וְאֵין שֵׁנִי.

The rules for imposing one stress on two words are rhythmical rather than syntactic. The length of the poem and the very possibility of reading it in this manner support such a reading.

(c) A 4-stress pattern is imposed on the line, though there are often less than four words, the long words getting two stresses each. This system is clearly opposed to the one mentioned in type (b). It creates a kind of alternating metre, which can be seen while a modern metrical scheme is applied, e.g. (p. 192):

בָּאֲרָזִים נָפְלָה שַׁלְהֶבֶת –
מַה יַּעֲשׂוּ אֱזוֹבֵי־הַקִּיר ?
לִוְיָתָן בְּחַכָּה הוֹעֲלָה –
מַה יַּעֲשׂוּ דְּגֵי־הָרְקָק ?

By imposing two stresses on 3-syllabic words as in modern poetry (and disregarding some half-syllables) we get something similar to a modern 4-trochee line. Applying similar principles (the details of which cannot be given here) we find that this metre is predominant throughout the writings of Ben Sira. It creates a regularity in the number of syllables not unlike the one found in Syriac poetry. It was, however, by no means a rigid syllabic order in the sense of latter-day systems.

THE PIYUT

In Palestine under Byzantine rule, somewhere between the second and the sixth century, an entirely new kind of formal poetry developed, named *piyut*, which served for liturgical purposes. In this tradition, highly formalized poetic cycles (*kerovot*, *yotserot*) were composed for the Sabbaths and holidays. Basically these were complex cycles of strophic poems with rigid norms for a variety of formal devices assigned separately to each part of the cycle. Most of the poems were stringed on an acrostic of the 22 letters of the Hebrew alphabet (sometimes incomplete or containing the name of the poet).

The major forms developed in this poetry were: a strictly observed strophic structure, a permanent rhythm based on a fixed number of words in each line, and obligatory rhyme. At first rhyme was everywhere and of all kinds – at the beginning of lines, at the end of lines, or throughout a line (like English and Germanic alliteration), rhyme based on repetition of either morphological endings or of words of the same root, or of semantic properties (e.g. all lines ending with names of rivers; or pairs of oppositions, see, for example, some of the rhymes in Yannai's כלו עינינו, p. 215: [Loving One – enemy] אוֹהֵב – אוֹיֵב, [is loved – hated] אָהוּב – שָׂנוּי [from within – from without] מִבַּיִת – מִחוּץ, [below – above] בְּמַטָּה – בְּמַעְלָה), or of a whole word recurring in all lines of a strophe or a poem. The basic and predominant innovation, however, was end-rhyme based on sound parallelism. It was a highly complex rhyme involving most of the sounds of the rhyming words. There were two complementary requirements: (1) in each rhyming word two out of the three consonants of the Hebrew root had to participate in the rhyme (with the sounds between them varying); (2) the last syllable of each rhyming word had to be identical as well. Each rhyme was repeated at the end of all the lines of a strophe, i.e. 4, 5, 8 or 9 times. For example, SHiRaTI – kaSHaRTI – SHoRaRTI – SHeRiRuTI; in this case SH and R are the rhyming root consonants, and TI the rhyming last syllable.

This rhyme, based on a discontinuous group of sounds yet including the entire last syllable, may be called 'discontinuous-terminal'.

Thus a metre based on the number of words created a rhyming system based on the sound patterns covering the whole word. Such a system, of course, was very demanding for the poet and it was only made possible due to the highly 'difficult' style of the poetry of Eleazar ben Kallir (? sixth century) and his followers (especially in Italy in the tenth century) based on almost unlimited word innovations, allusions, and ellipses. With the transition to a simpler style the difficult requirements of rhyme had to be dropped and only the last syllable repeated in all lines of a strophe remained as an absolute norm of Hebrew medieval rhyme. This process was complete by the eleventh century.

The rhyming system of the Hebrew *piyut* was the earliest known massive, systematic and obligatory use of rhyme in poetry, and it is very plausible that through the Christian Syriac church employing Aramaic (a cognate language to Hebrew), and via Latin liturgy, the principle of rhyme was transferred to European poetry.

The basic forms of the Palestinian *piyut* were carried through Italy to the whole of medieval central and eastern Europe (Ashkenaz), where they dominated the creation of liturgical poetry until modern times (notably in the genre of the *seliḥa* – 'supplication', which favoured 5-word lines in 4-line strophes, rhyming *aaaa bbbb cccc*). In medieval Spain such strophic *piyutim* were also written, supplemented however by religious poetry employing the new metrical system.

HEBREW QUANTITATIVE POETRY IN SPAIN

The Hebrew poetry that flourished in Spain from the tenth to the fifteenth century was based on the Arabic system of poetics adapted to the Hebrew language. In secular poetry the metre was quantitative, i.e. there was a pattern of long and short syllables throughout a line repeated in all the lines of a poem (similar to the system used in classical Greek poetry). Under Arabic influence the Hebrew language here emphasized a difference between 'short' vowels (*shva*, *ḥataf*, and the conjunction *u*) and the regular vowels, considered as 'long'. This distinction disregarded the stress which was the major rhythmical factor in biblical poetry. The typical secular poem was a long poem (*qasida*) consisting of a chain of lines, each composed of two metrically equivalent versets (the *delet*, 'door', and *soger*, 'lock'). Each poem had only one rhyme repeated throughout its dozens of lines as a string of beads (the metaphor used by the theoreticians; the Hebrew word for 'rhyme' means literally 'bead').

It should be noted that the schemes of such quantitative metres were of two types: the regular type, in which a short syllable alternates with a fixed number of long ones throughout the line except at the end of each *delet* and *soger*. For example, the most widespread metre was (from left to right)

∪ — — — / ∪ — — — / ∪ — — // ∪ — — — / ∪ — — — / ∪ — —

and the alternating type, such as Judah Halevi's Zionide (p. 347) where two basic feet alternate:

— — ∪ — / — ∪ — / — — ∪ — / — ∪ — //
— — ∪ — / — ∪ — / — — ∪ — / — —

There was also a kind of free metre, with an irregular order of short and long syllables, which was, however, fixed in a permanent scheme and repeated in all the lines of a poem, as in many of the girdle poems (see below).

The Hebrew poets also employed a metre of 'long' syllables, avoiding the short ones altogether (*mishkal hatenu'ot*). On the other hand they developed a syllabic metre, based on a regular number of syllables per line (6 or 8), which allowed the free use of short vowels but disregarded them as syllables.

At the same time, however, Hebrew poets in Spain favoured a new form that had developed in Spanish-Arabic poetry and was possibly based on Romance strophic songs. This was the so-called *muwashshaḥ* or girdle poem, comprising two kinds of strophes: (1) each basic strophe had its own rhyme (or rhyme pattern), but was alternated with (2) girdles, strophes of a separate form (and metre) repeating one rhyme (or rhyme pattern) throughout the whole poem (see p. 30). The last girdle usually employed colloquial Arabic or colloquial Romance, thus indicating the melody to be used for the poem.

The girdle poem combined the effects of the string which unified the whole poem in a refrain-like manner with the love for variation in rhyming typical of European poetry as well as of the earlier Hebrew *piyut*. Thus the poem by Ibn Ghiyyat (p. 317) rhymes in the following manner (capitals represent the permanent, girdle rhymes; lower case letters – the changing rhymes of the basic strophes): AA/BA cd/cd/cd AA/BA ef/ef/ef AA/BA.

ITALY AND OTHER COUNTRIES

Italy was located at the centre of the Jewish world of the Middle Ages. Influences from all directions, from all Hebrew centres, were exerted on the writings of Hebrew poets there, with Italian poetry as a major influence. Rhymed and strophic Hebrew poetry written in Byzantine southern Italy in the ninth century in the vein of the Palestinian *piyut* appeared far earlier than rhymed poetry in Latin or Italian. The tradition of the *piyut* was predominant here until the fourteenth century. When Immanuel of Rome set out to write sonnets, much in the fashion of his Italian contemporaries, he found a language for secular poetry only in the Hebrew verse of Spain. As a result he transferred from Spain not only the poetic language and imagery but the quantitative metrical system as well, writing perfect ('Italian') sonnets in quantitative ('Arabic') metres. Sonnets, *ottava rima*, *terza rima*, and other Italian strophic forms combined with the language and metre of Arabic Spain for several centuries.

Little by little Hebrew poetry in Italy lost its requirement for quantitative metre and became purely syllabic, much as Italian poetry was. In this case, however, unlike the Hebrew syllabic metre of Spain, all short vowels were counted as syllables. In fact, though the number of words with feminine endings is very small in Hebrew, these became the predominant rhyming form, activating rather artificial and archaic words in rhyming positions, all under the influence of Italian poetry. This syllabic system was adopted by the new movement of secular poetry known as the *Haskalah* (Enlightenment) which developed in Germany in the late eighteenth century and moved to Austria and Russia in the nineteenth century and which laid the foundations of modern Hebrew literature.

Elsewhere, in the Byzantine Empire and after it in the Balkans, the Turkish Empire, northern Africa and other countries, Hebrew poetry showed strong influences on the one hand of the Spanish centre and on the other of the traditional *piyut*, one based on a rigorous syllable counting and the other, on the contrary, on a fixed number of words per line. There were also influences of Turkish strophic forms, especially in songs. Rhyme was obligatory throughout, with very few exceptions.

ACCENTUAL-SYLLABIC METRES IN THE MODERN PERIOD

While accentual syllabic (or tonic-syllabic) metre has dominated European poetry for several centuries now, it was accepted only recently, in about 1890, as the main form for Hebrew poetry. The first major poet consistently to use this metrical system, strongly influenced by Russian versification, was Bialik. In Hebrew, as in English, German and Russian poetry, it is based on a regular pattern of stressed and unstressed syllables. The Hebrew language, however, unlike English, has a vast number of long words of three or more syllables each. Thus rhythmical variation is achieved by skipping some of the metrical stresses rather than by stressing weak positions. For example, Iago's opening words in Act 1, Scene 2 of Shakespeare's *Othello* are, in English:

Though in the trade of war I have slain men,
Yet do I hold it very stuff o' the conscience
to do no contriv'd murder: I lack iniquity . . .

and in Alterman's Hebrew translation:

אָמְנָם בַּעֲבוֹדַת־הַמִּלְחָמָה
שָׁפַכְתִּי דְּמֵי־אָדָם, אַךְ לְבָבִי
סוֹלֵד מֶרֶצַח־בְּמֵזִיד. אֲהָהּ...

Iambic pentameter is used in both versions but the rhythm is quite different. The following diagram divides the actual graphic words of each language by bars and uses a dash for each possible stress:

English

—	∪	∪	—	∪	—	—	—	—	—
—	—	—	—	—	— ∪	—	∪	— ∪
∪	—	—	∪ —	— ∪	∪	—	∪ — ∪ ∪

Hebrew (from left to right)

∪ —	∪ ∪ ∪ —	∪ ∪ ∪ —
∪ — ∪	—	∪ —	∪	∪ ∪ —
∪ —	∪ — ∪	∪ ∪ —	∪ —

Clearly, whereas the first line in English has ten words, in Hebrew it has only three, and whereas in English it is possible to stress seven of these, in Hebrew only three stresses are allowed. Such an irregular line as the third in Shakespeare's original is not permitted in Hebrew metrical verse which complies with the rules of the very rigorous Russian tradition. Its great variety is achieved by skipping stresses in various places and changing the divisions between words from line to line.

The example given here is in the Israeli (or Sephardic) pronunciation now dominant in Israel. The revival, however, of accentual-syllabic metres in Hebrew poetry, with Bialik and Tchernikhovsky in the last decade of the nineteenth century, was in a different dialect, that of the Ashkenazi pronunciation developed in medieval Europe. The basic rule of that pronunciation is that whenever possible stress should fall on the penultimate syllable. When the penultimate syllable is a half-syllable the stress recedes to the third from the end; only monosyllabic words are ultimately stressed. Thus Bialik's poem (p. 509) should be read as follows:

עִם דִּמְדּוּמֵי הַחַמָּה אֶל־הַחַלּוֹן נָא־גֹשִׁי
וְעָלַי הִתְרַפְּקִי
לִפְתִי הֵיטֵב צַוָּארִי, שִׂימִי רֹאשֵׁךְ עַל רֹאשִׁי —
וְכֹה עִמִּי תִּדְבָּקִי.

In the Israeli pronunciation the reading would be:

עִם דִּמְדּוּמֵי הַחַמָּה אֶל־הַחַלּוֹן נָא־גְשִׁי
וְעָלַי הִתְרַפְּקִי,
לִפְתִי הֵיטֵב צַוָּארִי, שִׂימִי רֹאשֵׁךְ עַל־רֹאשִׁי –
וְכֹה עִמִּי תִּדְבָּקִי.

and the metre is destroyed.

The shift from the Ashkenazi to the Israeli pronunciation caused an extremely painful crisis in Hebrew poetry, especially since the poetic values of Hebrew poetry in its modern phase were placed heavily on metre and sound in the best Russian tradition. Though for centuries European Jews had prayed and studied Hebrew from early childhood in one of several Ashkenazi dialects, the pioneers in the Land of Israel since the beginning of the twentieth century have spoken Sephardic. In Hebrew poetry, however, the Sephardic (or 'Israeli') dialect became dominant only in the late 1920s. The stress on the last syllables of most words sounded harsh and 'masculine' to the poets of the previous generation, who preferred 'melodious' poetry with feminine rhymes. Indeed, it was to them a new language and they wrote rather artificial poems in the spoken dialect. Some poets tried to translate their own poetry from Hebrew into new Hebrew, involving themselves in a reshuffling of sound-meaning relationships that rarely succeeded.

MODES OF MODERNISM

The dangers of a mechanical and overpronounced metre in a language with a strong ultimate stress were met by breaking away from the rigours of symmetry. The freeing of rhythm in Hebrew poetry took two major directions. Under Russian influence, a verse-form was developed, employing a metrical scheme with a large number of deviations, as if hovering between anapests and iambs. This poetry, influenced by the poetics of Akhmatova, Blok, Yesenin and Mayakovsky, relied heavily on sound effects and rich rhyming. Though the norm for Hebrew rhyme accepted one stressed syllable at the end of a line (as is common in English), poets in the Shlonsky tradition excelled in highly complex and very rich and innovatory rhymes based on a discontinuous set of sounds going from the end of a line far back into its middle. For example, Alterman uses rhymes such as:

> KSuMÁ HI – KoS HaMÁIm; LeKH uSHMÁ – haḤaSHMÁL; SiPuNÉKHA – kaSe PaNÉKHA.

Again Hebrew poetry, as in the *piyut* of Yannai and Kallir, moulded its rhymes not on the last syllable but on the whole word, based on the nature of the Hebrew word, which has only consonants as part of its lexical core and vowels belong merely to the morphological system. This rhyming principle, founded on the nature of the Hebrew language, created a tension between richness of sound on the one hand and discord on the other, in the best tradition of Mayakovsky and Pasternak. As the rhyming sounds are discontinuous, and require identity of the stressed vowels but not necessarily of the final sounds, it may be called 'discontinuous-accentual' rhyme.

A different trend was the free verse based on a paucity of rhymes and a stronger deviation from any metrical background, playing essentially on variation of phrases, long and short lines, and in general on local rhythmical effects or on the rhythms of prose. The first wave of this development appeared in the 1920s (notably with David Vogel) under the impact of German Expressionism. A second wave developed in the late 1950s and 1960s with the transition from a Russian-oriented metrical poetry to a poetry based on understatement and imagery, primarily under the influence of English modernism.

RHYME: A SURVEY

Rhyme was dominant in Hebrew poetry from the sixth to the twentieth century. In the eighteenth century, under European influence, unrhymed poetic drama and epic poetry appeared, and in the early twentieth century Tchernikhovsky's unrhymed idylls and some of Bialik's quasi-biblical unrhymed poems. In the second decade of this century, with the impact of Expressionism, the predilection for systematic rhyming in lyrical poetry disappeared. This trend has strengthened in the last generation.

Though often highly inventive under the constraints of rhyme, poets were never free to select the rhyming principles. In the rhymed *piyut* (and only in some genres) one could either repeat the same word throughout or find as many rhyming words as lines in a strophe (4, 5, 8 or 9), according to the requirements of the discontinuous-terminal rhyme of the 'difficult' Kallirian tradition (see p. 62).

At a later stage of the *piyut* the requirement for rhyming two root-consonants was dropped and only the last syllable remained mandatory in rhyme, including however the preceding consonant (*consonne d'appui*) but disregarding stress. E.g., kaROV-la'aROV, shéLEG-medaLÉG (though in other languages OV, EG is perfectly sufficient). This terminal rhyme became the obligatory Hebrew rhyme in Spain and elsewhere throughout the medieval period. As stress was disregarded in the metre, so it played no role in rhyme. Only in Italy did rhyme become stress-bound, involving all sounds from the stressed vowel onwards, with a distinction between feminine rhyme (shÉLEG-pÉLEG) and masculine rhyme (medalÉG-orÉG). This, basically, has remained the rhyme of modern Hebrew poetry in accentual-syllabic metres to this day.

In modernism, however, especially under Russian influence, a rich rhyme was developed, inexact in its final syllable, discontinuous in its set of sounds, covering the whole word again (as in the *piyut*) or even several words, but stress-bound, as the metre depends primarily on stress (as in Alterman's examples above).

The four major rhyming possibilities shown in the following diagram, moving clockwise, were employed in Hebrew poetry throughout its history.

	– continuous	+ continuous
– stress	1. discontinuous-terminal (*piyut*) aReMÁ – heḥRíMA – RuMÁ	2. terminal (Spain) shéLEG – medaLÉG
+ stress	4. discontinuous-accentual (Modernism) SHÉLEg – SHokÉLEt	3. terminal-accentual (modern age) shÉLEG – pÉLEG/medalÉG – orÉG

Similar radical changes occurred in rhyme-patterning. The *piyut* developed a very rigorous system of strophic structures. Each strophe, however, allowed for only one rhyme: *aaaa bbbb cccc*. In Spain the major tradition required one rhyme throughout the whole poem (of 10, 40 or 60 lines). Under the impact of Italian strophic poetry (with some Spanish precursors) alternation of several rhymes in one strophe was introduced: e.g. *abab*; *aba bcb cdc*. Reinforced by the Russian tradition of masculine-feminine alternation in rhyme, this has remained the predominant rhyme pattern.

SYNOPSIS

Thus Hebrew poetry turned full circle (see Table, p. 71). It started in the Bible (I) with a system of phrase parallelism based on several of the major components of the phrase: semantics, syntax, phrasal stress. In the *piyut* (II) a metre of a fixed number of words and a rhyme based on the sound pattern of the whole word was developed. In medieval Spain (III) the system went down to the lower unit of syllable, and rhyme was based on the last syllable only. Syllabic metre in Hebrew shifted from a quantitative principle (in Spain) to the number of syllables (in Italy, IV) to an accentual syllabic system (in modern poetry, V). Hence the system moved back (at an accelerated speed): at first to a poetry leaning strongly on the number of major stresses in the line (in Russian-influenced Hebrew modernism, VI) and a rhyme covering the whole sound structure of the rhyming words, then to an English-influenced free verse (VII) based on a changing balance of phrase groups. Of course, this schematic cycle is extremely abstract and simplified; the subordinated factors always played an additional and often important role. And in recent years a kaleidoscope of forms has existed concurrently, competing with and complementing each other.

The awareness which a Hebrew poet may have of the relativity of systems of versification and rhyming does not help him in choosing whatever he needs for his particular poem. Indeed biblical verse does seem 'free' from the point of view of the modern reader trained on strictly syllable-counting accentual-syllabic verse. It is, however, impossible to imitate, except for small passages or for specific stylistic purposes, as much as it is impossible for an English dramatist to write Shakespearean iambic pentameters. Each system has evolved major verse forms with very typical combinations of syn-

NOTE ON THE SYSTEMS OF HEBREW VERSIFICATION

The Major Systems of Hebrew Verse (in their logical and chronological order)

Length of Line	Free	Fixed	
Basis of Metre	Phrase	Word	Syllable
ANTIQUITY AND MEDIEVAL (From phrase to syllable)	I. *Bible*: free accentual metre varying semantic-syntactic-rhythmic parallelism in phrase groups	II. *Rhymed Piyut*: word-metre number of words	III. *Spain*: quantitative metre number of syllables + order of long/short
	Rhyme: sporadic	rich, discontinuous, based on whole word	based on last syllable
			IV. *Late Italy & Haskalah*: syllabic metre number of syllables
			Rhyme: stress-bound
MODERN AGE (From syllable to phrase)	VII. *Modernist*: Free Verse changing balance of phrase groups	VI. *Modernist*: accentual 'net' (in the Russian tradition) number of major stresses + deviating from syllabic order	V. *Modern*: accentual-syllabic metre number of syllables + order of stressed/unstressed
	Rhyme: not obligatory	rich, discontinuous, based on whole word	stress-bound

tactic and semantic, as well as rhythmical features. This combination, once automatized, has as it were 'exhausted' the possibilities of the system. Like their European and American contemporaries, Hebrew poets today either write basically free poetry, leaning heavily on the rhythmical formation of each line and passage, or are in search of a renewed form which would not sound epigonic on one hand and, at the same time, would be able to encompass the rhythms of the new spoken language.

NOTE ON THE TEXT

THE phonetic transcription in this volume is generally based on the current Israeli pronunciation, which has been characterized by Haim Blanc as 'native, Europeanized, moderately formal, and non puristic'.[1] No attempt has been made to formulate an accurate, 'scientific' transcription, if only because the selection represents a very wide range of Hebrew pronunciations, current in different geographical areas at different periods.

The symbol *ḥ* has been used to designate the sound of the Hebrew letter ח ; *kh* has been used to represent כ . In current Israeli pronunciation both letters approximate the sound of Scottish lo*ch*, Spanish *j*unta. No distinction has been made between א and ע . The combination *ts* corresponds to the letter צ . Thus the name of the sixteenth-century poet צרפתי is transcribed *Tsarfati* (in the *Encyclopaedia Judaica* – *Ẓarfati*), even though the צ was then pronounced as an aspirated *s*.

'The vowel symbols (vowels in Hebrew are indicated by vowel points written below, above, or next to the letter . . .) and their approximate English equivalents are as follows:

a	f*a*ther
e	b*e*t
i	mach*i*ne
o	sh*o*re
u	s*ou*p'

'The diphthongs are formed by adding the sound of *y* to each of the foregoing vowel sounds. Thus, with English equivalents:

ay	m*y*, m*i*ne
ey	gr*ey*, n*ei*gh
oy	b*oy*

The diphthong *uy* is closer to that of the German *pfui* or that of the French

1. H. Blanc, 'How to Read the Phonetic Transcriptions of the Poems', in S. Burnshaw, T. Carmi and E. Spicehandler (eds.), *The Modern Hebrew Poem Itself*, Schocken Books, New York, 1966, pp. 191–5. With few exceptions, our transcription follows the principles outlined in the above essay, from which all the following quotations, and some of the examples, are taken.

fouille than to that of the English *hooey*. The diphthong *iy* is closer to the sound of the French *fille* than to that of the English *fee*.'

'When two vowels adjoin, they are pronounced separately, so that each is given its true value.' Thus *sheol* ('the underworld') is pronounced as *she* followed by *ol*.

The symbol ' (apostrophe) has often been used to indicate a 'catch' or slight pause between vowels or between a consonant and a vowel belonging to different syllables. Thus *amora'im* (Talmudic 'interpreters') is pronounced as *amora* followed by *im*.

'When two consonants adjoin, they are pronounced without any intervening vowel sound' (e.g. *zmora*, 'vine-twig').

Consistency has proved impossible. I have respected the conventional English spelling of certain Hebrew words, works and proper names (e.g. Shekinah, Mishnah, Yannai, Heber; instead of *Shekhina*, *Mishna*, *Yanay*, *Hever*), even when they deviate from the principles outlined above.

The spelling of post-biblical poetry has been modernized except for those cases in which the original form is dictated by metrical, or other, considerations. Some rules of biblical vocalization have not been consistently observed in post-biblical poetry. Many of the medieval poems originate in unvocalized manuscripts and the vocalization supplied by the various editors is, in some respects (e.g. pausal forms), a matter of choice.

All deletions are indicated in the Hebrew text by three dots enclosed in square brackets [. . .] and are usually noted in the Table of Poems.

No special mention has been made of the few instances in which I have incorporated conjectural readings (by the scholars who edited the texts) in the body of the Hebrew poems. Unfortunately, it has proved impracticable to include a full list of the many sources (though occasionally the information is provided under the relevant headings).

The translator's additions and glosses are enclosed in square brackets. Needless to say, the distinction between an 'addition' and a meaning that is implicit in the Hebrew and immediately grasped by the reader is not always clear-cut.

The division into verse paragraphs of non-strophic poetry has been made by the editor to clarify the poem's thematic development. Many of the long non-strophic poems, especially of the Spanish period, are composed of independent, loosely connected units (which are governed by the conventions of the specific genre). I have felt that the loss in fidelity would be offset by a gain in clarity for the English reader. For typographical reasons, the two hemistichs which compose a single line of verse in the *qasida* poems of the Spanish school have often been printed consecutively.

The italicized superscriptions were written either by the author or by an early compiler. This is usually apparent from the context or is explained in the Table of Poems.

Biblical references follow the numbering of chapter and verse in the authorized Hebrew text. Scriptural quotations that serve as structural devices in a poem (i.e. as a refrain, as a transitional link or as part of a pattern of scriptural insertions) are italicized in the English translation.

Some of the poems included in the 'Anonymous' sections contain an acrostic of the author's name (e.g., 'Rain Song' on p. 241 which yields YeHUDA). However, when nothing is known of the poet, except his name, it is customary to relegate him to the company of the 'Anonymous'.

Ben, *bar* and *ibn* mean 'son of'. *T.B.* refers to the Babylonian Talmud.

In the Table of Poems, all the poems are identified by their opening words in English and in Hebrew. In the body of the book, the Hebrew titles generally consist of the opening words, whereas the English titles are explanatory, with a view to setting the scene for the reader. In the modern section, the titles are those given by the authors, unless otherwise indicated by their inclusion in square brackets.

TABLE OF POEMS

PART ONE: TO THE TENTH CENTURY

THE BIBLE was composed and compiled over a period extending from the thirteenth to the second century B.C.E. The canon of the Hebrew Scriptures, completed around 100 C.E., is divided into three parts. The first, the Law (*Torah*), comprises the five books of Moses, the Pentateuch. The second, Prophets (*Nevi'im*), is subdivided into the Former Prophets, which chronicle Israel's history from the conquest of Canaan (*c.* 1250 B.C.E.) to the destruction of the First Temple (587 B.C.E.); and the Latter Prophets, which include the great individual seers of the pre-exilic period, such as Amos, Isaiah, Micah, Jeremiah and Ezekiel. The third, Writings (*Ketuvim*), is a fairly random grouping of works, among them Psalms, Proverbs, Job, the five festival scrolls, and the apocalyptic book of Daniel (167–164 B.C.E.). The poetry of the Old Testament is rooted in the rich poetic literature of the ancient Near East: particularly Canaan (Ugaritic), Mesopotamia (Sumerian and Old Babylonian) and Egypt. The rhetorical forms and, to a certain degree, the content of Israelite poetry were derived from this milieu and adapted by Yahwism for its own purposes. The repertoire of literary types is extremely varied. G. Fohrer lists them under the following headings:

1. Songs of Everyday Life: vestiges of work songs, watchman's songs, drinking songs; elaborate taunt songs; love songs; war and victory songs; and personal or collective dirges. Early Israelite poetry was sung to the accompaniment of music and choral dancing.

2. Psalms: the two main literary types are the hymn (e.g. enthronement psalms, Zion songs, pilgrimage songs) and the communal or individual lament; there are also songs of thanksgiving, mainly of the individual, royal songs, and various forms belonging to the sphere of the priests and cult prophets. The psalms were chanted by the temple singers.

3. Wisdom Poetry and Didactic Poetry: these collections of sayings or single unified compositions, which embodied the views of the wisdom teachers, employ rhythmically structured proverbs, aphorisms, fables and allegories.

4. Prophetical Teaching: the prophets, whose messages were, for the most part, proclaimed orally, imitated many of the song types and often extended their use. They also introduced the prophetical dirge, which bewails a disaster to come, and developed distinctive rhetorical forms, such as the prophetical saying (oracles, threats and invectives; promises of divine intervention or salvation) and the prophetical report (of a vision, a call experience or a symbolic action). The various literary types of the Old Testament are often encountered in mixed form or are linked together to form a 'liturgy'. For example, the introduction of a lament may have hymnic character, or a thanksgiving song may often be formulated as a didactic poem. Some of the song types, such as the hymn, communal lament or royal song, were primarily composed for a specific cultic situation. However, religious or devotional

poetry written by individuals made its appearance very early and the distinction between cultic and non-cultic (or secular), or between communal and individual, is not always clear-cut.

The style of biblical poetry is characterized by a parallelism of line and thought and by the use of 'fixed pairs' of words set in parallel structure. The parallelism may be synonymous, antithetic, repetitive or synthetic (see Note on the Systems of Hebrew Versification, pp. 58 ff.). A verse can consist of one, two or three lines; the two-line verse, or bicolon, is the most common unit. Strophes, usually containing an equal or approximately equal number of verses, seem to have been common. Opinions concerning the character of Hebrew prosody are still divided. '. . . The correct pronunciation of ancient Hebrew, the syllabification of many words, and the quantity and accent of the syllables are uncertain' (S. Gevirtz). According to one major school of thought the metre is accentual: the verse is determined by the regular pattern of accented syllables; generally from one to three unaccented syllables fall between stresses. Some of the more common metric patterns are 3+2 (a bicolon with three stresses in the first colon and two in the second), 3+3 and 4+4. Other devices employed in biblical poetry include alliteration, vocalic and consonantal assonance, occasional rhymes, internal rhyme, key words and acrostics. The following examples of different types of biblical poetry are given in the sequence of the Hebrew canon:

'I shall sing to the Lord' אָשִׁירָה לַיהוה 147

Exodus 15.1b–18. 'The Song of the Sea', which celebrates the crucial event in Israel's history, is a hymn, incorporating elements of the victory song and thanksgiving song. Its archaic diction and stylistic affinities with Canaanite poetry have led scholars to date it as early as the Mosaic period (thirteenth century B.C.E.); others, however, believe it to be of post-exilic origin. The dominant metre is 2+2 but there are occasional shifts to 3+3 and, in common with Ugaritic poetry, verses with an additional colon. The translation of the tenses and the division into strophes present serious difficulties. It is noteworthy that the Song omits any reference to Moses. Yahweh alone performed the miracle at the Sea of Reeds.

'For the warriors, in Israel' בִּפְרֹעַ פְּרָעוֹת בְּיִשְׂרָאֵל 149

Judges 5.1–31. 'The Song of Deborah' (*c.* 1200 B.C.E.), noted for its dramatic vitality and rapid contrasts, is a religious victory song with a hymn-like beginning and conclusion, and motifs borrowed from taunt songs. It was composed soon after the battle it describes or it may have been sung while the campaign was still under way to muster the warriors. The archaic language and the 'impressionistic' technique – there is no attempt at logical, consecutive narration – often make the meaning and structure obscure. The verses are made up mainly of bicolons and tricolons, and the style is characterized by the urgency of repetitive, or 'climactic', parallelism. Scholars have pointed out the relationship of this song to nomadic war songs and to old Babylonian verse structure.

'All your glory, O Israel' הַצְּבִי, יִשְׂרָאֵל 154

2 Samuel 1.19–27. 'David's Lament over Saul and Jonathan' (*c.* 1000 B.C.E.) is a deeply moving masterpiece of early Hebrew poetry. It is a personal dirge (*kina*), marked by the absence of religious character. There is no reason for doubting David's authorship. Though the text is partly corrupt, it is clear that 'How the heroes have fallen!' is the refrain of the lament, which was probably sung antiphonally. *Ekh* or *ekha*, 'Ah, how . . .', is the formulaic introduction to a dirge (see Isaiah's taunt dirge, p. 160, and Lamentations 4, p. 179). The measure is predominantly 2+2, and the lament employs a great many 'fixed pairs' or 'stock parallels' (e.g. 'do not tell'//'do not proclaim', 'blood'//'fat', 'swift'//'strong').

'Hear, O heavens, and listen, O earth' שִׁמְעוּ, שָׁמַיִם 156

Isaiah 1.2–20 (second half of the eighth century B.C.E.). These verses are part of a collection of prophetic sayings which provide a cross-section of the prophet's message, and therefore have been placed at the beginning of the book (which actually comprises three independent groups of writings: Isaiah I, 1–39, Deutero-Isaiah, 40–55, and Trito-Isaiah, 56–66). Isaiah was probably of aristocratic origin and grew up in Jerusalem. His opening oracles consist of a 'prophetical judgement discourse' (lines 1–9), whose mode of speech is that of the law court. The invective (lines 10–39) was composed after the devastation of Judah by the Assyrian king Sennacherib (701 B.C.E.). The rejection of the cult as a means of salvation (lines 40–74) is a prophetical imitation of 'cultic torah', that is, instruction or advice given by a priest in questions involving cultic procedures. This section belongs to the first period of Isaiah's ministry (746/40–36 B.C.E.), in which he exposed the moral breakdown of Judah. The exhortation (lines 75–85) is another of the rhetorical forms employed by the great individual prophets.

'How the oppressor has met his end' אֵיךְ שָׁבַת נֹגֵשׂ 160

Isaiah 14.4b–21. This is the finest example in the Bible of the mocking prophetical dirge – usually directed against a foreign power – which fuses the taunt song (*mashal*) with the funeral lament. The poem probably does not derive from Isaiah; it is part of a collection of anonymous oracles against foreign nations (Moab, Egypt, Edom) which date from the sixth or fifth century. The tyrant referred to in the superscription as 'the king of Babylon' cannot be identified with any certainty. The dirge draws heavily on mythological elements in its detailed account of the underworld (*sheol*), its mention of Canaanite deities (line 30) and its references to the mountainous abode of the gods. The metre is almost uniformly 3+2. The 'prophetic perfect' tenses express future events as though they had already come to pass.

'I thought: I shall depart' אֲנִי אָמַרְתִּי : בִּדְמִי יָמַי 163

Isaiah 38.10–20. The so-called 'Psalm of Hezekiah' belongs to the category of individual songs of thanksgiving. Like 'The Song of the Sea' or Jonah's 'Thanksgiving Song' it was already extant as a finished composition and was interpolated by the compilers at a suitable place. It was probably added to the book of Isaiah during the final stage of its composition (*c.* fifth century B.C.E.). The poor repair of the text, especially in lines 9–27, has given rise to many conflicting interpretations.

'The Lord is my shepherd' יהוה רֹעִי – לֹא אֶחְסָר 165

Psalm 23 (? post-exilic; sixth or fifth century B.C.E.), an individual song of confidence, elaborates a motif that originally formed part of the introduction or body of a lament. It is included in the 'Davidic Psalter' (Psalms 3–41), the largest original collection of the five books into which the Psalter was divided, on the model of the Pentateuch. The Psalter (*Tehilim*, 'hymns of praise') contains a varied selection of songs, including wisdom poems, dating from several centuries. It assumed its final form in the fourth century and served as the hymnal of the post-exilic Temple and synagogue. The superscriptions are all secondary.

'As the deer longs for running waters' כְּאַיָּל תַּעֲרֹג 166

Psalms 42–43 (? pre-exilic; eighth or seventh century B.C.E.) constitute a single song. The division into strophes is clearly indicated by the regular repetition of the refrain 'Why are you so desolate . . .' This individual lament is part of the collection known as the 'Elohistic Psalter', in which the divine name 'Yahweh' is regularly replaced by the designation 'Elohim'. It has been suggested that this lament, 'unsurpassed in tenderness and depth' (H. Gunkel), was written by a refugee, living in exile in Northern Palestine (line 23). As in Psalm 23, the metre, with quite a few exceptions, is 3+2.

'O my soul, bless the Lord' בָּרְכִי, נַפְשִׁי 168

Psalm 104 (post-exilic) is a non-cultic devotional hymn, which derives many of its metaphors from Babylonian and especially Canaanite mythology. It is typical of the manner in which the Old Testament borrowed and demythologized pagan material. Leviathan, here the plaything of God (line 58), is the primeval dragon Lotan who, in Ugaritic literature, was the enemy of Ba'al. In the description of God's struggle with the powers of chaos (lines 11–20), the 'abyss', *tehom*, recalls Tiamat of the Babylonian Creation epic. It has been noted that this 'creation psalm' closely parallels the Egyptian Hymn to the Sun of Amenhotep IV (fourteenth century). The metre, with a few exceptions, is 3+3.

Job 28 (late post-exilic; fourth or third century B.C.E.), a wisdom poem with a charac-
teristic refrain, was composed as an independent lyrical unit. It probably does not
derive from the author of Job, who may have lived in Palestine in the fifth or fourth
century. The personification or hypostatization of 'Wisdom' (*ḥokhma*), which seems
to be rooted in a Gnostic myth, is also found in other Hebrew wisdom books, such as
Proverbs 1-9 and Ecclesiasticus 24. The last verse 'was probably a later addition to
bring to a practical conclusion this fine metaphysical flight' (E. P. Dhorme).

'*I was asleep but my heart was awake*'   אֲנִי יְשֵׁנָה וְלִבִּי עֵר   174

Song of Songs 5.2-6.3. The Song of Solomon (post-exilic; fifth or fourth century
B.C.E.) comprises a collection of profane love songs and epithalamia composed in
Palestine. Modern exegesis has rejected the many attempts to discover a coherent
plot in the collection which would assign the various sections to a fixed cast of
characters. The Song was probably taken into the canon as a result of the allegorical
interpretation – still dominant in orthodox Judaism – which equates the 'lover' or
'bridegroom' with God, and the 'beloved' or 'Shulammite' with Israel. However
'. . . in the second century A.D. the book still had to struggle for the recognition of its
canonicity . . . according to Tosephta Sanhedrin 12, 10² . . . Rabbi Akiba (A.D. 137)
cursed those who used to sing passages from the Song of Songs in the wine-shops –
evidently still understanding it in its literal sense . . .' (O. Eissfeldt). The Song is used
as the festival scroll for Passover. The first extract consists of a dream song (lines
1-31), a description of the lover's charms (lines 32-60) and a short dialogue.

'*Return, return, O Shulammite*'   שׁוּבִי, שׁוּבִי, הַשּׁוּלַמִּית   177

Song of Songs 7.1-10. The Shulammite's dance is one of the many echoes in the Song
of Syro-Palestinian marriage customs. On the eve of her wedding the bride performs
a sword dance to the rhythm of a descriptive song (known in Arabic as the *waṣf*) that
celebrates her beauty and her adornments. Then, during the 'royal week' following
the wedding, the couple are fêted as king and queen. Close associations with ancient
Egyptian love poetry have also been pointed out, especially in the presentation of the
lovers or bridal pair in the disguises of 'shepherd', 'gardener', 'king' and 'queen'.

'*Who is this coming up from the wilderness*'   מִי זֹאת עֹלָה   179

Song of Songs 8.5-7.

'*How the gold was tarnished*'   אֵיכָה יוּעַם זָהָב   179

Lamentations 4 (*c.* 550 B.C.E.) is a collective dirge, bewailing the misery and destruc-
tion of Jerusalem after its capture by the Babylonians. Written (in Palestine?) by an
eye-witness, it is structured as an alphabetic song: the first word of each strophe (con-
sisting of two bicolons) begins with the letter of the Hebrew alphabet in sequence.

This accounts for the relative looseness of the composition. Other alphabetic acrostics, of various types, which enable the author to display his skill and also serve as a mnemonic device, are found in Lamentations (1–3) and in Psalms (9–10, 25, 34, 111, 112). In Hebrew, the book is called by its initial word, *ekha*. Its dominant verse type is the '*kina* metre', 3+2, the 'rhythm that always dies away'. In fact, however, this metre is employed in a variety of poems having nothing to do with laments for the dead and, moreover, is not found in all funeral songs. Traditionally ascribed to Jeremiah, Lamentations is the festival scroll for the fast of the Ninth of Av, memorializing the destruction of Jerusalem.

SIMEON BEN SIRA or JESUS SIRACH (fl. late second century B.C.E.), a Jerusalemite scribe and scholar, was the author of a book of proverbial philosophy known since the fourth century as Ecclesiasticus. It is included in the Apocrypha. The original text had been lost, and the Wisdom of Ben Sira was preserved mainly through a Greek translation made by his grandson in Egypt. The first fragments of the Hebrew original were discovered in 1896 among manuscripts from the Cairo Genizah; within four years, two thirds of the Hebrew text was recovered. Additional fragments have turned up among the Dead Sea Scrolls and in the Masada excavations (1964). Though he probably spoke Mishnaic Hebrew, Ben Sira wrote his book in the idiom of biblical poetry, modelling himself on Psalms, Job, and especially the later sections of Proverbs. The following panegyric of the high priest, Simeon the Just, served as a paradigm for many later compositions commemorating the sacrificial service on the Day of Atonement in the Temple of Jerusalem.

THE DEAD SEA SCROLLS (*c.* 170 B.C.E.–*c.* 68 C.E.) were first discovered in 1947 by a Bedouin shepherd in a cave at Qumran, on the north-western shore of the Dead Sea. Excavations in adjacent caves later yielded additional texts. These manuscripts, which include the most ancient fragments of the Hebrew Scriptures, are probably the remnants of an extensive library which the Essene Brotherhood left behind when its isolated settlement was destroyed by the Romans. The language of the Scrolls is based on biblical Hebrew, but shows the influence of the Hebrew and Aramaic spoken at the time. The poetic passages employ parallelism very loosely, often varying the length of the corresponding cola.

Scholars have thus far been unable to elucidate this mysterious fragment. The 'birth-gates of evil' reappear, with slight variations, in the strange hymn describing the birth of the 'creatures of evil' (pp. 188–9).

This is the opening section of the sixteenth hymn of the *Hodayot* ('Thanksgiving Psalms'). These hymns imitate the style of the biblical Psalms, but their imagery is often over-elaborate and their vocabulary esoteric. The central religious experience of the *Hodayot*, which often have a personal tone, is the experience of election. The company of the elect, sequestered in the wilderness of Judea, is here represented by the tender 'Trees of Life', who are temporarily overshadowed by their thriving adversaries, the 'Well-Watered Trees'.

The birth of the Messiah, as described in the fifth hymn, will mark the onset of terrible pangs in the world's (or in Hell's) womb, culminating in the birth of the 'creatures of evil' and their final imprisonment. Like the preceding hymn, this one begins in the first person. But the incidental simile of the woman in labour is suddenly elaborated into an impersonal apocalyptic vision. J. Licht considers this to be 'undoubtedly the strangest and most difficult chapter of the Thanksgiving Scroll'.

THE TALMUD (completed *c.* 500 C.E.), a vast corpus of law, commentaries and legends, took shape in Palestine and Babylonia over a period of almost five centuries. It occasionally contains short poems: prayers designed for synagogal use, private devotions, elegies, and random snatches of popular verse. The personal prayers are often distinguished by great simplicity of diction and structure; the elegies, however, are highly stylized and because of their frequent use of epithets can sound like riddles. But both genres testify to a growing freedom from biblical models and to the evolution of new styles, under the impact of rabbinic Hebrew.

The *tanna* Abba Yose ben Ḥanin (second half of the first century) is said to have composed this complaint against the corruption and nepotism of the priestly ruling families.

Enumerates the woes which will precede the coming of the Messiah. Some scholars believe that this poem alludes to events that actually happened at the time of the Hadrianic persecutions, after Bar Kokhba's unsuccessful revolt (132–135).

A speech of condolence, improvised by the Palestinian *amora* Judah ben Naḥamani (third century) when he visited Hiyya bar Abba, whose child had died.

A funeral oration for the *amora'im* Rabba bar Huna ('the Scion') and Hamnuna Saba ('the Book'), both of whom died in Babylonia (early fourth century) and were brought to Palestine for burial. The long verse-line (here printed as two lines) is divided into four units, each consisting of two stressed words. This 'quadripartite rhythm', and the use of epithet and alliteration, are characteristic of Talmudic elegies.

A eulogy composed by the orator Bar Kipok (fourth century), when the Babylonian *amora* Ashi asked him: how will you eulogize me when I die? Rav Ashi was so outraged, presumably by the rhetoric of this improvisation, that he forbade Bar Kipok to attend his funeral.

This anonymous meditation became part of the morning benedictions in the liturgy.

Attributed to two different rabbis of the sixth century, this too is included in the liturgy, with the omission of lines 8–10.

Is grouped among the prayers to be recited at home before retiring at night. The formula 'May it be Your will' (line 5) and the opening 'My God' in the two preceding poems are typical of private prayers which were not part of the obligatory liturgy in Talmudic times.

This is quoted as the hymn of praise sung by the two milch-cows who, unguided, transported the Ark of the Covenant in a cart from Philistine to Israelite territory (1 Samuel 6.12). The Talmud attributes this unusual hymn to Isaac Napaḥa ('the smith'), a Palestinian sage of the middle of the third century, but it may be earlier in origin.

THE HEKHALOT HYMNS (*c.* third and fourth centuries) were composed by the *merkava* mystics in Palestine and later in Babylonia. The *hekhalot* ('palaces') are the seven heavenly halls through which the visionary aspires to pass; the *merkava* ('chariot') is the divine throne, situated in the inner recesses of the seventh heaven. Many of the hymns are addressed to the throne and to the divine glory seated upon it by 'the holy living creatures'; the mystic is instructed to recite them during his ecstatic ascent to heaven. The following sections are taken from the tract known as

The Greater Hekhalot, which describes – alternately in prose and verse – the angelic hosts in the 'Palaces of Silence', the celestial liturgy, and the techniques which enable the mystic to 'ascend' and 'descend' unharmed. The hymns have a characteristic rhythm and are often composed of double verses of 3 or 4 words to the line. They employ a consistent technical language, containing a great many bizarre words and phrases. In the opinion of G. Scholem, 'their immense solemnity of style is unsurpassed in Hebrew hymnology'.

'The beginning of praise' תְּחִלַּת שֶׁבַח 195

Is prefaced by the following instruction: 'Rabbi Ishmael said: "Which song should a man chant when he is about to descend to the *merkava*? He should begin by reciting this one."' The expression 'to descend to the *merkava*' refers to the ecstatic *ascent* to heaven. No explanation has been found for this paradoxical expression.

'You who revoke decrees' מְבַטְּלֵי גְזֵרָה 195

The 'living creatures' or 'heavenly beasts' (*ḥayot hakodesh*), who are the bearers of the throne in Ezekiel 1.5, are part of the angelic hierarchy at the celestial court. When they see that their King is angry at His children, they try to placate Him by invoking the memory of Abraham's devotion. They also 'hurl down their crowns, ungird their loins, beat their heads, fall on their faces and say, "forgive, forgive, O Holy One of Israel!"'

'Lovely face, majestic face' פָּנִים נָאִים 196

Based on the belief that 'day by day ministering angels are created from the stream of fire. They sing a paean and then pass away . . .' They are stationed at their posts as the throne revolves, so that those on the left find themselves on the right, etc.

'Day after day, at the break of dawn' בְּכָל יוֹם וָיוֹם 198

The celestial morning service. The last two lines refer to the belief that the angelic hosts are not permitted to sing in heaven before the congregation of Israel has begun to sing on earth.

'King of miracles, King of power' מֶלֶךְ נִסִּים 198

Describes in rhythmical prose the throne's daily service to God. Zohorariel (line 19), who is also involved in the next passage, is one of the secret names of God in His splendour (*zohar*).

'A quality of holiness' מִדָּה שֶׁל קְדֻשָּׁה 199

Celebrates the garment which God puts on when He descends to sit on His throne. From another hymn we learn that the stars and constellations were – and perhaps still are – created by the light that emanates from this cosmic robe.

Part of a long hymn which the throne addresses to God each day.

A recurrent theme of the *Hekhalot* is the danger facing the visionary of being consumed by fire as he ascends to the *merkava* sphere. Here, the mere mention of the names of the 'holy creatures', who minister to the divine manifestation in the Holy of Holies, calls forth the whirling flames. 'According to another fragment, the mystic must be able to stand upright "without hands and feet", both having been burned' (G. Scholem). Enoch, in one of the later *Hekhalot* manuscripts, was, more fortunately, transformed into fire: '. . . forthwith my flesh was changed into flames, my sinews into flaming fire, my bones into coals of burning juniper, my eye-lids into sparks of lightnings, my eye-balls into firebrands, the hair of my head into hot flames, all my limbs into wings of burning fire . . .' (translated by H. Odeberg).

ANONYMOUS (fourth century to the beginning of the seventh century). The *piyutim* in this section originated in Palestine during the Byzantine rule. All of them, except for the last one, are unrhymed and employ various forms of alphabetic acrostics. The metre is largely based on word-count.

This is the earliest known poem on the *akeda*, the binding of Isaac, which is one of the favourite themes of medieval Hebrew poetry. The poem is remarkable for its unadorned language and its hammer-like rhythm, three words to a line. It follows the narrative of Genesis 22, with occasional Midrashic allusions (e.g. the ten trials of Abraham in stanza 2). The mention of the 'ashes' (stanza 7) recalls the Midrashic statement that 'although Isaac did not die, Scripture regards him as though he had died and his ashes lay piled on the altar'. Two later and more elaborate versions of the *akeda* theme are printed on pp. 357 and 379.

The opening section of a long poem on the advent of spring. Its simple, lyrical style is typical of the pre-classical period of the *piyut*.

An excerpt from a prayer for rain, of which only a fragment has survived. Though the language is simple, the exact meaning of certain expressions (e.g. 'the birthplace of water') is uncertain.

'How long will there be weeping' עַד אָנָה בְּכִיָּה 204

The earliest known post-biblical dirge (*kina*) on the destruction of the Temple. It includes many references to Lamentations. The refrain, here printed at the head of the excerpts from the poem, is repeated after every two verses. The first eight signs of the zodiac bewail the fate of Jerusalem, while the last four are practically accused of betrayal. For some unknown reason, the author has changed the order of the signs by placing Capricorn after Aquarius. This poem is traditionally recited on the eve of the Ninth of Av.

'What is frail man' אֱנוֹשׁ מָה יִּזְכֶּה 206

Takes many of its phrases from Job. Its style is rich in word-play and alliteration.

'Now let us proclaim' וּנְתַנֶּה תֹּקֶף 207

This description of the heavenly court marks one of the most solemn moments in the service for New Year and the Day of Atonement. According to a well-known legend, the hymn was composed in the tenth century by Rabbi Amnon of Mainz, who, having been mutilated by the Archbishop for refusing to convert, spoke its words as he died in the synagogue on New Year's Day.

YOSE BEN YOSE (? fourth or fifth century) is the earliest Palestinian *paytan* known by name. Practically nothing else is known of him; even his traditional epithet, *hayatom*, 'the orphan', has not been clarified. He is best known for his masterful *avodot* (see Note on Medieval Hebrew Genres, p. 51). It is presumed that he is the author of many of the early, anonymous poems discovered in the Genizah. In contrast to the *paytanim* who follow him, his poetry is distinguished by its simplicity and almost total lack of rhyme.

'I shall proclaim the mighty deeds of God' אַזְכִּיר גְּבוּרוֹת אֱלוֹהַּ 209

(Excerpts.) The longest of Yose's three *avodot*. It consists of twenty-two ten-verse stanzas (the last stanza has an additional eight verses), composing a tenfold alphabetic acrostic. The verses (here printed as two lines) are in the 'quadripartite rhythm', previously encountered in Talmudic laments (p. 192). This is the most typical metre of the pre-classical period. The rapid succession of verbs, the rich musical texture and the asyndetic style enliven even the technicalities of the ritual. The prose passages in the poem, including the high priest's confession, are taken verbatim from the Mishnah.

YANNAI (? sixth century), the first *paytan* of the classical period, lived in Palestine and was probably a cantor by profession. He was virtually unknown fifty years ago when I. Davidson discovered several of his compositions among the Genizah manuscripts. Subsequently, the ingenious research of M. Zulay resulted in the publication of over eight hundred poems, remarkable for their force, originality, and variety. One of the clues that led scholars to track Yannai down was a legend in a twelfth-century manuscript according to which he was the master of Eleazar ben Kallir (p. 89), 'but in all of Lombardy it [the only poem by Yannai preserved in the Ashkenazi ritual] is not recited, for it is said of Yannai that he grew jealous of his disciple Eleazar and planted a scorpion in his shoe that killed him'. However, the chronicler is careful to add: 'May God forgive all those who say this of Yannai – if it did not really happen.'

Yannai is the first *paytan* known to have employed rhyme, name-acrostics, and the complicated form of the *kerova* (especially the *kedushta*; see p. 52), which was to dominate liturgical poetry until the ninth century. The subject-matter of the *kedushta* is drawn from the biblical portion read on the particular Sabbath or feast-day for which the sequence was composed. Yannai's vocabulary is predominantly biblical, though he draws freely from the idiom of the Mishnah and the Midrash and excels in linguistic innovations. In many instances, his poems cannot be thoroughly understood without reference to their Midrashic sources. All of the following poems are taken from *kedushta* sequences:

'*Our eyes are weak with longing*' כָּלוּ עֵינֵינוּ 215

Based on the story of the 'dulled-eyed' Leah who was unloved by Jacob, envied by her sister Rachel (Genesis 29.17ff.) and, according to the Midrash, hated even by sea-travellers and land-travellers for being deceitful.

'*See how we stand before You*' רְאֵה עֲמִידָתֵנוּ 215

'*Who are feared by faithful angels*' אֲשֶׁר אֵימָתָךְ 216

This well-known hymn, in double alphabetic acrostic, has been attributed to Yannai. It exhibits a brilliant use of elaborate phonetic patterns and structural devices.

'*What have I gained?*' מַה יִּתְרוֹן לִי 218

When God reassured Abraham: 'Fear not . . . Your reward shall be very great' – Abraham countered: 'O Lord God, what can You give me, seeing that I continue childless . . .' (Genesis 15.1ff.). This monologue elaborates on the complaint of Abraham who, in anticipation, is already called 'the father'.

'*From Heaven to the Heaven of Heavens*' מִשָּׁמַיִם לִשְׁמֵי הַשָּׁמַיִם 218

An unrhymed hymn in praise of God, whose mystery had been challenged by the builders of the Tower of Babel (Genesis 11). The hymn (whose conclusion has not been recovered) rises through the seven heavens, which are vaulted over the earth, and culminates in an agitated account of the metamorphoses of the angels when the moment comes for them to utter 'Holy, holy, holy!'

'Into the wilderness' אַחַר הַמִּדְבָּר 219

This is based on the episode of the burning bush in Exodus 3 and incorporates several Midrashic legends. Moses, tending a flock in the wilderness, is being tested as the future shepherd of his people. He and his sheep are miraculously transported (lines 3, 7) to the site of the burning bush on Mount Horeb-Sinai (line 9), where God fortifies him for his subsequent encounters with divine fire.

'A fire that devours fire' אֵשׁ אֹֽשֶׁר הִיא 221

Enumerates the peculiar qualities of the celestial fire revealed to Moses in the unconsumed thorn-bush. This is the very same fire that, in years to come, would descend upon the altar in the Temple. The poem contained a complete alphabetic acrostic, but the manuscript is damaged in parts.

ELEAZAR BEN KALLIR or KILLIR (? sixth century), the outstanding representative of the classical *piyut*, probably lived in Palestine before the Arab conquest (635). Though his poems have figured prominently in printed rituals, and hundreds more have come to light in manuscript collections, his biography remains one of the great mysteries of Hebrew literary history. His radical innovations in the diction, style, and structure of the *piyut* had a great influence on the poets who succeeded him in Palestine and in other lands of the Near East and Europe. The 'Kallir style' involves a highly allusive use of language, packed with references to written and oral traditions. Accordingly, the *dramatis personae* of his poems, as well as various objects and place-names, are often designated by epithets and periphrases, many of which became the stock-in-trade of liturgical writing. The enigmatic nature of Kallir's language, which draws on the full range of post-biblical Hebrew, is further complicated by a wealth of neologisms and morphological oddities (which probably did not seem odd to his contemporaries). The structure of his *kerovot*, the patterns of rhyme, acrostic, repetition, and refrain, are far more complex than those of Yannai.

The 'Kallir style' was severely criticized in the twelfth century by Abraham ibn Ezra for having corrupted 'classical' (i.e. biblical) Hebrew and for being unduly obscure and esoteric (see p. 34). But Kallir – like other great innovators of the classical and late Eastern periods – was also capable of writing simple and direct poetry, both lyrical and dramatic, as some of the following selections demonstrate.

'Bound by affection' אֲגוּדִים בְּשִׂמְחָה 221

Part of a '*Kedushta* for a Bridegroom', which was sung in the synagogue on the Sabbath following the wedding. In the fifth stanza, the bride and groom become personifications of Israel and of God. The metre (except for the refrain) is four words to a line.

'The mother of children' אֵם הַבָּנִים 223

The four-word verses of the monorhymed quatrains, composing an alphabetic acrostic, are paired off in parallelistic units. But a great deal of rhythmical variety is achieved by the shift of the caesura and the use of internal rhyme. God's 'garden bed' (line 14) is the Land of Israel.

'Then, when she had had her full measure' אָז בִּמְלֹאת סֶפֶק 224

One of a series of dirges (*kinot*) composed for the Ninth of Av and included in the Ashkenazi ritual.

'A king who says to the sea' מֶלֶךְ הָאוֹמֵר לַיָּם 226

The contrast between the upper and lower worlds is a common theme in medieval liturgical poetry (see pp. 216 and 263).

'Then shall the gates of the garden of Eden' וְיִפָּתְחוּ שַׁעֲרֵי עֵדֶן 227

(Excerpts.) A rare example of extended narrative based on mythological subject matter. It is part of the final section of a monumental *kerova* for the Ninth of Av, whose complex design has not yet been fully clarified. The preceding sections combine lyrical, dramatic, and didactic elements in a description of the fall of Jerusalem. This is followed by an ecstatic account of the coming of the Messiah and the marvels of the 'end of days', when 'the seven classes of the righteous', seated under the Tree of Life in the garden of Eden, will be treated to the spectacle of a ferocious duel between the two monsters Behemoth and Leviathan. Afterwards both beasts, as well as the delicious Ziz, king of the birds, will be cooked and served to the pious. The gladiatorial contest and the banquet, as the Midrash points out, are meant to compensate 'the people who are near to Him' for having shunned pagan sports and abstained from unclean flesh. The poem draws heavily on the description of the mythological monsters in Job 40 and 41. It is composed of irregular monorhymed sections, varying in length from three to twenty verses. The absence of any fixed metrical scheme, the frequent use of word-rhyme, and the introduction of a new rhyme even in the middle of a sentence – all enhance the free, flowing rhythm of the narrative.

PHINEHAS HAKOHEN (fl. late eighth century), the last of the classical *paytanim*, lived in the vicinity of Tiberias. A prolific poet, he wrote *kerovot* for the feast days and a series of poems commemorating each of the twenty-four classes (*mishmarot*) of priests who officiated in turn at the Temple.

'And from this day on' וּמֵהַיּוֹם וָהָלְאָה 232

An excerpt from a lengthy *siluk*. The 'male and female' (lines 3, 6) refer to the 'Male Upper Waters' and 'Female Lower Waters' which were separated from each other on the second day of creation.

A choral *zulat* (part of a *yotser*-sequence; see Note on Medieval Genres, p. 53), and one of the finest examples of a ballad-like *piyut* in the classical period. It is based on the climactic encounter between Joseph, now Viceroy of Egypt, and his brothers, after the 'stolen' silver goblet turns up in Benjamin's bag (Genesis 43-45). Judah is terrified by the Viceroy's uncanny knowledge of their crime: the sale of Joseph to the Ishmaelites (Genesis 37) for twenty pieces of silver (with which, according to legend, each of the brothers bought himself a pair of shoes; line 16). The irony of the exchange is heightened by Joseph's refrain: 'the Revealer' is the all-knowing God, but Judah takes it to mean the avenging Viceroy who is using the silver cup for divination.

AMITTAI BEN SHEPHATIAH (late ninth century) was born in Southern Italy, the first European centre of Hebrew poetry in the Middle Ages. Both his grandfather and father had been noted *paytanim*, and he succeeded the latter as head of the yeshiva in his native Oria. His poems, which are among the best of the period, continue the tradition of the Palestinian school. In many hymns he inveighs against the oppressive edicts, especially the forcible conversions, imposed during the Byzantine rule.

'*The Lord, who revealed the end*'   אָדוֹן מַגִּיד מֵרֵאשִׁית   235

First section of a 'Bridegroom's *Yotser*' in which the six days of Creation are described as a series of preparations culminating in the First Marriage, with God in the role of host and best man. Written in rhymed tercets, with five words to a line, the poem contains a complete alphabetic acrostic. The fourth stanza, a quatrain which contains the poet's name, may have served as a refrain after every three stanzas.

'*When the humble one*'   אֶל עִיר גִּבּוֹרִים   238

A dramatic account of the dangers that assailed Moses when he ascended to heaven to receive the Law. Angelology, derived from *Hekhalot* literature, is a favourite theme of early Hebrew poetry in Italy. According to the Midrashic source from which this *ofan* borrows many of its expressions, the Angel of Death (last stanza) taught Moses 'the secret of preserving life'.

'*A man draws a figure on a wall*'   אָדָם צָר בַּכֹּתֶל   240

An extract from a lengthy *siluk* describing the growth and movement of the foetus in the womb. It is part of the climax of a 'Bridegroom's *Kedushta*', which was sung on the Sabbath following the wedding.

ANONYMOUS (ninth to eleventh century). All the poems in this section, except for 'Open the gates' and 'We drew near', contain various types of alphabetic acrostics.

'Open the gates to us' פְּתַח לָנוּ שַׁעַר 241

This beautiful poem is chanted as the sun is setting on the Day of Atonement, during the *ne'ila* ('closing') service. The name referred to the closing of the Temple gates at dusk and, by extension, to the closing of the heavenly gates. The poem may be a fragment.

'The days of summer are gone' יְמֵי הַקַּיִץ עָבְרוּ 241

'He who revealed wisdom' אֲשֶׁר גִּלָּה חָכְמָה 241

Opening section of an unrhymed narrative of Palestinian origin which was patterned on an earlier Aramaic model. Like other hymns that celebrate Israel's miraculous passage through the Sea of Reeds, it was intended for the liturgy of the Seventh Day of Passover.

'Four saw visions of God' אַרְבָּעָה רָאוּ 243

An intricate *ofan* for the Feast of Weeks. Each of the monorhymed stanzas – the first and last employ word-rhyme – ends with a scriptural quotation. Line 10 alludes to the legend that, upon hearing the first commandment, the Israelites 'flew back in horror twelve miles, until their souls fled from them'. The Lord then revived them with the dew that will, one day, bring the dead back to life.

'The earth's foundations shook' אַדְנֵי אֲדָמָה 245

A *piyut* for the Feast of Weeks, 'the festival of the giving of our Law'. When God decided to reveal the Torah, the mountains vied with each other for the honour of receiving His glory. Mount Carmel (stanza 4) moved down to the seashore so that the Shekinah could descend upon it whether it chose to rest on the sea or on the mainland. The refrain is repeated after each stanza.

'The Angel of Death was dispatched' מַלְאַךְ הַמָּוֶת 246

In some Midrashic versions, the Angel of Death volunteers to seize Moses' soul, after the angels tearfully refuse to do so. His attempts end in humiliation; Moses almost batters him to death with his holy staff, when a heavenly voice is heard: 'Let him be, Moses, for the world is in need of him.' Infuriated, the Angel makes a third attempt, not knowing that God (last stanza) had already given Moses the kiss of death.

'You shall not withhold' לֹא תְאַחֵר לְהָשִׁיב 247

This unique poem echoes the tone of the Ten Commandments, but the imperatives are here addressed by the *paytan* to God.

A remorseless description, in rabbinic idiom, of the moment of death. The 'drop of poison' (line 23) falls from the tip of the sword that is brandished by the Plunderer. Lines 36–41 refer to the eschatological Aggadah of the 'beating in the grave', *ḥibut hakever*, according to which the Angel of Death revives the buried corpse and beats it with a chain which is 'half fire and half iron'.

One of the earliest known Karaite *piyutim*, probably composed in Jerusalem in the ninth century. Its child-like simplicity contrasts sharply with the customary rabbinate style. The poem originated in the circle of the 'mourners for Zion' (*aveley Tsiyon*), a group of ascetics who spent their time lamenting the destruction of 'mother-Zion' and the dispersion of Israel.

The quotations which conclude each stanza of this *Kedusha* follow the sequence of Isaiah 6.2–4.

SA'ADIAH GAON (882–942), the father of medieval Jewish philosophy, was born in the Faiyum district in Egypt. From 928, except for a period of conflict with the exilarch, he held the post of *gaon* ('eminence') of the Academy of Sura in Babylonia (Iraq). A bold innovator in many areas, he translated the Bible into Arabic (which had replaced Aramaic as the principal language spoken by the Jews); edited the first 'scientific' prayer-book; and compiled the first comprehensive Hebrew dictionary, including a rhyming dictionary for the use of poets. He was the first to wed Hebrew poetry and philosophy. He introduced alternating rhyme, new types of *piyut* and a complex diction which, though highly individual, reasserted the supremacy of biblical usages. The following excerpts are from a monumental philosophical hymn in ten sections (composed for the Day of Atonement), which is based on the opening verse of Psalm 104:

SAMUEL HASHELISHI (died after 1012) was 'the third' (*hashelishi*) in order of importance in the Jerusalem Academy. In some of his earlier poems, before he had risen to that rank, the acrostic reveals him as 'Samuel *Harevi'i*' ('the Fourth'). He died in Egypt, after having witnessed and recorded, in prose and verse, the Muslim riots against the Jews of Fostat. Though his poetry belongs to the 'Sa'adiah school', his musical qualities distinguish him as the finest lyricist of the late Eastern period. An extremely prolific poet, his favourite form was the classical *yotser*. Some of his *piyutim* observe a strict word count. The following selection consists of independent sections of *yotser* sequences:

(Excerpts.) The biblical verses that occur after every stanza and determine its recurrent rhyme are taken from the passage in 1 Kings 2.1–12 describing David's death.

EZEKIEL HAKOHEN (fl. late tenth century) is one of a large group of late Eastern *paytanim* of whom practically nothing is known. His euphemistic Arabic surname, Al-Baṣir ('the Seeing') would suggest that he was blind. Some of the allusions in the following poem are based on the allegorical interpretation of the Song of Songs. In the third stanza, for instance, 'the spice-bearing mountains' refer to Mount Moriah, the site of Isaac's sacrifice as well as of the Temple; the 'fawn' alludes to God who 'leapt from Egypt to the Red Sea . . . and from Sinai He leaps to the future redemption'; the 'myrrh and henna' represent Abraham and Isaac. Each stanza ends with a biblical verse which sets the rhyme for the quatrain. In addition to two acrostics (the complete alphabet and the author's name), the poem makes skilful use of the caesura and of internal rhyme.

JOSEPH ALBARDANI (tenth century) was chief *ḥazan* in the Great Synagogue of Baghdad, and was succeeded in this post by his son and grandson. The following poem, attributed to Albardani, is based on a Midrashic elaboration of the episode in Exodus 14:

MOSES BEN KALONYMUS (fl. late tenth century) is one of the first *paytanim* known in Germany. He was probably born in Lucca (Lombardy), where the extensive Kalonymus family had played a leading role in the development of Hebrew poetry. His family was moved by one of the Carolingian emperors to the Rhineland city of Mainz (Mayence, Magenza) and served as the link between the Italian and Central European *piyut*. Only two of his compositions have survived, including a long and spirited *kerova* for the last day of Passover, of which the concluding section is given here. The 'army of fire' (last line of stanza 4) recalls the legend that the Lord caused fiery steeds to swim out upon the sea in order to lure the Egyptian charioteers. The struggle between the 'Prince of the Sea' and the 'Prince of Egypt' (last stanza) accords with the tradition that God first vents his anger upon the 'guardian angels' before punishing the nations entrusted to their care.

SIMEON BEN ISAAC (b. *c.*950), a native of Mainz, was the outstanding synagogal
poet of Ashkenazi Jewry. His distinctive style clearly reflects the influence of the
Palestinian classical school, of *merkava* mysticism, and of his older contemporary,
Moses ben Kalonymus. In several of his *piyutim*, he introduced his son's name in the
acrostic. A venerated Talmudic authority, he became the hero of many folk legends.
One tradition has it that his son embraced Christianity and rose to the rank of Pope.
When Simeon the Great went to Rome to plead his people's cause, he played chess
with the Pope and, by the style of his game, recognized him as his son.

'This fool who tricks and provokes'	אֱוִילִי הַמַּתְעֶה	262

Opening section of a penitential hymn, composed of four-word lines, for the after-
noon service of the Day of Atonement. Line 7 borrows a Talmudic image: 'Man's evil
inclination resembles a fly and is seated between the two valves of the heart.'

'Supreme King: mighty, exalted'	מֶלֶךְ עֶלְיוֹן	263

The subject-matter, structure and metre of these excerpts from a *kerova* for the New
Year recall the famous hymn (p. 216) attributed to Yannai.

DAVID BEN NASI (? eleventh century). An Eastern *paytan* whose identity remains
uncertain. His poems have been preserved in the Karaite prayer-book as well as in
the 'Byzantine ritual' (*maḥzor Roumania*) which was used by the Jews in the Balkans
and in Constantinople. The metre of the following poem (excerpts) is four words to
a line:

'My poor heart burns'	אֲמוּלָה לִבָּתִי	265

THE DEATH OF MOSES (eighth to eleventh century). The poems forming this
unusual sequence, here given in abridged form, were written by various hands in the
Near East. They were grouped in their present order by an anonymous later editor,
and from the sixteenth century onwards have appeared in several synagogue rites
printed in Italy. They are part of the liturgy of *Simḥat Torah* ('Rejoicing of the Law')
which marks both the conclusion and the renewal of the annual cycle of readings from
the Pentateuch. The rejoicing is accompanied by laments over the death of Moses, a
custom which was already current in Babylonia in the tenth century. The death of
Moses (*petirat Moshe*), like the binding of Isaac, is one of the most popular subjects
of liturgical poetry. (See also pp. 246 and 445.)

'Who went up to heaven?'	מִי עָלָה לַמָּרוֹם	266

The first and last poems of the sequence, both of which have a popular flavour, are
the only ones without some form of acrostic. The second stanza alludes to the legend
(elaborated in the poem on p. 238) that the angels sought to scorch Moses with their

fiery breath, but God spread His 'mantle' over him (Job 26.9) and told him to cling to the Throne of Glory.

'While I was yet in my mother's womb' אָז מֵרֶחֶם אִמִּי 266

The 'perfection' of Moses (line 2) refers to the tradition that he came forth circumcised from his mother's womb and on that very day began to walk and speak. In the *Italian Maḥzor* (1856), edited by S. D. Luzzatto, this *piyut* is prefaced by the remark that it is designed to move the worshippers to profuse weeping.

'All creatures were formed' אָז כָּל בְּרִיּוֹת 268

The dialogue form is often employed in the many Midrashim on the death of Moses which are woven into these poems. The last stanza (in which the 'staff of life' is, literally, the 'tree of life') is based on the legend that Moses will continue to be the great leader and teacher of his people in the world to come.

'I will not die!' לֹא אָמוּת 269

This has recently been identified by E. Fleischer as part of a *kedushta* written by Phinehas Hakohen (see p. 90) for the last portion of Deuteronomy. In the original 115-line poem, Moses is told that he must die for having struck the rock instead of speaking to it (Numbers 20.8–13). The final stanza reads: '. . . accept My constraint / and die by My kiss. / Even My loved and trusted ones must perish. / Say no more. / I have regretted My decree, / but what can I do? – This has been decreed!'

'This man, who was graced with light' אִישׁ אֲשֶׁר הִקְרִן 270

'The road I am about to take' אֹרַח זוּ אֵלֵךְ 271

'Jokhebed went to Egypt' אָזְלַת יוֹכֶבֶד 273

A literal Hebrew translation of a much earlier Aramaic *piyut*, for which no source has been found in the Midrash. Jokhebed's futile search is closely paralleled by Samael's quest for Moses (p. 246).

PART TWO: FROM THE TENTH TO THE EIGHTEENTH CENTURY

MENAHEM IBN SARUK (fl. middle of the tenth century), apparently the earliest secular poet in Spain, was born in Tortosa and moved at an early age to Cordoba. There he engaged in important linguistic research under the patronage of Ḥisdai ibn Shaprut, the Jewish statesman and physician to the caliph 'Abd al-Raḥman III. For some unknown reason, possibly accusations of heresy, Ibn Saruk fell into disgrace.

His patron's agents broke into his house on the holy Sabbath, beat him mercilessly and led him off to prison where he composed an impassioned 'scroll' in epistolary form. The complaint, of which excerpts are given below, is written in cadenced biblical style, with occasional rhymed passages. It is prefaced by the words: 'I adjure you by the Lord, the God of heaven and earth, and by the bones of all the prophets and seers, that you read this scroll in its entirety until the very end.'

'I shall state my case'   אֲנִי אֶעֱרֹךְ מִשְׁפָּט   277

DUNASH BEN LABRAT (died *c.*990) changed the course of Hebrew poetry by introducing quantitative metres and secular genres, verse-forms and images borrowed from the Arabic. He was also the first to employ the new metrical technique in sacred poetry. A native of Fez, he studied in Baghdad under Sa'adiah Gaon and later settled in Cordoba, where he became the opponent of Ibn Saruk at Ibn Shaprut's court. His radical innovations aroused a fierce polemic, mostly in verse, between the disciples of the rival philologists, and he was accused of 'destroying the holy tongue'.

'He said: "Do not sleep!"'   וְאוֹמֵר: אַל תִּישַׁן   280

This is the first wine song, and reflects the new courtly setting of Hebrew poetry. Rhythmically, it testifies to the initial awkwardness of adapting Hebrew to quantitative metrics. Its rhyme scheme, aaab, cccb, became one of the preferred patterns of the Spanish school. It is conceivable that the moralistic conclusion was meant to forestall criticism.

JOSEPH IBN ABITUR (*c.* 950-after 1024) was born in Merida and achieved fame as a scholar in Cordoba. When his bid for the position of head of the yeshiva failed, he was placed under a ban by his opponents and fled to the East. He lived in Palestine and neighbouring countries from the end of the tenth century and is reported to have died in Damascus. The first great Spanish *paytan*, his many hundreds of *piyutim* continue the tradition of the Eastern school and are often indebted to Sa'adiah. Many of his formal and thematic innovations became standard practice in the Spanish *piyut*. He composed only one poem in the Arabic-inspired metre, a threnody on the persecutions that took place in Palestine when Bedouin tribes invaded the country in 1024. The following *seliha*, attributed to Ibn Abitur, is somewhat unusual for its personal tone. The rhyme of the first stanza is dictated by the biblical refrain, and recurs in the concluding 'couplet' of each subsequent stanza (bbbaa, cccaa).

'I know, my God'   יָדַעְתִּי, אֱלֹהַי   281

ISAAC IBN KHALFUN (*c.*965-after 1020). Born in Spain or North Africa, he lived in Cordoba for a long period, and travelled extensively, eking out a living by composing encomiums to capricious patrons. The first professional Hebrew poet, his verse is entirely secular and written in the Arabic *qasida* form (see Note on the Systems of Hebrew Versification, p. 63). He introduced a new note of elegance into Hebrew poetry and found biblical 'precedents' for motifs and metaphors taken from Arabic verse.

This was written to encourage his old friend Samuel Hanagid, after he had been deposed from a high-ranking post and two of his relatives had been murdered (1020). The 'spitting' and 'casting of the shoe' (lines 2–3) recall the degradation of the brother who refuses to perform a levirate marriage (Deuteronomy 25.9).

From a reply to a conciliatory 'song of friendship' by Hanagid, after the two had fallen out during a wine-feast. As was customary in such exchanges, the answer is cast in the same metre as the poem that prompted it.

SAMUEL HANAGID (993–1056), the first major poet of 'the golden age', was born in Cordoba and was among those who fled the capital when the Berber hordes destroyed it in 1013. A renowned Talmudist and statesman, he was the first Spanish Jew to be granted the title Nagid ('Prince'). He was appointed vizier shortly after the accession to the throne (1038) of Badis, the Berber ruler of Granada. In this capacity the Nagid, or Isma'il ibn Nagrela as he was known in Arab circles, commanded the armies of Granada in a series of victorious campaigns against Seville and her allies, which lasted from 1038 to 1056. The many poems he sent to his son from the battlefield constitute a unique poetic diary of his tempestuous life. He died after a strenuous campaign and was succeeded as vizier and commander by his son, Yehosef. Ten years later Yehosef Hanagid was assassinated and the Jewish community of Granada was massacred by the Muslims. Hanagid's vast knowledge of Hebrew and Arabic culture is apparent in his technical mastery and in his rich repertoire of forms and motifs. He excels in the fusion of epic and lyrical elements.

The conventional opening, as if in reply to an interlocutor, is also found in Ben Labrat's wine-song (p. 280). Here, the convention is somewhat modified by the poet's indirect answer.

Like the previous poem, this is taken from the collection *Ben Kohelet* ('Son of Ecclesiastes'), in which the dominant themes are the sorrows and vanities of life and the fear of death.

'Then Av – the month of ancient woe –' וַיֵּצֵא אָב 286

From a poem describing his first major battle, against the army of Almeria, which was ruled by the Slav eunuch Zuhair and his fanatical Arab vizier Ibn Abbas. The Nagid, who prided himself on being 'the David of his generation', borrowed the title of this poem (*Shira*, 'Song') from Psalm 18. It consists of 149 lines in order to correspond with the number of chapters in Psalms. The war poems were grouped, in his lifetime, in *Son of Psalms.*

'See my distress today' רְאֵה הַיּוֹם בְּצָרָתִי 288

The son referred to in the last line is Yehosef, who, at his father's request, began to copy and arrange the Nagid's poems when he was eight and a half years old. The superscriptions were written by Yehosef in Arabic.

'Good herald, now tell me' מְבַשֵּׂר טוֹב 289

The injunction at the end of these bloodthirsty verses, that they should be recited in synagogues and taught to children, stemmed from the Nagid's conviction that his personal success represented a triumph for the entire people. At the end of *Shira* he even requests that his victory be celebrated as a popular feast, 'a second Purim', throughout the Jewish world.

'Shall I forever live in a tent' הֲלָעַד אֲנִי שׁוֹכֵן 291

'War is at first' קְרָב דּוֹמֶה 291

From *Son of Proverbs*, a collection of over 1,000 aphorisms, many of which draw upon Arabic, Persian and Greek sources.

'No master will hire you' לֹא יַעֲבִידְךָ מוֹשְׁלְךָ 292

'The earth is a prison' אֶרֶץ לְאָדָם בֵּית כְּלוּא 292

'O you merry-makers' אוֹהֲבֵי יָמִים 292

'Reflect, and you will realize' שִׁית לִבְּךָ 292

'Is there a sea between me and you' הֲיָם בֵּינִי וּבֵינֶךָ 293

One of a series of dirges on the death of his elder brother Isaac to whom he was particularly devoted.

'Are you asleep, my friend?' רֵעִי, הֲתִישַׁן 293

(Opening section.) A younger Arab contemporary of the Nagid wrote that 'he was also proficient . . . in the various branches of mathematics, and his lore of astronomy also surpassed that of the astronomers . . .'. The long list of achievements is prefaced by the remark: 'This accursed Jew was in himself one of the most perfect men, although God had denied him His guidance' (quoted by J. Schirmann).

Appears both as an independent poem (in *Son of Ecclesiastes*) and as part of the 'introduction' or 'proem' to a panegyric (in *Son of Psalms*). It is a striking example of the autonomy of genres in the long poem, which often resembles a series of short poems on different themes.

Descriptions of nature often play an important role in the Nagid's wine songs, which are among the finest in Spanish Hebrew poetry.

The love poems are addressed not only to the female *ofra* or *tseviya* ('doe') but also, in the Arabic manner, to the male counterpart *ofer* or *tsevi* who, in this poem, is the cup-bearer. Apparently, there was still some opposition to love poems in the sacred tongue and Yehosef, in his Arabic introduction to the *diwan*, claimed that they were written allegorically (like Solomon's Song of Songs).

JOSEPH IBN ḤISDAI (fl. early eleventh century) was one of a group of scholars in Saragossa, which became a cultural centre after the destruction of Cordoba (1013). His son converted to Islam and served as vizier to three rulers of the Banu Hud dynasty. The following poem is the 'introduction' to a panegyric addressed to his childhood friend, Samuel Hanagid (who replied with a poem in the identical metre). Lines 21–24 are the surprising 'transition verse' which leads into the 'body', or actual theme, of the poem. Written around 1045, it is the only work of Ibn Ḥisdai which has survived. It was much admired for its involved rhetoric and, at a time when poems were rarely titled, came to be known as 'The Unique Song' (*Shira Yetoma*). This title was based on a bilingual pun in the poem, where *yetoma* means both 'orphan' (Hebrew) and 'unique' (Arabic).

HAYA GAON (939–1038), a halakhic scholar of immense authority, was the last *gaon* of the Academy in Pumbedita, a post which he held for forty years after succeeding his father, Sherira Gaon, in 998. All his secular poetry and some of his *piyutim* were written in quantitative metres. Though he may have been the first poet in Babylonia to employ the new Spanish prosody, he clearly adhered to the late Eastern tradition. The following *seliḥa* is one of a series of unrhymed, alphabetic compositions for the Ninth of Av, modelled after the Psalms. They describe the bitterness of exile with unusual power and boldness. He was the first to renounce rhyme in a composition intended for liturgical use.

ABRAHAM HAKOHEN (fl. early eleventh century), a Palestinian *paytan*, is known for his 'poems from prison', written in Egypt in 1024, after he was jailed for defaulting on a debt. These poems are of special interest because, like those of Samuel Hashelishi (p. 93), they record a personal experience in a classical, liturgical form, which could hardly have been intended for public service.

A striking description of the narcissus.

SOLOMON IBN GABIROL (1021/22–*c.* 1055), one of the greatest Hebrew poets of all time, was born in Malaga, lived most of his life in Saragossa and died in Valencia before 1058. Having decided to dedicate his life to the pursuit of poetry and philosophy, he depended on the precarious support of wealthy benefactors. He was conscious of his genius at an early age –

> I am the master and the song is my slave . . .
> and though I am only sixteen years of age
> my heart has the wisdom of an eighty-year old!

and his 'cantankerous soul' embroiled him in frequent conflicts. His secular poetry includes nature and love poems of unusual beauty; panegyrics, laments and riddles. But it was his turbulent personal poems, expressing his struggle against fate ('Time') and society, that struck a new note of introspective complexity. His liturgical poems, though entirely different in tone, are no less original. He was the first to introduce the full range of Hispano-Arabic conventions into the *piyut*. His compact and lyrical *reshuyot* (sing. *reshut*, 'prelude') served as a model for generations of poets. His monumental philosophic poem *Keter Malkhut* ('The Kingly Crown' – translated into English by B. Lewis) alternates rhymed, rhythmical prose and free, rhymed verse. It draws on early mystical Midrashim, neoplatonic cosmology and Muslim astronomy. His major theoretical prose work, *Mekor Ḥayim* ('The Source of Life'), enjoyed a curious history. Written in Arabic, but preserved only in a Latin translation (*Fons*

Vitae), it was attributed to Avicebron and regarded as the work of a Muslim or, in scholastic circles, Christian theologian. It was only in the nineteenth century that 'Avicebron' was shown to be a corruption of Gabirol's name.

(Excerpts.) The light of the moon is here equated with Wisdom. In an elegy on the death of his father, Wisdom appears and reproaches him for neglecting her by his prolonged mourning.

One of three elegies on the death of his friend and patron, Jekuthiel ibn Ḥasan, vizier in Saragossa, who was murdered by political rivals in 1040.

The opening and closing sections of a poem describing his illness, presumably a serious skin disease. In other poems he complains of his weak physique, small stature and ugliness.

'The paradox, which had served his predecessors as a rhetorical device, became in Gabirol's poems a means through which the poet expresses his divided soul' (D. Pagis).

Conclusion of a poem of self-praise. This was a conventional genre (see Ibn Khalfun's poem, p. 284), which suited Gabirol's temperament.

'Introduction' to a complaint on the departure of friends. Like the 'introductions' by Hanagid (p. 295) and Ibn Ḥisdai (p. 302), it has little to do with the theme of the poem.

This and the following five poems are *reshuyot* (preludes) to various prayers.

A dialogue between 'daughter-Zion' and God concerning the Messiah. According to Abraham ibn Ezra, Gabirol was among those who tried to predict the Day of Judgement on the basis of astronomical calculations.

The relationship between Zion, God and the Messiah is expressed in the form of a popular love poem. This seems to have been one of Gabirol's many innovations, like the direct address to the supreme 'soul' (Wisdom) in the following poem.

A prelude to *Nishmat*, the Sabbath morning prayer beginning 'The breath of (*nishmat*) every living being shall bless Your name . . .' As is customary, the last line of the *reshut* alludes to its liturgical function.

ISAAC IBN GHIYYAT (1038–89). As head of the yeshiva in his native town of Lucena, he was the teacher of the poets Joseph ibn Sahl and Moses ibn Ezra. His hundreds of *piyutim* (few secular poems have survived) are written almost entirely in the new Andalusian style. The last great innovator in the field of the *piyut*, he achieved special distinction in his melodious *muwashshaḥat* (girdle poems; see p. 30), a secular Arabic form first used as a vehicle for liturgical poetry by Gabirol.

An *ahava* in the form of a girdle poem employing internal rhymes.

The language of love poetry is used in this girdle poem to deplore the flight of the 'gazelle' (God) from the poet's 'dwelling' (Zion).

LEVI IBN ALTABBAN (fl. late eleventh century) lived in Saragossa. Little is known of his life. His talent for harmonious lyricism is manifest in his short *reshuyot* and in *ahavot* and *me'orot* which occasionally take the form of a dialogue between God and Israel.

Like others of his poems in which the acrostic yields LeVI, this philosophical *reshut* was mistakenly attributed to Judah Halevi.

Drought is a frequent theme in Spanish *piyutim*. The acrostic is incomplete and it is possible that a few verses have been lost.

BENJAMIN BEN ZERAH (fl. late eleventh century) is generally listed as an Ashkenazi *paytan*, but his style seems to indicate that he lived in the Byzantine Empire. He was called *Ba'al Hashem* ('Master of the Divine Name') probably because of his extensive usage of the names of God and the angels in his *merkava* poems. In the following *ofan*, the third stanza refers to the tradition that the 'song-uttering' angels are instantly consumed by fire if they deviate from the tempo by so much as a 'hair's breadth'. The 'gigantic beast' (last stanza) is an angel named Israel ('on his forehead is engraved ISRAEL'), who is stationed in the middle of heaven and who initiates the angelic song.

JOSEPH IBN SAHL (died *c.* 1123) occupied the position of *dayan* in Cordoba for the last ten years of his life. Only a few of his poems have been preserved. Moses ibn Ezra praised him for his biting satires.

MOSES IBN EZRA (*c.* 1055–after 1135), a consummate craftsman and the leading theoretician of the Spanish school, was born in Granada, where he was granted an honorific Arabic title. In 1090 the Jewish community was destroyed by the Berber Almoravids, and the members of his family dispersed. It is not known why Ibn Ezra, isolated and impoverished, remained in Granada. About five years later his life was endangered in a mysterious episode involving his elder brother's daughter, and he fled to Christian Spain. For the next forty years he wandered through 'the exile of Edom', an embittered refugee in search of patrons. Towards the end of his life he composed his Arabic treatise *The Book of Conversations and Memories*. This unique work, based on Arabic poetics, is an invaluable source for the history of Andalusian Hebrew poetry. It deals at length with poetics and the theory of 'ornamentation' and describes the rhetorical figures. In keeping with the ideal of *tsaḥot* ('purity' of rhetoric), these figures are primarily illustrated by reference to the Bible. Some of his long secular poems suffer from excessive ornamentation. However, his shorter meditative pieces and his sensual love poems are compact and beautiful. He was the first to write homonymic poems, on the model of the Arabic *tajnis*. In his extensive liturgical poetry, he deftly wove together Jewish religious and Arabic secular elements. He came to be known as *Hasalaḥ* ('the supplicant') in acknowledgement of his moving *seliḥot*, many of which found a place of honour in synagogue rites.

'The garden put on a coat' כְּתְנוֹת פַּסִּים 323

This description of spring, in terms of a royal procession, makes fleeting allusions to Joseph's ornamental tunic (line 1; Genesis 37.3); to the release from prison of King Jehoiachim who 'took off his prison garb' (lines 4–5; 2 Kings 25.27–29); and, by inference, to Joseph's appointment as vizier (Genesis 41.40–43) after being released from the dungeon and dressed in fine robes.

'The cold season' זְמַן הַקֹּר 323

Metaphors of growth and renewal in Ibn Ezra's poetry are almost always borrowed from the domain of the weaver or goldsmith (lines 5–6, 18). Many of these figures originate in biblical descriptions of the Tabernacle's ornaments and the priests' clothes.

'Caress the breasts' דַּדֵּי יְפַת תֹּאַר 324

This is, like the following poem, a *muwashshaḥ*. The poet must have had such passionate works in mind when, in old age, he renounced his love poems as the 'mistakes of unbridled youth'.

'My heart's desire' תַּאְוַת לְבָבִי 325

'Truly, God created the apple' וְתַפּוּחַ, אֱמֶת 326

'Love-sick, she weeps' חוֹלַת אֲהָבִים 326

The solution to this riddle is: a candle.

'Let man remember' יִזְכֹּר גֶּבֶר 327

'I shall always seek' פְּנֵי הָאֵל לְבַד 327

'My thoughts roused me' הֱקִיצוּנִי שְׂעִפַּי 327

The influence of Hanagid's *Son of Ecclesiastes* can be felt in Ibn Ezra's reflective poems.

'Who will take revenge' הֲדָמִי תִדְרְשׁוּ 328

The description of the suffering and insomnia of the abandoned lover during the 'night of wandering' is a stock element in love poems and complaints. In this instance, it is part of the proem to a panegyric.

'The runnels of this river' וְנָהָר, נְהָרוֹ 328

An invitation to a party in the poet's garden. The river is part of the conventional décor of wine feasts.

'Play for me, minstrel' בִּי, הַמְנַגֵּן 329

This address to the musician follows a detailed description of a wine feast. Lines 21–2 are the 'transition verse' which leads to an account of the poet's sorrows in exile.

'My thoughts rouse me' יְעִירוּנִי שְׂעִפַּי 330

A *pizmon* (strophic *seliḥa* with a refrain) for the Day of Atonement. Like many of the *piyutim* of the Spanish school, it is written in a syllabic, rather than quantitative, metre. Each line consists of nine syllables, divided into units of three and six. In the first three lines the shorter units are rhymed.

'With all my soul' נַפְשִׁי אִוִּיתִיךָ בַּלָּיְלָה 331

Excerpts from a *mustajab* (or *mustajib*) for the Day of Atonement. A Spanish type of *seliḥa*, it is composed of unmetrical, four-line stanzas. The biblical verse, which serves as the refrain, comes at the head of the poem. Its last word is then repeated in the rhyme position in the biblical quotation which concludes each stanza (x, aaax, bbbx). In the last stanza of this poem, 'my daughter' refers both to the soul and to the people of Israel; 'night' is also meant metaphorically as 'the darkness of exile'.

'I rouse my slumbering thoughts' הֱקִיצוֹתִי תְּנוּמַת רַעְיוֹנַי 333

Opening of a meditative poem, written in exile. The Arabic superscription in Ibn Ezra's *diwan* reads: 'And he said when he was comforting his soul and turning to abstinence.'

JUDAH HALEVI (before 1075–after 1141) was born in Muslim Tudela, on the borders of Christian Spain. At an early age he travelled to the centres of Jewish scholarship in Andalusia. In Granada, he formed a lasting friendship with Moses ibn Ezra which is recorded in a moving exchange of poems. Later, Halevi settled in Toledo, the capital of Castile under Alfonso VI, where he practised medicine, apparently in the service of the king. However, the murder in 1108 of his benefactor, Solomon ibn Ferrizuel, at the hands of Christian mercenaries, and the attacks upon the Jews in Toledo in the following year, prompted him to return to the Muslim area, where he made his home in Cordoba. His personal experiences in Christian and Muslim Spain during the Reconquest ('Between the armies of Seir and Kedar my army is lost . . . when they fight their wars, we fall in their downfall'), and his philosophical views concerning the meaning of diaspora and the path to redemption, culminated in his decision to emigrate to the Holy Land. Shortly before his departure he completed his influential treatise *The Book of Argument and Proof in Defence of the*

Despised Faith. Translated from Arabic into Hebrew in the twelfth century, it came to be known as *The Book of the Kuzari* because it is composed as a dialogue between a Jewish scholar (the *ḥaver*) and the king of the Khazars, who had converted to Judaism in the eighth century. In September 1140, after an arduous voyage, Halevi arrived in Alexandria and was received with great acclaim. He died six months later, after a period of intensive creativity. His poetic corpus of secular and sacred works consists of over a thousand compositions which attest to an unrivalled mastery of language and musical patterns and a profound lyrical expression of religious and national themes. His 'songs of Zion' are, perhaps, his most famous works. No Hebrew poet since the Psalmists had sung the praises of the Holy Land with such passion. The longing for Zion, the pain of parting from his cultural environment, the perilous sea voyage – all these topics were uncommon in the poetry of the time.

'Even since You were' מֵאָז מְעוֹן הָאַהֲבָה 333

This is the most extreme expression in Halevi's poetry of his view that the suffering of Israel is a sanctification of the name of God. In the *Kuzari* the *ḥaver* maintains that Israel could have hastened the deliverance by submitting willingly to the yoke of exile.

'My love, have you forgotten' יְדִידִי, הֲשָׁכַחְתָּ חֲנוֹתָךְ 334

'O sleeper, whose heart' יָשֵׁן – וְלִבּוֹ עֵר 334

The opening line of this *reshut* refers to Song of Songs 5.2 which was allegorically interpreted to mean that Israel 'slept' in the darkness of exile but its heart yearned to rejoin the Shekinah. The 'star' (line 3; Numbers 24.17) represents the Messiah. Various messianic movements were active in Halevi's time and he once dreamt that the redemption would come in 1130.

'The lovely doe' יַעֲלַת חֵן, מְמֻעוֹנָהּ 335

An *ahava* which, like the previous poem, employs the phraseology of the Song of Songs. The 'lover' and 'gazelle' represent God.

'O you that sleep' יְשֵׁנָה בְּחֵיק יַלְדוּת 335

A *reshut* for *Nishmat*.

'Lord, all my longing' אֲדֹנָי, נֶגְדְּךָ כָּל תַּאֲוָתִי 336

A metrical *bakasha* ('supplication'), a type of personal *seliḥa* introduced by early Spanish *piyut*. Characteristically, its ending repeats its beginning.

'I am running towards' לִקְרַאת מְקוֹר חַיֵּי אֱמֶת 337

Takes, as its point of departure, Psalms 36.10: 'With You is the fountain of life; by Your light do we see light.'

TABLE OF POEMS

'Lord, where shall I find You?' יָהּ, אָנָה אֶמְצָאֲךָ 338

An *ofan* in the rhyme-form of a *muwashshaḥ*, but written in the special syllabic metre which was exclusively used in Spain in strophic *piyutim*. In this case, there are twelve syllables to a line, divided into units of six and six by internal rhymes. It is based on Solomon's prayer (2 Chronicles 6.18), on a verse from the daily *Kedusha* ('Blessed be the glory of the Lord from His place'), and on the Midrashic paradox: 'The Lord is the place of His world, but the world is not His place'; that is, the world is contained in Him, not He in the world.

'Do these tears know' הֲיֵדְעוּ הַדְּמָעוֹת 339

An epitaph for the tombstone of an unidentified 'Rabbi Abraham'.

'Alas, my daughter' הָהּ, בִּתִּי, הֲשָׁכַחַתְּ 339

'On that day' יוֹם אַכְפִּי הִכְבַּדְתִּי 340

This lament, in the *muwashshaḥ* form, for the Ninth of Av elaborates on a Talmudic legend concerning the murder of the prophet Zechariah, who was stoned in the Temple-court by order of King Joash (2 Chronicles 24.21–22).

'O graceful doe' יַעֲלַת חֵן, רַחֲמִי לֵבָב 342

Vulgar Arabic – and sometimes Romance – was generally employed in the final couplet (*kharja*) of the secular Hebrew *muwashshaḥ*. The *kharja* was, in most cases, borrowed from popular Arabic or Romance songs.

'My love washes' עָפְרָה תְכַבֵּס 343

The Arabic superscription in the *diwan* reads: 'An improvisation composed upon passing by a river where washerwomen were laundering.'

'Why, O fair one' מַה לָּךְ, צְבִיָּה 343

Excerpts.

'O my fair youth' בִּי הַצְּבִי 344

Another *muwashshaḥ*, in a characteristic popular vein.

'Gently, my hard-hearted' אַט לִי, חֲזַק לֵבָב 346

Opening section of the reply to a song of friendship (by Solomon ibn al-Muallim) which had greeted Halevi's move to Granada.

'Why put your trust' מַה תַּאֲמִין בִּזְמַן 346

'Th slaves of Time' עַבְדֵי זְמַן 347

'My heart is in the East' לִבִּי בְמִזְרָח 347

Zion was 'in the domain of Edom' (line 4) after the conquest of Jerusalem by the Crusaders in 1099.

'O Zion, will you not ask'   צִיּוֹן, הֲלֹא תִשְׁאֲלִי   347

Excerpts from the most famous of Halevi's Zion poems. Though not intended for the liturgy, it was soon included in the laments for the Ninth of Av and gave rise to scores of imitations ('Zionides'), many of which entered the Ashkenazi rite. The sixteenth-century legend, that Halevi was trampled to death by an Arab horseman as he was reciting this poem at the gates of Jerusalem, is widely known from Heine's portrayal in *Hebrew Melodies* (1851). The gates of Zion 'face the gates of heaven' (line 12) because, according to rabbinic belief, there was a celestial Temple corresponding to, and exactly opposite, the earthly one.

'Let not your heart tremble'   וְאַל יִמּוֹט בְּלֵב יַמִּים   349

From a poem in which he exhorts himself to set forth on the voyage to Zion. The description of the storm at sea partly echoes Psalm 107.23-32.

'This wind of yours'   זֶה רוּחֲךָ, צַד מַעֲרָב   350

The western wind brings him closer to his destination. This, and the following poems, were written during the long sea journey.

'Greetings to the kinsfolk'   קִרְאוּ עֲלֵי בָנוֹת   351
'Has a flood come'   הֲבָא מַבּוּל   352

ABRAHAM IBN EZRA (1092-1167) was born in Tudela and lived for a time in Cordoba. In 1140 he left Spain and travelled extensively in Italy, Provence, Northern France and England. During these years he played a crucial role in disseminating the prosody and poetics of the Spanish school in Western Europe. His own poetry reveals some of the trends that began to emerge in the secular poetry of Christian Spain which, after the Almohad conquest of Andalusia, became the new centre of Hebrew creativity. In his liturgical poetry, Ibn Ezra favoured intricate varieties of the *muwash-shah*. He distinguished himself as a grammarian, biblical commentator and mathematician. He was also the author of a mystical allegory in rhymed prose.

'When I come to the patron's house'   אַשְׁכִּים לְבֵית הַשָּׂר   353

Ibn Ezra introduced the character of the penniless roving bard into Hebrew poetry.

'The heavenly sphere'   גַּלְגַּל וּמַזָּלוֹת   353
'However I struggle'   אִינַע לְהַצְלִיחַ   353

Both poems may reflect his belief in astrology, which he tried to reconcile with the faith in providence and free will; here, however, the tone is humorous.

'I have a cloak' מְעִיל יֶשׁ לִי 353

Generally attributed to Ibn Ezra.

'I bow down' אֶשְׁתַּחֲוֶה אַפַּיִם אַרְצָה 354

An unrhymed penitential prayer, in free biblical cadence (*rehuta*). The author's name is repeated twice in the acrostic.

ISAAC IBN EZRA (died middle of the twelfth century), one of Abraham's five sons, was born in Spain and seems to have accompanied Halevi on his voyage to Alexandria in 1140. He then proceeded to Baghdad where he converted to Islam (after 1143), probably under the influence of his patron, the philosopher-physician Abu al-Barakat, who had changed his faith at the age of sixty. Abraham composed two moving laments on his son's death.

'Go and weep' בְּכִי תִשְׂאוּ 356

Last section of a poem which was first published in 1965 by J. Schirmann in *New Hebrew Poems from the Genizah*, a collection of over 300 previously unknown compositions.

JUDAH SAMUEL ABBAS (died 1167), a native of Fez and resident of Aleppo, is the author of the most famous *akeda* in Hebrew poetry. It served as a model for many imitations, including one by Maimonides. It is chanted to an impressive melody in Sephardic communities before the blowing of the *shofar* during the New Year service.

'When the gates of mercy' עֵת שַׁעֲרֵי רָצוֹן 357

The binding of Isaac is portrayed as a ritual sacrifice, with Abraham performing 'his priestly office' (line 19). Isaac asks to be bound securely (lines 51–2) lest he shrink from the knife and make the offering unacceptable to God. These Midrashic motifs also appear in the *akeda* by Ephraim of Bonn (p. 379). According to legend, Elijah (last line) girded his loins with the ram's skin and its right horn will be blown in the days of the Messiah to proclaim the end of exile. The poem is in the form of a metrical *pizmon*: the last line of the opening quatrain serves as the refrain, and the quatrain's rhyme is repeated in the last line of each stanza.

MOSES DAR'I (fl. *c.* 1200), the foremost poet of medieval Karaism, was born in Alexandria and spent time travelling in Syria and Palestine. He skilfully cultivated the poetic genres of the Spanish school. Some of his poems were written in Hebrew and Arabic.

'I said to the spying lady' לַחֲבַצֶּלֶת שָׁרוֹן נַמְתִּי 360

TABLE OF POEMS

ANONYMOUS (eleventh to thirteenth century). This section is a miscellany of poems from Egypt, Spain, Italy, France and Germany.

'A mouth as round' וּפֶה עָגֹל כְּטַבַּעַת 360

A unique and unusually detailed description of woman's attributes by a poet who resided in Damietta, in northern Egypt. It serves as the 'introduction' to a song of friendship addressed to his benefactor.

'This gazelle' עֹפֶר אֲשֶׁר לִבִּי 361

'Put my cup' תְּנָה כוֹסִי כְּמוֹ יָדִי 362

'Lead your camels' לְאַט מִשְׁכָה גְמַלֶּיךָ 362

According to the superscription, this was written as the poet took leave of his friend.

'The fawn gives me' צְבִי – יֵין הָרֶקַח 362

A *muwashshaḥ* written by a member of the Spanish Ḥisdai family in praise of a fifteen-year-old 'fawn'.

'You might as well say' אִמְרוּ לְרֹאשׁ פֶּתֶן 364

A *me'ora* for the eighth day of the Feast of Booths.

'Creatures of flame' יְקוּדֵי אֵשׁ 365

An *ofan* for the fifth Sabbath after Passover.

'Shun the man' אֱנוֹשׁ רוֹצֶה 366

An extract from a long moralistic meditation, *The Foundation of Religious Fear*, in rhymed tercets, written in Italy.

'Like clay in the hands' כִּי הִנֵּה כַּחֹמֶר 367

A series of variations patterned on Jeremiah 18.6: '. . . like clay in the hand of the potter, so are you in My hand, house of Israel'. This *piyut*, believed to be of French origin, is chanted before the open Ark during the evening service of Yom Kippur.

'Come with us' קוּמִי לְכִי 368

A lament for the Ninth of Av, probably of German origin, which contrasts the troops of the Crusaders with the Israelite camps in biblical times. The invitation to the 'smitten' daughter of Zion to join in the march to the Holy Land has not been found elsewhere in the literature.

A beautiful hymn which is included in the morning 'Prayer Before Prayer' of some rites. Lines 19–21 refer to the Midrash that God, unlike man, never confuses the deposits in His trust: 'Has a man ever risen at dawn and looked for his soul and not found it?' In Hebrew, each stanza ends with the word 'morning'.

A mystical prayer traditionally attributed to the second-century *tanna* Neḥunya ben Hakana. It probably originated in the circles of *Ḥasidey Ashkenaz*, a pietist movement among the Jews of Germany and France. Each of the seven lines consists of six words; the forty-two words correspond to the forty-two-letter Name of God, which is formed by the initial letters of all the words.

Excerpts from a *seliḥa* describing the massacre of the Jews of Mainz by the Crusaders and burghers on 27 May 1096. After they had retreated to the bishop's fortified courtyard (stanza 5), more than 1,000 Jews met their deaths rather than submit to conversion.

DAVID BAR MESHULLAM OF SPEYER (twelfth century) was received in 1090 by the Emperor Henry IV as one of the representatives of the Jewish community. The following *seliḥa* for the eve of Yom Kippur describes the mass suicides in Speyer during the First Crusade (1096) in terms of ritual sacrifice. The 'royal purple' (line 6) is the garment which, according to tradition, God dips in the blood of the martyrs and which He will put on on the day of judgement. The joy of 'sanctifying the Name' (stanza 8) is a recurrent theme in the chronicles and *piyutim* of this period and is also found in late Midrashim on the *akeda*: ' While Abraham was building the altar, Isaac kept handing him the wood and the stones. Abraham was like a man who builds a wedding house for his son, and Isaac was like a man getting ready for the wedding feast . . .' (quoted by S. Spiegel).

EPHRAIM OF REGENSBURG (1110–75), a renowned Tosafist, studied in France in his youth, lived in Speyer and Worms, and finally settled in Regensburg, where he became a member of the *bet din*. His poetry reflects the horrors of the Regensburg massacre (1137), when the Jews were dragged to the Danube and forced to accept baptism, and of the Second Crusade (1146–7). He was influential in introducing Spanish quantitative metres into Ashkenazi liturgical poetry. His *piyutim*, and those of his disciples Ephraim of Bonn and Barukh of Mainz, represent the finest artistic achievements of the late Ashkenazi school.

Last section of a long alphabetic *zulat* in rhymed tercets. The metre is three words to a line, and the last line of each stanza alludes to a biblical verse.

EPHRAIM OF BONN (1132–1200) was thirteen when the violence of the Second Crusade erupted. He and his relatives found refuge in the fortress of Wolkenburg, under the protection of the Bishop of Cologne. In old age he again narrowly escaped death by leaving Neuss only three days before its Jews were massacred (1186). His *Sefer Zekhira* ('Book of Remembrance'), in which he recorded the decrees and persecutions of the Second and Third Crusades, is an important historical source for the martyrology of the Jews in Germany, France, Austria and England. In characteristic Ashkenazi fashion, his *piyutim* draw heavily on Talmudic and rabbinic idiom and employ stylistic devices of the Palestinian school. At the same time, he occasionally uses a limited range of quantitative metres. He is the author of a commentary on ancient *piyutim*.

An elaborate *akeda*, which weaves together many aggadic elements and introduces a surprising variant: Abraham's *second* attempt to perform the sacrifice after Isaac's resurrection (stanza 16). S. Spiegel, who first published this poem in a masterful essay on the binding of Isaac (subsequently published in English, in book-form, as *The Last Trial*), quotes striking parallels from the chronicles of the time which relate how the martyrs were 'killed a second time' or removed from the grave and then buried again. The last line of each stanza is a biblical verse, not necessarily related to the story of Isaac or the ritual of sacrifice. The metre is four words to a line and all the stanzas, except the last, rhyme aabb. The initial letters of the first and third line in each stanza form an *atbash* (AZBY) acrostic followed by the signature: 'Ephraim bar Jacob, be mighty in Torah and good deeds.'

Concluding section of a long, emotional lament on the massacre at Blois (see following poem).

BARUKH OF MAGENZA (MAINZ) (*c.* 1150–1221) was a noted scholar and *dayan*. Many of his powerful *piyutim* deal with the persecutions in the years before and during the Third Crusade. The subject of the following *seliḥa*, of which only excerpts are given, is the massacre at Blois in 1171, when all the members of the Jewish community were burned at the stake following a blood libel.

ELIEZER BAR JUDAH OF WORMS (*c.*1165–*c.*1230) was the last major scholar of the *Ḥasidey Ashkenaz* movement. Born in Mainz, he studied in the centres of learning in Germany and Northern France, and wrote important works in the fields of ethics and esoteric theosophy. In his *piyutim*, as well as in his important commentary on the prayers and his short *Memoirs*, he recorded the widespread persecutions that followed the fall of Jerusalem to Saladin (1187). The following excerpts, from a simple narrative in rhymed couplets, describe the tragedy that struck the author in 1197. The deep piety that informs the poem is one of the distinguishing traits of *ḥasidut*.

JUDAH AL-ḤARIZI (*c.* 1170–after 1235) was the master of the Hebrew *maqama*, a narrative in rhymed prose interspersed with metrical poems. A native of Christian Toledo, he lived for a while in Provence, then travelled extensively in the Near East. Before his departure from Spain (*c.* 1215) he completed his brilliant translation of the *maqamat* of the Arabic poet Al-Ḥariri (1054–1121), under the title *Maḥberot Iti'el* ('The Maqamas of Iti'el'). He then proceeded to use this form for his major work, *The Book of Taḥkemoni*, which shows the influence of his Arabic and Hebrew predecessors in this genre. Apart from its stylistic virtuosity, *Taḥkemoni* also records the author's impressions of Jewish communities in the Orient and his (often biased) evaluation of earlier and contemporary poets. The following poems are all taken from various episodes in *Taḥkemoni*, which consists of a series of fifty loosely-linked *maqamat*. The first three are part of a poetic duel between an old man, who claimed he could 'cleave rocks with his flinty tongue', and a young challenger. The youth sets the subject and the metre in the first two lines (ab), and the old man completes the quatrain with an appropriate simile and rhyme (cb).

Heber the Kenite, the roguish companion of the narrator of *Taḥkemoni*, chances upon a mountain village. His peasant host extends this rustic welcome.

This is the plea delivered by the 'big, soft, succulent' rooster, from the roof of a house of prayer, to the assembled villagers. The rooster was pursued for having kept Heber awake all night.

Heber is offered a beautiful young bride, sight unseen, for a price of 2,000 pieces of silver. When he unveils her after the wedding, he discovers that he has been duped, and addresses this song to her.

Al-Ḥarizi was a member of a wealthy family that became impoverished. He is known to have dedicated *Taḥkemoni* to four different patrons at different stages of his voyage through the East.

MEIR HALEVI ABULAFIA (*c.* 1170–1244), a renowned Talmudist and one of the early kabbalists of Toledo, wrote elegant secular verse which reflects his aristocratic background and his indebtedness to the works of Moses ibn Ezra. The following is an extract.

NAḤMANIDES (1194–1270). Moses ben Naḥman, also known as RaMBaN (an acronym for Rabbi Moses Ben Naḥman), the highest religious authority of his time in Spain, was born in Gerona. As a young man he joined the ranks of the kabbalists, who drew their inspiration from the mystics of Provence. In 1263, at the command of King James I, he took part in a public disputation in Barcelona with the apostate Pablo Christiani. Though he emerged victorious from the confrontation and was even commended by the king, he was forced to flee for his life after the intervention of Pope Clement IV. He emigrated to Palestine in 1267, seven years after the invasion of the Tatar hordes, and was active in founding yeshivot and synagogues in Acre and Jerusalem. It was during these years that he composed most of his classic commentary on the Pentateuch.

Excerpts from a *mustajab* (see p. 106) which may have been the first *piyut* to employ the distinctive images and figures of speech of the Kabbalah. Naḥmanides believed that 'the special soul of man . . . the "over-soul", was pre-existent to the creation of the world, treasured up as a wave in the sea or fountain of souls – dwelling in the eternal light and holiness of God' (S. Schechter). After death, it returns to its source. It is 'clothed again' (line 39) in a celestial garment which it wove from its good deeds during its earthly stay.

DAVID HAKOHEN (fl. late thirteenth century) probably lived in Avignon. The four metrical hymns that have been preserved in French and North African rituals show a high degree of artistry. The following *reshut* is in the form of a *muwashshah* with internal rhymes.

'Bow down, my soul'   הִשְׁתַּחֲוִי וּבָרְכִי   396

ISAAC HAGORNI (fl. late thirteenth century) was born in Aire ('threshing floor', Hebrew *goren*, hence his name ha-*Gorni*). The most original of the Hebrew poets in Provence, he led the life of an impecunious troubadour, wandering through the Jewish communities of Southern France in search of patrons. He was hounded by his compatriots because of his amorous adventures and complained bitterly about their boorishness and parsimony. He also engaged in several harsh literary quarrels. Only eighteen of his poems have survived, in a single manuscript.

'I shall now lament'   לְחָשְׁקִי הִנְנִי הוֹלֵךְ   397

The Andalusian tradition is apparent in the metre and form of this unusual poem, but the influence of the Christian environment is clearly felt, especially in the strange elaboration of the belief in relics.

'From its very first day'   עִיר אַרְלְדִי   399

Opening section of a poem against the notables of Arles. Hagorni wrote in a similar vein against the communities of Aix-en-Provence, Apt and Draguignan.

MOSES BEN JOSEPH (fl. *c.* 1250) lived in Rome. The following *tokhaha* ('rebuke') is written in the form of an Italian *quartina* (abab). The last line of each stanza is a biblical quotation which often acquires a surprising meaning in the new context. The disputation between body and soul after death, in the presence of God, is a traditional motif, already found in the Talmud.

'Listen to me, my limbs'   אִזְנוּ יְצוּרַי אֵלַי   400

IMMANUEL DEI ROSSI (late thirteenth century) also lived in Rome. His *tokhaha* follows one of the conventional Spanish patterns: it is written in rhymed tercets, each of which concludes with a biblical passage.

'Doomed, man gives vent'   אֱנוֹשׁ אָנוּשׁ   405

MESHULLAM DA PIERA or DE PIERA (died after 1260) was one of the main figures in the circle of kabbalists in Gerona and was chosen to head the *consilium* of the community. Though he adhered to the metrics and uniform rhyme of the Andalusian school, his innovations affected the language, structure and subject-matter of secular poetry in Christian Spain. Unlike his predecessors, he made extensive use of rabbinic Hebrew and did not hesitate to borrow the vocabulary of scientific and philosophic translations. His poems are often intentionally enigmatic and bear an affinity to the hermetic style (*trobar clus*) of the Provençal poets. He modified the accepted form of the panegyric by enlarging the 'introduction', omitting the elegant 'transition verse' and reducing the actual laudation to a short *envoi*-like dedication.

Introduction to a panegyric addressed to Abraham ibn Ḥasdai of Barcelona, a noted translator and *maqama* writer.

Two sections from a long poem sent to his close friend Naḥmanides.

TODROS ABULAFIA (1247–after 1295), a native of Toledo, was presented before King Alfonso X and offered him panegyrics in Hebrew. In 1281 he was among the Jews of Castile arrested by order of Alfonso the Wise. It is not known how the poet, whose possessions were confiscated, regained his status at court. But by 1289 he was in the service of Sancho IV and later headed a group of Jewish financiers who received important monopolies. Todros arranged his copious works in *Gan Hameshalim Vehaḥidot* ('The Garden of Poems and Songs'), which presents an unusually candid picture of his love affairs, his experiences at court and his literary controversies. Though he introduced new themes into secular poetry, such as the troubadour theme of spiritual love, and initiated some mannerist forms, he was to some extent an epigone of the Andalusian school.

Abulafia's thematic innovations included love poems about Arab and Christian women. In the general mood of repentance that swept the community after the release of the Jewish prisoners, a ban (*ḥerem*) was proclaimed in the synagogue against those who maintained liaisons with non-Jewish women. Abulafia, however, did not mend his ways.

The last line is a typical example of the humour achieved by displacing a biblical phrase. In the original, Lamentations 1.14, the reference is to God's hand which 'plaits' or 'knots' the author's sins about his neck.

From a cycle of forty-seven girdle poems written in imitation of Arabic and Hebrew models. Almost all the poems were set to popular Arabic tunes. The *kharjas* are generally in vulgar Arabic and sometimes in Romance.

Like Meshullam da Piera, Abulafia made extensive use of Talmudic idiom, even including legalistic expressions in Aramaic (line 10).

The last line refers to the fact that the Jewish prisoners were deprived of food in an attempt to force them into conversion.

ABRAHAM ABULAFIA (1240–after 1291), the leading exponent of 'ecstatic' Kabbalah, was born in Saragossa and raised in Tudela. In 1260 he travelled to Palestine in search of the mythical river Sambatyon and the ten lost tribes. In Barcelona, at the age of thirty-one, he experienced a prophetic vision. Urged by an inner voice, he undertook a voyage to Rome in 1280 to confer with Pope Nicholas III 'in the name of Jewry'. The sudden death of the Pope, on the eve of his arrival, saved him from the stake. After a month in prison, he was released and returned to Sicily. His messianic revelations aroused strong opposition in rabbinic circles and he was forced to flee to the desolate island of Comino, near Malta. His kabbalistic manuals, many of which were written during the latter period of his life, are systematic guides to the theory and practice of meditation leading to mystical ecstasy. He also wrote over twenty 'prophetic works' of which only one, *Sefer Ha'ot* ('The Book of the Sign', 1288), is extant. The following two excerpts are taken from this abstruse, but undeniably poetic, apocalypse.

The numerical value of the Herald's name, *Zekharyahu* (line 6) is the same as that of the author's name *Avraham*. Gematria, the method of interpretation based on the numerical value of Hebrew words, plays an important part in Abulafia's system.

ABRAHAM BEN SAMUEL (thirteenth century), the author of the following *seliḥa*, which J. Schirmann considers 'one of the finest Hebrew poems of all time', has not been identified. Some scholars have conjectured that he is the famous mystic, Abraham ben Samuel Abulafia. The *seliḥa* is unrhymed (except for the last couplet) and written in free biblical cadence.

NAHUM (? late thirteenth century) is known as the author of a dozen *piyutim* in Sephardic liturgical collections. His delicate lyricism and feeling for nature achieve an unusual fusion of secular elements and religious ecstasy.

A *me'ora* in the form of a *muwashshaḥ*. The spring landscape represents the time of redemption.

IMMANUEL OF ROME (*c.* 1261–*c.* 1332) was a source of inspiration for the Baroque poet Jacob Frances (p. 129), who called him 'the emperor of poets', as well as for Tchernikhovsky and Alterman in the twentieth century. Apparently he held the post of community scribe until he was forced to leave Rome temporarily because of some financial entanglement. He travelled extensively in Italy, devoting much of his time to writing biblical commentaries. In 1328 he returned to the home of his benefactor in Fermo and there edited his principal work *Maḥberot Imanu'el* ('The Maqamas of Immanuel'). It consists of twenty-eight *maḥbarot* (sing. *maḥberet*, Hebrew for *maqama*), alternating rhymed prose and metrical poetry, somewhat on the model of Al-Ḥarizi's *Taḥkemoni* (p. 114). The loose autobiographical framework of the book enabled Immanuel to group together poems, riddles, epigrams and epistles on a variety of subjects, written during different periods of his life. This work is unrivalled for its hilarious word-play and agile manipulation of the resources of the Hebrew language. The poetry combines the quantitative metres and ornaments of the Spanish school with strophic forms and motifs drawn from Italian verse. In the sonnet, a form which he introduced into Hebrew, he employed a new quantitative-syllabic metre. Known to his Christian friends as Manuello Giudeo, he also wrote poems in Italian and exchanged sonnets with his Italian colleagues. *Maḥberot Imanu'el* was among the first Hebrew books printed in Italy (Brescia, 1491). The following selection includes six sonnets, and two short poems in the Spanish style.

Like most of his thirty-eight sonnets, this is written in a Hebrew-Spanish metre, modified to correspond to the widespread Italian hendecasyllabic line. This became the favourite metrical scheme of Hebrew poetry in Italy.

This is prefaced by a long 'duel' in rhymed prose, in which the beautiful woman and the ugly woman (the daughter of the repulsive Gershom; line 2) are contrasted in great detail.

A love poem, written in the spirit of the *dolce stil nuovo.* In one of his sonnets, Immanuel included a final tercet adapted from Dante's *Vita Nuova.*

'Composed' by the virgin of the previous poem, after her marriage to an impotent mate.

Typical of Immanuel's ribald vein. Small wonder that the reading of his book 'on the Sabbath and even on week-days' was explicitly prohibited by the *Shulḥan Arukh* (The Standard Code of Jewish Law, *c.* 1569).

ISAAC ALḤADIB (died *c.* 1429), a native of Castile, was among the emigrants who sought refuge in Sicily towards the end of the fourteenth century. He lived in Syracuse and Palermo and gained fame as an astronomer. The following are excerpts from a thirty-five-stanza poem, extolling his mastery of all crafts, written in one of the Italian *ballata* forms (abababbccR). As in many of his satirical poems, the metre is eight 'long' syllables to the line.

DON VIDAL BENVENISTE (fl. early fifteenth century) was a member of a very influential family in Saragossa. The massacres of 1391, which destroyed practically all the Jewish communities of Catalonia and Aragon, by-passed Saragossa because of the king's presence in the town. It became the centre for the last circle of Hebrew poets in Spain, *Adat Nogenim* ('Band of Minstrels'), in which Vidal played the leading role. In 1413–14 he was one of the emissaries to the Disputation of Tortosa, initiated by the Antipope Benedict XIII. In the intensified persecution that followed the defeat of the Jews, Vidal and his teacher, the poet Solomon da Piera, were among the apostates. Vidal excels at satirical and aphoristic verse. His principal composition was the bawdy *maqama*, 'The Notebook of Epher and Dinah', from which the following poem is taken.

The beautiful but destitute Dinah is cajoled into marrying the old and impotent Epher. After objecting, 'Shall I in my youth . . . lie with my forefathers' – a pun on the biblical phrase meaning 'to die' – she sings this song.

(Excerpts.) This was plagiarized in the middle of the sixteenth century by David Onkinerah of Salonika (p. 125).

SOLOMON BONAFED (died after 1445), the last prominent poet in Christian Spain, was the youngest member of the *Adat Nogenim* in Saragossa. The defection of many of his friends and the deterioration of the Jewish community filled him with a sense of futility which is expressed in his personal poetry. He engaged in bitter polemics with his opponents and in old age was forced to flee to the town of Belchite. There he wrote a scathing satire in rhymed prose against the notables of Saragossa. His compositions include outspoken love lyrics, philosophical poems and *reshuyot*, some of which are set to Spanish melodies.

Written to comfort a friend who had lost his fortune.

MOSES DA RIETI (1388–after 1460) practised as a physician in his native town of Rieti. Later he served as rabbi to the local community in Rome and became private physician to Pope Pius II. At the age of twenty-four he wrote his most important work, *Mikdash Me'at* ('The Little Shrine'), an adaptation in *terza rima* of the *Divine Comedy*. His decasyllabic line (*endecasillabo tronco*) marks the first appearance of overt syllabic metre in Hebrew poetry in Italy. One of the cantos from this work was adopted into the ritual and sung in the synagogue in his lifetime. The following sections are from the second part of the epic which describes the celestial court.

MOSES GABBAI (died *c.* 1443) served as rabbi in Teruel (Aragon) and later settled in Majorca. During the riots of 1391 he escaped to Algeria, where he was appointed rabbi of Honein. The following poem is partly based on the Mishnah (*Ta'anith* 2) which details the ceremonies for invoking rain in time of drought. On the last seven days of fasting, it was customary to 'put wood-ashes on the Ark and on the heads of the President and the Father of the court' (last stanza). An unusual feature of the poem is the use of a refrain (lines 1-2) and narrative technique traditionally associated with certain *avodot* (poems describing the service of the high priest in the Temple).

'*Happy the eye that saw*'   אַשְׁרֵי עַיִן רָאֲתָה   436

MOSES REMOS (*c.* 1406-*c.* 1430) was born in Majorca, studied science and philosophy in Rome and practised medicine in Palermo. At the age of twenty-four he was condemned to death, ostensibly for having poisoned a Christian patient. He rejected an offer of pardon on condition that he renounce his faith. The following elegy, of which excerpts are given, was written on the eve of his execution. In other sections of the poem he describes how the ten *Sefirot*, the Active Intelligence, the planets and the Sciences all join in the lament.

'*Who could have believed*'   מִי הֶאֱמִין כִּי כְּמוֹת נָבָל   437

RAPHAEL DA FAENZA (fl. middle of fifteenth century) is known to have lived in Florence. The following poem may have been an adaptation of an Italian song.

'*Hear my words, my dearest*'   רַעְיָתִי, לִי אָזְנֵךְ הַטִּי־נָא   441

ANONYMOUS (thirteenth to sixteenth century). This section comprises a miscellany of poems from Spain (?), Provence, the Near East and Germany. The first four are written in classical Hispano-Arabic metres; the rest have a distinct popular tone.

'*Lord, how much longer*'   יָהּ, לְמָתַי פֵּרוּד יַנְדֵּנִי   443

An *ahava* for Passover, in the form of a *muwashshaḥ* with internal rhymes, probably of Spanish origin.

'*My heart goes out to Jokhebed*'   לִבִּי לְיוֹכֶבֶד   445

Has been attributed to Samuel ben Moses Dayan of Aleppo (Syria). It is one of the laments on the death of Moses that were sung in Aleppo on the holiday of the Rejoicing of the Law. It is in the form of a *muwashshaḥ*.

'*When I see that the rains*'   בִּרְאוֹתִי כִּי עָבַר   446

A melodious *piyut* for Passover which makes extensive use of secular love imagery. It is apparently of Provençal origin. It has a fixed line pattern of eight and seven syllables: $a_8b_7a_8b_7a_8b_7a_8a_8b_7a_4$. Two rhymes (a – masculine, b – feminine) recur throughout the poem. In line 11, the rhyme is formed by part of the word (*uvkir-*), a technique which is already found in eleventh-century Spanish poems.

The author of this wine song, who was probably of Eastern origin, introduced his name, Av(i)shay, in line 13. It can also be taken to mean 'father of (*Av*) gifts (*shay*)'.

A playful 'song of thanksgiving to a bridegroom' found in a liturgical collection from Tunis. (The English translation is freer than usual.)

A Provençal *piyut* in syllabic metre, for the night preceding the circumcision. It is put into the mouth of the seven-day-old child.

Several different versions are known of these popular 'Verses Against Gamblers'.

A loosely written satirical poem directed against the Jews of Germany. It is one of the few examples of secular verse during this period by Ashkenazi authors.

CALEB AFENDOPOLO (1465–1523), a Karaite scholar, lived most of his life in the vicinity of Constantinople and died in Belgrade. The following exchange is taken from a collection of poetry and prose, *The King's Garden*, which also includes elegies on the expulsion of the Jews from Lithuania and Kiev in 1495.

JOSEPH TSARFATI (ZARFATI) (died 1527), a native of Rome, was the most graceful Hebrew lyricist of the Renaissance. In his professional life as a physician, he was known as Giuseppe Gallo. An accomplished philosopher, mathematician and linguist, he was apparently the first to translate a play into Hebrew, the famous Spanish tragicomedy *La Celestina*; but only his own prologue in verse has survived. While in Constantinople, in the latter part of his life, he was imprisoned and tortured by the Turks, accused of being a papal spy. Upon his return to Rome, he was attacked by robbers during the sack of the city in 1527. He attempted to settle in Vicovaro, but since he had contracted a contagious disease he was refused entrance and died in misery in the open field. All of the following poems are octaves (*ottava rima*; abababcc), a form introduced into Hebrew poetry by Tsarfati.

JOSEPH HAKOHEN (1496–1578), a native of Avignon, practised medicine in Italy. He is noted for his historiographical works. In the following monorhymed poem he numerates the 'thirty-three conditions' of beauty in a woman. It is amusing to compare it to an earlier poem on the same theme (pp. 360–61).

SIMEON LABI (died *c.* 1585) was brought to Fez, probably from Spain, in the year of the expulsion. In 1549 he settled in Tripoli, where he engaged in teaching and kabbalistic studies.

A kabbalistic hymn in honour of Simeon ben (bar) Yoḥai, the second-century *tanna*, who, according to legend, hid from the Romans for twelve years in a cave, together with his son Eleazar, buried up to the neck in sand and studying the Torah. He is the classic hero of Jewish mysticism, to whom tradition attributed the authorship of the *Zohar* and other pseudepigrapha. The hymn consists of ten stanzas corresponding to the ten *Sefirot*, the powers that constitute the manifestations and emanations of God. In describing Bar Yoḥai's ascent to the supreme mystery, each stanza employs the highly charged symbols appropriate to the *Sefira* which it represents. This poem became the most popular kabbalistic hymn; it is still sung today by Oriental Jews during the festivities of *Lag Ba'omer* at the traditional site of Bar Yoḥai's tomb in Meron, near Safed.

SA'ADIAH LONGO (sixteenth century), born in Turkey, was the senior member of the *Ḥakhmey Hashir* ('Masters of Poetry'), a literary circle in Salonika. He was the author of ribald poems and versified polemics. One of the more spiteful exchanges was occasioned by his marriage, in old age, to a young wife. Like other members of the Greek-Turkish group, his poems are written partly in traditional Spanish forms and partly under the influence of the Italian school and local folk-songs.

This is set to the tune of a popular Ladino song. The opening verses serve as the refrain. It has been suggested that Longo was facetiously referring to himself as the 'scoundrel'.

DAVID ONKINERAH (sixteenth century), perhaps a native of Istanbul, was the youngest and most gifted member of the Salonika 'Academy'. Strangely enough, the first poem he sent Longo as a 'visiting-card' was a plagiarism. The 'master' rebuked him in verse, Onkinerah wrote a witty confession, and the two became firm friends.

A sonnet which clearly shows the influence of Immanuel of Rome.

Concluding section of a love poem.

Last section of a poem in praise of a virgin whose hair was 'black and golden'.

JUDAH ZARCO (sixteenth century) was born in Rhodes and for some time played an active role in the Salonika circle. The following poems are taken from his *maqama Leḥem Yehuda* ('Judah's Bread', Istanbul, 1560). It has an unusually complex structure, both formal and allegorical, and abounds in original, and often difficult, conceits.

Addressed by the suitor to his lady. The 'virgin' (line 8) also represents the last month of the Hebrew year (*Elul*).

Sung by the lover after he enters the lady's palace and is stunned by her splendour.

The message deposited by the 'captive' lover in the lady's home.

The prayer of the frustrated lover.

JOSEPH BIBAS (fl. early sixteenth century) lived in Constantinople. His jocular poem is written in syllabic metre, alternating lines of eight and seven syllables (abab):

SAMUEL ARCHEVOLTI (1515–1611) was born in Cesena and lived in Venice and Padua. He was influential as a grammarian and rhetorician. The last chapter of his major work, *Arugat Habosem* ('The Bed of Spices'), is devoted to theories of versification and cites many of his own poems to illustrate metrical forms.

The last tercet of this sonnet refers to Zachariah's prophecy (9.9): 'Lo, your king comes to you . . . humble and riding on an ass.'

MORDECAI DATO (1525–*c.* 1600), an Italian kabbalist, wrote biblical commentaries, messianic propaganda, and memoirs of a visit to Safed.

ISAAC LURIA (1534–72) is referred to as *Ha'ari* ('the lion'), an anagram of his Hebrew appellation 'the Divine Rabbi Isaac'. He was the most important kabbalistic figure after the expulsion from Spain. Born in Jerusalem and brought up in Egypt, he spent the last two years of his life in Safed. Here he exercised a profound influence on his select disciples, who propagated the Lurianic system after his death. He was at first known as a poet; his mystical hymns for Sabbath meals, written in Aramaic, are found in most prayer books. However, only a few of his poems make use of kabbalistic symbolism.

ELIEZER AZIKRI (1533–1600) was one of the outstanding poets among 'the lion whelps', the circle of Luria's disciples in Safed. His classical work on kabbalistic ethics, *Sefer Ḥaredim* ('The Book of the Devout', Venice, 1601), was widely read. The following 'prayer for Unification', in syllabic metre, contains the Tetragrammaton in its acrostic. Its gentle tone and purity of feeling have made it one of the favourite hymns in the prayer book.

ISRAEL NAJARA (?1555–?1625), apparently a native of Damascus, was the most significant poet in the revival of religious poetry under the impact of the Kabbalah. He travelled extensively in the Near East, lived at times in Safed and, in old age, served as a rabbi in Gaza. An extremely prolific poet, his work is noteworthy for its musical fluency and inventiveness. His devotional poems are set to popular Turkish, Armenian, Spanish and new Greek melodies. This fact, coupled with his bohemian wanderings and his erotic-mystical imagery, aroused the opposition of some prominent rabbis. But Luria's enthusiastic endorsement silenced the critics and the poetry achieved unusually wide circulation among the Oriental communities, spreading as far as Aden, Calcutta and Cochin.

'Now I shall raise'   נְהִי נִהְיָה אֲעוֹרֵר   472

A ballad-like dirge for the Ninth of Av which is based on the following legend: '. . . Doeg ben Joseph died and left a young son to his mother, who used to measure him by handbreadths and give his weight in gold to the Temple every year. When, however, the besieging army [of Babylonia] surrounded Jerusalem, his mother slaughtered him and ate him' (*Midrash Rabbah: Lamentations*, 1.51).

'Sleep deserts my eyes'   תֻּדַּד שְׁנַת עֵינִי   477
'Languishing in exile'   יְדִידִים לָאֵל נִבְחָרוּ   477

One of the many poems which reflect the feverish messianic currents of the time. Like most of his poems, it is written in a syllabic metre, in this case eight syllables to a line.

ANONYMOUS (fourteenth to seventeenth century). This section consists of poems written in Yemen. Early Yemenite poetry is dominated by the Spanish school. From the sixteenth century on, partly under the influence of the Kabbalah, it develops its distinctive regional flavour. All Yemenite poetry is meant to be sung, and certain categories are also accompanied by percussion and dancing.

'The love of the princely daughter'   אַהֲבַת בַּת נְדִבָה   478

This girdle poem was erroneously ascribed to Judah Halevi. It is included in W. Bacher's list of anonymous poems from Yemen.

'Shalom, I swear by you'   שָׁלוֹם, בָּךְ נִשְׁבַּעְתִּי   479

Stanzas 3 and 8 allude to the 'smooth words' of the adulteress in Proverbs 7.12-20. In a later manuscript version (*c.* 1661) these stanzas were deleted and the poem was read as a monologue addressed by a bride to her beloved.

'Old and grey as I am'   לִקְרַאת שַׁבָּת   481

One of a group of Yemenite poems written in alternating Hebrew and Aramaic stanzas. Only the Hebrew is printed here.

'The star looked down'   כּוֹכָב אֲשֶׁר הִשְׁקִיף   481

Wholly secular poems, such as this song of friendship, are comparatively rare in Yemenite poetry.

'She saw a figure' רָאֲתָה תְּמוּנָה בַּחֲלוֹם 482

Proem to a song of friendship.

'You are the Lord' אַתָּה אָדוֹן 483

Excerpts from a *piyut* containing a complete alphabetic acrostic.

SA'ADIAH BEN AMRAM (? sixteenth century) is the author of the following popular verses which are sung by Yemenite Jews to a merry Turkish tune. The meaning of the Arabic stanzas (3 and 4) is somewhat obscure. The majority of Yemenite poems were written in Hebrew-Arabic or entirely in Arabic. The poem is allegorical and employs kabbalistic terminology.

'Tell me, pure and perfect one' סַפְּרִי, תַּמָּה תְּמִימָה 484

SA'ADIAH (*c.* sixteenth century) also signed his poems SA'ID or ḤaZMaK. The last two names are identical if the letters of the Hebrew alphabet are listed in *atbash* order (i.e. Z = A, Y = B). Many of his poems are devoted to the favourite Yemenite themes: the Sabbath and the festivals. The following *havdala* is still sung today.

'My soul longs' לַנֵּר וְלִבְשָׂמִים 486

SHALEM SHABAZI (died after 1681), the foremost Yemenite poet, was born in Ta'izz, in South Yemen, and probably earned his livelihood as an itinerant weaver. His hundreds of poems, written in Hebrew, Arabic or Aramaic, deal primarily with religious themes and reflect the messianic expectations of the Jews of Yemen and the persecutions of 1679–81, which destroyed more than half the Jewish population. His poetry draws its inspiration from pre-Lurianic Kabbalah and owes much to Najara. Though it employs simple, almost prosaic, rabbinic diction, avoiding the rhetorical flourishes of the classical Spanish school, the meaning is often puzzling because of the mystical allusions and the abrupt transitions from one subject to another.

'My heart is bound' אַהֲבַת הֲדַסָּה 487

An allegorical epithalamium. In the first stanza the poet speaks for the congregation of Israel. The terrestrial wedding symbolizes the nuptials of God and Israel, the renewal of the ancient covenant, and the joy of redemption.

'Who kissed me' מִי נְשָׁקַנִי 488

The opening phrase, 'Who kissed me until/while I . . .' is a formula specific to Yemenite poetry. It usually introduces a religious allegory which, at first, seems to be a sensual love poem.

'From the far reaches' שָׁמַעְתִּי מִפַּאֲתֵי תֵימָן 489

Excerpts from a poem which Shabazi probably improvised during the ceremony of circumcision. The Yemenite *diwan* consists largely of such lyrical, semi-religious songs which are performed in the home on holidays and festivities.

JOSEPH JEDIDIAH CARMI (*c.* 1590–?) was appointed cantor of a private synagogue in Modena. For the 'Association for Vigils' (*Shomerim Laboker*) of this congregation he composed his kabbalistic *piyutim* and prayers in rhymed prose. The following is an excerpt from a rhythmical prayer. In his marginal glosses Carmi points out that the moon represents the people of Israel.

'Ehyeh-Asher-Ehyeh' אֶהְיֶה אֲשֶׁר אֶהְיֶה 490

JUDAH ARYEH (LEONE) MODENA (1571–1648) was born in Venice and studied under the poet-grammarian Samuel Archevolti in Padua. A child prodigy, he translated passages from Ariosto's *Orlando Furioso* at the age of twelve. He became famous as a rabbi and preacher in Venice and was the author of the first autobiography in Hebrew, *The Life of Judah*. In this unusually revealing narrative he lists twenty-six professions at which he tried his hand, among them: *maestro di cappella*, author of an Italian comedy, *dayan*, alchemist (his son died of lead poisoning after one of the experiments), writer of amulets and talismans, and matchmaker. He was addicted to gambling and, as a result, was perpetually on the verge of penury. At the request of the English Ambassador in Venice, he wrote *Historia de riti ebraici* for presentation to King James I. An avid polemicist, he wrote famous tracts against Christianity, Karaism and the Kabbalah, and a condemnation of games of chance.

'On this day, may the weight' יוֹם זֶה יְהִי מִשְׁקַל 491

A *seliḥa* for the eve of the new month, which, in the Hebrew calendar, coincides with the new moon. The custom of observing this day as a 'minor Day of Atonement' was instituted by the kabbalists of Safed towards the end of the sixteenth century. The poem is written in a quantitative-syllabic metre, alternating masculine and feminine rhymes, and has a *ballata*-like form.

JACOB FRANCES (1615–67) was the last major poet before the modern period. Born in Mantua, he acquired a thorough knowledge of Portuguese (which was his mother tongue), Italian, Aramaic and Latin. He courageously attacked the kabbalists and, later, the fervent followers of Shabbetai Tsevi (who proclaimed himself as the Messiah in 1665 and converted to Islam the following year). His anti-kabbalistic poems were banned and destroyed, he was stoned in the street and his house was ransacked. More than once, he was forced to seek refuge in Venice or Florence, where he eventually died. His collected works (published by P. Naveh in 1969 on the basis of a Bodleian autograph) comprise over 200 poems, including some fifty sonnets. However, only isolated poems were published during his lifetime. His satirical talent is matched only by that of Immanuel of Rome, whose influence he acknowledged. His love poems are among the finest in the baroque school of Hebrew poetry. A virtuoso technician, he employed many of the current Italian forms, but was equally skilful in the classical Spanish style. The close literary rapport between him and his younger brother, Immanuel, presents an unusual phenomenon: they collaborated in the writing of poems, and after Jacob's death, Immanuel added passages to some of his brother's poems, edited and revised them, and even completed them on the basis of rough drafts. He also compiled books which consisted of Jacob's poems and his own, suitably arranged and linked together by transitional passages in rhymed prose. There is still no definitive way of ascertaining the authorship of some of the poems by the Frances brothers.

'Up, Asmodeus! Rise up' קוּם, אַשְׁמְדַאי 493

One of several bitter poems against Rabbi Yeḥiel Norzi, a member of the Mantuan *bet-din* that banned his work. The sonnet is preceded by a note in Portuguese: 'For the death of Yeḥiel [the name is in code], a man who has not a single virtue, and is therefore the enemy of all good men.' Jacob often prefaced his poems with Portuguese comments and coded key words to avoid detection by the çommunity's spies and investigators. The code was deciphered by the Italian scholar and poet S. D. Luzzatto (1800–1865).

'My friends, all you wrynecks' מְבִין צְפִיִּים 493

The Portuguese note reads: 'For the marriage of two Germans.' It has been suggested that the sonnet refers to German Jews, whose excessive drinking was ridiculed by the Sephardim. The irony of this 'anti-epithalamium' is heightened by the bombastic biblical allusion in the last line (Exodus 15.11).

'Love, had I not known you' לוּלֵי יְדַעְתִּיךְ, אַהֲבָה 494

'Friends, let me praise' חֲסֵדַי שְׁנָתִי 495

In Greek mythology, sleep (Hypnos) and death (Thanatos) are twin brothers.

'Leave off, you poetasters' הִרְפּוּ, מְלִיצִים 496

Excerpts from a jesting epithalamium in *ottava rima*, written (and probably recited) in honour of his brother's second marriage in 1656. The superscription attributes the poem to a 'Hebrew Scapin', which, in Hebrew, is an anagram of the author's name. The poem, which employs popular Italian expressions, is a technical *tour de force*, alternating quantitative-syllabic and syllabic metrical patterns.

'What can I do, my friend' אֵיךְ אֶעֱשֶׂה, דּוֹד 497

'*Tell me, tableau*' לוּחַ, אֱמֹר 498

The sestet was written by Immanuel, probably after his brother's death. Jacob, it seems, had intended a different conclusion. The Portuguese note after the octave reads: 'Etc., to a beautiful portrait that will remain young forever.'

'*When I recall the day*' עֵת אֶזְכְּרָה יוֹם 499

Written after seeing 'a beautiful woman kissing the body of her young husband, who was taken away by Heaven'.

'*Friend, yesterday I was shown*' דּוֹד, מַרְאָה נוֹרָאָה 499

IMMANUEL FRANCES (1618–*c.* 1710) did not lag far behind his brother in poetic achievement. He was born and died in Leghorn. His wife – she was the sister of Jacob's wife – and two of his children died in 1654. Two years later he remarried (see Jacob's poem on p. 496). But the second wife and the son she bore him died in 1667. In the latter part of his life he served as a rabbi and highly regarded Talmudic authority in Florence. His poetry spans more than eighty years; it includes Italianate love poems, satirical dialogues against women and rabbis, and religious works of a dramatic and recitative character, some of which were commissioned by musical societies. Like Jacob, he set both secular and synagogal poems to popular Italian melodies. Though he occasionally used traditional Spanish patterns, he preferred Italian forms. He is best known for the collection of sarcastic poems *Tsevi Mudaḥ* ('The Banished Gazelle [*Tsevi*]'), a vehement denunciation of Shabbetai Tsevi and the messianic movement that engulfed the Jews of Italy. However, of the twenty-one poems in this book, seventeen are by Jacob. During a stay in Algiers in 1678 Immanuel composed the first draft of an important work on poetics and rhetoric, *Metek Sefatayim* ('Pleasing Speech'), which combined traditional and Baroque elements.

'*When I see Hannah*' עֵת אֶחֱזֶה חַנָּה 500

'*The girl's eyes*' עֵינֵי צְבִיָּה 501

'*O you paragon of glory*' שִׁמְעִי, כְּלִילַת הוֹד 501

Recalls the rustic imagery of Al-Ḥarizi's peasant-host (pp. 389–90).

'*Where are the merchants*' אֵי סוֹחֲרִים 502

The seventh section of a long poem in *ottava rima*, sung by 'an evil old hag'.

'*Only three exits*' לְבַד שָׁלוֹשׁ יְצִיאוֹת 502

This poem and the first of the following epitaphs are taken from 'The Dialogue of Itti'el and Ukhal', a mini-*maqama* against women. The 'Dialogue' consists of rhymed prose which links together sonnets, epigrams, and monorhymed verses in the Spanish manner. Six of the ten poems are by Jacob.

EPHRAIM LUZZATO (1729–92) was born in San Daniele and studied medicine in Padua. In 1763 he was appointed physician in London's Portuguese community hospital. His disregard for religious decorum (he wore his physician's sword on the Sabbath) attracted much criticism. He died in Lausanne, on his way back to Italy. In 1768 he published his collected poems in London in a limited edition of 100 copies. Entitled *Ele Bene Hane'urim* ('These Are the Sons of One's Youth') because most of them had been written in Italy, the volume contains over fifty poems, mostly sonnets in quantitative-syllabic metres. It was often republished and influenced the leading poets of the nineteenth-century Haskalah ('Enlightenment') movement. The lyrical quality of the love poems and the emphasis on individual experience made Luzzato a precursor of the modern period.

This sonnet limits itself to two alternating rhyme-words, 'water' and 'stone', and presents an amusing mosaic of scriptural allusions.

PART THREE: MODERN TIMES

ḤAYIM NAḤMAN BIALIK (1873–1934) was acclaimed as 'the poet of the national renaissance' with the publication of his first book (Warsaw, 1901). He created a rich and flexible diction, which broke the stranglehold of Haskalah rhetoric (see p. 41) and was largely responsible for the abandonment of the syllabic system in favour of tonic-syllabic (accentual) metres. Born in Radi (Southern Russia), his large family was left destitute after the death of his father in 1880. In his sixteenth year he was sent off to prepare for the rabbinate in the yeshiva of Volozhin (Lithuania), where he came into contact with a clandestine Zionist group and with Russian poetry. The resultant crisis of faith, the clash between traditional Judaism and Western secularism, was to become a central theme of his poetry. In 1891 he went to Odessa, to join the literary circle that had gathered around the philosopher Aḥad Ha'am. During the next two decades he composed all his major poems. His comprehensive anthology of rabbinic lore, *Sefer Ha'agada* ('The Book of Legends'), and his editions of medieval poets, all compiled in collaboration with H. J. Rawnitzki, played a crucial role in relinking Hebrew literature to its older sources. In 1921 he was one of a group of Hebrew writers who, thanks to the intervention of Maxim Gorky, were permitted to leave the Soviet Union. After three years in Hamburg and Berlin, which had become centres for Jewish emigré writers, he settled in Tel Aviv, where he devoted most of his energy to publishing and public affairs. He died in Vienna, where he had gone for medical treatment. His poetry includes long descriptive and allegorical works, 'prophetic' denunciations of the passivity of the Jewish people, an enigmatic, mystical prose poem *Megilat Ha'esh* ('The Scroll of Fire'), folk-songs of unusual charm and, above all, lyrical verse which is often marked by acute despair. All his poetry, except for some of his children's poems, was written in the Ashkenazi accent.

This is the first section of the poem. Cosmic and mythic images are a recurrent element in his poetry.

Written after the pogrom in Kishinev (Bessarabia) in Easter, 1903. Shortly afterwards Bialik was sent there, on behalf of the Jewish Historical Commission in Odessa, to interview survivors and prepare a report on the atrocity. The title of the poem, 'On the Slaughter', is the concluding phrase of the blessing employed in ritual slaughter; this blessing was used by the martyrs in medieval Germany and Spain who sacrificed each other rather than submit to conversion (see, for example, p. 373, line 4). The poem is tightly structured; each stanza is identical in metre and rhyme. It draws heavily on Judges 6 and on Psalms, often creating tension by a reversal of biblical meaning.

SAUL TCHERNIKHOVSKY (1875–1943) was the most 'European' poet of the Odessa group. Unlike most of his eastern European contemporaries, who received a thorough religious education, he was privately tutored in Russian and modern Hebrew in his native village of Mikhalovka (near Crimea). His first book of poems (Warsaw, 1898) was notable for its variety of verse-forms and its Romantic nature imagery. After several years in Heidelberg, he completed his medical studies in Lausanne (1905). Upon returning to Russia, he was imprisoned for six weeks in Melitopol as a 'political agitator'. He served as an army doctor throughout the First

World War. In 1931, after having lived mainly in Odessa and Berlin, he settled in Tel Aviv, where he was appointed physician to the municipal schools. He translated works from fifteen different languages, including the *Iliad* and the *Odyssey*; poems by Anacreon, Horace, Goethe, Byron and Shelley; plays by Sophocles, Shakespeare and Molière; and a series of national epics (*Gilgamesh*, *Kalevala*, and sections from Siberian, Georgian and Icelandic verse narratives). The Hellenic ideal of beauty and the Canaanite cult, as opposed to the strictures of Diaspora Judaism, figure largely in his poetry. At the same time, he celebrated traditional Jewish village life in a series of idylls in dactylic hexameter. Some of his best work was written in old age; it was cast in the Sephardic accent and expressed his awareness of the physical presence of the land. .

This is the seventh sonnet of a corona sequence (*sonnet redoublé*) entitled 'To the Sun' (1919). The scene is an underground operating-room at the front. The opening line is a powerful echo of Numbers 17.13: 'And he [Aaron] stood between the dead and the living, and the plague was checked . . .'

Included in 'The Ballads of Worms', a series of seven poems based on episodes from medieval Jewish history. The entire Jewish community of Worms, 350 souls, destroyed itself by fire during the persecutions of 1349. The 'Ballads' were written in 1942, in response to the horrors of the Holocaust.

JACOB FICHMAN (1881–1958), a native of Belz (Bessarabia), ran away from home at the age of fourteen and afterwards lived in Odessa, where he came in contact with the 'Bialik circle'. After working in Warsaw and Vilna, he settled in Palestine in 1912. An influential editor and anthologist, he gained recognition for his impressionistic critical essays and his conscientious artistry. Like many of his contemporaries, he later 'transposed' some of his poems from the Ashkenazi to the Sephardic pronunciation.

AVRAHAM BEN YITSḤAK (1883–1950) printed only eleven poems during his lifetime, nine of them before the First World War. Born in Przemysl (Galicia), he studied at the universities of Vienna and Berlin. After serving as general secretary of the Zionist Executive Council in London (1920), he headed the Hebrew Pedagogical Institute in Vienna up to the Nazi occupation of Austria, when he left for Jerusalem

(1938). His style is highly individual, combining biblical vocabulary with terseness and purity of expression and a rich musical texture. He wrote according to the Sephardic pronunciation long before it was adopted by other poets. He was 'rediscovered' with the publication of his collected poems in 1952, and 'is considered by many to be the first truly modern Hebrew poet' (Lea Goldberg).

This was the last poem he published (1930). The opening line evokes, and reverses the meaning of, Psalms 126.5 and Isaiah 32.20.

One of the few poems and fragments found among the author's effects.

JACOB STEINBERG (1887–1947), essayist and short-story writer, was born in Belaya Tserkov (the Ukraine). In Warsaw he wrote for Hebrew and Yiddish journals, and at the outbreak of the First World War emigrated to Palestine. Introspective and sceptical, his lyrical poetry reveals a persistent quest for the word that contains 'an epic of life'. Although he clung to Ashkenazi Hebrew and traditional techniques, his uncompromising individuality attracted the admiration of the poets of the fifties. The second of the following poems is typical of his passion for enigmatic affinities and paradoxes.

The first of a series of love poems.

DAVID VOGEL (1891–?1944), a native of Satanov (Russia), spent his youth in Vilna and Lvov, and settled in Vienna (1912). During the First World War he was imprisoned in Austrian detention camps as an enemy (Russian) national. From 1925 he lived mainly in Paris, and when the Second World War broke out, he was imprisoned by the French as an enemy (Austrian) alien. He was released after the capitulation of France (1941), then arrested by the Nazis (1944) and most likely perished in a concentration camp. Almost all his poems were written in free rhythm. Their imagery is startling and allusive, their tone restrained and dream-like. Like Ben Yitzḥak and Steinberg, his poetry became an active influence in the fifties. He published only one volume of poems, *Lifney Hasha'ar Ha'afel* ('Before the Dark Gate', Vienna, 1923), a few stories and a novel set in a TB sanatorium.

Published posthumously. It was one of his last poems, written in Hauteville, near Lyons, after his release from the French detention camp.

ISRAEL EFRAT (1891–1981) was born in Ostrog (the Ukraine) and emigrated to the United States in 1905. He founded the Baltimore Hebrew College and held chairs in medieval Jewish philosophy and modern Hebrew literature at various American universities. In 1955 he settled in Israel and served as rector of Tel Aviv University. He wrote some of his most intense lyrical poems in later years.

URI ZVI GREENBERG (1896–1981), a native of Bialykamien (Galicia), received a Hasidic upbringing in Lvov. In 1915 he was drafted into the Austrian army and served on the Serbian front. Two years later he deserted and returned to Lvov, where he witnessed the Polish pogroms. He published poems in both Yiddish and Hebrew and was a prominent member of a Yiddish *avant-garde* expressionist group centred in Warsaw and Berlin. He emigrated to Palestine in 1923 as a sympathizer of the Socialist Labour movement, but in the wake of the Arab riots of 1929 joined the extremist Revisionist Party. Two protracted stays in Poland (1931–5, 1939) strengthened his premonition of the impending tragedy. During Israel's struggle for national independence, he was active in the ranks of the Irgun Tseva'i Le'umi, and in 1949 was elected to the Knesset as a member of the Herut Party. His poetry reveals a passionate identification of personal experience with Jewish messianic destiny, and a deep-rooted belief in the eternal enmity between 'the Star of David' and 'the Cross and the Crescent'. His heavily charged idiom draws on the resources of biblical prophecy, medieval dirges and kabbalistic symbolism. In early manifestos and in some of his poetry he sharply rejected 'European aesthetics'.

Appears in Greenberg's third book of Hebrew poetry, *Anacreon at the Pole of Melancholy* (1928).

The first of a series of poems entitled 'At the Rim of Heaven', from *Reḥovot Hanahar* ('The Streets of the River', 1951), a monumental series of laments for the loss of European Jewry.

Line 11 (except for the word 'hearts') is in Aramaic; 'over there' refers to the destroyed European home.

SIMON HALKIN (1898–1960) emigrated from Bolsk (White Russia) to the United States in his fifteenth year. Except for seven years in Tel Aviv (1932–9), he lived in America, holding various academic posts, until 1949, when he returned to Israel to take up the chair of modern Hebrew literature at the Hebrew University of Jerusalem. He has been influential as a novelist and critic. His translations include Whitman's *Leaves of Grass* and works by Shelley and Seferis. His compressed and densely textured poetry bears the mark of his Hasidic background and his intimate knowledge of American and European literature. The title of the following poem is part of a blessing ('Blessed be the *true judge*, who causes death and life') which is recited at the burial service.

ABRAHAM SHLONSKY (1900–1973) spearheaded the revolt against the 'school of Bialik' and made a major contribution to the modernization of Hebrew poetry. Born in Karyokov (the Ukraine), he was sent to Palestine at the age of thirteen to study at the first secondary school in Tel Aviv. He completed his studies during the First World War in Russia, and in 1921 returned to Palestine with a group of pioneers. A year's stay in Paris (1925) left a deep imprint on his writing. A brilliant and prolific translator, he influenced the development of Hebrew poetry with his classic renditions of Blok (*The Twelve*), Pushkin (*Eugene Onegin*), and Shakespeare (*Hamlet*, *King Lear*). As editor, polemicist, popular lyricist and author of children's literature, he set the literary tone for an entire generation. From the early forties he headed the literary Left, but his own poetry is rarely overtly political. Of the following poems, the first two were written in the early twenties, when he worked as a road builder in the Valley of Jezreel (see p. 45), and the last represents his later 'prosaic' tone.

YOKHEVED BAT-MIRIAM (1901–80), a native of Keplits (White Russia), grew up in a traditional Hasidic home and later received a modern education in Russian and Hebrew. She settled in Palestine in 1929, following a brief stay in Paris. Her poetry is often marked by the elusive style of the Russian Symbolists.

The first of a cycle of thirteen poems inspired by memories of childhood in Southern Russia. The unnamed feminine singular 'you' (*at*), to whom the poem is addressed, is the country that the poet left behind.

AVOT YESHURUN (1904–92) was brought up in the devout Hasidic atmosphere of his grandfather's home in Krasnystaw (Poland). In 1925 he emigrated to Palestine, and for many years roamed the country's Jewish-Arab villages, working as a building-hand, fruit-picker and watchman. An identification of the eastern European Jew and the Palestinian Arab as victims of exile underlies much of his poetry, which is often studded with expressions in Yiddish and Arabic, bilingual puns and portmanteau words. Though his style is perhaps the most idiosyncratic in contemporary Hebrew poetry, his themes are often political and his tone ironically or elegiacally moralistic. The first three poems given below are extracted from *Thirty Pages*[1] *of Avot Yeshurun,* a series of letters exchanged between the poet and those in his home country whom he 'sentenced to the hard labour of endless longing':

ḤAYIM LENSKI (1905–?1942) was born in Slonim (White Russia). After two years (1921–3) at the Hebrew Teachers' Seminary in Vilna, he settled down in Leningrad, where he worked in a metal factory. In 1934 he was arrested for writing Hebrew and was sentenced to five years' hard labour in Siberia. While in the camps he continued to write lyrical poems, dramatic ballads and trenchant satires, remarkable for their bold imagery and musicality. He also translated the Vogul epic *The Tundra Book*. His poems managed to reach Palestine until 1937, when he was transferred to the notorious forced labour camp of Gornaya Shoriya, near the Mongolian border. Having served his time, he returned to Leningrad, but soon afterwards was again arrested and sent to the prison camp of Malaya Vyshera, and from there to Siberia, where, as far as can be ascertained, he died of hunger. His first collection was published in Palestine in 1939. In 1958 a manuscript in the poet's handwriting, containing 131 unpublished poems, reached Israel, and was published under the title *Beyond the River Lethe*. This title was taken from a late sonnet addressed to the Hebrew language:

1. Hebrew *amudim*, which also means 'synagogue lecterns' and 'pillars'.

'Queen! As I have transported your troops . . . beyond the Don, the Neva and the Neman . . . so will you transport my name beyond the river Lethe, like the names of the ancients, Heman [the singer] and Halevi.'

One of a series of ten sonnets written in Leningrad around 1931.

YONATAN RATOSH (1908–81), a controversial political and literary figure, was brought up in a Hebrew-speaking home in Warsaw, and emigrated with his family to Palestine in 1921. In the mid-thirties he edited the Revisionist Party newspaper and was active in right-wing underground movements. In 1939 he founded 'The Young Hebrews', or, as it was popularly known, the 'Canaanite' movement. This group rejected both the Jewish religion and Zionism in favour of a new identity which would share in the cultural heritage of the Fertile Crescent. The literary expression of this ideology, in the work of Ratosh and his followers, was an archaic 'pre-biblical' style, inspired by Canaanite mythology and Ugaritic epics. Although the movement was never broad, its emphasis on myth and its stylistic mannerisms had considerable impact on contemporary poetry. In his later books Ratosh went to the other extreme and cultivated a very colloquial diction. The following dirge, written for the poet's father, is intended as a hymn for the pall-bearers. It describes how the dead man is borne westward to the palace of El, who presides over the Canaanite pantheon:

NATHAN ALTERMAN (1910–70), for a time the most influential poet since Bialik, was born in Warsaw and settled in Tel Aviv in 1925. After completing his secondary school studies, he specialized in agronomy in Nancy, but upon his return took up a journalistic post. A disciple of Shlonsky and of Russian and French Modernism, he soon became the leading 'imagist' poet of his generation. His five books of poetry, each of which marks a distinct stage in his development, are noteworthy for their exhilarating wit, their adroit manipulation of traditional forms, and sensitivity to the rhythms of the spoken language. From 1943 onwards he wrote a weekly satirical column in verse ('The Seventh Column') which played an important role in expressing and shaping public opinion. As a translator, he set a new standard in his versions of Shakespeare, Racine, Molière and old English and Scottish ballads.

This is the fourth and last section of a market-scene entitled 'As Evening Falls'.

Taken from *Simḥat Aniyim* ('The Joy of the Poor'), one of the major works of modern

Hebrew poetry. This poem is spoken by the dead lover, who is the central figure of the sequence, to his living beloved. Line 3 is patterned on a well-known Talmudic saying: 'The poor man is regarded as dead.'

LEA GOLDBERG (1911–70) was born in Koenigsberg and spent the early years of her life in Kovno (Lithuania). After receiving her Ph.D. in Semitic languages at the University of Bonn, she emigrated to Palestine in 1935. Together with Abraham Shlonsky she edited an influential anthology of Russian poetry in translation. Subsequently she was chairman of the Department of Comparative Literature at the Hebrew University. Her poetry is characterized by clarity, universality and lyrical delicacy. Some of her finest love poems – often conversational – take the form of sonnet sequences. In addition to Lithuanian folk-songs, she translated poems by Petrarch, Dante, Baudelaire and Rilke. She also excelled as a writer for children in prose and verse.

The grandmother wears a wig (stanza 3) in keeping with Orthodox Jewish custom.

The first of six poems entitled 'The Shortest Voyage', written in the early sixties (see p. 46).

GABRIEL JOSHUA PREIL (1911–93), a native of Dorpat (Estonia) has lived in the United States since 1922, writing mainly in Hebrew, but also in Yiddish and English. His Hebrew translations include poems by Jeffers, Frost and Sandburg. His subtle, free-verse lyrical poetry is often set in the landscapes of New England.

ZELDA (MISHKOVSKY) (1914–85) emigrated from Chernigov (the Ukraine) to Palestine in 1925. She taught in Orthodox schools for girls. Her first collection was published in 1967 and brought her immediate recognition for its unique blend of deep religious feeling, drawing on Hasidic lore, with a modern poetic sensibility.

AMIR GILBOA (1917–84), a native of Razywilow (the Ukraine), studied in a Hebrew gymnasium and came to Palestine in 1937 as an illegal immigrant. He worked intermittently in kibbutzim, stone quarries and British army camps before joining the Jewish Brigade (1942). His experiences during the campaigns in Egypt, North Africa and Italy inspired many of the poems in his early books. He has consistently been one of the most original and experimental Israeli poets, combining traditional elements with colloquial usages, and personal concerns with national motifs.

This poem is discussed on pp. 48–50.

The title of the poem refers to the speaker's dead brother, to the biblical conqueror, and to the moon. The latter allusion is based on a Talmudic comparison: 'The face of Moses is like the face of the sun and the face of Joshua like the face of the moon.'

ABBA KOVNER (1918–88). From his native Sebastopol (Crimea) he moved to Vilna, where he graduated from the Hebrew Gymnasium. He was one of the organizers of the armed revolt in the Vilna Ghetto and later commanded Jewish partisan units in the neighbouring forests. He was imprisoned by the British in Cairo for his involvement in the *beriha* (rescue immigration) operations. In 1946 he settled in a kibbutz, and during the War of Independence served as a cultural officer. Most of his books of poetry are lyric-dramatic sequences, written in a highly-coloured and allusive style. The following poem is taken from the sequence *My Little Sister* (1967), which is set in a Dominican convent in Vilna. Stanza 2 refers to the bowl of broth which the newly-wed couple customarily drink after the ceremony. *Hala* (line 14) is the twisted loaf of Sabbath bread.

ḤAYIM GOURI (b. 1923) was born in Tel Aviv, studied at an agricultural school and served in the Palmaḥ. He was sent on various missions by the Haganah to the displaced persons' camps in Europe, and later saw active service in the Israeli forces during the War of Independence and succeeding campaigns. His later poetry is loosely-patterned and colloquial; it often reflects the volatile moods of the country.

TUVIA RUEBNER (b. 1924) was born in Bratislava (Czechoslovakia) and grew up under the influence of German literature. Soon after his arrival in Palestine, in 1941, he joined a kibbutz. A critic and university lecturer, he has translated medieval and modern German poets into Hebrew and Agnon's prose into German.

YEHUDA AMICHAI (b. 1924), a native of Würzburg, came to Jerusalem with his family in 1936. He served with the Jewish Brigade in the Second World War and as an infantryman in the War of Independence. He has played a leading role in the creation of the new idiom, which shows clear affinities to modern English poetry in its use of irony and understatement, and its juxtaposition of contrasting linguistic materials. His poems, novels and short stories have been widely translated.

The opening sonnet of a lengthy sequence from Amichai's first volume (1955).

The phrase *hakolot hanodedim* ('voices that are straying') in line 11 is a play on *haḥolot hanodedim*, meaning 'quicksand'.

This is included in the cycle 'Jerusalem 1967'. The letters of the Hebrew date (TASHKAḤ) in the opening line evoke the meaning 'you will [make] forget'.

AVNER TREININ (b. 1928), a native of Tel Aviv, is a professor of physical chemistry and Dean of the Faculty of Science at the Hebrew University. He has published three collections of poetry. His later work shows an increasing preoccupation with scientific themes.

DAN PAGIS (1930–86) was born in Radautz (Bukovina). During the Second World War he was interned for several years in a Ukrainian concentration camp. He escaped in 1944 and two years later came to Israel. He taught medieval Hebrew literature at the Hebrew University in his later years. His publications include important studies on the aesthetics of medieval secular poetry, as well as a critical edition of Vogel's collected poetry. All of the following poems are taken from his third book, *Gilgul* ('Transformations', 1970), in which, for the first time, he wrote explicitly of his European experiences.

Line 5 can also be understood as 'Cain, the human being'.

Refers, in the last two lines, to Genesis 37.30: 'The boy is gone! And I – what am I to do?'

NATHAN ZACH (b. 1930), a native of Berlin, came to Palestine with his family in 1935. After serving in the Israeli army, he worked in a publishing house and lectured at Tel Aviv University. As an editor and critic, he took an active, and often controversial, part in the re-evaluation of Hebrew poetry. His translations include plays by Frisch, Brecht and Dürrenmatt, as well as Arabic folk-songs (in collaboration with Rashed Ḥussein).

DALIA RAVIKOVITCH (b. 1936). A native of Ramat-Gan, she was educated in Haifa and Jerusalem, and later worked as a journalist and teacher. She published her first poems while still serving in the army. In addition to four collections of poetry, she is the author of children's books in verse and prose.

THE POEMS

PART ONE

TO THE TENTH CENTURY

שִׁירִים מִן הַמִּקְרָא

Biblical Poetry

שִׁירַת הַיָּם

THE SONG OF THE SEA

אז ישיר משה ובני ישראל את השירה הזאת
ליהוה ויאמרו לאמר:

Then Moses and the Israelites sang this song to the Lord:

אָשִׁירָה לַיהוה,
כִּי גָאֹה גָּאָה:
סוּס וְרֹכְבוֹ
רָמָה בַיָּם.

I shall sing to the Lord, for He has triumphed gloriously: horse and chariot[1] He has hurled into the sea.

עָזִּי וְזִמְרָת—יָהּ,
וַיְהִי לִי לִישׁוּעָה.
זֶה אֵלִי וְאַנְוֵהוּ,
אֱלֹהֵי אָבִי וַאֲרֹמְמֶנְהוּ.
יהוה—אִישׁ מִלְחָמָה;
יהוה שְׁמוֹ.

The Lord is my strength and my protection;[2] He has become my salvation. This is my God, and I shall praise Him; my father's God, and I shall extol Him. The Lord is a warrior; Lord is His name!

מַרְכְּבֹת פַּרְעֹה וְחֵילוֹ
יָרָה בַיָּם,
וּמִבְחַר שָׁלִשָׁיו
טֻבְּעוּ בְיַם סוּף.
תְּהֹמֹת יְכַסְיֻמוּ,
יָרְדוּ בִמְצוֹלֹת כְּמוֹ אָבֶן.

The chariots of Pharaoh and his army He cast into the sea; the pick of his officers were plunged into the Sea of Reeds. The abyss engulfed them; they went down into the depths like a stone.

יְמִינְךָ, יהוה,
נֶאְדָּרִי בַּכֹּחַ;
יְמִינְךָ, יהוה,
תִּרְעַץ אוֹיֵב.

Your right hand, O Lord, is majestic in power; Your right hand, O Lord, shattered the enemy! In Your great

1. Or 'rider'. 2. Or 'song'.

וּבְרֹב גְּאוֹנְךָ
תַּהֲרֹס קָמֶיךָ,
תְּשַׁלַּח חֲרֹנְךָ—
יֹאכְלֵמוֹ כַּקַּשׁ.
וּבְרוּחַ אַפֶּיךָ
נֶעֶרְמוּ מַיִם,
נִצְּבוּ כְמוֹ נֵד—נֹזְלִים,
קָפְאוּ תְהֹמֹת בְּלֶב־יָם.

splendour You destroyed Your foes. You let loose Your fury; it consumed them like straw. At the blast of Your nostrils, the waters were piled up, the waves stood like a wall,[1] the abyss congealed in the heart of the sea.

אָמַר אוֹיֵב:
'אֶרְדֹּף, אַשִּׂיג,
אֲחַלֵּק שָׁלָל,
תִּמְלָאֵמוֹ נַפְשִׁי;
אָרִיק חַרְבִּי,
תּוֹרִישֵׁמוֹ יָדִי.'
נָשַׁפְתָּ בְרוּחֲךָ,
כִּסָּמוֹ יָם;
צָלְלוּ כַּעוֹפֶרֶת
בְּמַיִם אַדִּירִים.

The enemy said: 'I shall pursue, I shall overtake them, I shall divide the spoils; my lust will have its fill; I shall draw my sword; my hand will ravage them.' You blew with Your breath and the sea engulfed them. They sank like lead in the mighty waters.

מִי כָמֹכָה בָּאֵלִם, יהוה?
מִי כָּמֹכָה נֶאְדָּר בַּקֹּדֶשׁ,
נוֹרָא תְהִלֹּת,
עֹשֵׂה פֶלֶא!

Who is like You among the gods, O Lord? Who is like You, majestic in holiness, awesome in fame, worker of miracles!

נָטִיתָ יְמִינְךָ—
תִּבְלָעֵמוֹ אָרֶץ.
נָחִיתָ בְחַסְדְּךָ
עַם, זוּ גָּאָלְתָּ,
נֵהַלְתָּ בְעָזְּךָ
אֶל נְוֵה קָדְשֶׁךָ.

You stretched out Your right hand and the earth[2] swallowed them. In Your love, You led the people whom You had redeemed; in Your strength, You guided them to Your holy abode.[3]

1. Or 'mound, bank, dyke'. 2. The underworld or the sea's floor. 3. This may denote Zion or the whole of Canaan.

שָׁמְעוּ עַמִּים – יִרְגָּזוּן;
חִיל אָחַז יֹשְׁבֵי פְּלָשֶׁת.
אָז נִבְהֲלוּ אַלּוּפֵי אֱדוֹם,
אֵילֵי מוֹאָב – יֹאחֲזֵמוֹ רָעַד,
נָמֹגוּ כֹּל יֹשְׁבֵי כְנָעַן.
תִּפֹּל עֲלֵיהֶם
אֵימָתָה וָפַחַד,
בִּגְדֹל זְרוֹעֲךָ
יִדְּמוּ כָּאָבֶן –
עַד יַעֲבֹר עַמְּךָ, יהוה,
עַד יַעֲבֹר עַם, זוּ קָנִיתָ.

The nations heard and quaked; anguish gripped the dwellers of Philistia. The clans of Edom were dismayed; trembling seized the tribes of Moab; all the dwellers of Canaan melted with fear. Terror and dread fell upon them; by Your mighty arm, they were struck dumb as stone – while Your people, O Lord, passed through, while the people whom You ransomed passed through them.

תְּבִאֵמוֹ וְתִטָּעֵמוֹ
בְּהַר נַחֲלָתְךָ,
מָכוֹן לְשִׁבְתְּךָ
פָּעַלְתָּ, יהוה,
מִקְּדָשׁ, אֲדֹנָי,
כּוֹנְנוּ יָדֶיךָ.
יהוה יִמְלֹךְ
לְעֹלָם וָעֶד!

You will bring them and plant them on the mount of Your inheritance, the place, O Lord, which You chose for Your dwelling, the sanctuary, O Lord, which Your hands established.
The Lord will reign for ever and ever!

שִׁירַת דְּבוֹרָה

THE SONG OF DEBORAH

ותשר דבורה וברק בן אבינעם ביום ההוא לאמר:

On that day, Deborah and Barak, the son of Abinoam, sang this song:

בִּפְרֹעַ פְּרָעוֹת בְּיִשְׂרָאֵל,
בְּהִתְנַדֵּב עָם –
בָּרְכוּ יהוה!

For the warriors, in Israel, who have flowing locks,[1] for the people who are answering the call – praise the Lord!

1. Warriors consecrated themselves by dedicating their hair to God and letting it grow untrimmed. Or, this obscure phrase may mean, 'when there were leaders in Israel, when the people acted nobly . . .'

שִׁמְעוּ, מְלָכִים,
הַאֲזִינוּ, רֹזְנִים!
אָנֹכִי לַיהוה,
אָנֹכִי אָשִׁירָה,
אֲזַמֵּר לַיהוה
אֱלֹהֵי יִשְׂרָאֵל.

Hear, O kings! Princes, give ear! I shall sing to the Lord, I shall sing to Him, I shall chant to the Lord, the God of Israel.

יהוה, בְּצֵאתְךָ מִשֵּׂעִיר,
בְּצַעְדְּךָ מִשְּׂדֵה אֱדוֹם –
אֶרֶץ רָעָשָׁה,
גַּם שָׁמַיִם נָטָפוּ,
גַּם עָבִים נָטְפוּ מָיִם.
הָרִים נָזְלוּ
מִפְּנֵי יהוה,
זֶה סִינַי מִפְּנֵי יהוה
אֱלֹהֵי יִשְׂרָאֵל.

Lord, when You set forth from Seir, when You marched from the land of Edom – the earth quaked and the heavens shook, the clouds poured down in torrents. Mountains melted before the Lord – even Sinai – before the Lord, the God of Israel.

בִּימֵי שַׁמְגַּר בֶּן עֲנָת,
בִּימֵי יָעֵל – חָדְלוּ אֳרָחוֹת;
וְהֹלְכֵי נְתִיבוֹת
יֵלְכוּ אֳרָחוֹת עֲקַלְקַלּוֹת.
חָדְלוּ פְרָזוֹן,
בְּיִשְׂרָאֵל חָדֵלּוּ –
עַד שַׁקַּמְתִּי, דְּבוֹרָה,
שַׁקַּמְתִּי אֵם בְּיִשְׂרָאֵל.
יִבְחַר אֱלֹהִים חֲדָשִׁים –
אָז לָחֶם שְׁעָרִים;
מָגֵן אִם יֵרָאֶה וָרֹמַח
בְּאַרְבָּעִים אֶלֶף בְּיִשְׂרָאֵל.

In the days of Shamgar, son of Anath, in the days of Jael – the highways were abandoned;[1] wayfarers went by roundabout paths. The unwalled towns of Israel were abandoned,[2] all abandoned, until I,[3] Deborah, arose, until I arose, a mother in Israel. Because they had chosen new gods, there was fighting at their gates. Not a shield could be seen, nor a lance, among the forty thousand of Israel.

1. Or 'caravans ceased'. 2. Or 'there were no champions in Israel'. 3. Or 'you'.

לִבִּי לְחוֹקְקֵי יִשְׂרָאֵל,
הַמִּתְנַדְּבִים בָּעָם –
בָּרְכוּ יהוה!

My heart goes out to the captains of Israel, who are answering the call among the people – praise the Lord!

רֹכְבֵי אֲתֹנוֹת צְחֹרוֹת,
יֹשְׁבֵי עַל מִדִּין,
וְהֹלְכֵי עַל דֶּרֶךְ –
שִׂיחוּ!
מִקּוֹל מְחַצְצִים בֵּין מַשְׁאַבִּים,
שָׁם יְתַנּוּ צִדְקוֹת יהוה,
צִדְקֹת פִּרְזוֹנוֹ בְּיִשְׂרָאֵל;
אָז יָרְדוּ לַשְּׁעָרִים עַם יהוה.

O you that ride on tawny donkeys, you that sit on caparisoned camels, you that voyage on foot – celebrate [His praises]! What is that sound of archers by the watering places?[1] There they recount the triumphs of the Lord, His triumphs that made Israel secure in the unwalled towns.[2] For then the people of the Lord marched down to the gates [to wage war].

עוּרִי, עוּרִי, דְּבוֹרָה!
עוּרִי, עוּרִי, דַּבְּרִי שִׁיר!
קוּם, בָּרָק
וּשֲׁבֵה שֶׁבְיְךָ,
בֶּן אֲבִינֹעַם!

Rouse, rouse yourself, Deborah! Rouse yourself, strike up a song! Arise, Barak! Seize your captives, son of Abinoam!

אָז יְרַד שָׂרִיד
לְאַדִּירִים־עָם,
יהוה יְרַד לִי בַּגִּבּוֹרִים.
מִנִּי אֶפְרַיִם, שָׁרְשָׁם בַּעֲמָלֵק;
אַחֲרֶיךָ בִנְיָמִין בַּעֲמָמֶיךָ.
מִנִּי מָכִיר יָרְדוּ מְחֹקְקִים,
וּמִזְּבוּלֻן מֹשְׁכִים בְּשֵׁבֶט סֹפֵר.
וְשָׂרַי בְּיִשָּׂשכָר עִם דְּבֹרָה,
וְיִשָּׂשכָר – כֵּן בָּרָק;
בָּעֵמֶק שֻׁלַּח בְּרַגְלָיו.

Then down marched the nobles, the chieftains of the people; the Lord Himself marched down for me among the valiant.[3] From Ephraim, the nobles came in force,[4] followed by the clans of Benjamin. From Machir, the captains marched down, and from Zebulun, those who bear the marshal's staff. The nobles of Isaschar joined with Deborah, and so did Barak; he sped into the valley on foot.[5]

1. Or 'To the strains of the musicians at the wells, there . . .' 2. Or 'the triumphs of His rule in Israel'.
3. Or 'then down came the remnant [of Israel to wage war] against the mighty [of Canaan]. The people of the Lord came down . . .'
4. Or 'came down to the valley'. 5. Or 'they rushed into the valley at his heels'.

בִּפְלַגּוֹת רְאוּבֵן
גְּדֹלִים חִקְקֵי לֵב.
לָמָּה יָשַׁבְתָּ בֵּין הַמִּשְׁפְּתַיִם
לִשְׁמֹעַ שְׁרִקוֹת עֲדָרִים ?
לִפְלַגּוֹת רְאוּבֵן
גְּדוֹלִים חִקְרֵי לֵב.
גִּלְעָד בְּעֵבֶר הַיַּרְדֵּן שָׁכֵן ;
וְדָן – לָמָּה יָגוּר אֳנִיּוֹת ?
אָשֵׁר יָשַׁב לְחוֹף יַמִּים
וְעַל מִפְרָצָיו יִשְׁכּוֹן.

Among the factions of Reuben there was much heart-searching. Why do you sit idly by the sheep-folds[1] listening to the whistling of the shepherds? Among the factions of Reuben there was much heart-searching! Gilead remained beyond the Jordan; and Dan – why does he tarry aboard his ships? Asher lingers along the sea-shore, remaining beside its coves.

זְבֻלוּן – עַם חֵרֵף נַפְשׁוֹ לָמוּת.
וְנַפְתָּלִי – עַל מְרוֹמֵי שָׂדֶה.

Zebulun – this tribe defied death in battle; and so did Naphtali, on the heights of the battle-field.

בָּאוּ מְלָכִים, נִלְחָמוּ,
אָז נִלְחֲמוּ מַלְכֵי כְנַעַן
בְּתַעְנָךְ, עַל מֵי מְגִדּוֹ ;
בֶּצַע כֶּסֶף לֹא לָקָחוּ.
מִן שָׁמַיִם נִלְחָמוּ,
הַכּוֹכָבִים מִמְּסִלּוֹתָם
נִלְחֲמוּ עִם סִיסְרָא.
נַחַל קִישׁוֹן גְּרָפָם,
נַחַל קְדוּמִים, נַחַל קִישׁוֹן !
תִּדְרְכִי, נַפְשִׁי, עֹז !
אָז הָלְמוּ עִקְּבֵי סוּס
מִדַּהֲרוֹת, דַּהֲרוֹת אַבִּירָיו.

The kings came, they fought; then the kings of Canaan fought at Ta'anach and by the waters of Megiddo; they took no silver booty. From the heavens they fought, the stars from their courses fought against Sisera. The Kishon River swept them away; that ancient river – the river of Kishon! O my soul, stride ahead mightily![2] Then the hoofs of [their own] horses crushed [them],[3] their galloping, galloping steeds.

1. Or 'bonfires'. 2. Or 'bless the Lord's might'. 3. Or 'hammered [the ground]'.

אוֹרוּ מֵרוֹז,
– אָמַר מַלְאַךְ יהוה –
אֹרוּ אָרוֹר יֹשְׁבֶיהָ!
כִּי לֹא בָאוּ לְעֶזְרַת יהוה,
לְעֶזְרַת יהוה בַּגִּבּוֹרִים.

A curse on Meroz! – said the angel of the Lord – a bitter curse on its inhabitants! For they did not come to the help of the Lord, to the help of the Lord in the ranks of the valiant.[1]

תְּבֹרַךְ מִנָּשִׁים יָעֵל,
אֵשֶׁת חֶבֶר הַקֵּינִי,
מִנָּשִׁים בָּאֹהֶל תְּבֹרָךְ!
מַיִם שָׁאַל –
חָלָב נָתָנָה;
בְּסֵפֶל אַדִּירִים
הִקְרִיבָה חֶמְאָה.
יָדָהּ לַיָּתֵד תִּשְׁלַחְנָה,
וִימִינָהּ – לְהַלְמוּת עֲמֵלִים,
וְהָלְמָה סִיסְרָא, מָחֲקָה רֹאשׁוֹ,
וּמָחֲצָה וְחָלְפָה רַקָּתוֹ.
בֵּין רַגְלֶיהָ כָּרַע, נָפַל, שָׁכָב,
בֵּין רַגְלֶיהָ כָּרַע, נָפָל;
בַּאֲשֶׁר כָּרַע –
שָׁם נָפַל שָׁדוּד.

Blessed above women be Jael, the wife of Heber the Kenite, blessed above all women dwelling in tents! He asked for water: she gave him milk; she offered him curds in a lordly bowl. Her left hand reached for the tent-peg, her right, for the workman's mallet. And she struck Sisera, she crushed his head, she shattered his temple and pierced it. At her feet he sank and fell; where he sank down, there he fell, slain.

בְּעַד הַחַלּוֹן נִשְׁקְפָה וַתְּיַבֵּב
אֵם סִיסְרָא, בְּעַד הָאֶשְׁנָב:
'מַדּוּעַ בֹּשֵׁשׁ רִכְבּוֹ לָבוֹא?
מַדּוּעַ אֶחֱרוּ פַּעֲמֵי מַרְכְּבוֹתָיו?'
חַכְמוֹת שָׂרוֹתֶיהָ תַּעֲנֶינָּה,
אַף הִיא תָּשִׁיב אֲמָרֶיהָ לָהּ:

She peered through the window, sobbing, Sisera's mother peered through the lattice: 'Why is his chariot so long in coming? Why is the clatter of his chariots delayed?' The wisest of her ladies reply, and she, too, answers

1. Or 'to the help of the Lord as warriors'.

׳הֲלֹא יִמְצְאוּ, יְחַלְּקוּ שָׁלָל –
רַחַם רַחֲמָתַיִם לְרֹאשׁ גֶּבֶר ;
שְׁלַל צְבָעִים לְסִיסְרָא ;
שְׁלַל צְבָעִים רִקְמָה,
צֶבַע רִקְמָתַיִם לְצַוְּארֵי שָׁלָל.׳

herself in kind: 'They must be finding and dividing the spoils: a girl or two for each man; spoils of dyed cloth for Sisera; spoils of dyed, embroidered cloth, a wealth of dyed embroideries for the victors' necks.'[1]

כֵּן יֹאבְדוּ כָל אוֹיְבֶיךָ, יהוה !
וְאֹהֲבָיו – כְּצֵאת הַשֶּׁמֶשׁ בִּגְבֻרָתוֹ.

May all Your enemies perish thus, O Lord! But those who love Him – they shall be like the sun rising in all its might!

קִינַת דָּוִד עַל מוֹת שָׁאוּל וִיהוֹנָתָן

DAVID'S LAMENT OVER SAUL AND JONATHAN

ויקנן דוד את הקינה הזאת על שאול ועל יהונתן בנו :

Then David chanted this lament over Saul and his son Jonathan:

הַצְּבִי, יִשְׂרָאֵל,
עַל בָּמוֹתֶיךָ חָלָל !
אֵיךְ נָפְלוּ גִבּוֹרִים !

All your glory, O Israel, lies slain upon your heights![2] How the heroes have fallen!

אַל תַּגִּידוּ בְגַת,
אַל תְּבַשְּׂרוּ בְּחוּצֹת אַשְׁקְלוֹן,
פֶּן תִּשְׂמַחְנָה בְּנוֹת פְּלִשְׁתִּים,
פֶּן תַּעֲלֹזְנָה בְּנוֹת הָעֲרֵלִים.

Do not tell of it in Gath, do not proclaim it in the streets of Ashkelon, lest the daughters of the Philistines rejoice, lest the daughters of the uncircumcised exult.

1. Or 'on the necks of the spoils', referring to the captive maidens; or 'for the queen', referring to Sisera's mother.

2. According to a different emendation: 'Raise up a dirge over your slain bodies'.

הָרֵי בַגִּלְבֹּעַ,
אַל טַל וְאַל מָטָר עֲלֵיכֶם
וּשְׂדֵי תְרוּמֹת!
כִּי שָׁם נִגְעַל מָגֵן גִּבּוֹרִים,
מָגֵן שָׁאוּל, בְּלִי מָשִׁיחַ בַּשָּׁמֶן.

You mountains of Gilboa – let there be no dew or rain upon you, no fertile fields![1] For there, the hero's shield[2] was defiled, the shield of Saul no longer anointed with oil.

מִדַּם חֲלָלִים,
מֵחֵלֶב גִּבּוֹרִים
קֶשֶׁת יְהוֹנָתָן לֹא נָשׂוֹג אָחוֹר
וְחֶרֶב שָׁאוּל לֹא תָשׁוּב רֵיקָם.

From the blood of the slain,[3] from the fat of the heroes – the bow of Jonathan never recoiled, the sword of Saul never returned unstained.

שָׁאוּל וִיהוֹנָתָן,
הַנֶּאֱהָבִים וְהַנְּעִימִם,
בְּחַיֵּיהֶם וּבְמוֹתָם לֹא נִפְרָדוּ.
מִנְּשָׁרִים קַלּוּ,
מֵאֲרָיוֹת גָּבֵרוּ.

Saul and Jonathan, beloved and cherished – in life and death they were not parted. They were swifter than eagles, stronger than lions.

בְּנוֹת יִשְׂרָאֵל, אֶל שָׁאוּל בְּכֶינָה,
הַמַּלְבִּשְׁכֶם שָׁנִי עִם עֲדָנִים,
הַמַּעֲלֶה עֲדִי זָהָב עַל לְבוּשְׁכֶן!

Daughters of Israel, weep for Saul, who dressed you in scarlet and finery, who decked your clothing with adornments of gold.

אֵיךְ נָפְלוּ גִבֹּרִים
בְּתוֹךְ הַמִּלְחָמָה!
יְהוֹנָתָן – עַל בָּמוֹתֶיךָ חָלָל!

How the heroes have fallen in the thick of the battle! O Jonathan – slain upon your heights!

1. Or 'no upsurging of the depths', that is, no water from springs or wells.
2. Or 'the shields of the heroes'. 3. Or 'of the valiant'.

צַר לִי עָלֶיךָ,
אָחִי יְהוֹנָתָן,
נָעַמְתָּ לִּי מְאֹד.
נִפְלְאַתָה אַהֲבָתְךָ לִי
מֵאַהֲבַת נָשִׁים.

I grieve for you, my brother, Jonathan. You were most dear to me. Your love for me was more wonderful than the love of women.

אֵיךְ נָפְלוּ גִבּוֹרִים
וַיֹּאבְדוּ כְּלֵי מִלְחָמָה!

How the heroes have fallen and the weapons of war perished.[1]

חֲזוֹן יְשַׁעְיָהוּ בֶּן־אָמוֹץ

THE INDICTMENT OF ISRAEL

שִׁמְעוּ, שָׁמַיִם,
וְהַאֲזִינִי, אֶרֶץ –
כִּי יהוה דִּבֵּר:

Hear, O heavens, and listen, O earth, for the Lord has spoken:

׳בָּנִים גִּדַּלְתִּי וְרוֹמַמְתִּי,
וְהֵם פָּשְׁעוּ בִי.
יָדַע שׁוֹר קֹנֵהוּ,
וַחֲמוֹר – אֵבוּס בְּעָלָיו;
יִשְׂרָאֵל לֹא יָדַע,
עַמִּי לֹא הִתְבּוֹנָן.׳

'I have raised children and reared them, but they have rebelled against me. The ox knows its owner and the ass its master's stall; but Israel does not know, My people has no understanding!

1. Saul and Jonathan are referred to as the 'instruments of war' which have been destroyed.

הוֹי, גּוֹי חֹטֵא,
עַם כֶּבֶד עָוֺן,
זֶרַע מְרֵעִים,
בָּנִים מַשְׁחִיתִים!
עָזְבוּ אֶת יהוה,
נִאֲצוּ אֶת קְדוֹשׁ יִשְׂרָאֵל,
נָזֹרוּ אָחוֹר.

O sinful nation, people heavy with crime, brood of evildoers, depraved children! They have forsaken the Lord, they have spurned the Holy One of Israel and turned their backs on Him.

עַל מֶה תֻכּוּ —
עוֹד תּוֹסִיפוּ סָרָה?
כָּל רֹאשׁ לָחֳלִי
וְכָל לֵבָב דַּוָּי.
מִכַּף רֶגֶל וְעַד רֹאשׁ
אֵין בּוֹ מְתֹם:
פֶּצַע וְחַבּוּרָה
וּמַכָּה טְרִיָּה,
לֹא זֹרוּ וְלֹא חֻבָּשׁוּ
וְלֹא רֻכְּכָה בַּשָּׁמֶן.
אַרְצְכֶם שְׁמָמָה,
עָרֵיכֶם שְׂרֻפוֹת אֵשׁ;
אַדְמַתְכֶם — לְנֶגְדְּכֶם
זָרִים אֹכְלִים אֹתָהּ;
וּשְׁמָמָה כְּמַהְפֵּכַת זָרִים.
וְנוֹתְרָה בַת־צִיּוֹן
כְּסֻכָּה בְכָרֶם,

Where can you still be struck, if you persist in your revolt?[1] Every head is diseased and every heart is in pain.[2] From head to foot there is not a sound spot: nothing but wounds and welts and festering sores which have not been drained or bandaged or softened with oil. Your country is desolate, your cities burnt to ashes; strangers devour your land before your very eyes; it is as desolate as Sodom[3] overthrown. Only the daughter of Zion[4] remains – like a watchman's hut in a vineyard, like a

1. Or 'Why would you be struck again? Why do you persist in your rebelliousness?'
2. Or 'The whole head . . . the whole heart . . .'
3. Lit. 'strangers, aliens'; 'Sodom' is conjectural. Or, the meaning could be: 'God has wreaked such desolation as He wreaks upon strangers.'
4. A common term for Jerusalem, 'daughter-Zion'.

כִּמְלוּנָה בְמִקְשָׁה,
כְּעִיר נְצוּרָה.
לוּלֵי יהוה צְבָאוֹת
הוֹתִיר לָנוּ שָׂרִיד כִּמְעָט –
כִּסְדֹם הָיִינוּ,
לַעֲמֹרָה דָּמִינוּ.

shed in a cucumber-field – a city under siege. If the Lord of hosts had not left us a scanty remnant, we should have been like Sodom, we should have become like Gomorrah.

שִׁמְעוּ דְבַר יהוה,
קְצִינֵי סְדֹם!
הַאֲזִינוּ תּוֹרַת אֱלֹהֵינוּ,
עַם עֲמֹרָה!
'לָמָּה לִּי רֹב זִבְחֵיכֶם?'
יֹאמַר יהוה.
'שָׂבַעְתִּי עֹלוֹת אֵילִים
וְחֵלֶב מְרִיאִים;
וְדַם פָּרִים וּכְבָשִׂים וְעַתּוּדִים
לֹא חָפָצְתִּי.
כִּי תָבֹאוּ לֵרָאוֹת פָּנָי –
מִי בִקֵּשׁ זֹאת מִיֶּדְכֶם
רְמֹס חֲצֵרָי?
לֹא תוֹסִיפוּ הָבִיא מִנְחַת שָׁוְא.
קְטֹרֶת – תּוֹעֵבָה הִיא לִי.
חֹדֶשׁ וְשַׁבָּת קְרֹא מִקְרָא –
לֹא אוּכַל אָוֶן וַעֲצָרָה.
חָדְשֵׁיכֶם וּמוֹעֲדֵיכֶם
שָׂנְאָה נַפְשִׁי,
הָיוּ עָלַי לָטֹרַח,
נִלְאֵיתִי נְשֹׂא.
וּבְפָרִשְׂכֶם כַּפֵּיכֶם,
אַעְלִים עֵינַי מִכֶּם;

Hear the word of the Lord, rulers of Sodom! Listen to the teaching of our God, people of Gomorrah! 'What need do I have of your countless sacrifices?' says the Lord. 'I have had my fill of burnt offerings of rams and the suet of fatlings; I take no delight in the blood of bulls, lambs and he-goats. When you come to appear before Me – who has required of you that you trample My courts? Bring no more worthless offerings; your incense is an abomination to Me. New moons and sabbaths and sacred assemblies – I cannot endure solemn congregations joined with evil. Your new moons and your festivals fill me with loathing; they have become a burden to me, I can bear them no longer. And when you spread out your hands, I shall avert My

גַּם כִּי תַרְבּוּ תְפִלָּה,
אֵינֶנִּי שֹׁמֵעַ;
יְדֵיכֶם דָּמִים מָלֵאוּ.

eyes from you. Though you pray continuously, I shall not listen: your hands are full of blood!

רַחֲצוּ, הִזַּכּוּ,
הָסִירוּ רֹעַ מַעַלְלֵיכֶם
מִנֶּגֶד עֵינָי!
חִדְלוּ הָרֵעַ,
לִמְדוּ הֵיטֵב,
דִּרְשׁוּ מִשְׁפָּט,
אַשְּׁרוּ חָמוֹץ,
שִׁפְטוּ יָתוֹם,
רִיבוּ אַלְמָנָה!'

'Wash yourselves, cleanse yourselves, put your evil deeds out of my sight! Cease doing evil, learn to do good, seek justice, sustain the oppressed, defend the fatherless, plead the widow's cause!

'לְכוּ נָא וְנִוָּכְחָה!'
יֹאמַר יהוה.
'אִם יִהְיוּ חֲטָאֵיכֶם כַּשָּׁנִים –
כַּשֶּׁלֶג יַלְבִּינוּ,
אִם יַאְדִּימוּ כַתּוֹלָע –
כַּצֶּמֶר יִהְיוּ.
אִם תֹּאבוּ וּשְׁמַעְתֶּם –
טוּב הָאָרֶץ תֹּאכֵלוּ;
וְאִם תְּמָאֲנוּ וּמְרִיתֶם –
חֶרֶב תְּאֻכְּלוּ' –
כִּי פִּי יהוה דִּבֵּר.

'Come now, let us settle our accounts,' says the Lord. 'Though your sins be like scarlet, they can yet turn white as snow; though they be red as crimson, they can yet become like wool. If you consent and obey, you will eat the fat of the land; but if you refuse and rebel, you will be consumed by the sword' – for the mouth of the Lord has spoken!

הַמָּשָׁל עַל מֶלֶךְ בָּבֶל

TAUNT DIRGE

והיה ביום הָנִיחַ יהוה לך מעצבך ומרגזֶךָ, ומן העבדה הקשה אשר עֻבַּד בך – ונשאת המשל הזה על מלך בבל, ואמרת:

When the day comes that the Lord gives you relief from your sorrow and anguish, and from the cruel servitude imposed upon you, you will take up this song of derision against the king of Babylon:

אֵיךְ שָׁבַת נֹגֵשׂ,
שָׁבְתָה מַדְהֵבָה!
שָׁבַר יהוה מַטֵּה רְשָׁעִים,
שֵׁבֶט מֹשְׁלִים.
מַכֶּה עַמִּים בְּעֶבְרָה
מַכַּת בִּלְתִּי סָרָה,
רֹדֶה בָאַף גּוֹיִם –
מֻרְדָּף בְּלִי חָשָׂךְ.
נָחָה, שָׁקְטָה כָּל הָאָרֶץ,
פָּצְחוּ רִנָּה;
גַּם בְּרוֹשִׁים שָׂמְחוּ לְךָ,
אַרְזֵי לְבָנוֹן:
'מֵאָז שָׁכַבְתָּ – לֹא יַעֲלֶה
הַכֹּרֵת עָלֵינוּ'.

How the oppressor has met his end! How his arrogance[1] has come to an end! The Lord has broken the staff of the wicked, the rod of the ruler, that struck peoples down in wrath, with ceaseless blows, and drove the nations in fury, with relentless tyranny. The whole earth is relieved and peaceful; all things break into song. Even the cypresses rejoice at your fate, even the cedars of Lebanon: 'Now that you have been laid to rest, no one will come to hew us down.'

שְׁאוֹל מִתַּחַת רָגְזָה לְךָ
לִקְרַאת בּוֹאֶךָ;
עוֹרֵר לְךָ רְפָאִים,
כָּל עַתּוּדֵי אָרֶץ;
הֵקִים מִכִּסְאוֹתָם
כֹּל מַלְכֵי גוֹיִם.
כֻּלָּם יַעֲנוּ
וְיֹאמְרוּ אֵלֶיךָ:

Sheol was all astir, awaiting your arrival: it roused the shades for you, all the leaders of the earth; it made the kings of all the nations rise from their thrones. They all speak out and say to

1. Or 'tyranny'; or 'imposition of taxes'.

׳גַּם אַתָּה חֻלֵּיתָ כָמוֹנוּ,
אֵלֵינוּ נִמְשָׁלְתָּ.
הוּרַד שְׁאוֹל גְּאוֹנֶךָ,
הֶמְיַת נְבָלֶיךָ;
תַּחְתֶּיךָ יֻצַּע רִמָּה,
וּמְכַסֶּיךָ תּוֹלֵעָה.׳

you: 'So you, too, have been enfeebled by disease, like us; you have become one of us. Your pomp has been brought down to Sheol, and the music of your lutes. Maggots will be your bedding, and worms your covering.'

אֵיךְ נָפַלְתָּ מִשָּׁמַיִם,
הֵילֵל בֶּן שָׁחַר!
נִגְדַּעְתָּ לָאָרֶץ,
חוֹלֵשׁ עַל גּוֹיִם!
וְאַתָּה אָמַרְתָּ בִלְבָבְךָ:
׳הַשָּׁמַיִם אֶעֱלֶה,
מִמַּעַל לְכוֹכְבֵי אֵל
אָרִים כִּסְאִי,
וְאֵשֵׁב בְּהַר־מוֹעֵד,
בְּיַרְכְּתֵי צָפוֹן;
אֶעֱלֶה עַל בָּמֳתֵי עָב,
אֶדַּמֶּה לְעֶלְיוֹן.׳
אַךְ אֶל שְׁאוֹל תּוּרָד,
אֶל יַרְכְּתֵי בוֹר.

How you have fallen from heaven, O radiant star of the dawn![1] How you have been felled to the ground – you who mowed down the nations! And you had said in your heart: 'I shall scale the heavens. I shall set my throne higher than the stars of God, and take my seat on the Mount of Assembly,[2] in the farthest reaches of the north. I shall scale the pinnacles of the clouds,[3] I shall be equal to the Most High!' But you have been brought down to Sheol, to the farthest reaches of the pit!

רֹאֶיךָ — אֵלֶיךָ יַשְׁגִּיחוּ,
אֵלֶיךָ יִתְבּוֹנָנוּ:
׳הֲזֶה הָאִישׁ מַרְגִּיז הָאָרֶץ,
מַרְעִישׁ מַמְלָכוֹת?

Those who see you stare at you, peer at you closely: Is this the man who shook the earth and made kingdoms tremble?

1. Lit. 'Shining One (*Helel*) son of Dawn (*ben Shaḥar*)', a minor Canaanite deity.
2. A mountain which, according to Mesopotamian belief, served as the meeting place of the gods.
3. Or 'I shall mount the backs of the clouds'.

שָׂם תֵּבֵל כַּמִּדְבָּר
וְעָרָיו הָרָס ?
אֲסִירָיו לֹא פָתַח בָּיְתָה ?׳

Who turned the world into a desert, and razed its cities? Who never set his captives free, to let them go home?

כָּל מַלְכֵי גוֹיִם כֻּלָּם
שָׁכְבוּ בְכָבוֹד אִישׁ בְּבֵיתוֹ ;
וְאַתָּה הָשְׁלַכְתָּ מִקִּבְרְךָ
כְּנֵצֶר נִתְעָב ;
לְבֻשׁ הֲרֻגִים מְטֹעֲנֵי חָרֶב,
יוֹרְדֵי אֶל אַבְנֵי בוֹר
כְּפֶגֶר מוּבָס.
לֹא תֵחַד אִתָּם בִּקְבוּרָה
כִּי אַרְצְךָ שִׁחַתָּ,
עַמְּךָ הָרָגְתָּ.

All the kings of the nations were laid to rest with honour, each in his sepulchre, but you were cast aside, unburied, like a rotten branch;[1] your clothes like those who are slashed to death by the sword; those who go down into a stony pit[2] like trampled carrion. You will not share their [royal] burial because you ravaged your land, you murdered your people!

לֹא יִקָּרֵא לְעוֹלָם
זֶרַע מְרֵעִים.
הָכִינוּ לְבָנָיו מַטְבֵּחַ
בַּעֲוֹן אֲבוֹתָם —
בַּל יָקֻמוּ וְיָרְשׁוּ אָרֶץ,
וּמָלְאוּ פְנֵי תֵבֵל עָרִים.

Let his brood of evildoers never again be named! Prepare a slaughterhouse for his sons, for the guilt of their father; lest they rise to possess the earth and cover the face of the world with despots![3]

1. Lit. 'contemptible branch'; the expression has also been interpreted as 'untimely birth' or 'loathsome carcass, putrefaction'.
2. A common grave in the battle-field.
3. This word has been variously translated as '[fortified] cities', 'ruins', or 'enemies'.

מִכְתָּב לְחִזְקִיָּהוּ

מכתב לחזקיהו מלך יהודה בחלתו, ויחי מֵחָליו:

אֲנִי אָמַרְתִּי:
בִּדְמִי יָמַי אֵלֵכָה,
בְּשַׁעֲרֵי שְׁאוֹל פֻּקַּדְתִּי
יֶתֶר שְׁנוֹתָי.
אָמַרְתִּי: לֹא אֶרְאֶה יָהּ,
יָהּ בְּאֶרֶץ הַחַיִּים;
לֹא אַבִּיט אָדָם עוֹד
עִם יוֹשְׁבֵי חָדֶל.
דּוֹרִי נִסַּע וְנִגְלָה מִנִּי
כְּאֹהֶל רֹעִי.
קִפַּדְתִּי כָאֹרֵג חַיַּי,
מִדַּלָּה יְבַצְּעֵנִי.
מִיּוֹם עַד לַיְלָה תַּשְׁלִימֵנִי.
שִׁוִּיתִי עַד בֹּקֶר,
כָּאֲרִי כֵּן יְשַׁבֵּר כָּל עַצְמוֹתָי.
מִיּוֹם עַד לַיְלָה תַּשְׁלִימֵנִי.
כְּסוּס, עָגוּר – כֵּן אֲצַפְצֵף,
אֶהְגֶּה כַּיּוֹנָה.
דַּלּוּ עֵינַי לַמָּרוֹם:
אֲדֹנָי, עָשְׁקָה לִּי – עָרְבֵנִי!

HEZEKIAH'S HYMN OF THANKSGIVING

A psalm by Hezekiah, king of Judah, upon recovering from his illness:

I thought: I shall depart in the midst[1] of my days; I am consigned to the gates of Sheol for the rest of my years. I thought: I shall never see the Lord again,[2] the Lord in the land of the living; I shall no more behold the face of men among the inhabitants of the earth. My dwelling,[3] like a shepherd's tent, is being pulled up and taken away from me. You are cutting off[4] my life, as a weaver severs the thrum. Between morning and nightfall, You will put an end to me. I cried out until daybreak: 'Like a lion, He[5] is crushing all my bones!' Between morning and nightfall, You will put an end to me. I twittered like a swallow, like a wryneck, I moaned like a dove. My wearied eyes were raised to heaven: 'O Lord, I am in misery, be my surety!' But what

1. Or 'stillness'.
2. I.e., visit His Temple.
3. Possibly, a reference to his body.
4. Or 'folding up'.
5. Or 'it [the illness]'.

מָה אֲדַבֵּר ? — וְאָמַר לִי ;
וְהוּא עָשָׂה.
אֶדַּדֶּה כָל שְׁנוֹתַי
עַל מַר נַפְשִׁי.
אֲדֹנָי ! עֲלֵיהֶם יִחְיוּ,
וּלְכָל בָּהֶן חַיֵּי רוּחִי,
וְתַחֲלִימֵנִי וְהַחֲיֵנִי !
הִנֵּה לְשָׁלוֹם —
מַר לִי מָר !

more can I say? He told me [this would come to pass], this is His doing.[1] I shall spend all my years wandering [through the underworld] with a bitter soul. 'O Lord, the days of my life are Yours, and Yours is the life of my spirit – restore me, bring me back to life! O give me peace, my lot is most bitter!'[2]

וְאַתָּה חָשַׁקְתָּ נַפְשִׁי
מִשַּׁחַת בְּלִי,
כִּי הִשְׁלַכְתָּ אַחֲרֵי גֵוְךָ
כָּל חֲטָאָי.
כִּי לֹא שְׁאוֹל תּוֹדֶךָּ,
מָוֶת — יְהַלְלֶךָּ ;
לֹא יְשַׂבְּרוּ יוֹרְדֵי בוֹר
אֶל אֲמִתֶּךָ.
חַי, חַי — הוּא יוֹדֶךָ
כָּמוֹנִי הַיּוֹם ;
אָב לְבָנִים יוֹדִיעַ
אֶל אֲמִתֶּךָ.

Then, loving me, You spared my life from the pit of destruction, when You cast all my sins behind Your back. For Sheol cannot praise you, Death cannot acclaim You. Those who sink into the pit cannot hope for Your kindness.[3] It is the living, only the living, who can give You praise, as I do this day. The [living] father proclaims Your kindness[3] to his sons.

יהוה לְהוֹשִׁיעֵנִי,
וּנְגִינוֹתַי נְנַגֵּן
כָּל יְמֵי חַיֵּינוּ
עַל בֵּית יהוה.

The Lord has come to my rescue, and we shall sing His praises, all the days of our life, in the House of the Lord.

1. Or 'What more can I say or tell Him? He has done it!' According to some interpretations, Hezekiah begins to celebrate his recovery at this point, and the following verses are rendered differently.
2. Or 'My great bitterness was transformed into peace'.
3. Or 'faithfulness, grace, truth'.

יהוה רֹעִי

THE LORD IS MY SHEPHERD

מזמור לדוד:

A psalm of David:

יהוה רֹעִי – לֹא אֶחְסָר:
בִּנְאוֹת דֶּשֶׁא יַרְבִּיצֵנִי,
עַל מֵי־מְנֻחוֹת יְנַהֲלֵנִי.
נַפְשִׁי יְשׁוֹבֵב,
יַנְחֵנִי בְמַעְגְּלֵי צֶדֶק
לְמַעַן שְׁמוֹ.
גַּם כִּי אֵלֵךְ
בְּגֵיא צַלְמָוֶת –
לֹא אִירָא רָע,
כִּי אַתָּה עִמָּדִי.
שִׁבְטְךָ וּמִשְׁעַנְתֶּךָ
הֵמָּה יְנַחֲמֻנִי.

The Lord is my shepherd, I lack nothing at all. He lays me down in green pastures, He leads me to calm waters.[1] He refreshes my soul. He guides me in straight paths for His own sake. Even when I walk through a valley of pitch darkness,[2] I fear no danger, for You are beside me. Your rod and Your staff – they give me comfort.

תַּעֲרֹךְ לְפָנַי שֻׁלְחָן
נֶגֶד צֹרְרָי;
דִּשַּׁנְתָּ בַשֶּׁמֶן ראשִׁי,
כּוֹסִי רְוָיָה.
אַךְ טוֹב וָחֶסֶד יִרְדְּפוּנִי
כָּל יְמֵי חַיָּי,
וְשַׁבְתִּי בְּבֵית יהוה
לְאֹרֶךְ יָמִים.

You spread a table for me in full view of my enemies. You anoint my head with oil; my cup is brim-full. Only goodness and mercy will follow me all the days of my life, and I shall live in the Lord's house for many, many years.

1. Or 'waters in places of repose'.
2. Or 'the valley of the shadow of death'.

כְּאַיָּל תַּעֲרֹג עַל אֲפִיקֵי־מָיִם

YEARNING FOR GOD

למנצח משכיל לבני קרח :

For the choirmaster ; a maskil *of the Korahites :*[1]

כְּאַיָּל תַּעֲרֹג עַל אֲפִיקֵי־מָיִם,
כֵּן נַפְשִׁי תַעֲרֹג אֵלֶיךָ, אֱלֹהִים!
צָמְאָה נַפְשִׁי לֵאלֹהִים,
לְאֵל חָי – מָתַי אָבוֹא וְאֵרָאֶה
פְּנֵי אֱלֹהִים?

As the deer longs for[2] running waters, so does my soul long for You, O God! My soul thirsts for God, for the living God; when shall I come before God?

הָיְתָה לִּי דִמְעָתִי לֶחֶם
יוֹמָם וָלָיְלָה,
בֶּאֱמֹר אֵלַי כָּל הַיּוֹם:
'אַיֵּה אֱלֹהֶיךָ?'
אֵלֶּה אֶזְכְּרָה
וְאֶשְׁפְּכָה עָלַי נַפְשִׁי:
כִּי אֶעֱבֹר בַּסָּךְ,
אֶדַּדֵּם עַד בֵּית־אֱלֹהִים
בְּקוֹל רִנָּה וְתוֹדָה,
הָמוֹן חוֹגֵג.

My tears have been my food day and night, as people taunt me, day after day: 'Where is your God?' I pour out my soul when I recall [the old days]: how I marched in the procession moving slowly[3] towards the house of God, with joyous shouts of praise, amid the festive throng.

מַה תִּשְׁתּוֹחֲחִי, נַפְשִׁי,
וַתֶּהֱמִי עָלָי?
הוֹחִלִי לֵאלֹהִים!
כִּי עוֹד אוֹדֶנּוּ,
יְשׁוּעוֹת פָּנָיו.

Why are you so desolate, my soul, why so distraught within me?[4] Hope in God. For I shall still praise Him for His saving presence.

1. *Maskil* is a type of song, perhaps 'artistic song, didactic poem'. The Korahites, or 'sons of Korah', were a guild of temple singers in the post-exilic period.
2. Or 'cries out for'.
3. The meaning of the Hebrew is uncertain.
4. Or 'why do you moan within me?'

אֱלֹהַי, עָלַי נַפְשִׁי תִשְׁתּוֹחָח —
עַל כֵּן אֶזְכָּרְךָ
מֵאֶרֶץ יַרְדֵּן וְחֶרְמוֹנִים,
מֵהַר מִצְעָר.
תְּהוֹם אֶל תְּהוֹם קוֹרֵא
לְקוֹל צִנּוֹרֶיךָ.
כָּל מִשְׁבָּרֶיךָ וְגַלֶּיךָ
עָלַי עָבָרוּ.

O God, my soul is desolate within me, and so from this land of the Jordan, the ranges of Hermon and Mount Mizar, I turn my thoughts to You. [Here] deep calls to deep in the roar of Your cataracts. All Your breakers and Your floods have swept over me.

יוֹמָם יְצַוֶּה יהוה חַסְדּוֹ,
וּבַלַּיְלָה שִׁירֹה עִמִּי:
תְּפִלָּה לְאֵל חַיָּי.
אוֹמְרָה לְאֵל־סַלְעִי:
'לָמָה שְׁכַחְתָּנִי?
לָמָּה קֹדֵר אֵלֵךְ
בְּלַחַץ אוֹיֵב?'
בְּרֶצַח, בְּעַצְמוֹתַי
חֵרְפוּנִי צוֹרְרָי,
בְּאָמְרָם אֵלַי כָּל הַיּוֹם:
'אַיֵּה אֱלֹהֶיךָ?'

May the Lord bestow his steadfast love by day, and may His song be with me every night: a prayer to the God of my life. I say to God, my Rock: 'Why have You forgotten me? Why must I go about in squalid black, tormented by the enemy?' My foes revile me, their jeers shatter my bones, as they taunt me, day after day: 'Where is your God?'

מַה תִּשְׁתּוֹחֲחִי, נַפְשִׁי,
וּמַה תֶּהֱמִי עָלָי?
הוֹחִילִי לֵאלֹהִים!
כִּי עוֹד אוֹדֶנּוּ,
יְשׁוּעֹת פָּנַי וֵאלֹהָי.

Why are you so desolate, my soul, why so distraught within me? Hope in God. For I shall still praise Him, my ever-present saviour, my God.

שָׁפְטֵנִי, אֱלֹהִים,
וְרִיבָה רִיבִי
מִגּוֹי לֹא־חָסִיד;

Grant me justice, O God, and champion my cause against impious people.

מֵאִישׁ מִרְמָה וְעַוְלָה תְפַלְּטֵנִי.
כִּי אַתָּה אֱלֹהֵי מָעוּזִּי,
לָמָה זְנַחְתָּנִי ?
לָמָּה קֹדֵר אֶתְהַלֵּךְ
בְּלַחַץ אוֹיֵב ?

Save me from treacherous and evil men. For You are my God, my stronghold; why, then, have You rejected me? Why must I go about in squalid black, tormented by the enemy?

שְׁלַח אוֹרְךָ וַאֲמִתְּךָ —
הֵמָּה יַנְחוּנִי,
יְבִיאוּנִי אֶל הַר קָדְשְׁךָ
וְאֶל מִשְׁכְּנוֹתֶיךָ.
וְאָבוֹאָה אֶל מִזְבַּח אֱלֹהִים,
אֶל אֵל שִׂמְחַת גִּילִי,
וְאוֹדְךָ בְכִנּוֹר, אֱלֹהִים אֱלֹהָי!

Send forth Your light and Your truth; they will guide me and bring me to Your dwelling place. Then I shall come to the altar of God, the God of my joy and my delight, and I shall praise You with the lyre, O God, my God!

מַה תִּשְׁתּוֹחֲחִי, נַפְשִׁי,
וּמַה תֶּהֱמִי עָלָי ?
הוֹחִילִי לֵאלֹהִים!
כִּי עוֹד אוֹדֶנּוּ,
יְשׁוּעֹת פָּנַי וֵאלֹהָי.

Why are you so desolate, my soul, why so distraught within me? Hope in God. For I shall still praise Him, my ever-present saviour, my God.

בָּרְכִי, נַפְשִׁי, אֶת יהוה

IN PRAISE OF THE CREATOR

בָּרְכִי, נַפְשִׁי, אֶת יהוה!

O my soul, bless the Lord!

יהוה אֱלֹהַי, גָּדַלְתָּ מְּאֹד,
הוֹד וְהָדָר לָבָשְׁתָּ:
עֹטֶה אוֹר כַּשַּׂלְמָה,
נוֹטֶה שָׁמַיִם כַּיְרִיעָה;

O Lord, my God, You are very great, clothed in majesty and splendour: You wrapped yourself in light as in a cloak; You spread out the heavens like a tent;

הַמְקָרֶה בַמַּיִם עֲלִיּוֹתָיו;
הַשָּׂם עָבִים רְכוּבוֹ,
הַמְהַלֵּךְ עַל כַּנְפֵי־רוּחַ;
עֹשֶׂה מַלְאָכָיו רוּחוֹת,
מְשָׁרְתָיו — אֵשׁ לֹהֵט.

You laid the beams of Your high chambers upon the waters;[1] You take the clouds for Your chariot, You ride on the wings of the wind; You make the winds Your messengers, and flaming fires Your servants.

יָסַד אֶרֶץ עַל מְכוֹנֶיהָ,
בַּל־תִּמּוֹט עוֹלָם וָעֶד.
תְּהוֹם כַּלְּבוּשׁ כִּסִּיתוֹ,
עַל הָרִים יַעַמְדוּ מָיִם.
מִן גַּעֲרָתְךָ יְנוּסוּן,
מִן קוֹל־רַעַמְךָ יֵחָפֵזוּן —
יַעֲלוּ הָרִים, יֵרְדוּ בְקָעוֹת,
אֶל מְקוֹם זֶה יָסַדְתָּ לָהֶם.
גְּבוּל שַׂמְתָּ, בַּל־יַעֲבֹרוּן,
בַּל־יְשׁוּבוּן לְכַסּוֹת הָאָרֶץ.

You fixed the earth on its foundations, so that it should never totter. You covered it with the abyss[2] as with a garment; the waters stood above the mountains. Then, at Your rebuke, they fled; at the blast of Your thunder they rushed away, streaming up the mountains and down into the valleys[3] to the place You had assigned them. You fixed their bounds: they may not pass them or cover the earth again.

הַמְשַׁלֵּחַ מַעְיָנִים בַּנְּחָלִים:
בֵּין הָרִים יְהַלֵּכוּן,
יַשְׁקוּ כָּל חַיְתוֹ־שָׂדָי,
יִשְׁבְּרוּ פְרָאִים צְמָאָם;
עֲלֵיהֶם עוֹף־הַשָּׁמַיִם יִשְׁכּוֹן,
מִבֵּין עֳפָאיִם יִתְּנוּ קוֹל.

You send forth springs into the gullies: they wind their way between the mountains, giving drink to all the animals; there the wild asses quench their thirst; the birds of the air dwell beside them, singing their songs from among the branches.

מַשְׁקֶה הָרִים מֵעֲלִיּוֹתָיו,
מִפְּרִי מַעֲשֶׂיךָ תִּשְׂבַּע הָאָרֶץ:
מַצְמִיחַ חָצִיר לַבְּהֵמָה
וְעֵשֶׂב — לַעֲבֹדַת הָאָדָם

You water the mountains from Your high chambers, the earth abounds with the fruit of Your works. You make grass grow for the cattle and grains for the service of man, bringing food out of

1. The royal palace of God was founded on the upper waters, above the firmaments.
2. Or 'You covered the depths [with water] as with a garment'.
3. Or 'as the mountains rose, they went down into the valleys'.

לְהוֹצִיא לֶחֶם מִן הָאָרֶץ;
וְיַיִן יְשַׂמַּח לְבַב־אֱנוֹשׁ,
לְהַצְהִיל פָּנִים מִשָּׁמֶן,
וְלֶחֶם לְבַב־אֱנוֹשׁ יִסְעָד.
יִשְׂבְּעוּ עֲצֵי־יהוה,
אַרְזֵי־לְבָנוֹן אֲשֶׁר נָטָע,
אֲשֶׁר שָׁם צִפֳּרִים יְקַנֵּנוּ.
חֲסִידָה – בְּרוֹשִׁים בֵּיתָהּ;
הָרִים הַגְּבֹהִים – לַיְּעֵלִים,
סְלָעִים – מַחְסֶה לַשְׁפַנִּים.

the earth; and wine that gladdens man's heart, oil that makes his face shine, and bread that strengthens man's heart. The trees of the Lord drink their fill, the cedars of Lebanon which He planted, where the birds build their nests. The stork makes her home among the junipers; the high mountains are for the wild goats; the cliffs are a refuge for rock-badgers.

עָשָׂה יָרֵחַ לְמוֹעֲדִים,
שֶׁמֶשׁ יָדַע מְבוֹאוֹ.
תָּשֶׁת חֹשֶׁךְ – וִיהִי לָיְלָה,
בּוֹ תִרְמֹשׂ כָּל חַיְתוֹ־יָעַר:
הַכְּפִירִים שֹׁאֲגִים לַטָּרֶף
וּלְבַקֵּשׁ מֵאֵל אָכְלָם;
תִּזְרַח הַשֶּׁמֶשׁ – יֵאָסֵפוּן
וְאֶל מְעוֹנֹתָם יִרְבָּצוּן;
יֵצֵא אָדָם לְפָעֳלוֹ
וְלַעֲבֹדָתוֹ – עֲדֵי עָרֶב.

You made the moon to mark the seasons; the sun knows when it must set. You bring on darkness, and night comes; then all the beasts of the forest prowl. The young lions roar for prey, looking to God for their food. When the sun rises, they steal away to lie down in their lairs. Then man goes out to his work and to his labours until nightfall.

מָה רַבּוּ מַעֲשֶׂיךָ, יהוה!
כֻּלָּם בְּחָכְמָה עָשִׂיתָ,
מָלְאָה הָאָרֶץ קִנְיָנֶךָ.
זֶה הַיָּם גָּדוֹל וּרְחַב־יָדָיִם –
שָׁם רֶמֶשׂ וְאֵין־מִסְפָּר,
חַיּוֹת קְטַנּוֹת עִם גְּדֹלוֹת;
שָׁם אֳנִיּוֹת יְהַלֵּכוּן,
לִוְיָתָן זֶה־יָצַרְתָּ לְשַׂחֶק־בּוֹ.

How manifold are Your works, O Lord! You made them all with wisdom; the earth is full of Your creatures. There is the sea, vast and wide, with innumerable beings in it, living things both small and great. There ships[1] move about, and Leviathan whom You created as Your plaything.

1. Some scholars read *emot* ('dreadful things, monsters') for the Masoretic text *oniyot* ('ships').

כֻּלָּם אֵלֶיךָ יְשַׂבֵּרוּן
לָתֵת אָכְלָם בְּעִתּוֹ.
תִּתֵּן לָהֶם – יִלְקֹטוּן,
תִּפְתַּח יָדְךָ – יִשְׂבְּעוּן טוֹב;
תַּסְתִּיר פָּנֶיךָ – יִבָּהֵלוּן,
תֹּסֵף רוּחָם – יִגְוָעוּן
וְאֶל עֲפָרָם יְשׁוּבוּן;
תְּשַׁלַּח רוּחֲךָ – יִבָּרֵאוּן,
וּתְחַדֵּשׁ פְּנֵי אֲדָמָה.

They all look hopefully to You, to give them their food in due time. When You give it to them, they gather it up; when You open Your hand, they eat their fill of it. When You hide Your face, they are appalled; when You take away their breath, they perish and return again to the dust. When You send forth Your breath, they are created; thus You renew the whole earth.

יְהִי כְבוֹד־יהוה לְעוֹלָם,
יִשְׂמַח יהוה בְּמַעֲשָׂיו!
הַמַּבִּיט לָאָרֶץ – וַתִּרְעָד,
יִגַּע בֶּהָרִים – וְיֶעֱשָׁנוּ.
אָשִׁירָה לַיהוה בְּחַיָּי,
אֲזַמְּרָה לֵאלֹהַי בְּעוֹדִי.
יֶעֱרַב עָלָיו שִׂיחִי,
אָנֹכִי אֶשְׂמַח בַּיהוה.
יִתַּמּוּ חַטָּאִים מִן הָאָרֶץ,
וּרְשָׁעִים עוֹד אֵינָם.

May the glory of the Lord endure forever! May the Lord rejoice in His works: He looks at the earth and it trembles; He touches the mountains and they smoke. I shall sing to the Lord all my life; I shall chant hymns to my God as long as I live. May my prayer be pleasing to Him; I shall rejoice in the Lord. May sinners disappear from the earth and the wicked be no more.

בָּרְכִי, נַפְשִׁי, אֶת יהוה!
הַלְלוּיָהּ!

O my soul, bless the Lord! Hallelujah!

וְהַחָכְמָה – מֵאַיִן תִּמָּצֵא ?

כִּי יֵשׁ לַכֶּסֶף מוֹצָא,
וּמָקוֹם לַזָּהָב יָזֹקּוּ.
בַּרְזֶל מֵעָפָר יֻקָּח,
וְאֶבֶן – יָצוּק נְחוּשָׁה.
קֵץ שָׂם לַחֹשֶׁךְ
וּלְכָל תַּכְלִית הוּא חוֹקֵר
אֶבֶן אֹפֶל וְצַלְמָוֶת.
פָּרַץ נַחַל מֵעִם גָּר,
הַנִּשְׁכָּחִים מִנִּי רָגֶל,
דַּלּוּ מֵאֱנוֹשׁ נָעוּ.
אֶרֶץ, מִמֶּנָּה יֵצֵא לָחֶם,
וְתַחְתֶּיהָ נֶהְפַּךְ כְּמוֹ אֵשׁ.
מְקוֹם־סַפִּיר אֲבָנֶיהָ,
וְעַפְרֹת זָהָב לוֹ.
נָתִיב – לֹא יְדָעוֹ עָיִט,
וְלֹא שְׁזָפַתּוּ עֵין־אַיָּה,
לֹא הִדְרִיכוּהוּ בְנֵי שָׁחַץ,
לֹא עָדָה עָלָיו שָׁחַל.
בַּחַלָּמִישׁ שָׁלַח יָדוֹ –
הָפַךְ מִשֹּׁרֶשׁ הָרִים.
בַּצּוּרוֹת יְאֹרִים בִּקֵּעַ
וְכָל יְקָר רָאֲתָה עֵינוֹ.
מִבְּכִי נְהָרוֹת חִבֵּשׁ
וְתַעֲלֻמָהּ יֹצִא אוֹר.

THE INACCESSIBILITY OF WISDOM

There is a source for silver, and a place where gold is refined. Iron is extracted from the earth and copper is smelted from stone. Man puts[1] an end to darkness, he probes the farthest confines for the stone [that is hidden in] gloom and pitch darkness. He breaks open a shaft far from human habitation, in sites forgotten by men's feet, forsaken by those who have wandered away. The very earth, from which bread comes forth, is convulsed underneath as if by fire. Its stones yield sapphires, its dust has gold in it.[2] No bird of prey knows the path to it, nor has the falcon's eye seen it; the proud beasts have not set foot on it, nor has the lion ever trodden it. Man sets his hand to the flinty rock, and overturns mountains by their roots. He hews out channels in the rocks and his eyes behold all that is precious. He dams[3] the springs of rivers, and brings hidden things to light.

1. Lit. 'He put'. The passage is obscure.
2. Or 'A place where stones are sapphires and whose dust is gold'.
3. Or 'probes, explores'.

וְהַחָכְמָה – מֵאַיִן תִּמָּצֵא,
וְאֵי זֶה מְקוֹם בִּינָה ?
לֹא יָדַע אֱנוֹשׁ עֶרְכָּהּ,
וְלֹא תִמָּצֵא בְּאֶרֶץ הַחַיִּים.
תְּהוֹם אָמַר: 'לֹא בִי הִיא,'
וְיָם אָמַר: 'אֵין עִמָּדִי.'

But where can Wisdom be found, and where is the home of understanding? No man knows the way to it[1] nor can it be found in the land of the living. The Abyss says 'It is not in me,' and the Sea says 'I do not have it.'

לֹא יֻתַּן סְגוֹר תַּחְתֶּיהָ,
וְלֹא יִשָּׁקֵל כֶּסֶף מְחִירָהּ.
לֹא תְסֻלֶּה בְּכֶתֶם־אוֹפִיר,
בְּשֹׁהַם יָקָר וְסַפִּיר.
לֹא יַעַרְכֶנָּה זָהָב וּזְכוֹכִית,
וּתְמוּרָתָהּ – כְּלִי פָז.
רָאמוֹת וְגָבִישׁ לֹא יִזָּכֵר;
וּמֶשֶׁךְ חָכְמָה – מִפְּנִינִים.
לֹא יַעַרְכֶנָּה פִּטְדַת־כּוּשׁ,
בְּכֶתֶם טָהוֹר לֹא תְסֻלֶּה.

It cannot be gotten in exchange for choice gold, nor can its price be weighed out in silver. It cannot be balanced against gold of Ophir, against precious onyx or sapphires. Gold and glass cannot equal it, nor can vessels of fine gold match its value. Coral and jasper are of no account; it is harder to acquire Wisdom than pearls. Arabian topaz cannot equal it, nor can it be balanced against pure gold.

וְהַחָכְמָה – מֵאַיִן תָּבוֹא,
וְאֵי זֶה מְקוֹם בִּינָה ?
וְנֶעֶלְמָה מֵעֵינֵי כָל חָי
וּמֵעוֹף הַשָּׁמַיִם נִסְתָּרָה.
אֲבַדּוֹן וָמָוֶת אָמְרוּ:
'בְּאָזְנֵינוּ שָׁמַעְנוּ שִׁמְעָהּ.'

Where, then, does Wisdom come from, and where is the home of understanding? It is hidden from the eyes of all the living, and concealed from the birds of the air. Hell and Death say 'We have heard of it, but only by rumour.'

אֱלֹהִים הֵבִין דַּרְכָּהּ
וְהוּא יָדַע אֶת מְקוֹמָהּ,
כִּי הוּא לִקְצוֹת הָאָרֶץ יַבִּיט,

Only God understands the way to it. He alone knows where it is, for He looks to the ends of the earth and

1. Lit. 'its worth' (*erka*). *Darka*, 'its way', is an accepted emendation.

תַּחַת כָּל הַשָּׁמַיִם יִרְאֶה.
לַעֲשׂוֹת לָרוּחַ מִשְׁקָל,
וּמַיִם תִּכֵּן בְּמִדָּה,
בַּעֲשֹׂתוֹ לַמָּטָר חֹק,
וְדֶרֶךְ לַחֲזִיז־קֹלוֹת –
אָז רָאָהּ וַיְסַפְּרָהּ,
הֱכִינָהּ וְגַם חֲקָרָהּ.
וַיֹּאמֶר לָאָדָם:
'הֵן יִרְאַת אֲדֹנָי – הִיא חָכְמָה,
וְסוּר מֵרָע – בִּינָה.'

surveys all that is under the heavens. When He determined the weight of the wind and set a measure to the waters; when He decreed a limit to the rain[1] and a path for the thunderstorm – it was then that He looked at Wisdom and appraised it, He established[2] it and fathomed its depths. And to man He said: 'To fear the Lord, that is Wisdom, and to avoid evil, that is understanding.'

אֲנִי יְשֵׁנָה – וְלִבִּי עֵר

THE LOST LOVER

אֲנִי יְשֵׁנָה – וְלִבִּי עֵר.
קוֹל דּוֹדִי דוֹפֵק:

I was asleep, but my heart was awake. I heard my lover knocking:

'פִּתְחִי לִי, אֲחֹתִי,
רַעְיָתִי, יוֹנָתִי תַמָּתִי!
שֶׁרֹּאשִׁי נִמְלָא טָל,
קְוֻצּוֹתַי – רְסִיסֵי לָיְלָה.'

'Let me in, my sister, my darling, my dove, my perfect one! For my head is wet with dew, my curls with the mist of the night.'

'פָּשַׁטְתִּי אֶת כֻּתָּנְתִּי –
אֵיכָכָה אֶלְבָּשֶׁנָּה?
רָחַצְתִּי אֶת רַגְלַי –
אֵיכָכָה אֲטַנְּפֵם?'

'I have already taken off my robe – shall I put it on again? I have bathed my feet – shall I now soil them?'

1. Or 'when he made rules for the rain'. 2. Or 'discerned'.

דּוֹדִי שָׁלַח יָדוֹ מִן הַחוֹר,
וּמֵעַי הָמוּ עָלָיו.
קַמְתִּי אֲנִי לִפְתֹּחַ לְדוֹדִי,
וְיָדַי נָטְפוּ מוֹר,
וְאֶצְבְּעֹתַי – מוֹר־עֹבֵר
עַל כַּפּוֹת הַמַּנְעוּל.
פָּתַחְתִּי אֲנִי לְדוֹדִי –
וְדוֹדִי חָמַק, עָבָר.
נַפְשִׁי יָצְאָה בְדַבְּרוֹ!
בִּקַּשְׁתִּיהוּ – וְלֹא מְצָאתִיהוּ,
קְרָאתִיו – וְלֹא עָנָנִי.

My lover drew back his hand from the latch, and my heart beat wildly for him. I rose to let my lover in; my hands dripped with myrrh, my fingers flowed with myrrh upon the handles of the bolt. I opened to my lover, but he had slipped away and was gone. My soul longed for his words![1] I looked for him, but could not find him; I called to him, but he did not answer me.

מְצָאֻנִי הַשֹּׁמְרִים,
הַסֹּבְבִים בָּעִיר,
הִכּוּנִי, פְצָעוּנִי,
נָשְׂאוּ אֶת רְדִידִי מֵעָלַי
שֹׁמְרֵי הַחֹמוֹת.
הִשְׁבַּעְתִּי אֶתְכֶם,
בְּנוֹת יְרוּשָׁלָם,
אִם תִּמְצְאוּ אֶת דּוֹדִי,
מַה תַּגִּידוּ לוֹ?
שֶׁחוֹלַת־אַהֲבָה אָנִי!

The watchmen, making the rounds of the city, came upon me; they beat me, they wounded me, they tore off my mantle – these guardians of the walls. I adjure you, daughters of Jerusalem, if you should find my lover, what will you say to him? Tell him that I am sick with love.

'מַה דּוֹדֵךְ מִדּוֹד,
הַיָּפָה בַּנָּשִׁים?
מַה דּוֹדֵךְ מִדּוֹד,
שֶׁכָּכָה הִשְׁבַּעְתָּנוּ?'

'O fairest of women, how does your lover excel other men, that you adjure us in this way?'

1. Or 'My soul had grown faint when he spoke'.

'דּוֹדִי צַח וְאָדוֹם,
דָּגוּל מֵרְבָבָה.
רֹאשׁוֹ כֶּתֶם פָּז,
קְוֻצּוֹתָיו תַּלְתַּלִּים,
שְׁחֹרוֹת כָּעוֹרֵב ;
עֵינָיו כְּיוֹנִים
עַל אֲפִיקֵי מָיִם —
רֹחֲצוֹת בֶּחָלָב,
יֹשְׁבוֹת עַל מִלֵּאת ;
לְחָיָו כַּעֲרוּגַת הַבֹּשֶׂם,
מִגְדְּלוֹת מֶרְקָחִים ;
שִׂפְתוֹתָיו שׁוֹשַׁנִּים,
נֹטְפוֹת מוֹר־עֹבֵר ;
יָדָיו גְּלִילֵי זָהָב,
מְמֻלָּאִים בַּתַּרְשִׁישׁ ;
מֵעָיו עֶשֶׁת־שֵׁן,
מְעֻלֶּפֶת סַפִּירִים ;
שׁוֹקָיו עַמּוּדֵי שֵׁשׁ,
מְיֻסָּדִים עַל אַדְנֵי פָז ;
מַרְאֵהוּ כַּלְּבָנוֹן,
בָּחוּר כָּאֲרָזִים ;
חִכּוֹ מַמְתַקִּים,
וְכֻלּוֹ מַחֲמַדִּים —
זֶה דוֹדִי וְזֶה רֵעִי,
בְּנוֹת יְרוּשָׁלָםִ !'

'My lover is fair and radiant, he is peerless among ten thousand. His head is the finest gold; his locks are palm fronds, black as the raven. His eyes are like doves beside flowing brooks: milk-white doves, perched by a brimming pool. His cheeks are like beds of spices, exhaling perfumes. His lips are lilies, flowing with liquid myrrh. His arms are rods of gold, inlaid with topaz. His body is a pillar of ivory, covered with sapphires. His legs are marble columns, set in sockets of fine gold. His bearing is like the trees of Lebanon, lofty as the cedars. His mouth is most sweet; all of him is pure delight. Such is my lover, such is my friend, O daughters of Jerusalem!'

'אָנָה הָלַךְ דּוֹדֵךְ,
הַיָּפָה בַּנָּשִׁים ?
אָנָה פָּנָה דוֹדֵךְ ? —
וּנְבַקְשֶׁנּוּ עִמָּךְ.'

'Where has your lover gone, O fairest of women? Which way has your lover turned? Let us seek him together.'

׳דּוֹדִי יָרַד לְגַנּוֹ,
לַעֲרֻגוֹת הַבֹּשֶׂם,
לִרְעוֹת בַּגַּנִּים
וְלִלְקֹט שׁוֹשַׁנִּים.
אֲנִי לְדוֹדִי וְדוֹדִי לִי,
הָרוֹעֶה בַּשּׁוֹשַׁנִּים.׳

'My lover has gone down to his garden, to the beds of spices, to tend his flock in the garden and to gather lilies. My lover is mine, and I am his; he tends his flock among the lilies.'

שׁוּבִי, שׁוּבִי, הַשּׁוּלַמִּית!

THE MAIDEN'S DANCE

׳שׁוּבִי, שׁוּבִי, הַשּׁוּלַמִּית,
שׁוּבִי, שׁוּבִי, וְנֶחֱזֶה בָּךְ!׳

'Return, return, O Shulammite, return, return, let us gaze at you!'

׳מַה תֶּחֱזוּ בַּשּׁוּלַמִּית
כִּמְחֹלַת הַמַּחֲנָיִם?׳

'What will you see in the Shulammite as she dances between the companies?'[1]

׳מַה יָּפוּ פְעָמַיִךְ בַּנְּעָלִים,
בַּת נָדִיב!
חַמּוּקֵי יְרֵכַיִךְ כְּמוֹ חֲלָאִים,
מַעֲשֵׂה יְדֵי אָמָּן;
שָׁרְרֵךְ אַגַּן הַסַּהַר
אַל יֶחְסַר הַמָּזֶג;
בִּטְנֵךְ עֲרֵמַת חִטִּים,
סוּגָה בַּשּׁוֹשַׁנִּים;
שְׁנֵי שָׁדַיִךְ כִּשְׁנֵי עֳפָרִים,
תָּאֳמֵי צְבִיָּה;
צַוָּארֵךְ כְּמִגְדַּל־הַשֵּׁן;
עֵינַיִךְ בְּרֵכוֹת בְּחֶשְׁבּוֹן,

'How beautiful are your sandalled feet, O royal daughter! Your curved thighs are like jewels fashioned by a master. Your navel is a round goblet, brim-full of wine.[2] Your belly is a heap of wheat, ringed with lilies. Your breasts are like two fawns – the twins of a gazelle. Your neck is like a tower of ivory. Your eyes are the pools of Heshbon, by the gate

1. Lit. 'the dance of Mahanaim'; the meaning is uncertain.
2. Or '– may it never lack mixed wine!'

עַל שַׁעַר בַּת־רַבִּים ;
אַפֵּךְ כְּמִגְדַּל הַלְּבָנוֹן,
צוֹפֶה פְּנֵי דַמָּשֶׂק ;
רֹאשֵׁךְ עָלַיִךְ כַּכַּרְמֶל,
וְדַלַּת רֹאשֵׁךְ כָּאַרְגָּמָן ;
מֶלֶךְ אָסוּר בָּרְהָטִים !'

of Bath-rabbim. Your nose is like the tower on Lebanon that looks towards Damascus. Your head rises like Mount Carmel,[1] your flowing locks are [lustrous] as purple; a king is held captive in these tresses!'

'מַה יָּפִית וּמַה נָּעַמְתְּ
אַהֲבָה בַּתַּעֲנוּגִים !
זֹאת קוֹמָתֵךְ דָּמְתָה לְתָמָר,
וְשָׁדַיִךְ – לְאַשְׁכֹּלוֹת.
אָמַרְתִּי : "אֶעֱלֶה בְתָמָר,
אֹחֲזָה בְּסַנְסִנָּיו !
וְיִהְיוּ נָא שָׁדַיִךְ
כְּאֶשְׁכְּלוֹת הַגֶּפֶן,
וְרֵיחַ אַפֵּךְ כַּתַּפּוּחִים,
וְחִכֵּךְ כְּיֵין הַטּוֹב !"'

[The Lover:] 'How fair you are, how pleasing, O rapturous love![2] Here is your figure, stately as a palm tree, and your breasts like clusters of fruit. I say: "Let me climb the palm tree and take hold of its branches! May your breasts be like clusters of grapes on the vine, the fragrance of your breath like apples, and your mouth like choice wine –"'

'הוֹלֵךְ לְדוֹדִי לְמֵישָׁרִים,
דּוֹבֵב שִׂפְתֵי יְשֵׁנִים.'

[The Maiden:] '– that will flow smoothly for my lover, gliding over his sleeping lips.'[3]

1. Or 'Your head adorns you like crimson'.
2. Or 'How beautiful you are, how pleasant, O Love with its delights!'
3. Or 'gliding over his lips and teeth'. The verse has also been understood as part of the lover's speech: '. . . choice wine that flows to give lovers vigour and stirs the lips of those who sleep'.

מִי זֹאת עֹלָה

מִי זֹאת עֹלָה מִן הַמִּדְבָּר,
מִתְרַפֶּקֶת עַל דּוֹדָהּ ?

׳תַּחַת הַתַּפּוּחַ עוֹרַרְתִּיךָ —
שָׁמָּה חִבְּלַתְךָ אִמֶּךָ,
שָׁמָּה חִבְּלָה יְלָדַתְךָ.
שִׂימֵנִי כַחוֹתָם עַל לִבֶּךָ,
כַּחוֹתָם עַל זְרוֹעֶךָ,
כִּי עַזָּה כַמָּוֶת אַהֲבָה,
קָשָׁה כִשְׁאוֹל קִנְאָה ;
רְשָׁפֶיהָ רִשְׁפֵּי אֵשׁ,
שַׁלְהֶבֶתְיָה.
מַיִם רַבִּים לֹא יוּכְלוּ
לְכַבּוֹת אֶת הָאַהֲבָה,
וּנְהָרוֹת לֹא יִשְׁטְפוּהָ.
אִם יִתֵּן אִישׁ
אֶת כָּל הוֹן בֵּיתוֹ בָּאַהֲבָה —
בּוֹז יָבוּזוּ לוֹ.׳

THE SEAL OF LOVE

Who is this coming up from the wilderness, leaning tenderly upon her lover?

[The Maiden:][1] 'Under the apple-tree I aroused you; it was there that your mother conceived you, there she conceived you and brought you forth. Set me as a seal upon your heart, as a seal upon your arm;[2] for love is as fierce as death, passion is as harsh as the grave; its flashes are raging fires, violent flames. Vast floods cannot quench love, nor can rivers sweep it away. If a man were to offer all his wealth for love, he would be laughed to scorn.'

אֵיכָה יוּעַם זָהָב

אֵיכָה יוּעַם זָהָב,
יִשְׁנֶא הַכֶּתֶם הַטּוֹב —
תִּשְׁתַּפֵּכְנָה אַבְנֵי־קֹדֶשׁ
בְּרֹאשׁ כָּל חוּצוֹת !

DIRGE ON THE FALL OF JERUSALEM

How the gold was tarnished, the finest gold debased! How the sacred gems[3] were strewn about at every street

1. Some translations ascribe the following verse to the Lover. The maiden's reply begins with 'Set me . . .'

2. Or 'like the seal which is upon your hand'.

3. I.e., the people of Jerusalem. Or 'the sacred stones [of the sanctuary]'.

בְּנֵי צִיּוֹן הַיְקָרִים,
הַמְסֻלָּאִים בַּפָּז –
אֵיכָה נֶחְשְׁבוּ לְנִבְלֵי־חֶרֶשׂ,
מַעֲשֵׂה יְדֵי יוֹצֵר!
גַּם תַּנִּים חָלְצוּ שַׁד,
הֵינִיקוּ גּוּרֵיהֶן;
בַּת עַמִּי לְאַכְזָר,
כַּיְעֵנִים בַּמִּדְבָּר.
דָּבַק לְשׁוֹן יוֹנֵק
אֶל חִכּוֹ בַּצָּמָא;
עוֹלָלִים שָׁאֲלוּ לֶחֶם,
פֹּרֵשׂ אֵין לָהֶם.
הָאֹכְלִים לְמַעֲדַנִּים –
נָשַׁמּוּ בַּחוּצוֹת;
הָאֱמֻנִים עֲלֵי תוֹלָע –
חִבְּקוּ אַשְׁפַּתּוֹת.
וַיִּגְדַּל עֲוֹן בַּת עַמִּי
מֵחַטַּאת סְדֹם,
הַהֲפוּכָה כְמוֹ־רָגַע,
וְלֹא חָלוּ בָהּ יָדָיִם.
זַכּוּ נְזִירֶיהָ מִשֶּׁלֶג;
צַחוּ מֵחָלָב;
אָדְמוּ־עֶצֶם מִפְּנִינִים,
סַפִּיר גִּזְרָתָם.
חָשַׁךְ מִשְּׁחוֹר תָּאֳרָם,
לֹא נִכְּרוּ בַּחוּצוֹת;
צָפַד עוֹרָם עַל עַצְמָם,
יָבֵשׁ הָיָה כָעֵץ.
טוֹבִים הָיוּ חַלְלֵי־חֶרֶב

corner! The precious sons of Zion, once worth their weight in gold – how they were disparaged as earthenware from a potter's hand! Even jackals bare their breasts and suckle their young; but the daughter of my people became as cruel as the desert ostrich. The tongue of the suckling cleaved to its palate for thirst; infants begged for bread, but no one offered them a crumb. Those who once fed on dainties lay stunned in the streets; those who were brought up in purple, clung to garbage-heaps. The punishment of the daughter of my people was far greater than the penalty of Sodom, which was overthrown in an instant, untouched by human hands. Her nobles were purer than snow, whiter than milk; their bodies were ruddier than coral, their limbs[1] were sapphire. Then their faces turned blacker than soot; none could recognize them in the streets. Their skin shrivelled on their bones, it became as dry as wood. Those who died by the sword were luckier than

1. Meaning uncertain.

מֵחַלְלֵי־רָעָב ;
שֶׁהֵם יָזֻבוּ מְדֻקָּרִים
מִתְּנוּבוֹת שָׂדָי.
יְדֵי נָשִׁים רַחֲמָנִיּוֹת
בִּשְּׁלוּ יַלְדֵיהֶן ;
הָיוּ לְבָרוֹת לָמוֹ
בְּשֶׁבֶר בַּת עַמִּי.
כִּלָּה יהוה אֶת חֲמָתוֹ,
שָׁפַךְ חֲרוֹן אַפּוֹ,
וַיַּצֶּת־אֵשׁ בְּצִיּוֹן
וַתֹּאכַל יְסֹדֹתֶיהָ.
לֹא הֶאֱמִינוּ מַלְכֵי אֶרֶץ,
כֹּל יֹשְׁבֵי תֵבֵל,
כִּי יָבֹא צַר וְאוֹיֵב
בְּשַׁעֲרֵי יְרוּשָׁלָם.
מֵחַטֹּאת נְבִיאֶיהָ,
עֲוֹנֹת כֹּהֲנֶיהָ,
הַשֹּׁפְכִים בְּקִרְבָּהּ
דַּם צַדִּיקִים.
נָעוּ עִוְרִים בַּחוּצוֹת,
נְגֹאֲלוּ בַּדָּם ;
בְּלֹא יוּכְלוּ יִגְּעוּ
בִּלְבֻשֵׁיהֶם.
'סוּרוּ, טָמֵא !' – קָרְאוּ לָמוֹ –
'סוּרוּ, סוּרוּ, אַל תִּגָּעוּ !'
כִּי נָצוּ גַּם נָעוּ, אָמְרוּ בַּגּוֹיִם :
'לֹא יוֹסִפוּ לָגוּר !'
פְּנֵי יהוה חִלְּקָם,

those who died of hunger; those who bled to death from their wounds than those who were deprived of all food.[1] Tender-hearted women cooked their children with their own hands; this was their fare when the daughter of my people met with disaster. The Lord vented all His wrath, He poured out His fury. He kindled a fire in Zion that consumed its foundations. The kings of the earth, all the world's inhabitants had never imagined that enemies could penetrate the gates of Jerusalem. But the sins of her prophets brought this to pass, the crimes of her priests, who in her midst shed the blood of the righteous! Defiled by blood, they staggered blindly through the streets; no one could bear to touch their garments. 'Away! Unclean!' people shouted at them,[2] 'Away! Away! Do not come near!' So they wandered, fugitives, and the nations said, 'They will never find a dwelling place.' The Lord Himself dispersed them, He no

1. Lit. 'the fruits of the field'.

2. Another possible interpretation is that they themselves are sounding the leper's cry; cf. Leviticus 13.46.

לֹא יוֹסִיף לְהַבִּיטָם ;
פְּנֵי כֹהֲנִים לֹא נָשָׂאוּ,
וּזְקֵנִים לֹא חָנָנוּ.
עוֹדֵינוּ תִּכְלֶינָה עֵינֵינוּ
אֶל עֶזְרָתֵנוּ הָבֶל ;
בְּצִפִּיָּתֵנוּ צִפִּינוּ
אֶל גּוֹי לֹא־יוֹשִׁעַ.
צָדוּ צְעָדֵינוּ
מִלֶּכֶת בִּרְחֹבֹתֵינוּ.
קָרַב קִצֵּנוּ, מָלְאוּ יָמֵינוּ,
כִּי בָא קִצֵּנוּ.
קַלִּים הָיוּ רֹדְפֵינוּ
מִנִּשְׁרֵי שָׁמָיִם ;
עַל הֶהָרִים דְּלָקֻנוּ,
בַּמִּדְבָּר אָרְבוּ לָנוּ.
רוּחַ אַפֵּינוּ, מְשִׁיחַ יהוה,
נִלְכַּד בִּשְׁחִיתוֹתָם –
אֲשֶׁר אָמַרְנוּ :
בְּצִלּוֹ נִחְיֶה בַגּוֹיִם.

longer took notice of them. He showed no regard for the priests, no favour to the elders. And still our eyes wasted away as we looked in vain for help; anxiously we watched for a nation[1] that would not save us. Men dogged our steps – we could not walk through our streets. Our end drew near; our days were numbered; our end had come. Our pursuers were swifter than eagles in the sky, they pursued us in the mountains, they waylaid us in the desert. The Lord's anointed[2] – the very breath of our life – was caught in their snares; it was under his wing that we had hoped to live on among the nations.

שִׂישִׂי וְשִׂמְחִי, בַּת אֱדוֹם,
יוֹשֶׁבֶת בְּאֶרֶץ עוּץ !
גַּם עָלַיִךְ תַּעֲבָר־כּוֹס,
תִּשְׁכְּרִי וְתִתְעָרִי.
תַּם עֲוֹנֵךְ, בַּת צִיּוֹן,
לֹא יוֹסִיף לְהַגְלוֹתֵךְ.
פָּקַד עֲוֹנֵךְ, בַּת אֱדוֹם,
גִּלָּה עַל חַטֹּאתָיִךְ !

Rejoice and be glad, O daughter of Edom, you who dwell in the land of Uz! The cup will yet pass to you as well; you will become drunk and expose your nakedness. Your punishment is now completed,[3] O daughter of Zion; He will not exile you again. But you, O daughter of Edom – He will make you pay for your crimes, He will lay bare all your sins!

1. Egypt, which gave no aid against Babylon.
2. King Zedekiah, who was captured in flight near Jericho, and afterwards blinded and imprisoned by Nebuchadnezzar (Jeremiah 52.7-11).
3. Or 'Your crime is absolved'.

בֶּן סִירָא

Simeon ben Sira

שִׁמְעוֹן כֹּהֵן גָּדוֹל

SIMEON THE HIGH PRIEST

גְּדוֹל אֶחָיו וְתִפְאֶרֶת עַמּוֹ,
שִׁמְעוֹן בֶּן יוֹחָנָן הַכֹּהֵן:
אֲשֶׁר בְּדוֹרוֹ נִבְדַּק הַבַּיִת
וּבְיָמָיו חֻזַּק הֵיכָל;
אֲשֶׁר בְּיָמָיו נִבְנָה קִיר,
פִּנּוֹת מָעוֹז בְּהֵיכַל מֶלֶךְ;
אֲשֶׁר בְּדוֹרוֹ נִכְרָה מִקְוֶה,
אָשִׁיחַ כַּיָּם בַּהֲמוֹנוֹ;
הַדּוֹאֵג לְעַמּוֹ מֵחֶתֶף
וּמְחַזֵּק עִירוֹ מִצָּר.

Chief among his brethren and pride of his people, Simeon son of Yohanan the priest: in whose time the House was repaired and in whose days the Temple was fortified; in whose days the wall was built, with battlements to secure the King's palace; in whose time a reservoir was dug, a cistern thundering with water like the sea. He safeguarded his people from marauders and strengthened his city against siege.

מַה נֶּהְדַּר בְּהַשְׁגִּיחוֹ מֵאֹהֶל
וּבְצֵאתוֹ מִבֵּית הַפָּרֹכֶת!
כְּכוֹכָב אוֹר מִבֵּין עָבִים
וּכְיָרֵחַ מָלֵא בִּימֵי מוֹעֵד;
כְּשֶׁמֶשׁ מַשְׂרֶקֶת אֶת הֵיכַל הַמֶּלֶךְ
וּכְקֶשֶׁת נִרְאֲתָה בֶּעָנָן;
כְּנֵץ בַּעֲנָפִים בִּימֵי מוֹעֵד
וּכְשׁוֹשָׁן עַל יִבְלֵי מָיִם;
כְּפֶרַח לְבָנוֹן בִּימֵי קַיִץ
וּכְאֵשׁ לְבוֹנָה עַל הַמִּנְחָה;
כְּזַיִת רַעֲנָן מָלֵא גַּרְגֵּר
וּכְעֵץ שֶׁמֶן מַרְוֶה עָנָף;
כִּכְלִי זָהָב בְּבֵית אָצִיל
הַנֶּאֱחָז עַל אַבְנֵי חֵפֶץ —

How glorious he was as he looked out from the Tent of the Presence, as he emerged from the curtained shrine! Like a star shining through the clouds, or the full moon on feast days; like the sun glittering on the King's palace or the rainbow seen in the cloud; like a blossom on the bough at spring time, or a lily by a flowing stream; like a flower of Lebanon on a summer's day, or the fire of frankincense upon the offering; like a spreading olive-tree laden with fruit, or an oleaster whose branches drink their fill; like a golden vessel in the house of a nobleman, encrusted with precious stones.

בַּעֲטוֹתוֹ בִּגְדֵי כָבוֹד
וְהִתְלַבְּשׁוֹ כְּלִיל תִּפְאֶרֶת;
בַּעֲלוֹתוֹ עַל מִזְבַּח הוֹד
וַיֶּהְדַּר עֲזָרַת מִקְדָּשׁ;
בְּקַבְּלוֹ נְתָחִים מִיַּד אֶחָיו
וְהוּא נִצָּב עַל מַעֲרָכוֹת;
סָבִיב לוֹ עֲטֶרֶת בָּנִים
כִּשְׁתִילֵי אֲרָזִים בַּלְּבָנוֹן;
וַיַּקִּיפוּהוּ כְּעַרְבֵי נָחַל
כָּל בְּנֵי אַהֲרֹן בִּכְבוֹדָם
וְאִשֵּׁי אֲדֹנָי בְּיָדָם,
נֶגֶד כָּל קְהַל יִשְׂרָאֵל —
עַד כַּלּוֹתוֹ לְשָׁרֵת מִזְבֵּחַ
וּלְסַדֵּר מַעַרְכוֹת עֶלְיוֹן.
וַיִּשְׁלַח יָדוֹ עַל הַקַּשְׂוָה
וַיַּסֵּךְ מִדַּם עֵנָב,
וַיִּצֹק עַל יְסוֹד הַמִּזְבֵּחַ
לְרֵיחַ נִיחֹחַ לְמֶלֶךְ עֶלְיוֹן.

When he clothed himself in his splendid robes and put on his glorious diadem; when he ascended the majestic altar and filled the Temple Court with his splendour; when he received the portions of the offering from his fellow-priests as he stood by the wood-stacks on the altar; a garland of sons was around him, like shoots of a cedar in Lebanon; all the sons of Aaron in their priestly garments surrounded him like willows of the brook, with the Lord's offerings in their hands, before the whole assembly of Israel, until he completed the rites at the altar and set in order the fire for the Most High. Then he held out his hand for the libation cup and poured out the blood of the grape, poured it at the base of the altar, as a soothing odour to the Most High King.

אָז יָרִיעוּ בְּנֵי אַהֲרֹן הַכֹּהֲנִים
בַּחֲצֹצְרוֹת מִקְשָׁה.
וַיָּרִיעוּ וַיַּשְׁמִיעוּ קוֹל אַדִּיר,
לְהַזְכִּיר לִפְנֵי עֶלְיוֹן.
כָּל בָּשָׂר יַחְדָּו נִמְהָרוּ
וַיִּפְּלוּ עַל פְּנֵיהֶם אַרְצָה
לְהִשְׁתַּחֲוֹת לִפְנֵי עֶלְיוֹן,
לִפְנֵי קְדוֹשׁ יִשְׂרָאֵל.
וַיִּתֵּן הַשִּׁיר קוֹלוֹ
וְעַל הָמוֹן הֶעֱרִיבוּ רִנָּה.
וַיָּרֹנּוּ כָּל עַם הָאָרֶץ

At this, the sons of Aaron, the priests, blew their trumpets of beaten silver, sounding a mighty fanfare as a reminder before the Most High. Instantly all the people as one man fell on their faces to worship before the Most High, the Holy One of Israel. Then the song [of the Levites] resounded, sweetly sung to the sound of instruments. And all the common people cried out in prayer

בִּתְפִלָּה לִפְנֵי רַחוּם –
עַד כַּלּוֹתוֹ לְשָׁרֵת מִזְבֵּחַ
וּמִשְׁפָּטָיו הִגִּיעַ אֵלָיו.

to the Merciful One, until he completed the rites at the altar and placed the offerings upon it in due order.

אָז יָרַד וְנָשָׂא יָדָיו
עַל כָּל קְהַל יִשְׂרָאֵל,
וּבִרְכַּת אֲדֹנָי בִּשְׂפָתָיו
וּבְשֵׁם אֲדֹנָי יִתְפָּאָר.
וַיִּשְׁנוּ לִנְפֹּל שֵׁנִית
הָעָם כֻּלּוֹ מִפָּנָיו.

Then he came down from the altar and, raising his hands over the whole assembly of Israel, he pronounced the Lord's blessing,[1] he gloried in the Name of the Lord. And a second time they all prostrated themselves before Him.

עַתָּה, בָּרְכוּ־נָא אֶת אֲדֹנָי אֱלֹהֵי יִשְׂרָאֵל
הַמַּפְלִיא לַעֲשׂוֹת בָּאָרֶץ,
הַמְגַדֵּל אָדָם מֵרֶחֶם
וַיַּעֲשֵׂהוּ כִּרְצוֹנוֹ.

Now bless the Lord God of Israel who works wonders on the earth, who raises a man from the womb and moulds him as He wills.

יִתֵּן לָכֶם חָכְמַת לֵבָב
וִיהִי בְשָׁלוֹם בֵּינֵיכֶם.
יֵאָמֵן עִם שִׁמְעוֹן חַסְדּוֹ
וְיָקֶם־לוֹ בְּרִית פִּינְחָס:
אֲשֶׁר לֹא יִכָּרֶת לוֹ וּלְזַרְעוֹ
כִּימֵי שָׁמָיִם.

May He give you wisdom of the heart and may peace reign among you. May His gracious word stand fast with the house of Simeon, may He make good His promise to Phinehas: that neither he nor his descendants shall be cut off [from the priesthood] for as long as the heavens endure.

1. The 'Lord's blessing' is found in Numbers 6.24–26.

שִׁירִים מִן הַמְּגִלּוֹת הַגְּנוּזוֹת

Poems from the Dead Sea Scrolls

וְלֹא יָדְעוּ רָז נִהְיָה

THE MYSTERY TO COME

. . . וְלֹא יָדְעוּ רָז נִהְיָה
וּבְקַדְמוֹנִיּוֹת לֹא הִתְבּוֹנָנוּ.
וְלֹא יָדְעוּ מָה אֲשֶׁר יָבוֹא עֲלֵיהֶמָה
וְנַפְשָׁמָה לֹא מִלְּטוּ מֵרָז נִהְיָה.

. . . and they do not know the mystery to come; they have not brooded over the past; they do not know what will befall them; they have not saved their lives from the mystery to come.

וְזֶה לָכֶם הָאוֹת,
כִּי יִהְיֶה בְּהִסָּגֵר מוֹלְדֵי־עַוְלָה:
וְגָלָה הָרֶשַׁע מִפְּנֵי הַצֶּדֶק
כִּגְלוֹת חֹשֶׁךְ מִפְּנֵי אוֹר;
וּכְתֹם עָשָׁן וְאֵינֶנּוּ עוֹד –
כֵּן יִתַּם הָרֶשַׁע לָעַד
וְהַצֶּדֶק יִגָּלֶה כַּשֶּׁמֶשׁ,
תִּכּוֹן תֵּבֵל.
וְכָל תּוֹמְכֵי רָזֵי־פֶשַׁע אֵינָמָה עוֹד
וְדֵעָה תִּמְלָא תֵבֵל
וְאֵין שָׁם לָעַד אִוֶּלֶת.

And this shall be the sign for you, for it will come to pass when the birth-gates of evil are shut: wickedness will then fly before righteousness as darkness flies before light; and as smoke disappears and is no more, so shall wickedness disappear forever and righteousness be revealed like the sun. The earth will be fixed and firm. All those who support the mysteries of sin will be no more. Knowledge will fill the earth, and never again will there be folly on earth.

נָכוֹן הַדָּבָר לָבוֹא וֶאֱמֶת הַמַּשָּׂא!

This word is sure to come; this oracle is true!

וּמִזֶּה יִוָּדַע לָכֶמָה כִּי לֹא יָשׁוּב אָחוֹר:
הֲלֹא כָּל הָעַמִּים שָׂנְאוּ עָוֶל?
וּבְיַד כֻּלָּמָה יִתְהַלָּךְ.
הֲלֹא מִפִּי כָל לְאֻמִּים שֵׁמַע הָאֱמֶת?
הֲיֵשׁ שָׂפָה וְלָשׁוֹן מַחֲזֶקֶת בָּהּ?
מִי גוֹי חָפֵץ אֲשֶׁר יַעַשְׁקֶנּוּ חָזָק מִמֶּנּוּ?
מִי יַחְפֹּץ כִּי יִגָּזֵל בְּרֶשַׁע הוֹנוֹ?

And by this shall you know that it will not fail: Do not all peoples hate injustice? Yet all of them commit it. Do not all nations mouth the praises of truth? But is there a lip or tongue that keeps it? Which nation would wish to be oppressed by a stronger rival? Who would wish to have his wealth wickedly plundered? Which nation has not

מִי גוֹי אֲשֶׁר לֹא עָשַׁק רֵעֵהוּ ?
אֵיפֹה עָם אֲשֶׁר לֹא גָזַל הוֹן לְאַחֵר . . .

oppressed its neighbour? Where is the people that has not plundered another's wealth? . . .

מְשַׁל הַגַּן

THE PARABLE OF THE TREES

אוֹדְךָ, אֲדֹנָי,
כִּי נְתַתַּנִי בִּמְקוֹר נוֹזְלִים בַּיַּבָּשָׁה
וּמַבּוּעַ מַיִם בְּאֶרֶץ צִיָּה
וּמַשְׁקֶה גַּן רָוֶה אֲשֶׁר נָטַעְתָּ,
מַטַּע בְּרוֹשׁ וְתִדְהָר עִם תְּאַשּׁוּר יַחַד לִכְבוֹדֶךָ:
עֲצֵי חַיִּים בְּמַעְיַן רָז,
מְחֻבָּאִים בְּתוֹךְ כָּל עֲצֵי מָיִם.

I will praise You, O Lord, for You have put me by a source of streams on the dry ground, by bubbling springs on the parched land, by the waters that irrigate Your luxuriant garden – a grove of pine together with fir and box – which You planted for Your glory. These are the Trees of Life, set beside a secret spring, concealed among all the Well-Watered Trees.

וְהָיוּ לְהַפְרִיחַ נֵצֶר לְמַטַּעַת־עוֹלָם,
לְהַשְׁרִישׁ טֶרֶם יַפְרִיחוּ
וְשָׁרָשֵׁיהֶם לְיוּבַל יְשַׁלֵּחוּ.
וְיִפְתַּח לְמַיִם חַיִּים גִּזְעוֹ
וִיהִי לִמְקוֹר־עוֹלָם,
וּבְנֶשֶׁר עָלָיו יִרְעוּ כָּל חַיַּת יָעַר,
וּמִרְמָס גִּזְעוֹ לְכָל עוֹבְרֵי דֶרֶךְ,
וְדָלִיָּתוֹ לְכָל עוֹף כָּנָף.

One day the Trees of Life will put forth a shoot which will become the Everlasting Plant, for they take root before they grow and extend their roots towards the stream. And the Plant will open its stem to the living waters; it will become an everlasting source [of blessing]. All the wild creatures will graze among its fallen leaves; all the wayfarers will pass by its stem; all the winged birds will nest in its boughs.

וַיָּרֹמּוּ עָלָיו כָּל עֲצֵי־מָיִם
כִּי בְּמַטַּעְתָּם יִתְשַׂגְשָׂגוּ,
וְאֶל יוּבַל לֹא יְשַׁלְּחוּ שֹׁרֶשׁ.
וּמַפְרִיחַ נֵצֶר־קֹדֶשׁ לְמַטַּעַת־אֱמֶת סֻתָּר,
בְּלֹא נֶחְשַׁב וּבְלֹא נוֹדַע חוֹתַם רָזוֹ.

But now all the Well-Watered Trees tower over it, for they grow as soon as they are planted; but their roots do not extend towards the stream. And the trees that will one day put forth the holy shoot of the Plant of truth – these trees are hidden away; their secret is sealed, it is not valued, it is not known.

וְאַתָּה, אֵל, שַׂכֹתָ בְּעַד פִּרְיוֹ
בְּרָז גִּבּוֹרֵי כֹחַ וְרוּחוֹת קֹדֶשׁ
וְלַהַט אֵשׁ מִתְהַפֶּכֶת.
בַּל יָבוֹא זָר בְּמַעְיַן־חַיִּים
וְעִם עֲצֵי־עוֹלָם לֹא יִשְׁתֶּה מֵי־קֹדֶשׁ.
בַּל יְנוֹבֵב פִּרְיוֹ עִם מַטַּע־שְׁחָקִים
כִּי רָאָה בְּלֹא הִכִּיר
וַיַּחֲשֹׁב בְּלֹא הֶאֱמִין לִמְקוֹר־חַיִּים
וַיִּתֵּן יָדוֹ בְּפֶרַח־עוֹלָם.

For You, O God, have hedged in its fruit on every side with the mystery of angels, creatures of might, and of holy spirits, with a whirling, flashing fire. No stranger can approach the spring of life; he cannot drink the holy waters together with the everlasting trees; he cannot bear fruit together with the heavenly Plant – because he saw but did not understand, he considered but did not believe in the source of life, he dared to lay hands upon the eternal flower.

חֶבְלֵי מָשִׁיחַ

THE BIRTH OF THE MESSIAH

...וַיָּשִׂימוּ נַפְשִׁי כָּאֳנִיָּה בִּמְצוּלוֹת יָם,
וּכְעִיר מִבְצָר מִלִּפְנֵי אוֹיֵב.
וָאֶהְיֶה בְצוּקָה כְּמוֹ אֵשֶׁת לֵדָה מַבְכִּירָה
כִּי נֶהֶפְכוּ צִירֶיהָ
וְחֶבֶל נִמְרָץ עַל מִשְׁבָּרֶיהָ
לְהָחִיל בְּכוּר־הָרִיָּה,
כִּי בָאוּ בָנִים עַד מִשְׁבְּרֵי־מָוֶת.

They have made my life like a ship in the depths of the sea, like a fortified town facing the enemy. I was in anguish, like a woman bearing her first child, when her labour suddenly begins and she is seized with cruel pangs which hasten the birth in her womb,[1] when the child is about to be born with deadly pangs.

וְהָרִיַּת גֶּבֶר הֵצֵרָה בַּחֲבָלֶיהָ
כִּי בְמִשְׁבְּרֵי־מָוֶת תַּמְלִיט זָכָר,
וּבְחֶבְלֵי־שְׁאוֹל יָגִיחַ מִכּוּר־הָרִיָּה
פֶּלֶא יוֹעֵץ עִם גְּבוּרָתוֹ.
וְיִפָּלֵט גֶּבֶר מִמִּשְׁבָּרִים.

Then she who bears the man will be gripped by spasms, for she will give birth to a son in deadly pangs. He will burst from her womb[1] in hellish spasms – a wonderful, mighty counsellor. Thus will the man spring forth amid pangs.

1. Lit. 'crucible of pregnancy'.

בְּהָרִיָּתוֹ הֵחִישׁוּ כָּל מִשְׁבָּרִים
וְחֶבְלֵי־מֶרֶץ בְּמוֹלְדֵיהֶם
וּפַלָּצוּת לְהוֹרוֹתָם.
וּבְמוֹלָדָיו יֵהָפְכוּ כָּל צִירִים בְּכוּר־הָרִיָּה.

At his conception all the [world's] pangs will redouble; wherever they spring up there will be cruel spasms, wherever they are bred there will be agony. At his birth, the womb [of Hell] will suddenly be gripped by all its throes.

וְהָרִיַּת אֶפְעֶה לְחֶבֶל נִמְרָץ
וּמִשְׁבְּרֵי־שַׁחַת לְכָל מַעֲשֵׂי פַלָּצוּת.
וַיֵּרֹעוּ אֻשֵּׁי־קִיר כָּאֳנִיָּה עַל פְּנֵי מָיִם
וַיֶּהֱמוּ שְׁחָקִים בְּקוֹל הָמוֹן.
וְיוֹשְׁבֵי עָפָר כְּיוֹרְדֵי יַמִּים
נִבְעָתִים מֵהֲמוֹן מָיִם,
וַחֲכָמֶיהָ כֻלָּמוֹ כְּמַלָּחִים בִּמְצוּלוֹת
כִּי תִתְבַּלַּע כָּל חָכְמָתָם
בַּהֲמוֹת יַמִּים,
בִּרְתֹחַ תְּהוֹמוֹת עַל נְבוּכֵי מָיִם.
וַיִּתְרַגְּשׁוּ לְרוּם גַּלִּים
וּמִשְׁבְּרֵי־מַיִם בַּהֲמוֹן קוֹלָם.
וּבְהִתְרַגְּשָׁם יִפָּתְחוּ שְׁאוֹל וַאֲבַדּוֹן,
וְכָל חִצֵּי־שַׁחַת עִם מִצְעָדָם
לִתְהוֹם יַשְׁמִיעוּ קוֹלָם.
וַיִּפָּתְחוּ שַׁעֲרֵי־שְׁאוֹל לְכָל מַעֲשֵׂי־אֶפְעֶה.

Then she who bears evil will suffer cruel spasms, as the infernal pangs bring forth all the creatures of havoc. The earth's foundations will rock like a ship upon the waters, the skies will roar with a thunder of waters. All the inhabitants of the dust, like men who sail the sea, will be terrified by the roar of waters. All the wise men will be like sailors on the ocean; their seamanship will be in vain, as the sea thunders and the abyss boils with swirling waters, as billows are cast up and breakers roar. Then, as they rage, Hell and Perdition will gape open, and the arrows of the Pit, let loose, will cry out to the abyss. Thus will the gates of Hell open up to all the creatures of evil.

וַיִּסָּגְרוּ דַּלְתֵי־שַׁחַת בְּעַד הָרִיַּת־עָוֶל
וּבְרִיחֵי־עוֹלָם בְּעַד כָּל רוּחֵי־אֶפְעֶה.

But then the doors of the Pit will shut upon the children of wickedness, and the eternal bolts will close upon all the spirits of evil.

שִׁירִים מִן הַתַּלְמוּד

Poems from the Talmud

אוֹי לִי מִבֵּית בַּיְתוֹס

אוֹי לִי מִבֵּית בַּיְתוֹס,
אוֹי לִי מֵאַלָּתָן.
אוֹי לִי מִבֵּית קַתְרוֹס,
אוֹי לִי מִקֻּלְמוֹסָן.
אוֹי לִי מִבֵּית חָנָן,
אוֹי לִי מִלְּחִישָׁתָן.
אוֹי לִי מִבֵּית יִשְׁמָעֵאל בֶּן פִּיאָבִי,
אוֹי לִי מֵאֶגְרוֹפָן —
שֶׁהֵם כֹּהֲנִים גְּדוֹלִים,
וּבְנֵיהֶם גִּזְבָּרִין,
וַחֲתְנֵיהֶן אֲמַרְכָּלִין,
וְעַבְדֵיהֶן בָּאִין
וְחוֹבְטִין עָלֵינוּ בְּמַקְלוֹת.

SONG OF PROTEST

Woe to me from the house of Boethus: woe to me from their cudgels. Woe to me from the house of Kathros: woe to me from their quills. Woe to me from the house of Hanin: woe to me from their slanders. Woe to me from the house of Ishmael son of Phabi: woe to me from their fists. For they are the High Priests, their sons are the treasurers, their sons-in-law are the trustees, and their slaves come and beat us with their sticks.

בְּעִקְבוֹת מְשִׁיחָא

בְּעִקְבוֹת מְשִׁיחָא
חֻצְפָּא יִסְגֵּא
וְיֹקֶר יַאֲמִיר.
הַגֶּפֶן תִּתֵּן פִּרְיָהּ,
וְהַיַּיִן בְּיֹקֶר.
וְהַמַּלְכוּת תֵּהָפֵךְ לְמִינוּת,
וְאֵין תּוֹכָחַת.
בֵּית־וַעַד יִהְיֶה לִזְנוּת,
וְהַגָּלִיל יֶחֱרַב

THE ADVENT OF THE MESSIAH

At the advent of the Messiah, impudence will increase and prices will soar. The vine will yield its fruit, yet wine will be costly. The empire will fall into heresy, and no one will protest. The meeting-place of scholars will be given over to harlotry; the Galilee will

וְהַגַּבְלָן יְשֹׁם.
וְאַנְשֵׁי־הַגְּבוּל
יְסוֹבְבוּ מֵעִיר לְעִיר,
וְלֹא יְחוֹנָנוּ.
וְחָכְמַת־סוֹפְרִים תִּסְרַח,
וְיִרְאֵי־חֵטְא יִמָּאֲסוּ,
וְהָאֱמֶת תְּהֵא נֶעְדֶּרֶת.
נְעָרִים פְּנֵי זְקֵנִים יַלְבִּינוּ,
זְקֵנִים יַעַמְדוּ מִפְּנֵי קְטַנִּים.
׳בֵּן מְנַבֵּל אָב,
בַּת קָמָה בְאִמָּהּ,
כַּלָּה בַּחֲמֹתָהּ,
אֹיְבֵי אִישׁ אַנְשֵׁי בֵיתוֹ.׳
פְּנֵי הַדּוֹר כִּפְנֵי הַכֶּלֶב.
הַבֵּן אֵינוֹ מִתְבַּיֵּשׁ מֵאָבִיו.
וְעַל מִי יֵשׁ לָנוּ לְהִשָּׁעֵן ?
עַל אָבִינוּ שֶׁבַּשָּׁמַיִם !

be laid waste, the Golan made desolate. Those who live on the frontier will roam from town to town, and no one will take pity on them. The wisdom of the scribes will decay, sin-fearing men will be despised, and truth will be gone. The young will shame their elders; the aged will stand up in the presence of youngsters. *For son maligns father, daughter rebels against mother, daughter-in-law against mother-in-law, and a man's household are his enemies.*[1] The face of this generation is like a dog's face; the son feels no shame before his father. On whom then can we rely? On our Father in heaven!

אַחֵינוּ הַמְיֻגָּעִים

אַחֵינוּ הַמְיֻגָּעִים,
הַמְּדֻכָּאִים בָּאֵבֶל הַזֶּה,
תְּנוּ לְבַבְכֶם לַחְקֹר אֶת זֹאת –
זֹאת הִיא עוֹמֶדֶת לָעַד,
נָתִיב הוּא מִשֵּׁשֶׁת יְמֵי בְרֵאשִׁית:
רַבִּים שָׁתוּ, רַבִּים יִשְׁתּוּ,
כְּמִשְׁתֵּה רִאשׁוֹנִים כָּךְ מִשְׁתֵּה אַחֲרוֹנִים.
אַחֵינוּ,
בַּעַל הַנֶּחָמוֹת יְנַחֵם אֶתְכֶם!

ON THE DEATH OF A CHILD

O wearied brethren, weighed down by this grief, set your hearts to consider this, for this is eternally so, the way of the world since the six days of creation: many have drunk, many will drink, and the last will drink as the first drank. Our brethren, may the Master of Comfort comfort you!

1. Micah 7.6.

גֶּזַע־יְשִׁישִׁים

גֶּזַע־יְשִׁישִׁים עָלָה מִבָּבֶל
וְעִמּוֹ סֵפֶר מִלְחֲמוֹת אֲדֹנָי.
קָאָת וְקִפּוֹד הָכְפְּלוּ לִרְאוֹת
בְּשֹׁד וָשֶׁבֶר הַבָּא מִשִּׁנְעָר.
קָצַף עַל עוֹלָמוֹ וְחָמַס נְפָשׁוֹת,
וְשָׂמַח בָּהֶם כְּכַלָּה חֲדָשָׁה.
רוֹכֵב־עֲרָבוֹת שָׂשׂ וְשָׂמֵחַ
בְּבוֹא אֵלָיו נֶפֶשׁ צַדִּיק!

FUNERAL ORATION

The Scion of an Ancient Stock has come from Babylon together with the Book of the Wars of the Lord. Both vulture and raven rush to see this ravage and ruin, which has come from Shinear.[1] When He raged at His world, He plundered souls, then delighted in them as in a new bride. He who rides upon the highest heaven rejoices and exults when the souls of the righteous come to Him.

בָּאֲרָזִים נָפְלָה שַׁלְהֶבֶת

בָּאֲרָזִים נָפְלָה שַׁלְהֶבֶת –
מַה יַּעֲשׂוּ אֵזוֹבֵי־הַקִּיר?
לִוְיָתָן בְּחַכָּה הֹעֲלָה –
מַה יַּעֲשׂוּ דְּגֵי־הָרְקָק?
בְּנַחַל שׁוֹטֵף נָפְלָה חָרָבָה –
מַה יַּעֲשׂוּ מֵי־גֵבִים?

LAMENT

If the cedars have caught fire, what hope is there for the moss on the wall? If Leviathan has been hauled in by a fish-hook, what hope is there for the minnows? If the mighty river has been struck by drought, what hope is there for the waterholes?

אֱלֹהַי, נְשָׁמָה שֶׁנָּתַתָּ בִּי

אֱלֹהַי,
נְשָׁמָה שֶׁנָּתַתָּ בִּי – טְהוֹרָה.
אַתָּה בְרָאתָהּ,
אַתָּה יְצַרְתָּהּ,

THANKSGIVING UPON AWAKENING

My God, the soul which You set within me is pure. You created it, You

1. Babylon.

אַתָּה נְפַחְתָּהּ בִּי
וְאַתָּה מְשַׁמְּרָהּ בְּקִרְבִּי.
וְאַתָּה עָתִיד לִטְּלָהּ מִמֶּנִּי
וּלְהַחֲזִירָהּ בִּי לֶעָתִיד לָבוֹא.

formed it, You breathed it into me, and You preserve it within me. One day You will reclaim it from me, but then You will restore it to me in the days to come.

כָּל זְמַן שֶׁהַנְּשָׁמָה בְּקִרְבִּי,
מוֹדֶה אֲנִי לְפָנֶיךָ,
יהוה אֱלֹהַי וֵאלֹהֵי אֲבוֹתַי,
רִבּוֹן כָּל הַמַּעֲשִׂים,
אֲדוֹן כָּל הַנְּשָׁמוֹת:
בָּרוּךְ אַתָּה יהוה
הַמַּחֲזִיר נְשָׁמוֹת לִפְגָרִים מֵתִים.

As long as the soul is within me, I shall give thanks to You, Lord my God and God of my fathers, Master of all creation, Lord of all souls. Blessed are You, O Lord, who restore souls to dead bodies.

אֱלֹהַי, נְצֹר לְשׁוֹנִי מֵרָע

PRAYER

אֱלֹהַי,
נְצֹר לְשׁוֹנִי מֵרָע
וּשְׂפָתַי מִדַּבֵּר מִרְמָה.
וְלִמְקַלְלַי נַפְשִׁי תִדֹּם
וְנַפְשִׁי כֶּעָפָר לַכֹּל תִּהְיֶה.
פְּתַח לִבִּי בְּתוֹרָתֶךָ
וּבְמִצְווֹתֶיךָ תִּרְדֹּף נַפְשִׁי.
וְתַצִּילֵנִי מִפֶּגַע רָע,
מִיֵּצֶר הָרָע וּמֵאִשָּׁה רָעָה,
וּמִכָּל רָעוֹת הַמִּתְרַגְּשׁוֹת בָּעוֹלָם.
וְכָל הַחוֹשְׁבִים עָלַי רָעָה –
מַהֵר הָפֵר עֲצָתָם
וְקַלְקֵל מַחְשְׁבוֹתָם!

My God, keep my tongue from evil and my lips from speaking guile. May my soul be silent before those who revile me; may my soul be as lowly to all as the dust. Open my heart to Your law, so that my soul may pursue Your commandments. Deliver me from mishap, from the evil urge and from an evil wife, from all the misfortunes that occur in the world. And as for those who scheme against me – quickly thwart their counsels and frustrate their designs!

הַמַּפִּיל חַבְלֵי־שֵׁנָה

PRAYER BEFORE SLEEP

בָּרוּךְ אַתָּה יהוה
אֱלֹהֵינוּ מֶלֶךְ הָעוֹלָם,
הַמַּפִּיל חַבְלֵי־שֵׁנָה עַל עֵינַי
וּתְנוּמָה עַל עַפְעַפַּי.
וִיהִי רָצוֹן מִלְּפָנֶיךָ,
יהוה אֱלֹהַי וֵאלֹהֵי אֲבוֹתַי,
שֶׁתַּשְׁכִּיבֵנִי לְשָׁלוֹם
וְתַעֲמִידֵנִי לְשָׁלוֹם.
וְאַל יְבַהֲלוּנִי רַעְיוֹנַי
וַחֲלוֹמוֹת רָעִים וְהַרְהוֹרִים רָעִים,
וּתְהִי מִטָּתִי שְׁלֵמָה לְפָנֶיךָ.

Blessed are You, Lord our God, king of the universe, who weigh down my eyes with bonds of sleep and my eyelids with slumber. May it be Your will, Lord my God and God of my fathers, to lay me down in peace and raise me up in peace. Do not let my thoughts, or evil dreams, or sinful fancies alarm me. Grant that [the fruit of] my bed be perfect before You.

וְהָאֵר עֵינַי
פֶּן אִישַׁן הַמָּוֶת,
כִּי אַתָּה הַמֵּאִיר לְאִישׁוֹן בַּת־עָיִן.
בָּרוּךְ אַתָּה יהוה,
הַמֵּאִיר לָעוֹלָם כֻּלּוֹ בִּכְבוֹדוֹ.

Give light to my eyes lest I sink into the sleep of death, for it is You who illuminate the pupil of the eye. Blessed are You, O Lord, whose glory illuminates all the world.

רָנִּי, רָנִּי הַשִּׁטָּה!

THE COWS' HYMN TO THE ARK OF THE LORD

רָנִּי, רָנִּי הַשִּׁטָּה!
הִתְנוֹפְפִי בְּרֹב הֲדָרֵךְ —
הַמְחֻשֶּׁקֶת בְּרִקְמֵי־זָהָב,
הַמְהֻלָּלָה בִּדְבִיר־אַרְמוֹן,
הַמְפֹאָרָה בַּעֲדִי־עֲדָיִים.

Sing, oh sing, acacia! Tower in all your splendour, you who are decked with golden embroidery, praised in the inmost sanctuary, resplendent with the finest adornments!

שִׁירִים מֵהֵיכָלוֹת רַבָּתִי

Hekhalot Hymns

תְּהִלַּת שֶׁבַח

HYMN FOR THE DESCENT TO THE MERKAVA

תְּהִלַּת שֶׁבַח וְרֵאשִׁית שִׁירָה,
תְּהִלַּת גִּילָה וְרֵאשִׁית רִנָּה
מְשׁוֹרְרִים הַשָּׂרִים הַמְשָׁרְתִים
בְּכָל יוֹם לַיהוה אֱלֹהֵי יִשְׂרָאֵל.
לְכִסֵּא כְבוֹדוֹ הֵם מְנַשְּׂאִים:
'גִּיל, גִּיל, כִּסֵּא כָבוֹד,
רַנֵּן, רַנֵּן, מוֹשַׁב־עֶלְיוֹן!
הָרִיעַ, הָרִיעַ, כְּלִי־חֶמְדָּה,
שֶׁנַּעֲשָׂה בְּהַפְלֵא וָפֶלֶא.
שַׂמֵּחַ תְּשַׂמַּח מֶלֶךְ שֶׁעָלֶיךָ
כְּשִׂמְחַת חָתָן בְּבֵית חֻפָּתוֹ!'

The beginning of praise and the start of song, the beginning of joy and the start of jubilation – these are sung by the princes[1] who daily serve the Lord God of Israel. They exalt His throne of glory: 'Rejoice, rejoice, throne of glory! Sing, sing for joy, seat of the Most High! Exult, exult, O precious vessel, so marvellously fashioned! You will gladden the king upon you, as a bridegroom is gladdened in his bridal-chamber!'

מְבַטְּלֵי גְזֵרָה

HYMN TO THE HOLY LIVING CREATURES

מְבַטְּלֵי גְזֵרָה, מְפֵרֵי שְׁבוּעָה,
מַעֲבִירֵי חֵמָה, מְשִׁיבֵי קִנְאָה,
מַזְכִּירֵי אַהֲבָה, מְסַדְּרֵי רֵעוּת
לִפְנֵי הֲדַר־גָּאוֹן־הֵיכַל־נוֹרָא:

You who revoke decrees, undo vows, remove wrath, soothe fury, recall love, restore friendship before the splendour of the glory of the palace of the Dread One –

מַה לָּכֶם שֶׁאַתֶּם נוֹרָאִים,
וּפְעָמִים לָכֶם שֶׁאַתֶּם שְׂמֵחִים?

Why is it that sometimes you take fright and at other times you are merry?

1. The Holy Living Creatures.

מַה לָּכֶם שֶׁאַתֶּם מְרַנְּנִים,
וּפְעָמִים לָכֶם שֶׁאַתֶּם מְבֹהָלִים ?

Why is it that sometimes you exult and at other times you are terrified?

אָמְרוּ : 'כְּשֶׁפְּנֵי גְבוּרָה מַקְדִּירִין,
עוֹמְדִים אָנוּ בְּבֶהָלָה גְדוֹלָה ;
וּכְשֶׁזָּהֳרֵי שְׁכִינָה מְאִירִין,
אָנוּ שְׂמֵחִים שִׂמְחָה רַבָּה !'

They said: 'When the face of the Divine Majesty grows dark, we stand in great terror. But when the sparks of the Shekinah[1] radiate, we are full of mirth!'

פָּנִים נָאִים

THE FACE OF GOD

פָּנִים נָאִים, פָּנִים הֲדוּרִים,
פָּנִים שֶׁל יֹפִי, פָּנִים שֶׁל לֶהָבָה,
פְּנֵי יהוה אֱלֹהֵי יִשְׂרָאֵל
כְּשֶׁהוּא יוֹשֵׁב עַל כִּסֵּא כְבוֹדוֹ
וְסִלְסוּלוֹ מְתֻקָּן בְּמוֹשַׁב הֲדָרוֹ.
יָפְיוֹ נָאֶה מִיָּפְיִ גְבוּרוֹת,
הֲדָרוֹ מְעֻלֶּה מֵהֲדַר חֲתָנִים וְכַלּוֹת
בְּבֵית חֻפָּתָם.

Lovely face, majestic face, face of beauty, face of flame, the face of the Lord God of Israel when He sits upon His throne of glory, robed in praise upon His seat of splendour. His beauty surpasses the beauty of the aged, His splendour outshines the splendour of newly-weds in their bridal chamber.

הַמִּסְתַּכֵּל בּוֹ מִיָּד נִקְרָע,
וְהַמֵּצִיץ בְּיָפְיוֹ מִיָּד מִשְׁתַּפֵּךְ כְּקִיתוֹן.
הַמְשָׁרְתִים אוֹתוֹ הַיּוֹם
שׁוּב אֵין מְשָׁרְתִים אוֹתוֹ לְמָחָר,
וְהַמְשָׁרְתִים אוֹתוֹ לְמָחָר
שׁוּב אֵין מְשָׁרְתִים לְפָנָיו —
כִּי תָשַׁשׁ כֹּחָם וְהֻשְׁחֲרוּ פְנֵיהֶם,
תָּעָה לִבָּם וְנֶחְשְׁכוּ עֵינֵיהֶם
אַחַר הֲדַר־זִיו־יֹפִי שֶׁל מַלְכָּם.

Whoever looks at Him is instantly torn; whoever glimpses His beauty immediately melts away.[2] Those who serve Him today no longer serve Him tomorrow; those who serve Him tomorrow no longer serve Him afterwards; for their strength fails and their faces are charred, their hearts reel and their eyes grow dim at the splendour and radiance of their king's beauty.

1. God's 'immanence' or 'indwelling' in the world.
2. Lit. 'is emptied out like a ladle'.

מְשָׁרְתִים אֲהוּבִים, מְשָׁרְתִים נָאִים,
מְשָׁרְתִים מְמַהֲרִים, מְשָׁרְתִים קַלִּים!
הָעוֹמְדִים עַל אֶבֶן כִּסֵּא הַכָּבוֹד
וְהַנִּצָּבִים עַל גַּלְגַּל הַמֶּרְכָּבָה;
כְּשֶׁאֶבֶן כִּסֵּא הַכָּבוֹד מְחַזֵּר עֲלֵיהֶם,
כְּשֶׁגַּלְגַּל הַמֶּרְכָּבָה מַחְטִיף אוֹתָם –
הָעוֹמְדִים לְיָמִין,
חוֹזְרִים וְעוֹמְדִים לִשְׂמֹאל;
וְהָעוֹמְדִים לִשְׂמֹאל,
חוֹזְרִים וְעוֹמְדִים לְיָמִין;
וְהָעוֹמְדִים לְפָנִים,
חוֹזְרִים וְעוֹמְדִים לְאָחוֹר;
וְהָעוֹמְדִים לְאָחוֹר,
חוֹזְרִים וְעוֹמְדִים לְפָנִים.

Beloved servants, lovely servants, swift servants, light-footed servants, who stand before the stone of the throne of glory, who wait upon the wheel of the chariot. When the sapphire of the throne of glory whirls at them, when the wheel of the chariot hurls past them, those on the right now stand again to the left, those on the left now stand again to the right, those in front now stand again in back, those in back now stand again in front.

הָרוֹאֶה אֶת זֶה, אוֹמֵר: זֶה הוּא זֶה.
וְהָרוֹאֶה אֶת זֶה, אוֹמֵר: זֶה הוּא זֶה.
כִּי קְלַסְתֵּר פָּנָיו שֶׁל זֶה
דּוֹמֶה לִקְלַסְתֵּר פָּנָיו שֶׁל זֶה;
וּקְלַסְתֵּר פָּנָיו שֶׁל זֶה
דּוֹמֶה לִקְלַסְתֵּר פָּנָיו שֶׁל זֶה.

He who sees the one says, 'That is the other'. And he who sees the other says, 'That is the one'. For the visage of the one is like the visage of the other; and the visage of the other is like the visage of the one.

אַשְׁרֵי הַמֶּלֶךְ שֶׁאֵלּוּ מְשָׁרְתָיו,
וְאַשְׁרֵי מְשָׁרְתִים שֶׁזֶּה מַלְכָּם.
אַשְׁרֵי עַיִן הַנִּזּוֹנֶת וְהַמִּסְתַּכֶּלֶת
בָּאוֹר הַמֻּפְלָא הַזֶּה,
רְאִיָּה מֻפְלָאָה וּמְשֻׁנָּה מְאֹד.

Happy the King who has such servants, and happy the servants who have such a King. Happy the eye that sees and feeds upon this wondrous light – a wondrous vision and most strange!

בְּכָל יוֹם וָיוֹם

בְּכָל יוֹם וָיוֹם בְּהַגִּיעַ עֲלוֹת־הַשַּׁחַר,
מֶלֶךְ הָדוּר יוֹשֵׁב וּמְבָרֵךְ לַחַיּוֹת:
'לָכֶם, חַיּוֹת, אֲנִי אוֹמֵר,
לָכֶם, בְּרִיּוֹת, אֲנִי מַשְׁמִיעַ —
חַיּוֹת, חַיּוֹת נוֹשְׂאוֹת כִּסֵּא כְבוֹדִי
בְּלֵב שָׁלֵם וּבְנֶפֶשׁ חֲפֵצָה —
תִּתְבָּרֵךְ הַשָּׁעָה שֶׁבְּרָאתִי אֶתְכֶם בָּהּ,
יִתְרוֹמֵם הַמַּזָּל שֶׁיָּצַרְתִּי אֶתְכֶם בּוֹ;
יָאִיר אוֹרוֹ שֶׁל אוֹתוֹ הַיּוֹם
שֶׁעֲלִיתֶם בְּמַחֲשָׁבָה עַל לְבָבִי;
שֶׁאַתֶּם כְּלֵי־חֶמְדָּה שֶׁהֵכַנְתִּי
וְשִׁכְלַלְתִּי אֶתְכֶם בּוֹ.
הַחֲרִישׁוּ לִי קוֹל כָּל יְצוּרִים שֶׁבָּרָאתִי
וְאֶשְׁמַע וְאַאֲזִין לְקוֹל תְּפִלַּת בָּנַי.'

THE CELESTIAL MORNING SERVICE

Day after day, at the break of dawn, the majestic King sits and blesses the Holy Beings: 'To you, Holy Beings, I say; to you, Living Creatures, I proclaim – Holy Beings, Holy Beings, who carry My throne of glory with whole heart and willing mind – blessed be the hour in which I created you; exalted be the zodiacal sign under which I fashioned you; radiant be the light of the day on which you first occurred to Me. For you are the precious vessels that I prepared and perfected on that day. Now silence the voice of all the heavenly beings I have made, so that I may listen to the voice of My children praying.'

מֶלֶךְ נִסִּים

מֶלֶךְ נִסִּים, מֶלֶךְ גְּבוּרוֹת,
מֶלֶךְ נִפְלָאוֹת, מֶלֶךְ פְּרִישׁוּת —
כִּסְאֲךָ מְעוֹפֵף וְעוֹמֵד תַּחְתָּיו
מִשָּׁעָה שֶׁתָּקַעְתָּ יְתַד אֲרִיגַת הַמַּסֶּכֶת,
שֶׁשִּׁכְלוּל הָעוֹלָם וּמַסְלוּלוֹ עוֹמֵד עָלֶיהָ
שָׁנִים רַבּוֹת, דּוֹרוֹת עַד אֵין קֵץ.
וַעֲדַיִן לֹא הִנִּיחַ רַגְלָיו
עַל קַרְקַע עֲרָבוֹת רָקִיעַ
אֶלָּא כְּעוֹף מְעוֹפֵף וְעוֹמֵד תַּחְתָּיו.
גֵּאֵי־גֵאִים, קְשׁוּרֵי־כְתָרִים

THE THRONE OF GLORY ADDRESSES THE KING

King of miracles, King of power, King of wonders, King of marvels: Your throne hovers yet does not move, ever since You set the peg of the loom which fixes the world's course and its perfection, all these many years and endless generations. Your throne has never set foot on the floor of the seventh heaven, but hovers like a bird and does not move. The proudest of the proud, adorned with crowns, and

וְכָל מַלְכֵי רָאשֵׁי־מִדּוֹת שֶׁבָּרָאתָ
חֲבוּשִׁים וְעוֹמְדִים תַּחַת כִּסֵּא כְבוֹדֶךָ
וְהָיוּ מְנַטְּלִין אוֹתוֹ בְּעֹז, תֹּקֶף וּגְבוּרָה.
וְאַף הֵם לֹא הִנִּיחוּ רַגְלֵיהֶם
עַל קַרְקַע עֲרָבוֹת רָקִיעַ
אֶלָּא כָּעוֹף מְעוֹפְפִים וְעוֹמְדִים תַּחְתֵּיהֶם.
וְשָׁלשׁ פְּעָמִים בְּכָל יוֹם וָיוֹם
כִּסֵּא כְבוֹדְךָ מִשְׁתַּטֵּחַ לְפָנֶיךָ וְאוֹמֵר לְךָ:
'זֲהָרָרִיאֵל יהוה אֱלֹהֵי יִשְׂרָאֵל,
הִתְכַּבֵּד וְשֵׁב עָלַי, מֶלֶךְ מְפֹאָר,
לְפִי שֶׁמַּשָּׂאֲךָ חָבִיב עָלַי וְיָקָר
וְאֵין כָּבֵד עָלַי.'

all the royal living creatures whom You created stand close together beneath Your throne of glory, bearing it with might, strength, and power. They too have never set foot upon the floor of the seventh heaven, but hover like a bird and do not move. Thrice daily Your throne of glory prostrates itself before You and says: 'Zoharariel, Adonai, God of Israel, sit upon me in glory, resplendent King, for Your burden is most dear to me and does not weigh me down.'

מִדָּה שֶׁל קְדֻשָּׁה

GOD'S ROBE OF GLORY

מִדָּה שֶׁל קְדֻשָּׁה, מִדָּה שֶׁל גְּבוּרָה,
מִדָּה נוֹרָאָה, מִדָּה מְבֹהָלָה,
מִדָּה שֶׁל רְתֵת, מִדָּה שֶׁל זִיעַ,
מִדָּה שֶׁל בַּהַל, מִדָּה שֶׁל חַלְחָלָה –
מִדָּה שֶׁל חָלוּק
שֶׁל זֲהָרָרִיאֵל יהוה אֱלֹהֵי יִשְׂרָאֵל,
שֶׁמְּעֻטָּר וּבָא עַל כִּסֵּא כְבוֹדוֹ,
וְחָקוּק וּמָלֵא כֻּלּוֹ, מִבִּפְנִים וּמִן הַחִיצוֹן,
יהוה יהוה.
וְעֵינֵי כָּל בְּרִיָּה אֵינָהּ יְכוֹלָה לְהִסְתַּכֵּל בּוֹ,
לֹא עֵינֵי בָּשָׂר וָדָם וְלֹא עֵינֵי מְשָׁרְתָיו.
כִּי הַמִּסְתַּכֵּל בּוֹ וְהַמֵּצִיץ וְהָרוֹאֶה אוֹתוֹ,
אוֹחֲזוֹת מַחֲזוֹרִיּוֹת לְגַלְגַּלֵּי עֵינָיו,
וְגַלְגַּלֵּי עֵינָיו מְפַלְּטִין וּמוֹצִיאִין לַפִּידֵי אֵשׁ

A quality of holiness, a quality of power, a fearful quality, a dreaded quality, a quality of awe, a quality of shuddering, a quality of dismay, a quality of terror – such is the quality of the garment of Zoharariel, Adonai, God of Israel, who, crowned, comes to the throne of His glory; His garment is engraved inside and outside and entirely covered with YHWH YHWH. No eyes are able to behold it, neither the eyes of flesh and blood nor the eyes of His servants. Whoever beholds it, whoever glimpses and sees it, his eye-balls are seized by balls of fire, his eye-balls discharge fiery torches which

וְהֵן מְלַהֲטִין אוֹתוֹ וְהֵן שׂוֹרְפִין אוֹתוֹ;
כִּי הָאֵשׁ הַיּוֹצֵא מִן הָאָדָם הַמִּסְתַּכֵּל
הִיא מְלַהֶטֶת אוֹתוֹ וְהִיא שׂוֹרֶפֶת אוֹתוֹ.
מִפְּנֵי מָה?
מִפְּנֵי דְמוּת עֵינַיִם שֶׁל חָלוּק
שֶׁל זְהַרְרִיאֵל יהוה אֱלֹהֵי יִשְׂרָאֵל,
שֶׁמְּעֻטָּר וּבָא עַל כִּסֵּא כְבוֹדוֹ.

burn him and consume him. For the very fire that springs out of the man beholding the garment burns him and consumes him. Why? Because of the image of eyes in the garment of Zoharariel, Adonai, God of Israel, who, crowned, comes to the throne of His glory.

מֶלֶךְ הַמְּלָכִים

CREATION HYMN

כיון שעמד לפני כסא כבוד, פותח ואומר שירה שכסא כבוד משורר בכל יום ויום:

מֶלֶךְ הַמְּלָכִים,
אֱלֹהֵי הָאֱלֹהִים וַאֲדוֹנֵי הָאֲדוֹנִים –
הַמְסוּבָב בְּקִשְׁרֵי כְתָרִים,
הַמֻּקָּף בְּעַנְפֵי נְגִידֵי נֹגַהּ,
שֶׁבְּעַנְפוֹ הוֹדוֹ כִּסָּה שָׁמַיִם
וּבַהֲדָרוֹ הוֹפִיעַ מִמְּרוֹמִים.
מִיָּפְיוֹ נִתְבַּעֲרוּ תְהוֹמוֹת,
וּמִתָּאֳרוֹ נִתְּזוּ שְׁחָקִים.
וְגֵאִים מַפְלִיט תָּאֳרוֹ,
וְאֵיתָנִים מְפוֹצֵץ כִּתְרוֹ,
וִיקָרִים טוֹרֵד חֲלוּקוֹ.
וְכָל עֵצִים יִשְׂמְחוּ בִּדְבָרוֹ,
וִירַנְּנוּ דְשָׁאִים בְּשִׂמְחָתוֹ –
וּבְדַבְּרוֹ יִזְּלוּ בְשָׂמִים.

When [the man who has made the ascent] *stands before the throne of glory, he begins by reciting the hymn that the throne of glory sings each day:*

King of Kings, God of Gods and Lord of Lords, encircled by wreaths of crowns, surrounded by boughs of glowing princes – He who covered the heavens with His glorious bough and appeared from the heights in His majesty. The deeps were set ablaze by His beauty, the firmaments were kindled by his radiant stature. The proud angels burst out of His stature, the mighty explode from His crown, the precious erupt from His garment. And all the trees rejoice in His word, the grasses exult in His joy, and as He speaks perfumes flow forth.

עֲטוּרֵי פְאֵר

THE ATTENDANTS OF THE INNERMOST CHAMBER

עֲטוּרֵי פְאֵר, מְכֻתָּרֵי כְתָרִים,
מְרַנְּנֵי עֶלְיוֹן בְּשִׁיר גִּילָה –
רוֹמְמוּ אַתֶּם לַאֲדוֹן לֶהָבָה,
כִּי בִשְׁכִינַת שְׁכִינָה, הֲדַר הַדְרֵי
חַדְרֵי חֲדָרָיו אַתֶּם חוֹנִים.
הִפְלִיא אֶת שִׁמְכֶם מִשֵּׁם מְשָׁרְתָיו,
הִבְדִּיל אֶתְכֶם מִמְּשָׁרְתֵי מֶרְכָּבָה.
הַמַּזְכִּיר שֵׁם אֶחָד מִכֶּם –
אֵשׁ לוֹהֶטֶת, לֶהָבָה סוֹבֶבֶת, שַׁלְהֶבֶת מַקֶּפֶת,
גַּחֲלֵי אֵשׁ, גַּחֲלֵי רוּחַ, גַּחֲלֵי זִיו מִנַּתְּזוֹת.

You who are crowned in grandeur, who are wreathed in crowns, who celebrate the Most High with hymns of jubilation – now glorify the Master of flame, for you are stationed within the very heart of the Shekinah, in the innermost glory of the chamber of chambers. He has exalted your names above those of His other servants; He has singled you out from among the servants of the chariot. Whoever mentions any of you by name – fire consumes him, flames surround him, torches whirl about him and glaring coals, coals of wind, coals of splendour shower upon him!

עֲלוּמֵי שֵׁם

Anonymous

אֵיתָן לִמֵּד דַּעַת

AKEDA: THE SACRIFICE OF ISAAC

אֵיתָן לִמֵּד דַּעַת
בְּטֶרֶם יְדָעֲךָ כֹּל,
גִּלָּה לְכָל יָצוּר
דֶּרֶךְ לְהִתְהַלֶּךְ־בָּהּ.

Abraham, the steadfast one, made You known, before You were known by the world; he revealed to all creatures the path which they should take.

הֻבְחַן מֵעֶשְׂרִים דּוֹר,
וְעָמַד בְּכָל נִסָּיוֹן.
זֶה, נִסִּיתוֹ בְּעֶשֶׂר,
חֲנַנְתּוֹ לְמֵאָה פֶּרִי.

He was designated from among twenty generations[1] and withstood every trial. Lord, you put him to the test ten times; You granted him offspring in his hundredth year.

1. The book of Genesis records twenty generations from Adam to Abraham.

טוֹב, בְּאָמְרְךָ לוֹ:
'יֶלֶד לְנִיחוֹחַ חָשַׁקְתִּי' –
כְּמָה צִוּוּי שָׁקַד,
לֹא אֵחַר דָּבָר!

Benign One, when You said to him: 'I desire your child as a fragrant offering' – he rushed to fulfil the command, he lost no time at all.

מִהַר וּבִקַּע עֵצִים,
נָשָׂא אֵשׁ וּמַאֲכֶלֶת,
שָׂם עַל יְחִידוֹ
עֶרֶךְ עֲצֵי עוֹלָה.

Quickly he split the wood, took up the fire and the knife, loaded his favoured one, Isaac, with the faggot for the burnt offering.

פָּנָה וּבָנָה מִזְבֵּחַ,
צָג וְהֶעֱלָה כֶּבֶשׂ;
קַח בְּיָדוֹ חֶרֶב –
רַחֲמָיו לֹא נִכְמָרוּ.

Then he went on to build the altar, stood up and placed his lamb upon it; he took the sword in his hand and took no pity at all.

שַׁדַּי הִשְׁמִיעַ לוֹ:
'הֶרֶף יָדְךָ מְהֵרָה!
תְּמוּר בִּנְךָ רָצִיתִי
תָּפוּשׂ בַּסְּבָךְ בְּקֶרֶן.'

The Almighty cried out to him: 'Drop your hand at once! Instead of your son, I desire the ram caught by his horns in the thicket.'

תֵּפֶן, אֵל, בָּאֵפֶר,
תִּזְכֹּר־לָנוּ בְּרִיתוֹ,
תִּנְצֹר־לָנוּ עֲקֵדָתוֹ,
תַּעַן עִנּוּי נַפְשֵׁנוּ.

O God, heed these ashes, credit us with his covenant, favour us for his binding, reward our self-denial!

תִּגְאָלֵנוּ גָּאוֹל, חָזָק.

Redeem us, Mighty One!

ANONYMOUS

אַבִּיעָה זְמִירוֹת

GO IN PEACE, COME IN PEACE

אַבִּיעָה זְמִירוֹת בְּהַגִּיעַ עֵת זָמִיר
וּבְזִמְרָה אֶעֱן:
לֵךְ לְשָׁלוֹם גֶּשֶׁם.
בְּמִפְעֲלוֹת צוּרִי אַבִּיטָה כִּי נְעִימִים בְּעִתָּם
וּבְנֹעַם אֲמַלֵּל:
בֹּא בְשָׁלוֹם טַל.
גֶּשֶׁם חָלַף וּסְתָיו עָבַר
וְהַכֹּל בְּצִבְיוֹן נוֹצָר:
לֵךְ לְשָׁלוֹם גֶּשֶׁם.
דּוּדָאִים נָתְנוּ רֵיחַ בְּגִנַּת דּוֹדִים
וְחָלְפוּ דְוָיִים:
בֹּא בְשָׁלוֹם טַל.
הָאָרֶץ עֻטְּרָה דָּגָן וְתִירוֹשׁ
וְכָל יָצוּר צוֹוֵחַ:
לֵךְ לְשָׁלוֹם גֶּשֶׁם. [...]

I shall sing praises now that the time of the singing of birds has come, and I shall answer in song: go in peace, rain. I shall look at the deeds of my God, so pleasant in their season, and sweetly say: come in peace, dew. The rains are over and gone, the winter is past; everything is created with beauty: go in peace, rain. The mandrakes give forth their perfume in the lovers' garden; sorrows are past: come in peace, dew. The earth is crowned with new grain and wine, and every creature cries: go in peace, rain!

זְמַנֵּי חָרוֹן

PRAYER FOR RAIN

זְמַנֵּי חָרוֹן תִּמְחֶה מֶנּוּ,
יוֹדֵעַ זְמַנֵּי עוֹלָם,
וְנִדְבוֹת פִּינוּ קַבֵּל מֶנּוּ,
בּוֹרֵא מַיִם בְּיַלְדוּת־מַיִם.

O You who know the times of the universe, avert from us the times of wrath. Accept our offerings of praise, You who create water in the birthplace of waters.

זַךְ בְּלִי עָוֹן אַתָּה
וְחַי בְּלִי מָוֶת אַתָּה,
זַכֵּנוּ לְמַעַנְךָ וְהַחֲיֵנוּ
וְהַרְאֵנוּ בְּנִדְבַת מַיִם.

You are pure, untouched by sin; You are alive, untouched by death. Purify us[1] for Your sake, and revive us. Let us see bounteous waters.

1. Also: 'acquit us'.

וְאֵין אֵל יְקַדְּמֶךָ
וְאֵין מֶלֶךְ מוֹלְכֶךָ,
מַלְכוּתְךָ מוֹשְׁלָה בַכֹּל,
מוֹלִיךְ בְּלַהַב וּבְמַּיִם.

There is no god before You, no king who reigns over You. Your kingdom has dominion over all – You who lead us through fire and through water.

וְאֵין לְךָ גּוֹי כָּמוֹנוּ,
וְאֵין לָנוּ אֵל כָּמוֹךָ,
פּוֹתֵחַ יָדוֹ לִתְשׁוּבָה,
וְאַחֶרֶת לְאוֹצַר מַיִם.

You have no other people like us; we have no other god like You, who open Your one hand to those who repent, while the other opens the storehouse of water.

הֲלִכָךְ בְּלַהֲבֵי אֵשׁ,
יְשִׁבְךָ בְּנַהֲרֵי מַיִם,
קְדֻשָּׁתְךָ בְּרִבְבוֹתֵי אֵשׁ,
סְפִירָתְךָ בְּנִטְפֵי מַיִם.

Your path is in flames of fire, Your dwelling in streams of water. You are sanctified by myriad fires, Your *Sefira*[1] is in drops of water.

הֵן מַלְאָכִים לְךָ יַמְלִיכוּ
וְגַם שָׂרִים לְךָ יָשִׁירוּ.
מְלֹךְ מְהֵרָה בְצִיּוֹן,
וְנָגִיל בְּמַלְקוֹשׁ מַיִם. [...]

Angels crown You; princes enthrone You. Reign speedily in Zion, and let us rejoice in showers of water.

עַד אָנָה בְּכִיָּה בְּצִיּוֹן

DIRGE FOR THE NINTH OF AV

עַד אָנָה בְּכִיָּה בְּצִיּוֹן וּמִסְפֵּד בִּירוּשָׁלָיִם ?
תְּרַחֵם צִיּוֹן וְתִבְנֶה חוֹמוֹת יְרוּשָׁלָיִם !

How long will there be weeping in Zion and lamentation in Jerusalem? Have mercy on Zion and build anew the walls of Jerusalem!

1. The ten *Sefirot* are the ideal numbers which contain the forces of creation. The third and fourth *Sefirot* are water and fire. In later kabbalistic usage (e.g. Simeon Labi, pp. 124, 457) the term was understood differently.

אָז בַּחֲטָאֵינוּ חָרַב מִקְדָּשׁ
וּבַעֲווֹנוֹתֵינוּ נִשְׂרַף הֵיכָל.
בָּעִיר שֶׁחֻבְּרָה לָּהּ קָשְׁרוּ מִסְפֵּד
וּצְבָא הַשָּׁמַיִם נָשְׂאוּ קִינָה: [...]

Because of our sins the Temple was destroyed, because of our crimes the Palace was burnt. In the city that once was bound firmly together[1] lamentations were heard, and the host of heaven sounded a dirge.

טָלֶה רִאשׁוֹן בָּכָה בְּמַר נֶפֶשׁ
עַל כִּי כְבָשָׂיו לַטֶּבַח הוּבָלוּ:
יִלְלָה הִשְׁמִיעַ שׁוֹר בַּמְּרוֹמִים
כִּי עַל צַוָּארֵנוּ נִרְדַּפְנוּ כֻלָּנוּ:

The Ram, first of all, wept bitterly, for his sheep were being led to the slaughter. The Bull howled on high, for we were all driven hard, with yokes upon our necks.

כּוֹכַב תְּאוֹמִים נִרְאֶה חָלוּק
כִּי דַּם אַחִים נִשְׁפַּךְ כַּמָּיִם.
לָאָרֶץ בִּקֵּשׁ לִנְפֹּל סַרְטָן
כִּי הִתְעַלַּפְנוּ מִפְּנֵי צָמָא.

The Twins were seen to split asunder, for the blood of brothers was shed like water. The Crab would have fallen down to earth, for we were fainting from thirst.

מָרוֹם נִבְעַת מִקּוֹל אַרְיֵה
כִּי שַׁאֲגָתֵנוּ לֹא עָלְתָה לַמָּרוֹם.
נֶהֶרְגוּ בְתוּלוֹת וְגַם בַּחוּרִים
כִּי עַל כֵּן בְּתוּלָה קָדְרוּ פָנֶיהָ.

The Lion's roar filled heaven with terror, for our cry did not ascend to heaven. Virgins and young men were slaughtered, and the Virgin's face grew dark with grief.

סִבֵּב מֹאזְנַיִם וּבִקֵּשׁ תְּחִנָּה
כִּי נִבְחַר לָנוּ מָוֶת מֵחַיִּים.
עַקְרָב לָבַשׁ פַּחַד וּרְעָדָה
כִּי בְעַקְרַבִּים יִסְּרוּנוּ צָרֵינוּ.

The Balance tipped in supplication, for we preferred death to life. The Scorpion shuddered, for our enemies whipped us with lashes.[2]

פְּנֵי הַקֶּשֶׁת נֶהֶפְכוּ לְאָחוֹר
כִּי צוּר דָּרַךְ קַשְׁתּוֹ כְּאוֹיֵב.
צָפוּ מַיִם עַל רֹאשֵׁנוּ
וּבִדְלִי מָלֵא חִכֵּנוּ יָבֵשׁ.

The Archer turned his bow away, for the Lord had drawn His bow like an enemy. The water rose high above our head, yet in the month of the Water Bearer[3] our palates were parched.

1. Jerusalem (see Psalms 122.3).
2. In Hebrew, 'scorpions'.
3. Lit. 'in a full pail'. 'Pail' is the Hebrew sign of the zodiac for the rainy month.

קָרַבְנוּ קָרְבָּן וְלֹא נִתְקַבָּל
וּגְדִי פָּסַק שְׂעִיר חַטָּאתֵנוּ.
רַחֲמָנִיּוֹת בִּשְּׁלוּ יַלְדֵיהֶן
וּמַזַּל דָּגִים הֶעְלִים עֵינָיו.

We offered a sacrifice, but it was not accepted; the Goat would not present a he-goat as our sin-offering.[1] Tender-hearted women boiled their own children, yet the Fish turned a blind eye.

שָׁכַחְנוּ שַׁבָּת בִּלְבוֹת שׁוֹבָבִים –
שַׁדַּי שָׁכַח כָּל צִדְקוֹתֵינוּ.
תְּקַנֵּא לְצִיּוֹן קִנְאָה גְדוֹלָה
וְתָאִיר לְרַבָּתִי עָם מְאוֹר נָגְהֶךָ!

With wayward hearts we forgot the Sabbath, and so the Lord did not remember our merits. O Lord, be most jealous for Zion's honour, and let Your radiance shine upon the city once so full of people!

אֱנוֹשׁ מַה יִּזְכֶּה

BEAR THIS IN MIND

אֱנוֹשׁ מַה יִּזְכֶּה – וּצְבָא דֹק לֹא זַכּוּ בְעֵינֶיךָ?
בְּלַחִים אִם תִּבְעַר הָאֵשׁ – מַה בְּחָצִיר יָבֵשׁ?
גָּלוּי לְךָ חֹשֶׁךְ כְּמוֹ אוֹר, מְשׁוֹטֵט כֹּל בְּעָיִן.
דִּירָתְךָ בַּסֵּתֶר, וּגְלוּיוֹת לְךָ כָּל נִסְתָּרוֹת.
הַדָּן יְחִידִי, וְהוּא בְאֶחָד וּמִי יְשִׁיבֶנּוּ,
וְעַל גּוֹי וְעַל אָדָם יַחַד יִנְטֶה קָו וְאֵין מִי יַרְשִׁיעַ.
זֹאת יָבִין יְצִיר, וְלֹא יַתְעוּ יֵצֶר – לַחֲטֹא לְיוֹצֵר:
חֲתֻלַּת בְּאֵרוֹ, חֲפִירַת בּוֹרוֹ, חֶשְׁבּוֹן בּוֹרְאוֹ;

What is frail man, that he should be innocent when even the host of heaven are not innocent in Your sight? If fire consumes the green trees, surely the withered grass will perish. Darkness is as clear to You as light; Your eyes range over all the earth. Though Your dwelling is hidden, all hidden things are revealed to You. He alone is judge; He decides, and who can turn Him from His purpose? Upon nations and men alike He stretches His measuring line, and no one can condemn Him. Man would not be tricked by his passions into sinning against his Maker, if he bore these things in mind: that he was swaddled in his mother's womb,[2] that a grave will be dug for him, that he will have to answer to his Creator;

1. See Leviticus 16.6 ff.
2. Lit. 'his well'.

טָמֵא מִשְּׁאֵרוֹ, וּמְטַמֵּא בְּעוֹדוֹ, וּמְטַמֵּא בְּמוֹתוֹ;
יְמֵי חַיָּיו תֹּהוּ, וְלֵילוֹתָיו בֹּהוּ, וְעִנְיָנָיו הָבֶל;
כַּחֲלוֹם מֵהָקִיץ נִדְמֶה, בַּלָּהוֹת יְבַעֲתוּהוּ תָמִיד;
לַיְלָה לֹא יִשְׁכָּב, יוֹמָם לֹא יָנוּחַ, עַד יֵרָדֵם בַּקֶּבֶר.
מַה יִּתְאוֹנֵן אָדָם חָי – דַּיּוֹ אֲשֶׁר הוּא חָי! [...]

that his flesh exudes impurity: alive – he becomes defiled, dead – [his body] defiles others; that the days of his life are desolate, and his nights are chaos, and all his labours come to nothing; like a dream when a man awakens, he is always beset by the terrors of death. He finds no rest at night, no repose during the day, until at last he is put to sleep in the grave. Why, then, should any man who is alive complain? It should be enough for him that he is alive!

וּנְתַנֶּה תֹּקֶף

THE DAY OF JUDGEMENT

וּנְתַנֶּה תֹּקֶף קְדֻשַּׁת הַיּוֹם
כִּי הוּא נוֹרָא וְאָיֹם
וּבוֹ תִנָּשֵׂא מַלְכוּתֶךָ
וְיִכּוֹן בְּחֶסֶד כִּסְאֶךָ
וְתֵשֵׁב עָלָיו בֶּאֱמֶת.

Now let us proclaim how majestic is the holiness of this day, for it is a day of terror and of awe. On this day, Your kingdom is lifted high, Your throne established in mercy, as You sit upon it in truth.

אֱמֶת כִּי אַתָּה הוּא דַיָּן
וּמוֹכִיחַ וְיוֹדֵעַ וָעֵד
וְכוֹתֵב וְחוֹתֵם וְסוֹפֵר וּמוֹנֶה
וְתִזְכֹּר כָּל הַנִּשְׁכָּחוֹת
וְתִפְתַּח סֵפֶר הַזִּכְרוֹנוֹת
וּמֵאֵלָיו יִקָּרֵא
וְחוֹתַם יַד כָּל אָדָם בּוֹ.

Truly it is You who are judge and plaintiff, knower and witness; You record and set the seal; You count and number; You recall all forgotten things; You open the Book of Remembrance, which reads itself aloud; the signature of every [dying] man is in this book.

וּבְשׁוֹפָר גָּדוֹל יִתָּקַע
וְקוֹל דְּמָמָה דַקָּה יִשָּׁמַע
וּמַלְאָכִים יֵחָפֵזוּן

Then a great trumpet is sounded; a still, small voice is heard; angels scurry,

וְחִיל וּרְעָדָה יֹאחֵזוּן
וְיֹאמְרוּ: ׳הִנֵּה יוֹם הַדִּין
לִפְקֹד עַל צְבָא־מָרוֹם בַּדִּין׳ –
כִּי לֹא יִזְכּוּ בְעֵינֶיךָ בַּדִּין.

seized with pain and trembling, as they declare: 'Behold the Day of Judgement, come to punish the host of heaven in judgement!' – for they are not innocent in Your sight, when You sit in judgement.

וְכָל בָּאֵי־עוֹלָם יַעַבְרוּן לְפָנֶיךָ כִּבְנֵי־מָרוֹן:
כְּבַקָּרַת רוֹעֶה עֶדְרוֹ,
מַעֲבִיר צֹאנוֹ תַּחַת שִׁבְטוֹ –
כֵּן תַּעֲבִיר וְתִסְפֹּר וְתִמְנֶה
וְתִפְקֹד נֶפֶשׁ כָּל חָי,
וְתַחְתֹּךְ קִצְבָה לְכָל בְּרִיָּה
וְתִכְתֹּב אֶת גְּזַר דִּינָם.

And all that come into the world pass before You like troops[1] on parade: as a shepherd seeks out his sheep, then passes his flock under the counting rod, so do You parade, count, number and remember the life of every living thing, as you sentence all creatures and record their verdict.

בְּרֹאשׁ הַשָּׁנָה יִכָּתֵבוּן
וּבְיוֹם צוֹם כִּפּוּר יֵחָתֵמוּן:
כַּמָּה יַעַבְרוּן וְכַמָּה יִבָּרֵאוּן
מִי יִחְיֶה וּמִי יָמוּת
מִי בְקִצּוֹ וּמִי לֹא בְקִצּוֹ
מִי בַמַּיִם וּמִי בָאֵשׁ
מִי בַחֶרֶב וּמִי בַחַיָּה
מִי בָרַעַשׁ וּמִי בַמַּגֵּפָה
מִי יָנוּחַ וּמִי יָנוּעַ
מִי יַשְׁקִיט וּמִי יִטָּרֵף
מִי יִשָּׁלֵו וּמִי יִתְיַסָּר
מִי יָרוּם וּמִי יִשָּׁפֵל
מִי יַעֲשִׁיר וּמִי יַעֲנִי:

On New Year's Day their fate is inscribed, and on the Fast-Day of Atonement it is sealed:[2] how many will pass away, and how many will be born; who is to live, and who is to die; who will come to the end of his time, and who to an untimely end; who will perish by fire, and who by water; who by the sword, and who by wild beasts; who by earthquake, and who by plague; who will rest, and who will stagger; who will be serene, and who will be harassed; who will be at ease, and who will suffer; who will be lifted up, and who will be brought low; who will be rich, and who will be poor.

וּתְשׁוּבָה וּתְפִלָּה וּצְדָקָה
מַעֲבִירִין אֶת רֹעַ הַגְּזֵרָה!

But penitence, charity, and prayer can revoke the harsh decree.

1. Or 'flocks of sheep'.
2. There are ten 'days of awe' or 'penitence' between the first day of the year and the Day of Atonement.

[...] אֱמֶת כִּי אַתָּה הוּא יוֹצְרָם
וְיוֹדֵעַ יִצְרָם
כִּי הֵם בָּשָׂר וָדָם:
אָדָם יְסוֹדוֹ מֵעָפָר
וְסוֹפוֹ לֶעָפָר,
בְּנַפְשׁוֹ יָבִיא לַחְמוֹ.
מָשׁוּל כַּחֶרֶס הַנִּשְׁבָּר
כְּחָצִיר יָבֵשׁ וּכְצִיץ נוֹבֵל
כְּצֵל עוֹבֵר וּכְעָנָן כָּלֶה
וּכְרוּחַ נוֹשָׁבֶת וּכְאָבָק פּוֹרֵחַ
וְכַחֲלוֹם יָעוּף!

Truly it is You who fashioned them and You know their nature: they are but flesh and blood; man comes from dust and to dust returns; he gets his food at the peril of his life; he is like broken earthenware; like withering grass and fading flowers; like a fleeting shadow and a driven cloud; like a puff of wind, like vanishing dust, like a dream that flies away.

וְאַתָּה הוּא מֶלֶךְ, אֵל חַי וְקַיָּם.

But You are the King, the living, everlasting God!

יוֹסֵי בֶּן־יוֹסֵי

Yose ben Yose

סֵדֶר עֲבוֹדַת יוֹם הַכִּפּוּרִים

AVODA: THE SERVICE ON THE DAY OF ATONEMENT

[פתיחה בשבח האל]

Prologue: In Praise of God

אַזְכִּיר גְּבוּרוֹת אֱלוֹהַּ נֶאְדָּרִי בַּכֹּחַ,
יָחִיד וְאֵין עוֹד, אֶפֶס וְאֵין שֵׁנִי.
אַחֲרָיו אַיִן בַּחֶלֶד, לְפָנָיו בַּשַּׁחַק,
אֵין בִּלְתּוֹ קֶדֶם, זוּלָתוֹ בְּעֵקֶב.
אָדוֹן לַחְשֹׁב, אֱלֹהִים לַעֲשׂוֹת,

I shall proclaim the mighty deeds of God, who is glorious in power. He alone is God and there is no other; there is none besides Him, none second to Him; there will be none after Him on earth, there was none before Him in heaven; there was none but He of old, nor shall there be in the end. Lordly in thought, godly in action –

נִמְלָךְ וְאֵין נֶעְדָּר, שָׂח וְאֵין מְאַחֵר.
אוֹמֵר וְעוֹשֶׂה, יוֹעֵץ וּמֵקִים,
אַמִּיץ לָשֵׂאת וְגִבּוֹר לִסְבֹּל.
אֲשֶׁר לוֹ רְנָנוֹת מִפִּי יְצוּרָיו,
מִמַּעְלָה וּמִמַּטָּה יִשָּׂא תְהִלָּה.
אֵל אֶחָד בָּאָרֶץ וְקָדוֹשׁ בַּשָּׁמַיִם,
אַדִּיר בַּמָּרוֹם – מִמַּיִם יִשָּׂא שִׁיר,
אֶדֶר מִתְּהוֹמוֹת, שֶׁבַח מִמְּאוֹרוֹת,
אֹמֶר מִיָּמִים, זֶמֶר מִלֵּילוֹת;
אֵשׁ תּוֹדִיעַ שְׁמוֹ, עֲצֵי־יַעַר יְרַנֵּנוּ,
בְּהֵמָה תְלַמֵּד עֱזוּז נוֹרְאוֹתָיו.

when He takes counsel,[1] no one is absent; when He orders, no one delays. He speaks and does, designs and fulfils, bearing the world with strength, carrying it with might. He is celebrated in song by His creatures; from above and from below He is given praise. The only God on earth, the Holy One in heaven, the Mighty One on high – He receives songs from the waters, paeans from the deeps, adoration from the luminaries, speech from the days, melody from the nights. Fire shouts out His name, the trees of the forest sing for joy, the animals teach the might of His terrible acts.

[אהרן, משה ומרים]

Aaron, Moses, and Miriam

יִחַד שְׁלִישִׁי לִרְאוֹת פְּנֵי־מֶלֶךְ,
לְשׁוֹרֵר, לְשָׁרֵת, לָבוֹא חֲדָרָיו.
כְּגֶפֶן אַדֶּרֶת, יְפַת פְּרִי וְעָנָף,
הִצְמִיחַ עַמְרָם מִשֹּׁרֶשׁ לֵוִי,
כִּי שִׁלְּחָה שְׁלֹשֶׁת שָׂרִיגֵי חֶמֶד:
מְכַהֵן וְרוֹעֶה וְאִשָּׁה נְבִיאָה.
כְּגֶשֶׁת עֵת דּוֹדִים, פִּרְחוֹ הוּקַם
לְשַׁבֵּר מוֹסְרוֹת צֹעַן, לִפְרֹץ גֶּדֶר שֹׁעַל.
כֻּסָּה בֶּעָנָן וְנִתְקַדֵּשׁ שָׁבוּעַ,
נִצָּב בַּתָּוֶךְ בְּעֵת מַתַּן אֹמֶר.
כֹּחַ אַדִּירִים לְפָנָיו נִכְנָעוּ,
מִמּוֹרָאוֹ לֹא עָמַד אִישׁ.
כִּלְכֵּל צֹאן קֹדֶשׁ שְׁאֵר בִּישִׁימוֹן,

Levi, the third son of Jacob, was singled out to see the face of the King, to sing, to serve, to enter His chambers. Like a noble vine, lovely with fruit and branch, Amram – of the root of Levi – blossomed, putting forth three beautiful branches: priest, shepherd, and prophetess. When the hour of deliverance came, Moses, the flower of Amram, arose to break the bonds of Egypt, to breach the wall of the Sea. He was hidden by the cloud [on Mount Sinai] for a week and was purified, then stood between God and Israel when the word was given. The mighty angels yielded before him; no mortal could withstand his awe. He fed the holy flock with flesh in the desert and bread from the skies, until they came

1. A reference to the Midrashic legend that God consulted the ministering angels before creating Adam.

מִלֶּחֶם שְׁחָקִים עַד בּוֹאָם לָאָרֶץ.
כָּרְתָה בְרִית עִם עַלְמָה תּוֹפֶפֶת,
גָּוְעָה וְנֶאֶסְפָה וְלֹא הָיָה מָיִם.

to the land. A covenant was made with the girl who played on the tambourine; when she breathed her last and was gathered to her kin, there was no more water.[1]

[בגדי הכהן הגדול]

The Vestments of the High Priest

שַׂר פָּקִיד, נְגִיד מְלֶאכֶת הַקֹּדֶשׁ
שָׁלַח לְקָדִים צִירֵי אֱמוּנָה,
שָׂח לָמוֹ: ׳הַבִּיטוּ אִם עָלָה הַשַּׁחַר,
אִם הֵפִיץ אוֹר קָדִים עֲלֵי אָרֶץ.׳
סִפְּרוּ לוֹ כִּי בָרַק נֹגַהּ —.
וְרָץ לְמִקְוֵה טֹהַר לְבֵית הָעֲזָרָה;
סָכוּ מְחִיצַת שֵׁשׁ בֵּינוֹ לְבֵין עָם
לִנְהָג־בּוֹ בְּגֹדֶל, בְּלִי חֲזוֹת מַעֲרֵהוּ.
שִׂמְלַת עוֹרוֹ יְמַהֵר וְיִפְשֹׁט,
וְיֵרֵד וְיִטְבֹּל וְיַעַל וְיִסְתַּפָּג.
סֶגֶן הַמַּלְבּוּשׁ יַעֲטֵהוּ בַדִּים,
וְיוֹסִיף לְגַדְּלוֹ בַּעֲדִי בִגְדֵי־פָז.
שָׂשׂ בְּמַעֲטֵה הוֹד וְלֵב לֹא יַגְבִּיהַּ,
לְבֵשָׁם לִכְבוֹד אֵל, וְלֹא לְמַעֲנֵהוּ.
סֵדֶר מִלְחָמוֹת בָּהֶם יִשְׁאַל,
וְעֵינָיו לְמוֹרֵהוּ כְּתַלְמִיד לָרָב.
סוֹד יְגַלֶּה לוֹ בְּמִשְׁפַּט הָאוּרִים,
אִם עָלֹה אִם חָדוֹל, אִם לְחֶרֶב אִם לְיֶשַׁע.
סֹלּוּ לֵאלֹהִים, בְּנֵי גוֹי גָּדוֹל,
קָרוֹב בְּכָל עֵת לְבַשֵּׂר יְשׁוּעוֹת!

Then the officer, the overseer in charge of the holy service, sends faithful messengers to the East, saying to them: 'See if the dawn has risen, if light from the East has spread over the earth.' As soon as they tell him that the light is gleaming, the high priest rushes to the pool of purification in the Temple court. They spread a screen of fine linen between him and the people, thus dignifying him, so that none should see his nudity. Quickly he strips off his clothes, goes down and bathes, comes up and dries himself. The prefect, in charge of his vestments, clothes him in linen, then further adorns him with golden ornaments. He rejoices in his majestic garments but does not become proud, having put them on for the glory of God, not for his own. He consults the Urim[2] about the order of battle, raising his eyes to his Master, as a pupil to his teacher. Then He reveals the secret to him in the decision of the Urim: should they go forth or desist; will they fall by the sword or be victorious. Oh, sing out God's praise, sons of a great nation, for He is always close at hand, bearing tidings of salvation!

1. According to legend, a well, granted because of the merits of Miriam, followed the Israelites for forty years on their wanderings through the desert and disappeared when she died.

2. A kind of oracle, set within the 'breastpiece of decision', worn by the high priest over his heart.

עָלַץ כְּמַלְאָךְ בְּשִׁבּוּץ מִכְנְסֵי־בָד,
כְּפָרָשׁ מוּכָן, צִיר אֱמֶת לְשׁוֹלְחָיו:
עֶרְוַת זִמָּה בָּהֶם יְכַסֶּה,
כִּי כֵן מִצְוָתָם לְכַסּוֹת עֶרְוָה.
עַלְמוּת קוֹמָה יְמַלֵּא בְּכֻתֹּנֶת
כְּפוּלָה, מְשֻׁבֶּצֶת עַד פַּסֵּי יָד:
עֲוֹן בֵּית יַעֲקֹב יְכַפֵּר בְּזֹאת,
מוֹכְרֵי צַדִּיק עַל כְּתֹנֶת פַּסִּים.
עֹז אַבְנֵט הִתְאַזֵּר בְּמֵזַח אֲרוּג־בָּד,
וְלֹא כִלְאַיִם כְּכָל יְמֵי שָׁנָה.
עֲטֶרֶת רֹאשׁוֹ כְּהוֹד הַמְּלוּכָה,
צָנִיף צְפִירַת שֵׁשׁ לְכָבוֹד וּלְתִפְאָרֶת.
עָטוּי מְעִיל תְּכֵלֶת כְּזוֹהַר הָרָקִיעַ,
מְמַלֵּא בֵּית־יָד גְּלִילֵי זְרוֹעוֹתָיו;
עָגֹל שְׂפַת־פִּיו, רֹאשׁוֹ כְּתַחְרָא,
מֵסַב קֶלַע, בְּלִי לְהִקָּרַע;
עַל פְּאַת שׁוּלָיו רִמּוֹנֵי צְבָעִים,
וּפַעֲמוֹנֵי פָז סָבִיב בְּתָוֶךְ:
עֵת יַשִּׁיקוּ קוֹל זֶה בָּזֶה,
יְכַפֵּר בְּעַד קוֹל מַכֵּה רֵעַ בַּסָּתֶר.

He exults in the fringed linen pants – like an envoy, like a horseman on the alert, a messenger faithful to those who dispatch him. By wearing the pants he atones for lechery, for they were prescribed[1] to cover his nakedness. He completes the concealment of his body with a double tunic, fringed, reaching down to the wrists. Thus he atones for the sin of the house of Jacob, who sold the righteous Joseph because of his ornamented tunic.[2] Then he girds himself with a splendid sash, a belt entirely woven of linen, and not of linen mixed with wool as is the custom throughout the year. The crown on his head is like a sovereign's glory, a turban-diadem of fine linen, for dignity and beauty. Wrapped in a robe of blue, bright as the firmament, his rounded arms fill the sleeves. The opening for the head has a binding around it, as in a coat of mail, which deflects the slingstones, without being torn. All around the hem there are multi-coloured pomegranates, with golden bells between them; when they strike each other and tinkle, the high priest atones for the voice of him who strikes down his neighbour in secret.[3]

[הַוִּדּוּי וְהַטָּלַת הַגּוֹרָלוֹת]

The Confession and Casting of Lots

קָרַב אֵצֶל פַּר חַטָּאתוֹ,
וְהוּא עוֹמֵד בֵּין הָאוּלָם וְלַמִּזְבֵּחַ —

He draws near to the bull, his sin-offering, which stands between the porch and the altar and,

1. Exodus 28.42.
2. Joseph's 'coat of many colours' (Genesis 37.3).
3. I.e., the sin of slander.

וסומך שתי ידיו עליו ומתודה. וכך היה אומר:
'אנא השם, חטאתי עויתי פשעתי לפניך, אני וביתי.
אנא בשם, כפר נא לחטאים ולעוונות ולפשעים
שחטאתי ושעויתי ושפשעתי לפניך, אני וביתי.
ככתוב בתורת משה עבדך מפי כבודך:
"כי ביום הזה יכפר עליכם לטהר אתכם.
מכל חטאתיכם לפני יי –"'
והכוהנים והעם העומדים בעזרה,
כשהיו שומעים את השם הנכבד והנורא
מפורש יוצא מפי כוהן גדול בקדושה ובטהרה,
היו כורעים ומשתחוים ונופלים על פניהם
ואומרים: 'ברוך שם כבוד מלכותו לעולם ועד!'
ואף הוא היה מתכון לגמור את השם כנגד המברכים
ואומר להם: '"תטהרו!"'

laying both his hands upon it, confesses; and he says: 'O Lord,[1] I have sinned, I have committed iniquity, I have transgressed against You, I and my household. I beseech You, by Your Name,[1] absolve me of the sins, iniquities, and transgressions which I have committed against You, I and my household, as it is written in the Law of Your servant Moses[2] from the mouth of Your Glory: *For on this day atonement shall be made for you to cleanse you, of all your sins before the Lord.*' And when the priests and the people, who stand in the court, hear the glorious and awesome Ineffable Name come forth from the mouth of the high priest, in sanctity and purity, they kneel, bow down and prostrate themselves, saying: 'Blessed be the name of His glorious kingdom for ever and ever!' – while the high priest takes care to complete the utterance of the Name as they end the blessing, and then says to them: '*– you shall be clean!*'

קִדְמָה לְשַׁעַר אֵיתָן, לִצְפוֹן הַמִּזְבֵּחַ,
יְלַוּוּהוּ בְּכָבוֹד כֹּהֲנֵי מִשְׁנֶה.
קִימַת שְׂעִירִים הֲלוֹא שָׁם הָיְתָה
וּכְלִי בֵּית הַנַּחַת גּוֹרָלוֹת זָהָב.
קוֹבְצָם עַל־יָד וְטוֹרֵף וּמַעֲלֶה:
זֶה לְחֵי עוֹלָם, וְזֶה לְמִיתַת צוּק.
קָחְתּוֹ בְּיָמִין פּוּר חָקוּק לַשֵּׁם,
סֶגֶן יַשְׁמִיעַ לוֹ: 'הַגְבֵּהַ יְמִינֶךָ!'
קְשִׁי מַעַלְלֵי־דוֹר בִּשְׂמֹאל אִם יַעַל,

Then he goes towards the Eastern gate [of the Temple court], to the north of the altar, accompanied with pomp by his lieutenants. For there the two he-goats stand in waiting and the casket in which the golden lots are kept. He takes them in his hand, shuffles and draws them out – one marked for the Eternal and the other for death in a ravine. If he takes up the lot inscribed 'For the Lord' in his right hand,[3] the prefect says to him: 'Raise your right hand.' But if this lot[4] comes up in his

1. The high priest uttered the Tetragrammaton.
2. Leviticus 16.30.
3. This was considered a good omen.
4. Lit. '[the lot marked for] the stubbornness of the generation's doings'.

רֹאשׁ בֵּית אָב יָשִׂיחַ לוֹ: 'הַגְבֵּהַּ שְׂמֹאלְךָ!'
קָפַץ וּנְתָנָם עַל שְׁנֵי הַשְּׂעִירִים
וְהִצְרִיחַ בְּקוֹל רָם: 'לַשֵּׁם חַטָּאת!'
קָשַׁר שָׁנִי בְּרֹאשׁ הַמְּשֻׁתַּלֵּחַ,
דְּחָפוֹ לְמִדְבָּר – וְזֶה לְבֵית שְׁחִיטָה.

left hand, the chief of the priestly division tells him: 'Raise your left hand.' At once he places the lots on the two goats, crying with a loud voice: 'A sin offering to the Lord!' He binds a thread of scarlet wool onto the head of the scapegoat, dispatching it to the wilderness, and the other to the place of slaughter.

[הַמּוֹפֵת]

The Sign

תַּכְלִית מַעֲשִׂים – נֵרוֹת הִבְעִיר,
פָּרַשׂ כַּפַּיִם, קִדֵּשׁ וּפָשַׁט.
תִּלְבֹּשֶׁת שְׁאֵרוֹ חֲנִיכָיו יָרִיצוּ,
לְבֵשָׁם בְּכָבוֹד וְיָצָא בְּמָשׂוֹשׂ.
תָּאֳרוֹ הִקְרִין כְּצֵאת הַשֶּׁמֶשׁ בִּגְבוּרָתוֹ,
מְשַׁלֵּחַ לְשׁוֹלְחָיו צְדָקָה וּמַרְפֵּא.
תְּחִלָּה הִשְׁמִיעָם: 'לְכוּ שְׁתוּ בְּלֵב טוֹב,
אֵל נוֹשֵׂא עָוֹן וְעוֹבֵר עַל פֶּשַׁע!'
תְּמִימִים יְשָׁרִים לְנָוֵהוּ יְלַוּוּהוּ,
שִׂמְחָה יַעֲשׂוּ בְּצֵאתוֹ בְּלִי פֶגַע.
'תֶּן לָנוּ מוֹפֵת', בְּאָזְנָיו יֹאמֵרוּ,
'וְנֵדַע בַּמֶּה יְכֻפַּר עָוֹן.'
תִּתּוֹ צִיר שָׂעִיר, וְהוּא מְבַשֵּׂר יְשׁוּעוֹת:
'הִלְבִּין כַּשֶּׁלֶג אֹדֶם הַשָּׁנִי!'

Finally, he lights the lamps, spreads his hands, laves and removes the golden garments. His acolytes quickly bring him his own clothes; he puts them on triumphantly and joyously steps forth. His face is radiant, like the sun rising in all its grandeur, as he grants deliverance and healing to those who dispatched him. At first he says to them: 'Go drink with a good heart, for God has forgiven iniquity and pardoned transgression!' Now, perfect and pure of heart, they accompany him to his house, rejoicing that he has come forth from the Sanctuary without mishap. 'Give us a sign,' they say to him, 'by which we shall know that our sins have been atoned for.' Whereupon he shows them the messenger who dispatched the goat; he bears tidings of salvation: 'The scarlet thread has turned as white as snow[1]!'

1. The thread of scarlet yarn was tied to the door of the Sanctuary; when the scapegoat reached the wilderness, the thread would turn white.

יַנַּאי
Yannai

כָּלוּ עֵינֵינוּ לְאַהֲבָתְךָ

כָּלוּ עֵינֵינוּ לְאַהֲבָתְךָ, אוֹהֵב,
נִשְׂנָאִים מִשִּׂנְאַת אוֹיֵב.
רְאֵה־נָא בְּעָנְיֵנוּ מִבַּיִת
וְשׁוּר שִׂנְאָתֵנוּ מִבַּחוּץ,
כְּלֵאָה אֲשֶׁר רָאִיתָ בְּעָנְיָהּ
וְשַׁרְתָּ בְּשִׂנְאַת עֲנוּיָהּ;
מִבַּיִת הָיוּ לָהּ שׂוֹנְאִים,
וּבַחוּץ הָיוּ לָהּ מַשְׂנִיאִים.
וְלֹא כָּל אָהוּב אָהוּב
וְלֹא כָּל שָׂנוּי שָׂנוּי –
יֵשׁ שְׂנוּאִים בְּמַטָּה וַאֲהוּבִים בְּמַעְלָה.
שְׂנוּאֶיךָ שְׂנוּאִים וַאֲהוּבֶיךָ אֲהוּבִים.
שְׂנְאָתֵנוּ כִּי אֲהַבְנוּךָ, קָדוֹשׁ!

PRAYER FOR LOVE

Our eyes are weak with longing for Your love, O Loving One, for we are hated by the enemy. Look how afflicted we are from within, see how hated we are from without – as You looked on the affliction of Leah and saw her tormented by hate. She was hated within the house and detested without. But not every loved one is loved, nor every hated one hated: there are some who are hated below, yet beloved above. Those whom You hate are hated; those whom You love are loved. We are hated because we love You, O Holy One!

רְאֵה עֲמִידָתֵנוּ

רְאֵה עֲמִידָתֵנוּ מִכַּף וְעַד קָדְקֹד,
מִגִּיד וְעַד עֶצֶם, מִנֶּפֶשׁ וְעַד בָּשָׂר:

יָחֵף כַּפֵּינוּ, נִגּוֹף אֶצְבְּעוֹתֵינוּ.
נָדוּ רַגְלֵינוּ וְהָלְמוּ עֲקֵבֵינוּ.
מָעֲדוּ קַרְסֻלֵּינוּ וְדַלְיוּ שׁוֹקֵינוּ.
כָּשְׁלוּ בִּרְכֵּינוּ וְקָטְנוּ יְרֵכֵינוּ.
חַלְחֲלוּ מָתְנֵינוּ וְנֶעֶצְבוּ כְּסָלֵינוּ.
הָמוּ מֵעֵינוּ וְנִתַּר לִבֵּנוּ.

FROM SOUL TO FLESH

See how we stand before You from foot to head, from sinew to bone, from soul to flesh:

The soles of our feet are sore, our toes bruised; our feet wobble, our heels are battered; our ankles totter, our legs hang useless; our knees stagger, our thighs are thin; our hips quiver, our loins are in anguish; our entrails howl, our heart leaps out; our arms are fallen,

מָטָה זְרוֹעֵנוּ וְלֹא הִשִּׂיגָה יָדֵנוּ.
הֻכְחַשׁ שִׁכְמֵנוּ בְּעֹל צַוָּארֵנוּ.
נִסְקַד גְּרוֹנֵנוּ בְּמַכַּת לְחָיֵינוּ.
יָבְשׁוּ שְׂפָתֵינוּ וְקֵהוּ שִׁנֵּינוּ —
וְתִפְאַרְתָּךְ בְּפִינוּ וְצִדְקָךְ בִּלְשׁוֹנֵנוּ.

our hands grasp nothing; our shoulders are shrunken because of the yoke upon our neck; our throat is twisted, because of the blows upon our cheeks; our lips are parched, our teeth set on edge. Yet Your praise is in our mouths and Your righteousness on our tongues.

קָצַר נֶשֶׁם־אַפֵּינוּ וְצָלוּ אָזְנֵינוּ.
נִכְלַם מִצְחֵנוּ וְחָוְרוּ פָּנֵינוּ.
כָּלוּ עֵינֵינוּ וְנֶעֶצְבוּ רַקּוֹתֵינוּ.
אַגְמַן רֹאשֵׁנוּ וְסָמַר שְׂעָרֵנוּ.
נִבְהֲלוּ עֲצָמֵינוּ וְצָפַד עוֹרֵנוּ.
נָקְטָה נַפְשֵׁנוּ, קָפְדָה רוּחֵנוּ.
נִצְרַפְנוּ בָּאֵשׁ, נִבְחַנְנוּ בַּמַּיִם.
בְּשִׂמְחָה, בְּצָרָה, בַּבַּיִת וּבַגָּלוּת,
הַשְׁכֵּם וְהַעֲרֵב פַּעֲמַיִם אוֹמְרִים:
'שְׁמַע יִשְׂרָאֵל יהוה אֱלֹהֵינוּ יהוה אֶחָד.'

The breath of our nostrils is cut short, our ears ring; our forehead is shamed, our face is pale; our eyes dim, our temples are in pain; our head bends down, our hair stands on end; our bones are frightened, our skin is shrivelled; our soul is sick, our spirit is restless; we have been tried by fire and tested by water. Yet in joy and sorrow, at home and in exile, morning and evening, twice daily, we proclaim: *'Hear O Israel! The Lord is our God, the Lord alone.'*

אֲשֶׁר אֵימָתָךְ

AND THAT IS YOUR GLORY

ולך כֹּל יכתירו:

And all shall wreathe crowns for You –

אֲשֶׁר אֵימָתָךְ
בְּאֶרְאֶלֵּי אֹמֶן, בְּאַבִּירֵי אֹמֶץ,
בִּבְרוּאֵי קֶרַח, בִּבְלוּלֵי קֶדַח —
וּמוֹרָאָךְ עֲלֵיהֶם;

who are feared by faithful angels, mighty heroes, creatures of ice mingled with fire – and Your dread is upon them;

וְאָבִיתָ תְּהִלָּה
מִגְּלוּמֵי גוּשׁ, מְגָרֵי גַיְא,

yet You desire glory from those made of dust, sojourners of the valley,

מְדֻלּוּלֵי פֹּעַל, מְדַלֵּי מַעַשׂ –
וְהִיא תְּהִלָּתֶךָ.

destitute of deeds, lacking in good works – and that is Your glory;

אֲשֶׁר אֵימָתָךְ
בַּהֲמוֹן מַלְאָכִים, בְּהִלּוּךְ מַחֲנוֹת,
וּבְאַלְפֵי אֲלָפִים וּבְרִבְבֵי רְבָבוֹת –
וּמוֹרָאֲךָ עֲלֵיהֶם;

who are feared by multitudes of angels, armies on the move, thousands of thousands, myriads of myriads – and Your dread is upon them;

וְאָבִיתָ תְּהִלָּה
מִזִּיו שׁוֹנֶה, מִזֹּהַר כָּבֶה,
מֵחַסְרֵי שֶׂכֶל, מֵחוֹרְשֵׁי רֶשַׁע –
וְהִיא תְּהִלָּתֶךָ [...]

yet You desire glory from those whose radiance changes, whose lustre fades, devoid of sense, devising evil – and that is Your glory;

אֲשֶׁר אֵימָתָךְ
בִּשְׁבִיבֵי אֵשׁ, בִּשְׁבִילֵי מַיִם,
בְּתִלּוּלֵי רוּם, בִּתְלוּיֵי גֹבַהּ –
וּמוֹרָאֲךָ עֲלֵיהֶם;

who are feared by flaming fires, watery paths, celestial steeps, suspended stars – and Your dread is upon them;

וְאָבִיתָ תְּהִלָּה מִבָּשָׂר וָדָם,
מֵהֶבֶל וָתֹהוּ, מֵחָצִיר יָבֵשׁ,
מִצֵּל עוֹבֵר, מִצִּיץ נוֹבֵל;
מַשְׁלִימֵי נֶפֶשׁ וּמַפְרִיחֵי רוּחַ
וּמְעִיפֵי חַיָּה וְחוֹנְטֵי נְשָׁמָה
וּמוֹצִיאֵי יְחִידָה וְנִשְׁמָעִים בַּדִּין
וּמֵתִים בְּמִשְׁפָּט וְחַיִּים בְּרַחֲמִים –
וְנוֹתְנִים לְךָ פְּאֵר, חֵי עוֹלָמִים!

yet You desire praise from flesh and blood, vanity and nothingness, withering grass, fleeting shadow, fading flower; from those who surrender their soul, fling away their breath, cast up their life, disgorge their spirit, expel their soul; who are heard in judgement, die by Your sentence, live by Your mercy, and acclaim Your splendour, O Life Eternal!

מַה יִּתְרוֹן לִי

ABRAHAM'S COMPLAINT

'מַה יִּתְרוֹן לִי?' אָב נִתְחַנָּן,
'נַפְשִׁי עֲגוּמָה וְלִבִּי מִתְאוֹנָן.
שִׂמְחָה בְּלִבִּי מַה יְּרַנֵּן?
עֵץ סְרָק אָנֹכִי וְלֹא רַעֲנָן.

'What have I gained?' the father cried. 'My soul is mournful and my heart laments. How can joy sing in my heart? I am a barren tree, bearing no fruit.

פְּעָלַי מַה בְּכָל יְקָרִי?
צִיץ עִקָּרִי עֲקָרִי בִּמְקוֹרִי.
קִנְיַן בִּרְכָתִי יִירַשׁ אֲרוּרִי,
רֵיק אִם אֶפְנֶה וַעֲרִירִי.

'What does all my honour avail me? The blossom of my root is cut off at the source. The accursed one[1] will inherit all the wealth given to me as a blessing if I die empty and childless.

שֵׁם צֶדֶק יֶשׁ לִי,
שֶׁתֶל צֶדֶק אֵין לִי.
תַּתִּי לָךְ וְנָתַתָּ לִי —
מָה אֶתֵּן לָךְ וּמַה תִּתֵּן לִי?'

'I have a good name but have no good seedling. You have given to me, I have given to You – what can I give You, what can You give me?

אָזְנֶיךָ קַשּׁוּבוֹת
לְכָל מַחֲשָׁבוֹת
מַטְלִיל תְּחִי בְּרוּחוֹת נִשָּׁבוֹת!

'Your ears are attentive to all thoughts, O You who revive us with dew carried on the wind!'

מִשָּׁמַיִם לִשְׁמֵי הַשָּׁמַיִם

HYMN FROM THE HEAVENS

מִשָּׁמַיִם לִשְׁמֵי הַשָּׁמַיִם,
מִשְּׁמֵי שָׁמַיִם לַעֲרָפֶל,
מֵעֲרָפֶל לִזְבוּלָה,
מִזְּבוּלָה לִמְעוֹנָה,
מִמְּעוֹנָה לִשְׁחָקִים,

From Heaven to the Heaven of Heavens; from the Heaven of Heavens to the Dark Clouds; from the Dark Clouds to the Abode; from the Abode to the Dwelling-place; from the Dwelling-place to the Skies; from the

1. His servant, Eliezer.

מִשְּׁחָקִים לַעֲרָבוֹת,
מֵעֲרָבוֹת לְרוּם כִּסֵּא,
וּמֵרוּם כִּסֵּא לַמֶּרְכָּבָה –

Skies to the Plains; from the Plains to the height of the Throne; and from the height of the Throne to the Chariot –

מִי יִדְמֶה לָּךְ, מִי יִשְׁוֶה לָּךְ,
מִי רָאָה, מִי הִגִּיעַ,
מִי יִתְלֶה רֹאשׁ, מִי יָרִים עַיִן,
מִי יַקְשֶׁה, מִי יָעֵז,
מִי יָזִיד, מִי יְחַשֵּׁב בַּלֵּב,
מִי יִגְאֶה, מִי יִגַּס,
מִי יַעֲרֹךְ –

who can be compared to You, who is Your equal? who has seen You, who has reached You? who can hold his head high, who can lift up his eyes? who can question, who can defy? who can fathom, who can calculate? who can be proud, who can be haughty? who is like You?

וּרְכוּבְךָ עַל כְּרוּב וְדִיאָתְךָ עַל רוּחַ,
וְאָרְחָךְ בְּסוּפָה וְדַרְכָּךְ בִּסְעָרָה,
וּשְׁבִילָךְ בְּמַיִם וּשְׁלִיחוּתָךְ בָּאֵשׁ –
אֶלֶף אֲלָפִים וְרִבֵּי רְבָבוֹת,
נַעֲשִׂים אֲנָשִׁים, נַעֲשִׂים נָשִׁים,
נַעֲשִׂים רוּחוֹת, נַעֲשִׂים זִקִּים,
נַעֲשִׂים כָּל דְּמוּת וְעוֹשִׂים כָּל שְׁלִיחוּת,
בְּאֵימָה, בְּיִרְאָה, בְּפַחַד, בְּרַעַד, בְּרֶתֶת, בְּזִיעַ
יִפְתְּחוּ...

For You ride on a cherub and fly on a wind; Your road is in whirlwind, Your way is in storm; Your path is through waters. Fires are Your emissaries – thousands of thousands and myriads of myriads, who are changed into men, changed into women, changed into winds, changed into demons; who assume all shapes and fulfil every mission, with fear, dread, awe, trembling, terror, trepidation, they open . . .

אַחַר הַמִּדְבָּר

MOSES THE MESSENGER

אַחַר הַמִּדְבָּר צִיר נָהַג צֹאן;
אַחַר הַמִּדְבָּר הִנְהִיג עַמּוֹ כַּצֹּאן.

Into the wilderness the Messenger drove his flock; into the wilderness he would lead his people like a flock.

בְּלֹא רַגְלַיִם רָץ וְהֵרִיץ מַרְעִיתוֹ,
לָלֶכֶת לִמְקוֹם חֶזְיוֹן מַרְאִיתוֹ.

Without feet he ran, rushing his herd to the place where he would see his vision of God.

גְּדוּלֵי דֶשֶׁא הָיוּ נִבְרָאִים לְפָנָיו
וְאַחַר כָּךְ הָיוּ נִבְלָעִים מִלְּפָנָיו.

Green crops sprang up before him,
then were swallowed in his wake.

דֶּרֶךְ גְּדוֹלָה לְיוֹם אֶחָד הִלֵּךְ
כִּי אוֹהֵב מֵישָׁרִים יִשֵּׁר לוֹ הֶלֶךְ.

In a single day he travelled a long
distance, for He who loves straightness
straightened the path before him.

הַר הָאֱלֹהִים עֵת כִּי הִגִּיעַ,
מִטָּרְחוֹ הוּנַח וּמִיגִיעוֹ הֻרְגַּע.

When he reached the mountain of God,
he was eased of his hardship and
relieved of his toil.

וּתְחִלָּה נִרְאָה לוֹ כִּדְמוּת מַלְאָךְ,
לַעֲשׂוֹת דְּמוּתוֹ כִּדְמוּת מַלְאָךְ.

At first an angel appeared before him to
change his form into that of an angel.

זֶה, לְפִי דַרְכּוֹ חִנְּכוֹ לִרְאוֹת,
לִהְיוֹת בָּקִי בְּכָל מַרְאֵי מַרְאוֹת:

Then the Lord taught him to look at
fire, to be expert in fiery visions.

חִזֵּק לִבּוֹ כְּשֶׁר לַבַּת אֵשׁ –
בַּעֲבוּר לְלַבְּבוֹ בְּכָל מִינֵי אֵשׁ.

His heart was strengthened by looking
at the flame, so that he might be able to
withstand all manner of fire.

טָהוֹר בְּתוֹךְ טֻמְאָה יְקָרוֹ הוֹפִיעַ,
גָּבֹהַּ עַל סְנֶה כְּבוֹדוֹ הוֹדִיעַ;

The Pure One revealed His splendour
in the midst of Egypt's defilement; the
High One proclaimed His glory from
the lowly bush –

יַעַן כִּי צָרַת עַמּוֹ הִיא צָרָתוֹ
וִישׁוּעָתָם הִיא יְשׁוּעָתוֹ.

For His people's distress is His distress,
and their salvation is His own.

אֵשׁ אֲשֶׁר הִיא

ובכן וַיֵּרא מלאך יהוה אליו בלַבַּת אש:

אֵשׁ אֲשֶׁר הִיא אוֹכְלָה אֵשׁ
אֵשׁ בּוֹעֶרֶת בְּיִבֵשִׁים וּבְלַחִים
אֵשׁ גּוֹחֶלֶת בְּשֶׁלֶג וְקִיטוֹר
אֵשׁ דּוֹמָה לַאֲרִי רוֹבֵץ
אֵשׁ הַמַּרְאָה כַּמָּה מַרְאוֹת
אֵשׁ וַדַּאי כִּי לֹא כָבָה
אֵשׁ זוֹרַחַת וּמְשׁוֹטֶטֶת
אֵשׁ חוֹשֶׁשֶׁת וּמִתְלַקַּחַת
אֵשׁ טָסָה בְּרוּחַ סְעָרָה
אֵשׁ יוֹקֶדֶת בְּאֶפֶס עֵצִים
אֵשׁ כִּי כָל יוֹם מִתְחַדֶּשֶׁת
אֵשׁ לֹא נֻפְּחָה מֵאֵשׁ
אֵשׁ מַעֲלָה לוּלַבִּין
אֵשׁ נִיצוֹצֶיהָ הֵם הַבְּרָקִים [...]
אֵשׁ שְׁחוֹרָה כָּעוֹרֵב
אֵשׁ תַּלְתַּלִּים כְּצִבְעֵי קֶשֶׁת.

THE CELESTIAL FIRE

Now an angel of the Lord appeared to Moses in a blazing fire –

a fire that devours fire; a fire that burns in things dry and moist; a fire that glows amid snow and ice; a fire that is like a crouching lion; a fire that reveals itself in many forms; a fire that is, and never expires; a fire that shines and roars; a fire that blazes and sparkles; a fire that flies in a storm wind; a fire that burns without wood; a fire that renews itself every day; a fire that is not fanned by fire; a fire that billows like palm branches; a fire whose sparks are flashes of lightning; a fire black as a raven; a fire, curled, like the colours of the rainbow!

אֶלְעָזָר בֵּירַבִּי קַלִּיר (קִילִיר)

Eleazar ben Kallir

אֲגוּדִים בְּשִׂמְחָה

'אֲגוּדִים בְּשִׂמְחָה, תָּעֳצַם שִׂמְחַתְכֶם
בְּאַהֲבָה וּבְגִיל הַיּוֹם בְּהִתְחַתֶּנְכֶם;
גִּילוּ וְשִׂמְחוּ בַּייָ אֱלֹהֵיכֶם.

EPITHALAMIUM

[The Poet:] 'Bound by affection, may your joy increase, as you are wed today in love and gladness; be glad and rejoice in the Lord your God.

דּוּץ חָתָן בְּחֻפַּת הֲדָרֶךָ
הִנָּוֵה בְּלִפִי בֵּין חֲבֵרֶיךָ,
וְיִשְׂמַח לִבְּךָ מֵאֵשֶׁת נְעוּרֶיךָ.

'Bridegroom, delight in your glorious marriage chambers; excel in beauty among your companions; may your heart rejoice in the wife of your youth.

זֹהַר פָּנַיִךְ יַצְהִיר כְּיַיִן.
חוֹרְשַׁיִךְ יִהְיוּ כְּאֶפֶס וּכְאַיִן.
טִירָתִי, טֹבוּ דוֹדַיִךְ מִיַּיִן.'

'Your radiant face [O bride,] shall glow like wine; your enemies shall be as nothing; My [silver] parapet,[1] your love is sweeter than wine.'

כְּהַשָּׁפַת עָסִיס,
כְּעָגוּר וָסִיס,
שׂוֹשׂ אָשִׂישׂ בְּקָדוֹשׁ!

Like one drinking wine or hearing the song of a swallow or a crane, I shall revel in the Holy One!

'יוֹנָתִי בְּחֵן וָחֶסֶד אֲכַלְּלָה
כְּהִגָּלוֹתִי בְּלַהַב אֵשׁ אוֹכֵלָה;
לָכֵן לִבַּבְתִּנִי, אֲחוֹתִי כַלָּה.

[God to Israel:] 'I shall crown My dove with grace and kindness, as once I did when I revealed Myself in the flame of the consuming fire [on Mount Sinai]; for you have ravished My heart, My sister, My bride.

מְקוֹם מַיִם חַיִּים מַעְיָנַיִךְ.
נִעַרְתִּי מִמֵּךְ כָּל מְעַנַּיִךְ.
סְגֻלָּתִי, שְׂאִי סָבִיב עֵינַיִךְ.

'Your fountains are a place of running water; I have shaken all your tormentors from you; My treasured one,[2] lift up your eyes and look about you.

עוֹלָה־מִמִּדְבָּר טוֹבוֹת אֲדַשֵּׁן.
פִּנָּתִי בְּעַנְנֵי כָבוֹד אֲעַשֵּׁן.
צַוָּארֵךְ דִּמִּיתִי כְּמִגְדַּל הַשֵּׁן.

'I shall shower her who comes up from the wilderness[2] with favours; I shall envelop My cornerstone[3] with clouds of glory; I have likened your neck to an ivory tower.'

כְּהַשָּׁפַת עָסִיס,
כְּעָגוּר וָסִיס,
שׂוֹשׂ אָשִׂישׂ בְּקָדוֹשׁ!

Like one drinking wine or hearing the song of a swallow or a crane, I shall revel in the Holy One!

1. An epithet for the bride (Song of Songs 8.9).
2. Epithets for the people of Israel, derived from biblical expressions.
3. Jerusalem.

קוּמִי, רַעְיָתִי, בְּאַהֲבָה הִתְחַתְּנִי,
רִנָּה וְתוֹדָה לְמַלְכֵּךְ תְּנִי.
שִׁיר הָפִיקִי בְּחֻפַּת חִתּוּנִי,
תּוֹפְפִי: ״תַּחַת הַתַּפּוּחַ עוֹרַרְתַּנִי.״׳

'Arise, My beloved, and be married in love; give hymns and thanks to your King; sing and make music in My bridal chamber: "under the apple tree You have awakened me!"'

אֵם הַבָּנִים

THE DIALOGUE OF ZION AND GOD

אֵם הַבָּנִים כְּיוֹנָה מְנַהֶמֶת,
בַּלֵּב מִתְאוֹנֶנֶת וּבַפֶּה מִתְרַעֶמֶת,
גּוֹעָה בִּבְכִי וּבְמַר נוֹאֶמֶת,
דְּמָעוֹת מַזֶּלֶת וְדוֹמֶמֶת וְנִדְהֶמֶת:

The mother of children moans like a dove; she mourns in her heart and complains out loud; she cries bitterly, calls out desperately; she sheds tears, she is silent and stunned:

׳הִשְׁלִיכַנִי בַּעְלִי וְסָר מֵעָלַי,
וְלֹא זָכַר אַהֲבַת כְּלוּלַי,
זֵרַנִי וּפִזְּרַנִי מֵעַל גְּבוּלַי,
חִדָּה עָלַי כָּל תּוֹלָלַי.

'My husband has abandoned me and turned away, and has not remembered my love as a bride; he has scattered and dispersed me far from my land; he has let all my tormentors rejoice at my downfall.

טְרָפַנִי כְּנִדָּה וּמִפָּנָיו הִדִּיחַנִי,
יְקָשַׁנִי בְּכֹבֶד וְלֹא הֱנִיחַנִי,
כָּלוּ עֵינַי בְּתוֹכָחוֹת וְכִחֲנִי,
לָמָּה לָנֶצַח עֲזָבַנִי, שְׁכֵחַנִי?׳

'He has cast me off like an unclean woman, banished me from his presence; he has harshly ensnared me, given me no respite; he has chastised me till my eyes failed. Why has he forsaken me, forgotten me forever?'

׳מַה תִּתְאוֹנְנִי עָלַי, יוֹנָתִי,
נֶטַע חֶמֶד עֲרוּגַת גַּנָּתִי?
שִׂיחַ פִּלּוּלַיִךְ כְּבָר עָנִיתִי,
עָטוּר בָּךְ כְּאָז חָנִיתִי.

'O my dove, O plant of delight in my garden bed, why do you cry out against me? I have already answered your prayer, as I did in days of old, when I dwelt crowned in your midst.

פָּנִיתִי אֵלַיִךְ בְּרַחֲמֵי הָרַבִּים,
צָעוֹד בְּשַׁעַר בַּת רַבִּים,
קָמַיִךְ, אֲשֶׁר עָלַיִךְ מִתְרַבִּים,
רִעַשְׁתִּי הֱיוֹת כֶּעָשָׁן כָּבִים.

'I have turned to you with great compassion, and now I march through the gate of Bath-Rabbim [Jerusalem]. Your enemies, ever more numerous – I shook them till they were snuffed out like smoke.

שְׁחוֹרָתִי, לָעַד לֹא אֶזְנָחֵךְ,
שֵׁנִית אוֹסִיף יָד וְאֶקָּחֵךְ.
תַּמּוּ וְסָפוּ דִּבְרֵי וִכּוּחֵךְ,
תַּמָּתִי, לֹא אֶעֶזְבֵךְ וְלֹא אֶשְׁכָּחֵךְ.'

'My dark one, I shall never desert you; I shall reach out again and take you to myself. Your complaint has come to an end: my perfect one, I shall not forsake you or forget you.'

אָז בִּמְלֹאת סֶפֶק

JEREMIAH AND THE BEAUTIFUL WOMAN

אָז בִּמְלֹאת סֶפֶק יָפָה כְּתִרְצָה,
הֵן אֶרְאֶלָּם צָעֲקוּ חוּצָה.
בֶּן חִלְקִיָּהוּ מֵאַרְמוֹן כְּיָצָא,
אִשָּׁה יְפַת תֹּאַר מְנֻוֶּלֶת מָצָא:

Then, when she had had her full measure of grief – she who was as beautiful as Tirzah[1] – the valiant angels cried aloud. As Jeremiah son of Hilkiah came out of the Temple, he met the beautiful woman, in filthy attire.

'גּוֹזְרַנִי עָלַיִךְ בְּשֵׁם אֱלֹהִים וְאָדָם –
אִם שֵׁד לַשֵּׁדִים אַתְּ אוֹ לִבְנֵי אָדָם?
דְּמוּת יָפְיֵךְ כְּבָשָׂר וָדָם,
פַּחְדֵּךְ וְיִרְאָתֵךְ כְּמַלְאָכִים לְבַדָּם.'

'In the name of God and man, I charge you to tell me: are you a demon among demons or a human being? Your beauteous form is like that of flesh and blood; but the dread and fear of you is like that of angels alone!'

'הֵן לֹא שֵׁד אֲנִי וְלֹא גֹּלֶם פַּחַת.
יְדוּעָה הָיִיתִי בְּשׁוּבָה וָנַחַת.
וְהֵן לְשָׁלוֹשׁ אֲנִי, וּלְשִׁבְעִים וְאֶחָד,
וְלִשְׁנֵים עָשָׂר, וְשִׁשִּׁים, וְאֶחָד.

'I am neither a demon nor a thing of base matter. I was renowned for my peace and repose; for I belonged to *three* and to *seventy-one*, to *twelve*, to *sixty* and to *one*.

1. Song of Songs 6.4.

זֶה הָאֶחָד – אַבְרָהָם הָיָה,
וּבֶן הַשְּׁלוֹשָׁה – אָבוֹת שְׁלִישִׁיָּה;
חֹק שְׁנֵים עָשָׂר – הֵן הֵן שִׁבְטֵי יָהּ,
וְשִׁשִּׁים – רִבּוֹא, וְשִׁבְעִים וְאֶחָד – סַנְהֶדְרֵי יָהּ.'

'The *one* was Abraham, who was one of the *three*, the Patriarchs three; the *twelve* were the tribes of the Lord; the *sixty* were the myriads [who came out of Egypt]; and the *seventy-one* were the elders of the Lord.'[1]

'טַעְמִי הַקְשִׁיבִי וַעֲשִׂי תְשׁוּבָה.
יַעַן הֱיוֹתֵךְ כָּל כָּךְ חֲשׁוּבָה,
יָפֶה לִיךְ בְּעֶלֶץ וְלִשְׂמֹחַ בְּטוֹבָה
וְלֹא תִקָּרֵא עוֹד "בַּת הַשּׁוֹבֵבָה".'

'Heed my advice and repent. Since you were once so esteemed, it is fitting that you exult and rejoice in goodness, so that you may no longer be called "the faithless daughter".'[2]

'כִּי אֵיךְ אֶשְׂמַח וְקוֹלִי מָה אָרִים –
הֵן עוֹלָלַי נִתְּנוּ בְּיַד צָרִים!
לָקוּ נְבִיאַי וְהִנָּם מְגֹרָרִים,
גָּלוּ מְלָכַי וְשָׂרַי, וְכֹהֲנַי בְּקוֹלָרִים.

'How can I rejoice, how sing out loud? My infants are delivered into the enemies' hands, my prophets beaten and dragged away, my kings and nobles exiled, my priests in chains.

מְלוֹן מִקְדָּשִׁי בַּעֲווֹנִי נִבְדָּד,
דּוֹדִי מֵאָז בָּרַח וַיִּדַּד,
נֹעַם אָהֳלִי בְּעַל־כָּרְחִי שֻׁדַּד,
רַבָּתִי עָם – אֵיכָה יָשְׁבָה בָדָד.

'On account of my sins my abode is desolate; my beloved[3] of old was driven away and fled; my lovely tabernacle was ravaged; she that was full of people, *how lonely she dwells!*[4]

סִיחַ לֵאלֹהֶיךָ, נְבִיא יִרְמְיָה,
בְּעַד סֹעֲרָה, מֻכָּה, עֲנִיָּה,
עַד יַעֲנֶה אֵל וְיֹאמַר: "דַּיָּהּ."
וְיַצִּיל בָּנַי מֵחֶרֶב וְשִׁבְיָה.'

'Pray to your God, prophet Jeremiah, for the one who is storm-tossed, flogged, afflicted – till God hearken and say, "She has had her fill!"; till He save my children from captivity and the sword.'

פִּלֵּל תְּחִנָּה לִפְנֵי קוֹנוֹ:
'מָלֵא רַחֲמִים, רַחֵם כְּאָב עַל בְּנוֹ!'

Whereupon he entreated his Creator: 'O You who are full of pity, have pity – as a father upon his son!' Then God

1. The members of the *Sanhedrin*, the Supreme Council.
2. Jeremiah 31.22.
3. The Shekinah (Divine Majesty), which accompanied Israel wherever they went as exiles.
4. I.e. Jerusalem: Lamentations 1.1.

צָעַק: ׳אוֹי לָאָב שֶׁהֶגְלָה נִינוֹ
וְגַם אוֹי לַבֵּן שֶׁבְּשֻׁלְחַן אָב אֵינוֹ!

cried out: 'Woe to the father who has banished his son, and woe to the son who is not at his father's table!

קוּם לָךְ, יִרְמְיָה, לָמָּה תֶחֱשֶׁה?
לֵךְ קְרָא לָאָבוֹת וְאַהֲרֹן וּמֹשֶׁה.
רוֹעִים יָבוֹאוּ קִינָה לְהִנָּשֵׂא
כִּי זְאֵבֵי עֶרֶב טָרְפוּ אֶת הַשֶּׂה.׳

'Arise, Jeremiah! Why are you so silent? Go summon the Patriarchs and Aaron and Moses. Let the shepherds come and raise a lament, for desert wolves have devoured the lamb.'

שׁוֹאֵג הָיָה יִרְמְיָה הַנָּבִיא,
עַל מַכְפֵּלָה נוֹהֵם כְּלָבִיא:
׳תְּנוּ קוֹל בִּבְכִי, אֲבוֹת הַצְּבִי,
תָּעוּ בְנֵיכֶם, הֲרֵי הֵן בַּשֶּׁבִי!׳

Then the prophet Jeremiah growled out loud; by the Double Cave[1] he roared like a lion: 'Weep aloud, you fathers of splendour; for your children have strayed, and are captives!'

מֶלֶךְ הָאוֹמֵר לַיָּם

HE SHALL BE KING!

לך יהוה הממלכה והמתנשׂא לכל לראש:

Yours, O Lord, is the sovereignty and You are exalted over all.

מֶלֶךְ הָאוֹמֵר לַיָּם: ׳עַד פֹּה תָּבוֹא׳ –
הוּא יִמְלֹךְ מֶלֶךְ!
מֶלֶךְ הַתִּעוּב, מִלֵּחָה סְרוּחָה וְעַד בּוֹר יָבוֹא,
לָמָּה יִמְלֹךְ מֶלֶךְ?

A king who says to the sea: 'Thus far shall you come' – He shall be king! A king of abomination, who comes from a stinking drop and goes no further than the grave – why should he be king?

מֶלֶךְ הַבּוֹנֶה בַשָּׁמַיִם מַעֲלוֹתָיו וְכֵס רְכוּבוֹ,
הוּא יִמְלֹךְ מֶלֶךְ!
מֶלֶךְ הַשָּׁב לַעֲפָרוֹ כַּנֵּר בְּהִכָּבוֹ,
לָמָּה יִמְלֹךְ מֶלֶךְ?

A king who builds his upper chambers and his chariot-throne in the heavens – He shall be king! A king who returns to the dust like an expiring candle – why should he be king?

1. The Cave of *Makhpelah* in Hebron, the burial place of the Patriarchs and their wives.

מֶלֶךְ הַגּוֹאֵל מִכָּל רָע כָּל בּוֹטְחֵי בוֹ,
הוּא יִמְלֹךְ מֶלֶךְ!
מֶלֶךְ הָרָדוּף כְּעָלֶה נִדָּף מִפַּחַד לְבָבוֹ,
לָמָּה יִמְלֹךְ מֶלֶךְ?

A king who redeems from harm all those who trust in him – He shall be king! A king who flees like a driven leaf because of his heart's dread – why should he be king?

מֶלֶךְ הַדָּגוּל מֵרְבָבָה בְּהַאֲלִיפוֹ וּבְהַרְבִּיבוֹ,
הוּא יִמְלֹךְ מֶלֶךְ!
מֶלֶךְ הַקָּץ נָגַר, וְיָרֵא מִדִּין רִבּוֹ,
לָמָּה יִמְלֹךְ מֶלֶךְ?

A king distinguished among ten thousand, who brings forth thousands and ten thousands of angels – He shall be king! A king who fears, dreads, and is terrified at the judgement of his Master – why should he be king?

מֶלֶךְ הֶהָיָה וְהוּא יִהְיֶה בְּחַסְדּוֹ וּבְטוּבוֹ,
הוּא יִמְלֹךְ מֶלֶךְ! [...]

A king Who ever was and shall be, in His grace and in His bounty – He shall be king!

וַיִּפָּתְחוּ שַׁעֲרֵי עֵדֶן גָּן

THE BATTLE BETWEEN BEHEMOTH AND LEVIATHAN

וַיִּפָּתְחוּ שַׁעֲרֵי עֵדֶן גָּן,
וְשֶׁבַע כִּתִּים מְשֹׁעָרִים בַּגָּן,
וְעֵץ הַחַיִּים בְּתוֹךְ הַגָּן.
וְיִשְׁמְעוּ קוֹל צוֹרָם בַּגָּן;
וּכְמוֹ לְשֶׁעָבַר נִתְהַלֵּךְ בַּגָּן
כֵּן יִתְהַלֵּךְ בְּתוֹכָם בְּתוֹךְ הַגָּן.

Then shall the gates of the garden of Eden be opened, and the seven preordained companies of righteous men shall be revealed within the garden, and the tree of life in the middle of the garden. They shall hear the sound of their Creator in the garden; and as once He moved about in the garden, so shall He now move amongst them in the garden.

וְיִרְאוּ וְיַרְאוּ בְּאֶצְבַּע וּבִדְמוּת
וְיֹאמְרוּ: 'זֶה אֱלֹהִים אֱלֹהֵינוּ וְלֹא נָמוּת.
הוּא יְנַהֲגֵנוּ עַל מוּת!'

They shall see, and pointing a finger at His likeness, they shall say: 'Such is God, our God, and we shall not die. He shall be our guide forever!'

וְאָז יַרְאֵם שָׁלוֹשׁ נֶחָמוֹת:
זִיז וְלִוְיָתָן וּבְהֵמוֹת.

Whereupon He shall show them the three rewards: Ziz, Leviathan and

זִיז הַמַּטְעִים כָּל מִין מַטְעַמּוֹת,
פּוֹרֵשׂ כְּנָפָיו בְּתַעֲצוּמוֹת
וּמַכְהֶה מְאוֹרוֹת עַד תְּהוֹמוֹת.
וְיוֹצִיא לָהֶם בְּכֹחַ בְּהֵמוֹת –

Behemoth. Ziz: his flesh has many different flavours; when, with great might, he unfurls his wings, he darkens the lights of heaven, down to the very deeps. And then, for their pleasure, He shall bring out Behemoth by force.

אֲשֶׁר רִבְצוֹ אֶלֶף הָרִים
וַאֲבוּסוֹ מֵאֶלֶף הָרִים ;
מַשְׁקֵהוּ מֵאֹסֶם נְהָרִים,
יוּבַל הַיּוֹצֵא מֵעֵדֶן לְאַרְבַּעַת נְהָרִים ;
מִגְּעִיָּתוֹ מְפָרֵק הָרִים.

Behemoth: his lair is upon the Thousand Mountains; he daily feeds upon the produce of the Thousand Mountains; and he drinks from the abundant waters of the River Yuval, which issues from Eden to become four rivers; his roar rends the mountains.

הִנֵּה נָא בְּמָתְנָיו כֹּחוֹ
וּמְעִידִין מַעֲשָׂיו עַל כָּרְחוֹ
וְאוֹנוֹ בִּשְׁרִירֵי בִטְנוֹ מוֹכִיחוֹ.
וּמִי יוּכַל לַעֲמֹד נִכְחוֹ ?

See the strength in his loins; his deeds testify to his might; the power in the muscles of his belly proves it. Who can stand up to him?

יַחְפֹּץ כְּמוֹ אֶרֶז לְהַגְבִּיהַּ זְנָבוֹ
וְכָל חַיְתוֹ שָׂדַי יַשְׁכִּין לְקַנֵּן בּוֹ.
וְאַחֲרֵי כֵן יוֹרִיד בְּנַחַת זְנָבוֹ
וְיַשְׁכִּין מְעוֹפְפִים בְּאִבּוֹ,
לְבַל יִנָּזְקוּ מֵחַיּוֹת הַיּוֹשְׁבוֹת בְּקִרְבּוֹ.
כִּי רַחֲמָן הוּא בְּכָל מִדּוֹת שֶׁבּוֹ,
וְיוֹשֵׁב כַּמֶּלֶךְ בִּמְסִבּוֹ –
עַד בּוֹא יוֹם מוּכָן לְשַׂחֶק בּוֹ
וִיגַלֶּה לְעַם קְרוֹבוֹ.

When he so wills, he raises his tail like a cedar, making room for all the beasts of the field to nestle there. Then he gently lowers his tail, in the thicket of which he shelters the birds of the air, so that none shall be harmed by the beasts dwelling within him – for he is merciful in all his ways. Thus he reclines like a king on his couch, till the appointed day, on which God shall sport with him and reveal him to the companies of the pious.[1]

וְנֶגְדּוֹ יֻצַּג לִוְיָתָן –

And against him shall Leviathan be pitted:

1. Lit. 'the people who are near to Him'.

מִלְּמַטָּה יְחוֹלְלוּ לוֹ דָּגִים גְּדוֹלִים
וּמִלְמַעְלָה יְצַלְצְלוּ לוֹ אֶרְאֶלִּים,
הוֹדוֹ וְשִׁבְחוֹ מְמַלְּלִים.

Big fish dance for him below, angels sing for him above, chanting his glory and his praise.

תַּחְתָּיו חַדּוּדֵי חֶרֶשׂ,
סְנַפִּירָיו מַכְהֶה גַּלְגַּל חֶרֶס,
יִרְפַּד חָרוּץ עַל טִיט חֶרֶס.

His undersides are jagged shards; his radiant fins obscure the sun; he sprawls on the mud like a threshing-sledge.

מִנְּחִירָיו יֵצֵא עָשָׁן,
מַרְתִּיחַ כָּל מֵי בָּשָׁן.
מַטְרִיד בְּעָקְצוֹ וּמַדְאִיג חַיּוֹת וְרוֹמְסָן
וּמֵהֶן יִשְׂבַּע וִידֻשָּׁן.
יַחְשֹׁב תְּהוֹם לְשֵׂיבָה בּוֹ לְכָבְשָׁן.

Smoke issues from his nostrils, making all the waters of Bashan seethe; he lashes the sea-beasts with his tail, terrifies and tramples them, then eats them and grows fat; he makes the ocean foam and look white-haired, as he crushes the beasts with his tail.

כְּעַפְעַפֵּי שַׁחַר מְכֻנֶּה בְּעֵינַיִם.
בִּשְׁלוֹשׁ מֵאוֹת וְשִׁשִּׁים וְחָמֵשׁ עֵינַיִם.
סָבוּב אֵימוֹת שִׁנַּיִם.
מְשֻׁבָּח בְּמִינִים שִׁשִּׁים וּשְׁנַיִם
וְיֵשׁ לוֹ זוּוּגִים שְׁנַיִם:
בָּרִיחַ, עֲקַלָּתוֹן וְתַנִּינִים שְׁנַיִם;
וְהוּא עֲלֵיהֶם כְּמֶלֶךְ בְּמַחֲנַיִם,
מוּכָן לְמִשְׁתֵּה־נְצָחִים, לְבֶן שִׁנַּיִם.

His three hundred sixty-five eyes gleam like the shimmer of dawn;[1] he has rings of terrifying teeth; he is the finest of the sixty-two species; he has two couples in his retinue: the Fleeing Serpent and the Coiled Serpent, and a pair of dragons; he is over them like a king over two armies, and open-mouthed[2] awaits the final banquet.

וְהוּא מִכֻּלָּם כָּבֵד וְגָדוֹל.
זְנָבוֹ סְמוּכָה בְּפִיהוּ בְּחַיִל גָּדוֹל,
מַסְבִּיב כְּטַבַּעַת הַיָּם הַגָּדוֹל.
וּבְבוֹא יוֹם הַגָּדוֹל,
יֹאמַר מֶלֶךְ הַגָּדוֹל

He is the heaviest and greatest of them all. His tail, mightily gripped in his mouth, girds the Great Sea like a ring. And when the great day comes, the great King will ordain that he be served

1. Lit. 'are called "the eyelids of dawn"'; a reference to Job 41.10.
2. Lit. 'whose teeth are white'.

לְתִתְּנוֹ מַאֲכָל לְגוֹי גָּדוֹל.
וִישַׁלַּח בּוֹ הַשַּׂר הַגָּדוֹל
— וְאִתּוֹ גְדוּדִים הָמוֹן גָּדוֹל —
לִפְרֹס עָלָיו חֵרֶם גָּדוֹל,
לְמָשְׁכוֹ בְחַכָּה בְּכֹחוֹ הַגָּדוֹל.

up as a delicacy to the great people.
He will dispatch the great prince
Gabriel against him, accompanied by
a great throng of hosts, to spread a
great net over him and, with great
force, to draw him out with a hook.

וִירְמְחוּ בוֹ רְמָחִים —
וַיַּחְשֹׁב לְתֶבֶן בַּרְזֶל מֵרְמָחִים.
וְעוֹד יַרְתִּיחוּ בוֹ רְתָחִים
וּלְקַשׁ נֶחְשְׁבוּ לוֹ תוֹתָחִים.

They throw spears at him, but he
regards the iron spears as straws; they
batter him and beat him, but he
considers the clubs as splinters.

וְיוֹרוּ חִצֵּי קֶשֶׁת —
וְלֹא יַבְרִיחֶנּוּ בֶן־קֶשֶׁת;
לְעֵץ רִקָּבוֹן נְחֹשֶׁת.

They shoot arrows at him, but no
arrow can put him to flight; bronze to
him is rotten wood.

וִיקַלְּעוּ בוֹ אֲבָנִים כְּסֶלַע —
וּלְקַשׁ נֶהֶפְכוּ לוֹ אַבְנֵי קֶלַע.
וְאָז יֶחֱרֶה לְשִׁיתָם לְבֶלַע!

They sling stones at him, huge as rocks,
but slingstones turn to chaff on him.
Then, seized with rage, he rears about
to slaughter them.

וַיַּגְבִּיהַּ רֹאשׁ מוּל אֵלִים,
וּמִשֵּׂתוֹ יָגוּרוּ אֶרְאֶלִּים
וּמִפָּנָיו בְּחִיל נִבְהָלִים.

He raises his head against the mighty
ones, and at his majesty the angels are
struck with dread and flee from him in
dismay.

וְיִוָּדַע אֶל מָעוֹז
וְיִתֵּן בְּקוֹלוֹ, קוֹל עֹז,
לְשַׁלֵּחַ בּוֹ מַתַּן עֹז,
לְהִתָּפֵשׂ בְּלִי מָעוֹז —
בְּצַוָּארוֹ יָלִין עֹז.

When this becomes known to God the
Stronghold, He sends forth His voice,
His mighty voice, to assault him with
great force. Leviathan, in whose neck
dwells strength, can find no refuge and
is caught.

וְאֶחָד בְּאֶחָד יִגְּשׁוּ שְׁנֵיהֶם
וְרוּחַ לֹא יָבֹא בֵינֵיהֶם;
וּקְדוֹשִׁים יִרְאוּם בְּעֵינֵיהֶם
אֵיךְ יִנָּצוּ לִפְנֵיהֶם
וְצוּר יְשַׂחֶק בָּם לִפְנֵיהֶם.

Now they press so close to each other, that air cannot pass between them. The holy ones, with their own eyes, behold the combat, as the Lord sports with the beasts.

וַיַּתְחִיל מַקְרִין לְנַגֵּחַ בּוֹ בְּקַרְנָיו,
וְזֶה בְּגַאֲוַת אֲפִיקֵי מָגִנָּיו.
וְיִבְעַר אֵשׁ עֲשׁוּנָיו
וַיֶּאֱחֵז בַּגִּזָּה אֲשֶׁר בְּמָתְנָיו
וְיָנוּס מִצַּעַר לְבֵין עֲצֵי עֲדָנָיו
וְיָרוּץ וְיִבְרַח מִפָּנָיו;
וַיֶּאֱחֹז בְּקִיטוֹר עֲשָׁנָיו
בַּעֲצֵי בֹשֶׂם וְשׁוֹשַׁנָּיו
וַיַּעֲלֶה רֵיחַ קְטֹרֶת עַד שְׁמֵי מְעוֹנָיו
וְכָל גַּן תְּעֶשַׁן בְּעִנְיָנָיו.

The horned Behemoth begins by thrusting with his horns, and Leviathan parries with the rows of shields on his back. Then his smoking fire flares up, catching hold of the fleece on Behemoth's loins. In pain, he runs away to the shelter of Eden's trees, and escapes from Leviathan. But the smoke billowing out of him kindles the spice trees and lilies of Eden, and the odour of incense is wafted to His heavenly abode. The whole garden fills with smoke because of Behemoth.

וּבַת קוֹל תְּפוֹצֵץ מִמְּרוֹמָיו:
'הָפִיחִי גַנִּי, יִזְּלוּ בְשָׂמָיו!'
לְהָפִיחַ בּוֹ רֵיחַ סַמָּיו.

Whereupon a divine voice calls out from the heights: 'Blow upon my garden, let its fragrance be wafted abroad'[1] to disperse the odour of its perfumes.

וְאָז יְעוֹרֲרוּ צָפוֹן וְתֵימָן
וִיסוֹבְבוּ לְאוֹת וְסִימָן.
וַיֶּאֱזֹר עָז־חַיִל וְיֶאֱמָן
וְיָשׁוּב עַל בָּרִיחַ מְזֻמָּן
וַיֵּצֵא לִקְרָאתוֹ מְיֻמָּן.
וְיִלָּפְתוּ שֵׁנִית בּוֹ בַזְּמָן:
וְיִתְמַרְמַר אֵלָיו מַכְמָן

Then, at this signal, the north wind and the south wind awake and blow in all directions. Behemoth girds himself with strength and, gaining courage, turns back to Leviathan,[2] who is prepared for battle. He moves at him, tensed for the combat, and again they grapple with each other. Behemoth,[3] mad with rage, encircles him with his

1. Song of Songs 4.16. 2. Lit. 'the fleeing [serpent]'. 3. Lit. 'the concealed one'.

וַיְסַבְּבוּ בְקַרְנָיו כְּאָמָּן ;
וְדָג לְעֻמָּתוֹ יִתְיַמָּן
וּסְנַפִּירָיו יַשְׁחִיז לִזְמָן
וּלְשַׁחֲטוֹ בָּם יִתְאַמָּן ;
זֶה קַרְנָיו לְמוּלוֹ יְעַקְמָן,
וְזֶה סְנַפִּירָיו לְמוּלוֹ יְקִימָן —
וּמִתּוֹךְ כָּךְ שְׁנֵיהֶם יַשְׁלִימָן
לְשַׁחֲטָם וּלְטָבְחָם וּלְהַחֲרִימָן.
וְיִנָּתְנוּ מַאֲכָל לְעַם נֶאֱמָן
וְיָבִינוּ כִּי לֹא אַלְמָן,
וְיֹאמְרוּ : ׳בָּרוּךְ הַנֶּאֱמָן !
כִּי כָל דָּבָר אֲשֶׁר מֵאָז זִמֵּן,
הֱקִיצוֹ לְקֵץ וּזְמָן.׳

horns like a master warrior; while the Fish, facing him, wheels to the right, whetting his fins again and again, as he tries to gash him. Behemoth arches his horns, Leviathan rears his fins – but now He makes an end of the pair, to slaughter, prepare, and consecrate them. They shall be served up as a dish to the faithful people. Seeing that Israel has not been forsaken, they shall say: 'Blessed is the Steadfast One. For everything that he ordained long ago, he accomplishes now, at the end of time!'

פִּינְחָס הַכֹּהֵן

Phinehas Hakohen

וּמֵהַיּוֹם וָהָלְאָה

WATER

וּמֵהַיּוֹם וָהָלְאָה יֵרָאוּ הֲמוֹנֵי מַיִם :
מִלְּמַטָּה סִילוֹנֵי מַיִם וּמִלְמַעְלָה קִילוֹנֵי מַיִם ;
זְכָרִים וּנְקֵבוֹת עֲרוּבֵי מַיִם ;
מְתוּקִים, מְלוּחִים — מַיִם עִם מַיִם.
וּבִשְׂאֵת עֲנָנִים מַיִם —
יָרִיקוּ זְכָרִים עַל נְקֵבוֹת, לְהַרְבִּיעַ מַיִם ;
מְתוּקִים עַל מְלוּחִים, לְהֵיטִיב מַיִם.
וּמֵהֶם תְּעֻבַּר אֶרֶץ, מֵעֵרוּבֵי מַיִם,
לְהוֹלִידָהּ וּלְהַצְמִיחָהּ מִשְּׁמֵי שָׁמַיִם. [...]

And from this day on, teeming waters shall be seen: jets of water from below and torrents of water from above; male and female – mingled waters; sweet and salty – waters with waters. And when the clouds are laden with water, they shall empty the male upon the female waters, to inseminate the waters; the sweet upon the salty, to improve the waters. And by them shall the earth conceive, by these mingled waters, to give birth and to sprout, from the heaven of heavens.

אָח בְּנַעֲלֵיכֶם

JOSEPH REVEALS HIMSELF TO HIS BROTHERS

’אָח בְּנַעֲלֵיכֶם מְכַרְתֶּם.
בְּשִׂטְמַתְכֶם עַל דָּמוֹ קַמְתֶּם.
גְּדִי עִזִּים בְּמִרְמָה שְׁחַטְתֶּם.
דִּאַגְתֶּם לֵב אֲבִיכֶם וְסוֹד הֶעֱרַמְתֶּם.
אוֹי לָכֶם מִדִּין חוֹשֵׂף!’
אָמַר לָהֶם יוֹסֵף.

‘You sold a brother for the price of shoes. Full of hate, you set upon him to shed his blood. Deceitfully, you slaughtered a kid. You pained your father's heart, you plotted to delude him. Woe to you from the judgement of the Revealer!’ – said Joseph to them.

’הֶאָח, חָלִילָה לְּךָ מֵעֲשׂוֹת זֹאת,
וְתָמַהְנוּ כְּשָׁמַעְנוּ מִמְּךָ כָּזֹאת.
זְקֹף עֵינֶיךָ לַמָּרוֹם וְאַל תְּגַלֶּה רָזוֹת.
חוֹבָתֵנוּ גָּרְמָה, עַל כֵּן בָּאָה עָלֵינוּ הַצָּרָה הַזֹּאת.
בִּי אֲדוֹנִי, בִּדְבָרְךָ הֲמַמְתָּנוּ בִּרְעָדָה!’
אָמַר לוֹ יְהוּדָה.

‘O far be it from you to do such a thing! We are amazed to hear all this from you. Lift your eyes to heaven; do not reveal the secrets [of our past]. It is our crime that has brought this trouble upon us. My lord, your words have filled us with trembling!’ – said Judah to him.

’טְרַחְתּוּהוּ בְּיַד עוֹשֵׂי חֲבָלִים.
יְעַצְתֶּם לָשׂוּם רַגְלוֹ בִּכְבָלִים.
כְּאַכְזָרִים מְכַרְתּוּהוּ לַאֲנָשִׁים מְחַבְּלִים,
לְיִשְׁמְעֵאלִים, בַּעֲבוּר נְעָלִים.
אוֹי לָכֶם מִדִּין חוֹשֵׂף!’
אָמַר לָהֶם יוֹסֵף.

‘You tormented him at the hands of schemers. You conspired to have his feet shackled. Merciless, you sold him to violent men, to the Ishmaelites, for shoes. Woe to you from the judgement of the Revealer!’ – said Joseph to them.

’מְלַּלְנוּ אֵלֶיךָ כְּדַל וָרָשׁ.
נַדְנוּ כְּנִמְצָא הַגָּבִיעַ הַנִּדְרָשׁ.
סוֹדֵנוּ אַל תְּגַל, וְרִיבְךָ יִפְרָשׁ.
עַל דָּמֵנוּ אַל תַּעֲמֹד, כִּי הַדָּם מִיַּד מְאַבְּדוֹ יִדָּרֵשׁ.
בִּי אֲדוֹנִי, בִּדְבָרְךָ הֲמַמְתָּנוּ בִּרְעָדָה!’
אָמַר לוֹ יְהוּדָה.

‘Most humbly we pleaded with you. We grieved when the sought-for goblet was found. Do not disclose our secret, or mix our past in this [present] quarrel. Do not allow our blood to be spilled, for blood shall be revenged on the murderer's head. My lord, your words have filled us with trembling!’ – said Judah to him.

׳פָּתַר לָכֶם אֶת חֲלוֹמוֹ.
צְפִיתֶם בְּקִנְאַתְכֶם לְהַחֲרִימוֹ.
קַמְתֶּם וְהִתְמַכַּרְתֶּם לִשְׁפֹּךְ אֶת דָּמוֹ.
רִמִּיתֶם בַּאֲבִיכֶם בְּ״זֹאת מָצָאנוּ״, וְקַמְתֶּם לְנַחֲמוֹ.
אוֹי לָכֶם מִדִּין חוֹשֵׂף!׳
אָמַר לָהֶם יוֹסֵף.

'He interpreted his dream to you.
Envious, you lay in wait to destroy him.
Then you eagerly rose to shed his blood.
You deceived your father, saying:
"*We found this*",[1] and then sought to
comfort him. Woe to you from the
judgement of the Revealer!' – said
Joseph to them.

׳שִׁנַּנְתָּ לְשׁוֹנְךָ כְּחִצִּים לְשַׁכֵּל.
תָּמַהְנוּ מִדְּבָרֶיךָ וּלְהָשִׁיב לֹא נוּכַל.
פְּנֵה אֶל בּוֹרְאֶךָ, אַל תֵּלֶךְ בָּנוּ רֶכֶל.
נָא, בִּי אֲדוֹנִי, רִיבָה רִיבֵנוּ בְּשֶׂכֶל.
בִּי אֲדוֹנִי, בְּדָבְרְךָ הֲמַמְתָּנוּ בִּרְעָדָה!׳
אָמַר לוֹ יְהוּדָה.

'You have sharpened your tongue like
arrows to destroy us. We are terrified
by your words and cannot answer.
O turn to your Creator, and do not
bear old tales against us. If you please,
my lord, contend with us reasonably.
My lord, your words have filled us with
trembling!' – said Judah to him.

׳חֲיַּבְתֶּם מִיתָה מְשֻׁנָּה.
שָׂב – דַּרְכּוֹ סְכַרְתֶּם מִשְּׁכִינָה.
הָאֵל יִמְחֹל לָכֶם מִשְּׁמֵי מְעוֹנָה.
כֻּלְּכֶם בֹּאוּ אֵלַי גֹּשְׁנָה.
הֵן לְמִחְיָה שְׁלָחַנִי חוֹשֵׂף.׳
נָם: ׳אֲנִי אֲחִיכֶם יוֹסֵף!׳

'You have merited an unnatural death.
You blocked the old man's way to the
prophetic spirit.[2] May God, in his
heavenly abode, forgive you. Now
come, all of you, to Goshen; it was the
Revealer who sent me ahead to save
men's lives.' And he said: 'I am your
brother Joseph!'

חֲלְחֲלוּ כְּשָׁמְעוּ מִלָּתוֹ.
זָעוּ וְנִבְהֲלוּ וְלֹא יָכְלוּ לַעֲנוֹתוֹ.
קוֹל נָתַן בִּבְכִי וּבָכוּ לְעֻמָּתוֹ.
וְאַחֲרֵי כֵן דִּבְּרוּ אֶחָיו אִתּוֹ.

They shuddered at his words. They
shook, dumbfounded, and could not
answer him. Then he wept aloud, and
they too wept. *And afterwards his
brothers talked with him.*

1. Joseph's ornamental tunic, dipped in the kid's blood; Genesis 37.32.
2. Legend has it that the spirit of prophecy deserted Jacob as long as he was separated from Joseph.

אֲמִתַּי בַּר־שְׁפַטְיָה

Amittai ben Shephatiah

אָדוֹן מַגִּיד מֵרֵאשִׁית

FOR THE MARRIAGE OF CASSIA, THE POET'S SISTER

אָדוֹן מַגִּיד מֵרֵאשִׁית אַחֲרִית שָׁנִים
וּמִקֶּדֶם אֲשֶׁר לֹא נַעֲשׂוּ מְזֻמָּנִים,
אוֹמֵר: 'עֲצָתִי תָקוּם לְדוֹרוֹת אַחֲרוֹנִים.'

The Lord, who revealed the end from the beginning and from ancient times prepared what is yet to be, says: 'My design shall last for generations to come.'

בְּמַחֲשַׁבְתּוֹ אָז כְּעָלָה לִבְרֹאוֹת חֲתָנִים,
בְּטֶרֶם יְצָרָם הִקְדִּים כָּל תִּקּוּנִים
לְלַמֵּד תַּכְסִיסֵי חֻפָּה לִבְנֵי־בָנִים.

When He resolved to create the Bridegroom and Bride, He first made all the necessary provisions, so that their descendants would be instructed in the order of marriage.

גָּדַר וְקֵרָה בָּרִאשׁוֹן גַּג תִּקְרָתָם,
תָּכַף וְיָסַד אֶת בֵּית חֲתֻנָּתָם,
וְאוֹר לְהָאִיר עֲלֵי הַסִבַּת סְעֻדָּתָם.

He built the frame of the celestial roof and laid its beams; then quickly constructed their bridal bower and created light to shine upon their banquet.

אֱמֶת, מַה נּוֹרָאִים מַעֲשֶׂיךָ, נוֹרָא!
מִדַּת בָּשָׂר וָדָם צָר צוּרָה —
תְּפִיסַת רֵיק בְּלֹא רְאוּת וַחֲקִירָה;
יוֹצֵר צָר צוּרָה בְּתוֹךְ צוּרָה. קָדוֹשׁ!

In truth, most fearsome are Your deeds, O Fearful One! When a human being makes a form, he can do nothing without sight and study; but You, O Creator, can make a form within a form [in the womb], O Holy One!

וִיבֵּק בַּשֵּׁנִי עֲלִיָּה נָאָה וּמְיֻפָּה
וּבָהּ הֵכִין שׁוֹשְׁבִינִים לְצַלְצֵל וּלְתוֹפְפָה
וְהִסִּיק אַתּוּנָא מְעַרְבְּבֵי סְעֻדָּתָם לִשְׂרֵפָה.

On the second day, He added an upper storey, beautifully adorned, and created the groomsmen,[1] to sing and strike the timbrels; and He stoked a fiery furnace to burn the adulterers.[2]

הִקְוָה בַּשְּׁלִישִׁי וּפִנָּה תֵיאַטְרוֹן לִמְשַׂחֲקִים
וְהֵצִיץ אִילָנוֹת תְּמוּר פַּרְפְּרָיוֹת וּפִנּוּקִים
וְגִנַּת בִּיתָן גְּנוּנִים בּוֹ לְהָקִים.

On the third day, He assembled the waters, thus clearing a stage for the players; He brought forth trees, for pleasure and delight, and made a royal garden for their bridal chambers.

1. Angels. 2. Lit. 'those who disrupt their feast'.

וּבָרְבִיעִי הִדְלִיק שְׁנֵי נֵרוֹת כְּפָנָסִיּוֹת
מִלְּהִכָּבוֹת מֵהֲפָּחַת רוּחַ וּמְטַר מֵיוֹת
וְהַשְּׁאָר לְנוֹי כְּעִטּוּרֵי סֻכָּה לִהְיוֹת.

On the fourth day, He lit up two torch-like lamps, which even gusts of wind and pouring rain could not put out; and He lit all the others for beauty's sake, to adorn the bridal canopy.

זִמֵּן בַּחֲמִישִׁי מִינֵי עוֹפוֹת וְדָגִים
וְהִתְקִין מֵהֶם לְמַאֲכַל יְשִׁישִׁים וּמְעֻנָּגִים
וְזִיז וְלִוְיָתָן לְחַבֵּא לַחֲבוּרַת זוּגִים.

On the fifth day, He summoned every kind of bird and fish, with which He would prepare a meal for the venerable celebrants; and He hid away Ziz and Leviathan for the companies of the pious.[1]

חִיֵּל בַּשִּׁשִּׁי מִינֵי חַיָּה וּבְהֵמָה
תַּבְשִׁילֵי שֹׂבַע וְהוֹתֵר לַעֲשׂוֹת מֵהֵמָּה
וּבְהֵמוֹת גָּנַז לַצַּדִּיקִים לְיוֹם נֶחָמָה.

On the sixth day, He mustered all kinds of beasts and cattle to provide abundant food; and He stored away Behemoth for the righteous on the day of redemption.[1]

טוֹב שָׁר וְהִנֵּה הַכֹּל נִתְיַפָּה
וְכָל מִינֵי סְעֻדָּה צְרוּרִים בַּמַּפָּה
וַעֲדַיִן אֵין חָתָן וְכַלָּה בַּחֻפָּה.

The Benign One saw that everything was now beautiful, and the table set with many fine dishes, but as yet no bride and groom stood under the canopy.

יִפָּה זִיו חָתָן מִגַּלְגַּל חַמָּה
נִשָּׂא גָלְמוֹ מֵהֲדוֹם וְעַד רוֹמָה
וְאַחֲרֵי כֵן הֶעֱמִידוֹ לְאֶלֶף אַמָּה.

He made the groom more radiant than the globe of the sun, made his body tower from earth to heaven; but later [after the Fall] reduced him to a thousand ells.

כּוֹנֵן שְׁתֵּים עֶשְׂרֵה חֻפּוֹת מָלוֹן
שֶׁל אֹדֶם פִּטְדָה זָהָב תַּרְשִׁישׁ וְיַהֲלֹם
וְהִכְרִיזוּ לוֹ מַלְאָכִים: 'בֹּאֲךָ לְשָׁלוֹם!'

He set up twelve bridal chambers of carnelian, topaz, gold, chrysolite and diamond; and the angels called to him: 'Welcome!'

לְעֵת הִכְנִיסוֹ בְּכִלַּת חֲתָנִים הַמְיֻקָּרָה
הִרְדִּימוֹ וְלָקַח צַלְעוֹ וְקִשְּׁטָהּ כְּנַעֲרָה
הִרְחִיצָהּ וְסָכָהּ וּפִרְכְּסָהּ וְקָלַע שְׂעָרָהּ.

Then, placing him in the precious bridal bed, He put him to sleep. He took one of his ribs and dressed it up as a girl; He bathed her, anointed and adorned her, and plaited her hair.

1. To be eaten by them at the end of time; see 'The Battle Between Behemoth and Leviathan', p. 232.

מְסָרָהּ לַאֲלָפִים וְלִרְבָבוֹת לַהֲבִיאָהּ בִּזְמִירוֹת
וְכָל שַׁמָּשִׁים עוֹמְדִים שׁוּרוֹת־שׁוּרוֹת
חַמָּה וּלְבָנָה לְעֻמָּתָם מְרַקְּדוֹת כִּנְעָרוֹת.

He entrusted her to the thousands and myriads of angels who ushered her in with song. All the attendants arranged themselves in rows, the sun and the moon dancing like maidens before them.

נָשְׂאָה חֵן וָחֶסֶד לִפְנֵי בַעְלָהּ
וְהוּא בִּכְבוֹדוֹ בֵּרְכָם בְּרָכָה מֻכְלָלָה
וְהַכֹּל עָנוּ: 'יִשְׂמַח חָתָן עִם כַּלָּה!'

Her husband found her lovely and delightful, and God Himself gave them His perfect blessing. And all responded: 'Let the groom rejoice with his bride!'

סָח לְשׁוֹשְׁבִינָיו לְסַדֵּר שֻׁלְחָן שֶׁל מַרְגָּלִיּוֹת
וְסָבִיב־סָבִיב הוֹשֵׁב סַפְסָלִים וְקָתֶדְרָיוֹת
וּלְשַׁמֵּשׁ בְּבָשָׂר וְלִמְזֹג יַיִן עֲסִיסִיּוֹת.

He told His groomsmen to set the jewelled table, to put benches and soft chairs all around it, to serve the meat and pour out fine wine.

עוֹדָם בְּחֻפָּתָם הִתְרָם הַתְרָיָה אַחַת
וְלֹא קִיְּמוּהָ וְכִמְעַט יָרְדוּ לַשַּׁחַת
לוּלֵי מִזְמוֹר שִׁיר לְיוֹם נַחַת.

While still in their bridal bower, He imposed upon them a single prohibition [not to eat of the tree of knowledge]. They did not heed it and, but for the intervention of the Sabbath-Day,[1] would have been doomed to the Pit.

פֻּקַּד זְמַנָּם וְגָע קֵץ עִתָּם
וּמֵאָז וְעַד עַתָּה נִמְסַר לְתוֹלְדוֹתָם
לִפְרוֹת וְלִרְבּוֹת וְסוֹף לָמוּת אַחֲרִיתָם.

A limit was set to their time, and the end of their life arrived. Ever since then their offspring are fated to be fertile and increase, and then in the end to die.

צְנוּעִים נָהֲגוּ אֵלֶּה לְדוֹרֵי דוֹרוֹתָם
לְשַׁדֵּךְ בְּעֵת אֵרוּסִין וּלְקַדֵּשׁ בְּטַבַּעְתָּם
וּבְעֵת חֻפָּתָם לִשְׂמֹחַ בְּשִׂמְחַת חֲתֻנָּתָם.

The 'pure ones'[2] have made this their custom for all generations: to betroth, to consecrate with a ring, and to rejoice in their marriage within the bridal chamber.

1. The Sabbath persuaded God not to send Adam to Gehenna. In gratitude he composed 'A Psalm, a Song for the day of rest' (Psalm 92).

2. Epithet for the children of Israel.

קְרֵבִים בְּשִׂמְחָתָם עָדֶיךָ עֲמוּסֵי מֵעַיִם,
לָגִיל בְּמוֹרָא וְלֹא בְּעַזּוּת אַפַּיִם,
מְסַיְּמִים בִּרְכָתָם: ׳כְּהַיּוֹם הַזֶּה בִּירוּשָׁלַיִם!׳

Now, 'those whom You carried since birth'[1] approach You joyfully to celebrate – with awe, not with arrogance – and they conclude their blessing thus: 'If only we were in Jerusalem on this day!'

רַחֲמִים מְבַקְשִׁים מִמְּךָ, נוֹרָא וְנִקְדָּשׁ,
לֶאֱסֹף נִדָּחִים וְלָשִׁיר שִׁיר חָדָשׁ,
שָׂשִׂים וּשְׂמֵחִים בְּבִנְיַן בֵּית הַמִּקְדָּשׁ.

They beg You for mercy, O Hallowed and Fearful One. Gather the exiles, so that they may sing a new song as they rejoice in the restored Temple.

שֶׁבַח וּגְדֻלָּה לְשִׁמְךָ, אֵלִי זֶה,
אֲשֶׁר רִחַמְתָּ דוֹר עָנִי וְנִבְזֶה,
וְנֹאמַר: ׳שֶׁהֶחֱיָנוּ וְהִגִּיעָנוּ לַזְּמַן הַזֶּה!׳

Praise and glory to Your name, O my God, for You have shown mercy to a lowly, wretched generation. Now let us say: 'He has kept us alive, He has brought us to the present moment!'

תָּמִיד הֵיטִיבָה אַחֲרִית עֲלֵי יְדִידִים
לְדוֹרֵי דוֹרִים הֱיוֹת שִׁמְךָ מְיַחֲדִים;
לְהַקְדִּישְׁךָ בְּרַעַד וּבִרְתֵת כֻּלָּם עוֹמְדִים.

May You always grant Your loved ones a happy end, so that they may declare Your unity forever. Now all rise to sanctify You with fear and trembling.

אֶל עִיר גִּבּוֹרִים

MOSES' JOURNEY THROUGH HEAVEN

אֶל עִיר גִּבּוֹרִים כְּעָלָה עָנָו,
פְּגָעוֹ קְמוּאֵל, הַשּׁוֹעֵר, עִם צְבָא שִׁנְאַנָּיו.
גָּעַר בּוֹ נֶאֱמָן וְנָס מִפָּנָיו,
וְהוּא מִתְהַלֵּךְ בָּרָקִיעַ כְּבִשְׁכוּנַת שְׁכֵנָיו.
וּמֵאֲחוֹרֵי הַפַּרְגּוֹד שָׁמַע קוֹל־רַעַשׁ בְּאָזְנָיו,
אוֹמְרִים: ׳קָדוֹשׁ קָדוֹשׁ קָדוֹשׁ יְיָ צְבָאוֹת!׳

When the humble one scaled the city of the mighty angels, he was met by Kemuel, the gate keeper, with his dread legions. The faithful one rebuked him and he fled. Then Moses walked about on the firmament as a man walks in his own neighbourhood. And he heard tumultuous voices from behind the Curtain, saying: '*Holy, holy, holy is the Lord of hosts!*'

1. Epithet for the children of Israel.

מַרְאֵה הֲדַרְנִיאֵל כְּחָזוּ, נִבְהַל מִתָּאֳרוֹ,
שֶׁשְּׁמוֹנֶה מֵאוֹת פַּרְסָה גָּדוֹל מֵחֲבֵרוֹ
וּשְׁנֵים־עָשָׂר בְּרָקִים יוֹצְאִים מִפִּיו בְּדַבְּרוֹ.
וּלְבַסּוֹף הָלַךְ לְפָנָיו כְּתַלְמִיד לִפְנֵי מוֹרוֹ,
וּבַת קוֹל שָׁמַע מֵהֵיכַל דְּבִירוֹ,
אוֹמְרִים: ׳קָדוֹשׁ קָדוֹשׁ קָדוֹשׁ יְיָ צְבָאוֹת!׳

When he beheld Hadarniel, he was terrified by his stature, for he was taller than his fellows by eight hundred parasangs, and twelve lightning flashes leapt from his mouth as he spoke; but in the end, he went before him as a disciple goes before his master. And Moses heard a divine voice from within the palace sanctuary, saying: '*Holy, holy, holy is the Lord of hosts!*'

תְּמוּנַת סַנְדַּלְפוֹן כְּרָאָה, אֲחָזוּהוּ חֲבָלִים,
שֶׁאִשּׁוֹ שׂוֹרֶפֶת לַפִּידִים וְגֶחָלִים
וְהוּא מְשַׁמֵּשׁ אַחַר־הַמֶּרְכָּבָה בְּכֶתֶר הִלּוּלִים.
וּבְשָׁעַת הַכְתֵּר כָּל חֵילֵי מָרוֹם חָלִים
וְכָל אַדְנֵי שְׁרַפְרַף רוֹעֲשִׁים וּמִתְגַּלְגְּלִים,
אוֹמְרִים: ׳קָדוֹשׁ קָדוֹשׁ קָדוֹשׁ יְיָ צְבָאוֹת!׳

When he saw the figure of Sandalfon, anguish struck him, for his fire consumes torches and burning coals. He stands behind the Chariot, wreathing a crown of praises for Him, and when the crown rests on His head, all the armies of heaven shudder. The supports of His footstool roar and roll, saying: '*Holy, holy, holy is the Lord of hosts!*'

יְפִי־כַנְפֵי גַלִּיצוּר נֶגֶד הַחַיּוֹת מַעֲמָדָם
שֶׁלֹּא יִשָּׂרְפוּ מַלְאָכִים מִלַּהַב לַפִּידָם.
וְאוּדֵי־רִגְיוֹן אוֹחֵז מוּל מַלְכֵי אָדָם
לְהַפִּיל עַל כֹּל אֵימָתָם וּפַחְדָּם —
וּכְקוֹל מַיִם רַבִּים שָׁמַע מֹשֶׁה כְּנֶגְדָּם,
אוֹמְרִים: ׳קָדוֹשׁ קָדוֹשׁ קָדוֹשׁ יְיָ צְבָאוֹת!׳

The glorious wings of Gallizur screen the creatures of the chariot, so that their fiery torches shall not consume the angels. He holds fire-brands from the Rigyon[1] up to the faces of human kings, so that their radiant faces strike the world with terror and dread. And Moses heard a sound there like the rush of many waters, saying: '*Holy, holy, holy is the Lord of hosts!*'

חַשְׁרַת מַיִם מִתְוַעֲדִים בַּחֲבוּרָתָם
זִקּוּק נוּר וְלַפִּידִים בְּשׁוּב אִשּׁוֹתָם;
קוֹרְאִים שַׂר הַחֹשֶׁךְ לְהִתְוַעֵד בְּוַעִידָתָם,
קוֹפֵץ מַלְאַךְ הַמָּוֶת לְהִזְדַּוֵּג אִתָּם —
וְכָל צִבְאוֹתָם בִּקְרִיאָתָם עוֹנִים לְעֻמָּתָם,
אוֹמְרִים: ׳קָדוֹשׁ קָדוֹשׁ קָדוֹשׁ יְיָ צְבָאוֹת!׳

Masses of water merge with the angelic companies. Torches and flares, back from their missions, join them. They call on the Prince of Darkness to enter their ranks. The Angel of Death leaps forward to be united with them. And the heavenly legions all cry out in answer, saying: '*Holy, holy, holy is the Lord of hosts!*'

1. The river of fire which is formed by the sweat of the creatures of the chariot (see p. 244, line 13).

אָדָם צָר בַּכֹּתֶל

GOD THE ARTIST

[...] אָדָם צָר בַּכֹּתֶל צוּרָה,
מְיַפָּהּ בְּסַם וּבְסִקְרָא.
בַּאֲשֶׁר שָׂמָהּ שָׁם דָּרָה
וְאֵינָהּ זָזָה מִמְּקוֹם סְדוּרָהּ,
כִּי רַגְלָהּ מְקֻפַּחַת וּשְׁבוּרָה
וְלֹא שׁוֹמַעַת קוֹל אֲמִירָה
וְאֵינָהּ רוֹאָה וְלֹא מְדַבְּרָה —
אֲבָל צוּר צַיָּר הַנּוֹרָא,
צָר צוּרָה בְּתוֹךְ צוּרָה,
בְּכָל מִדּוֹתֶיהָ שְׁלֵמָה וּגְמוּרָה,
בְּמַרְאֶה וּבְמִשְׁמָע סְדוּרָה
וְגַם בַּהֲלִיכָה וּבַחֲזִירָה,
שֶׁהוּא צָר וָלָד בִּמְעֵי־עֻבָּרָה.

A man draws a figure on a wall, embellishing it with yellows and with reds. Where he has put it, there must it stay. It cannot move from its fixed place, for its foot is twisted and broken; it cannot hear speech, or see, or speak. But God is an awesome artist who can shape form within form, flawless and perfect in all its dimensions, able to see and hear, to move back and forth. Thus does he shape the embryo in the womb of a pregnant woman.

אָדָם הוֹלֵךְ אֵצֶל צַיָּר לְהַשְׂכִּירוֹ,
אִיקוֹנִין שֶׁל אָבִיו לְצַיְּרוֹ,
וְהוּא מְשִׁיבוֹ כָּכָה בְּדִבּוּרוֹ:
'מִיָּמַי לֹא רְאִיתִיו וְאֵינִי מַכִּירוֹ,
הַרְאֵנִי דְמוּתוֹ וַאֲנִי אַתְאִירוֹ' —
אֲבָל צוּר צַיָּר יוֹצֵר יִצְרוֹ:
מַטִּיף מֵאִישׁ טִפַּת מְקוֹרוֹ
וּפוֹתֵחַ רֶחֶם לִקְלֹט הֶרְיוֹן עִבּוּרוֹ
וּמַקְרִישׁ עֲצָמָיו וּמַגְלִיד עוֹרוֹ
וּמְדַמֶּה פָּנָיו כְּנֶגֶד פַּרְצוּף הוֹרוֹ. [...]

A man goes to an artist to commission a portrait of his father. This is what he says in reply: 'I have never seen him and do not know him, but if you show me his likeness, I will make an image of him.' But God is an artist who can make his creation: He makes a man emit a drop of semen from his source, makes the womb open to conceive the embryo, makes its bones congeal, coats it with skin, and forms its features in the father's image.

עֲלוּמֵי־שֵׁם

Anonymous

פְּתַח לָנוּ שַׁעַר

THE CLOSING OF THE GATES

פְּתַח לָנוּ שַׁעַר
בְּעֵת נְעִילַת שַׁעַר,
כִּי פָנָה יוֹם.

הַיּוֹם יִפְנֶה,
הַשֶּׁמֶשׁ יָבוֹא וְיִפְנֶה,
נָבוֹאָה שְׁעָרֶיךָ.

Open the gates to us when the gates are being closed, for the day is about to set.

The day shall set, the sun shall go down and set – let us enter Your gates!

יְמֵי הַקַּיִץ עָבְרוּ

RAIN SONG

יְמֵי הַקַּיִץ עָבְרוּ.
הַסְּתָיו בָּא, מְטְרוֹתָיו יְחַשְׁרוּ
וְעַל הָאָרֶץ יָרִיקוּ וְיִגְבְּרוּ.
דָּגָן, תִּירוֹשׁ וְיִצְהָר מְהֵרָה יִפְרוּ.
הֶעָבִים גֶּשֶׁם יַמְטִירוּ,
חֶלֶד עֲשָׂבִים לָצֵאת יְמַהֵרוּ.
זֵרְעוֹנֶיהָ וְנִצֶּיהָ יֻשְׁפְּרוּ.
קוֹלוֹת רְעָמִים יְבַשְּׂרוּ:
׳הַזּוֹרְעִים בְּדִמְעָה בְּרִנָּה יִקְצֹרוּ!׳

The days of summer are gone. The rainy season is here. Its showers will gather, then pour themselves, more and more, upon the earth. Grain, wine, and oil will flourish quickly. The clouds will send down rain, and urge the earth to bring forth grass. Seeds and buds will grow in beauty. Voices of thunder will herald: '*Those who sow in tears shall reap with songs of joy!*'

אֲשֶׁר גִּלָּה חָכְמָה

MOSES OVERCOMES THE SEA

אֲשֶׁר גִּלָּה חָכְמָה לְיַעֲקֹב
וְהִתְקִין בִּינָה לִבְנוֹ בְּכוֹרוֹ –

He who revealed wisdom to the sons of Jacob and bestowed knowledge upon

בַּחֲרוֹן אַפּוֹ עַל מִצְרַיִם הִשְׁקִיף,
הוֹפִיעַ בְּחֵמָה עַל בְּכוֹרֵיהֶם,
גָּזַר יַם־סוּף לִגְזָרִים
וּבֵין חוֹמוֹת־מַיִם עָבְרוּ שְׁבָטִים.

His first-born,[1] He looked down in anger upon the Egyptians, appeared in wrath to their first-born, split the Red Sea asunder, so that the tribes could pass between walls of water.

דִּינִים אָמַר הַיָּם לְמֹשֶׁה:
׳לָמָּה, מֹשֶׁה, תַּעֲשֶׂה לִּי כָּכָה?
הֲלֹא אֲנִי נִבְרֵאתִי בַּיּוֹם הַשְּׁלִישִׁי
וְאַתָּה נִבְרֵאתָ בַּיּוֹם הַשִּׁשִּׁי,
וַאֲנִי גָּדוֹל מִמְּךָ בִּשְׁלֹשֶׁת יָמִים,
וְאַתָּה מְבַקֵּשׁ לַעֲבֹר בְּתוֹכִי?
זְכָר־נָא מֹשֶׁה שֶׁאֲנִי הֶחְכַּמְתִּיךָ.
וּמַדּוּעַ תֹּאמַר: ״הִבָּקְעָה לִּי!״׳

The sea berated Moses: 'Why, Moses, are you doing this to me? After all, I was created on the third day, while you were created on the sixth; I am three days older than you, and yet you wish to pass through me? Remember, Moses, that I am wiser than you. Then how dare you say: "Divide before me!"'

חָרָה אַף מֹשֶׁה וְהֵשִׁיב כְּנֶגְדּוֹ:
׳שְׁמָעֵנִי, הַיָּם, וְקַבֵּל אֲמָרַי!׳
טַפֵּי יַעֲקֹב רָאָה אֱלֹהִים
נְתוּנִים בְּצָרָה לִפְנֵי אוֹיֵב –
יַעַמְדוּ מֵימֶיךָ חוֹמָה גְּבֹהָה,
וּבְדֶרֶךְ סְלוּלָה, יָמִין וּשְׂמֹאל.
כִּי הוּא אָמַר, אֶעֱבֹר בְּגַלָּךְ.
הִבָּקְעָה לִּי וְאַל תִּתְעַכָּב!׳

The anger of Moses was kindled and he replied: 'Listen to me, O sea, and heed my words! God has seen that the children of Jacob are imperilled by the enemy. So let your waters arise like a great wall, on the right and on the left, with a paved path in their midst. For He has ordained that I shall pass through your waves. Now divide before me and do not delay!'

לֵאלֹהִים נַעֲשָׂה הַיָּם,
וּמַרְכְּבוֹת כְּרוּב אֵלָיו נִגְלָה.
מִמְּקוֹם תָּקְפּוֹ הִתְמוֹטְטָה אֶרֶץ,
כִּי פְּדוּיֵי יהוה רָאוּ אֲפִיקִים.

God, Who had created the sea, now revealed Himself to it, riding on a cherub. From His mighty seat He made the earth heave, and the children of the Lord, redeemed, beheld the sea's

1. The people of Israel.

’נֵלְכָה סִינַי לִשְׁמֹעַ תּוֹרָה!’
אָמְרוּ פְּדוּיִים לְמֹשֶׁה יָדִיד.
סָגַר הַיָּם בִּתְפִלָּתוֹ
וְעַל יַד שְׁלוּחוֹ חֲרוֹן־אַף הֵשִׁיב.
עָנָהוּ יהוה מִתּוֹךְ לַהֲבֵי אֵשׁ וַיֹּאמֶר לְעַמּוֹ:
’אָנֹכִי יהוה אֱלֹהֶיךָ אֲשֶׁר הוֹצֵאתִיךָ
מֵאֶרֶץ מִצְרַיִם מִבֵּית עֲבָדִים.’ [...]

bed. ‘Let us go to Sinai to hear the Law!’ said the redeemed ones to Moses, the beloved, whose prayer had closed the sea,[1] whose emissary[2] placated His wrath. Then the Lord spoke to him from the midst of blazing fires and said to His people: “*I am the Lord your God who brought you out of Egypt, out of the land of slavery!*”[3]

אַרְבָּעָה רָאוּ

FOUR SAW VISIONS OF GOD

אַרְבָּעָה רָאוּ מַרְאוֹת אֱלֹהִים:
עָנָיו וּבֶן אָמוֹץ וּבֶן בּוּזִי וְאִישׁ חֲמוּדוֹת –
בִּדְבַר הָאֱלֹהִים;
וְלֹא יָכְלוּ אַרְבַּעְתָּם לִרְאוֹת דְּמוּת אֱלֹהֵי הָאֱלֹהִים
כִּי אֵל גָּדוֹל יְיָ וּמֶלֶךְ גָּדוֹל עַל כָּל הָאֱלֹהִים.

Four saw visions of God – the humble one (Moses), the son of Amoz (Isaiah), the son of Buzi (Ezekiel), and the man greatly beloved (Daniel) – at the command of God. Yet none of the four could see the image of the God of gods, *for the Lord is a great God, and a great king over all gods.*

עָנָיו, אֱמָר־נָא מָה רָאִיתָ!
’רָאִיתִי אֵשׁ בַּסְּנֶה וְאֵינָהּ בּוֹעֲרָה.
בְּהִסְתַּכְּלִי לִרְאוֹת זָחַלְתִּי וָאִירָא.
גֵּאֶה קוֹלוֹ בְּהַר חָמַד קָרָא,
דְּבַר יְיָ נָכוֹן וְהִרְתִּיעָה בָרָה.
וְלֹא יָכֹלְתִּי לִרְאוֹת דְּמוּת אָיֹם וְנוֹרָא,
מוֹנֶה מִסְפָּר לַכּוֹכָבִים, לְכֻלָּם שֵׁמוֹת יִקְרָא.’

O humble one, tell what you saw. ‘I saw a flame in the thorn-bush, but it did not burn. When I gazed at it, I recoiled in fear. The Proud One called out from His cherished mountain. The word of the Lord rang out and the people drew back. But I could not see the image of Him, dread and terrible, *who numbers the stars one by one, and calls each one by its name.*’

בֶּן אָמוֹץ, אֱמָר־נָא מָה רָאִיתָ!
’רָאִיתִי הַיּוֹשֵׁב עַל כֵּס, מְשׁוֹטֵט חִקְרֵי נְשִׁיָּה,
וְשׁוּלָיו מְלֵאִים הֵיכַל שְׁמֵי עֲלִיָּה.

O son of Amoz, tell what you saw.
‘I saw Him who sits upon a throne, scanning the limits of the earth, as His train filled the temple of the uppermost

1. Over the drowning Egyptians.
2. Aaron, who later checked the plague; Numbers 17.11.
3. Exodus 20.2; the first sentence of the Ten Commandments.

זֶה לָזֶה קוֹרְאִים קְדֻשָּׁתוֹ לְשְׁעִיָּה,
חַתִּים אַמּוֹת הַסִּפִּים מֵאֵימָתוֹ בְּיִרְאָה.
וְלֹא יָכֹלְתִּי לִרְאוֹת אֱלוֹהַּ כָּל בְּרִיָּה,
גְּדֹל הָעֵצָה וְרַב הָעֲלִילִיָּה.׳

heavens. The seraphim called one to another, saying the Thrice Holy[1] so that He should heed them. For fear of Him, the threshold trembled to its foundations. But I could not see the God of all creatures, who is *great in counsel and mighty in deed.*'

בֶּן בּוּזִי, אֱמָר־נָא מָה רָאִיתָ!
׳רָאִיתִי טַפְסְרֵי חַיָּלֵי גְדוּדֵי צְבָאוֹת,
יַחַד כְּמַרְאֵה הַבָּזָק רָצוֹא וָשׁוֹב בְּנוֹרָאוֹת.
כְּקוֹל מַיִם רַבִּים כַּנְפֵיהֶם דָּאוֹת.
לְמוּלָם נִרְאוֹת נוֹשְׂאוֹת וְהֵם נִשָּׂאוֹת.
וְלֹא יָכֹלְתִּי לִרְאוֹת דְּמוּת עוֹשֵׂה נוֹרָאוֹת,
קָדוֹשׁ קָדוֹשׁ קָדוֹשׁ יְיָ צְבָאוֹת.׳

O son of Buzi, tell what you saw. 'I saw the angels – legions, armies, and hosts – like a flash of lightning, all fearfully darting to and fro, their beating wings like the sound of many waters. And the holy creatures, facing them, seemed to be bearing the throne though they were borne by it. But I could not see the image of Him who does awesome deeds, the *holy, holy, holy Lord of Hosts.*'

אִישׁ־חֲמוּדוֹת, אֱמָר־נָא מָה רָאִיתָ!
׳רָאִיתִי מִזֵּעַת חַיּוֹת נַהֲרֵי לַהַב מוֹשְׁכִים,
נִשְׂגָּב חָן עַל כִּסְאוֹ – מִפַּחְדּוֹ הֵם נִמְשָׁכִים;
שְׂעַר רֵאשֵׁהּ כַּעֲמַר נְקֵא וְהוּא מַחֲלִיף
וּמַעֲבִיר מְלָכִים,
עַל חוּג הָאָרֶץ יוֹשֵׁב מֶלֶךְ מַלְכֵי הַמְּלָכִים.
וְלֹא יָכֹלְתִּי לִרְאוֹת דְּמוּת הַנּוֹתֵן תְּשׁוּעָה לַמְּלָכִים,
מַשְׁגִּיחַ מִן הַחַלּוֹנוֹת, מֵצִיץ מִן הַחֲרַכִּים.׳

O man greatly beloved, tell what you saw. 'I saw fiery rivers streaming from the sweat of the holy creatures. The Lofty One rested upon His throne; it was His dread that made them stream forth. The hair of His head was like pure wool. He replaced kings, removed kings – the King of all kings, throned on the vaulted roof of the earth. But I could not see the image of Him who gives victory to kings, *who looks in at the windows, gazes through the lattice.*'

מִימִינוֹ אֵשׁ דָּת וּמִשְּׂמֹאלוֹ אֵשׁ
וּלְפָנָיו אֵשׁ וְאַחֲרָיו אֵשׁ
וְהוּא אֵשׁ אוֹכְלָה אֵשׁ, וְעַמּוֹ בֵּית אֵשׁ
וּמַלְאָכָיו חֶצְיָם מַיִם וְחֶצְיָם אֵשׁ
וְהֵם טוֹבְלִים בְּנַהֲרֵי אֵשׁ
וְעוֹנִים וְאוֹמְרִים: ׳בָּרוּךְ כְּבוֹדוֹ מִמְּקוֹמוֹ!׳

There are flaming fires at His right and fires at His left; fire before Him and fire behind Him; He is a fire that devours fire, His people are a house of fire; his angels are half water and half fire; they immerse themselves in rivers of fire, then proclaim: '*Blessed be His glory from His place!*'

1. The *Kedusha*: 'Holy, holy, holy is the Lord of Hosts' (Isaiah 6.3).

אַדְנֵי אֲדָמָה

אַדְנֵי אֲדָמָה הָיוּ מִתְפָּרְקִים
בְּרֶדֶת מִשָּׁמַיִם שׁוֹכֵן שְׁחָקִים.
בָּנִים, מִקּוֹל בְּרָקִים, לֹא הָיוּ יוֹנְקִים
בְּשָׁמְעָם דְּבַר אֵל חַי מְפָרֵשׁ חֲקוּקִים.

יֵקַר תְּיֻקַּר בַּבֹּקֶר בַּבֹּקֶר
כְּוַיְהִי בַיּוֹם הַשְּׁלִישִׁי בִּהְיוֹת הַבֹּקֶר;
וְכֵן לְעֵת עֶרֶב יִהְיֶה אוֹר בֹּקֶר
לַמְתַנִּים שִׁבְחָךְ עֶרֶב וָבֹקֶר.

גָּעֲשׁוּ וְרָעֲשׁוּ מִמְּקוֹמָם הָרִים
וְנָמוּ: ׳אַיֵּה שׁוֹקֵל בְּפֶלֶס הָרִים?׳
דִּבֶּר תָּבוֹר: ׳אֲנִי גָבֹהַּ מִכָּל הָרִים
וְעָלַי נָאֶה לַחֲנוֹת יוֹצֵר הָרִים.׳

הָמָה כַרְמֶל וּבְתוֹךְ יָם בָּא
וְנָם: ׳בִּי יַחֲנֶה נַעֲרָץ בְּסוֹד קְדוֹשִׁים רַבָּה.׳
וְגַבְהוּתוֹ אוֹתוֹ תְּעֲבָה,
וְלֹא נֶאֱמַר לוֹ ׳בָּרוּךְ הַבָּא׳.

זָע סִינַי וְלֹא דִבֶּר מְאוּמָה
וְנָם: ׳אֵיךְ בִּי יַחֲנֶה שׁוֹכֵן רוּמָה?׳
חַי הֱשִׁיבוֹ: ׳עָלֶיךָ אֲקַדְּמָה,
כִּי הִשְׁפַּלְתָּ אֶת עַצְמָךְ אוֹתָךְ אֲרִימָה.׳

THE CONTEST OF THE MOUNTAINS

The earth's foundations shook when He who dwells in the clouds descended from heaven. At the sound of the lightning, infants ceased suckling, as they heard the word of the living God pronounce the Law on the Tablets.

You shall be cherished ever more, morning after morning, as *on the third day, when morning came.*[1] And in the evening, let there be morning light for those who say Your praise evening and morning.

The mountains heaved and quaked, leaped from their places and said: 'Where is He who weighs the mountains on a balance?' Mount Tabor declared: 'I am the highest of the mountains; by right, the maker of mountains should rest upon me.'

Mount Carmel spoke softly, as it moved down to the sea, and said: 'He who is feared in the council of the holy ones, He shall rest upon me!' But, for his pride, he was spurned and was not told 'Welcome'.

Mount Sinai shuddered but did not speak. 'How could He who dwells on high rest upon me?' The Living One answered him: 'Upon you shall I greet my people. Since you lowered yourself, I shall raise you up.'

1. The day the Lord came down upon Mount Sinai (Exodus 19.16) to give the Torah.

טָהוֹר מָאַס כָּל הֶהָרִים הַגְּדוֹלִים,
כִּי מִקּוֹל אֵימָתוֹ נָפְלוּ חֲלָלִים.
יָרַד לְסִינַי וְעִמּוֹ כָּל חֲיָלִים
וְהִנְחִיל לְמֹשֶׁה פְּרָטִים וּכְלָלִים.

The Pure One disdained all the high mountains. At His dread voice, they were struck down. Then He descended upon Sinai, with all His host, and bestowed the Law[1] upon Moses.

יֵיקַר תְּיֻקַּר בַּבֹּקֶר בַּבֹּקֶר
כְּוַיְהִי בַיּוֹם הַשְּׁלִישִׁי בִּהְיֹת הַבֹּקֶר;
וְכֵן לְעֵת עֶרֶב יִהְיֶה אוֹר בֹּקֶר
לַמְתַנִּים שִׁבְחָךְ עֶרֶב וָבֹקֶר.

You shall be cherished ever more, morning after morning as *on the third day, when morning came*. And in the evening, let there be morning light for those who say your praise evening and morning.

מַלְאַךְ הַמָּוֶת

THE ANGEL OF DEATH SEEKS MOSES

[...] מַלְאַךְ הַמָּוֶת שֻׁלַּח בְּמֹשֶׁה:
'נְאַם פִּיּוּסִים דַּבֵּר לְמֹשֶׁה,
אֱמָר־לוֹ: "רַבָּנִי, רַבְּךָ אֶצְלְךָ שְׁלָחַנִי
נַפְשְׁךָ לְבַקֵּשׁ."'
וְלֹא קָם נָבִיא עוֹד בְּיִשְׂרָאֵל כְּמֹשֶׁה.

The Angel of Death was dispatched against Moses: 'Speak soothing words to Moses. Say to him, "O master, your Master has sent me to you to request your soul."' *Never again did there arise in Israel a prophet like Moses.*[2]

סָעוּר יָצָא הַמַּלְאָךְ וְהָלַךְ אֶל הַסְּנֶה,
עָן: 'שֶׁמָּא רָאִיתָ לְמֹשֶׁה רֹאשׁ רַבָּנָי?'
פָּתַח לוֹ: 'מִיּוֹם שֶׁהִלְהִיבַנִי בָאֵשׁ לֹא רְאִיתִיו לְפָנָי.'
וְלֹא קָם נָבִיא עוֹד בְּיִשְׂרָאֵל כְּמֹשֶׁה.

The Angel stormed forth, came to the bush of thorns and said: 'Have you, perchance, seen Moses, the chief master?' It answered him: 'I have not seen him since the day I was set ablaze.' *Never again did there arise in Israel a prophet like Moses.*

1. Lit. 'specific and general [precepts]'.
2. Deuteronomy 34.10.

צָעַד וְהָלַךְ אֶל הַיָּם הַגָּדוֹל,
קָרָא: ׳שֶׁמָּא רָאִיתָ לְמשֶׁה הָרַב הַגָּדוֹל?׳
רָחַשׁ: ׳לֹא רְאִיתִיו מִיּוֹם שֶׁקְּרָעַנִי
וְהִרְעִיץ הַתַּנִּין הַגָּדוֹל.׳
וְלֹא קָם נָבִיא עוֹד בְּיִשְׂרָאֵל כְּמשֶׁה.

He marched and came to the Great Sea, shouting: 'Have you, perchance, seen Moses, the great teacher?' It murmured: 'I have not seen him since the day he tore me apart and shattered the Great Serpent (Pharaoh).' *Never again did there arise in Israel a prophet like Moses.*

שָׁאַג וְהָלַךְ אֶל הַר סִינָי,
שְׁאֵלוֹ: ׳שֶׁמָּא רָאִיתָ לְמשֶׁה הָעַנְוְנָי?׳
תְּנָּה לוֹ: ׳לֹא רְאִיתִיו מִיּוֹם שֶׁקִּבֵּל תּוֹרָה מִסִּינָי.׳
וְלֹא קָם נָבִיא עוֹד בְּיִשְׂרָאֵל כְּמשֶׁה.

Roaring, he went on to Mount Sinai and asked: 'Have you, perchance, seen Moses, the humble one?' It told him: 'I have not seen him since the day he received the Law on Sinai.' *Never again did there arise in Israel a prophet like Moses.*

וְנַפְשׁוֹ בִּנְשִׁיקָה קִבֵּל הַנִּקְדָּשׁ בְּפִי חַיּוֹת וְאוֹפַנִּים.

But He had already taken his soul with a kiss – He who is hallowed by the holy creatures and the angels of the chariot.

לֹא תְאַחֵר לְהָשִׁיב

THE POET'S COMMANDMENTS TO GOD

לֹא תְאַחֵר לְהָשִׁיב שְׁאֵלַת קוֹרְאֲךָ בְּכָל לִבּוֹ.
לֹא תִבְזֶה עֱנוּת עָנִי בְּהִתְחַנְנוֹ אֵלֶיךָ בְּנִיבוֹ.
לֹא תִגְעַר בְּרָשׁ וְאִישׁ תְּכָכִים לְפָנֶיךָ בְּהִתְיַצְּבוֹ.
לֹא תִדְחֶה אֶת יְצוּרְךָ מִפִּתְחָךְ רֵיקָם לַהֲשִׁיבוֹ.
לֹא תַהְכְּרֵהוּ וְתַכְלִימֵהוּ עַל חַטָּאתוֹ וְחוֹבוֹ.
לֹא תוֹכִיחֶנּוּ בְּאַפְּךָ אֶת דְּרָכָיו בְּעָזְבוֹ.
לֹא תִזְכָּר־לוֹ עֲוֹנוֹתָיו הָרִאשׁוֹנִים הַטְּמוּנִים בְּחֻבּוֹ
לֹא תַחֲבֹל עֲבוֹטוֹ עַל פִּשְׁעוֹ אֲשֶׁר נִגְאַל בּוֹ.
לֹא תִטְרֹד הָרָחוֹק בְּשִׁיבָתוֹ, כִּי קָרוֹב תְּקָרְבוֹ.

You shall not withhold Your answer from him who cries to You with all his heart. You shall not despise the afflicted wretch when he implores You for mercy. You shall not berate the poor and downtrodden, when he appears before You. You shall not turn Your creature away from Your door empty-handed. You shall not grieve him or shame him for his sin and guilt. You shall not rebuke him in Your anger once he forsakes his ways. You shall not remember against him his early sins, buried in his bosom. You shall not take his pledge in pawn for having defiled himself with crime. You shall not banish him who strays afar, but

לֹא תְיַסְּרֶנּוּ בַחֲמָתְךָ, כִּי רַפּוֹא תְרַפֵּא מַכְאוֹבוֹ.
לֹא תְכַלֶּה רָשָׁע וְסוֹרֵר מִדְּרָכָיו בְּשׁוּבוֹ.
לֹא תִלְחָצֶנּוּ לְגָמְלוֹ כְּרֹעַ מַעֲלָלוֹ וְאָרְבּוֹ.
לֹא תִמְשֹׁךְ אַפְּךָ עַל עַמְּךָ בְּדוֹר וָדוֹר בְּעָצְבּוֹ.
לֹא תִנְטְשֵׁהוּ וְתַזְנִיחֵהוּ כִּי גָדַל לִמְאֹד כְּאֵבוֹ.
לֹא תַסְגִּירֵהוּ לָעַד בְּיַד צָרוֹ וְאוֹיְבוֹ.
לֹא תַעֲזֹב אֶת נְוֵה קָדְשְׁךָ לְשִׁמְמוֹ וְחָרְבּוֹ.
לֹא תָפִיג אֶת שֵׁם קָדְשְׁךָ לְחַלְּלוֹ בְּיַד לוֹעֲבוֹ.
לֹא תַצְמִית וּתְבַיֵּשׁ מִסִּבְרְךָ יִשְׂרָאֵל עַם קְרוֹבוֹ.
לֹא תָקוּץ בְּשִׂיחִי בְּעָמְדִי לְפָנֶיךָ כְּעָנִי לָבוֹא.
לֹא תִרְחַק מֶנִּי, אֵלִי צוּרִי אֶחֱסֶה בּוֹ.
לֹא תִשְׁכַּח אֶת צָרוֹתַי אֲשֶׁר עָבְרוּ עָלַי
וְעֶלְבּוֹנִי מִי יַחְשְׁבוֹ!
לֹא תִתְעַלַּם מִתְּחִנָּתִי, וְאֶנְקָתִי אֵלֶיךָ תָבוֹא!

shall draw him near when he returns. You shall not chasten him in anger, but shall remedy his pain. You shall not destroy the wicked and rebellious when he turns from his course. You shall not oppress him and requite him for his evildoing and deceit. You shall not prolong Your anger with Your sorrowing people to all generations. You shall not forsake them or cast them off, for their suffering is very great. You shall not deliver them forever into the hands of their foes. You shall not abandon Your holy abode to desolation and ruin. You shall not enfeeble Your holy name, and let it be profaned by those who flout it. You shall not frustrate or put to shame the hope placed in You by the people of Israel, who are close to You. You shall not abhor my complaint when I come to stand before You like a pauper. You shall not be far from me, my God, my Rock, in whom I take refuge. You shall not forget the troubles that have swept over me, for who can measure my humiliation? You shall not hide Yourself when I beseech You: let my sighs come before You!

אֵבֶל וּבְכִי

אֵבֶל וּבְכִי
אֵין מוֹעִילִין לוֹ לְאָדָם בִּמְלֹאות סִפְקוֹ.
בְּזָהָב לֹא יִפָּדֶה וּבְכֶסֶף לֹא יִנָּצֵל מִיּוֹם הַדִּין.
בִּרְאוֹתוֹ שׁוֹדֵד לוֹבֵשׁ אַף וּמְכַסֶּה חֵמָה,
גַּם הוֹכִיחוֹ
עֲקֹב לִבּוֹ וּפֹעַל כַּפָּיו.
דְּמָעוֹת מוֹרִיד
בְּשָׁמְעוֹ תַּחְבּוּלוֹתָיו מִפִּי שׁוֹדְדוֹ.

DEATH THE PLUNDERER

Mourning and weeping do not avail a man when his measure is full. Gold cannot ransom him or silver save him from the Day of Judgement. He beholds the Plunderer clothed in anger, covered in wrath, rebuking him for his heart's deceit and the works of his hands. He weeps as he hears his treacherous acts from the mouth of the

הוּא מִתְחַנֵּן:
׳לְקַח־נָא כֹּפֶר וְאַל תַּשְׁחִיתֵנִי!׳
וּמֵשִׁיחַ לוֹ שׁוֹדֵד:
׳מַה לְּךָ לְשַׁטּוּת? מִי זֶה אָדָם שֶׁנִּפְדָּה בְּכֹפֶר?
זוֹ הִיא מִדָּה וְזֹאת הִיא דֶּרֶךְ
לְכָל בְּנֵי זֶרַע אָדָם, שֶׁלֹּא יִנָּצֵל מִן הַמִּיתָה.׳
חֲבָלִים מַשִּׂיגִין אוֹתוֹ,
צִירֵי מָוֶת מִפֹּה וּמִפֹּה.
טֶרֶם אָבָד,
וְנוֹתֵן בּוֹ עֵינָיו וּמַרְאִיתוֹ נֶהְפֶּכֶת.
יָדוֹ מוֹשִׁיט וְחוֹתֵם עַל כָּל מַה שֶּׁקּוֹרִין לְפָנָיו.
בְּגִשְׁתּוֹ אֵלָיו, יַעֲמֹד מְרַאֲשׁוֹתָיו.
כִּרְאוֹתוֹ חֶרֶב שְׁלוּפָה – כְּיֵדַע, זָע וּפוֹתֵחַ פִּיו.
לְתוֹךְ פִּיו מַשְׁלָךְ
טִפָּה מָרָה, שֶׁהִיא עֲצוּמָה מִכָּל מָר:
מִמֶּנָּה מֵת,
מִמֶּנָּה מַסְרִיחַ וּמִמֶּנָּה פָּנָיו מוֹרִיקוֹת.
נֶאֱנָחִים עָלָיו
אוֹהֲבָיו וּקְרוֹבָיו וְהוּא מֻשְׁלָךְ כְּאָבֶן.
סָאִין אוֹתוֹ עַל הַמִּטָּה
לְהוֹלִיכוֹ לַקֶּבֶר.
עִמּוֹ מִתְלַוִּין
שְׁנֵי מַלְאֲכֵי שָׁרֵת שֶׁמְּלַוִּין לוֹ בְּחַיָּיו.
פּוֹנִין הֵנָּה וָהֵנָּה,
מַקְשִׁיבִין מַה מְּשִׂיחִין אַחֲרֵי מִטָּתוֹ,
צִדְקוֹ וְכִזְבוֹ
כּוֹתְבִין וְחוֹתְמִין וּמַעֲלִין לְחֶשְׁבּוֹן.
קָרֵב לַקֶּבֶר –
רָעֲשׁוּ מָאתַיִם וְאַרְבָּעִים וּשְׁמוֹנָה אֵבָרָיו.

Plunderer. He begs him: 'Oh, take ransom and do not destroy me.' But the Plunderer replies: 'Don't be foolish. Has a man ever been redeemed by ransom? This is the rule and the road for all who are born of the seed of man: none may be saved from death.' Then the throes of death overtake him, the pangs of death beset him from all sides. About to perish, he fixes his gaze on the Plunderer, and his face changes. He reaches out and signs everything that is read to him. Then the Plunderer draws near and stands at the head of his bed. When he sees the drawn sword, he knows. Trembling, he opens his mouth. A drop of poison is thrust into his mouth, more bitter than any bitterness. From that drop he dies, from that he putrefies, from that his face turns green. His friends and kinsmen mourn over him as he lies there like a stone. He is carried on a bier and led to the grave. Two ministering angels – his escorts during his lifetime – now escort him to the grave. They turn here and there, listening to what is said around his bier. They note down his just deeds and his falsehoods, and affix their seal; this will be part of the final reckoning. As he approaches the grave, all the organs of his body[1]

1. Lit. 'his 248 organs', a conventional Talmudic phrase.

רַעַד וָפַחַד אוֹחֲזוּ
בְּהַסִּיעוּ מִן הַמִּטָּה לְהוֹרִידוֹ לַקָּבֶר.
שִׁכְּנוּהוּ בַקֶּבֶר וְהִשְׁלִיכוּ עָפָר עַל פָּנָיו.
שִׁבְעַת יָמִים קָשִׁין לַגּוּף יוֹתֵר מִן הַמִּיתָה.
תָּמְהוּ וְנֶחְפְּזוּ
כָּל טוֹמְנָיו וְחוֹזְרִין מֵאַחֲרָיו.

quiver. Terror and trembling seize him when he is removed from the bier to be lowered into the grave. They lodge him in the grave, throw dirt on his face. The seven days to come are more painful to the body than the moment of death. All those who buried him now shudder and run away from him.

זְכָר־זֹאת, אֱלוֹהַּ מָעֻזֵּנוּ,
וְהִתְנַהֵג עִמָּנוּ בְּמִדַּת רַחֲמִים.
אַתָּה רַחֲמָן, מָלֵא רַחֲמִים!

Remember this, God our Stronghold, and favour us with Your mercy. For You are merciful, Most Merciful One!

נִגַּשְׁנוּ לָדַעַת

LAMENT FOR ZION

נִגַּשְׁנוּ לָדַעַת אֶת שְׁלוֹם אִמֵּנוּ,
עָמַדְנוּ עַל פִּתְחָהּ וּבָכִינוּ.
מְצָאוּנוּ הַשּׁוֹמְרִים, הִכּוּנוּ, פְּצָעוּנוּ —
'סוּרוּ, טָמֵא!' קָרְאוּ לָנוּ.

We drew near to find out how our mother was faring. We stood at her door and wept. The watchmen found us, beat us, wounded us: 'Away, unclean ones!' they shouted.

אָתָאנוּ שֵׁנִית וְלֹא נִגָּשְׁנוּ,
וְעַל רֹאשׁ הָהָר מֵרָחוֹק עָמָדְנוּ.
יוֹשֶׁבֶת־בָּדָד יָצְאָה לִקְרָאתֵנוּ,
נִשְׁקְפָה מִכִּלְאָהּ וְעָמְדָה נֶגְדֵּנוּ.

Again we came but did not draw near; from afar, we stood at the top of the Mount [of Olives]. The solitary one[1] appeared before us; she looked out from her prison as she faced us.

נָשָׂאנוּ עֵינֵינוּ לִרְאוֹתָהּ
וְלֹא הִכַּרְנוּהָ מֵרֹעַ מַרְאִיתָהּ.
סָר תָּכְנִיתָהּ וְכָל תַּבְנִיתָהּ,
אֲסוּרָה בַכֶּבֶל וְהִכְבִּידוּ נְחֻשְׁתָּהּ.

We raised our eyes to see her but could not recognize her, so wasted did she look. She had lost her shape, her form was gone; she was bound in chains and weighed down by her fetters.

1. An epithet for the captive Zion, derived from Lamentations 1.1.

נָשָׂאנוּ קוֹלֵנוּ בִּבְכִיָּה
עַל חִלּוּל הַר הַמּוֹרִיָּה
וְעַל אִמֵּנוּ הָעֲנִיָּה,
כִּי לֹא נִשְׁאַר לָהּ מִחְיָה.

We raised our voices in lament for the desecration of Mount Moriah and for our poor mother, who had nothing left to sustain her.

צַעֲקָתֵנוּ עָלְתָה בְאָזְנָהּ,
אַף הִיא קוֹלָהּ נָתָנָה.
בָּכְתָה בְתַחֲנוּנִים וְנָשְׂאָה קִינָה:
׳הִנְנִי יוֹשֶׁבֶת כְּאַלְמָנָה.

Our cries reached her ears and she too wept aloud. She wept and implored and lamented: 'How like a widow am I!

בָּנַי הָלְכוּ בַשִּׁבְיָה
וּמִקְדָּשִׁי נִתַּן לִשְׁאִיָּה
וְנִשְׁאַרְתִּי עֵרֹם וְעֶרְיָה –
עַל אֵלֶּה אֲנִי בוֹכִיָּה.׳

'My children have gone into captivity, my sanctuary is laid waste, and I am left naked and bare – *for these things do I weep!*'[1]

אוֹר נֹגַהּ

THE SANCTIFICATION

אוֹר נֹגַהּ עֲטִיַּת מְעִילוֹ,
בָּרוּךְ שֵׁם כְּבוֹד גָּדְלוֹ,
גִּבּוֹר כֹּחַ וְשַׂגִּיא חֵילוֹ:
שְׂרָפִים עוֹמְדִים מִמַּעַל לוֹ.

He wraps Himself in a cloak of morning light. Blessed is the name of His great glory. His hosts are very mighty. *Seraphim stand above Him.*

דָּר בְּשִׁבְעָה וְהוּא בְאֶחָד:
הוּא לְבַדּוֹ בְּיִחוּד נִתְיַחָד,
וְעִמּוֹ צְבָא הַמְּשֵׁל וָפַחַד,
שֵׁשׁ כְּנָפַיִם שֵׁשׁ כְּנָפַיִם לְאֶחָד.

He dwells in the seven heavens, yet is one. No one but He is one. With Him are the legions of dominion and fear. *Each has six wings.*

1. Lamentations 1.16.

זָהֳרֵי שְׁבִיבֵי אוּר בִּפְנִינָיו,
חֶסֶד וֶאֱמֶת יְקַדְּמוּ פָנָיו,
טְכוּסֵי גַלְגַּל הֵם אוֹפַנָּיו,
בִּשְׁתַּיִם יְכַסֶּה פָנָיו.

Flames glow in his angels of pearl. Love and truth herald His coming. His ofanim[1] are arrayed like wheels. *With two he covers his face.*

יְקוֹד סוּפָה וָסַעַר מַעְגָּלָיו,
כְּלוּל עָנָן אֲבַק רַגְלָיו,
לַהֲטַת אֵשׁ בּוֹעֶרֶת גַּלְגִּלָּיו,
וּבִשְׁתַּיִם יְכַסֶּה רַגְלָיו.

Flaming storm and whirlwind are His paths. The crests of clouds are the dust at His feet. His wheels are blazing fire. *And with two he covers his feet.*

מַלְאָךְ בְּתֻפֵּי לַהַב מְתוֹפֵף,
נְגִינוֹת חֲדָשׁוֹת לְחַדֵּשׁ וּלְנוֹפֵף;
שִׂיחַ כַּנֶּשֶׁר יַשְׁמִיעַ וִיצַפְצֵף,
וּבִשְׁתַּיִם יְעוֹפֵף.

An angel beats fiery drums, waving new songs to Him, soars screaming like an eagle. *And with two he flies.*

עִמּוֹ כָּל מִינֵי זְמָר,
׳פֶּלְאִי׳ הוּא שְׁמוֹ, נֶאֱמַר;
צִלְצוּל קְדֻשָּׁתוֹ לַעֲנוֹת וְלוֹמַר:
וְקָרָא זֶה אֶל זֶה וְאָמַר.

Singing of every kind attends Him. It is written[2] that 'His name is a mystery'. To celebrate His sanctity in song, *one calls to the other and says –*

קוֹל יַשְׁמִיעוּ מֵאַרְבַּע תּוֹצָאוֹת,
רְבוּעִים וּמְרֻבָּעִים לְכָל יְצִיאוֹת;
שׁוֹאֲגִים בְּקוֹל צָבָא וָאוֹת:
׳קָדוֹשׁ קָדוֹשׁ קָדוֹשׁ יְיָ צְבָאוֹת׳.

Four-sided, facing in all directions, they cry out from the four quarters. Legions and standards roar: *Holy, holy, holy is the Lord of the hosts.*

תַּחַת וָמַעַל יָסְדָה יָדוֹ,
תּוֹלֶה תֵבֵל בִּזְרוֹעַ יָדוֹ,
תַּקִּיף, וְאֵין עוֹד מִלְּבַדּוֹ:
׳מְלֹא כָל הָאָרֶץ כְּבוֹדוֹ׳.

His hand founded earth and heaven. The universe hangs upon His mighty arm. The power is His, there is no other. *The whole earth is full of His glory!*

1. Angels attending the chariot. 2. Judges 13.18.

סְעַדְיָה גָאוֹן

Sa'adiah Gaon

גָּדַלְתָּ מְאֹד

YOU ARE GREAT INDEED!

גָּדַלְתָּ מְאֹד מִכָּל הַתּוֹכְנִים,
כִּי הֵמָּה יְתַכְּנוּ הַתַּחְתּוֹן וְעָלָיו יִבְנוּ הָעֶלְיוֹן –
וְאַתָּה תִכַּנְתָּ הַשָּׁמַיִם תְּחִלָּה וְתַחְתֵּימוֹ
רָקַעְתָּ הָאָרֶץ לְחֶבְיוֹן.
יְיָ אֱלֹהַי, גָּדַלְתָּ מְאֹד!

You are far greater than all architects: for they fix the lower, then erect the upper part above it; but You first fixed the heavens, then stretched the earth beneath them as a haven. *O Lord my God, You are great indeed!*

גָּדַלְתָּ מְאֹד מִכָּל הַשּׁוֹמְעִים,
כִּי כֻלָּם לֹא יָבִינוּ דִּבְרֵי שְׁנַיִם מְדַבְּרִים
כְּאֶחָד לְמוּלָם –
וְאַתָּה שׁוֹמֵעַ דִּבְרֵי כָּל קַצְוֵי אֶרֶץ וְאִיֵּי הַיָּם,
וְדָבָר מִמְּךָ לֹא נֶעֱלָם.
יְיָ אֱלֹהַי, גָּדַלְתָּ מְאֹד!

You are far greater than all those who have hearing: for they cannot grasp the words of two people who address them at the same time; but You hear what is said by all the ends of the earth, as well as the islands of the sea; nothing escapes You. *O Lord my God, You are great indeed!*

גָּדַלְתָּ מְאֹד מִכָּל הָרָמִים,
כִּי הֵמָּה רוֹמָם וְגָבְהָם יֵשׁ לְמַעְלָה מִמֶּנּוּ
רוּם וָגֹבַהּ –
וְאַתָּה רָם עַל כָּל רָמִים, וְאֵין רוּם לְפָנֶיךָ לְכָל גֹּבַהּ.
יְיָ אֱלֹהַי, גָּדַלְתָּ מְאֹד!

You are far greater than all the lofty ones: for though they are lofty and high, yet is there loftiness and height beyond them; but You are the highest of the high; no loftiness is high to You. *O Lord my God, You are great indeed!*

גָּדַלְתָּ מְאֹד מִכָּל הַקּוֹבְעִים מַחַן,
כִּי כֻלָּם בָּאָרֶץ יִקְבְּעוּן, וּבְהָרֵי תוֹעָפוֹת –
וְאַתָּה קָבַעְתָּ בָּאֲוִיר מַחַן לְכָל עֵיט צִפּוֹר וְלָעוֹפוֹת.
יְיָ אֱלֹהַי, גָּדַלְתָּ מְאֹד!

You are far greater than all those who set up encampments: for they set them up on the earth, even on steep mountains; but You made the birds of prey and winged creatures encamp in the air. *O Lord my God, You are great indeed!*

גָּדַלְתָּ מְאֹד מִכָּל הַצַּיָּרִים,
כִּי הֵמָּה יָצוּרוּ בָאוֹר וּבְפַלְדּוֹת אוּרִים –

You are far greater than all artists: for they can only make forms by the light of day or fire; but You form all life

וְאַתָּה צַרְתָּ אֶת כָּל הַחַיִּים בְּמֵעַיִם וּבִסְתָרִים
וּבְחַדְרֵי חֲדָרִים.
יְיָ אֱלֹהַי, גָּדַלְתָּ מְאֹד! [...]

within the entrails, in the hidden recesses and innermost chambers.
O Lord my God, You are great indeed!

שְׁמוּאֵל הַשְּׁלִישִׁי

Samuel Hashelishi

שָׁאַפְנוּ צֵל

THE MESSAGE

שָׁאַפְנוּ צֵל מְקַוִּים לְיִשְׁעָךְ,
כְּשָׂכִיר פָּעֳלוֹ יְקַוֶּה.
מְצַפֶּה הֶעֱמַדְנוּ,
אֲשֶׁר יִרְאֶה — יַגִּיד, יְחַוֶּה.
וַנְּיַחֲלָה לְהִתְבַּשֵּׂר: 'בָּא גוֹאֵל
כְּמַסְתִּיר פָּנָיו בַּמַּסְוֶה.'
אָמוֹר אָמַר: 'שׁוּבוּ אֵתָיוּ,
וְאִם אַיִן — בְּעִתּוֹ יִנְוֶה.'
לִבֵּנוּ אֲזַי נִשְׁבָּר
וְכָל הַדָּוֶה — עַל כָּךְ יִדְוֶה.

We longed for Your salvation as one sighs for the shade, as a servant pines for his wages. We posted a lookout who would report whatever he saw. We hoped to hear good tidings: 'The redeemer has come! He is like the one who covered his face with a veil![1]' But the lookout said: 'Come back again; and if he is not yet here, he will appear in due time.' Then our hearts broke. All those who grieve – it is this that they grieve for.

דַּכָּא תָּשֵׁב אֱנוֹשׁ

RESURRECTION

דַּכָּא תָּשֵׁב אֱנוֹשׁ וְתָשׁוּב תָּחֹן וְתַחֲנֹן.
גְּרָמִים תְּדַבֵּק, גִּידִים תִּמְתַּח, וְגָנוֹן תִּגְנֹן,
בָּשָׂר תַּעֲלֶה, וְהָעוֹר תַּקְרִים בְּנוֹן יִנּוֹן.
אֲהוּבְךָ יִפְרַח כַּשּׁוֹשַׁנָּה, יַךְ שָׁרָשָׁיו כַּלְּבָנוֹן.

You turn man back into dust, but You will turn to him again with compassion. You will join his bones, stretch his sinews and protect him. You will put flesh upon him, cover him with skin – when the Messiah comes. Then Your loved one will blossom like the lily, and strike root like the poplar.

1. I.e. Moses; Exodus 34.33 ff.

אִישׁ מְשׁוֹרֵר

אִישׁ מְשׁוֹרֵר,
שַׁחַר מְעוֹרֵר,
צֶדֶק בּוֹרֵר
וּתְמִימוּת;
בְּבוֹא קִצּוֹ
פְּנוֹת לְרִבְצוֹ,
הֵיטִיב יָעֲצוֹ
בִּנְאִימוּת;
גִּלָּה חֶפְצוֹ
וְחִזֵּק נִצּוֹ
הֱיוֹת בְּמַעֲרִיצוֹ
עָמוּת.
׳וַיִּקְרְבוּ יְמֵי דָוִד לָמוּת׳ [...]

DAVID'S LAST WORDS TO SOLOMON

On his last day, about to go to his resting place, the singer who awoke the dawn with song, who cherished justice and righteousness, raised his voice to give good counsel. He disclosed his heart's desire and urged his offshoot to cling to his dread God. *Then the time of David's death drew near.*

׳יְרָא בְּרַעַד
מְשׁוֹכֵן עַד,
הַמְכוֹנֵן מִצְעַד
גָּבֶר.
כָּל דְּבָרַי אֵלֶּה
נְצֹר וּמַלֵּא,
וְכַנְּשָׁרִים תַּעֲלֶה
אֵבֶר.
לְדַכָּא מְיַחֶלֶת
הַלְאֵט מְנַהֶלֶת,
וְתִמְצָא תּוֹחֶלֶת
וָסֵבֶר.׳
׳לְמַעַן יָקִים יְיָ אֶת דְּבָרוֹ אֲשֶׁר דִּבֶּר׳ [...]

'Fear and tremble before the Dweller of Eternity, who orders the steps of man. If you heed all my words, you will grow wings like an eagle. The Daughter of Zion is contrite, filled with longing; lead her gently, so that she may find hope and cheer' *so that the Lord may fulfil the promise that He made.*

תַּצְמִיחַ חָטְרוֹ
וְתָחֹק מִשְׁטָרוֹ
וְנֵזֶר תְּעַטְּרוֹ
בְּמֵישָׁרִים.
תְּהַדֵּר מוֹשָׁבוֹ
וּבֶטַח תּוֹשִׁיבוֹ
וְיִמְסֹךְ מַשְׁאַבּוֹ
לַיְשָׁרִים.
תִּזְכֹּר לְשַׁכּוּלָה
אַהֲבַת כְּלוּלָה
וְתַעְדֶּה כַּכַּלָּה
קִשּׁוּרִים.
תּוֹצִיא בַּכְּשָׁרוֹת
בַּכּוֹשָׁרוֹת,
וִיקַדְּמוּךְ שָׁרוֹת
וְשָׁרִים.

Oh spread David's branch, impose his rule, and crown him with his rightful diadem. Glorify his throne, make him sit securely. Let him water the righteous from his wellspring. The Daughter of Zion is bereaved; remember the love of her bridal days, and let her adorn herself with ribbons like a bride. When the time has come, bring out the prisoner safe and sound. Then will men and women, singing, welcome You.

יִפָּתְחוּ קִבְרוֹת מְתֵי מִסְפָּר

PRAYER FOR RESURRECTION

יִפָּתְחוּ קִבְרוֹת מְתֵי מִסְפָּר,
יְגֻלֶּה מֵעֵינֵיהֶם עָפָר.
זָב גּוּפָם וְנִתְעַפָּר,
זָעַךְ עַצְמָם וּפֻרְפָּר.
כִּלְאָם – עַד אָנָה יוּפַר?
כֵּהָיָם – מָתַי יְצֻפָּר?
הַעִירֵם בְּקוֹל שׁוֹפָר,
הֵן בְּהָקִצָם שִׁבְחֲךָ יְסֻפָּר.
'וִידַעְתֶּם כִּי אֲנִי יְיָ בְּפִתְחִי אֶת קִבְרוֹתֵיכֶם.'

Let the graves of the few[1] be opened; let the dust be removed from upon their eyes. Their bodies have wasted away in the dust; their bones have been crushed and battered. When will their prison crumble? When will their darkness turn to dawn? Arouse them with a trumpet blast; for when they awaken, Your glory will be told. '*You shall know that I am the Lord when I open your graves.*'

1. The children of Israel.

יְחֶזְקֵאל הַכֹּהֵן

Ezekiel Hakohen

אָמַרְתִּי לָאֲבָנִים

I SAID TO THE STONES

אָמַרְתִּי לָאֲבָנִים בְּשִׁגָּיוֹן גָּלוּי, לֹא לָחוּשׁ:
'הָבוּ לִי מִכֹּחֲכֶם, אוּלַי אוּכַל לָחוּשׁ,
כִּי יְגוֹנִים כִּלּוּנִי וַיְשִׂימוּנִי כָּחוּשׁ –
אִם כֹּחַ אֲבָנִים כֹּחִי, אִם בְּשָׂרִי נָחוּשׁ?'

I said to the stones distinctly, not in a whisper: 'Give me of your strength, so that I may feel again; for griefs have consumed me and made me lean. *Is my strength the strength of stones? Is my flesh made of bronze?'*

אָמַרְתִּי לְגִבְהֵי נֶשֶׁר הַדָּאִים לְכָל פִּנָּה:
'הַדְאוּנִי עִמָּכֶם וְאֶרְאֶה דּוֹדִי אָנָה פָּנָה,
כִּי חוֹלַת אַהֲבָה אָנִי וְנַפְשִׁי מְסֻכָּנָה –
מִי יִתֶּן לִי אֵבֶר כַּיּוֹנָה, אָעוּפָה וְאֶשְׁכֹּנָה!'

I said to the loftiest eagles, who soar in all directions: 'Lift me with you in flight, so that I may see where my Beloved is gone; for I am faint with love, and my soul is in agony. *If only I had the wings of a dove, to fly away and find rest!'*

אָמַרְתִּי לְהַרְרֵי בְשָׂמִים, מְקוֹם דִּלּוּג הָעֹפֶר:
'הִוָּסְרוּ וְאַל תִּתְגָּאוּ בַּאֲשֶׁר מִכֶּם הַמֹּר וְהַכֹּפֶר,
כִּי זְרוֹעוֹתַי נָטְפוּ מֹר בְּדוֹד הֶחָסֹן וְהַשָּׁפֶר –
וַיַּגְרֵס בֶּחָצָץ שִׁנַּי, הִכְפִּישַׁנִי בָּאֵפֶר.'

I said to the spice-bearing mountains, where the fawn leaps: 'Take heed; do not be proud that you are favoured with myrrh and henna. My arms too once dripped with myrrh for my strong and graceful lover, *but he broke my teeth on gravel, and trampled me in ashes.'*

אָמַרְתִּי לְזִרְמֵי עָבוֹת אֲשֶׁר צִיָּה מְמוֹגְגוֹת:
'הָחִישׁוּ וּרְאוּ אֵיךְ עֵינַי מַזְלִיגוֹת,
כִּי קָדַח בָּרָק בָּבוֹתַי, לְבָבִי שָׂם כִּפְלַגּוֹת –
עֵינִי נִגְּרָה, וְלֹא תִדְמֶה, מֵאֵין הֲפֻגוֹת.'

I said to the flowing clouds that soften deserts: 'Come quickly, see how my eyes are streaming; for lightning has seared my eyeballs, and split my heart into runnels of water. *My eyes flow unceasingly, without respite.'*

אָמַרְתִּי לְטַרְפֵּי אִילָנוֹת וָאַשְׁבִּיעֵם בְּאֵלִי:
'הֱיוּ סֵתֶר לִי פֶּן הַחֶרֶב יְשַׁכְּלִי,
כִּי אָהֳלִי שֻׁדַּד וְנֶהֱרַס הֵיכָלִי –
בָּנַי יְצָאֻנִי וְאֵינָם, אֵין נֹטֶה עוֹד אָהֳלִי.'

I said to the leaves of the trees, I adjured them by my God: 'Be my refuge, lest the sword destroy me; for my tent[1] is despoiled, my temple in ruins. *My sons have left me and are gone; there is none to pitch my tent again.'*

1. The land of Israel.

אָמַרְתִּי לַכְּפִירִים וּלְכָל בְּנֵי לָבִיא :
׳הַלְווּנִי מִכֹּחֲכֶם אוּלַי אֲכַלְכֵּל כְּאֵבִי,
כִּי לִבִּי נָמַס בְּקִרְבִּי, לֹא יִשָּׂא עָצְבִּי —
כִּי עָנִי וְאֶבְיוֹן אָנֹכִי וְלִבִּי חָלַל בְּקִרְבִּי.׳

I said to the lions and to all their young: 'Lend me your prowess, so that I may endure my pain; for my heart is melted within me, and cannot bear my anguish. *I am downtrodden and poor; my heart is sorely tormented.*'

אָמַרְתִּי לִמְלוֹנֵי מִדְבָּר וּמִקְלְטֵי בוֹרְחִים :
׳הַנְווּנִי בַּלֵּילוֹת מִקֹּרֵי קְרָחִים,
כִּי הָיִיתִי כִּצְבִי מֻדָּח מִפְּנֵי אֹחִים —
מִי יִתְּנֵנִי בַמִּדְבָּר מְלוֹן אֹרְחִים.׳

I said to the desert havens and places of refuge: 'Shelter me at night from the freezing cold; for I am like a gazelle pursued by howling beasts. *If only I could find a haven in the desert!*'

אָמַרְתִּי לִסְפִינוֹת הַיָּם בִּנְהִי וּמַאֲמָר מָר :
׳הַעֲבִירוּנִי עִמָּכֶם וַאֲבַקֵּשׁ צֳרִי לִבְשָׂרִי הַנִּסְמָר,
כִּי כְסָלַי מָלְאוּ נִקְלֶה, עַל כֵּן אֶזְעַק כְּתוֹא מִכְמָר —
הֲיָם אָנִי, אִם תַּנִּין, כִּי תָשִׂים עָלַי מִשְׁמָר?׳

I said to the sailing ships, crying out bitterly: 'Take me with you to seek a balm for my bristling flesh; for my loins burn with fever, and I shriek like an antelope trapped in a net. *Am I the sea or the Serpent, that you build barriers around me?*'

אָמַרְתִּי לִפְלִיאֵי הַדּוֹר הַמְרַשְּׁלִים אֶזְרוֹעִי :
׳הָצִינוּ וְהַרְאוּנִי הַדֶּרֶךְ אֲשֶׁר בָּהּ נָסַע דּוֹדִי וְרֵעִי,
כִּי הָרִים סִבְּכוּנִי וָאֶשְׁכַּח אָרְחִי וְרִבְעִי —
דּוֹדִי נִסַּע וְנִגְלָה מִנִּי כְּאֹהֶל רֹעִי.׳

I said to the illustrious men of my generation, who have crushed my spirit:[1] 'Set up sign-posts; show me the path that my Beloved, my Darling, has taken; for I am bewildered by mountains, and have forgotten my journey and my resting place. *My home has been taken from me, pulled up like a shepherd's tent.*'

אָמַרְתִּי לַקּוֹנְנוֹת בַּשַּׁחַר לְהַשְׁכִּים :
׳הַרְבֶּינָה עָלַי נְהִי כְּיוֹנֵי חֲרַכִּים,
כִּי נִכְסָף אֲנִי לְקוֹלְכֶן וְאֶל נְהִיכֶן אַסְכִּים —
וַיְהִי לְאֵבֶל כִּנֹּרִי וְעֻגָבִי לְקוֹל בֹּכִים.׳

I said to the wailing-women who rise at dawn: 'Raise a long lament for me, like doves moaning in a lattice. I long to hear your voices, to join in your lament. *My harp is tuned to a dirge, my flute to the voice of those who weep.*'

1. Lit. 'who weaken my arm'. The meaning is not clear.

אָמַרְתִּי לְשׁוֹמְרֵי פֶּתַח אֵל מַצִּיל וּפוֹדֶה:
'הִתְעַשְּׁתוּ לִפְדוּתִי מִפֶּתַח צוֹדֶה,
כִּי תוֹעֲבוֹתַי וּפְשָׁעַי בָּאתִי לְהִתְוַדֵּה —
פִּתְחוּ לִי שַׁעֲרֵי צֶדֶק אָבֹא בָם אוֹדֶה!'

I said to the door-keepers of God the Saviour: 'Devise a way to free me from the evil at my door; for I have come to confess my abominations and my crimes. *Open to me the gates of righteousness; I will enter through them and praise Him.*'

יוֹסֵף אַלְבַּרְדָּאנִי

Joseph Albardani

אָמְנָם שָׁלוֹשׁ כִּתּוֹת

THE THREE FACTIONS

אָמְנָם שָׁלוֹשׁ כִּתּוֹת נֶחְלְקוּ עַמּוֹ
בְּצֵאתָם מִמִּצְרַיִם וּרְדָפָם פַּרְעֹה בְּעַצְמוֹ.
גַּלֵּי יָם כְּחִפָּה צִבְאוֹתֵיהֶם, שׁוֹרְרוּ לִשְׁמוֹ:
'יהוה אִישׁ מִלְחָמָה יהוה שְׁמוֹ.'

As they were leaving Egypt, pursued by Pharaoh himself, His people divided into three factions. But when the waves of the sea engulfed Egypt's armies, they all sang to His name: '*The Lord, the warrior – Lord is His name!*'

כִּתָּה רִאשׁוֹנָה דִּבְּרָה: 'נִטְבַּע בְּמֵי זֵידוֹנַי',
הִגִּידָה: 'כִּי רַבִּים רַחֲמָיו, נִפְּלָה נָּא בְּיַד יְיָ.'
וְאָמַר לָהֶם מֹשֶׁה עֶבֶד יְיָ:
'הִתְיַצְּבוּ וּרְאוּ אֶת יְשׁוּעַת יְיָ.'

The first faction spoke up: 'Let us drown in the seething waters.' They insisted: 'Let us fall into the hands of the Lord, for His mercy is great.' But Moses, the servant of the Lord, replied: '*Stand firm and see the Lord's deliverance.*'

כִּתָּה שְׁנִיָּה זָמְמָה לַחֲזוֹר לְמִצְרַיִם וּלְשִׁעְבּוּדָם וְעֻלָּם.
חַי הֱשִׁיבָם: 'אֲנִי תַּחְתֵּיכֶם אַשְׁפִּילָם'.
טָהוֹר נָם לָהֶם: 'זֹאת קָשָׁה מִכֻּלָּם,
כִּי אֲשֶׁר רְאִיתֶם אֶת מִצְרַיִם הַיּוֹם
לֹא תֹסִפוּ לִרְאֹתָם עוֹד עַד עוֹלָם.'

The second faction wanted them to go back to Egypt, back to servitude and the yoke. To them the Eternal spoke: 'I shall strike down the Egyptians before you.' And Moses, the pure one, said to them: 'What you wish is worst of all; *but as sure as you see the Egyptians now, you will never see them again.*'

כִּתָּה שְׁלִישִׁית יָזְמָה: 'נַעֲשֶׂה מִלְחָמָה בַּיָּם וְיֵבוֹשׁוּן,
כֻּלָּם עַל צַוְּארֵיהֶם דְּגָלֵינוּ יִרְגָּשׁוּן.'
לָהֶם הֵשִׁיב עָנָו: 'נִפְלְאוֹת אֵל תַּרְחִישׁוּן,
יהוה יִלָּחֵם לָכֶם וְאַתֶּם תַּחֲרִשׁוּן.'

The third faction proposed: 'Let us give battle in the sea and abase them; our standards will rage above their necks!' To them the humble Moses said: 'Rather extol God's wonders; *the Lord will fight for you; so you hold your peace!*'

שָׁלוֹשׁ כִּתּוֹת נֶחְלְקָה אֲיֻמָּה.
אַחַת נָמָה: ׳נִתְּנָה רֹאשׁ וְנָשׁוּבָה מִצְרָיְמָה.׳
וְאַחַת נָמָה: ׳נִטְבַּע בְּתוֹךְ הַיָּמָּה.׳
וְאַחַת נָמָה: ׳נַעֲשֶׂה בָּם מִלְחָמָה.׳
הֵשִׁיב עָנָו בְּשָׂפָה נְעִימָה:
׳יְמִין יהוה רוֹמֵמָה.׳

Thus did the noble people split up into three factions, the one saying: 'Let us head back for Egypt'; the other: 'Let us drown in the sea'; and the last: 'Let us give them battle'. To all of which the humble one joyfully replied: '*The right hand of the Lord raises up!*'

מֹשֶׁה בַּר־קָלוֹנִימוֹס

Moses ben Kalonymus

אָז פָּתַח אוֹצְרוֹת

[...] אָז פָּתַח אוֹצְרוֹת גִּנְזֵי מַטְמוֹנִים,
אֲשֶׁר גָּנַז הוּא וּמְלָכִים קַדְמוֹנִים,
וְהוֹצִיא כְּלֵי יְקָר וְדַרְכְּמוֹנִים
וְחִלֵּק לְכָל אֶחָד וְאֶחָד כְּפִי הֲגוּנִים
וְשִׁדְּלָם בִּדְבָרִים וְהִסְבִּיר לָמוֹ פָּנִים.
וְכֹה אָמַר לָהֶם בְּשִׂיחַ מַעֲנִים:
׳מִשְׁפַּט הַמֶּלֶךְ – כָּל הָעָם בּוֹזְזִים וּלְפָנָיו נוֹתְנִים,
וַאֲנִי כְּאֶחָד מִכֶּם אֶטֹּל מָנִים;
מִשְׁפַּט הַמֶּלֶךְ – עֲבָדָיו יוֹצְאִים רִאשׁוֹנִים,
וַאֲנִי אֵצֵא רִאשׁוֹן וְאַתֶּם צְאוּ אַחֲרוֹנִים;
מִשְׁפַּט הַמֶּלֶךְ – עֲבָדָיו אוֹסְרִים
מֶרְכַּבְתּוֹ וּמְתַקְּנִים,
וַאֲנִי בְּעַצְמִי אֶאְסֹר רִכְבִּי וְאָשִׂים רְסָנִים!׳

וְנִתְרַצּוּ יַחַד גְּדוֹלִים וּקְטַנִּים
וַיָּשִׂימוּ כּוֹבַע עַל רָאשֵׁיהֶם וְלָבְשׁוּ שִׁרְיוֹנִים
וַיַּחְגְּרוּ אִישׁ חַרְבּוֹ וְנָטְלוּ כִידוֹנִים

PHARAOH PURSUES THE ISRAELITES

Then he opened the hoards of hidden treasures which he and kings of old had stored away. He brought out precious vessels and gold Darics and presented them to his chieftains, to each according to his rank. He enticed them with words, with a show of kindness, and appealed to them thus: 'It is the royal custom that all the people yield their plunder to the king; but I shall share with you on equal terms. It is the royal custom that subjects go first into battle; but I shall go first and you will follow me. It is the royal custom that subjects harness the king's chariot and make it ready; but I shall harness my chariot and secure the reins with my own hands.'

Then all of them, the lowly and the high alike, assented. They put helmets on their heads, arrayed themselves in armour, girt on their swords, seized

וַיִּקְחוּ אִישׁ רֹמַח בְּיָדוֹ וַיַּחֲזִיקוּ מָגִנִּים
וְנָשְׂאוּ קֶשֶׁת וּמִלְאוּ שִׁלְטֵיהֶם חִצִּים שְׁנוּנִים,
וְהַקַּלָּעִים, אִישׁ קַלְעוֹ בְּיָדוֹ, לְקַלַּע בָּאֲבָנִים.
וַיֵּצְאוּ יַחַד בְּלֵב שָׁלֵם וּבִצְבְיוֹנִים,
וְלֹא נִכְשַׁל אֶחָד מֵהֶם וְלֹא אֶרְעוּהוּ סִימָנִים,
לְבִלְתִּי לְנַחֵשׁ לָשׁוּב לִמְלוֹנִים –
כִּי חֻקּוֹת הָעַמִּים מְנַחֲשִׁים וּמְעוֹנְנִים.

their javelins, gripped their lances, equipped themselves with shields. They took their bows, filled their quivers with keen arrows, and the slingers held their slings ready to cast stones. Thus did they set forth together, eagerly and wholeheartedly. None met with any accident, none was beset by evil omens, lest they turn back because of some foreboding (for the heathen resort to augurs and to soothsayers).

וְאִישׁ יִשְׂרָאֵל עַל שְׂפַת יָם חוֹנִים.
וַיִּשְׂאוּ עֵינֵיהֶם וְהִנֵּה מִצְרַיִם נוֹסְעִים כַּעֲנָנִים
וְאֵין מָקוֹם לָנוּס, לֹא לְאָחוֹר וְלֹא לְפָנִים,
וְאַף לֹא מִדְּפָנוֹת מִפְּנֵי חַיּוֹת וּפְתָנִים –
וַיִּצְעֲקוּ אֶל יְיָ וְהִפִּילוּ לְפָנָיו תַּחֲנוּנִים.
וַיִּמָּצֵא לָהֶם הַמָּצוּי בְּכָל עִדָּנִים
וַיִּגְעַר בְּיַם סוּף וְחָרְבוּ זֵידוֹנִים,
וַיֵּלְכוּ בַתְּהוֹמוֹת כְּעַל דְּרָכִים מְפֻנִּים.
מִזֶּה וּמִזֶּה הֶעֱלָה אִילָנוֹת טְעוּנִים
וּבְתוֹךְ תְּהוֹמוֹת הִמְתִּיק לָמוֹ מַעְיָנִים
וְעִשֵּׁן לִפְנֵיהֶם קְטֹרֶת סַמְמָנִים
וַיַּנְחֵם אֶל מְחוֹז חֶפְצָם שַׁאֲנַנִּים. [...]

The Israelites were encamped on the sea-shore. When they looked up, they saw the Egyptians advancing like clouds. There was nowhere to flee, neither in front nor in back nor to the sides, which were blocked by vipers and wild beasts. They cried out to the Lord, appealing to Him; and He, who is ever-present, presented Himself to them. He rebuked the Red Sea, and the seething waters dried up. Then they walked through the deeps as through cleared paths. On either side He raised up trees laden with fruit; within the deeps He made sweet fountains flow. He perfumed their way with clouds of incense; and He led them, safe and serene, to their destination.

וְהִנֵּה כְּבוֹד יְיָ אֱלֹהֵי יִשְׂרָאֵל בָּא בְּרֹב לִגְיוֹנִים.
וַיִּרְכַּב עַל כְּרוּב וַיֵּדֶא מוּל בַּעֲלֵי מְדָנִים
וְעִמּוֹ שַׂרְפֵי הַקֹּדֶשׁ וְחַיּוֹת וְאוֹפַנִּים
וְאֶלֶף אַלְפִין וְרִבּוֹ רִבְוָן גְּדוּדֵי שִׁנְאַנִּים
וְרֶכֶב אֵשׁ וְסוּסֵי אֵשׁ וְכָל דִּמְיוֹנִים,
כַּמַּרְאֶה אֲשֶׁר רָאָה צִיר בְּחֶזְיוֹנִים:
סוּסִים אֲדֻמִּים וְסוּסִים שְׁחֹרִים, שְׂרֻקִּים וּלְבָנִים.

And the glory of the Lord God of Israel appeared among a multitude of legions. Riding on a cherub, He swooped down upon the men of strife. In His company were the seraphim, the holy creatures, the ofanim,[1] and thousands upon thousands, myriads upon myriads of angelic troops, with fiery chariots, fiery horses, and all the other apparitions which the prophet[2] beheld in his ecstatic vision: red horses

1. A class of chariot-angels. 2. Zechariah; see 1.8.

וַיַּחֲנוּ אֵלֶּה נֹכַח אֵלֶּה אֲפוּנִים:
מַחֲנֵה אֵשׁ מוּל מַחֲנֵה קַשׁ פָּנִים בְּפָנִים. [...]

and black, sorrel and white. Thus they camped opposite each other, wheels ready to roll, face to face: an army of fire and an army of straw.

וְאָז שַׂר יָם עִם שַׂר חָם יַחַד נִדּוֹנִים:
זֶה לְעֻמַּת זֶה נֶאֶבְקוּ בִּמְעוֹנִים.
וַיֶּחֱזַק רַהַב עַל שַׂר אֲוֵינִים
וַיַּשְׁלִיכֵהוּ אַרְצָה וַיִּרְמְסֵהוּ בְּעֶזְרַת דָּר אוֹפַנִּים.
וְעַם וּו בְּשׁוּרָם בְּאֵלֶּה דִינִים,
עוֹזֵר וְעָזוּר בְּקַו נִדּוֹנִים,
פָּתְחוּ פִיהֶם בְּשִׁיר וּבִרְנָנִים:
'עָזִּי וְזִמְרָת יָהּ!' פָּצְחוּ בְרִנּוּנִים,
לְרָם עַל רָמִים וּמִתְגָּאֶה עַל גֵּיוֹתָנִים,
לְשׁוֹמֵעַ אֶנְקַת אֶבְיוֹנִים,
לְמַשְׁפִּיל רָמִים וּמֵרִים מִסְכֵּנִים.
וְקִדְּמוּ שָׁרִים אַחַר נוֹגְנִים
וּבְתוֹךְ עֲלָמוֹת תּוֹפֵפוּ נִגּוּנִים.
וְאַחַר כָּךְ הֻרְשׁוּ שִׁנְאַנִּים.

Then the Prince of the Sea and the Prince of Egypt[1] came to grips, struggling with each other in the heavens. Rahav, the Prince of the Sea, with the help of the Chariot-Dweller, overpowered the Prince of the Egyptians, hurled him down to earth and trampled him. And when the Israelites witnessed these judgements, how the protector and those he protected met their doom, they shouted and sang songs of praise. 'The Lord is my refuge and my defence,' they chanted, in honour of the highest of the high, who rules over the proud, who heeds the groans of the needy, who brings down the haughty and raises up the poor. The singers went first, then came the musicians, and among them maidens playing timbrels. Only afterwards were the angels permitted to sing.

שִׁמְעוֹן בַּר־יִצְחָק

Simeon ben Isaac

אֱוִילִי הַמַּתְעֶה

AGAINST THE EVIL INCLINATION

אֱוִילִי הַמַּתְעֶה, מַרְגִּיז וּמַחֲטִיא –
בַּלְּעֵהוּ, קַלְּעֵהוּ וְעוֹד בַּל יַסְטִיא.
גִּעוּל הַמְגָאֵל וּמְטַנֵּף טְהוֹרִים –

This fool who tricks and provokes and seduces to sin – destroy him, cast him away, so that he may no more mislead us! This abomination that defiles and

1. The tutelary angel of the Egyptians.

דְּחֵהוּ, מְחֵהוּ מִלְּבּוֹת וְהַרְהוֹרִים.
הוֹתַל הַמְהַתֵּל וּמְפַתֵּל יְשָׁרִים –
וַכְּחֵהוּ, שַׁכְּחֵהוּ וְלֹא יַשֶּׁה אֲשׁוּרִים.
זְבוּב הַמְאָרֵב בְּמִפְתְּחֵי הַלֵּב –
חַנְּקֵהוּ, נַקֵּהוּ, וְלֵב חָדָשׁ תְּלַבְלֵב. [...]

befouls the pure – repulse it, erase it from heart and mind. This dupe who deludes and perverts the righteous – punish him, obliterate him, so that he may not lead us astray. This fly that lurks in the doorway of the heart – strangle it, blot it out, and make a new heart blossom forth!

מֶלֶךְ עֶלְיוֹן

THE TWO KINGS

ובכן נמליכך, מלך.

Let us declare Your dominion, O King!

מֶלֶךְ עֶלְיוֹן :
אַמִּיץ הַמְנֻשָּׂא, לְכֹל לְרֹאשׁ מִתְנַשֵּׂא,
אוֹמֵר וְעוֹשֶׂה, מָעוֹז וּמַחְסֶה,
נִשָּׂא וְנוֹשֵׂא, מוֹשִׁיב מְלָכִים לַכִּסֵּא –
לַעֲדֵי־עַד יִמְלֹךְ.

Supreme King: mighty, exalted, raised over all; ordaining, fulfilling; refuge and stronghold; lofty, bearing the world aloft; setting kings on their thrones – He shall reign for ever!

מֶלֶךְ אֶבְיוֹן :
בָּזוּי וּמְשֻׁסֶּה, פְּשָׁעָיו מְכַסֶּה,
בָּהוּל וּמִתְשֶׁה, עָווֹן פּוֹשֶׂה,
נִבְחָן בְּכָל מַעֲשֶׂה, וְאוֹצָרוֹ יְשֻׁסֶּה –
וְאֵיךְ יִמְלֹךְ ? [...]

Abject king: vile, despoiled; concealing his crimes; frantic, enfeebled, spread in sin; tested at every step, his treasure doomed to plunder – how shall he reign?

מֶלֶךְ עֶלְיוֹן :
טָהוֹר בִּזְבוּלָיו, אוֹת הוּא בְּאֶרְאֶלָּיו,
אֵין עֲרֹךְ אֵלָיו, לִפְעֹל כְּמִפְעָלָיו,
חוֹל שָׂם גְּבוּלָיו כַּהֲמוֹת יָם לְגַלָּיו –
לַעֲדֵי־עַד יִמְלֹךְ.

Supreme King: pure in His dwelling; eminent among his legions; none can compare with Him, none match His works; He bounded the sea with sand, even as its waves roared – He shall reign for ever!

מֶלֶךְ אֶבְיוֹן :
יָהִיר בְּזָדוֹן, מְגָרֶה מָדוֹן,
בְּחַיָּיו נִדּוֹן, בְּמוֹתוֹ לַאֲבַדּוֹן,
רוּחוֹ יָדוֹן וְיֵדַע שַׁדּוּן —
וְאֵיךְ יִמְלֹךְ ? [. . .]

Abject king: haughty, wilful, stirring up discord; alive – he is judged, dead – the pit awaits him; his spirit lives on to know that there is a judgement – how shall he reign?

מֶלֶךְ עֶלְיוֹן :
שׁוֹמֵעַ אֶל אֶבְיוֹנִים וּמַאֲזִין חִנּוּנִים,
מַאֲרִיךְ רְצוֹנִים וּמְקַצֵּר חֲרוֹנִים,
רִאשׁוֹן לָרִאשׁוֹנִים וְאַחֲרוֹן לָאַחֲרוֹנִים —
לַעֲדֵי־עַד יִמְלֹךְ.

Supreme King: He listens to the poor, heeds their pleading; prolongs His favour, curtails His wrath; first of the first, last of the last – He shall reign for ever!

מֶלֶךְ אֶבְיוֹן :
תּוֹחַלְתּוֹ נִכְזָבָה, תִּקְוָתוֹ נֶעֱלָבָה,
גְּוִיָּתוֹ נִרְקָבָה, נִשְׁמָתוֹ נִכְאָבָה,
נִשְׁבָּר וְנִשְׁבָּה מִלַּהַט הַיּוֹם הַבָּא —
וְאֵיךְ יִמְלֹךְ ?

Abject king: his hopes are empty, his wishes put to shame; his body rots, his soul is in pain; he is broken and captive, dreading the flames of the day that will come – how shall he reign?

אֲבָל מֶלֶךְ עֶלְיוֹן :
שׁוֹפֵט הָאֱמֶת, מַעְבָּדָיו אֱמֶת,
עוֹשֶׂה חֶסֶד וֶאֱמֶת וְרַב־חֶסֶד וֶאֱמֶת,
נְתִיבָתוֹ אֱמֶת וְחוֹתָמוֹ אֱמֶת —
לַעֲדֵי־עַד יִמְלֹךְ.

But the Supreme King is a truthful judge, His works are truth; He does right, with unfailing love, ever constant and true; truth is His way and truth His seal – He shall reign for ever!

דָּוִד בֶּן־נָשִׂיא

David ben Nasi

אֲמוּלָה לִבָּתִי

A REPROACH

אֲמוּלָה לִבָּתִי כְּמוֹ אֵשׁ מִתְלַהֶטֶת,
וְנֹכַח תּוֹעֲבוֹתַי עֵינִי מַבֶּטֶת,
לַעֲשׂוֹת אוֹתָם בָּאוֹר וּבָעֲלָטֶת,
מַעֲשֵׂה אִשָּׁה זוֹנָה שַׁלָּטֶת.

My poor heart burns, as if it were on fire, when I look at my own abominations, done in darkness and in light – *the deeds of a bold-faced whore!*

בְּפִי וּבִלְשׁוֹנִי פִּתּוּי קַשׁוּב,
וְתַחַת שְׂפָתַי חֲמַת עַכְשׁוּב.
וְשָׂרַי וּזְקֵנַי וְכָל נִכְבָּד וְחָשׁוּב
הֶחֱזִיקוּ בַּתַּרְמִית, מֵאֲנוּ לָשׁוּב. [...]

Lures lie in wait in my mouth, on my tongue; on my lips is spiders' poison; my lords and elders, all the honoured and important men *cling to deceit, refusing to repent.*

זְקֵנַי וִישִׁישַׁי, שַׁחֲרִית וְעַרְבִית,
זוֹלְלֵי בָשָׂר וְסוֹבְאֵי יַיִן חָבִית.
וְסוֹחֵר וּמוֹכֵר, לְהוֹסִיף מַגְבִּית,
מַרְבֶּה הוֹנוֹ בְּנֶשֶׁךְ וְתַרְבִּית. [...]

From morning to evening my aged leaders gorge themselves on meat and guzzle wine from the barrel; while the dealers and merchants augment their hoard, *grow rich by lending at discount or at interest.*

דְּחֵה מְזֵי רָעָב מִבָּתִּים וּמִתְּחוּמִים,
וְכַבֵּה רֶשֶׁף וְגַם קֶטֶב לְחוּמִים.
יְהִי־נָא חַסְדְּךָ לְשַׂבְּעֵנוּ מִמְּרוֹמִים
דְּבָרִים טוֹבִים, דְּבָרִים נִחוּמִים.

Oh, banish the pangs of hunger from our homes and realms, and quench the burning heat, the ravaging pestilence. May Your never-failing love nourish us from on high, *with kind words, with words of consolation.*

עֲלוּמֵי־שֵׁם
Anonymous

פְּטִירַת מֹשֶׁה
THE DEATH OF MOSES SEQUENCE

מי עלה למרום
1. The Angels Try to Block His Way

מִי עָלָה לַמָּרוֹם,
מִי עָלָה לַמָּרוֹם,
מִי עָלָה לַמָּרוֹם,
וּמִי הוֹרִיד עֹז מִבְטֶחָה?

Who went up to heaven? Who went up to heaven? Who went up to heaven and brought down the mighty mainstay?[1]

הִתְקַבְּצוּ מַלְאָכִים זֶה אֶל זֶה,
לְקָבֶל־זֶה,
וְאָמַר זֶה אֶל זֶה:
'מִי הוּא זֶה וְאֵיזֶה הוּא,
מְאַחֵז פְּנֵי כִסֵּה,
פַּרְשֵׁז עָלָיו עֲנָנוֹ?'

The angels banded together against this man; and they said one to another: 'Who is he and what is he, that he dares cling to the Throne, and God spreads His radiant cloud over him?'

מֹשֶׁה עָלָה לַמָּרוֹם,
מֹשֶׁה עָלָה לַמָּרוֹם,
מֹשֶׁה עָלָה לַמָּרוֹם,
וְהוּא הוֹרִיד עֹז מִבְטֶחָה!

Moses went up to heaven. Moses went up to heaven. Moses went up to heaven and brought down the mighty mainstay!

אז מרחם אמי
2. He Pleads with God for His Life

'אָז מֵרֶחֶם אִמִּי
בְּחַנְתָּ תֻּמִּי
וּבָחַרְתָּ נְאֻמִּי –
וְלָמָּה אֲנִי מֵת?'

'While I was yet in my mother's womb You marked my perfection and chose me as Your spokesman – why then

1. I.e. the Torah, in which the angels put their trust and which they refused to relinquish to mortals.

'פֶּן יֵאָמַר: אִישׁ הָאֱלֹהִים
עָלָה אֶל הָאֱלֹהִים,
וְהִנּוֹ כֵּאלֹהִים.'

should I die?' 'Lest it be said: the man of God went up to God, and he has become like God.'

'בְּעֵת טִיט וָחֹמֶר
נִתַּתִּי בְּתֵבַת גֹּמֶא,
וְשָׁמַרְתִּי אֹמֶר —
וְלָמָּה אֲנִי מֵת?'
'פֶּן יֵאָמַר: בִּיטָּה אֵל פָּנִים בְּפָנִים,
וְקָרַן לוֹ עוֹר פָּנִים,
וְהִנּוֹ כֵּאלֹהִים.'

'When Israel laboured with clay and with mortar, I was put into a wicker basket. And I fulfilled Your word – why then should I die?' 'Lest it be said: He spoke to God face to face and then the skin of his face shone, and he has become like God.'

'גַּם הֻשְׁלַכְתִּי לַיְאוֹר
מִפְּנֵי מוֹרְדֵי אוֹר,
וּדְבָרְךָ הָיָה לִי אוֹר —
וְלָמָּה אֲנִי מֵת?'
'פֶּן יֵאָמַר: גָּדַע חָם בְּעֶשֶׂר מַכּוֹת,
וְגָאַל עֵינֶיהָ־בְּרֵכוֹת,
וְהִנּוֹ כֵּאלֹהִים.'

'I was cast into the Nile for fear of those who rebelled against the light, but Your word was my light – why then should I die?' 'Lest it be said: He felled Egypt with ten plagues and redeemed her whose eyes are like pools,[1] and he has become like God.'

'דִּהַרְתָּ בַּת מַפְרִיךְ
עַל יַד הַיְאוֹר לְהַדְרִיךְ,
יָמַי לְהַאֲרִיךְ —
וְלָמָּה אֲנִי מֵת?'
'פֶּן יֵאָמַר: דָּץ כְּנִשְׁתַּלַּח אֶל סְגֻלָּה
וְהוֹצִיאָם בְּגִילָה,
וְהִנּוֹ כֵּאלֹהִים.'

'You led the tyrant's daughter to the Nile, brought her in haste, so that my life might be prolonged – why then should I die?' 'Lest it be said: He exulted when he was sent to the treasured people and brought them out of Egypt joyfully, and he has become like God.'

1. Israel; see Song of Songs 7.5.

אז כל בריות

3. God Bargains with Him

'אָז כָּל בְּרִיּוֹת נוֹצְרוּ מֵאֲדָמָה,
וְסוֹפָם לְתוֹלֵעָה וְרִמָּה.
כִּי נִשְׁבַּעְתִּי:
בְּגוּפְךָ לֹא תִשְׁלֹט רִמָּה,
וְלֹא כְּמוֹת כָּל הָאָדָם תָּמוּת.'

'All creatures were formed out of earth and are doomed to be food for maggots and worms. By My own self I swear: no maggot shall have sway over your body, and you shall not die as all men die.'

'וְאֵיךְ אָמוּת?'

'How then shall I die?'

'גְּדוּדִים וּשְׂרָפִים יַעַמְדוּ מִפֹּה וּמִפֹּה
וְיַעֲשׂוּ שֵׁרוּתֶךָ,
וַאֲנִי אַצְהִיר בְּתוֹךְ שׁוּרָתֶךָ.
כִּי נִשְׁבַּעְתִּי:
וְלֹא יֵדַע אִישׁ אֶת קְבוּרָתֶךָ,
וְלֹא כְּמוֹת כָּל הָאָדָם תָּמוּת.'

'Bands of angels and seraphim, standing on either side, shall wait upon you, and My splendour shall shine in your ranks. By My own self I swear: no one shall know your burial place, and you shall not die as all men die.'

'וְאֵיךְ אָמוּת?'

'How then shall I die?'

'הֵן אֲנִי בִּכְבוֹדִי אֶשָּׂאֲךָ אַרְבָּעָה מִילִים,
וְתַרְשִׁישִׁים חַסְדְּךָ יִהְיוּ גוֹמְלִים.
כִּי נִשְׁבַּעְתִּי:
וְאַנִּיחֲךָ אֵצֶל שְׁלֹשֶׁת הַגְּדוֹלִים,
וְלֹא כְּמוֹת כָּל הָאָדָם תָּמוּת.'

'I Myself will carry you for four miles, and gleaming angels shall shower you with favours. By My own self I swear: I will place you next to the three Patriarchs, and you shall not die as all men die.'

'וְאֵיךְ אָמוּת?'

'How then shall I die?'

'מַלְאֲכֵי־מַעַל אֲשֶׁר בֵּינֵיהֶם שָׁלוֹם
יֵצְאוּ לִקְרָאתְךָ בְּדִבְרֵי שָׁלוֹם.
כִּי נִשְׁבַּעְתִּי:

'The angels on high, who dwell in peace, shall go forth to greet you with words of peace. By My own self I

נוֹאֲמִים לְפָנֶיךָ: ״יָבוֹא שָׁלוֹם״ –
וְלֹא כְּמוֹת כָּל הָאָדָם תָּמוּת.׳

swear: they shall salute you: "Enter into peace!", and you shall not die as all men die.'

׳וְאֵיךְ אָמוּת?׳

'How then shall I die?'

׳קְדוֹשֵׁי מַעְלָה יֹאמְרוּ: ״מָתַי יָבוֹא בְּרֹאשׁ עַם
לִתְשׁוּעַת עֲדָתוֹ,
הָאִישׁ אֲשֶׁר לֹא קָם בְּיִשְׂרָאֵל כְּמוֹתוֹ?״
בִּי נִשְׁבַּעְתִּי:
רוֹגְשִׁים וְאוֹמְרִים: ״יְהִי שָׁלוֹם בִּמְנוּחָתוֹ״ –
וְלֹא כְּמוֹת כָּל הָאָדָם תָּמוּת.׳

'The holy ones on high shall say: "When will he come again at the head of his flock to bring salvation to all his people – this man, whose like has never yet arisen in Israel?" By My own self I swear: they shall all cry out: "Peace be upon his resting place!", and you shall not die as all men die.'

׳וְאֵיךְ אָמוּת?׳

'How then shall I die?'

׳שְׁמוּרָה תִהְיֶה אֶצְלְךָ דָּת עֵץ הַחַיִּים,
וְאַתָּה תָּבוֹא בְּרֹאשׁ חֲבוּרָתְךָ בְּבִנְיַן
מוֹצָא מַיִם חַיִּים.
בִּי נִשְׁבַּעְתִּי:
תִּשְׁמַע מִפִּי ״תְּהִי נִשְׁמָתְךָ צְרוּרָה בִּצְרוֹר הַחַיִּים״,
וְלֹא כְּמוֹת כָּל הָאָדָם תָּמוּת.׳

'The Law, that staff of life, shall be entrusted to you; you shall come at the head of your company when Jerusalem, the source of living waters, is rebuilt. By My own self I swear: you shall hear Me say: "May your soul be treasured in the treasury of life", and you shall not die as all men die.'

׳וְאֵיךְ אָמוּת?׳

'How then shall I die?'

לא אמות

4. He Refuses to Die

׳לֹא אָמוּת! לָמָּה אָמוּת?

'I will not die! Why should I die?

אִם גָּרַמְתִּי בְּעָוֶל פֶּה
בַּסְּנֶה בְּדִבּוּר פֶּה,

'If it is because of my perverse words, spoken at the burning bush, when I

כְּשָׁמְעִי פֶּה אֶל פֶּה
"וְאַתָּה תִּהְיֶה לּוֹ לְפֶה",
בְּעַוְתִי כִּי כְבַד פֶּה
לְחַר בְּמִי שָׂם פֶּה –
אִם עָוֹן הוּא מְחֵהוּ,
וְאַל תִּזְכְּרֵהוּ.'

heard You say, mouth to mouth, "You shall put the words in Aaron's mouth"; when I sinfully answered: "I am slow of speech", and angered You who give man speech – if this is my crime, blot it out and do not call it to mind!'

וְהֱשִׁיבוֹ אָיֹם
בְּעֶצֶם הַיּוֹם:
'דְּבָרֶיךָ הָחְמְדוּ
בַּסְּנֶה, וְאִם כָּבְדוּ,
לְדוֹרוֹת יֻתְמְדוּ.
וְאֵיךְ לְעָוֹן יִפָּקְדוּ?

And the Dread One answered him that very day: 'Your words were sweet to me, and though they faltered at the bush they will be remembered for many generations. How can such words be counted a crime?

זאת לֹא זאת.'

'That is not why.'

'לָמָּה זֹאת – אֵין זאת?'

'If that is not why, why then should I die?'

'מֹשֶׁה, עֲלֵה וָמוּת,
כִּי גְזֵרָה הִיא שֶׁתָּמוּת!'

'Moses, go up and die, for it has been decreed that you shall die!'

איש אשר הֻקרן

5. *He Cries Out to His Mother*

אִישׁ אֲשֶׁר הֻקְרַן לוֹ אוֹרָה,
אִישׁ בְּחָרוֹ אֵל נוֹרָא,
אִישׁ גָּשׁ לְעַרְפִלֵּי־נוֹרָא –
יֵאָמֶר לוֹ: 'עֲלֵה וּמוּת בָּהָר'?
צָעַק צְעָקָה גְדוֹלָה וּמָרָה:
'יוֹכֶבֶד, אִמִּי!'

This man, who was graced with light, who was chosen by the dread God, who approached the dark clouds of terror – shall he now be told: 'Go up and die on the mountain'? He cried out, loud and bitter: 'Jokhebed, my mother!'

אִישׁ דָּשׁ עַנְנֵי נְהוֹרָא,
אִישׁ הֵשִׁיךְ עֶבְרָה,
אִישׁ וִתֵּר מֵעָם עֶבְרָה –
יֵאָמֶר לוֹ: 'עֲלֵה וּמוּת בָּהָר'?
צָעַק צְעָקָה גְדוֹלָה וּמָרָה:
'יוֹכֶבֶד, אִמִּי!'

This man, who walked on the glowing clouds, who stilled God's anger, who averted His wrath from the people – shall he now be told: 'Go up and die on the mountain'? He cried out, loud and bitter: 'Jokhebed, my mother!'

אִישׁ קָרָא עַל הַיָּם שִׁירָה,
אִישׁ רָאָה וַיִּירָא,
אִישׁ שְׁכִינָה שָׁרָהּ,
אִישׁ תִּנָּה מִשְׁנֵה תוֹרָה –
יֵאָמֶר לוֹ: 'עֲלֵה וּמוּת בָּהָר'?
צָעַק צְעָקָה גְדוֹלָה וּמָרָה:
'יוֹכֶבֶד, אִמִּי!'

This man, who sang out by the shores of the Red Sea, who looked, terrified, at the burning bush, who beheld the Shekinah, who expounded the Law[1] – shall he now be told: 'Go up and die on the mountain'? He cried out, loud and bitter: 'Jokhebed, my mother!'

אֹרח זו אלך

6. He Takes Leave of His People

'אֹרַח זוּ אֵלֵךְ
גָּזַר עָלַי הַמֶּלֶךְ.
הִנְנִי הַיּוֹם מֻבְדָּל וְהוֹלֵךְ.
קְהָלִי, הֱיֵה לְשָׁלוֹם.'

'The road I am about to take was decreed by the King; I am set apart today, and take my leave. My people, be at peace.'

'בְּזֹאת לֹא נֵדַע מַה נַּעֲשֶׂה,
כִּי כָל אֲשֶׁר יַחְפֹּץ יַעֲשֶׂה,
וְאֵין מִי יֹאמַר לוֹ: "מַה תַּעֲשֶׂה?"
רוֹעֵנוּ, לֵךְ לְשָׁלוֹם.'

'As for this, we do not know what to do, for He does what He chooses, and none can say to Him: "What are you doing?" Our shepherd, go in peace.'

1. Lit. 'a copy of the Law', the traditional name of the fifth book of Moses, Deuteronomy.

'הַיּוֹם לִי אַחֲרוֹן,
חַק לִי רִאשׁוֹן וְאַחֲרוֹן.
אֵאָסֵף כְּנֶאֱסַף אָחִי אַהֲרֹן.
קְהָלִי, הֱיֵה לְשָׁלוֹם.'

'This day is my last; thus has He ordained, who is both First and Last; I shall be gathered to my kin as was my brother Aaron. My people, be at peace.'

'וְנָתִיב מוּכָן הוּא,
קָטֹן וְגָדוֹל שָׁם הוּא.
מִי יִחְיֶה וְלֹא יִרְאֵהוּ?
רוֹעֵנוּ, לֵךְ לְשָׁלוֹם.'

'Such is the fated course; both high and low must take it; who shall live and not see death? Our shepherd, go in peace.'

'זֶה הוּא לִי אָמַר:
"עֲלֵה וּמוּת בָּהָר" –
וְנַפְשִׁי לִמְאֹד הֵמַר.
קְהָלִי, הֱיֵה לְשָׁלוֹם.'

'This is what He said to me: "Go up and die on the mountain"; and He made my soul most bitter. My people, be at peace.'

'חָקַק לִבְנֵי אָדָם מִיתָה.
לַחֲסִידָיו יָקָר הַמָּוְתָה –
וֶעֱנוּתְךָ לָעָם הִבָּעְתָּ.
רוֹעֵנוּ, לֵךְ לְשָׁלוֹם.'

'He has doomed all men to death, but the death of His faithful ones is precious in His sight. Now that you have told the people of your grief, our shepherd, go in peace.'

'כָּבַד עָלַי רָעָה,
כִּי הַמָּוֶת לִי הִגְעָה.
מָה אֶעֱשֶׂה – לֹא אֵדְעָה.
קְהָלִי, הֱיֵה לְשָׁלוֹם.'

'Disaster weighs me down, for death is close upon me. What shall I do? I do not know. My people, be at peace.'

'לֹא יִחַר לָךְ
וְלֹא יֵצֶר לָךְ,
כָּבוֹד בְּגַן עֵדֶן מוּכָן לָךְ,
רוֹעֵנוּ, לֵךְ לְשָׁלוֹם.'

'Do not be angry, do not be grieved; glory awaits you in the Garden of Eden. Our Shepherd, go in peace.'

ויקבֹּר אתו בגַּי בארץ מואב מול בית פעור,
ולא ידע איש את קְבֻרתו עד היום הזה.

He was buried in a valley in Moab opposite Beth-peor, but to this day no one knows his burial-place.[1]

אזלת יוכבד

7. *His Mother Looks for His Grave*

אָזְלַת יוֹכֶבֶד מְפַיֶּסֶת לְמִצְרָיִם:
'מִצְרַיִם, מִצְרַיִם, אוּלַי רָאִיתָ לִי לְמֹשֶׁה?'
'בְּחַיַּיִךְ, יוֹכֶבֶד, לֹא רָאִיתִי אוֹתוֹ
מִן הַיּוֹם שֶׁהָרַג כָּל בְּכוֹר.'

Jokhebed went to Egypt and implored it: 'Egypt, Egypt, have you by chance seen Moses?' 'On your life, Jokhebed, I have not seen him since the day he slew all my first-born.'

אָזְלַת יוֹכֶבֶד וְשָׁאֲלָה לְנִילוּס:
'נִילוּס, נִילוּס, אוּלַי רָאִיתָ לִי לְמֹשֶׁה?'
'בְּחַיַּיִךְ, יוֹכֶבֶד, לֹא רָאִיתִי אוֹתוֹ
מִן הַיּוֹם שֶׁהָפַךְ מֵימַי לְדָם.'

Jokhebed went to the Nile and asked it: 'Nile, Nile, have you by chance seen Moses?' 'On your life, Jokhebed, I have not seen him since the day he turned my water to blood.'

אָזְלַת יוֹכֶבֶד מְפַיֶּסֶת לַיָּם:
'יָם, יָם, אוּלַי רָאִיתָ לִי לְמֹשֶׁה?'
'בְּחַיַּיִךְ, יוֹכֶבֶד, לֹא רָאִיתִי אוֹתוֹ
מִן הַיּוֹם שֶׁהֶעֱבִיר בִּי שְׁנֵים עָשָׂר שְׁבָטִים.'

Jokhebed went to the Red Sea and implored it: 'Sea, sea, have you by chance seen Moses?' 'On your life, Jokhebed, I have not seen him since the day he led the twelve tribes through me.'

אָזְלַת יוֹכֶבֶד וְשָׁאֲלָה לַמִּדְבָּר:
'מִדְבָּר, מִדְבָּר, אוּלַי רָאִיתָ לִי לְמֹשֶׁה?'
'בְּחַיַּיִךְ, יוֹכֶבֶד, לֹא רָאִיתִי אוֹתוֹ
מִן הַיּוֹם שֶׁהִמְטִיר עָלַי מָן לְיִשְׂרָאֵל.'

Jokhebed went to the desert and asked it: 'Desert, desert, have you by chance seen Moses?' 'On your life, Jokhebed, I have not seen him since the day he showered manna upon me for Israel.'

אָזְלַת יוֹכֶבֶד מְפַיֶּסֶת לְסִינַי:
'סִינַי, סִינַי, אוּלַי רָאִיתָ לִי לְמֹשֶׁה?'
'בְּחַיַּיִךְ, יוֹכֶבֶד, לֹא רָאִיתִי אוֹתוֹ
מִן הַיּוֹם שֶׁהוֹרִיד עָלַי שְׁנֵי לוּחוֹת הַבְּרִית.'

Jokhebed went to Mount Sinai and implored it: 'Sinai, Sinai, have you by chance seen Moses?' 'On your life, Jokhebed, I have not seen him since the day he descended upon me with the two tablets of the Law.'

1. Deuteronomy 34.6.

אָזְלַת יוֹכֶבֶד וְשָׁאֲלָה לַסֶּלַע :
'סֶלַע, סֶלַע, אוּלַי רָאִיתָ לִי לְמשֶׁה ?'
'בְּחַיַּיִךְ, יוֹכֶבֶד, לֹא רָאִיתִי אוֹתוֹ
מִן הַיּוֹם שֶׁהִכָּה עָלַי שְׁנֵי שַׁרְבִיטִין.' [...]

Jokhebed went to the rock and asked it:
'Rock, rock, have you by chance seen
Moses?' 'On your life, Jokhebed, I have
not seen him since the day he struck
me twice with the staff.'

ולא קם נביא עוד בישראל כמשה
אשר ידעו יהוה פנים אל פנים.

There has never yet arisen in Israel a
prophet like Moses, whom the Lord knew
face to face.[1]

1. Deuteronomy 34.10.

PART TWO

FROM THE TENTH TO THE EIGHTEENTH CENTURY

מְנַחֵם אִבְּן־סָרוּק

Menahem ibn Saruk

אֲנִי אֶעֱרֹךְ מִשְׁפָּט

THE POET PLEADS HIS CASE

[...] אֲנִי אֶעֱרֹךְ מִשְׁפָּט וְיָדַעְתִּי כִּי אֲנִי אֶצְדָּק.
כֹּה חַקּוֹתָ לִי בִּתְשׁוּבַת אִגַּרְתִּי
אֲשֶׁר שָׁלַחְתָּ אֵלַי לֵאמֹר:
'אִם הֶעֱוֵיתָ –
כְּבָר הֲבִיאוֹתִיךָ לְמוּסָר,
וְאִם לֹא הֶעֱוֵיתָ –
כְּבָר הֲבִיאוֹתִיךָ לְחַיֵּי הָעוֹלָם הַבָּא'.
הֲזֹאת חָשַׁבְתָּ לְמִשְׁפָּט? הַלְהוֹכֵחַ מִלִּין תַּחְשֹׁב?
הֲלֹא אֱלֹהִים יַחֲקָר־זֹאת,
הֲנוֹטַע אֹזֶן הֲלֹא יִשְׁמָע,
אִם יוֹצֵר עַיִן הֲלֹא יַבִּיט!
וְכִי תַחְסֹם אֶת פִּי בְּרוּחַ קָדִים
וְתַאֲלִים אֶת לְשׁוֹנִי בְּהַבְלֵי מַהֲתַלּוֹת?
הֲלֹא מֵעֲפָרְךָ עֲפָרִי וֵאלֹהֶיךָ אֱלֹהָי,
חוֹפֵשׂ כָּל תַּעֲלוּמוֹת וְחוֹפֵשׂ כָּל חַדְרֵי בָטֶן. [...]

I shall state my case, and I know that I shall be acquitted. This is what you wrote in reply to my letter, this is what you dispatched to me: 'If you have sinned, I have already repaid you as you merit; but if you have not sinned, I have made you merit eternal life in the world beyond.' Do you consider this a judgement? Do you think such words are proof enough? Will not God find this out? He that planted the ear, will He not hear? He that moulded the eye, will He not see? Will you muzzle my mouth with an east wind, and silence my tongue with taunting lies? Is not my dust the same as yours, and your God mine – He who searches out all secrets and delves into man's inmost being?

שְׁמַע נָא, בֶּן אָדָם, כִּי עוֹד יֵשׁ לְעַבְדְּךָ מִלִּים.
דַּע אַתָּה, אֲדוֹנִי, כִּי אֱלֹהִים הָיִיתָ בְמִשְׁפָּטִי,
מִשְׁפַּט אֱלֹהִים שְׁפַטְתָּנִי, דִּין עֶלְיוֹן דַּנְתָּנִי:
אֲשֶׁר הוּא הָעֵד – הוּא הַדַּיָּן,
וְלוֹ הַנִּסְתָּרוֹת וְהוּא יוֹדֵעַ תַּעֲלוּמוֹת לֵב.
וְלֹא צִוָּה כֵן לְנוֹחֲלֵי מִשְׁפָּט לַעֲשׂוֹת פְּלִילָה.
וַאֲנִי יָדַעְתִּי כִּי לֹא יְיָ הֱסִיתְךָ בִי,
כִּי אִם בְּנֵי הָאָדָם,
כִּי גֵרְשׁוּנִי הַיּוֹם מֵהִסְתַּפֵּחַ בְּנַחֲלַת יְיָ. [...]

Listen, man, for your servant still has something more to say. Know, my lord, that you have taken the role of God in my trial. You have judged me as though you were God, sentenced me as though you were the Most High, who is both witness and judge. All the hidden things are His; He knows the secrets of the heart. But this is not how He ordained that mortal judges should sit in judgement. I know that it is not God, but men, who set you against me; it is they who have deprived me of my share in the Lord's inheritance.

עַל חָמָס עוֹשְׁקַי אָשִׂיחַ אֶל אָרֶץ:
אֶרֶץ, אַל תְּכַסִּי דָמִי! [...]
מֵאַרְבַּע הָרוּחוֹת בּוֹאִי, רוּחַ,
אֲשֶׁר מִמֶּנָּה רוּחִי נֻפָּחָה!
הִתְאַבְּלִי – הֵימִינִי, הִתְאַנְּנִי – הַשְׂמִילִי,
לִבְשִׁי עָלַי שָׂק וְהִתְפַּלְּשִׁי בָּאֵפֶר.
עַל תּוּגַת מֶחֱצָתֵךְ – הַרְחִיבִי קָרְחָתֵךְ,
וְעַל מַר רוּחִי – חוּלִי וָגֹחִי.
אֱלִי נָא עָלַי כָּל יְמֵי הָאָרֶץ
וְחָלִילָה לָּךְ תֵּת לְזַעֲקָתֵךְ דֹּמִי.
שְׂאִי עַל כַּפַּיִךְ – אוּלַי תּוּכְלִי הוֹעִיל,
וְגַם שִׁפְכִי שִׂיחַ – אוּלַי תַּעֲרֹצִי:
כִּי גוֹאֲלִי חָי, לֹא שָׁכַח חַנּוֹת,
וּלְהַסְתִּיר פָּנִים – לֹא גָמַר אֹמֶר.

My oppressors have done me violence, and I shall cry out to the earth: O earth, cover not my blood! From the four quarters come, O wind, from which my spirit drew its breath! Mourn, turn right. Lament, turn left. Put on sackcloth for me, roll in ashes. In grief for me, who am half of you, pluck out your hair. Lie writhing on the ground for my embittered soul. Wail for me through all the years of the earth. Never let your cry abate. Lift up your hands on high: you may yet help. Pour out your complaint: you may inspire awe. For my vindicator lives, He has not forgotten to be gracious, He has not resolved to hide His face.

גַּם קוֹלִי אֱלֵי מַיִם עַל יַבֶּשֶׁת לֵחוּתִי –
הֲלֹא בְמֵימֵי מוּצָק בְּצֵקִי הוּלָשׁ.
גַּם אַתֶּם צַעֲקוּ בְּקוֹל שָׁאוֹן
וְאַל תִּדֹּם הֶמְיַת צְוָחַתְכֶם.
גַּם אַתֶּם לוּ שְׁמָעוּנִי,
הֵן לָכֶם יְכֹלֶת לִנְקֹם נִקְמָתִי:
בִּשְׁתוֹת אֶתְכֶם חוֹמְסַי – הֱיוּ נָא לְמָרִים,
בְּבוֹאֲכֶם בְּמֵעֵימוֹ – הֱיוּ לַצְבּוֹת בֶּטֶן,
וְכָל מַשְׁקֶה אֲשֶׁר יִשְׁתֶּה – יֵמַר לְשׁוֹתָיו,
וְעוֹלְלוּ לָמוֹ – וְיִהְיוּ כָמוֹנִי!

I shall cry out to the waters too, for my body has been parched. Was not my dough kneaded from the waters that freeze fast? Now you too roar and boom; let your thundering cry never cease. Oh, if only you too would heed me, for you have it in your power to avenge me. When my despoilers drink you, turn bitter; when you enter their bowels, swell their bellies. Let every liquid that they drink be bitter to them. Torment them till they become like me!

וְלִשְׁמֵי קֶדֶם אָמַרְתִּי: שְׁמָעוּנִי!
וְלִצְבָא מָרוֹם חַנֹּתִי בְּמוֹ פִי,
וּלְגִבּוֹרֵי כֹחַ, אֵלֵי פֶלֶא,
אֲשֶׁר מִשְׁכְּנוֹתָם גָּבְהֵי מְרוֹמִים –

And to the ancient heavens I shall say: listen to me! I shall entreat the host of heaven, the creatures of night, the wondrous angels who dwell in the uppermost heavens. To all of them I

לְכֻלָּם אֶפְרֹשׂ כַּפַּי וְאֶשְׁפֹּךְ שִׂיחִי:
אוּלַי יָעִידוּ חֲמָתִי לְשָׂהֲדִי בַּמְּרוֹמִים
הַשַּׁלִּיט עַל כֻּלָּם!

shall spread out my hands and pour out my prayer: may they attest my wrath before my Witness on high, who rules over all!

וְגַם לְשׁוֹכְנֵי עָפָר עֵינִי דוֹמַעַת,
הָעֲתִידִים לַעֲמֹד בַּדִּין לִפְנֵי יוֹצֵר כֹּל.
הָעֲשׁוּקִים כָּמוֹנִי הַיּוֹם –
דִּמְעוֹת אַנְחוֹתַי יָשׁוּ לְדִמְעוֹתָם,
וְעַל חֲמָסִי אֶל אֵל יְשַׁוֵּעוּ:
אוּלַי מִמֶּנִּי אוֹ מֵהֶם יַקְשִׁיב אֹזֶן.

They that sleep in the earth, they that are destined to stand on trial before the Creator of all – to them too will my tears flow. And they that are wronged as I am today – let them join my tears and my sighs to their weeping, and bemoan the violence done to me before God. Perhaps He will listen to me, or to them.

עוֹד אֲנִי מְדַבֵּר וְאֶעֱרֹךְ מִלִּים – וְלֹא לְהוֹכִיחַ;
וְאַזְכִּיר קַדְמוֹנִיּוֹת – לֹא לְהוֹעִיל.
אַךְ עַתָּה הֱצִיקַתְנִי רוּחִי:
עוּרָה, אֲדוֹנִי, וְהִתְבּוֹנֵן וְהַט אֹזֶן לְשַׁוְעַת מִתְחַנֵּן,
וְלֵב עָגוּם תַּרְנִין, אִם פָּנֶיךָ לֹא תַעֲנִין!
מְאוּמָה לֹא אֲבַקֵּשׁ – בִּלְתִּי קֶשֶׁב.
וְאִם אֶל כָּמוֹנִי יִפְנֶה כָמוֹךָ – אֵינֶנּוּ תִּמָּהוֹן,
וְאִם תֵּט אֵלַי סְכוּת חִין עֶרְכִּי – כְּבוֹדְךָ לֹא יֵחָל
וְאֵין לְמַעֲלָתְךָ גֵּרָעוֹן.
אָעִיר זִכְרוֹנֵי קֶדֶם אֲשֶׁר צִדְקִי בָם,
וְאִם תִּבְחַר אֱמוּנָה, תּוֹדֶה לִּי עֲלֵיהֶם. [...]

Though I am still speaking, stringing words together, it is not to rebuke you. Though I recall days gone by, it is not to profit by them.[1] But now my spirit constrains me to say: Arise, my lord, and behold, listen to the suppliant's cry. You will make the sad heart sing for joy if you do not cover your face with clouds. I ask nothing but an attentive ear. If a man of your rank were to turn to the likes of me, none would wonder. And if you were to bend down to me and heed my prayer, your glory would not be diminished, nor your eminence lessened. I shall awaken memories of the past in which my righteousness is manifest. If you choose the path of truth, you will thank me for having done so!

1. A reminder of the services he rendered Ḥisdai as his court poet and secretary.

דּוּנָשׁ בֶּן־לַבְרָט

Dunash ben Labrat

וְאוֹמֵר: אַל תִּישָׁן

וְאוֹמֵר: 'אַל תִּישָׁן! שְׁתֵה יַיִן יָשָׁן,
עֲלֵי מֹר עִם שׁוֹשָׁן וְכֹפֶר וַאֲהָלִים,
בְּפַרְדֵּס רִמּוֹנִים וְתָמָר וּגְפָנִים
וְנִטְעֵי נַעֲמָנִים וּמִינֵי הָאֲשָׁלִים,
וְרֶגֶשׁ צִנּוֹרִים וְהֶמְיַת כִּנּוֹרִים
עֲלֵי פֶה הַשָּׁרִים בְּמִנִּים וּנְבָלִים.
וְשָׁם כָּל עֵץ מוּנָף, יְפֵה פְרִי עָנָף,
וְצִפּוֹר כָּל כָּנָף יְרַנֵּן בֵּין עָלִים,
וְיֶהְגּוּ הַיּוֹנִים כְּהוֹגִים נִגּוּנִים,
וְהַתּוֹרִים עוֹנִים וְהוֹמִים כַּחֲלִילִים.
וְנִשְׁתֶּה בַעֲרוּגוֹת בְּשׁוֹשַׁנִּים סוּגוֹת,
וְנָנִיס הַתּוּגוֹת בְּמִינֵי הִלּוּלִים,
וְנֹאכַל מַמְתַקִּים וְנִשְׁתֶּה מִזְרָקִים
וְנִנְהַג כַּעֲנָקִים וְנִשְׁתֶּה בִסְפָלִים.
וְאָקוּם בִּבְקָרִים אֲנִי לִשְׁחֹט פָּרִים
בְּרִיאִים נִבְחָרִים, וְאֵילִים וַעֲגָלִים,
וְנִמְשַׁח שֶׁמֶן טוֹב וְנַקְטִיר עֵץ רָטֹב.
בְּטֶרֶם יוֹם קָטֹב יְבוֹאֵנוּ — נִשְׁלִים!'

THE POET REFUSES AN INVITATION TO DRINK

He said: 'Do not sleep! Drink old wine, amidst myrrh and lilies, henna and aloes, in an orchard of pomegranates, palms, and vines, full of pleasant plants and tamarisks, to the hum of fountains and the throb of lutes, to the sound of singers, flutes and lyres. There every tree is tall, branches are fair with fruit, and winged birds of every kind sing among the leaves. The doves moan melodiously, and the turtle-doves reply, cooing like reed pipes. There we shall drink among flower-beds fenced in by lilies, putting sorrow to rout with songs of praise. We shall eat sweets as we drink by the bowlful. We shall act like giants, drinking out of huge goblets. And in the mornings I shall rise to slaughter fat choice bulls and rams and calves. We shall anoint ourselves with fragrant oil and burn aloe incense. Oh, before doom overtakes us, let us enjoy ourselves in peace!'

גְּעַרְתִּיהוּ: 'דֹּם, דֹּם! עֲלֵי זֹאת אֵיךְ תִּקְדֹּם —
וּבֵית קֹדֶשׁ וַהֲדוֹם אֱלֹהִים לָעֲרֵלִים!
בְּכִסְלָה דִּבַּרְתָּ וַעֲצָלָה בָּחַרְתָּ
וְהֶבֶל אָמַרְתָּ כְּלֵצִים וּכְסִילִים,
וְעָזַבְתָּ הֶגְיוֹן בְּתוֹרַת אֵל עֶלְיוֹן
וְתָגִיל — וּבְצִיּוֹן יְרוּצוּן שׁוּעָלִים.
וְאֵיךְ נִשְׁתֶּה יַיִן וְאֵיךְ נָרִים עַיִן —
וְהָיִינוּ אַיִן, מְאוּסִים וּגְעוּלִים!'

But I reproached him thus: 'Silence! How dare you – when the Holy House, the footstool of God, is in the hands of the gentiles. You have spoken foolishly, you have chosen sloth, you have uttered nonsense, like the mockers and fools. You have forsaken the study of the Supreme God's law. Even as you rejoice, jackals run wild in Zion. Then how could we drink wine, how even raise our eyes – when we are loathed and abhorred, and less than nothing?'

יוֹסֵף אִבְּן־אֲבִיתוֹר

Joseph ibn Abitur

יָדַעְתִּי, אֱלֹהַי

CONFESSION

יָדַעְתִּי, אֱלֹהַי, כִּי אֲנִי חָמַסְתִּי נַפְשִׁי
וְאָנֹכִי סִבַּבְתִּי חָרְבָּן עַל מִקְדָּשִׁי.
פְּשָׁעַי הֵם לְכָדוּנִי וַיָּקָם בִּי כַחֲשִׁי,
כִּי עֲוֹנוֹתַי עָבְרוּ רֹאשִׁי.

I know, my God, that I have done violence to myself, that I have brought destruction upon my Temple. My own crimes have trapped me, my lies have risen up against me; *for my sins have swept over my head.*

אָנֹכִי הַחוֹטֵא וְהָרַע מִתְּחִלָּתִי,
כִּי לְבַדִּי הֶעָוֹן וְאֵין בְּאַחֵר זוּלָתִי,
גַּם לֹא יִתְעָרַב זָר עִמִּי בִּנְפִילָתִי
וְהַבֹּשֶׁת הִיא סוּתִי וּכְלִמָּה מַלְבּוּשִׁי
כִּי עֲוֹנוֹתַי עָבְרוּ רֹאשִׁי.

I am the sinner, the evil-doer, from my very inception. I alone am guilty, no other is at fault; no stranger shall have any part in my downfall. Shame is my garment, disgrace my clothing; *for my sins have swept over my head.*

דְּבָרַי יַרְשִׁיעוּנִי וּשְׂפָתַי יַעֲנוּ בִי,
הֵן בְּעָווֹן חוֹלָלְתִּי וְעִמִּי נוֹלַד חוֹבִי,
וּבוֹ יֶחֱמַתְנִי אִמִּי וּבוֹ גִּדְּלַנִי אָבִי.
אֵין פֶּשַׁע כְּמוֹ פִשְׁעִי אֲשֶׁר הוּא לִי לְמוֹקְשִׁי
כִּי עֲוֹנוֹתַי עָבְרוּ רֹאשִׁי.

My very words convict me, my lips bear witness against me. Indeed, I was brought to birth in iniquity, and my guilt was born with me. My mother conceived me in guilt, my father reared me in it. There is no crime like mine, it sets a snare for me; *for my sins have swept over my head.*

זוּלָתִי עֲוֹן כָּל יוֹם, דַּיֵּנִי עֲוֹן הַיּוֹם.
חֵטְא יוֹם אֶחָד אִלּוּ פָּקַד עָלַי אָיֹם,
טָבַעְתִּי בְּאֵין מָקוֹם וְלֹא אֶמְצָא לִי פִּדְיוֹם.
רְאוּ מֶה עָשָׂה חֶטְאִי וּמַה שִּׁלֵּם לִי טִפְּשִׁי
כִּי עֲוֹנוֹתַי עָבְרוּ רֹאשִׁי.

This day's crimes alone – not even counting those of other days – would suffice. If the Dread One were to punish me for the sins of a single day, I would sink without any foothold, and would find no redemption. See what my crime has done, how my folly has repaid me; *for my sins have swept over my head.*

יַד אוֹיְבִי מְצָאַתְנִי וְנָפַלְתִּי בְּיַד צוֹרְרִי,
כִּי הִכְעַסְתִּי לְיוֹצְרִי וְגַם מָרַדְתִּי בְצוּרִי,

My assailant found me out, I fell into the hands of my enemies, because I angered my Creator and rebelled

לֹא מָשַׁלְתִּי בְיִצְרִי לָכֵן מָשַׁל בִּי צָרִי.
אֵין עָוֹן כַּעֲווֹנִי וְאֵין יֹקֶשׁ כְּיָקְשִׁי
כִּי עֲוֹנוֹתַי עָבְרוּ רֹאשִׁי.

against my Rock. I did not curb my passion; now my enemy curbs me. There is no guilt like mine, no trap like the trap set for me; *for my sins have swept over my head.*

מִי הָאִישׁ הֶחָפֵץ לְהָמִית נַפְשׁוֹ בְּיָדוֹ –
נִהְיֶה לוֹ אֲנִי וַעֲווֹנִי, וְלֹא יִהְיֶה הוּא לְבַדּוֹ;
סוֹף וְרֹאשׁ לֹא יִרְצֶה כָּזֶה לֹא אִישׁ וְלֹא עַבְדּוֹ,
אֲנִי שָׂחִתִּי בְּמֵי פִשְׁעִי, מִי יְדַלֵּנִי מֵרִפְשִׁי?
כִּי עֲוֹנוֹתַי עָבְרוּ רֹאשִׁי.

If any man should wish to die by his own hands, my sin and I shall join him, and he will not be alone. No man, not even a slave, would desire to live from such a beginning to such an end. I swim in a sea of crime; who will lift me up out of my filth? *For my sins have swept over my head.*

עֲשׁוּקִים הֵם בְּנֵי אִמִּי, חֲמָסָם וְדִינָם עָלַי,
פָּטוֹר לֹא יִפְטְרֵנִי דַּם טַפִּי וְעוֹלָלַי,
צוּרִי, כִּי אֲנִי הֲרַגְתִּים בְּחַטֹּאתַי וּמַעֲלָלַי,
וְיָדִי הִיא פְצָעַתְנִי וַחֲמָסִי עֲלֵי נַפְשִׁי
כִּי עֲוֹנוֹתַי עָבְרוּ רֹאשִׁי.

My mother's sons are oppressed; I must answer for the violence done to them. O my Lord, I shall never be purged of the blood of my children and infants, for I killed them with my sins and misdeeds. My own hand wounded me, my own self did me wrong; *for my sins have swept over my head.*

קָמוּ בִי עֲוֹנוֹתַי וְלֹא מָצָאתִי תְקוּמָה,
רָמָה יָדָם עָלַי וּבָאוּנִי בְּיָד רָמָה.
שָׁמַיִם וָאָרֶץ אָז רָאוּ בִי נְקָמָה.
אֲנִי אֶבְכֶּה בְּלֵילֵי שָׁנָה, בְּשַׁבְּתִּי וּבְחָדְשִׁי
כִּי עֲוֹנוֹתַי עָבְרוּ רֹאשִׁי.

My iniquities stood up against me, I could not stand my ground. They raised their hand high over me, charged at me defiantly. Then heaven and earth saw their vengeance upon me. Now I weep every night, all year long, and on Sabbaths too, and on New Moons; *for my sins have swept over my head.*

תִּעֲבוּנִי מְתֵי תָחַת, שְׂנֵאוּנִי צְבָא מְגֹעָל,
יָדְעוּ כִּי אֲנִי נִתְעָב, רָאוּ כִּי אֲנִי נִגְעָל.
צוּרִי, מָה אֲשֶׁר אֶעֱשֶׂה, מָה אֲשֶׁר אֶפְעַל?
שְׁעֵה שַׁוְעִי וּפִלּוּלִי וְהַט אָזְנְךָ לְמוֹ רַחֲשִׁי
כִּי עֲוֹנוֹתַי עָבְרוּ רֹאשִׁי.

The dwellers of the underworld detest me, even the host of the impure abhor me. They sense that I am loathsome, they see that I am soiled. My Lord, what shall I do, what can I do? Oh, turn to my cry and my plea, listen to my prayer; *for my sins have swept over my head.*

חֵפֶץ מַה לִּי בַּחַיִּים, הֲנָאָה אֵין לִי בְּמוֹתִי,
חֶטְאִי עָלַי בְּחַיַּי, וּבְמוֹתִי אַשְׁמָתִי.

I have no pleasure in life, I have no enjoyment in death. My sin afflicts me in life, my guilt in death. Hasten to me

חוּשָׁה לִּי וְעָזְרֵנִי, אֵל יוֹצֵר נִשְׁמָתִי,
סְלַח פְּשָׁעִי וְחִישׁ יִשְׁעִי, מַלְכִּי גוֹאֲלִי וּקְדוֹשִׁי
כִּי עֲוֹנוֹתַי עָבְרוּ רֹאשִׁי.

and help me, O God, maker of my soul. Forgive my crime, speed my salvation, O my King, my Redeemer, my Holy One; *for my sins have swept over my head.*

יִצְחָק אִבְּן־כַ׳לְפוּן

Isaac ibn Khalfun

בְּעֵת חֵשֶׁק יְעִירֵנִי

THE RETREAT

בְּעֵת חֵשֶׁק יְעִירֵנִי, אֲדַלֵּג
כְּאַיָּל לַחֲזוֹת עֵינֵי כְבוּדָּהּ.
וְאָבוֹאָה, וְהֵן אִמָּהּ לְנֶגְדָּהּ –
וְאָבִיהָ וְאָחִיהָ וְדוֹדָהּ!
אֲשׁוּרֶנָּה, וְאֶפְנֶה לַאֲחוֹרָי,
כְּאִלּוּ לֹא אֲנִי רֵעֶהָ־יְדִידָהּ.
יְרֵא מֵהֶם, וְעָלֶיהָ לְבָבִי
כְּלֵב אִשָּׁה מְשַׁכֶּלֶת יְחִידָהּ.

When desire arouses me, I leap like a deer to see my lady's eyes. But when I come, I find her mother there – and her father and her brother and her uncle![1] I look at her, then quickly turn away, as though I were not her beloved. I am afraid of them, and my heart mourns for her like the heart of a woman bereft of her only son.

פְּנֵי תֵבֵל

THE WORLD AND HER CHILDREN

פְּנֵי תֵבֵל כְּצַוַּאר הַמְּצֹרָע –
לְכֵן הָרֵק בְּפָנֶיהָ צְדָקָה;
וְהַנְּעֵל בְּעֹרֶף אוֹהֲבֶיהָ,
וְגִלּוּי מַעֲרָם – חֻקָּה חֲקוּקָה.
לְכֵן רַוֵּם לְלַעֲנָה, אִם תְּהָכִיל,
וְהַרְאֵם כִּי תְרַוֵּמוֹ מְתִיקָה,
וְרַוֵּה חַרְבְּךָ מִדַּם בְּנֵי אִישׁ,
וְלֹא תִשְׁמַע אֲלֵיהֶם קוֹל נְאָקָה.

The World's face is like a leper's neck. Therefore, it is only right to spit in her face; it is fitting and proper to cast one's sandals at the nape of her lovers and to strip them bare. So, if you can, make them drink deep of wormwood, but pretend to satisfy them with sweet drinks. Then make your sword drink deep of men's blood, and do not heed their groans. Show no mercy to high or

1. Or 'betrothed'.

וְלֹא תַחְמֹל עֲלֵי קָטֹן וְגָדוֹל,
וְתֹאמַר: ׳כִּי בְזֶה יֶשׁ לִי חֲשִׁיקָה.׳
נְחָשִׁים הֵם וְעַקְרַבִּים, וְלוּ תַ־
עֲנִיק לָהֶם יְחִידָתְךָ עֲנִיקָה,
בְּנֵי תֵבֵל לְעוֹלָם יִבְגְּדוּ כַּ־
אֲשֶׁר תִּבְגֹּד בְּעֵת צָרָה וְצוּקָה.
אֱמֶת, הֵמָּה כְּאִמָּם, כֵּן הֲבִיאֵם
בְּרֶחֶם הָרְחָבָה, הָעֲמֻקָּה.
הֲרֹג אוֹתָם בְּמוֹ סֵתֶר וְגָלוּי,
וְאֵל עָרֵב לְלֹא תֵרֵד עֲלוּקָה.

low, but say outright: 'This is what I wish to do'. They are snakes and scorpions, these children of the World, and even if you offer them your precious life as a gift, they will always betray you, as does the World herself in time of anguish and distress. Yes, they are just like their mother – so put them back into her deep, wide womb; kill them, either secretly or in the open. God is your pledge that you will not go down to hell.

אֲרַדֵּף מַחֲנֶה גָדוֹל

[...] אֲרַדֵּף מַחֲנֶה גָדוֹל לְבַדִּי
וְאָנִיס, וַאֲנִי אֶחָד, רְבָבָה.
רְכֹב עַל בָּמֳתֵי עָב קַל רְצוֹנִי,
וְאֶבְעַט בַּמְּלָכִים לָרְכִיבָה.
אֲנִי עוֹלֵב לְכָל מַמְרֶה אֲמָרַי,
וְנִשְׁמָתִי בְּכַף רֵעַי עֲלוּבָה.
יְדִיבֵנִי כְּמוֹ דוֹנַג לְשׁוֹן רַךְ,
וְרוּחַ פִּי לְכָל בַּרְזֶל מְדִיבָה.
נְהָרוֹת יִמְחֲאוּ הַכַּף בְּעָבְרִי,
וְלִפְעָמַי מְצוּלַת יָם חֲרֵבָה.
אֲנִי אוֹהֵב וְגַם חוֹשֵׁק לְכָל בָּר,
וְכֵן נַפְשִׁי לְכָל גֶּבֶר אֲהוּבָה.
וְלֹא מִרְמָה לְכָל אָדָם עֲלֵי פִי,
וְחַיָּתִי לְכָל עָצֵב עֲצֵבָה.
וְאִלּוּ יֻלְּדוּ מֵאֵין נְקֵבוֹת
גְּבָרִים – לֹא יְלָדַתְנִי נְקֵבָה. [...]

THE POET'S BOAST

I can hunt down great armies by myself and, single-handed, rout ten thousand. Whenever I want, I ride upon swift cloud-banks, kicking the kings as I ride by. I humble all those who disobey me, but I humble my soul and submit to my friends. A soft tongue melts me like wax, though the breath of my mouth eats away iron. Rivers clap their hands as I pass by; deep waters dry up under my feet. I have great love for the pure of heart and am myself beloved by the innocent. I speak no word of treachery to any man; I am heartbroken for all the brokenhearted. If a man could be born not of a woman, I would be that man!

שְׁמוּאֵל הַנָּגִיד

Samuel Hanagid

אָמְרָה: שְׂמַח

THE MOMENT

אָמְרָה: 'שְׂמַח, בַּעֲבוּר הִגִּיעֲךָ אֵל אֱלֵי
שָׁנִים חֲמִשִּׁים בְּעוֹלָמְךָ!' – וְלֹא יָדְעָה
כִּי אֵין חֲלֻקָּה בְּעֵינַי בֵּין יְמוֹתַי אֲשֶׁר
עָבְרוּ וּבֵינוֹת יְמֵי נֹחַ אֲשֶׁר אֶשְׁמְעָה.
אֵין לִי בְעוֹלָם לְבַד שָׁעָה אֲנִי בָהּ, וְהִיא
תַעְמֹד כְּרֶגַע – וְאַחַר כֵּן כְּעָב נָסְעָה.

She said: 'Rejoice, for God has brought you to your fiftieth year in the world!' But she had no inkling that, for my part, there is no difference at all between my own days which have gone by and the distant days of Noah in the rumoured past. I have nothing in the world but the hour in which I am: it pauses for a moment, and then, like a cloud, moves on.

הֲלִינוֹתִי גְדוּד כָּבֵד

IN THE RUINED CITADEL

הֲלִינוֹתִי גְדוּד כָּבֵד בְּבִירָה
הֲרָסוּהָ יְמֵי קֶדֶם קְצִינִים.
וְיָשַׁנּוּ עֲלֵי גַבָּהּ וְצִדָּהּ –
וְתַחְתֵּינוּ בְּעָלֶיהָ יְשֵׁנִים.
וְדִבַּרְתִּי לְלִבִּי: אֵי קְהָלִים
וְעַמִּים שָׁכְנוּ בָזֹאת לְפָנִים?
וְאֵי בוֹנִים וּמַחְרִיבִים, וְשָׂרִים
וְדַלִּים, וַעֲבָדִים וַאֲדוֹנִים,
וּמוֹלִידִים וְשַׁכּוּלִים, וְאָבוֹת
וּבָנִים, וַאֲבֵלִים וַחֲתָנִים?
וְעַם רַב נוֹלְדוּ אַחַר אֲחֵרִים,
בְּיָמִים אַחֲרֵי יָמִים וְשָׁנִים,
וְהָיוּ עַל פְּנֵי אֶרֶץ שְׁכֵנִים –
וְהֵם הַיּוֹם בְּלֶב אֶרֶץ שְׁכוּנִים,
וְקֶבֶר חָלְפוּ מֵאַרְמְנוֹתָם,
וְעָפָר – מֵחֲצֵרִים נַעֲמָנִים.

I billeted a strong force overnight in a citadel laid waste in former days by other generals. There we slept upon its back and flanks, while under us its landlords slept. And I said to my heart: Where are the many people who once lived here? Where are the builders and vandals, the rulers and paupers, the slaves and masters? Where are the begetters and the bereaved, the fathers and the sons, the mourners and the bridegrooms? And where are the many people born after the others had died, in days gone by, after other days and years? Once they lodged upon the earth; now they are lodged within it. They passed from their palaces to the grave, from pleasant courts to dust.

וְאִלּוּ הֶעֱלוּ רֹאשָׁם וְיָצְאוּ –
שְׁלָלוּנוּ נְפָשִׁים וַעֲדָנִים.
אֱמֶת, נַפְשִׁי, אֱמֶת, כָּהֵם לְמָחָר
אֱהִי אָנִי, וְאֵלֶּה הַהֲמוֹנִים!

Were they now to raise their heads and emerge, they would rob us of our lives and pleasures. Oh, it is true, my soul, most true: tomorrow I shall be like them, and all these troops as well!

וְיָצָא אָב

THE BATTLE OF ALFUENTE

...וכאשר הצילו האל אמר שירה זאת...והתרחש הנצחון הנכבד הזה ביום הששי, יום ראשון באלול, שנת שבע מאות ותשעים ושמונה.

. . . When God came to his rescue he spoke this song . . . The great victory took place on Friday, the first of Elul, in the year 4798 [4 August 1038].

[...] וְיָצָא אָב בְּרָעָה הַקְּדוּמָה,
וּבָא אֱלוּל בְּטוֹבָה לֹא אֲחוּרָה.
וְתָקַע אָהֳלוֹ בָּהָר בְּעֵבֶר,
וְתָקַעְנוּ בְּדֶרֶךְ הָעֲבָרָה,
וְלֹא שַׁתְנוּ לְבָבֵנוּ לְחֵילוֹ,
חֲשַׁבְנוּהוּ כְּאִלּוּ הוּא שְׁיָרָה.
וְהִרְבָּה, כַּאֲשֶׁר בָּא, הַדְּבָרִים,
וְשִׁסָּה בִי אֲנָשֵׁינוּ וְגֵרָה.
וּבִרְאוֹת צוֹרְרִי כִּי עַל לְשׁוֹנִי,
בְּפֶה אֶחָד, תְּדַבֵּר הַחֲבוּרָה –
אֲזַי הֵרִיק חֲנִית, רֹמַח וְחֶרֶב,
וְגַם סָגַר לְהִלָּחֵם סְגִירָה.

Then Av – the month of ancient woe[1] – departed, and Elul arrived, speeding good fortune. Ibn Abbas pitched his tents on the mountain side, and we pitched ours in the pass, taking no heed of his army, as though it were a passing caravan. Then he drew near and, with many words, tried to incite my men against me. But when my adversary saw that my company spoke with my voice, as one man, he uncovered spears, swords, and lances, and prepared his weapons for battle.

וְקָם הַצָּר – וְקָם הַצּוּר לְנֶגְדּוֹ;
וְאֵיךְ תָּקוּם, בְּקוּם צוּר, הַיְצִירָה?
וְעָמְדוּ הַחֲיָלוֹת מַעֲרָכָה
לְעֻמַּת מַעֲרֶכֶת צָר בְּשׁוּרָה.
אֲנָשִׁים יַחְשְׁבוּ, יוֹם אַף וְחֵמָה

My enemy rose – and the Rock rose against him. How can any creature rise up against his Creator? Now my troops and the enemy's drew up their ranks opposite each other. On such a day of anger, jealousy, and rage, men

1. The first and second Temples were both destroyed on the ninth of Av.

וְקִנְאָה, אֶת בְּכוֹר מָוֶת – בְּכוֹרָה,
וְכָל אֶחָד יְבַקֵּשׁ לוֹ קְנוֹת שֵׁם,
וְנַפְשׁוֹ, בַּאֲשֶׁר יִקְנֶה, מְכוּרָה.
וְנָעָה הָאֲדָמָה מִיְּסוֹדָהּ
וְנֶהֶפְכָה כְּמַהְפֵּכַת עֲמֹרָה,
וּפָנִים קִבְּצוּ פָארוּר וְהָדָר,
וְנֶהֶפְכוּ אֱלֵי שׁוּלֵי קְדֵרָה.
וְהַיּוֹם – יוֹם עֲרָפֶל וַחֲשֵׁכָה,
וְהַשֶּׁמֶשׁ, כְּמוֹ לִבִּי, שְׁחֹרָה,
וְקוֹל הָמוֹן – כְּקוֹל שַׁדַּי, כְּקוֹל יָם
וּמִשְׁבָּרָיו בְּעֵת יִסְעַר סְעִירָה.
וְהָאָרֶץ, בְּצֵאת שֶׁמֶשׁ, נְמוֹגָה
בְּעַמְדֶיהָ, כְּאִלּוּ הִיא שְׁכוּרָה,
וְהַסּוּסִים יְרוּצוּן גַּם יְשׁוּבוּן
כְּצִפְעוֹנִים נְטוּשִׁים מִמְּאוּרָה,
כְּאִלּוּ הָרְמָחִים הַשְּׁלוּחִים –
בְּרָקִים מִלְּאוּ אֲוִיר בְּאוֹרָה,
וְהַחִצִּים כְּמוֹ נִטְפֵי גְשָׁמִים,
וְהַגַּבּוֹת כְּאִלּוּ הֵם כְּבָרָה,
וְקַשְׁתוֹתָם בְּכַפָּם כַּנְּחָשִׁים,
וְכָל נָחָשׁ בְּפִיו יָקִיא דְבוֹרָה,
וְהַחֶרֶב עֲלֵי רֹאשָׁם כְּלַפִּיד,
בְּנָפְלוֹ כָּהֲתָה בוֹ הַנְּהָרָה.
וְדַם אִישִׁים עֲלֵי אֶרֶץ מְהַלֵּךְ
כְּדַם אֵילִים בְּצִדֵּי הָעֲזָרָה,
וְקָצוּ הַגְּבָרִים הַגְּבִירִים
בְּחַיֵּיהֶם, וְהַמִּיתָה בְחוּרָה.
כְּפִירִים יֶחֱזוּ מַכָּה טְרִיָּה
עֲלֵי רֹאשָׁם כְּאִלּוּ הִיא עֲטָרָה,
וְהַמִּיתָה בְדָתֵיהֶם יְשָׁרָה,
וְחַיָּתָם בְּעֵינֵיהֶם אֲסוּרָה.

deem the Prince of Death a princely prize; and each man seeks to win renown, though he must lose his life for it. The earth's foundations, overthrown like Gomorrah, reeled to and fro. Every face turned red, or black as the bottom of a pot. It was a day of darkness and thick fog. The sun was as black as my heart. The tumult was like that of a cloudburst, like the roar of breakers when the sea is swept by a storm. As the sun came out, the earth rocked on its pillars as if it were drunk. The horses lunged back and forth like vipers darting out of their nests. The hurled spears were like bolts of lightning, filling the air with light. Arrows pelted us like raindrops, as if our shields were sieves. Their strung bows were like serpents, each serpent spewing forth a stinging bee. Their swords above their heads were like glowing torches which darken as they fall. The blood of men flowed upon the ground like the blood of rams on the corners of the altar. Still, my gallant men scorned their lives, preferring death. These young lions welcomed each raw wound upon their heads as though it were a garland. To die – they believed – was to keep the faith; to live – they thought – was forbidden.

וּמָה אֶעְשֶׂה ? וְאֵין מָנוֹס וּמַשְׁעֵן
וּמַשְׁעֵנָה, וְהַתִּקְוָה עֲקוּרָה !
מְשַׂנְאִים יִשְׁפְּכוּ דָמִים כְּמַיִם
בְּיוֹם צָר – וַאֲנִי אֶשְׁפֹּךְ עֲתָרָה
לְאֵל מַשְׁפִּיל וּמַפִּיל כָּל מְעַוֵּל
בְּגֻמָּצוֹ אֲשֶׁר חָפַר וְכָרָה,
וּמֵשִׁיב, יוֹם קְרָב, חֶרֶב וְחִצִּים
בְּלֵב אוֹיֵב אֲשֶׁר הֵכִין וְיָרָה. [...]

(1038)

And what was I to do with no escape, no prop or stay, and all hope gone? While my foes, on this bitter day, poured out blood like water, I poured out my prayer to God, who degrades all evildoers and makes them fall into the pit which they have dug; to God, who on the day of battle will make the enemy's drawn swords and darting arrows pierce his own heart!

רְאֵה הַיּוֹם בְּצָרָתִי

SHORT PRAYER IN TIME OF BATTLE

...והמלחמה [בין צבאות הנגיד ובין צבאות אסמעיל אבן עבאד] התלקחה ביניהם בקרבת הנחל ג׳ניל. אז אמר את הבתים האלה ושׂמם במקום תפילת המנחה ליום ההוא.

. . . *The battle* [between the forces of the Nagid and the army of Seville under Isma'il ibn Abbad] *flared up near the Sengil river. It was then that he composed these verses, which he recited instead of the afternoon service on that day.*

רְאֵה הַיּוֹם בְּצָרָתִי, שְׁמַע וּשְׁעֵה עֲתָרָתִי,
זְכָר־דָּבָר לְעַבְדֶּךָ וְאַל אֵבוֹשׁ בְּשִׂבְרָתִי.
הֲתַגִּיעַ לְרַע לִי יָד וְאַתְּ יָדִי וְסִתְרָתִי ?
יְעַדְתַּנִי וְהֵיטַבְתָּ בְּיַד צִירִים בְּשׂוֹרָתִי.
אֲנִי עוֹבֵר בְּתוֹךְ מַיִם – דְּלֵנִי מִמְּגוּרָתִי,
אֲנִי הוֹלֵךְ בְּמוֹקֵד אֵשׁ – פְּצֵנִי מִבְּעֵרָתִי.
וְאִם יֶשׁ לִי מְרוּרוֹת, מָה אֲנִי אוֹ מַה מְּרוֹרָתִי ?
אֲנִי בַצַּר וְלֹא אוּכַל לְהַרְבּוֹת אֶת אֲמִירָתִי.
עֲשֵׂה לִי תַּאֲוַת לִבִּי וְחוּשָׁה נָּא לְעֶזְרָתִי,
וְאִם אֵינִי כְדַאי אֶצְלָךְ, עֲשֵׂה לִבְנִי וְתוֹרָתִי !

(1039)

See my distress today; listen to my prayer, and answer it. Remember Your promise[1] to Your servant; do not disappoint my hope. Can any hand do me violence, when You are my hand and my shelter? You once made me a pledge and sent me good tidings with Your angels. Now I am passing through deep waters – lift me out of my terrors. I am walking through searing fire – snatch me from the flames. If I have sinned – what am I, what are my sins? I am in danger, and cannot pray at length. Give me my heart's desire; oh, hasten to my aid. If I am not deserving in Your eyes – do it for the sake of my son and my sacred learning.

1. In his childhood the Nagid had a vision, in which the archangels Michael and Gabriel brought him God's promise of protection.

מְבַשֵּׂר טוֹב, הֲבִינֵנִי

ON LEARNING OF HIS ENEMY'S DEATH

והיה הרופא אבו מדין לן אצלו ויעוררו והודיעו על מה שראה בחלום ולא פקפק עוד בקצו של אבן אבי מוסי. ואכן נהרג הלה כעבור ימים מועטים. ויאמר הנגיד כשנתבשׂר במותו, והיה זה בשנת ת״ת, ויקרא לשירו בשם ׳בשורה׳.

One night, when the doctor Abu Medin was sleeping in his house, the Nagid woke him up and told him what he had dreamt; he was now certain that Ibn Abi Musa's death was imminent. And, indeed, the latter was killed a few days later. When the Nagid was informed of his death – this was in the year 4800 [1040] – he composed the following verses, which he entitled 'The Tidings'.

[...] ׳מְבַשֵּׂר טוֹב, הֲבִינֵנִי וְהָרִים קוֹל בְּחַסְדֶּךָ,
וְצַפְצֶף לִי כְּסוּס עָגוּר וְאַל תַּמְעִיט אֲמָרֶיךָ:
הֲצֶדֶק הוּא אֲשֶׁר אֶשְׁמַע, וְאֵיךְ הָיָה וְאֵיכָכָה?
הֲבִינֵנִי, הֲגְוִיַּת בֶּן־אֲבִי־מוּסִי מְחֻתָּכָה?
וְנִבְלָתוֹ – הֲנִסְחָבָה עֲלֵי חוּצוֹת וְהָשְׁלָכָה?׳

'Good herald, now tell me and, if you please, speak up. Twitter at me like a swallow, do not spare your words. Is what I hear true indeed? And how, how did it happen? Tell me, was the corpse of Ibn Abi Musa mangled? Was his carcass dragged through the streets, then flung away?'

הֱשִׁיבַנִי: ׳חֲדֵה וּשְׂמַח וְיַעֲלֹץ לְבָבֶךָ,
וְקוּם וּרְקַע עֲלֵי רֶגֶל וְשׁוּב וּמְחָא בְכַפֶּךָ!
וְהֵרָפֵד בְּתַפּוּחִים וְהִסָּמֵךְ בְּיֵינֶךָ,
וְגַדֵּל שֵׁם אֱלֹהֶיךָ וּמַלֵּא מִשְׂחוֹק פִּיךָ!
וְקוּם וּקְרָא בְּ״שִׁיר שִׁירִים״
וְאַל תִּקְרַב אֱלֵי ״אֵיכָה״.
וְתֵן לִי בַבְּשׂוֹרָה אֶת חֲלִיצָתְךָ וּמַדֶּיךָ –
לְמַעַן בֶּן־אֲבִי־מוּסִי כְּבָר נָפַל בְּמַהְפֵּכָה,
כְּמוֹ נִכְסַף לְבֶן־עַבָּאס אֲשֶׁר בִּקֵּשׁ לְהָרְגֶךָ,
וְהָלַךְ לַחֲזוֹת פָּנָיו בְּצַלְמָוֶת וּבַחֲשֵׁכָה.
וְהָעִיר מִמְּשׂוֹשׂ קָמָיו מְשַׂמַּחַת כְּמוֹתֶךָ,
וּמְשׁוֹאַת בְּנֵי בֵיתוֹ מְבֹהָלָה וְנָבוֹכָה׳.

He answered: 'Rejoice and let your heart exult! Arise and stamp your feet, then clap your hands! Indulge yourself in apricots, refresh yourself with wine, glorify the name of your God, fill your mouth with laughter, go and read the Song of Songs, and stay away from Lamentations. And, for my news, give me your belt and clothes. Know that Ibn Abi Musa has already fallen into the pit, as though he were longing for Ibn Abbas – who tried to kill you[1] – and went to see his face in darkness, dark as death. The city, full of his rivals' joy, is as elated as you are, but stunned and dazed as well by his kinsmen's ruin.'

1. Ibn Abbas, another enemy of the Nagid, was captured and executed the previous year, after the battle of Alfuente (p. 286).

הֲשִׁיבוֹתִיו: ׳דְּבַשׁ מָתוֹק וְחָלָב עַל לְשׁוֹנֶךָ,
וְתִתְבַּשֵּׂר מְהֵרָה כִּי כְּמוֹ זֹאת בָּא לְצָרֶיךָ!
קְחָה מַדִּי וּמַלְבּוּשִׁי וְשִׂים נִזְרִי בְּרֹאשֶׁךָ,
וְלֵךְ אֶל כָּל מְיֻדָּעַי וְהַשְׂמִיחֵם בְּמִלֶּיךָ –
וְיֵדְעוּ כִּי יְחִידָתוֹ לְגֵיהִנֹּם מְמֻשָּׁכָה
וְכִי מֶלֶךְ הֲרָגָהוּ וְרָאָה בוֹ אֲשֶׁר חִכָּה׳.

I said to him: 'Sweet syrup and milk are on your tongue! May you quickly learn that a like fate has struck down your enemies! Now take my clothes, my robes, put my diadem on your head, go to all my friends and gladden them with your words. Let them know that his soul has been dragged down to hell, that he was killed by a king[1] who is now gloating over him, as he had hoped.'

בְּנוֹ עַבָּאס, שְׂמַח כִּי בָא לְשַׁחֶרְךָ חֲבֵרֶךָ!
שְׁבוּ יַחַד, וְהַכֵּהוּ בְּצַלְמָוֶת – וְיַכֶּכָּה.
וְאִם תַּחְפֹּץ, קְשֹׁר חֶבֶל עֲלֵי רֹאשׁוֹ וְרֹאשֶׁךָ,
וְיָנוּד עַל אֲשֶׁר הָיָה – וְתָשִׁיב לוֹ בְּקִינֶיךָ,
וְיִהְיֶה לָּךְ כְּמוֹ פֶסֶל – וְתִהְיֶה לּוֹ כְּמוֹ מִיכָה.
וְחִרְשׁוּ עַל בְּנֵי שַׁחַת שְׁנֵיכֶם רַע וְתַהְפּוּכָה.
וְיִרְקַב בֶּן־אֲבִי־מוּסַי כְּמוֹתֶךָ בְּקִבְרֶךָ,
וְיִשָּׁכַח, כְּמוֹ נִשְׁכַּח שִׁמְךָ הָרַע וְזִכְרֶךָ.
כְּבָר בָּאתֶם אֱלֵי צַוָּאר בְּפַח יָקוּשׁ וּבִשְׂבָכָה,
וְנָחָה הַמְּלוּכָה מִן מְשׁוֹאַתְכֶם וְשָׁכְכָה,
וְאֵין בָּכֶם אֲשֶׁר יִצְלַח לְמוֹעֵצוֹת וְלִמְלוּכָה.

Ibn Abbas, be happy that your friend has come to visit you! Sit together in the gloom of death, hit him and he will hit you back. Or, if you wish to mourn, wind ropes around his head and yours. He will lament what is past, and you will answer him with your dirges. He will be for you a graven image, and you will be like a father[2] to him. Now the pair of you can plot your evil and subversion against the progeny of the pit. Ibn Abi Musa will rot, as you did in your grave; he will be forgotten, as your evil name and memory have been forgotten. Now that you are up to your necks in nets and snares, the kingdom will at last be rid of your havoc and find peace, for none of you is fit for the councils of kings.

וְאַתְּ, חוֹפֵר, אֲשֶׁר תַּחְפֹּר קְבוּרָתוֹ בְּיָדֶיךָ –
כְּרֵה לוֹ כַּאֲשֶׁר כָּרָה, בְּדִינְךָ וֵאלֹהֶיךָ,
וְהַעְמִיק עַד תְּהוֹם לוֹ – וַאֲנִי אֶתֵּן שְׂכָרֶךָ,
וְהַךְ בָּאֵת לְכָל עַיִן אֲשֶׁר עָלָיו תְּהִי בוֹכָה!

And you, O gravedigger, whose hands will dig his grave, I charge you by your God and by your creed: make a pit for him, as he made for others. Dig down to the very abyss – I will pay you for it myself – and with your mattock strike any eye that sheds a tear for him!

1. Nega, king of the Slavs.
2. Lit. 'Micah' (Judges 17.4 ff.), who made an idol and installed a young Levite in his house as priest.

לְזֹאת אֶלְבַּשׁ וְאֶתְעַטֵּף וְאֶתְבַּשֵּׂם וְאָסוּכָה
וְאֶתְנַהֵג בְּטוּב לֵבָב וְאָשׁוּבָה וְאֵלֵכָה
וְאֶדַּמֶּה אֱלֵי יוֹנִים עֲלֵי מְלֵאת וּבִבְרֵכָה,
וְאֶתְאַמֵּץ כְּשִׁמְשׁוֹן עַל יְתַד אֹהֶל וּמַסֵּכָה,
וְאָגִילָה בְּמוֹת צָרַי בְּבֵיתָם אוֹ בְמַעֲרָכָה.

As for me, I will put on festive clothing, I will perfume and anoint myself. I will move about with a glad heart, coming and going, as happy as a dove beside a brook or splashing in a pool. I will become as strong as Samson, who pulled away the tent pin and the warp.[1] I will make merry when my enemies die, whether it be in their homes or in battle!

וְאוֹמֵר: ׳מִי אֲשֶׁר עָשָׂה לְךָ אֶת זֹאת כְּנַפְשֶׁךָ?׳
עֲנִיתִיהוּ: ׳הֲלֹא תֵדַע, אֱלֹהִים יַעֲשֶׂה כָּכָה!
שְׁתֹק, וּכְתֹב לְךָ טוּרִים לְזִכָּרוֹן בְּסִפְרֶךָ,
וְתִקְרָאֵם קְרִיאָתְךָ בְּיוֹם שַׁבָּת בְּדָתֶךָ,
וְיִהְיוּ עַל לְבָבֶךָ וְהוֹדַעְתָּם לְבָנֶיךָ.

(1040)

If anyone should ask me, 'Who was it that made your wish come true?', I will answer, 'Don't you know? It was God who did all this! Now be quiet, and write down these verses! Read them aloud, as the portion of the Law is read on Sabbath. Keep them in your heart and teach them to your sons.'

הֲלָעַד אֲנִי שׁוֹכֵן

COMPLAINT

הֲלָעַד אֲנִי שׁוֹכֵן בְּאֹהֶל, כְּמוֹ עֲרָב,
וְתַחַת יְרִיעָה כָּל יְמוֹתַי מְדוֹרִי?
כְּבָר שִׁכְּחוּנִי הָעֲרָבָה וְהַזְּמַן
חֲצֵרִי בְּעִירִי — אָן יְדִידֵי חֲצֵרִי?

Shall I forever live in a tent, like a Bedouin? Must all my days be passed beneath tent-curtains? Time and the desert have already made me forget my court back in town. Oh, where are my courtier friends?

קְרָב

WAR

קְרָב דּוֹמֶה בְרֹאשׁוֹ אֶל יְפֵיפִיָּה
אֲשֶׁר כָּל אִישׁ לְשַׂחֵק בָּהּ יְאַוֶּה,
וְסוֹפוֹ כִּזְקֵנָה הַמְּאוּסָה
אֲשֶׁר כָּל שׁוֹחֲרָהּ יִבְכֶּה וְיִדְוֶה.

War is at first like a beautiful girl with whom all men long to play, but in the end like a repulsive hag whose suitors all weep and ache.

1. Judges 16.4.

לֹא יַעֲבִידְךָ

THE MASTER

לֹא יַעֲבִידְךָ מוֹשְׁלְךָ עַד יְקַוֶּה כִּי
יִשְׁקֹט וְאַתְּ תִּיגַע וְתִיעַף בְּמַעֲבָדָיו.
אַתָּה כְּמֶלְקָחָיו: בְּיָדוֹ יְבִיאֲךָ תּוֹךְ
הָאוּר – וְיִשְׁמֹר מִשְּׂרֵפָה בְּךָ יָדָיו!

No master will hire you, unless he can expect to be idle while you tire and become weary in his service. You are for him like tongs: with his hands he pushes you into the fire, but he takes great care not to burn himself on you.

אֶרֶץ לְאָדָם

THE PRISON

אֶרֶץ לְאָדָם בֵּית כְּלוּא כָּל יָמָיו,
לָכֵן אֲנִי אוֹמֵר אֱמֶת לַסָּכָל:
תָּרוּץ – וְשָׁמַיִם סְבִיבוֹתֶיךָ
מִכָּל עֲבָרִים; קוּם וְצֵא אִם תּוּכָל.

The earth is a prison to man all his life. Therefore I say this truth to the fool: though you rush about, the sky surrounds you on all sides. Try to get out, if you can.

אוֹהֲבֵי יָמִים

THE ROOT

אוֹהֲבֵי יָמִים עַל גַּב אָרֶץ,
הַיְדַעְתֶּם כִּי חַיֵּיכֶם שָׁוְא?
אַתֶּם מִשֹּׁרֶשׁ מָוֶת: כָּל
עָנָף יָשׁוּב אֶל שָׁרָשָׁיו!

Oh, you merry-makers on earth's back, do you know that your life is nothing? You grew from the root of death – and every branch to its own root returns!

שִׁית לִבְּךָ

THE TWO CRIES

שִׁית לִבְּךָ, תָּבִין קְלוֹן שִׂמְחַת
לֵב בֵּין שְׁתֵּי בְכִיּוֹת לְךָ נִמְצֵאת:
תִּבְכֶּה בְּעֵת בּוֹאֲךָ אֱלֵי עוֹלָם
אַתָּה, וְאַחֵר יִבְכְּךָ עֵת צֵאת.

Reflect, and you will realize how shameful is your heart's delight, which comes between two cries: you cry when you come into the world, and others cry for you when you leave it.

הַיָּם בֵּינִי וּבֵינֶךָ

ונסע עד שהתקרב למקום קברו והפסיק את נסיעתו ופנה אליו ואמר בענין זה:

הֲיָם בֵּינִי וּבֵינְךָ וְלֹא אֶטֶּה לְחַלּוֹתְךָ
וְלֹא אָרוּץ בְּלֵב חָרֵד וְאֵשֵׁב עַל קְבוּרָתְךָ ?
אֱמֶת, אִם אֶעֱשֶׂה כָזֹאת אֱהִי בוֹגֵד בְּאַחְוָתְךָ,
אֲהָהּ, אָחִי, אֲנִי יוֹשֵׁב עֲלֵי קִבְרְךָ לְעֻמָּתְךָ,
לְךָ מַכְאוֹב בְּתוֹךְ לִבִּי כְּמַכְאוֹבִי בְמִיתָתְךָ.
וְאִם אֶתֵּן לְךָ שָׁלוֹם – וְלֹא אֶשְׁמַע תְּשׁוּבָתְךָ,
וְלֹא תֵצֵא לְפָגְשֵׁנִי בְּיוֹם בּוֹאִי לְאַדְמָתְךָ,
וְלֹא תִשְׂחַק בְּקִרְבָתִי וְלֹא אֶשְׂחַק בְּקִרְבָתְךָ,
וְלֹא תִרְאֶה תְמוּנָתִי וְלֹא אֶרְאֶה תְמוּנָתְךָ,
לְמַעַן כִּי שְׁאוֹל בֵּיתְךָ וּבַקֶּבֶר מְעוֹנָתְךָ.
בְּכוֹר אָבִי וּבֶן אִמִּי, שְׁלוֹמִים לָךְ בְּאַחֲרִיתְךָ,
וְרוּחַ אֵל תְּהִי נָחָה עֲלֵי רוּחָךְ וְנִשְׁמָתְךָ!
אֲנִי הוֹלֵךְ לְאַרְצִי, כִּי בְאֶרֶץ סָגְרוּ אוֹתְךָ.
וְאָנוּם עֵת וְאִיקַץ עֵת – וְאַתְּ לָעַד בְּנוּמָתְךָ,
וְעַד בּוֹא יוֹם חֲלִיפָתִי בְּלִבִּי אֵשׁ פְּרִידָתְךָ!

LAMENT FOR HIS BROTHER

On one of his journeys, he passed by his brother's burial-place. There he paused and addressed him as follows:

Is there a sea between me and you, that I should not turn aside to be with you, that I should not run with a troubled heart to sit at your grave-side? Truly, if I did not do so, I would be a traitor to our brotherly love. O my brother, here I am, facing you, sitting by your grave, and the grief in my heart is as great as on the day you died. If I greeted you, I would hear no reply. You do not come out to meet me when I visit your grounds. You will not laugh in my company, nor I in yours. You cannot see my face, nor I yours, for the pit is your home, the grave your dwelling-place! First-born of my father, son of my mother, may you have peace in your final rest, and may the spirit of God rest upon your spirit and your soul! I am returning to my own soil, for you have been locked under the soil. Sometimes I shall sleep, sometimes wake – while you lie in your sleep forever. But until my last day, the fire of your loss will remain in my heart!

רֵעִי, הֲתִישַׁן

ובסוף כסלו של שנת תת"ה שר שירה וסיפר בה שתי הלקיות, השמשי והירחי...

רֵעִי, הֲתִישַׁן ? קוּם וְהָעִירָה
שַׁחַר, וּבִשְׁמֵי מַעְלָה שׁוּרָה:

THE TWO ECLIPSES

At the end of the year 1044, the Nagid composed this song, in which he described the two eclipses, the solar and the lunar.

Are you asleep, my friend? Rise and awake the dawn, look up to heaven.

תִּרְאֵם כְּעוֹר נָמֵר אֲשֶׁר אֵין בּוֹ
מָקוֹם אֲשֶׁר אֵין בּוֹ חֲבַרְבּוּרָה;
וּרְאֵה חֲצִי סַהַר בְּלֵיל תֻּמּוֹ
קוֹדֵר כְּפִי כִבְשָׁן וְכִקְדֵרָה,
כִּדְמוּת פְּנֵי עַלְמָה אֲשֶׁר חֶצְיָם
אָדְמוּ וְעַל חֶצְיָם שְׁקַעֲרוּרָה.

See, it is like a leopard's skin, all covered with spots. And see how the half-moon – which should be full on this night – is as black as the mouth of an oven or the rim of a pot; like the face of a girl, half flushed and half in shadow.

שׁוּב וַחֲזֵה שֶׁמֶשׁ אֲשֶׁר רֻבָּהּ
הוּבָא בְּסוֹף חֹדֶשׁ בְּשַׁעֲרוּרָה,
וּדְמוּת מְעַט אוֹרָהּ עֲלֵי חָשְׁכָּהּ
נֵזֶר בְּרֹאשׁ לוּדִית שְׁחַרְחָרָה,
וּדְמוּת אֲדָמָה, עַל אֲשֶׁר בָּא עַל
שִׁמְשָׁהּ, כְּבוֹכִיָּה חֲמַרְמָרָה.

Now look again, at this month's end, and see the sun, almost engulfed by gloom. What little light remains upon its darkness is like a diadem on the head of a Negress. And the earth, as if in mourning for its sun, is like a woman disfigured by tears.

הִכָּה שְׁנֵי אוֹרָיו בְּתוֹךְ חֹדֶשׁ
אֶחָד אֲשֶׁר לוֹ עֹז וְתִפְאָרָה:
כִּסָּה פְּנֵי סַהַר בְּחוּג אַרְצוֹ,
וּבְסַהֲרוֹ שִׁמְשׁוֹ מְסֻתָּרָה.
כָּל זֹאת פְּעֻלַּת אֵל, וְהוּא יַעַשׂ
חֶפְצוֹ בְּמִפְעָלָיו אֲשֶׁר בָּרָא.

He who is master of might and beauty, He struck both His luminaries in the very same month. He covered the face of the moon with His terrestrial globe and blocked off the sun with His moon. All this was done by God, who does as He wishes with His works.

נִבְרָא בְּתוֹךְ סַהַר מְעַט אֹפֶל
מֵרֹאשׁ, וְחַמָּה נִבְרְאָה בָרָה;
לָכֵן אֲדַמֵּמוֹ, בְּהִקָּדְרָם
עַתָּה בְּחֹשֶׁךְ זֶה אֲשֶׁר קָרָה,
לִשְׁתֵּי שְׁכוּלוֹת: זֹאת בְּפָנֶיהָ
פֶּצַע, וְזֹאת פֶּצַע וְחַבּוּרָה.

From the very beginning He put some shadow in the moon, but the sun He created pure. Therefore – as they now dim, in this darkness that has come to pass – I compare them to two bereaved women: the one with bruises on her face, the other with bruises and sores.

אוֹר יוֹם בְּיוֹם הָקְדַּר, וְאוֹר לַיִל
הִקְדִּיר בְּעֶרֶב יוֹם וְאַשְׁמוּרָה –
כְּגְבִיר אֲשֶׁר קָצַף וְהֵבִיא כָּל

He darkened the light of day in mid-morning, and the light of night at midnight, like a raging king who

שָׂרָיו בְּאַרְצוֹתָם בְּתוֹךְ צָרָה.
הִכָּה מְאוֹר לַיִל תְּחִלָּה, אַךְ
מַכַּת מְאוֹר הַיּוֹם מְאֻחָרָה –
כִּגְבִיר אֲשֶׁר יַשְׁקֶה לְאָמָה כּוֹס
רַעַל, וְאַחַר יַשְׁקְ לִגְבִירָה. [...]

harasses all his lords in their own domains. First He struck the night-light, and only later did He strike the light of day, like a king who gives a stupefying drink first to his maid-servant and afterwards to his queen.

אֲצַפֶּה אֱלֵי שַׁחַק

HEAVEN AND EARTH

אֲצַפֶּה אֱלֵי שַׁחַק וְכוֹכָבָיו
וְאַבִּיט בְּאֶרֶץ אֶת רְמָשֶׂיהָ,
וְאָבִין בְּלִבִּי כִּי יְצִירָתָם
יְצִירָה מְחֻכָּמָה בְּמַעְשֶׂיהָ.
רְאוּ אֶת שְׁמֵי מָרוֹם כְּמוֹ קֻבָּה,
תְּפוּרִים בְּלוּלָאוֹת קְרָסֶיהָ.
וְסַהַר וְכוֹכָבָיו כְּמוֹ רוֹעָה,
תְּשַׁלַּח בְּתוֹךְ אָחוּ כְּבָשֶׂיהָ.
כְּאִלּוּ לְבָנָה בֵּין נְשִׂיאֵי עָב
סְפִינָה מְהַלֶּכֶת בְּנִסֶּיהָ.
וְעָנָן כְּעַלְמָה עַל פְּנֵי גַנָּה
תְּהַלֵּךְ וְתַשְׁקֶה אֶת הֲדַסֶּיהָ.
וְעָב טַל כְּמוֹ נַעֲרָה, תְּנַעֵר מִן
שְׂעָרָהּ עֲלֵי אֶרֶץ רְסִיסֶיהָ.
וְשׁוֹכְנִים כְּמוֹ חַיָּה אֲשֶׁר נָטְתָה
לְלִינָה, וְחַצְרוֹתָם אֲבוּסֶיהָ –
וְכֻלָּם יְנוּסוּן מֵחֲתַת מָוֶת
כְּיוֹנָה אֲשֶׁר הַנֵּץ יְנִיסֶהָ,
וְסוֹפָם לְהִדָּמוֹת לְצַלַּחַת
אֲשֶׁר שִׁבְּרוּ כָתִית חֲרָסֶיהָ.

I survey the heavens and the stars; I look at the earth with its creeping creatures; and I understand in my heart that they were all intricately fashioned. Look up at the sky – like a tent, whose clasps[1] are joined to it by loops; the moon and its stars – like a shepherdess grazing her flock in a pasture; the moon among the sweeping clouds – like a ship sailing with raised pennants; a cloud – like a girl walking through a garden, watering the myrtles; a cloud of dew – like a maiden shaking the drops from her hair onto the ground. But the earth's inhabitants are like an army pitching its tents for a night, looting the local granaries.[2] And all flee before the terror of death – like a dove chased by a hawk. All are doomed to be like an earthenware plate which has been smashed to bits.

1. The gold fasteners in the Tabernacle hangings (Exodus 26.6) were traditionally compared to the stars.
2. Lit. 'the dwellings [of the inhabitants] are the food-stores [of the army]'. This may also mean 'their dwellings are as temporary and transient as an army's stores or mess'.

בְּעִתּוֹת עָצְבְּךָ

בְּעִתּוֹת עָצְבְּךָ חַזֵּק לְבָבְךָ,
וְאִם תַּעְמֹד עֲלֵי שַׁעַר הֲרֵגָה:
לְנֵר – מָאוֹר בְּטֶרֶם הַדְּעִיכָה,
וְלִכְפִירִים מְדֻקָּרִים – שְׁאָגָה.

TAKE HEART

In times of sorrow, take heart, even though you stand at death's door: the candle flares up before it dies, and wounded lions roar.

עֲלֵיכֶם לְפוֹעַלְכֶם

עֲלֵיכֶם לְפוֹעַלְכֶם לְיַשֵּׁר פְּעָלֵיכֶם –
וְלָכֶם יְהִי עָלָיו לְשַׁלֵּם גְּמוּלֵיכֶם.
וְאַל בַּעֲבוֹדָתוֹ תְּבַלּוּ יְמוֹתֵיכֶם,
אֲבָל עֵת עֲשׂוּ לָאֵל, וְעִתִּים עֲשׂוּ לָכֶם.
תְּנוּ לוֹ חֲצִי הַיּוֹם, וְחֶצְיוֹ לְמַעֲשֵׂיכֶם –
וְאַל תִּתְּנוּ פוּגַת לְיַיִן בְּלֵילֵיכֶם!
וְכַבּוּ מְאוֹר הַנֵּר וְאוֹרוּ בְכוֹסֵיכֶם,
וְקוּצוּ בְּקוֹל שָׁרִים וְשִׁירוּ בְנִבְלֵיכֶם.
וְאִם אֵין בְּקֶבֶר שִׁיר וְחֶמֶר וְחֶבֶר – הוֹי
פְּתָאִים, יְהִי זֶה חֶלְקְכֶם מֵעֲמָלֵיכֶם!

THE REWARD

You owe it to your Maker to pursue a righteous course, and He must give you your just deserts. But do not pass all your days in His service: set aside a time for God and times for yourselves. Give half the day to Him, half to your own needs – and then give wine no respite all night long! Put out the candle light – let your goblets shine instead. Scorn the voice of singers – let your jugs sing for you. Since you will not find wine, song, or company in the grave – let this, O fools, be your reward for all your labours!

מֵת אָב

מֵת אָב וּמֵת אֱלוּל וּמֵת חֻמָּם,
גַּם נֶאֱסַף תִּשְׁרִי וּמֵת עִמָּם.
בָּאוּ יְמֵי הַקֹּר, וְהַתִּירוֹשׁ
אָדַם, וְקוֹלוֹ בִכְלִי דָמָם.
לָכֵן, יְדִידִי, סֹב אֱלֵי רֵעִים,
כָּל אִישׁ וְאִישׁ יַעַשׂ אֲשֶׁר זָמָם.

WINTER WINE SONG

Av[1] has died and Elul has died, and so has their warmth. Tishri, too, has died and been gathered to them. The cold days have come, the must has grown red and is now silent in its barrel.[2] Therefore, my friend, go find companions – and let each man fulfil his own desire! They said: 'Behold the

1. Av, Elul and Tishri are the autumn months.
2. After fermentation is complete.

אָמְרוּ: ׳חֲזֵה עָבִים בְּהַגְשִׁימָם
וּשְׁמַע שְׁמֵי מָרוֹם בְּהַרְעִימָם
וּרְאֵה כְפוֹר וּלְשׁוֹן מְדוּרָה – זֶה
יֵרֵד וְזֶה יַעַל וְיִתְרוֹמָם.
קוּמָה שְׁתֵה בַכּוֹס, וְשׁוּב וּשְׁתֵה
בַּכַּד, וּבַלַּיִל וְגַם יוֹמָם.׳

clouds pouring down, listen to the heavens thundering. See the frost and the tongues of fire: one falls down as the others rise and swirl. Arise, drink from the cup, and then again out of the jug; drink night and day!'

מְאָדָּם בְּמַרְאֵהוּ

WINE

מְאָדָּם בְּמַרְאֵהוּ וְעָרֵב לְשׁוֹתֵהוּ
וּמָזוּג בְּאִסְפַּמְיָא – וְזִכְרוֹ אֱלֵי הֹדּוּ.
וְחַלָּשׁ בְּאַגָּנָיו, אֲבָל בַּעֲלוֹתוֹ אֶל
רָאשִׁים – אֲזַי יִרְדֶּה בְרָאשִׁים אֲשֶׁר יֵרְדוּ.
וְשַׁכּוּל אֲשֶׁר דָּמָיו מְסוּכִים בְּדִמְעוֹתָיו –
יְגוֹנָיו בְּדַם אֶשְׁכּוֹל יְנוּסוּן וְיִדּוּ.
כְּאִלּוּ יְדִידִים, עֵת יְסַבּוּם אֲשִׁישׁוֹתָיו
מִיָּד לְיָד, גּוֹרָל עֲלֵי יַהֲלֹם יַדּוּ.

Red to the eye, sweet to the drinker, it is poured out in Spain but its bouquet reaches India. When it is in the bowls, it is feeble; but once it goes to the head, it holds sway over swaying heads.[1] The wretch whose heart's blood is mixed with his tears banishes his sorrows with the grape's blood. As the goblets make the rounds, passing from hand to hand, it seems as if the friends are casting lots for a diamond.

רְאֵה יַסְמִין

THE JASMINE

רְאֵה יַסְמִין אֲשֶׁר בַּדָּיו יְרֻקִּים
כְּמוֹ פִטְדָה וְעָלָיו וַאֲגַפָּיו,
וְצִצָּיו כַּבְּדֹלָחִים לְבָנִים,
וְכָאֹדֶם מְאָדָּמִים סְעִפָּיו –
כְּמוֹ עֶלֶם לְבֶן פָּנִים וְשׁוֹפֵךְ
דְּמֵי אִישִׁים נְקִיֵּי כַף בְּכַפָּיו.

Look at the jasmine, whose branches, leaves, and stems are green as chrysolite, whose flowers are white as rock crystal, whose tendrils are red as carnelian – like a white-faced youth whose hands are shedding the blood of innocent men.

1. Or, according to another reading, 'it rules the heads of states'.

אֱהִי כֹּפֶר לְעֹפֶר

אֱהִי כֹּפֶר לְעֹפֶר קָם בְּלֵיל
לְקוֹל כִּנּוֹר וְעוּגָבִים מְטִיבִים,
אֲשֶׁר רָאָה בְּיָדִי כוֹס וְאָמַר:
'שְׁתֵה מִבֵּין שְׂפָתַי דַּם עֲנָבִים!'
וְיָרֵחַ כְּמוֹ יוֹד נִכְתְּבָה עַל
כְּסוּת שַׁחַר בְּמֵימֵי הַזְּהָבִים.

INVITATION

I would lay down my life for the fawn who, rising at night to the sound of melodious harp and flute, saw a cup in my hand and said: 'Drink your grape's blood from between my lips.' And the moon was like a C[1] inscribed in golden ink upon the robes of night.

אֱהִי כֹּפֶר צְבִי

אֱהִי כֹּפֶר צְבִי הֵפֵר בְּרִיתִי,
וְאַהֲבָתוֹ בְּתוֹךְ לִבִּי שְׁמוּרָה,
אֲשֶׁר אָמַר לְסַהַר בַּעֲלוֹתוֹ:
'הֲתִרְאֶה אֶת מְאוֹר פָּנַי, וְתֵרָא?'
וּמַרְאֵה הַלְּבָנָה בָּאֲפֵלָה
כְּבָרֶקֶת בְּכַף עַלְמָה שְׁחֹרָה.

THE BEAUTIFUL BOY

I would lay down my life for that gazelle (even though he betrayed me, my heart still keeps his love) who said to the rising moon: 'You see my radiant face, and yet you dare to show yourself?' And in the dark the moon looked like an emerald in the palm of a black girl.

הֲנִמְצָא בְרֵעַי

ומצאהו – יוקירהו האל! – חלישות הכח והגוף מדרך הזקנה במלחמה אשר היתה בקיץ של שנת תתי"ד ואמר בזה שיר כמתאונן:

הֲנִמְצָא בְרֵעַי מַר לְבָבוֹ לְמָרוֹתַי,
וְאִם אֶמְצְאָה בַּעֲלַת נְהִי רַב בְּגָרוֹתַי?
וְאִם יַחֲלִיף רַגְלָיו צְבִי לִי, וְאָרוּץ בָּם
לְתַנִּים וְיוֹרוּנִי סְפֹד עַל בְּחוּרוֹתַי?

THE FEAR OF DEATH

He – may God cherish him – was suddenly beset by the weakness of old age during a battle which took place in the summer of 1054. Then he composed this complaint:

Is there anyone among my friends whose heart hurts for my hurt? Can I find, among my neighbours, a woman skilled in keening? Will the deer lend me his feet, so that I may run to the jackals and learn from them how to

1. In Hebrew, the letter *yod*.

הֲיֵשׁ – אַחֲרֵי אַחַת וְשִׁשִּׁים עֲבַרְתִּימוֹ –
בְּנַפְשִׁי מְקוֹם חֵפֶץ כְּשַׂעֲרָה בְשָׁרוֹתַי?
וְאַחַר עֲצֹר שַׁחַק עֲנַן אוֹר עֲלוּמַי – טַל
עֲלוּמִים זְמַן יוֹרִיד וְיַשְׁכִּיב בְּאוֹרוֹתַי?
וְאַחַר כְּהוֹת נֵרוֹת בְּחוּרַי – הֲיֵשׁ לִיצֹק
כְּמֵאָז מְאוֹר שֶׁמֶן בְּחוּרִים בְּנֵרוֹתַי?

bewail my youth? Now that I have passed my sixty-first year, is there any room in my heart – even a hair's breadth – for the delights of singing-women? Now that heaven has locked up the rain-clouds of my youth, will time bring down the dew of youth upon my blossoms? Now that the light of my manhood has dimmed, is there an oil of manhood that can be poured again into my lamps?

קְבוּרוֹת חֲבֵרַי דִּבְּרוּ כִּי אֲנִי בָהֶם
לְמָחָר, וְעִמָּם אָהֳלִי אֵט בְּגֵרוּתַי.
וְאִם אֵין אֲנִי שָׁב אֶל נְעוּרַי אֲחוֹרַנִּית –
קְחוּ אֵת וְהָחֵלּוּ לְהָכִין קְבוּרוֹתַי!
יְגוֹנֵי זְקוּנִים הֶעֱלוּ עַל לְבָבִי אֵשׁ
יְקוֹדִים, לְשׁוֹנוֹתָם מְאִירוֹת בְּשַׂעֲרוֹתַי,
וְצִירֵי חֲלוּשָׁה עוֹרְרוּ מַחֲלֵי בִרְכַּי,
וְהִנֵּה אֲנִי כּוֹשֵׁל בְּמִישׁוֹר בְּחַצְרוֹתַי!
אֲנִי אֵבְךְּ נַפְשִׁי, כִּי יְקָרָה מְאֹד נַפְשִׁי,
וְלִי נָאֲוֶה לִסְפֹּד וְלִבְכּוֹת יְקָרוֹתַי.
וְאֶרְאֶה, בְּהִתְלַבֵּן זְקָנִי, בְּמוֹרָשִׁי
מְקוֹם שַׁחֲרוּת זֹקֶן כְּפִיחַ בְּסִירוֹתַי.
וְלוּ אֵרֶךְ בּוֹ – כִּמְעַט אֲסַרְתִּיו בְּמֵיתָר, עַד
אֲשֶׁר לֹא יְנוֹפֵף יָד לְהַלְבִּין שְׁחָרוֹתַי.
וְלוּ אֵשׁ יְגוֹנִים לְהַטָּה קָדְקֳדִי, הָיוּ
צְרִי אֵשׁ יְגוֹנִים – מֵי עֲנָבִים בְּפוּרוֹתַי.
וְאוּלָם בְּזִקְנָה נִנְעֲרוּ מֵי נְעוּרַי מִן
זְקָנִי, וְזִקְנָה נִאֲצַתְנִי לְנַעֲרוֹתַי!

I have heard the graves of my companions say that I shall be in them tomorrow, that in this alien land I shall pitch my tent with my companions. And indeed if I cannot go backwards to my youth, take a mattock and begin to prepare my grave! The sorrows of age set my heart aflame, and the tongues of fire brighten my hair. Pangs of weakness plague my knees. I stumble even on level ground, in my own courtyard. I shall grieve for my soul – it is so precious! – and it befits me to grieve and lament my treasures. As my beard turns white, I see in my heart a spot black with age, like soot on a pot. Oh, if I had power over old age, I would quickly bind him with a rope, till he no longer raised his hand to shame my beard with grey. If it were only the fire of sorrow that scorched my head, grape-water from my wine press would be the cure for this fire. But old age has shaken all the water of youth out of my beard and made me loathsome to women!

וּמִי יִתְּנֵנִי כֶאֱלֹהִים וְאֶתְבּוֹנֵן:
הֲקָרוֹב וְאִם רָחוֹק יְהִי יוֹם מְגוּרוֹתַי,

If only I were like God and knew: is my day of dread near or far; how long

וְכַמָּה אֱהִי עָפָר בְּקִבְרִי בְּלִי רוּחַ,
וּמָתַי תְּחִי רוּחִי וְתוּפַח בְּעַפְרוֹתַי.
וְיֹאמַר לְבָבִי כִּי אֶחְיֶה עוֹד, וְאִם יִכְאַב
בְּשָׂרִי – יְרַפֵּא אֵל אֱלֹהִים חַבּוּרוֹתַי,
וְיִתֵּן אֱיָל חֵלֶף לְחָלְשִׁי, וְיִתֵּן לִי
כְּכֹחַ בְּאֶבְרוֹת הַנְּשָׁרִים בְּאֶבְרוֹתַי.
וְכֵן יַעֲשֶׂה לִּי אֵל בְּטוּבוֹ וְחַסְדּוֹ, כִּי
בְּאֵל מַחֲסִי שַׂמְתִּי בְּעוֹדִי, וְשִׂבְרוֹתַי.

am I to rest in my grave, dust without spirit, and when will my spirit be breathed into my dust? Still, my heart tells me that I shall go on living, and when my flesh is in pain, the God of Gods will heal my wounds. He will replace my weakness with strength; He will give my limbs the power of eagle's wings. In His goodness and His love He will do all this for me, because all my life I made Him my refuge and my hope.

וְיֹאמְרוּ אֲנָשִׁים כִּי מְנוּחָה בְקֶבֶר יֵשׁ –
וְאֶדְאַג אֲנִי פֶּן אֶפְגְּעָה בוֹ בְּסָרוֹתַי.
וְהֵם יִקְרְאוּ מָוֶת 'הֲלִיכָה אֱלֵי אָבוֹת' –
וְצָדְקוּ, לְמַעַן שָׁם אֲבוֹתַי וְהוֹרוֹתַי.
עֲלֵי מַה בְּיוֹם מוֹתִי תְּחִישׁוּן בְּגוּפָתִי
אֱלֵי צֵל שְׁאוֹל מֵצֵל מְעוֹנִי וְקוֹרוֹתַי?
וְלָמָּה תְּצוּרוּן עַל בְּשָׂרִי בְּתַכְרִיכֵי
קְבוּרָה – וְשָׁם אֶבְלֶה אֲנִי עִם צְרוֹרוֹתַי?
וְלָמָּה בְמַיִם תִּטְבְּלוּנִי לְהִטַּהֵר –
וּמָחָר תְּטַנֵּף צַחֲנָתִי חֲגוֹרוֹתַי?

People say that the grave is a quiet place, but I fear that I may encounter my sins there. They call death 'joining one's forefathers', and that is true enough: all my fathers and mothers are there. But why, when I am dead, will you hurry my body from under the shelter of my roof into the shadows of the underworld? Why wrap my body in winding-sheets, when both I and my wrapping will rot in the grave? Why bathe me with water to purify me, when on the very next day my stench will foul my sashes?

אֱלֹהִים, כְּבָר עָבְרוּ זְמַנִּים וְדוֹרוֹת עַל
אֲדָמָה, וְהָיִיתִי כְּאַיִן בְּדוֹרוֹתַי.
וְאַחַר פְּקַדְתַּנִי לְרָצוֹן וְיָצָאתִי
– לְבַל אֶשְׁאֲלָה צֵאת מִמְּךָ – אֶל מְכוּרוֹתַי.
וְאַחַר יְצִיאָתִי לְהַוּוֹת נְתַתָּנִי
וּמָקוֹר לְמִקְרוֹתַי וְכִצְרוֹר לְצָרוֹתַי.
וְאַתָּה יְצַרְתַּנִי בְּעוֹלָם יְפֵה מַרְאֶה –
וְאַתָּה בְאַחֲרִיתִי תְּשַׁנֶּה יְצִירוֹתַי.
וְאוּלָם צְדָקָה מַעֲשֶׂיךָ, וְאִמְרָתְךָ
אֱמוּנָה, וְרוּחַ פִּי מְעֻקָּל, וְאִמְרוֹתַי.

O God, so many ages and generations passed over the earth, and I was nothing in all these ages. Then You remembered me with kindness, and without my asking to come I came forth into my family. And then You handed me over to adversity, made me the root of my disasters, a stone to be slung by my calamities. And though You made me handsome at my birth, in the end You will misshape my limbs. But Your acts are just and Your word is true; only my spirit and my words are crooked.

קְחוּ לִי מְגִלָּה וַעֲשׂוּ לִי דְּיוֹ וָעֵט
לְיָדִי, וַאֲשַׁחִירָה כְּהַיּוֹם בְּקוֹרוֹתַי.
וְאֶקְרָא וְתִזַּלְנָה כְּעֵינֵי מְאוֹרוֹתַי,
לְמַעַן בְּקֶבֶר לֹא אֲדַמַּע מְאוּרוֹתַי.
וְאֶבְכֶּה עֲלֵי צוּרָה יְפֵיפָה, יְאִיצוּן בָּהּ
לְמוֹעֵד בְּנֵי אָדָם חֲבֵרַי וַחֲבֵרוֹתַי;
וְיִפְעָה כְבוּדָּה – כָּל כְּבוֹדָהּ בְּכַסּוֹתָהּ
בְּעָפָר וּבִסְתֹם פִּי וְעַצֵּם שְׁמוּרוֹתַי;
וְכִי אָז יְהִי דוּמָם בְּאָרוֹן, כְּמוֹ אֶבֶן
בְּלֶב יָם, לְשׁוֹנִי הַמְסַפֵּר גְּבוּרוֹתַי;
וְעֵינַי אֲשֶׁר חָזְתָה פְלָאִים אֲזַי תֶּעַשׁ
בְּחֹרָהּ בְּרִקָּבוֹן וְתִמַּק בְּנִקְרוֹתַי;
וְכִי אֵין בְּחֵךְ טַעַם וְשִׂיחַ, וְאֵין שֵׁמַע
לְאָזְנִי, וּבָטְלָה יָד וּבָטְלוּ מְמַהֲרוֹתַי.
וְרָעָה אֲשֶׁר רָעָה וּמָרָה עֲלֵי כָּל זֹאת –
עֲלוֹתִי לְמִשְׁפָּט מִן רְגָבַי וְקִבְרוֹתַי,
וְכִי כָל פְּעֻלּוֹתַי שְׁקוּלוֹת בְּמֹאזְנַיִם:
בְּכַף זֹאת זְכִיּוֹתַי, וּבָזֹאת מְרוֹרוֹתַי.

Bring me a scroll, get me ink and a quill, and I shall blacken it today with my tale of woe. When I read it, my eyes will flow like fountains, for in the grave I shall not shed any tears. I shall bewail this lovely form, which my friends, both men and women, will rush to the charnel house; and shall bewail this glorious beauty, which can expect no glory but to be covered with dust, mouth stopped and eye-lids shut. For then my tongue, which once told my exploits, will lie still in the coffin, like a stone in the depths of the sea. And my eyes, which once beheld wonders, will rot in their sockets and decay in the pit. For then taste and speech will be gone from my palate, my ears will have no hearing, my hands will be idle, my swift feet idle. And worst of all, most bitter fate of all: I shall have to rise from my dusty grave to stand in judgement, while all my deeds are weighed in a balance, my merits on this scale and my sins on the other.

וְאוּלַי יְהִי מַלְאָךְ וּמֵלִיץ בְּדָבָר טוֹב
לְהָרִים עֲווֹנוֹתַי וְהַשְׁפֵּל יְשָׁרוֹתַי,
וְיַזְכִּיר בְּהִשָּׁפְטִי לְצוּרִי חֲקִירוֹתַי
בְּדָתֵי תְעוּדוֹתַי וְדָרְשִׁי בְתוֹרוֹתַי,
וְאֶשְׁמַע: 'כְּבָר רָצָה אֱלֹהִים פְּעָלֶיךָ' –
וְתֵרֵד בְּבָזֹאת מֵעֲבָרֵי כְּשׁוּרוֹתַי.
וְאֶשְׂמַח בְּצֵאתִי אֶל כְּבוֹד אֵל לְאָסְפֵנִי,
וְאֶשְׂמַח בְּהֵאָסֵף יְרֵחִי וְאוֹרוֹתַי.

(1054)

But perhaps an angel will speak up in my favour to lighten my sins and add weight to my virtues. He will remind my Rock, as I am being judged, that I pored over the Scriptures and expounded the Law. And I shall then hear: 'God has already approved what you have done!' Thus shall the scales be tipped, and my good deeds will outweigh my crimes. Dying, I shall rejoice that I am being taken by the glory of God. And I shall rejoice as my moon and my sun are taken away.

יוֹסֵף אִבְּן־חִסְדַּאי

שִׁירָה יְתוּמָה

הֲלִצְבִי חֵן גְּבוּרַת אוֹן וְעָצְמָה
לְהִתְעַטֵּף רְדִיד אֹפֶל כְּשַׂלְמָה,
וְלִרְעוֹת כּוֹכְבֵי נֶשֶׁף, וְלִתְעוֹת
בְּעִי מִדְבָּר, מְעוֹן פַּחַד וְאֵימָה,
וְלָצֵאת מֵחֲדָרִים אֶל חֲרָדָה,
וּמֶהֶמְיַת נְבָלִים אֶל מְהוּמָה? –
עֲדֵי נִלְכַּד בְּחַבְלֵי הַחֲלוֹמוֹת,
וְנִצְטַיַּד בְּפַחֵי הַתְּנוּמָה.
וְאָרִיתִי – וְהוּא נִרְדָּם – בְּרָצוֹן
אֲשֶׁר יִמְנַע – וְהוּא מֵקִיץ – בְּחֵמָה,
וְהִשְׁקַנִי, בְּיַד שֵׁנָה עֲרֵבָה,
עֲסִיס פִּיהוּ בְּכוֹסֵי אַחְלָמָה.
וְשָׁכַבְתִּי – וּבֵין שָׁדַי קְוֻצּוֹת
מְרִיקוֹת מֹר עֲלֵי רַקָּה אֲדֻמָּה,
וְהַיָּמִין מְחַבֶּקֶת לְבָנָה,
וְהַשָּׂפָה מְנַשֶּׁקֶת לְחַמָּה,
וְהַמִּטָּה מְקֻטֶּרֶת לְבוֹנָה,
וְהָעֶרֶשׂ בְּכָל בֹּשֶׂם פְּטוּמָה.
וְנָעַמְתִּי בְחֶזְיוֹנִי, עֲדֵי כִּי
הֱקִיצֹתִי – וְהִנֵּה אֵין מְאוּמָה
אֲבָל רֵיחַ יְשׁוֹבֵב הַנְּפָשׁוֹת
וּמֹר עוֹבֵר יְחַיֶּה הַנְּשָׁמָה –
כְּשֵׁם נָגִיד וְיָחִיד רַב שְׁמוּאֵל,
אֲשֶׁר מִלֵּא פְּנֵי כָל הָאֲדָמָה! [...]

Joseph ibn Ḥisdai

HOMAGE TO SAMUEL THE PRINCE

How did the lovely gazelle find such courage and strength to wrap himself in a veil of darkness as in a robe; to tend the flocks of the stars; to wander amid desert ruins, haunts of fear and terror; to abandon his home for horrors, the music of lutes for turmoil – till he was caught in the net of dreams, and trapped in the snares of slumber? And as he slept I plucked, with his consent, that which he angrily refuses me when awake. With the hand of sweet sleep, he gave me the nectar of his mouth to drink in ruby bowls. I lay down, and on my breast were locks flowing with myrrh over blushing cheeks. My right hand embraced the white moon, my lips kissed the warm sun. Our bed was perfumed with frankincense, our couch fragrant with many spices. Oh, I revelled in my vision until I awoke to find nothing but an aroma that delights the spirit and a trace of liquid myrrh that revives the soul – like the name of Rabbi Samuel, the one and only, the Prince, whose fragrance fills the whole earth!

הַאיְי גָּאוֹן

Haya Gaon

אָכֵן סָר מַר הַמָּוֶת

SWEET DEATH

אָכֵן סָר מַר הַמָּוֶת, נִמְתַּק מִדְּבַשׁ הֵיטֵב –
בַּל לְכָל הָעַמִּים וְלֹא לְכָל הַלְּשׁוֹנוֹת.
גּוֹי אֶחָד עָרֵב לוֹ – אֵלֶּה הֵם עַם אֲדֹנָי,
דִּגְלֵי שְׁלֹשֶׁת אָבוֹת, אַבְרָהָם, יִצְחָק וְיַעֲקֹב,
הַמְחַכִּים לַמָּוֶת וְאֵינֶנּוּ, פֶּן יִמְצְאוּ חֶפְצָם.
וּלְבַל יֵעָדֵר בָּם יָגוֹן הָנְחֲלוּ אֹרֶךְ יָמִים.

Yes, the bitterness of death is past, and death is far sweeter than honey, but not for all nations, not for all races. There is only one people to whom death is pleasant – the people of God, the offspring of the three patriarchs, Abraham, Isaac, and Jacob, who wait for death but it does not come. Not even this wish is granted them. They have been allotted a long life, so that no sorrow shall escape them.

זֶה הָעָם לֹא הָיָה. אֲכָלַתְהוּ כָּל פֶּה,
חִלְּקוּהוּ פַּאֲתֵי אֶרֶץ, שְׁלָלוּהוּ כָּל הַגּוֹיִם.
טֶרֶם תַּדִּיחֶנּוּ מָדַי, כִּלַּתְהוּ בָבֶל,
יָוָן הִיא בְלָעַתּוּ וְיִשְׁמָעֵאל לֹא הֱקִיאַתּוּ.
כִּי תוֹסִיף עַל עֻלּוֹ, כִּי תַכְפִּיל עָנְיוֹ ?
לֹא חַיִל וְלֹא כֹחַ, מַה יּוּכַל שְׂאֵת.

This is the people that is as though it had never been. Every mouth devoured it; it was scattered to the corners of the earth, plundered by all nations. Before Media toppled it, Babylon consumed it; Greece swallowed it up, Ishmael did not spew it out. Why do You make its yoke heavier; why do You multiply its misery? It has neither weapons nor strength; it can no longer bear the burden.

מַהֲרוּ וַעֲלוּ אֶל אָבִי וַאֲמַרְתֶּם אֵלָיו :
'נֶפֶשׁ בִּנְךָ קָרְבָה לָצֵאת, הֲלֹא תָבוֹא וּתְבַקְּרֶנּוּ ?
שִׂיחַ לָאָרֶץ וְתֹרֶךָּ אֵיךְ נָד לַאֲפָסֶיהָ.
עֲפָרָהּ גַּם הוּא יוֹדִיעֲךָ אֵיךְ נִגְבַּל מִדָּמָיו.
פָּנֶיךָ בְּאֶרֶץ עֲרָבָה אֵיךְ רֻוְּתָה מִדִּמְעָתוֹ.
צִיָּה הוֹצִיאָה זֶרַע מִדַּם חַלְלֵי עַמּוֹ.'

Make haste, go up to my Father and say to Him: 'Your son is about to die. Will You not come to visit him? Speak to the earth and it will tell You how he has wandered to its limits. Its dust will inform you how it was kneaded with his blood. Go to the wilderness and see how it was drenched with his tears. The blood of Your murdered people has made the desert bring forth grain.'

קוּם קְרָא אֶל אֱלֹהֶיךָ, קַבֵּץ הֲדוּגֶיךָ וֶאֱמָר־לוֹ:
׳רַחוּם וְחַנּוּן אֲדֹנָי, הַעַל אֵלֶּה תִּתְאַפָּק?
שִׁכַּלְתָּם גַּם שִׁבַּלְתָּם, וְלֹא הִשְׂכַּלְתָּ אֲלֵיהֶם.
תַּתָּם כְּצֹאן מַאֲכָל, וְעַד הֵנָּה לֹא חֲנַנְתָּם.
הֲגַם עַל הָאַלְמָנָה, אֲשֶׁר הָיְתָה רַבָּתִי עָם,
יִקְשֶׁה בְעֵינֶיךָ לְרַחֵם? יְמָאֲנוּ חֲסָדֶיךָ לְבוֹאָהּ?׳

Get up, call on your God, gather all your dead and say to Him: 'O Lord, You are compassionate and gracious; after all this, will You hold back? You have ravaged them, You have ridiculed them, You have paid them no heed. You have given them up to be butchered like sheep and till now You have shown them no pity. Is it so hard for You to have mercy even on the widowed city which was once so full of people?[1] Will You refuse to comfort her with Your love?'

אַבְרָהָם הַכֹּהֵן

Abraham Hakohen

יְפֵה תֹאַר

THE NARCISSUS

יְפֵה תֹאַר וְטוֹב רֹאִי
כְּרִקּוּחִים וְרֹאשׁ סַמִּים,
כְּכוֹס זָהָב בְּכוֹס כֶּסֶף,
כְּמִזְרָקוֹת מְרֻקָּמִים,
אֲשֶׁר אֶחָד כְּמוֹ שֶׁלֶג,
וְהַשֵּׁנִי כְּכַרְכֻּמִּים
וְשֵׁשׁ עָלִים סְבוּבִים לוֹ,
כְּמוֹ שַׁבָּת בְּתוֹךְ יָמִים. [...]

Lovely and fair, like blended perfumes and choicest spices; like richly coloured jugs; or like a bowl of gold in a bowl of silver: the one is like snow, and the other is like saffron and is encircled by six petals, as the Sabbath is by the week-days.

שְׁלֹמֹה אִבְּן־גַּבִּירוֹל

Solomon ibn Gabirol

אֲנִי הָאִישׁ

NIGHT STORM

אֲנִי הָאִישׁ אֲשֶׁר שִׁנֵּס אֱזוֹרוֹ
וְלֹא יֶרֶף עֲדֵי יָקִים אֱסָרוֹ,

I am the man who braced himself and will not desist until he fulfils his vow –

1. Jerusalem; see Lamentations 1.1.

אֲשֶׁר נִבְהַל לְבָבוֹ מִלְּבָבוֹ
וְנַפְשׁוֹ מָאֲסָה לִשְׁכֹּן בְּשָׂרוֹ,
וּבָחַר בַּתְּבוּנָה מִנְּעוּרָיו —
וְאִם כּוּר הַזְּמַן שֶׁבַע בְּחָרוֹ
וַיַּהֲרֹס כָּל אֲשֶׁר יִבְנֶה, וְיִתֹּשׁ
אֲשֶׁר יִטַּע, וְיִפְרֹץ אֶת גְּדֵרוֹ. [...]

whose heart recoiled from his heart, whose spirit scorned to dwell in his flesh, who chose wisdom even as a youth – though he be tested seven times in the crucible of Time, though it pull down whatever he has built, though it uproot whatever he has planted and breach all his barriers.

בְּעֵת לוּנִי, וְהַשַּׁחַק נְקִי־כַף,
וְהַסַּהַר טְהָר־לֵבָב וּבָרוֹ,
נְהָגַנִי עֲלֵי אָרְחֵי תְבוּנוֹת
וְהוֹרַנִי בְּאוֹר נָהוֹג וְהוֹרוֹ.
וְחָמַלְתִּי, בְּפַחֲדִי מִתְּלָאוֹת,
עֲלֵי אוֹרוֹ כְּאָב עַל בֵּן בְּכוֹרוֹ.

As I slept – and the skies were spotless – the radiant, pure-hearted moon led me over the paths of wisdom and, as he led me, instructed me in his light. And I, fearing some misfortune, was filled with pity for his light, as a father for his first-born son.

וְרוּחַ שִׁלְּחָה בוֹ מִפְרְשֵׂי עָב,
וּפָרַשׂ עַל פְּנֵי סַהַר אֲפֵרוֹ,
כְּאִלּוּ אִוְּתָה זֶרֶם גְּשָׁמִים,
וְתִשָּׁעֵן לְעָב עַד כִּי תְקֵרוֹ.
וְשַׁחַק הֶעֱטָה קַדְרוּת, וְסַהַר
כְּאִלּוּ מֵת, וְהֶעָנָן קְבָרוֹ,
וּבָכוּ אַחֲרָיו עָבֵי שְׁחָקִים
בְּכוֹת, כִּבְכוֹת אֲרָם עַל בֶּן־בְּעוֹרוֹ.

Then the wind assailed the moon with sailing clouds, and they covered his face with a mask. It was as if the wind craved for streams of rain and pressed upon the clouds to make them flow. The skies robed themselves in darkness. It seemed as if the moon had died, and the cloud had buried him. And all the other clouds of heaven wept for him, as the people of Aram wept for the son of Beor.[1]

וְלָבַשׁ לַיְלָה שִׁרְיוֹן אֲפֵלָה,
וְרַעַם בַּחֲנִית בָּרָק דְּקָרוֹ,
וְהַבָּרָק עֲלֵי שַׁחַק מְעוֹפֵף
כְּאִלּוּ הוּא מְשַׂחֵק עַל דְּבָרוֹ,
אֲשֶׁר פֵּרַשׂ כְּנָפָיו כַּעֲטַלֵּף

Then the night put on an armour-plate of darkness; thunder, with a spear of lightning, pierced it; and the lightning flew about the skies, as if it were jousting with the night, spreading its wings like a bat; the ravens of the

1. Balaam; Numbers 22.5 ff.

וְצָפוּ עוֹרְבֵי חֹשֶׁךְ בְּשׁוּרוֹ.
וְסָגַר מַחְשְׁבוֹתַי אֵל, וְחֵפֶץ
לְבָבִי מִשְּׁנֵי פָנִים אֲסָרוֹ,
וְאָסַר בַּעֲבוֹת חֹשֶׁךְ לְבָבִי –
וְהִתְעוֹרֵר כְּגִבּוֹר מִמְּצוּרוֹ.

dark fled when they saw it. And God closed in my thoughts. He barred my heart's desire from all sides. He bound my heart with ropes of darkness. Yet it arose like a warrior breaking out of a siege.

וּבַל אוֹחִיל, יְדִידַי, וַאֲקַוֶּה
לְאוֹר סַהַר, אֱשׁוּן חֹשֶׁךְ הֱמִירוֹ,
כְּאִלּוּ קִנְאוּ עָבִים לְנַפְשִׁי,
וְעַל כֵּן מָנְעוּ מִנִּי מְאוֹרוֹ.
וְאַשְׁקִיף עֵת יְגַל פָּנָיו, וְאָגִיל
כְּגִיל עֶבֶד אֲשֶׁר אָדוֹן זְכָרוֹ.
בְּהִלָּחֵם אֱנוֹשׁ יֻכַּת חֲנִיתוֹ,
וְעֵת יָרוּץ אֲזַי יִמְעַד אֲשׁוּרוֹ.
וְכֵן אִישׁ – יַדְבִּקוּ אוֹתוֹ תְּלָאוֹת,
וְלוּ יָשִׂים בְּבֵית נֹגַהּ דְּבִירוֹ!

But I dare not hope, my friends, for the light of the moon, which has turned into pitch-black darkness, as though the clouds were jealous of my soul and therefore deprived me of his light. And when I chance to see his face revealed, I rejoice like a slave who sees that his master remembers him. When a mortal wages war, his spear is beaten down; and when he tries to run, his steps falter. And even the man whose spirit dwells in the shining heavens – misfortune overtakes him.

רְאֵה שֶׁמֶשׁ

LAMENT

רְאֵה שֶׁמֶשׁ לְעֵת עֶרֶב אֲדֻמָּה,
כְּאִלּוּ לָבְשָׁה תוֹלָע לְמִכְסֶה.
תְּפַשֵּׁט פַּאֲתֵי צָפוֹן וְיָמִין
וְרוּחַ יָם בְּאַרְגָּמָן תְּכַסֶּה.
וְאֶרֶץ – עֲזָבָה אוֹתָהּ עֲרֻמָּה –
בְּצֵל הַלַּיְלָה תָּלִין וְתֶחְסֶה.
וְהַשַּׁחַק אֲזַי קָדַר, כְּאִלּוּ
בְּשַׂק עַל מוֹת יְקוּתִיאֵל מְכֻסֶּה.

See the sun at evening time: red, as though it clothed itself in scarlet. It disrobes the north and the south, it covers the west with purple. And the earth, now left naked, seeks refuge in the shadow of the night, and sleeps. Then the skies darken, as if covered with sackcloth, mourning the death of Jekuthiel.

רְבִיבֵי דִמְעֲךָ

THE POET'S ILLNESS

׳רְבִיבֵי דִמְעֲךָ הָיוּ רְסִיסִים
וְהָיוּ הַבְּקָעוֹת כָּרְכָסִים.
וְאֵיכָה לֹא תְזַמֵּר הַזְּמוֹרָה
וְלָמָּה לֹא תְהַלֵּל הָעֲסִיסִים,
אֲשֶׁר רָדְפוּ יְגוֹנֶיךָ, וְנָסוּ
מְנוּסַת בֶּן־נְבָט אֶל תַּחְפַּנְחֵס ?׳

'Your showers of tears, like a torrent, have made the plains rise like mountain ranges. Why not celebrate the grape-vine, why not sing the praises of wine, which could pursue your sorrows and make them flee as Jeroboam son of Nebat fled to Egypt[1]?'

עֲנִיתִיו : ׳הַלְּבָבוֹת שָׁכְחוּ רִישׁ
וְשָׂמְחוּ בָם כְּשִׂמְחָה בִנְכָסִים. [...]
וְהִנֵּה הֶחֳלִי כִּלָּה בְשָׂרִי
וְשָׂם בִּשְׁאָר שְׁאֵרִי אֵשׁ הֲמָסִים,
עֲדֵי הָיוּ נְזָמֵינוּ עֲטָרוֹת
וְהָיוּ טַבְּעוֹתֵינוּ עֲכָסִים.
וּבִעֵר הַקְּרָבִים עַל יְקוֹד אֵשׁ
וְדִמִּינוּ עֲצָמֵינוּ נְמַסִּים.
קְרָבִים שִׁלְּחוּ בָהֶם חֲלָיִים
וּמִצְוַת הַזְּמָן שׁוֹמְרִים וְעוֹשִׂים.
וְאֵיךְ לֹא יִהְיוּ אֶפֶס וְתֹהוּ
עֲצָמוֹת בַּתְּלָאוֹת הֵם אֲבוּסִים ?
חֲמָסִי עַל חֳלִי כִּלָּה שְׁאֵרִי
וְשָׂם אַלּוֹן בְּעֵינַי עֵץ הֲדַסִּים,
וְעַל הַלַּיְלָה אָשִׁית חֲמָסִי
אֲשֶׁר שָׁת אָהֳלֵי חֹשֶׁךְ פְּרוּשִׂים.׳ [...]

I answered him: 'Yes, the heart forgets its trouble and rejoices in wine as does a man in riches. But disease has consumed my flesh and set the shreds of my body ablaze like brushwood. [I have grown so thin] that a nose-ring could serve me as a crown and a ringlet as an ankle-band. Sickness burned my innards with a fever like fire, till I thought my bones would melt. Sores infested my innards and carried out Time's orders faithfully. Bones that are filled with suffering – how should they not disintegrate? I rage against the disease that has wasted away my body. [It has made me so weak] that a myrtle looks to me like an oak. And I rage against the night that spreads out its tents of gloom.'

בְּאָמְרִי : ׳מַה לְּבוּשׁ קָדִים ?׳ יְשִׁיבוּן :
׳תְּכֵלֶת וַעֲלוֹת שַׁחַר מְכַסִּים.׳
וְעֵת כִּי הֶעֱלָה שַׁחַר דְּגָלָיו

Then when I asked: 'How is the East robed?', they answered: 'Covered with blue and dawning light.' And at last, when the dawn lifted its flags and raised

1. 1 Kings 11.40.

וְהֵרִים כּוֹכְבֵי בֹקֶר כְּנִסִּים —
קְרָבַי שָׁקְטוּ כִּי נִמְלְאוּ טָל,
וְעָלַי נִגְּרוּ נִטְפֵי רְסִיסִים.

its morning stars like banners, my innards were soothed, for they were filled with dew, and drops of water flowed upon me.

נִחַר בְּקָרְאִי גְרוֹנִי

ON LEAVING SARAGOSSA

נִחַר בְּקָרְאִי גְרוֹנִי, דָּבַק לְחִכִּי לְשׁוֹנִי,
הָיָה לְבָבִי סְחַרְחַר מֵרֹב כְּאֵבִי וְאוֹנִי,
גָּדַל יְגוֹנִי, וְחָדַל מֵתֵת תְּנוּמָה לְעֵינִי.
כַּמָּה אֲיַחֵל, וְכַמָּה יִבְעַר כְּמוֹ אֵשׁ חֲרוֹנִי?
אֶל מִי אֲדַבֵּר וְאָעִיד וּלְמִי אֲסַפֵּר יְגוֹנִי?

My throat is parched with crying, my tongue clings to my palate. My heart reels from so much pain and suffering. My grief has become so great that it will not let sleep close my eyes. How much longer must I wait? How long will my fury burn like a fire? To whom can I speak and complain? To whom can I tell my sorrow?

לוּ יֵשׁ מְנַחֵם, מְרַחֵם עָלַי וְיֹאחֵז יְמִינִי,
אֶשְׁפֹּךְ לְבָבִי לְפָנָיו, אַגִּיד קְצֵה עִצְּבוֹנִי:
אוּלַי, בְּזָכְרִי יְגוֹנִי, אֶשְׁקֹט מְעַט מִשְּׁאוֹנִי.

If only there were someone to comfort me, someone to pity me and hold my right hand. I would pour out my heart to him, I would tell him a small part of my woes. Perhaps by giving vent to my sorrow, I would find some relief from the turmoil inside me.

שׁוֹאֵל שְׁלוֹמִי, קְרַב־נָא וּשְׁמַע כְּמוֹ יָם הֲמוֹנִי!
אִם יֵשׁ לְבָבְךָ כְּשָׁמִיר — יֵרַךְ לְרֹב דִּרְאוֹנִי.
אֵיךְ תַּחֲשֹׁב כִּי אֲנִי חַי עַל דַּעְתְּךָ דַּאֲבוֹנִי?
הַמְעַט הֱיוֹתִי בְּתוֹךְ עַם יַחְשֹׁב שְׂמֹאלוֹ יְמִינִי?
נִקְבָּר — אֲבָל לֹא בְמִדְבָּר, כִּי אִם בְּבֵיתִי אֲרוֹנִי!
נִכְאָב, בְּלִי אֵם וְלֹא אָב, צָעִיר וְיָחִיד וְעָנִי,
נִפְרָד בְּלִי אָח, וְאֵין לִי רֵעַ לְבַד רַעְיוֹנִי.
אֶמְסֹךְ בְּדָמִי דְּמָעַי, אֶמְסֹךְ דְּמָעַי בְּיֵינִי,

O you who wish me well, come closer and listen to my tumult, which is like the sea. Though your heart be adamant, it will soften at the tale of my debasement. How will you believe that I am alive once you have learnt of my distress? Is it a small thing to live among boors who cannot tell their right hand from their left? I am buried, but not in a graveyard: my house is my coffin! I am full of pain. I am motherless and fatherless, young and lonely and oppressed. I am alone, I have no brother, and I have no friend except my thoughts. I mix my tears with my blood, and my wine with my tears.

אֶצְמָא לְרֵעַ – וְאֶכְלֶה טֶרֶם כְּלוֹת צִמְּאוֹנִי,
כְּאִלּוּ שְׁחָקִים וְחֵילָם בֵּין תַּאֲוָתִי וּבֵינִי!
נֶחְשָׁב כְּמוֹ גֵר וְתוֹשָׁב, יוֹשֵׁב בְּשֶׁבֶת יַעֲנִי,
בֵּין כָּל פְּתַלְתֹּל וְסָכָל – לִבּוֹ כְּלֵב תַּחְכְּמוֹנִי.
זֶה יַשְׁקְךָ רֹאשׁ פְּתָנִים, זֶה יַחֲלִיק רֹאשׁ וְיָנִי,
יָשִׂים אָרְבּוֹ בְקִרְבּוֹ, יֹאמַר לְךָ: 'בִּי אֲדוֹנִי'.
עָם – נִמְאֲסוּ לִי אֲבוֹתָם מִהְיוֹת כְּלָבִים לְצֹאנִי.
לֹא יַאְדִּימוּ פְנֵיהֶם – כִּי אִם צְבָעוּם בְּשָׁנִי.
הֵם כַּעֲנָקִים בְּעֵינָם – הֵם כַּחֲגָבִים בְּעֵינִי!
בִּשְׂאֵת מְשָׁלַי, יְרִיבוּן עִמִּי כְּמוֹ עִם יְוָנִי:
'דַּבֵּר שְׂפַת־עָם וְנִשְׁמַע, כִּי זֶה לְשׁוֹן אֶשְׁקְלוֹנִי!'
עַתָּה אֲדִקֵּם כְּמוֹ טִיט, כִּי קִלְּשׁוֹנִי לְשׁוֹנִי.
אִם אָזְנְכֶם הִיא עֲרֵלָה, מַה יַּעֲשֶׂה פַּעֲמוֹנִי?
לֹא יוּכְלוּ צַוְּארֵיכֶם לָשֵׂאת זְהַב שַׂהֲרוֹנִי.
לוּ פָעֲרוּ הַפְּתָיִים פִּיהֶם לְמַלְקוֹשׁ עֲנָנִי –
נָטַף בְּשָׂמִי עֲלֵיהֶם, בֹּשֶׂם עֲנַן קִנְּמוֹנִי.
אוֹי לַתְּבוּנָה וְאוֹי לִי, כִּי גוֹי כְּמוֹ זֶה שְׁכֵנִי!
דַּעַת אֱלֹהִים יְשִׂימוּן כָּאוֹב וְכַיִּדְּעוֹנִי. [...]

I thirst for a friend and am quenched before my thirst is quenched, as though the heavens and their host stood between me and my desire. I am considered an alien or a stranger. I live among cruel ostriches, among the crooked and the foolish, who think that their hearts are the seat of wisdom. One man gives you asps' poison to drink; another, fawning, pats your head. In his heart he sets a trap for you, but out loud he says: 'If you please, my lord.' These people – I would disdain to make their fathers the dogs of my flock. Their faces never blush, except if they paint them scarlet. They are like giants in their own eyes, but like grasshoppers in mine. When I utter my sayings, they chide me as if I were a Greek.[1] 'Speak an intelligible language, so that we may understand, for this is gibberish!'[2] Now I shall step on them like dirt! My tongue will be my pitchfork! If your ears are uncircumcised, how can my bell be heard? Your necks are not fit to wear my golden crescents. If the fools were to open their mouths to my rainclouds, my fragrance would fall gently upon them, the cinnamon fragrance of my cloud. Woe to wisdom and woe to me, that I live in the midst of such people! They think that the knowledge of God is witchcraft and sorcery.

נַפְשִׁי בְמוֹתִי תְרַנֵּן, לוּ מָצְאָה צוּר מְעוֹנִי.
אָקוּץ בְּחַיַּי וְאֶמְאַס לִהְיוֹת בְּשָׂרִי מְכוֹנִי,
כִּי יוֹם שְׂשׂוֹנִי – אֲסוֹנִי, וּבְיוֹם אֲסוֹנִי – שְׂשׂוֹנִי.
אִיגַע לְהָבִין וְאֵדַע, כִּכְלוֹת בְּשָׂרִי וְאוֹנִי,

Oh, my soul would rejoice in death, if it could find refuge in the Rock. I am sick of my life, I loathe this house of flesh. For here all joy is sorrow, but my final sorrow will be my joy. I struggle to understand, and I shall learn, when my flesh and vigour are spent, that the

1. Possibly an allusion to the fact that his philosophical views were in part derived from the Greeks.
2. Lit. 'the language of an Ashkelonite'.

כִּי סוֹף אֲנָחָה – הֲנָחָה, עֵקֶב רְזוֹנִי – מְזוֹנִי.
אֶדְרֹשׁ בְּעוֹדִי, אֲחַפֵּשׂ כְּמִצְוַת שְׁלֹמֹה זְקֵנִי:
אוּלַי מְגַלֶּה עֲמוּקוֹת יְגַלֶּה תְבוּנָה לְעֵינַי,
כִּי הִיא מְנָתִי לְבַדָּהּ מִכָּל עֲמָלִי, וְהוֹנִי.

end of all this grief is relief, that my nourishment[1] is the fruit of my leanness. But as long as I live, I shall delve, I shall search, as my forefather Solomon bade me.[2] Perhaps He who uncovers mysteries will reveal wisdom to my eyes; for that is my only wealth and the only reward for all my labours.

כָּתַב סְתָיו

EARTH'S EMBROIDERY

כָּתַב סְתָיו בִּדְיוֹ מְטָרָיו וּבִרְבִיבָיו
וּבְעֵט בְּרָקָיו הַמְּאִירִים וְכַף עָבָיו
מִכְתָּב עֲלֵי גַן מִתְּכֵלֶת וְאַרְגָּמָן,
לֹא נִתְכְּנוּ כָהֵם לְחוֹשֵׁב בְּמַחְשְׁבָיו.
לָכֵן, בְּעֵת חָמְדָה אֲדָמָה פְּנֵי שַׁחַק,
רָקְמָה עֲלֵי בַדֵּי עֲרוּגוֹת כְּכוֹכָבָיו.

With the ink of its showers and rains, with the quill of its lightning, with the hand of its clouds, winter wrote a letter upon the garden, in purple and blue. No artist could ever conceive the like of that. And this is why the earth, grown jealous of the sky, embroidered stars in the folds of the flower-beds.

עָבֵי שְׁחָקִים

TEMPEST AT DAWN

עָבֵי שְׁחָקִים כַּשְּׁוָרִים גָּעוּ,
כִּי הַסְּתָיו זָעַף וּפָנָיו רָעוּ,
וּכְמוֹ תְרָנִים יִרְדְּפֵם סַעַר, כְּמוֹ
סַרְנֵי בְּקַרְנֵי יוֹבְלִים תָּקְעוּ.
וּפְנֵי שְׁחָקִים בַּעֲרָפֶל חָשְׁכוּ,
אַף כּוֹכְבֵי בֹקֶר בְּאוֹרָם לָעוּ.
שֶׁמֶשׁ נְשָׂאָם עַל כְּנָפָיו עַל פְּנֵי

The heavy clouds of heaven lowed like oxen, for the winter was scowling with rage. They were like ship-masts[3] driven on by a tempest, like captains sounding their horns in alarm. Then the face of heaven was darkened by fog, and the morning-stars stammered out their light. The sun bore the clouds on its

1. His spiritual food; or, his reward in the world to come.
2. The reference is to King Solomon (Proverbs 2.3–5), whose name the poet bears.
3. Another version has 'like light clouds'.

אֶרֶץ, וְעֵת כִּי נִבְקְעוּ – נִבְקָעוּ.
אֵיךְ עָמְדוּ, אֵיךְ כָּבְדוּ נֶגְדָּהּ, וְעֵת
קַלּוּ – כְּמוֹ נֶשֶׁר אֲזַי נָסָעוּ!
פַּחֵי גְשָׁמִים רִקְּעָה רוּחַ, וְעָב
קֵצֵּץ פְּתִילִים עַד שְׁאוֹל נָגָעוּ.
הוּא בִגְדוּד נִחַת גְּדוּדֶיהָ וְגַם
הֵכִין תְּלָמֶיהָ עֲדֵי נִזְרָעוּ.
גִּלָּה יְבוּל הָרִים אֲשֶׁר נִסְתַּר, כְּמוֹ
סוֹדוֹת יְדָעָם אִישׁ וְלֹא נוֹדָעוּ.
כָּל הַסְּתָיו בָּכוּ עֲנָנָיו, עַד אֲשֶׁר
חָיוּ עֲצֵי שָׂדֶה אֲשֶׁר גָּוָעוּ.

wings over the earth, and when they burst, the face of the earth burst open. How still they stood, how heavily they faced the earth, where once they were swift and flew like eagles! The wind beat the plates of rain, cut the cloud into strips which reached down to the abyss. The cloud and its battalions levelled the earth's ridges, prepared its furrows for sowing. Then the harvest of the hills, hidden away, like a secret known to one man but not disclosed to the many, was revealed. All winter long its clouds wept until the trees of the field, which had been dead, lived again.

אֱמֹר לַפְּתָיִים

[...] אֱמֹר לַפְּתָיִים: 'שְׁבוּ, אַל תְּנוּעוּן
לְהָעִיר חֲמַת אִישׁ כְּנוֹעַ כְּבָרָה,
אֲשֶׁר שָׁת תְּבוּנָה לְמַקֵּל בְּיָדוֹ
וּמֵזַח מְזִמּוֹת לְמָתְנָיו חֲגוֹרָה.'
וְאַל תַּאֲמֵן בָּם, אֲבָל כִּי בְעֵדוּת
יְעִידוּן לְאִמָּם אֲשֶׁר הִיא עֲקָרָה.
וְאֵיךְ יִפְרְצוּ לַעֲלוֹת אֶל מְקוֹמִי –
וְיָדַם לְהַשִּׂיג לְגָדֵר קְצָרָה?
וְגֻלַּת שְׁחָקִים צְצוּרָה בְלִבִּי,
וְתֵבֵל בְּגֻלַּת שְׁחָקִים צְצוּרָה!
וְאִם הֵם יְקַלּוּ דִבְרֵי אֲשֶׁר עַז,
וְחוֹלָה תְּחַלֵּל וְאִשָּׁה מְצֵרָה?
וְאִם הֵם כְּשַׁיִת – אֲנִי הַמְּדוּרָה,
וְאִם הֵם כְּרוּחַ – אֲנִי הַסְּעָרָה,

TO THE FOOLS

Say to the fools: 'Sit still, do not stir, lest you rouse the anger of a man who will shake you to and fro like a sieve, a man who has taken wisdom for his staff and has girt his loins with a belt of knowledge.' Do not believe a word they say, unless they testify that their mothers were childless. How can they hope to force their way up to my station, when they cannot even reach the fence? My heart contains the vault of heaven, and the vault of heaven contains the wide world. Then how dare they, who are weak as a sick and wretched woman, revile and debase my fierce words? If they are like a thorn-bush, I am the fire. If they are like a wind, I am the whirlwind. If they are dogs,

וְאִם הֵם כִּלְבִים – אֲנִי הַמְגָרָה
וְאִם הֵם כְּשָׁמִיר – אֲנִי הַמְגֵרָה.
וְלוּ יֵדְעוּן כָּל יְפִי הַוְּרָדִים –
עֲזָבוּם וְלֹא נִשְׂרְפוּ בַבְּעֵרָה.
וְאִם נָשְׁכָה הַדְּבוֹרָה בְּשַׂר אִישׁ –
וְלֹא יָדְעָה אַחֲרִיתָהּ דְּבוֹרָה.

I am he who sets them on. And if they are like a thistle, I am the scythe. If the rose's thorns knew its beauty, they would let it be and thus escape the fire. The bee which stings a man's flesh does not know that it has sealed its own fate.

מַה לַּאֲבִיגַיִל

THE OFFERINGS OF LOVE

מַה לַּאֲבִיגַיִל – אֲשֶׁר לָקְחָה
נַפְשִׁי בְּעֵינֶיהָ וְשָׁם הִנִּיחָה ?
כָּל חוֹשְׁקֶיהָ דִּבְּרוּ לָהּ כִּי שְׂנֵא־
תִיהָ וְשִׂנְאָתִי מְאֹד נִצְּחָה !
עִם זֹאת וְאִם שָׁכְחָה יְדִידוּתַי, הֲלֹא
אֶשְׁמֹר בְּרִית אַהֲבָה וְלֹא אֶשְׁכָּחָה :
שָׁלַח בְּנוֹ יִשַׁי לְבֵיתָהּ – וַאֲנִי
אֵלֵךְ אֱלֵי בֵיתָהּ, וְלֹא אֶשְׁלָחָה.
אִם אֵין בְּיוֹם גָּלוּת לְאֵל קָרְבָּן – הֲלֹא
עוֹלוֹת וְקָרְבָּנוֹת לְזֹאת אֶזְבָּחָה !

What is the matter with Abigail, that first she took my soul with her eyes and then forsook it? All her suitors told her that I hate her with a most enduring hatred. Yet despite this slander, and though she has forgotten my affection, I shall keep love's pact, I shall not forget. The son of Jesse sent messengers to Abigail's house;[1] but I shall go to her in person, not by proxy. In time of exile no sacrifices can be offered to God; then I shall slaughter whole offerings and sacrifices to this woman!

עֲזָבַתְנִי

THE FAITHLESS WOMAN

עֲזָבַתְנִי וְעָלְתָה לַשְּׁחָקִים,
אֲשֶׁר יָפוּ בְצַוָּארָהּ עֲנָקִים,
אֲשֶׁר תֵּמַר – וְתִמְשֹׁךְ הַלְּבָבוֹת –
וְאִם הָיוּ שְׂפָתֶיהָ מְתוּקִים.

She left me and went up to heaven, she whose neck is so lovely with its ornaments. But though her lips are sweet, and she entices men's hearts, yet she is

1. To ask for her hand in marriage; see 1 Samuel 25.39.

חֲרָבוֹת מִדְּנֶיהָ שְׁלוּפוֹת,
רְמָחִים לַהֲרֹג דַּלִּים מְרוּקִים.
תְּיָעֵץ לִי בְּעֵינֶיהָ וְתַעֲרֹג
כְּאַיָּלָה צְמֵאָה אֶל אֲפִיקִים.
אֲשֶׁר תַּזְכִּיר בְּרִית נֹחַ בְּקַשְׁתָּהּ –
וְתַבְרִק מִלְּחָיֶיהָ בְּרָקִים.
וְעֵת תִּצְמָא – עֲנָנֶיהָ תְּצַוֶּה
וְהֵמָּה הַבְּדֹלָחִים מְרִיקִים. [...]

bitter. Swords are unsheathed from the scabbards of her eyes, lances are burnished to kill unlucky men. Her eyes beckon to me; she is as full of longing as a deer thirsting for the running stream. Her arched eyebrow[1] calls to mind the covenant with Noah; she flashes lightning from her cheeks. And when you thirst, she orders her clouds to flood you with crystals.

אִמְרוּ לְמִי חִבֵּק

THE TESTIMONY OF BEAUTY

אִמְרוּ לְמִי חִבֵּק שְׂעָרוֹ לְחָיָו:
׳אֵיכָה יְחַבֵּק צָהֳרַיִם בֹּקֶר?׳
אַל תַּחֲשֹׁב עָוֹן לְאָגוּר בֶּאֱמֹר
כִּי הַיֳּפִי הֶבֶל וְהַחֵן שֶׁקֶר.
דַּי כִּי לְחָיֶיךָ יְעִידוּן בֶּאֱמֶת
כִּי אֵין לְמַעֲשֵׂי הָאֱלֹהִים חֵקֶר.

Say to the youth whose hair enfolds his cheeks: 'How can yellow noon enfold the rosy dawn?' Agur said, 'Beauty is vain, and charm a delusion',[2] but do not hold it against him. Clearly, your cheeks bear true witness that the acts of God are unfathomable.

שַׁעַר פְּתַח, דּוֹדִי

TO GOD

שַׁעַר פְּתַח, דּוֹדִי, קוּמָה פְּתַח שַׁעַר,
כִּי נִבְהֲלָה נַפְשִׁי, גַּם נִשְׂעֲרָה שַׂעַר.
לִי לַעֲגָה שִׁפְחַת אִמִּי, וְרָם לִבָּהּ
יַעַן שְׁמֹעַ אֵל קוֹל צַעֲקַת נַעַר.
מִנִּי חֲצוֹת לַיְלָה פֶּרֶא רְדָפַנִי,
אַחֲרֵי אֲשֶׁר רָמַס אוֹתִי חֲזִיר־יַעַר.

Open the gate, my love, arise and open the gate! My soul is dismayed and shaken with terror. Hagar, my mother's slave-girl, laughed me to scorn; she grew haughty because God heard the outcry of her child Ishmael.[3] In this midnight of exile, I was trampled by the wild boar[3] of the thickets, then pursued by the wild ass.[3] When the

1. Lit. 'bow'; also 'rainbow', the sign which God gave Noah that the flood would not recur (Genesis 9.15).
2. Proverbs 31.30.
3. Ishmael (Genesis 21.17) and the wild ass represent Islam; the wild boar, Christianity.

הַקֵּץ אֲשֶׁר נֶחְתַּם הוֹסִיף עֲלֵי מַכְאוֹב
לִבִּי וְאֵין מֵבִין לִי – וַאֲנִי בַעַר.

time of the end was sealed,[1] my agony redoubled. There is no one to guide me, and I am like a beast.

שַׁעַר אֲשֶׁר נִסְגַּר

THAT IS MY BELOVED

'שַׁעַר אֲשֶׁר נִסְגַּר – קוּמָה פְּתָחֵהוּ,
וּצְבִי אֲשֶׁר בָּרַח – אֵלַי שָׁלְחֵהוּ!
לְיוֹם בּוֹאֲךָ עָדַי לָלִין בְּבֵין שָׁדַי,
שָׁם רֵיחֲךָ הַטּוֹב עָלַי תְּנִיחֵהוּ.'

[Zion:] 'The gate that was shut – oh, arise and open it! The gazelle[2] that ran away – oh, send him to me! On the day You come to me and lie between my breasts, Your fragrance will rest upon me.'

'מַה זֶּה דְּמוּת דּוֹדֵךְ, כַּלָּה יְפֵה־פִיָּה,
כִּי תֹאמְרִי אֵלַי: "שָׁלְחָה וְקָחֵהוּ"?
הַהוּא יְפֵה עַיִן, אָדֹם וְטוֹב רֹאִי?'

[God:] 'Lovely bride, what shape has your beloved, that you say to Me: "Send for him and bring him"? Is he the bright-eyed one, ruddy and handsome?'

'רֵעִי וְדוֹדִי זֶה – קוּמָה מְשָׁחֵהוּ!'

[Zion:] 'That is my darling, that is my beloved. Oh, rise and anoint him!'

שׁוֹכֵב עֲלֵי מִטּוֹת

ZION LONGING FOR THE MESSIAH

שׁוֹכֵב עֲלֵי מִטּוֹת זָהָב בְּאַרְמוֹנִי,
מָתַי יְצוּעִי, יָהּ, תָּכִין לְאַדְמוֹנִי?
לָמָּה, צְבִי נֶחְמָד, תִּישַׁן – וְהַשַּׁחַר
עָלָה כְּנֵס עַל רֹאשׁ שְׂנִירִי וְחֶרְמוֹנִי?
מֵעַל פְּרָאִים סוּר, וּנְטֵה לְיַעֲלַת־חֵן.
הִנְנִי לְכָמוֹךָ, וְאַתְּ טוֹב לְכָמוֹנִי.
הַבָּא בְּאַרְמוֹנִי יִמְצָא בְמַטְמוֹנִי
עֲסִיס וְרִמּוֹנִי, מוֹרִי וְקִנְמוֹנִי.

Lord, You who reclined upon couches of gold in my palace,[3] when will You prepare my bed for the rosy-cheeked youth?[2] O lovely Gazelle, why are You still sleeping? The dawn has already risen like a banner over the mountains of Senir and Hermon. Turn away from the wild asses of Ishmael, come to Your graceful deer. I am Yours and You are fit for such as me. He who enters my palace will find in its treasures the juice of my pomegranates and my cinnamon and my myrrh.

1. The end of the period of exile; see Daniel 12.9.
2. The Messiah.
3. An allusion to the golden cherubim in the Temple.

שְׁחִי לָאֵל

THE SOUL AND ITS MAKER

שְׁחִי לָאֵל, יְחִידָה הַחֲכָמָה,
וְרוּצִי לַעֲבֹד אוֹתוֹ בְּאֵימָה.
לְעוֹלָמֵךְ פְּנִי לֵילֵךְ וְיוֹמֵךְ,
וְלָמָּה תִרְדְּפִי הֶבֶל וְלָמָּה ?
מְשׁוּלָה אַתְּ בְּחַיּוּתֵךְ לְאֵל חַי,
אֲשֶׁר נֶעְלָם כְּמוֹ אַתְּ נַעֲלָמָה.
הֲלֹא אִם יוֹצְרֵךְ טָהוֹר וְנָקִי –
דְּעִי כִּי כֵן טְהוֹרָה אַתְּ וְתַמָּה.
חֲסִין יִשָּׂא שְׁחָקִים עַל זְרוֹעוֹ –
כְּמוֹ תִשְׂאִי גְּוִיָּה נֶאֱלָמָה.
זְמִירוֹת קַדְּמִי, נַפְשִׁי, לְצוּרֵךְ
אֲשֶׁר לֹא שָׂם דְּמוּתֵךְ בָּאֲדָמָה.
קְרָבַי, בָּרְכוּ תָמִיד לְצוּרְכֶם,
אֲשֶׁר לְשְׁמוֹ תְהַלֵּל כֹּל נְשָׁמָה !

Bow down before God, my precious thinking soul, and make haste to worship Him with reverence. Night and day think only of your everlasting world. Why should you chase after vanity and emptiness? As long as you live, you are akin to the living God: just as He is invisible, so are you. Since your Creator is pure and flawless, know that you too are pure and perfect. The Mighty One upholds the heavens on His arm, as you uphold the mute body. My soul, let your songs come before your Rock, who does not lay your form in the dust. My innermost heart, bless your Rock always, whose name is praised by everything that has breath.

שַׁדַּי אֲשֶׁר יַקְשִׁיב

THE REQUEST

שַׁדַּי אֲשֶׁר יַקְשִׁיב לְדַל וְיֵעָתֵר –
עַד אָן תְּהֵא רָחוֹק מִנִּי, וְתִסָּתֵר ?
לַיִל וְיוֹם אֶעְטֹף, אֶקְרָא בְּלֵב נָכוֹן,
אוֹדֶה לְךָ תָמִיד, כִּי חַסְדְּךָ יָתֵר.
מַלְכִּי, לְךָ אוֹחִיל, לִבִּי בְךָ יִבְטַח,
חוֹלֵם חֲלוֹם סָתוּם יִבְטַח עֲלֵי פוֹתֵר.
הִנֵּה שְׁאֵלָתִי : הַקְשֵׁב תְּחִנָּתִי.
אוֹתָהּ אֲבַקֵּשׁ, לֹא פָחוֹת וְלֹא יוֹתֵר.

God Almighty, You who listen to the wretched and grant their desire, how long will You remain far from me and hidden? Night and day I entreat You, I cry out with a confident heart. I shall always praise You, for Your love is never-ending. My King, I wait for You, I put my trust in You, like one who has dreamt an obscure dream and places his trust in the interpreter. All I ask is that You listen to my plea. This is my request, neither more nor less.

שְׁחַרְתִּיךָ

IN PRAISE OF GOD

שְׁחַרְתִּיךָ בְּכָל שַׁחְרִי וְנִשְׁפִּי
וּפָרַשְׂתִּי לְךָ כַּפַּי וְאַפִּי.
לְךָ אֶהְמֶה בְּלֵב צָמֵא, וְאֶדְמֶה
לְדַל שׁוֹאֵל עֲלֵי פְתָחַי וְסִפִּי.
מְרוֹמוֹת לֹא יְכִילוּךָ לְשִׁבְתָּךְ —
וְאוּלָם יֵשׁ מְקוֹמְךָ תּוֹךְ סְעִפִּי!
הֲלֹא אֶצְפֹּן בְּלִבִּי שֵׁם כְּבוֹדְךָ,
וְגָבַר חִשְׁקְךָ עַד יַעֲבָר־פִּי:
אֲנִי עַל כֵּן אֲהוֹדֶה שֵׁם אֲדֹנָי
בְּעוֹד נִשְׁמַת אֱלֹהִים חַי בְּאַפִּי.

Morning and evening I seek You, spreading out my hands, lifting up my face in prayer. I sigh for You with a thirsting heart; I am like the pauper begging at my doorstep. The heights of heaven cannot contain Your presence, yet You have a dwelling in my mind. I try to conceal Your glorious name in my heart, but my desire for You grows till it bursts out of my mouth. Therefore I shall praise the name of the Lord as long as the breath of the living God is in my nostrils.

טֶרֶם הֱיוֹתִי

BEFORE I WAS

טֶרֶם הֱיוֹתִי חַסְדְּךָ בָאַנִי,
הַשָּׂם לְיֵשׁ אַיִן וְהִמְצִיאַנִי.
מִי הוּא אֲשֶׁר רִקַּם תְּמוּנָתִי? וּמִי
עַצְמִי בְּכוּר יָצַק וְהִקְפִּיאַנִי?
מִי הוּא אֲשֶׁר נָפַח נְשָׁמָה בִי? וּמִי
בֶּטֶן שְׁאוֹל פָּתַח וְהוֹצִיאַנִי?
מִי נְהָגַנִי מִנְּעוּרַי עַד הֲלֹם?
מִי לִמְּדַנִי בִין וְהִפְלִיאַנִי?
אָמְנָם אֲנִי חֹמֶר בְּקֶרֶב יָדְךָ.
אַתָּה עֲשִׂיתָנִי, אֱמֶת, לֹא אָנִי.
אוֹדֶה עֲלֵי פִשְׁעִי וְלֹא אֹמַר לְךָ
כִּי הֶעֱרִים נָחָשׁ וְהִשִּׁיאַנִי.
אֵיכָה אֲכַחֵד מִמְּךָ חֶטְאִי? הֲלֹא
טֶרֶם הֱיוֹתִי חַסְדְּךָ בָאַנִי!

Before I was, Your enduring love came to me, O You who make being out of nothingness, and You created me. Who was it that designed my form? Who cast my body in a crucible and then made it congeal? Who was it that breathed into me the breath of life? Who opened the belly of Sheol[1] and brought me forth? Who has been my guide from boyhood to this day? Who taught me wisdom and showed me wonders? Yes, I am like clay in Your hands. Truly, it was You, not I, that made me. And so I shall confess my guilt; nor shall I say, 'It was the serpent[2] who conspired to deceive me.' How could I ever conceal my sin from You? Even before I was, Your enduring love came to me!

1. Here, the womb. 2. An epithet for the 'evil inclination'.

יִצְחָק אִבְּן־גִּ׳יאַת

שַׁדַּי, שׁוֹבֵבָה

שַׁדַּי, שׁוֹבֵבָה חוֹלַת אַהֲבָה,
הוֹמָה לָרְגָעִים עַל דָּת הַכְּזָבָה.

יוֹם רָחַק יְדִידָהּ, נַפְשָׁהּ מֵאֲנָה
הִנָּחֵם, וְיָדָהּ עַל רֹאשׁ נָתְנָה,
וּבְיַד מַעֲבִידָהּ דוּמָה שָׁכְנָה.
עַל כִּי שׁוֹבֵבָה, עֵינָהּ דָּאֲבָה,
וּבְצוּרֵי רְגָעִים בֵּיתָהּ חָצְבָה.

צוֹעֶקֶת וְהוֹמָה מִיַּד לוֹחֲצִים,
כִּי מִשְׁמָע וְדוּמָה אוֹתָהּ קוֹלְסִים,
גַּם גָּדֵר וְחוֹמָה יַחַד פּוֹרְצִים.
אֵיךְ לֹא־עֲזוּבָה פִּתְאֹם עֻזָּבָה,
בֵּין שִׁנֵּי רְשָׁעִים לוֹהֲטִים שָׁכְבָה.

חֶזְיוֹנֵי כְתָבָהּ הֵן מַה נֶּחְתְּמוּ!
רַעְיוֹנֵי לְבָבָהּ לִמְאֹד נִפְעֲמוּ.
כָּל יוֹשְׁבֵי סְבִיבָהּ בָּהּ יִלָּחֲמוּ.
עַל כִּי אוֹהֲבָהּ פִּתְאֹם עָזְבָה,
בֵּין זֶרַע מְרֵעִים בָּדָד יָשְׁבָה.

׳קוֹרְאָה מִמְּצָרִים, לָמָּה תִירְאִי?
עַל כַּנְפֵי נְשָׁרִים עוֹד תִּנָּשְׂאִי.
הֵן אֵשֶׁת נְעוּרִים לִי עוֹד תִּקָּרְאִי,
רַעְיָה נֶעְצָבָה – אוֹתָהּ אוֹהֲבָה,
כִּי עַל כָּל פְּשָׁעִים תְּכַסֶּה אַהֲבָה!׳

Isaac ibn Ghiyyat

THE PROMISE

O Lord, bring back the one who is faint with love, who constantly bewails the broken pledge.

The day her beloved forsook her, she refused all comfort. She put her hands on her head and silently submitted to the hands of her enslaver. She has been wayward; she has carved her home in the treacherous cliffs of time. For this her eyes grow dim with sorrow.

She cries and groans at the hands of her oppressors; Mishma and Dumah[1] gloat over her and breach all her barriers and walls. She who had never been forlorn – how she was suddenly abandoned, to lie among the teeth of ravenous villains!

Her book of visions was sealed. Oh, how this troubled her heart's thoughts! Now those on every side of her attack her. Because she had betrayed her beloved, she now sits alone among a race of evil men.

[God:] 'O you who call out in distress, why should you fear? You will again be carried on eagles' wings. I shall again call you "My youthful bride".[2] My sad beloved, it is you I love, for love overlooks all offences!'

1. The sons of Ishmael (Genesis 25.4), i.e. the Muslims. 2. Isaiah 54.6.

הֲיְדַעְתֶּם, יְדִידַי?

ZION'S PLEA FOR PARDON

הֲיְדַעְתֶּם, יְדִידַי? הַצְּבִי בָּרַח מִמְּלוֹנִי!
מָתַי יָשׁוּב מְעוֹנִי?

Have you heard, my friends? The Gazelle has fled from my dwelling. When will He come home to me?

יַגִּיד לָכֶם כְּרוּבִי:
אַחֲרֵי נָשָׂא לְבָבִי
אֵיךְ אֶשָּׂא מַעֲצָבִי?
לֹא יָדַע, בְּעֵת שֶׁהֶעֱלָה עִמּוֹ כָּל שְׂשׂוֹנִי,
עַל מִי נָטַשׁ יְגוֹנִי.

If only my Cherub would tell you how I am to bear my sorrow after He bore away my heart! When He flew away with all my joys, He did not know whose hands I would fall into, grief-stricken.

צַר לִי צַר עַל נְדוּדוֹ:
סָר מֵעָלַי כְּבוֹדוֹ,
אוֹר יִפְעָתוֹ וְהוֹדוֹ.
אֵי יָמִים שְׂפָתָיו יִטְּפוּ נֹפֶת עַל לְשׁוֹנִי,
וַעֲנָקָיו עַל גְּרוֹנִי?

I am in anguish because He is gone. His glory has left me, and the glow of His beauty and splendour. Where are the days when His lips dropped sweetness on my tongue like the honeycomb and His necklaces hung on my throat?

חַנּוֹתִי אֵיךְ שְׁכֵחָם?
שַׁעֲשׁוּעַי אֵיךְ זְנָחָם?
וִידִידוּת, בֵּין בְּנֵי חָם
הֶרְאָה לִי בְּאָמוֹן, עֵת אֲשֶׁר מוֹפְתָיו שָׂם בְּמוֹנִי
וַיּוֹצֵא אֶת הֲמוֹנִי?

How could He forget His favours to me? How could He forsake my delights and the love He showed me in Egypt, among the sons of Ham, when He sent His portents against my enemies and led my people out?

קָרַע יַם סוּף לְפָנַי,
הֶרְאָה אוֹרוֹ לְעֵינַי,
דִּבֶּר דּוֹדָיו בְּאָזְנַי,
וּלְחַדְרוֹ אֲהוּבִי סָר, אֱלֵי חִין קוֹל פַּעֲמוֹנִי
וּלְרֵיחַ קִנְּמוֹנִי.

He split the Red Sea before me; He revealed His light to my eyes; He spoke words of love in my ear and He came – my Beloved – into His room,[1] to the lovely sound of my bells and the fragrance of my cinnamon.

1. The Tabernacle.

עָבְרִי חֻקִּים וְעֵדוֹת,
הֶעֱבִיר מִנִּי יְדִידוֹת
נִכְבָּדוֹת וַחֲמוּדוֹת.
הָשֵׁב לִי שְׂשׂוֹן יִשְׁעֲךָ, וְאִם עָבַר רֹאשׁ זְדוֹנִי –
נָא הַעֲבֵר אֶת עֲווֹנִי!

Because I did not keep His statutes and commands, He did not keep His precious love for me. Oh, restore to me the joy of Your deliverance; and though my insolence has swept over my head – I pray You, sweep away my guilt!

לֵוִי אִבְּן־אַלְתַּבָּאן

Levi ibn Altabban

לִקְרַאת מְקוֹר חַיַּי

THE AWAKENING

לִקְרַאת מְקוֹר חַיַּי אֶתֵּן מְגַמָּתִי,
טֶרֶם יְשִׁיבוּנִי יָמִים לְאַדְמָתִי.
לוּ חָכְמָה נֶפֶשׁ, רוּחַ מְרַדֶּפֶת,
כִּי הִיא לְבַדָּהּ מִתֵּבֵל תְּרוּמָתִי!
וִיהִי לְבָבִי עֵר מֵבִין לְאַחֲרִיתִי
כִּי יוֹם תְּנוּמָתִי תִּהְיֶה תְקוּמָתִי –
יוֹם יַעֲמִיד מַעֲשֵׂה יָדַי לְעֻמָּתִי,
יוֹם יֶאֱסֹף אֵלָיו רוּחִי וְנִשְׁמָתִי.

I shall turn to the fountain of my life, before time returns me to the earth. If only my soul, which is bent on folly, had the wisdom to know that it alone is my treasure in this world! If only my heart would rouse itself and understand my end: that the very day on which I sleep will be my awakening – the day He summons all my deeds to face me, the day He recalls my spirit and my soul to Himself.

יְיָ, לְבָבוֹת נִמְהָרוּ

PRAYER IN TIME OF DROUGHT

יְיָ, לְבָבוֹת נִמְהָרוּ וּנְפָשׁוֹת קָדְרוּ,
כִּי שָׁמַיִם נֶעֶצְרוּ וַיֶּחְסְרוּ הַמָּיִם.
וְכִסְּתָה כְלִמָּה פָּנֵינוּ, כִּי רַבּוּ עֲווֹנֵינוּ,
וְתֵרַדְנָה עֵינֵינוּ דִּמְעָה וְעַפְעַפֵּינוּ יִזְּלוּ מָיִם.
בְּהֵעָצֵר עֲנָנִים בָּאנוּ בְּבֹשֶׁת פָּנִים,
הָעֲנִיִּים וְהָאֶבְיוֹנִים, מְבַקְשִׁים מָיִם.

Lord, our hearts are filled with fear and our souls with gloom, for the sky is locked *and there is no water*. Shame covers our faces, so great is our guilt; *our eyes run with tears, our eyelids are moist with water*. Now that the clouds are stopped up, we come shamefacedly, *paupers and wretches, to beg for water*.

רְעֵבִים גַּם צְמֵאִים הִתְעַטְּפוּ כִּפְרָאִים,
עָמְדוּ עַל שְׁפָיִים וַיֹּאמְרוּ: ׳תְּנוּ לָנוּ מַיִם!׳
עָבְשׁוּ פְּרֻדוֹת, וְעַל כָּל יָדַיִם גְּדֻדוֹת,
וּנְפָשׁוֹת מְאֹד חֲרֵדוֹת, כִּי קַלּוּ הַמָּיִם.
קוֹל רַעַמְךָ בַּגַּלְגַּל צַוֵּה, וְחַסְדְּךָ יִגַּל
לְהָנִיף בְּקָצִיר מַגָּל, לְקוֹל תִּתּוֹ הֲמוֹן מַיִם.
בְּרִנָּה יִקְצְרוּ וּבִתְרוּעָה הַזּוֹרְעִים בְּדִמְעָה
וְקוֹל רִנָּה וִישׁוּעָה, כִּי נִבְקְעוּ בַמִּדְבָּר מַיִם.
חֶרְפַּת רָעָב הָסֵר, וְאַל תּוֹסֶף לְיַסֵּר,
וְעַל עַם דַּל וְאֶבְיוֹן בַּשֵּׂר:
׳אַשְׁרֵיכֶם זוֹרְעֵי עַל כָּל מָיִם!׳

The hungry and the thirsty faint like wild asses [in a drought]. They stand on the bare heights *and say: 'Give us water!'* The soil is parched and all our hands are gashed in mourning; our hearts are in anguish *because they are gone, the waters.* Order Your thunder to resound in the whirlwind; let Your steadfast love reveal itself, so that we may lift our sickles at harvest-time, as Your love *gives us the sound of tumultuous waters.* Those who sow in tears will reap with songs of joy and triumph; there will be shouts of deliverance *when the wilderness gushes with water.* Oh remove the reproach of hunger, and torment us no more; declare to Your poor and helpless people: '*Happy shall you be who sow beside all waters!*'

בִּנְיָמִין בֶּן־זֶרַח

Benjamin ben Zerah

בְּלוּלֵי אֵשׁ וּמֵימוֹת

PRAISE IN HEAVEN AND ON EARTH

בְּלוּלֵי אֵשׁ וּמֵימוֹת,
גִּבּוֹרֵי עִיר מְרוֹמוֹת,
נִצָּבִים כְּחוֹמוֹת.
בִּרְתָתִים וְאֵימוֹת
מַרְבִּים תַּעֲצוּמוֹת
לָאֵל יוֹסֵד הֲדוֹמוֹת —
וַאֲנִי, אֹם מֵאֻמּוֹת,
בְּחֵךְ וְגָרוֹן רוֹמֵמוֹת.

Fashioned of fire and water, warriors of the lofty city – they stand before Him like walls. With trembling and dread, again and again, they celebrate the power of God, who built the earth. And I, chosen of all people – His high praises are in my throat.

נוֹהֵם מִיכָאֵל
וְגוֹעֶה גַּבְרִיאֵל,

Michael roars and Gabriel clamours.

זוֹעֵק אוּרִיאֵל
וְגוֹעֵשׁ רְפָאֵל,
וּמְהַדֵּר הֲדַרְנִיאֵל
הוֹד לְיָהּ אַכְתְּרִיאֵל –
וַאֲנִי, כְּנֶסֶת יִשְׂרָאֵל,
מְעִידָה כִּי אֵין כָּאֵל.

Uriel shouts and Raphael bellows. Hadarniel extols and Akhteriel acclaims God's majesty. And I, the assembly of Israel, declare: there is none like God!

יְרוֹצְצוּ כִּבְרָקִים
חֵיל זְוָעוֹת וְזִקִּים,
לַפִּידִים דּוֹלְקִים
וְכַבָּזָק בּוֹזְקִים,
תִּשְׁבָּחוֹת מְפִיקִים
וְשִׁעוּר רֹן מְדַקְדְּקִים –
וַאֲנִי, שׁוֹשַׁנַּת הָעֲמָקִים,
עֲשׁוּקָה בְּמִצְווֹת וְחֻקִּים.

Quivering hosts of firebrands streak like lightning, flaming torches dart like rays of light, uttering songs of praise, keeping the rhythm with care. And I, the lily of the valley, devote myself to His precepts and statutes.

מֵאָה וְאַלְפֵי רְבָבוֹת,
מַרְכְּבוֹת אֵשׁ וְשַׁלְהָבוֹת
מַקִּיפוֹת וְסוֹבְבוֹת
עִלּוּי כֵּס עֲרָבוֹת.
שָׁלוֹשׁ קְדֻשּׁוֹת דּוֹבְבוֹת,
וְקוֹל דְּמָמָה מַקְשִׁיבוֹת –
וַאֲנִי, בַּת שְׁלֹשֶׁת אָבוֹת,
תָּמִיד תְּפִלּוֹתַי עֲרֵבוֹת.

Thousands and myriads of angels, chariots of flame and bolts of fire circle and whirl around the throne, raised upon the seventh heaven. Three times they say 'Holy!', and they listen to the low murmuring sound. And I, daughter of the three patriarchs – my prayers always please Him.

נַהֲרֵי אֵימָה וְחִילָה
זֵעַת חַיּוֹת מַגְדִּילָה,
וְעַל אַרְבַּעְתָּן מִלְמַעְלָה
חַיָּה חֲמִישִׁית גְּדוֹלָה,

The sweat of the four Heavenly Beasts swells the rushing river of terror,[1] and above them stands a fifth gigantic Beast. He begins to chant God's glory,

1. The fiery Rigyon; see p. 239.

לְסַלְסֵל הִיא מְתְחִילָה
וְאַחֲרֶיהָ פָּמַלְיָא כֻלָּהּ –
וַאֲנִי בְּבֵית הַתְּפִלָּה
תַּבַּעְנָה שְׂפָתַי תְּהִלָּה.

and all the attendants join in. And I, in the house of prayer – my lips pour forth Your praise.

יוֹסֵף אִבְּן־סַהְל

Joseph ibn Sahl

וּפַרְעוֹשִׁים כְּפָרָשִׁים

THE FLEAS

וּפַרְעוֹשִׁים כְּפָרָשִׁים יְרוּצוּן,
וְכָעוֹף לֶאֱכֹל עוֹרִי יְאוּצוּן,
וְכִשְׂעִירִים יְרַקֵּדוּן סְבִיבִי,
וְאוֹתִי מִתְּנוּמָתִי יְקִיצוּן.
וְנִלְאֵיתִי הֲרֹג קָטָן וְגָדוֹל
לְהַכְנִיעָם – וְהֵם לֹא יַעֲרִיצוּן.
כְּגִבּוֹרִים בְּמִלְחַמְתָּם קְשֵׁי לֵב,
אֲשֶׁר בִּנְפֹל אֲחֵיהֶם יַאֲמִיצוּן.
וְאִם יִהְיוּ מְעַט בַּיּוֹם עֲצֵלִים,
בְּבוֹא לַיִל כְּגַנָּב יֶחֱרָצוּן.
וְהֵן נַפְשִׁי בְּכָל יוֹם קָצְרָה בָם,
וְיָדַי מֵהֲרֹג אוֹתָם יְקוּצוּן –
וְהַסַּף מִנְּשִׁיכָתָם בְּשָׂרִי
חֲבַרְבּוּרוֹת, כְּמוֹ רִמּוֹן יְנַצּוּן.
אֱלֹהִים, הַחֲרִימֵם, כִּי בְלִי נוּם
אֲנִי, דָוֶה – וְהֵמָּה יַעֲלֹצוּן!

And the fleas charge like war-horses; they swoop down like birds to devour my skin. They caper around me like he-goats, and rouse me out of my sleep. I have become weary of killing both young and old to rout them; yet they know no fear. They are stout-hearted like warriors in battle who pluck up their courage when their comrades fall. Though they are a bit lazy during the day, when night comes they are as nimble as thieves. Day after day I loathe them, and my hands are sick of killing them; but their bites have covered my flesh with sores that blossom like pomegranates. O God, wipe them out, for I am in anguish and cannot sleep – while they exult!

מֹשֶׁה אִבְּן־עֶזְרָא

Moses ibn Ezra

כָּתְנוֹת פַּסִּים לָבַשׁ הַגַּן

כָּתְנוֹת פַּסִּים לָבַשׁ הַגַּן, וּכְסוּת רִקְמָה מַדֵּי דִשְׁאוֹ,
וּמְעִיל תַּשְׁבֵּץ עָטָה כָל עֵץ, וּלְכָל עַיִן הֶרְאָה פִלְאוֹ.
כָּל צִיץ חָדָשׁ לִזְמַן חֹדֶשׁ יָצָא, שׂוֹחֵק לִקְרַאת בּוֹאוֹ –
אַךְ לִפְנֵיהֶם שׁוֹשָׁן עָבַר, מֶלֶךְ, כִּי עַל הוּרַם כִּסְאוֹ.
יָצָא מִבֵּין מִשְׁמַר עָלָיו, וַיְשַׁנֶּה אֵת בִּגְדֵי כִלְאוֹ.
מִי לֹא יִשְׁתֶּה יֵינוֹ עָלָיו – הָאִישׁ הַהוּא יִשָּׂא חֶטְאוֹ!

THE ROSE[1]

The garden put on a coat of many colours, and its grass garments were like robes of brocade. All the trees dressed in chequered tunics and showed their wonders to every eye. The new blossoms all came forth in honour of Time renewed, came gaily to welcome him. But at their head advanced the rose, king of them all, for his throne was set on high. He came out from among the guard of leaves and cast aside his prison-clothes. Whoever does not drink his wine upon the rose-bed – that man will surely bear his guilt!

זְמַן הַקֹּר

זְמַן הַקֹּר כְּצֵל בָּרַח, וְגִשְׁמוֹ
כְּבָר חָלַף, וּפָרָשָׁיו וְרִכְבּוֹ,
וְחָל שֶׁמֶשׁ בְּרֹאשׁ טָלֶה, עֲלֵי חֹק
תְּקוּפָתוֹ, כְּמֶלֶךְ עַל מְסִבּוֹ.
וְחָבְשׁוּ מִגְבְּעוֹת צִצִּים גְּבָעוֹת,
וּמִישׁוֹר – כָּתְנוֹת דִּשְׁאוֹ וְעֶשְׂבּוֹ,
יְשַׁלַּח אֶל נְחִירֵינוּ קְטֹרֶת,
יְמוֹתֵי הַסְּתָיו טָמַן בְּחֻבּוֹ.

תְּנָה הַכּוֹס, אֲשֶׁר יָשִׁיר מְשׂוֹשִׂי
וְיָסִיר מִלְּבָבִי מַעֲצָבוֹ,
וְכַבֵּה אֶת יְקוֹד אִשּׁוֹ בְּדִמְעִי,
לְמַעַן כִּי חֲמָתוֹ בָּעֲרָה בוֹ.

WINE SONG FOR SPRING

The cold season has slipped away like a shadow. Its rains are already gone, its chariots and its horsemen.[2] Now the sun, in its ordained circuit, is at the sign of the Ram, like a king reclining on his couch. The hills have put on turbans of flowers, and the plain has robed itself in tunics of grass and herbs; it greets our nostrils with the incense hidden in its bosom all winter long.

Give me the cup that will enthrone my joy and banish sorrow from my heart. The wine is hot with anger; temper its fierce fire with my tears. Beware of

1. Or 'The Lily'. 2. The storms of winter.

וְגוּר מֵהַזְּמָן, כִּי מַתְּנוֹתָיו
כְּרֹאשׁ פֶּתֶן מְעַט נֹפֶת בְּקִרְבּוֹ,
וְהַשֵּׁא נַפְשְׁךָ בֹּקֶר בְּטוּבוֹ –
וְיַחֵל תַּהְפּוּכוֹתָיו בְּעַרְבּוֹ!

Fortune: her favours are like the venom of serpents, spiced with honey. But let your soul deceive itself and accept her goodness in the morning, even though you know that she will be treacherous at night.

שְׁתֵה בַיּוֹם – עֲדֵי יִפֶן, וְשֶׁמֶשׁ
עֲלֵי כַסְפּוֹ יְצַפֶּה אֶת זְהָבוֹ,
וּבַלַּיְלָה – עֲדֵי יִבְרַח כְּשָׁחוֹר,
וְיַד־שַׁחַר מְאַחֵז אֶת עֲקֵבוֹ.

Drink all day long, until the day wanes and the sun coats its silver with gold; and all night long, until the night flees like a Moor, while the hand of dawn grips its heel.

דַּדֵּי יְפַת תֹּאַר

YOUR RIGHTFUL PORTION

דַּדֵּי יְפַת תֹּאַר לַיִל חֲבֹק,
וּשְׂפַת יְפַת מַרְאֶה יוֹמָם נְשֹׁק!

Caress the breasts of the lovely girl at night, and kiss the lips of the beautiful girl all day long!

וּגְעַר בְּכָל מֵרִיב, יוֹעֵץ לְפִי
דַרְכּוֹ, וְקַח יֹשֶׁר נִמְצָא בְּפִי:
אֵין הַחַיּוּת רַק עִם יַלְדֵי יֳפִי
כִּי גָנְבוּ מֵעֵדֶן לַעֲשֹׁק
חַיִּים – וְאֵין אִישׁ חַי לֹא יַחְשֹׁק!

Spurn those who chide you for loving, who counsel you to their own advantage; and heed my words of truth: there is no life but in the company of beauty's daughters, who stole out of Eden to torture the living, and there is no man living who is not full of desire.

נַסֵּךְ לְבָבְךָ בְּשְׂמָחוֹת, וְשִׂישׂ,
וּשְׁתֵה עֲלֵי יֵבַל גֶּבֶל עֲסִיס־
יַיִן, לְקוֹל נֵבֶל עִם תּוֹר וְסִיס,
וּרְקֹד וְגִיל, גַּם כַּף עַל כַּף סְפֹק,
וּשְׁכַר, וְדֶלֶת יַעֲלַת חֵן דְּפֹק.

Plunge your heart into pleasures, make merry, drink out of wine-skins by the riverside to the sound of lyres, doves, and swifts; dance and rejoice, clap your hands, get drunk, and knock on the door of the lovely girl!

זֶה הוּא נְעִים תֵּבֵל – קַח חֶלְקְךָ
מֶנּוּ כְּאֵיל מִלּוּאִים, חָקְךָ
שִׂימָה מְנָת רָאשֵׁי עַם צִדְקְךָ:
אַל תֶּחֱשֶׁה לִמְצֹץ שָׂפָה וְרֹק,
עַד תֶּאֱחֹז חָקְךָ – חָזֶה וְשׁוֹק!

These are the delights of the world; take your part as [did the priests] from the ram of installation. Always allot yourself the very portion that was your leaders'[1] due; do not stop sipping the moist lips until you hold your rightful portion – the breast and the thigh!

תַּאֲוַת לְבָבִי

THE TREACHEROUS FAWN

תַּאֲוַת לְבָבִי וּמַחְמַד עֵינַי –
עֹפֶר לְצִדִּי וְכוֹס בִּימִינִי!

My heart's desire and my eyes' delight: the hart beside me and a cup in my right hand!

רַבּוּ מְרִיבַי – וְלֹא אֶשְׁמָעֵם.
בּוֹא, הַצְּבִי, וַאֲנִי אַכְנִיעֵם,
וּזְמַן יְכַלֵּם וּמָוֶת יִרְעֵם.
בּוֹא, הַצְּבִי, קוּם וְהַבְרִיאֵנִי
מִצּוּף שְׂפָתְךָ וְהַשְׂבִּיעֵנִי!

Many denounce me for loving, but I pay no heed. Come to me, fawn, and I shall vanquish them. Time will consume them and death will shepherd them away. Oh come to me, fawn, let me feast on the nectar of your lips until I am satisfied.

לָמָּה יְנִיאוּן לְבָבִי, לָמָּה?
אִם בַּעֲבוּר חֵטְא וּבִגְלַל אַשְׁמָה
אֶשְׁגֶּה בְיָפְיָךְ – אֲדֹנָי שָׁמָּה!
אַל יֵט לְבָבְךָ בְּנִיב מְעַנְּנִי,
אִישׁ מַעֲקַשִּׁים, וּבוֹא נַסֵּנִי.

Why, why would they discourage me? If there be any sin or guilt in being ravished by your beauty – let the Lord be my judge![2] Do not let your heart be swayed by the words of my tormentor, that obstinate man. Oh, come put me to the test!

נִפְתָּה – וַקַּמְנוּ אֱלֵי בֵית אִמּוֹ,
נַיֵּט לְעֹל סֻבֳּלִי אֶת שִׁכְמוֹ,
לַיְלָה וְיוֹמָם אֲנִי רַק עִמּוֹ.
אֶפְשֹׁט בְּגָדָיו – וַיַּפְשִׁיטֵנִי,
אִינַק שְׂפָתָיו – וַיֵּינִיקֵנִי.

He was lured and we went to his mother's house. There he bent his back to my heavy yoke. Night and day I alone was with him. I took off his clothes and he took off mine, I sucked at his lips and he suckled me.

1. Lit. 'the heads of the righteous people'; the breast and the leg of the ram of installation were the perquisite of Aaron and his descendants the priests (Exodus 26.27–28).
2. Lit. 'the Lord is there'.

כַּאֲשֶׁר לְבָבִי בְּעֵינָיו נִפְקַד,
גַּם עֹל פְּשָׁעַי בְּיָדוֹ נִשְׂקַד —
דָּרַשׁ תְּנוּאוֹת וְאַפּוֹ פָקַד,
צָעַק בְּאַף: 'רַב לְךָ, עָזְבֵנִי,
אַל תְּהַדְּפֵנִי וְאַל תַּתְעֵנִי!'

But once his eyes had done away with my heart, his hand fastened the yoke of my sin, and he looked for grievances against me. He raged and shouted in fury: 'Enough! Leave me alone! Do not drive me to crime, do not lead me astray!'

אַל תֶּאֱנַף בִּי, צְבִי, עַד כַּלֵּה.
הַפְלֵא רְצוֹנְךָ, יְדִידִי, הַפְלֵא,
וּנְשַׁק יְדִידְךָ וְחֶפְצוֹ מַלֵּא.
אִם יֵשׁ בְּנַפְשְׁךָ חַיּוֹת — חַיֵּנִי,
אוֹ חֶפְצְךָ לַהֲרֹג — הָרְגֵנִי!

Oh, do not be unrelenting in your anger, fawn. Show me the wonders of your love, my friend; kiss your friend and fulfil his desire. If you wish to let me live – give me life; but if you would kill – then kill me!

וְתַפּוּחַ

THE APPLE

וְתַפּוּחַ, אֱמֶת, אֵל לֹא בְרָאוֹ
לְבַד עֹנֶג לְמֵרִיחַ וְנוֹשֵׁק:
חֲשַׁבְתִּיהוּ — בְּשׁוּר יָרֹק וְאָדֹם
קְבוּצִים בּוֹ — פְּנֵי חָשׁוּק וְחוֹשֵׁק.

Truly, God created the apple only to delight those who smell and fondle it. Seeing how green and red are joined in it, I imagine it to be the faces of the wan lover and the blushing beloved.

חוֹלַת אֲהָבִים

RIDDLE

חוֹלַת אֲהָבִים לַיְלָה בָּכֹה
תִבְכֶּה, וְדִמְעָתָהּ עֲלֵי לֶחְיָהּ.
תִּשְׂחַק פְּנֵי הַיּוֹשְׁבִים לְרַנֵּן
אוֹתָם — וְאֵשׁ יֹאכַל שְׁאֵר גְּוִיָּהּ.
תִּתְחַל, וְאִם יָגֹז אֱנוֹשׁ רֹאשָׁהּ,
תָּעִיד — הֲכִי מֵהֶחֳלִי חִיָּהּ!

Love-sick, she weeps bitterly in the night, tears running down her cheeks. She laughs before the company to make them merry, while fire eats away her flesh. Then she looks ill; but should a man shave her head, she would clearly show that he has cured her of her illness.

יִזְכֹּר גֶּבֶר

THE JOURNEY

יִזְכֹּר גֶּבֶר בִּימֵי חַיָּיו
כִּי לַמָּוֶת הוּא לָקוּחַ.
וּלְאַט יִסַּע כָּל יוֹם מַסָּע,
אָכֵן יַחְשֹׁב כִּי יָנוּחַ:
דּוֹמֶה אֶל אִישׁ שׁוֹקֵט עַל צִי –
אַף יִדֶּא עַל כַּנְפֵי רוּחַ.

Let man remember all the days of his life that he is being led to death. Stealthily he journeys on, day after day; he thinks he is at rest, like a man who is motionless on board ship, while the ship is flying on the wings of the wind.

פְּנֵי הָאֵל לְבַד

THE TWO SONS

פְּנֵי הָאֵל לְבַד תָּמִיד אֲחַלֶּה,
וְסוֹד לִבִּי לְאָדָם לֹא אֲגַלֶּה.
וּמַה בֶּצַע בְּיַד גֶּבֶר לְגֶבֶר?
וּמַה הוֹעִיל בְּשִׂפְתֵי רָשׁ לְנִקְלֶה?
מְאַס תֵּבֵל, אֲשֶׁר תַּשְׁפִּיל גְּאוֹנָהּ
בְּיָדֶיהָ, וְקִנְיָנָהּ תְּבַלֶּה,
וּבָנִים יָלְדָה הֵמָּה שְׁנַיִם:
בְּבִטְנָהּ – מֵת, וְעַל גַּבָּהּ – מְחֻלֶּה.

I shall always seek God's favour, His alone; I shall never reveal the secret of my heart to any mortal. Can any man help his fellow-man? What use are the words of a wretch to a pauper? Scorn the World, who with her hands debases her own glory and wears out her treasures. She has given birth to two sons: the one in her belly is dead, and the one on her back is dying.

הֶקִיצוּנִי שְׂעִפַּי

IN THE GRAVEYARD

הֶקִיצוּנִי שְׂעִפַּי לַעֲבֹר עַל
מְלוֹן הוֹרַי וְכָל אַנְשֵׁי שְׁלוֹמִי.
שְׁאֶלְתִּימוֹ – וְאֵין מַקְשִׁיב וּמֵשִׁיב –
הֲבָגְדוּ בִי עֲדֵי אָבִי וְאִמִּי?
בְּלִי לָשׁוֹן קְרָאוּנִי אֲלֵיהֶם
וְהֶרְאוּנִי לְצִדֵּיהֶם מְקוֹמִי.

My thoughts roused me to stop by the resting-place of my parents and my friends. I asked them, though none could listen or reply: have you all betrayed me, even my father and my mother? Mouthlessly they summoned me to them, and showed me my place at their side.

הֲדָמִי תִדְרְשׁוּ

A NIGHT OF GRIEF

הֲדָמִי תִדְרְשׁוּ מִפִּי לְבָאִים,
וְנוּמִי תִשְׁאֲלוּ מִידֵי צְבָאִים ?
וְדַם חוֹשֵׁק, הֲיִגָּאֵל ? וְשֵׁנָה,
הֲתֶעֱרַב לוֹ ? וּמַכְאוֹבָיו מְנִיאִים !
כְּאִלּוּ כָחֲלוּ עֵינָיו בְּרֶשֶׁף,
וְאִישׁוֹנָיו בְּקוֹץ מַכְאִיב מְלֵאִים,
וְעַפְעַפָּיו לְהִתְקָרֵב רְחוֹקִים,
כְּאִלּוּ הֵם בְּגַבּוֹתָם תְּלוּאִים.
וְהַלַּיִל בְּיָם אָפְלוֹ מְגֻדָּח
בְּלִי רַעַשׁ, וְגַלָּיו לֹא נְשׂוּאִים.
וּמַיִם רָחֲבוּ יָדָיו בְּעֵינַי,
וְאֵין לוֹ חוֹף וְלֹא עֵבֶר לְבָאִים.
וְסַהַר יְהַלֵּךְ יָקָר כְּרוֹעֶה,
יְנַהֵל אַט בְּכַר נִרְחָב טְלָאִים ;
וְאִם שֶׁמֶשׁ שְׁלָחָהוּ מְאַסֵּף
לְמַחְנוֹתָיו וְשָׂמוֹ שַׂר צְבָאִים.
וְלֹא אָבִין הֲיֶאֱרַךְ אוֹ הֲיִקְצַר ;
וְאֵיךְ יָבִין אֱנוֹשׁ, יִשָּׂא חֳלָאִים ? [...]

Who will take revenge upon the lions[1] for my blood? Who will demand my sleep from the gazelles? Is there vengeance for a lover's blood? Can he ever savour sleep? His pain will not allow it! It is as if his eyes were painted with burning embers and his pupils filled with painful briars. His eyelids cannot come together; it is as if they were tied to their brows. My night is plunged into a silent sea of darkness, where no waves rise – a sea that is to me far wider than the sea; for it has no coast, no shore for those who voyage. The moon, in his glory, moves like a shepherd, slowly grazing his lambs in broad pastures; or like a general, commissioned by the sun, to be the rearguard of his armies. And I do not know if this night is long or short: how can a man who is oppressed with grief know such a thing?

וְנָהָר, נְהָרוּ

TO MY DISTANT FRIEND

וְנָהָר, נְהָרוּ מֵימֵי פְלָגָיו
לְמוּל עֵינַי וְאֶל עֻמַּת עֲמִיתִי,
וְיָנוּעַ עֲלֵי יָמִין וְלִשְׂמֹאל,
כְּמוֹ שִׁכּוֹר וְיִתְרוֹנֵן כְּדָתִי.
וְעֵת רוּחַ עֲלֵי פָנָיו תְּרַחֵף,
אֲדַמֶּה כִּי יְשַׂחֵק לַהֲמוֹתִי.

The runnels of this river flow before my eyes and towards my friend. It reels right and left like a drunken man, and moans just as I do. When the wind sweeps over its face, it seems to be mocking my sighs. The tumult of

1. Lit. 'the mouth of the lions'; the 'lions' and 'gazelles' are the cruel friends who deserted the poet.

שְׁאוֹן מֵימָיו – שְׁאוֹן לִבִּי לְרֵעִי,
וּמֵי דִמְעִי לְאַנְשֵׁי אַחֲוָתִי.
מְיֻדָּעִי, הֲכִי רוּחַ תְּרַגֵּל?
וְהַנָּהָר מְשַׂחֵק מִבְּכוֹתִי?

its waters is the tumult of my heart for my comrade; its waves are my tears for my dear companions. O my friend, will not the wind inform [on me and tell you of my longing]? Is the river really laughing at my tears?

בִּי, הַמְנַגֵּן

TO THE MINSTREL

[...] בִּי, הַמְנַגֵּן הַמְמַגֵּן מַחְשְׁבוֹת
עֲצָבַי וְתוּגָתִי – כְּצֵל יִבְרָחוּ!
כִּנּוֹר – דְּמוּת פַּעַם לְיַד פַּחַד בְּלִי
שׁוֹק, דָּבְקוּ יַחַד וְלֹא נִתָּחוּ –
יִתַּר לְבָבִי אֶל יְתָרָיו, עֵת אֲשֶׁר
נָעוּ וְלִקְרָאתָם אֲחֵרִים נָחוּ.
אֶתְמַהּ לְהוֹד יָדָיו אֲשֶׁר הָדוּ וְעַל
קַו קָפְצוּ בְּסֵפֶר וְגַם שִׁלֵּחוּ:
הַקּוֹל וְהַפֹּעַל בְּמוֹ מִשְׁקָל וְעַל
מִסְפָּר בְּמוֹפֵת הָאֱמֶת הֻנָּחוּ.
גִּיל הַנְּשָׁמוֹת הַנְּשַׁמּוֹת וַעֲלֵי
אִישִׁים אֲנוּשִׁים מִנֶּגֶף פָּסְחוּ.
יִסָּגְרוּ דַלְתֵי אֹפֶל, אַךְ מִשְׁכְּנֵי
עֶלְיוֹן לְעֵינֵי יוֹדְעִים נִפְתָּחוּ,
יַעֲלוּ לְעוֹלַם הַנְּפָשִׁים מִבְּלִי
מַעֲלוֹת וְנַחֲלֵי הַיְקָר יִצְלָחוּ,
זַכּוּ שְׂעִפֵּיהֶם וְכִמְעַט יֹאמְרוּ:
רוּחוֹת מְשָׁרְתֵי אֵל עֲלֵיהֶם נָחוּ.
עִם תּוֹפְשֵׂי כִנּוֹר וְעוּגָב יִצְהֲלוּ
אוֹנִים, וְלָהֶם מִבְּכִי יִרְוָחוּ –
בִּלְתִּי כְאֵבִי עַל בְּנֵי אָבִי אֲשֶׁר
סָפוּ וּמוֹדָעַי אֲשֶׁר הֻדָּחוּ. [...]

Play for me, minstrel, for you vanquish my thoughts of grief and sorrow, and they disappear like a shadow. Your lute is like a leg joined to a hip, without a thigh to divide them. My heart leaps out to the lute's strings – now some of them are in motion and some are at rest. I marvel at the grace of the plectrums which roam the lute and, keeping time, pounce upon the strings, then set them free. The melody and the gestures accord in measure and in number and have been established by veritable proof; they are the joy of desolate souls and they hover over[1] the afflicted to shield them from torment. Now the doors of darkness are closed, and the heavenly dwellings open before the initiates. They ascend, without stairs, to the realm of souls, and cross the rivers of delight. Their thoughts become so pure that people almost say: the spirit of the Lord's angels is resting upon them. The wretched rejoice with those who play the lute and pipe, finding relief from their tears. And only my pain persists: for my father's sons who have perished and for my friends who have gone far away.

1. Lit. 'they pass over'; an allusion to Exodus 12.13.

יְעִירוּנִי שְׂעִפַּי

יְעִירוּנִי שְׂעִפַּי לַחֲזוֹתֶךָ,
וְיַרְאוּנִי בְּעֵין לֵב נוֹרְאוֹתֶיךָ,
וְיוֹרוּנִי לְהַגִּיד נִפְלְאוֹתֶיךָ –
כִּי אֶרְאֶה שָׁמֶיךָ, מַעֲשֵׂה אֶצְבְּעוֹתֶיךָ.

מִתְהַלֵּךְ עֲלֵי קַו חוּג שָׁמַיִם,
וּמְסַבֵּב מְסִבָּתוֹ כָּאָבְנַיִם,
וּמְסַפֵּר כְּבוֹדְךָ בְּלִי שְׂפָתַיִם.
וְהָאָרֶץ עוֹמֶדֶת בְּנַתַּיִם,
וְהִיא תְלוּיָה בְּחַבְלֵי אַהֲבָתֶךָ.

שָׁם שׁוֹאֵף הַשֶּׁמֶשׁ וְזוֹרֵחַ,
וְהוּא אוֹצֵל מֵאוֹרוֹ לְיָרֵחַ,
וְהַגַּלְגַּל כְּמוֹ אֹהֶל מוֹתֵחַ,
וְכוֹכָבִים עָלָיו כְּגַן פּוֹרֵחַ –
לְהוֹדִיעַ עֹמֶק מַחְשְׁבוֹתֶיךָ.

הֶאָפֵס חֶסֶד אֵל לַעֲדֵי עַד?
וְאִם גָּבַהּ דְּבַר נִחוּמִים וּמִסְעָד?
אִם רוֹפֵא אוֹ הַצֳּרִי אֵין בְּגִלְעָד
יְהִי מַחְזִיק לֵב יֶלֶד יִמְעַד,
וְהוּא דוֹפֵק שַׁעֲרֵי חֶמְלָתֶךָ?

THE GATES OF COMPASSION

My thoughts rouse me to behold You; they show Your fearsome deeds to my heart's eye; they teach me to recite Your wonders – when I look up at Your heavens, the work of Your fingers.

The heavenly spheres move in their course, turning like a potter's wheel, telling Your glory without lips. And the earth is fixed in the centre, suspended from the cords of Your love.

The sun hastens to its place to rise again; it bestows some of its light on the moon; the dome of heaven is spread out like a tent, with stars upon it like a flowering garden – all to display Your fathomless thoughts.

Is God's love gone for ever? Is the word of comfort and support so far from us? Is there no healer, no balm in Gilead, to strengthen the heart of a faltering child who knocks at the gates of Your compassion?

נַפְשִׁי אִוִּיתִיךָ בַּלַּיְלָה

THE SOUL

נַפְשִׁי אִוִּיתִיךָ בַּלַּיְלָה!

With all my soul I long for You in the night.

אִוְּתָה נַפְשִׁי אֶל מְקוֹם נַפְשָׁהּ
וְכָלְתָה אֶל מְקוֹר שָׁרְשָׁהּ
וְנִכְסְפָה לִנְוֵה קָדְשָׁהּ –
לָלֶכֶת יוֹמָם וָלַיְלָה!

My soul longs for the home of her soul,[1] she yearns for her fountainhead, she pines for her holy dwelling – *she would travel there day and night.*

נֹעַם הַכָּבוֹד בְּעֵין הַדַּעַת תִּרְאֶה
וּמִבְּלִי אֵבֶר אֵלָיו תִּדְאֶה
וְתִשְׁאַף עָדָיו וְתִשְׁתָּאֶה –
בְּנֶשֶׁף, בְּעֶרֶב יוֹם, בְּאִישׁוֹן לַיְלָה.

There, with her mind's eye, she would look on the delights of His glory; she would fly to Him without wings; she would hasten to Him and marvel – *at twilight, as the day fades, and in the dark of night.*

יְקָרוֹ תָשׁוּר עַל יְדֵי פְעָלָיו
וְתִתְאַו לָגֶשֶׁת אֵלָיו,
יוֹם לְיוֹם תַּבִּיעַ אֹמֶר מְהַלְּלָיו
וְלַיְלָה לְלַיְלָה.

She would see His splendour in His handiwork; she would long to approach Him; day after day she would speak His praises, *and night after night.*

מֵעוֹדִי עָלַי דֶּגֶל חַסְדְּךָ נוֹדַע,
וְאֹהֶל יִרְאָתְךָ מִלִּבִּי בַּל נִגְדַּע.
אֲדֹנָי, חֲקַרְתַּנִי וַתֵּדַע,
בָּחַנְתָּ לִבִּי פָּקַדְתָּ לַּיְלָה!

You have always kept the banner of Your love over me; Your awe is never absent from my heart.[2] O Lord, You have examined me and known me, *You have tested my heart and watched me by night.*

שָׂבַעְתִּי נְדוּדִים עַל עַרְשׂוֹת אֲנוּשִׁים,
הֱרִיצוּנִי פְעָמַי לִמְעוֹנוֹת קְדוֹשִׁים,
בִּנְפֹל תַּרְדֵּמָה עַל אֲנָשִׁים
בִּשְׂעִפִּים מֵחֶזְיוֹנוֹת לַיְלָה.

I have had my fill of sleepless nights, tossing on my sick-bed. My feet have hurried me to the holy houses of worship even *when deep sleep falls upon men and they have visions in the night.*

1. I.e. God, the all-encompassing soul.
2. Lit. 'the tent of Your awe has never been cut off from my heart'.

הִסְכַּלְתִּי וָאֶשְׁגֶּה כָּל יְמֵי שַׁחֲרוּתִי
וְנִכְלַמְתִּי כִּי הֶבֵלְתִּי זְמַן יַלְדוּתִי.
לְזֹאת הָיְתָה לִּי דִמְעָתִי
לֶחֶם יוֹמָם וָלַיְלָה!

I was a fool, I blundered all the days of my childhood; I am ashamed that I wasted my youth; that is why *tears are now my food, day and night.*

בָּרָה, בִּכְלוּא הַגּוּף נֶעֱצֶרֶת,
הִתְבּוֹנְנִי כִּי הָעוֹלָם מַעְבֶּרֶת,
עוּרִי, עוּרִי לְרֹאשׁ אַשְׁמֹרֶת,
קוּמִי, רֹנִּי בַלַּיְלָה!

O pure one, held in the body's prison, observe that this world is nothing but a passageway. Then rouse, rouse yourself at the beginning of every watch, *rise and cry aloud in the night.*

חָלְפוּ כְצֵל יְמֵי עֲלוּמוֹתַי,
וְקַלּוּ מִנְּשָׁרִים שְׁנוֹתַי,
וְלֹא אֶזְכֹּר מִזְּמַן שְׂמְחוֹתַי
לֹא יוֹם וְלֹא לַיְלָה!

My youthful days vanished like a shadow, my years flew away more swiftly than eagles. Of all my joys I cannot remember *a single day or night.*

זֵדִים הֱצִיקוּנִי וְהִגְדִּילוּ עָלַי בְּפִיהֶם,
דּוֹבְרִים שָׁלוֹם וְנוֹשְׁכִים בְּשִׁנֵּיהֶם.
נָא יִזָּכֵר רֹעַ מַעַלְלֵיהֶם
לְפָנֶיךָ הַיּוֹם, יוֹמָם וָלַיְלָה!

Proud men oppress me and gloat over me; they speak words of peace as their teeth bite into me. Let their evil doings be remembered *before You day and night!*

קַדְּשׁוּ עֲצָרָה וְרַחֲצוּ וְהִתְקַדָּשׁוּ,
הָבֵרוּ סִיג לְבָבוֹת וְהִתְאוֹשָׁשׁוּ,
הַמַּזְכִּירִים אֶת אֲדֹנָי, אַל תֶּחֱשׁוּ
כָּל הַיּוֹם וְכָל הַלַּיְלָה.

You who invoke the Lord's name – call a solemn assembly, wash yourselves, hallow yourselves, purge your hearts of dross, stand fast, do not be silent *day or night.*

'הִתְבַּשְּׂרִי, בִּתִּי, כִּי עוֹד אַנְחִילֵךְ חִנִּי
וּלְאַט אַנְחֵךְ וְאַנִּיחֵךְ בִּמְעוֹנִי,
כִּי אֵין גּוֹאֵל קָרוֹב מִמֶּנִּי:
לִינִי הַלַּיְלָה!'

[God:] 'My daughter, know that I shall yet endow you with My grace; I shall gently lead you to My dwelling and instal you there. You have no kinsman[1] closer than I: *now go and sleep through the night.*

1. Also, 'saviour'.

הֶקִיצוֹתִי תְּנוּמַת רַעֲיוֹנַי

IN OLD AGE

הֶקִיצוֹתִי תְּנוּמַת רַעֲיוֹנַי,
לְיַשֵּׁן תַּאֲוַת נַפְשִׁי וְעֵינַי,
וְחוּלְפוֹת הַזְּמָן תַּרְתִּי בְלִבִּי,
לְהַשְׁמִיעַ עֲתִידוֹתָיו לְאָזְנָי.
וּפִי דֵעִי יְחַוֶּנִּי גְדוֹלוֹת,
וְיַצִּיב מִפְלְאוֹת צוּרִי לְפָנַי,
וְיַגֶּד לִי צְפוּנֵי תַעֲלוּמוֹת,
עֲדֵי אֶחְשֹׁב בְּנֵי עֶלְיוֹן שְׁכֵנַי.
וְאַחַז מַחֲזֵה שַׁדַּי בְּשִׂכְלִי,
וְאָבִין כִּי בְקִרְבִּי יֵשׁ אֲדֹנָי,
אֲשֶׁר נִסְתַּר יְקָר עַצְמוֹ, וְנִגְלָה
בְמִפְעָלָיו לְעֵינֵי רַעֲיוֹנַי.
בְּפִגְרִי הֶעֱלָה נֵר מִכְּבוֹדוֹ,
יְשִׂיחֵנִי שְׁבִילֵי תַחְכְּמוֹנַי,
וְהוּא הָאוֹר, אֲשֶׁר יֵלֵךְ וְיֵאוֹר
יְמֵי נֹעַר, וְיוֹסִיף עֵת זְקוּנַי. [...]

I rouse my slumbering thoughts to lull the cravings of my heart and eyes. I delve into the past to tell my ears what the future will be. Then my mind's lips tell me of great things, and set the marvels of my Rock before me. They disclose to me deep mysteries, until I believe that I dwell among the angels. My intellect beholds visions from the Almighty and I understand that the Lord is within me; that His Precious Self is hidden, but His works reveal Him to the eye of thought. He kindled a lamp, lit with His glory, in my body; it shows me the ways of the ancient sages. And this is the light that grew brighter in youth, and shines even more now that I am old.

יְהוּדָה הַלֵּוִי

Judah Halevi

מֵאָז מְעוֹן הָאַהֲבָה

THE HOME OF LOVE

מֵאָז מְעוֹן הָאַהֲבָה הָיִיתָ –
חָנוּ אֲהָבַי בַּאֲשֶׁר חָנִיתָ.
תּוֹכְחוֹת מְרִיבַי עָרְבוּ לִי עַל שְׁמָךְ;
עָזְבֵם – יְעַנּוּ אֶת אֲשֶׁר עִנִּיתָ.
לָמְדוּ חֲרוֹנְךָ אוֹיְבַי – וָאֹהֲבֵם,
כִּי רָדְפוּ חָלָל אֲשֶׁר הִכִּיתָ.

Ever since You were the home of love for me, my love has lived where You have lived. Because of You, I have delighted in the wrath of my enemies; let them be, let them torment the one whom You tormented. It was from You that they learned their wrath, and I love them, for they hound the wounded one whom You struck down. Ever

מִיּוֹם בְּזִיתַנִי בְּזִיתִינִי אֲנִי,
כִּי לֹא אֲכַבֵּד אֶת אֲשֶׁר בָּזִיתָ.
עַד יַעֲבָר־זַעַם, וְתִשְׁלַח עוֹד פְּדוּת
אֶל נַחֲלָתְךָ זֹאת אֲשֶׁר פָּדִיתָ.

since You despised me, I have despised myself, for I will not honour what You despise. So be it, until Your anger has passed, and again You will redeem Your own possession, which You once redeemed.[1]

יְדִידִי, הֲשָׁכַחְתָּ

ZION COMPLAINS TO GOD

יְדִידִי, הֲשָׁכַחְתָּ חֲנוֹתְךָ בְּבֵין שָׁדַי –
וְלָמָּה מְכַרְתַּנִי צְמִיתוּת לְמַעְבִדַי?
הֲלֹא אָז בְּאֶרֶץ לֹא זְרוּעָה רְדַפְתִּיךָ?
וְשֵׂעִיר וְהַר פָּארָן וְסִינַי וְסִין עֵדַי!
וְהָיוּ לְךָ דוֹדַי, וְהָיָה רְצוֹנְךָ בִּי –
וְאֵיךְ תְּחַלֵּק עַתָּה כְּבוֹדִי לְבִלְעָדַי?
דְּחוּיָה אֱלֵי שֵׂעִיר, הֲדוּפָה עֲדֵי קֵדָר,
בְּחוּנָה בְּכוּר יָוָן, מְעֻנָּה בְּעֹל מָדַי:
הֲיֵשׁ בִּלְתְּךָ גּוֹאֵל, וּבִלְתִּי – אֲסִיר־תִּקְוָה?
תְּנָה עֻזְּךָ לִי, כִּי לְךָ אֶתְּנָה דוֹדַי!

My love, have you forgotten how you lay between my breasts? Then why have you sold me forever to my enslavers? Did I not follow you[2] through a barren land? Let Mount Seir and Mount Paran, Sinai and Sin be my witnesses! There my love was yours, and I was your delight. Then how can you now bestow my glory upon others? I am thrust into Seir,[3] driven towards Kedar,[4] tested in the furnace of Greece, crushed under the yoke of Media. Is there any saviour but you? any prisoner of hope but I? Give me your strength, for I shall give you my love!

יָשֵׁן – וְלִבּוֹ עֵר

TO ISRAEL, IN EXILE

יָשֵׁן – וְלִבּוֹ עֵר, בּוֹעֵר וּמִשְׁתָּעֵר –
צֵא נָא וְהִנָּעֵר וּלְכָה בְּאוֹר פָּנַי.
קוּמָה, צְלַח וּרְכַב! דָּרַךְ לְךָ כּוֹכָב,
וַאֲשֶׁר בְּבוֹר שָׁכַב עָלָה לְרֹאשׁ סִינַי.
אַל תַּעֲלֹז נַפְשָׁם, הָאוֹמְרִים 'תֶּאְשַׁם

O sleeper, whose heart is awake, burning and raging, now wake and go forth, and walk in the light of My presence. Rise, and ride on! A star has come forth for you, and he who has lain in the pit will go up to the top of Sinai. Let them not exult, those who

1. From the bondage of Egypt. 2. After the exodus from Egypt.
3. The Christian nations. 4. The Muslim nations.

צִיּוֹן !' וְהִנֵּה שָׁם לִבִּי וְשָׁם עֵינַי.
אֶגָּל וְאֶסָּתֵר, אֶקְצֹף וְאֵעָתֵר –
מִי יַחְמֹל יוֹתֵר מִנִּי עֲלֵי בָנַי ?

say, 'Zion is desolate!' – for My heart is in Zion and My eyes are there. I reveal Myself and I conceal Myself, now I rage, now I consent – but who has more compassion than I have for My children?

יַעֲלַת־חֵן

TO THE RIVALS

יַעֲלַת חֵן, מִמְּעוֹנָהּ רָחֲקָה,
אוֹהֲבָהּ כּוֹעֵס – וְלָמָּה צָחֲקָה ?
צָחֲקָה עַל בַּת אֱדוֹם וּבְנוֹת עֲרָב
הַמְבַקְשׁוֹת לַחֲשֹׁק דּוֹד חָשְׁקָה.
הֵן פְּרָאִים הֵם – וְאֵיךְ יִדְמוּ אֱלֵי
יַעֲלָה עַל הַצְּבִי הִתְרַפְּקָה ?
אֵי נְבוּאָה, אֵי מְנוֹרָה, אֵי אֲרוֹן
הַבְּרִית, אֵי הַשְּׁכִינָה דְּבֵקָה ?
אַל, מְשַׂנְאַי, אַל תְּכַבּוּ אַהֲבָה,
כִּי תְכַבּוּהָ – וְהִיא אֵשׁ נִשָּׂקָה !

The lovely doe, far from her home, whose lover is angry – why did she laugh? She laughed at the daughter of Edom and the daughter of Arabia who covet her beloved. Why, they are nothing but wild asses, and how can they compare to the doe who nestled against her gazelle? Where is the spirit of prophecy found, where the lamp-stand, the Ark of the Covenant, the ever-present Shekinah? No, my rivals, do not try to quench love, for if you do, it will blaze up like fire!

יְשֵׁנָה בְּחֵיק יַלְדוּת

TO THE SOUL

יְשֵׁנָה בְּחֵיק יַלְדוּת, לְמָתַי תִּשְׁכְּבִי ?
דְּעִי כִּי נְעוּרִים כַּנְּעֹרֶת נִנְעֲרוּ.
הֲלָעַד יְמֵי הַשַּׁחֲרוּת ? קוּמִי צְאִי,
רְאִי מַלְאֲכֵי שֵׂיבָה בְּמוּסָר שִׁחֲרוּ.
וְהִתְנַעֲרִי מִן הַזְּמָן, כַּצִּפֳּרִים
אֲשֶׁר מֵרְסִיסֵי לַיְלָה יִתְנַעֲרוּ.
רְאִי כַדְּרוֹר לִמְצֹא דְרוֹר מִמַּעֲלָךְ
וּמִתּוֹלְדוֹת יָמִים כְּיַמִּים יִסְעֲרוּ.
הֲיִי אַחֲרֵי מַלְכֵּךְ מְרַדֶּפֶת, בְּסוֹד
נְשָׁמוֹת אֲשֶׁר אֶל טוּב יְיָ נָהֲרוּ.

Oh, you that sleep in the bosom of childhood, how long will you rest there? Know that youth is shaken off like straw! Do you think boyhood lasts for ever? Get up, go out and see the grey heralds, who have come to rebuke you. Shake off Time as birds shake off the dew-drops of the night. Soar like a swallow to find freedom from your sins and from the vagaries of Fortune, that rage like a sea. Pursue your King, at one with the souls who flock towards the bounty of God.

אֲדֹנָי, נֶגְדְּךָ כָל תַּאֲוָתִי

FOR THE DAY OF ATONEMENT

אֲדֹנָי, נֶגְדְּךָ כָל תַּאֲוָתִי,
וְאִם לֹא אַעֲלֶנָּה עַל שְׂפָתִי.
רְצוֹנְךָ אֶשְׁאֲלָה רֶגַע – וְאֶגְוַע,
וּמִי יִתֵּן וְתָבוֹא שֶׁאֱלָתִי,
וְאַפְקִיד אֶת שְׁאָר רוּחִי בְּיָדְךָ,
וְיָשַׁנְתִּי, וְעָרְבָה לִי שְׁנָתִי!
בְּרָחְקִי מִמְּךָ – מוֹתִי בְחַיַּי,
וְאִם אֶדְבַּק בְּךָ – חַיַּי בְּמוֹתִי.
אֲבָל לֹא אֵדְעָה בַּמָּה אֲקַדֵּם,
וּמַה תִּהְיֶה עֲבוֹדָתִי וְדָתִי.

Lord, all my longing is before You, even though it does not pass my lips. Grant me Your favour for even a moment, and I will die. If only You would grant my wish! I will commit my spirit into Your keeping, I will sleep, and my sleep will be pleasant. When I am far from You my life is death; but if I cling to You, my death is life. But I do not know what to offer You, what my service and my worship should be.

דְּרָכֶיךָ, אֲדֹנָי, לַמְּדֵנִי,
וְשׁוּב מִמַּאֲסַר סִכְלוּת שְׁבוּתִי.
וְהוֹרֵנִי בְּעוֹד יֵשׁ בִּי יְכֹלֶת
לְהִתְעַנּוֹת, וְאַל תִּבְזֶה עֱנוּתִי,
בְּטֶרֶם יוֹם אֱהִי עָלַי לְמַשָּׂא,
וְיוֹם יִכְבַּד קְצָתִי עַל קְצָתִי,
וְאֶכָּנַע בְּעַל־כָּרְחִי, וְיֹאכַל
עֲצָמַי עָשׁ וְנִלְאוּ מִשְּׂאֵתִי,
וְאֶסַּע אֶל מְקוֹם נָסְעוּ אֲבוֹתַי
וּבִמְקוֹם תַּחֲנוֹתָם תַּחֲנוֹתִי.
כְּגֵר תּוֹשָׁב אֲנִי עַל גַּב אֲדָמָה,
וְאוּלָם כִּי בְּבִטְנָהּ נַחֲלָתִי.

Show me Your ways, O Lord, restore me from the bondage of folly. Teach me while I still have the strength to endure – do not scorn my plight! – before I become a burden to myself and my limbs weigh heavy on each other; before I yield unwillingly, and my bones wither and are unable to bear me; before I journey to where my fathers have gone, and come to rest where they are resting. I am like a stranger upon the earth, but my true home is in her womb.

נְעוּרַי עַד הֲלֹם עָשׂוּ לְנַפְשָׁם,
וּמָתַי גַּם אֲנִי אֶעְשֶׂה לְבֵיתִי?
וְהָעוֹלָם אֲשֶׁר נָתַן בְּלִבִּי
מְנָעַנִי לְבַקֵּשׁ אַחֲרִיתִי.

My youth has thus far had its pleasure, but when shall I, too, provide for my household? The world and its delights, which He put in my heart, have kept

וְאֵיכָה אֶעֱבֹד יוֹצְרִי – בְּעוֹדִי
אֲסִיר יִצְרִי וְעֶבֶד תַּאֲוָתִי?
וְאֵיכָה מַעֲלָה רָמָה אֲבַקֵּשׁ –
וּמָחָר תִּהְיֶה רִמָּה אֲחוֹתִי?
וְאֵיךְ יִיטַב בְּיוֹם טוֹבָה לְבָבִי,
וְלֹא אֵדַע – הֲיִיטַב מָחֳרָתִי?
וְהַיָּמִים וְהַלֵּילוֹת עֲרֵבִים
לְכַלּוֹת אֶת שְׁאֵרִי עַד כְּלוֹתִי,
וְלָרוּחַ יְזָרוּן מַחֲצִיתִי,
וְלֶעָפָר יְשִׁיבוּן מַחֲצִיתִי.

me from seeking my aim. And how can I worship my Maker while I am still captive to my lust, slave to my desire? How can I aspire to a high rank, when tomorrow the worm will be my sister? How can I be cheerful on a happy day, when I do not know if there will be happiness tomorrow? The days and nights have pledged to consume my flesh, to scatter half of me to the winds and return the other half to the dust.

וּמָה אֹמַר – וְיִצְרִי יִרְדְּפֵנִי
כְּאוֹיֵב מִנְּעוּרַי עַד בְּלוֹתִי?
וּמַה לִּי בַּזְּמָן – אִם לֹא רְצוֹנְךָ?
וְאִם אֵינְךָ מְנָתִי – מַה מְּנָתִי?
אֲנִי מִמַּעֲשִׂים שׁוֹלָל וְעָרֹם,
וְצִדְקָתְךָ לְבַדָּהּ הִיא כְסוּתִי.
וְעוֹד מָה אַאֲרִיךְ לָשׁוֹן וְאֶשְׁאַל?
אֲדֹנָי, נֶגְדְּךָ כָּל תַּאֲוָתִי!

What more can I say? My passions hound me like an enemy from youth to withered old age. Does Time hold anything for me except Your favour? And if You are not my lot, what other lot do I have? I am stripped naked, devoid of good works, and only Your righteousness is my covering. Then why do I go on wagging my tongue and pleading? O Lord, all my longing is before You!

לִקְרַאת מְקוֹר חַיֵּי אֱמֶת

THE TRUE VISION

לִקְרַאת מְקוֹר חַיֵּי אֱמֶת אָרוּצָה –
עַל כֵּן בְּחַיֵּי שָׁוְא וָרִיק אָקוּצָה.
לִרְאוֹת פְּנֵי מַלְכִּי מְגַמָּתִי לְבַד,
לֹא אֶעֱרֹץ בִּלְתּוֹ וְלֹא אַעְרִיצָה.
מִי יִתְּנֵנִי לַחֲזוֹתוֹ בַחֲלוֹם!
אִישַׁן שְׁנַת עוֹלָם וְלֹא אָקִיצָה.
לוּ אֶחֱזֶה פָנָיו בְּלִבִּי בָיְתָה,
לֹא שָׁאֲלוּ עֵינַי לְהַבִּיט חוּצָה.

I am running towards the fountain of true life; therefore, I spurn the life of lies and trifles. To look at the face of my King – that is my only wish. None but Him do I fear and venerate. If only I could see Him in a dream! Oh, I would sleep forever and never wake up. If I could see His face inside my heart, my eyes would no more wish to look outside.

יָהּ, אָנָה אֶמְצָאֲךָ?

LORD, WHERE SHALL I FIND YOU?

יָהּ, אָנָה אֶמְצָאֲךָ? מְקוֹמְךָ נַעֲלֶה וְנֶעְלָם!
וְאָנָה לֹא אֶמְצָאֲךָ? כְּבוֹדְךָ מָלֵא עוֹלָם!

Lord, where shall I find You? Your place is lofty and secret. And where shall I not find you? The whole earth is full of Your glory!

הַנִּמְצָא בַקְּרָבִים, אַפְסֵי אֶרֶץ הֵקִים.
הַמִּשְׂגָּב לַקְּרוֹבִים, הַמִּבְטָח לָרְחוֹקִים.
אַתָּה יוֹשֵׁב כְּרוּבִים, אַתָּה שׁוֹכֵן שְׁחָקִים.
תִּתְהַלֵּל בִּצְבָאֲךָ – וְאַתְּ עַל רֹאשׁ מְהֻלָּלָם.
גַּלְגַּל לֹא יְשָׂאֲךָ – אַף כִּי חַדְרֵי אוּלָם!

You are found in man's innermost heart, yet You fixed earth's boundaries. You are a strong tower for those who are near, and the trust of those who are far. You are enthroned on the cherubim,[1] yet You dwell in the heights of heaven. You are praised by Your hosts, but even their praise is not worthy of You. The sphere of heaven cannot contain You; how much less the chambers of the Temple!

וּבְהִנָּשְׂאֲךָ עֲלֵיהֶם עַל כֵּס נִשָּׂא וָרָם,
אַתָּה קָרוֹב אֲלֵיהֶם מֵרוּחָם וּמִבְּשָׂרָם.
פִּיהֶם יָעִיד בָּהֶם, כִּי אֵין בִּלְתְּךָ יוֹצְרָם.
מִי זֶה לֹא יִירָאֲךָ – וְעֹל מַלְכוּתְךָ עֻלָּם?
אוֹ מִי לֹא יִקְרָאֲךָ – וְאַתָּה נוֹתֵן אָכְלָם?

Even when You rise above Your hosts on a throne, high and exalted, You are nearer to them than their own bodies and souls. Their mouths attest that they have no Maker except You. Who shall not fear You? All bear the yoke of Your kingdom. And who shall not call to You? It is You who give them their food.

דָּרַשְׁתִּי קִרְבָתְךָ, בְּכָל לִבִּי קְרָאתִיךָ,
וּבְצֵאתִי לִקְרָאתְךָ – לִקְרָאתִי מְצָאתִיךָ,
וּבְפִלְאֵי גְבוּרָתְךָ בַּקֹּדֶשׁ חֲזִיתִיךָ.
מִי יֹאמַר לֹא רָאָךְ? הֵן שָׁמַיִם וְחֵילָם
יַגִּידוּ מוֹרָאֲךָ בְּלִי נִשְׁמָע קוֹלָם!

I have sought to come near You, I have called to You with all my heart; and when I went out towards You, I found You coming towards me. I look upon Your wondrous power with awe. Who can say that he has not seen You? The heavens and their legions proclaim Your dread – without a sound.

1. Above the Ark.

הַאֻמְנָם כִּי יֵשֵׁב אֱלֹהִים אֶת הָאָדָם?
וּמָה יַּחְשֹׁב כָּל חוֹשֵׁב, אֲשֶׁר בֶּעָפָר יְסוֹדָם –
וְאַתָּה, קָדוֹשׁ, יוֹשֵׁב תְּהִלּוֹתָם וּכְבוֹדָם!
חַיּוֹת יוֹדוּ פִּלְאָךְ, הָעוֹמְדוֹת בְּרוּם עוֹלָם.
עַל רָאשֵׁיהֶם כִּסְאָךְ – וְאַתָּה נוֹשֵׂא כֻלָּם!

But can God really dwell among men? Their foundations are dust – what can they conceive of Him? Yet You, O Holy One, make Your home where they sing Your praises and Your glory. The living creatures, standing on the summit of the world, praise Your wonders. Your throne is above their heads, yet it is You who carry them all!

הֲיֵדְעוּ הַדְּמָעוֹת

TOMBSTONE INSCRIPTION

הֲיֵדְעוּ הַדְּמָעוֹת מִי שְׁפָכָם,
וְיֵדְעוּ הַלְּבָבוֹת מִי הֲפָכָם?
הֲפָכָם בּוֹא מְאוֹרָם תּוֹךְ רְגָבִים,
וְלֹא יֵדְעוּ רְגָבִים מָה בְּתוֹכָם.
בְּתוֹכָם שַׂר וְגָדוֹל, תָּם וְיָשָׁר,
יְרֵא הָאֵל וְאִישׁ נָבוֹן וְחָכָם.

Do these tears know who made them fall? Do these hearts know who made them recoil? Oh, they recoiled because their sun sank into the dust, and the dust does not know what it holds. It holds a princely man, blameless and upright, a God-fearing man, discreet and wise.

הָהּ, בִּתִּי

A MOTHER'S LAMENT

'הָהּ, בִּתִּי, הֲשָׁכַחַתְּ מִשְׁכָּנֵךְ?
כִּי לִשְׁאוֹל נָסְעוּ נוֹשְׂאֵי אֲרוֹנֵךְ,
וְאֵין חֶלְקִי מִמֵּךְ רַק זִכְרוֹנֵךְ.
וַאֲחוֹנֵן אֶת עַפְרוֹת צִיּוּנֵךְ
עֵת אָסוּר לִשְׁאֹל שְׁלוֹמֵךְ – וְאֵינֵךְ:
כִּי הַמָּוֶת יַפְרִיד בֵּינִי וּבֵינֵךְ.

'Alas, my daughter, have you forgotten your home? The coffin bearers have taken you to the grave, and I have nothing left of you but your memory. When I come to greet you, and do not find you, I take pity on the dust of your tomb; for death has parted us.

בַּת מוּצֵאת מֵחֶדֶר הוֹרָתָהּ –
אֵיךְ אֶחְיֶה וּמִנַּפְשִׁי גְזָרָתָהּ?
צוּר אֲבַקַּע עֵת אֶרְאֶה צוּרָתָהּ.
אֵיךְ תִּשְׁנֶה לְבָנָה מֵהֲדָרָתָהּ!

'O the daughter is taken from her mother's room! How can I live? Her limbs were part of me. My tears cleave rocks when I remember her. How the lustre of the moon has been tarnished!

שָׁם בִּשְׁאוֹל אֶרְאֶה אֶת חֲתֻנָּתָהּ,
אֵיךְ תָּשִׂים גּוּשׁ עָפָר חֻפָּתָהּ,
אֵיךְ מָתְקוּ לָהּ רִגְבֵי קְבוּרָתָהּ.
מַר לִי מָר, בִּתִּי, עַל חֶסְרוֹנֵךְ:
כִּי הַמָּוֶת יַפְרִיד בֵּינִי וּבֵינֵךְ. [...]

There, in the grave, I see her being wed: clods of earth are her canopy, and the dust of the pit is sweet to her. O my daughter, your loss is bitter to me; for death has parted us.

הָהּ, בִּתִּי, הַכְרֵעַ הִכְרַעְתִּנִי!'
'אוֹי, אִמִּי, אוֹי לִי כִּי יְלִדְתִּנִי.
אַךְ הַיּוֹם אֵיךְ מָאוֹס מְאַסְתִּנִי?
כִּי לִבְכוֹר מָוֶת גִּדַּלְתִּנִי.
בְּהַגִּיעַ תּוֹר, לְנַפְשִׁי שְׁלַחְתִּנִי,
וּבַעֲטֶרֶת עָפָר עִשַּׂרְתִּנִי,
וּבְחֻפַּת אֲבַדּוֹן הוֹשַׁבְתִּנִי.
בְּעַל־כָּרְחֵךְ, אִמִּי, לֹא בִרְצוֹנֵךְ:
כִּי הַמָּוֶת יַפְרִיד בֵּינִי וּבֵינֵךְ.' [...]

'Alas, my daughter, what sorrow you have brought me!' 'Alas, alas, my mother, that you ever gave me birth. How, on this day, how could you cast me off? Oh, you brought me up to be Death's bride! When my turn came, you sent me away alone; you crowned me with a garland of dust; you set me down in the bridal-bower of destruction. O my mother, it was against your will, it was not of your doing, for death has parted us.'

יוֹם אַכְפִּי הִכְבַּדְתִּי

THE MURDER OF ZECHARIAH

יוֹם אַכְפִּי הִכְבַּדְתִּי וַיִּכָּפְלוּ עֲווֹנַי,
בְּשָׁלְחִי יָד בְּדַם נָבִיא בַּחֲצַר מִקְדַּשׁ אֲדֹנָי.
וְלֹא כִסַּתְהוּ אֲדָמָה עַד בּוֹא חֶרֶב מוֹנַי,
וְלֹא שָׁקַט עֲדֵי הֵקַם וְעַד הִפְלִיא פְּלִילִיָּה –
וַיֶּרֶב בְּבַת יְהוּדָה תַּאֲנִיָּה וַאֲנִיָּה.

On that day I made my burden heavier and multiplied my crimes when I shed the prophet's blood in the court of the Lord's temple. The earth would not cover it until my enemies[1] came with the sword; it would not rest until it was avenged, wreaking terrible judgements. Oh, He brought sorrow upon sorrow to the daughter of Judah.

הָיָה הוֹלֵךְ וְסוֹעֵר עַד בּוֹא רַב טַבָּחִים,
וּבָא אֶל מִקְדַּשׁ אֲדֹנָי וְרָאָה דָמִים רוֹתְחִים.
וַיִּשְׁאַל בַּעֲבוּר זֹאת לַכֹּהֲנִים הַזּוֹבְחִים,

The blood grew more and more tempestuous until Nebuzaradan, the commander of the guard, arrived. When he entered the Lord's temple, he discovered the seething blood. He asked the priests who were offering

1. The Babylonian armies, under the command of Nebuzaradan (2 Kings 25.8).

וַיַּעֲנוּהוּ: ׳אֵין זֶה כִּי אִם דַּם הַזְּבָחִים׳.
גַּם הוּא זָבַח לַחֲקֹר מַה זֶּה וְעַל מֶה הָיָה –
וָאֹמַר לְנַפְשִׁי: זֹאת חַטָּאתֵךְ וְזֶה פִּרְיָהּ!

sacrifices, what it signified; and they replied: 'It is nothing but the blood of the sacrifices.' Then he, too, slaughtered a beast to see if this was so and how it came about; and I said to myself: 'This is your sin, and this is its fruit.'

וּבְכָל זֹאת לֹא שָׁקַט וְעוֹדוֹ כַּיָּם נִגְרָשׁ.
וַיְבֻקַּשׁ הַדָּבָר וַיִּמָּצֵא מְפֹרָשׁ,
כִּי דַּם אִישׁ הָאֱלֹהִים עַל לֹא חָמָס שֹׁרַשׁ.
וַיֹּאמֶר נְבוּזַרְאֲדָן: ׳וְגַם דָּמוֹ הִנֵּה נִדְרָשׁ!
אִסְפוּ לִי הַכֹּהֲנִים וְהוֹצִיאוּם מִבֵּית יָהּ,
וְלֹא אֶשְׁקֹט עַד יִשְׁקֹט דַּם הַנָּבִיא זְכַרְיָה׳.

Still, the blood would not rest; it surged like the sea. Then, after questioning, the truth came to light: this was the blood of the man of God, cut down though he had done no wrong. Nebuzaradan said: 'The time has come to pay for his blood. Gather all the priests, take them out of the house of God. I shall not rest until the blood of the prophet Zechariah finds rest.'

דָּקַר יְשִׁישִׁים לְמֵאוֹת וּבַחוּרִים לְרִבּוֹאוֹת,
וַיּוֹרֶד לַטֶּבַח כֹּהֲנֵי אֲדֹנָי צְבָאוֹת,
וְתִינוֹקוֹת שֶׁל בֵּית רַב, וְעֵינֵי אָבוֹת רוֹאוֹת.
וְאֵין שֶׁקֶט לְדַם נָבִיא, וַיְהִי לְמוֹפֵת וּלְאוֹת!
וְחֶרֶב צַר נוֹקֶמֶת וְהַקִּרְיָה הוֹמִיָּה –
בְּכָל זֹאת לֹא שָׁב אַפּוֹ וְעוֹד יָדוֹ נְטוּיָה.

He murdered old men by the hundreds, and young men by the tens of thousands. He slaughtered the priests of the Lord of hosts, and school-children before the very eyes of their fathers. Still the blood of the prophet would not rest. This was a sign and a portent. The enemy's sword wreaked vengeance, the city was filled with uproar – yet His anger was not turned back and His hand was stretched out still!

הוֹסִיף לַהֲרֹג נָשִׁים עִם יוֹנְקֵי שָׁדַיִם,
וְדָם עוֹלֶה בֵּינֵיהֶם כַּיָּם וִיאוֹר מִצְרַיִם,
עֲדֵי נָשָׂא נְבוּזַרְאֲדָן עֵינָיו לַשָּׁמַיִם
וַיֹּאמַר: ׳הַאֵין דַּי לְדָם בִּבְנוֹת יְרוּשָׁלַיִם?
הֲכָלָה אַתָּה עוֹשֶׂה אֶת שְׁאֵרִית הַשְּׁבִיָּה?׳
וְאָז שָׁקַט דַּם נָקִי, וְחֶרֶב נָקָם רָוְיָה.

Then he killed women as well as babes at the breast, and the blood rose among them like a sea, like the river of Egypt, until Nebuzaradan raised his eyes to heaven and said: 'Will this blood not be content with the blood of Jerusalem's daughters? Are You going to wipe out the remnant of Israel?' Only then did the innocent blood come to rest; the sword of vengeance had drunk its fill.

יַעֲלַת־חֵן, רַחֲמִי לֵבָב

יַעֲלַת חֵן, רַחֲמִי לֵבָב שְׁכַנְתִּיו מֵעוֹדֵךְ.
תֵּדְעִי כִּי יוֹם תָּנוּדִי – אֲסוֹנִי בִּנְדוֹדֵךְ.
גַּם בְּעֵת יֶהֶרְסוּ עֵינַי לְהַבִּיט אֶל הוֹדֵךְ,
מִלְּחָיַיִךְ פָּגְעוּ בִי נְחָשִׁים יַפְרִישׁוּ,
כִּי חֲמָתָם כָּאֵשׁ יַחְתּוּ, וְאוֹתִי יְגָרְשׁוּ.

שָׁלְלָה לִבִּי בְּדַדִּים עֲלֵי לֵב מֻנָּחִים:
לֵב כְּמוֹ אֶבֶן וְרַק יִגְמֹל שְׁנֵי תַפּוּחִים!
נִצְּבוּ וַיִּהְיוּ לִשְׂמֹאל וְיָמִין כִּרְמָחִים.
מוֹקְדֵיהֶם הֵם בִּלְבָבִי – וְהֵם לֹא נִגָּשׁוּ,
גַּם בְּפִיהֶם דָּמִי שָׁתוּ – וְלֹא הִתְבּוֹשָׁשׁוּ!

יַעֲלָה חֻקֵּי דָת הָאֵל בְּעֵינֶיהָ תָפֵר,
כִּי תְמִיתֵנִי בִצְדִיָּה אֲבָל אֵין לִי כֹפֶר.
הַרְאִיתֶם עוֹד לֵב אַרְיֵה וְעַפְעַפֵּי עֹפֶר?
לָמְדוּ לִטְרֹף כַּלָּבִיא, וְחִצִּים יְלַטְּשׁוּ,
דַּם לְבָבִי יִמְצוּ יִשְׁתּוּ, וְנַפְשִׁי בִּקֵּשׁוּ.

יוֹם אֲנִי מִיֵּין דּוֹדֶיהָ כְּשִׁכּוֹר מִתְרוֹנֵן,
כִּי שְׁלוֹמֶיהָ תַפְגִּיעַ וְעָלַי תִּתְלוֹנֵן
עַל יְדֵי צִירִים; וּבְבוֹאָם, אֲלֵיהֶם תִּתְחַנֵּן:
׳מַלְאֲכֵי שָׁלוֹם, פִּגְעוּ בִי, שְׁנוּ גַּם שַׁלֵּשׁוּ!׳
מַאֲמָרָם לִבִּי פִתּוּ וְרוּחִי חִדֵּשׁוּ.

THE SENSITIVE DOE

O graceful doe, pity this heart in which you have dwelled all your life. Know that the day you leave me, your going will be my ruin. And even now, when my eyes dare to glance at your splendour, I am stung by the serpents that guard your cheeks, for their poison burns like fire and they drive me out.

She ensnared my heart with the breasts that lie upon her heart – a heart of stone, and yet it put forth two apples! They stand guard, to the left and to the right, like lances. Their fiery [nipples burn] in my heart, though they have never come near me. Their mouths have drunk my blood, they felt no shame at all!

This doe violates the laws of God with her eyes: she kills me with malice aforethought, yet no one avenges me. Have you ever seen the heart of a lion joined to the eyelids of a gazelle? Her eyelids have learned to tear like a lion, they hurl sharpened arrows at me, they drain my heart's blood to the dregs. They are out for my life.

One day, when I was reeling like a drunkard, longing for the wine of her love, she dispatched envoys to me bearing greetings and complaints; and when they returned to her, she begged them: 'O messengers of peace, come again and yet again!' These tidings seduced my heart and revived my spirit.

יוֹם בְּגַנָּהּ רָעוּ יָדַי וְדַדֶּיהָ עִשּׂוּ,
אָמְרָה: ׳הֶרֶף יָדֶיךָ – הֲכִי עוֹד לֹא נֻסּוּ!׳
וַאֲמָרִים לִי הֶחְלִיקָה לְבָבִי הֵמַסּוּ:
׳גן מתא נקש, יא חביבי, פאנכר דנאשו
אלג׳לאלה רכיצה בשתאת הפרמשו.׳

But one day when my hands were grazing in her garden and fondling her breasts, she said: 'Now take away your hands – they are not skilful enough.'[1] And her words were so seductive that they melted my heart: 'Do not touch me, friend, I do not like those who hurt me. My breasts are soft and sensitive. Enough! I shall refuse one and all!'[2]

עָפְרָה תְּכַבֵּס

THE LAUNDRESS

עָפְרָה תְּכַבֵּס אֶת בְּגָדֶיהָ בְּמֵי
דִמְעִי וְתִשְׁטָחֵם לְשֶׁמֶשׁ זָהֳרָהּ:
לֹא שָׁאֲלָה מֵי הָעֲיָנוֹת – עִם שְׁתֵּי
עֵינַי, וְלֹא שֶׁמֶשׁ – לְיֹפִי תָאֳרָהּ.

My love washes her clothes in the water of my tears and spreads them out in the sun of her beauty. She has no need of spring-water – she has my two eyes; nor of the sun – she has her own radiance.

מַה לָּךְ, צְבִיָּה

SONG OF FAREWELL

מַה לָּךְ, צְבִיָּה, תִּמְנְעִי צִירַיִךְ
מְדּוֹד, צְלָעָיו מָלְאוּ צִירַיִךְ?
לֹא תֵדְעִי כִּי אֵין לְדוֹדֵךְ מְזֻמָּן
בִּלְתִּי שְׁמֹעַ קוֹל שְׁלוֹמוֹתַיִךְ?
אִם הַפְּרִידָה עַל שְׁנֵינוּ נִגְזָרָה –
עִמְדִי מְעַט עַד אֶחֱזֶה פָּנַיִךְ.
לֹא אֵדְעָה אִם בֵּין צְלָעַי נֶעֱצַר
לִבִּי, וְאִם יֵלֵךְ לְמַסָּעַיִךְ.

Why, O fair one, do you withhold your envoys from the lover whose heart is filled with pain of you? Do you not know that Time means nothing to your beloved, unless he hear your welcoming voice? If we two are doomed to parting, stay a while and let me look at your face. I do not know if my heart has come to a stop between my ribs, or else has wandered off with you. Oh,

1. Or, 'they [my breasts] have not yet experienced such things'.
2. The last two lines are in mixed Arabic and Romance. The meaning is uncertain.

חֵי אַהֲבָה, זִכְרִי יְמֵי חִשְׁקֵךְ כְּמוֹ
אֶזְכֹּר אֲנִי לֵילוֹת תְּשׁוּקוֹתַיִךְ.
כַּאְשֶׁר דְּמוּתֵךְ בַּחֲלוֹמִי יַעֲבֹר,
כֵּן אֶעְבְּרָה־נָּא בַחֲלוֹמוֹתַיִךְ.
בֵּינִי וּבֵינֵךְ יָם דְּמָעוֹת יֶהֱמוּ
גַּלָּיו, וְלֹא אוּכַל עֲבֹר אֵלַיִךְ.
אַךְ לוּ פְּעָמַיִךְ לְעָבְרוֹ קָרְבוּ,
אָז נִבְקְעוּ מֵימָיו לְכַף רַגְלַיִךְ.
לוּ אַחֲרֵי מוֹתִי בְּאָזְנִי יַעֲלֶה
קוֹל פַּעֲמוֹן זָהָב עֲלֵי שׁוּלַיִךְ!
אוֹ תִשְׁאֲלִי לִשְׁלוֹם יְדִידֵךְ, מִשְּׁאוֹל
אֶשְׁאַל בְּדוֹדַיִךְ וּבִשְׁלוֹמַיִךְ! [...]

for the life of love, remember the days of your desire, as I remember the nights of your passion. And just as your image moves through my dreams, let mine move through yours. A sea of tears roars between us, and I cannot cross its waves to reach you. But if your steps approached to cross them, the waters would divide before your feet. Oh, after my death, let me still hear the sound of the golden bells on the hem of your skirt. And if you then ask how your beloved is, I, from the grave, will send you my love and my blessings!

מִי יִתְּנֵנִי אֶחְיֶה עַד אֶאֱרֶה
בֹּשֶׂם וּמֹר מִבֵּין הֲלִיכוֹתַיִךְ.
לֹא אֶשְׁמְעָה קוֹלֵךְ, אֲבָל אֶשְׁמַע עֲלֵי
סִתְרֵי לְבָבִי קוֹל צְעָדוֹתַיִךְ. [...]

If only I could live until I gather myrrh and spices from among your footprints! I cannot hear your voice, but in the covert of my heart I hear the sound of your steps.

בִּי הַצְּבִי, בִּי אֲדוֹנִי

THE CRUEL LOVER

בִּי הַצְּבִי, בִּי אֲדוֹנִי,
יֵקַר בְּעֵינֶךָ יְגוֹנִי,
פֶּן יִקְרֵנִי אֲסוֹנִי.
אַט, אַט, אַט בְּדָמִי,
כִּי רַק בְּיָדְךָ שְׁלוֹמִי!

O my fair youth, my lord, take my grief to heart, lest disaster overtake me. Oh, gently, deal gently with my blood, for my fate is in your hands alone.

יֵרַךְ לְבָבְךָ לְנִדְכֶּה
יָצוּם לְזַעְמְךָ וְיִבְכֶּה
וּלְמָן רְצוֹנְךָ יְחַכֶּה.
מָן, מָן מַן לְצוֹמִי,
וּתְנָה שְׂכָרִי בְּיוֹמִי.

Pity the forlorn one, fasting and weeping because of your anger, waiting for the manna of your favour. Oh, give me manna, manna for my hunger and pay me my wages every day.

אִם תַּעֲלֹז עַל חֳלָיַי —
אֶשְׁטַח לְךָ אֶת לְחָיַי,
וַתַּעֲנֵנִי: 'וְחַיַּי!
אֵין, אֵין, אֵין בְּחֶרְמִי
רַק הַהֲרוּגִים לְתֻמִּי'.

When you laugh at my suffering, I show you my tear-stained cheeks. But you answer: 'Truly, there are none in my trap, none but those whom I captured unwittingly.'

אָרִיב בְּנַפְשִׁי לְכִילַי:
לוּ יְפַחֲדֵנִי וְאֵלַי
יָשִׁיב שְׁנָתִי, וְאוּלַי
עָף, עָף, עָף בְּנוּמִי,
יָבוֹא בְּכֶפֶל חֲלוֹמִי!

I reproach myself because of this miserly youth: if he were to fear me, he might give me back my slumber; he might fly, Oh fly to me in my sleep, and be caught in the mesh of my dreams.

אִם אֶשְׁאֲלָה צוּף שְׂפָתוֹ,
יַאְדִּים כְּשֶׁמֶשׁ בְּצֵאתוֹ —
עַד אֶחֱזֶה מִדְּמוּתוֹ
אֵיךְ, אֵיךְ, אֵיךְ אֲרַמִּי
יֵהָפֵךְ דְּמוּתוֹ אֲדוֹמִי!

When I ask for the nectar of his lips, he blushes like the rising sun, until I see in his face how, Oh how the Aramean turns into an Edomite![1]

שִׁירוֹ יְפַלַּח כְּבֵדִי.
יָשִׁיר לְעוֹרֵר יְקוֹדִי:
'שַׁק פִּי וְרַב לָךְ, יְדִידִי,
בס, בס, בס בפמי
ודע סואדך, יא עמי!'

His song pierces my heart. He sings to fan my flames: 'Kiss my mouth, and no more, my friend. Kiss me on the mouth, kiss me, and forget your melancholy, love.'[2]

1. A play on words: i.e. how Laban (*lavan*, 'white') the Aramean turns into an Edomite (*adom*, 'red').
2. The last couplet is in Arabic.

אַט לִי, חֲזַק לֵבָב

אַט לִי, חֲזַק לֵבָב, רְפֵה מָתְנַיִם,
אַט לִי עֲדֵי אֶשְׁתַּחֲוֶה אַפַּיִם!
שָׁגוּ בְךָ עֵינַי לְבַדָּם, וַאֲנִי
אָמְנָם טְהָר־לֵב, לֹא טְהוֹר עֵינַיִם.
הֶרֶף לְצִיר תְּאָרֵה מִתָּאֳרָךְ
וֶרֶד וְשׁוֹשָׁן נִזְרְעוּ כִּלְאַיִם.
אֵשׁ לֶחְיְךָ אֶחְתֶּה לְכַבּוֹת אֵשׁ בְּאֵשׁ.
עֵת אֶצְמָאָה כִּי אֶמְצְאָה בוֹ מַיִם.
מָצֹה שְׂפַת אֹדֶם אֲשֶׁר תִּיקַד כְּמוֹ
רִצְפָּה, וּמַלְקוֹחַי כְּמֶלְקָחַיִם.
חַיַּי תְּלוּאִים בֵּין שְׁנֵי חוּטֵי שְׁנִי
תוֹלָע, אֲבָל מוֹתִי בְּבֵין עַרְבַּיִם.
לֹא אֶמְצְאָה עַתָּה לְלֵילוֹת קֵץ, וְאָז
לֹא בָא אֱשׁוּן לַיִל בְּתוֹךְ יוֹמַיִם —
בִּהְיוֹת זְמַנִּי בֵּין יְדֵי חֶפְצִי כְּמוֹ
חֹמֶר, וְהַגַּלְגַּל כְּמוֹ אָבְנַיִם.

THE PURE LOVER

Gently, my hard-hearted, soft-hipped one, deal gently with me and let me bow down before you. It is only my eyes that were ravished by you; my heart is pure, yes, but my eyes are not. Oh, let my eyes pluck the roses and lilies that were sown together in your face![1] I rake the fire of your cheeks, to put out fire with fire: and when I am thirsty, it is there that I look for water. Oh, I would suck your red lips that flame like glowing coals, and my jaws would be like tongs. My life hangs upon the two scarlet threads [of your lips], but my death lurks in the twilight [of your hair]. Now the nights are endless, though once no darkness came between the days; Time was like clay in my hands, and the zodiac turned like a potter's wheel.

מַה תַּאֲמִין בִּזְמַן

מַה תַּאֲמִין בִּזְמַן אֲשֶׁר אֵין בּוֹ אֱמֶת?
הָהּ, כִּי עֲמָלִי רַב וְיוֹמִי קָצֵר!
כָּל אִישׁ יְצַו אָחִיו לְבִלְתִּי יֶחֱטָא,
לֵאמֹר: 'שְׁמָר־לְךָ פֶּן יְסִיתְךָ יֵצֶר.'
וּבְעֵת חֲטֹא, שָׂח: 'מַה בְּיַד אִישׁ לַעֲשׂוֹת?
הַיְצוּר וְהַיֵּצֶר בְּיַד הַיּוֹצֵר!'

THE EXCUSE

Why put your trust in Time, which has no truth in it? Alas, my labours are so great and my day is so short. Each man urges his neighbour not to sin, saying: 'Don't let your passions lead you astray.' But when he himself sins, he says: 'What can a man do? All creatures and their passions are in the hands of the Creator'.

1. A playful allusion to the scriptural prohibition: 'You shall not plant your field with two kinds of seed' (Leviticus 19.19).

עַבְדֵי זְמַן

THE LORD IS MY PORTION

עַבְדֵי זְמַן עַבְדֵי עֲבָדִים הֵם –
עֶבֶד אֲדֹנָי הוּא לְבַד חָפְשִׁי.
עַל כֵּן, בְּבַקֵּשׁ כָּל אֱנוֹשׁ חֶלְקוֹ,
'חֶלְקִי אֲדֹנָי!' אָמְרָה נַפְשִׁי.

The slaves of Time are the slaves of a slave; only the slave of the Lord is free. Therefore, while other men seek their portion, 'The Lord is my portion,' says my soul.

לִבִּי בְמִזְרָח

MY HEART IS IN THE EAST

לִבִּי בְמִזְרָח, וְאָנֹכִי בְּסוֹף מַעֲרָב –
אֵיךְ אֶטְעֲמָה אֵת אֲשֶׁר אֹכַל וְאֵיךְ יֶעֱרַב?
אֵיכָה אֲשַׁלֵּם נְדָרַי וֶאֱסָרַי, בְּעוֹד
צִיּוֹן בְּחֶבֶל אֱדוֹם וַאְנִי בְּכֶבֶל עֲרָב?
יֵקַל בְּעֵינַי עֲזֹב כָּל טוּב סְפָרַד, כְּמוֹ
יֵקַר בְּעֵינַי רְאוֹת עַפְרוֹת דְּבִיר נֶחֱרָב.

My heart is in the East and I am at the edge of the West. Then how can I taste what I eat, how can I enjoy it? How can I fulfil my vows and pledges[1] while Zion is in the domain of Edom, and I am in the bonds of Arabia? It would be easy for me to leave behind all the good things of Spain; it would be glorious to see the dust of the ruined Shrine.

צִיּוֹן, הֲלֹא תִשְׁאֲלִי

ODE TO ZION

צִיּוֹן, הֲלֹא תִשְׁאֲלִי לִשְׁלוֹם אֲסִירַיִךְ,
דּוֹרְשֵׁי שְׁלוֹמֵךְ, וְהֵם יֶתֶר עֲדָרָיִךְ?
מִיָּם וּמִזְרָח וּמִצָּפוֹן וְתֵימָן שְׁלוֹם
רָחוֹק וְקָרוֹב שְׂאִי מִכֹּל עֲבָרָיִךְ,
וּשְׁלוֹם אֲסִיר תַּאֲוָה, נוֹתֵן דְּמָעָיו כְּטַל-
חֶרְמוֹן וְנִכְסָף לְרִדְתָּם עַל הֲרָרָיִךְ!
לִבְכּוֹת עֱנוּתֵךְ – אֲנִי תַנִּים, וְעֵת אֶחֱלֹם
שִׁיבַת שְׁבוּתֵךְ – אֲנִי כִנּוֹר לְשִׁירָיִךְ.

O Zion, will you not ask how your captives are – the exiles who seek your welfare, who are the remnant of your flocks? From west and east, north and south, from every side, accept the greetings of those near and far, and the blessings of this captive of desire, who sheds his tears like the dew of Hermon and longs to have them fall upon your hills. I am like a jackal when I weep for your affliction; but when I dream of your exiles' return, I am a lute for your songs.

1. The poet had made a vow to leave Spain for Zion.

לִבִּי לְבֵית־אֵל וְלִפְנִיאֵל מְאֹד יֶהֱמֶה
וּלְמַחֲנַיִם וְכָל פִּגְעֵי טְהוֹרָיִךְ.
שָׁם הַשְּׁכִינָה שְׁכֵנָה לָךְ, וְהַיּוֹצְרֵךְ
פָּתַח לְמוּל שַׁעֲרֵי שַׁחַק שְׁעָרַיִךְ,
וּכְבוֹד אֲדֹנָי לְבַד הָיָה מְאוֹרֵךְ, וְאֵין
שֶׁמֶשׁ וְסַהַר וְכוֹכָבִים מְאִירַיִךְ.
אֶבְחַר לְנַפְשִׁי לְהִשְׁתַּפֵּךְ בְּמָקוֹם אֲשֶׁר
רוּחַ אֱלֹהִים שְׁפוּכָה עַל בְּחִירַיִךְ.
אַתְּ בֵּית מְלוּכָה וְאַתְּ כִּסֵּא אֲדֹנָי, וְאִם
יָשְׁבוּ עֲבָדִים עֲלֵי כִסְאוֹת גְּבִירַיִךְ!

My heart longs for Bethel and Penuel, for Mahanaim[1] and for all the shrines of your pure ones. There the Shekinah dwelled within you, and your Maker opened your gates to face the gates of heaven. There the glory of the Lord was your only light; it was not the sun, moon, or stars that shone over you. Oh, I would pour out my life in the very place where once the spirit of God was poured out upon your chosen ones. You are the seat of royalty, you are the throne of the Lord – though slaves now sit upon your princes' thrones!

מִי יִתְּנֵנִי מְשׁוֹטֵט בִּמְקוֹמוֹת אֲשֶׁר
נִגְלוּ אֱלֹהִים לְחוֹזַיִךְ וְצִירַיִךְ.
מִי יַעֲשֶׂה לִּי כְנָפַיִם וְאַרְחִיק נְדֹד,
אָנִיד לְבִתְרֵי לְבָבִי בֵּין בְּתָרַיִךְ.
אֶפֹּל לְאַפַּי עֲלֵי אַרְצֵךְ וְאֶרְצֶה אֲבָ־
נַיִךְ מְאֹד וַאֲחוֹנֵן אֶת עֲפָרַיִךְ.
אֶבְכֶּה בְּעָמְדִי עֲלֵי קִבְרוֹת אֲבוֹתַי וְאֶשְׁ־
תּוֹמֵם בְּחֶבְרוֹן עֲלֵי מִבְחַר קְבָרַיִךְ.
אֶעְבֹּר בְּיַעְרֵךְ וְכַרְמִלֵּךְ וְאֶעְמֹד בְּגִלְ־
עָדֵךְ וְאֶשְׁתּוֹמְמָה אֶל הַר עֲבָרַיִךְ –
הַר הָעֲבָרִים וְהֹר הָהָר, אֲשֶׁר שָׁם שְׁנֵי
אוֹרִים גְּדוֹלִים, מְאִירַיִךְ וּמוֹרַיִךְ.
חַיֵּי נְשָׁמוֹת – אֲוִיר אַרְצֵךְ, וּמִמָּר־דְּרוֹר
אַבְקַת עֲפָרֵךְ, וְנֹפֶת צוּף – נְהָרַיִךְ!
יִנְעַם לְנַפְשִׁי הֲלֹךְ עָרֹם וְיָחֵף עֲלֵי
חָרְבוֹת שְׁמָמָה אֲשֶׁר הָיוּ דְבִירַיִךְ,

If only I could roam through those places where God was revealed to your prophets and heralds! Who will give me wings, so that I may wander far away? I would carry the pieces of my broken heart over your rugged mountains.[2] I would bow down, my face on your ground; I would love your stones; your dust would move me to pity. I would weep, as I stood by my ancestors' graves, I would grieve, in Hebron, over the choicest of burial places![3] I would walk in your forests and meadows, stop in Gilead, marvel at Mount Abarim; Mount Abarim and Mount Hor, where the two great luminaries [Moses and Aaron] rest, those who guided you and gave you light. The air of your land is the very life of the soul, the grains of your dust are flowing myrrh, your rivers are honey from the comb. It would delight my heart to walk naked and barefoot among the desolate ruins where your shrines once stood; where

1. All sites figuring in the life of Jacob.
2. The hills of Bether (Song of Songs 2.17), in the vicinity of Jerusalem.
3. The burial cave of the Patriarchs (Genesis 23.17).

בִּמְקוֹם אֲרוֹנְךָ אֲשֶׁר נִגְנַז, וּבִמְקוֹם כְּרוּ־
בֶיךָ אֲשֶׁר שָׁכְנוּ חַדְרֵי חֲדָרֶיךָ.
אָגֹז וְאַשְׁלִיךְ פְּאֵר נִזְרִי וְאֶקֹּב זְמָן,
חִלֵּל בְּאֶרֶץ טְמֵאָה אֶת נְזִירֶיךָ. [...]

אַשְׁרֵי מְחַכֶּה וְיַגִּיעַ וְיִרְאֶה עֲלוֹת
אוֹרֵךְ וְיִבָּקְעוּ עָלָיו שְׁחָרָיִךְ,
לִרְאוֹת בְּטוֹבַת בְּחִירַיִךְ, וְלַעְלֹז בְּשִׂמְ־
חָתֵךְ בְּשׁוּבֵךְ אֱלֵי קַדְמַת נְעוּרָיִךְ!

your Ark was hidden away,[1] where your cherubim once dwelled in the innermost chamber. I shall cut off my glorious hair and throw it away, I shall curse Time that has defiled your pure ones in the polluted lands [of exile].

Happy is he who waits and lives to see your light rising, your dawn breaking forth over him! He shall see your chosen people prospering, he shall rejoice in your joy when you regain the days of your youth.

וְאַל יִמּוֹט

[...] וְאַל יִמּוֹט בְּלֵב יַמִּים לְבָבְךָ
וְהָרִים תֶּחֱזֶה מָטִים וּמָשִׁים,
וּמַלָּחִים יְדֵיהֶם כִּמְלָחִים,
וְחַכְמֵי הַחֲרָשִׁים מַחֲרִישִׁים.
שְׂמֵחִים הוֹלְכִים נֹכַח פְּנֵיהֶם —
וְשָׁבִים אֶל אֲחוֹרֵיהֶם וּבוֹשִׁים.
וְאֶקְיָנוּס לְפָנֶיךָ לְמָנוֹס —
וְאֵין מִבְרָח לְךָ כִּי אִם יְקוּשִׁים!
וְיָמוּטוּ וְיָנוּטוּ קְלָעִים,
וְיָנוּעוּ וְיָזוּעוּ קְרָשִׁים,
וְיַד רוּחַ מְצַחֶקֶת בְּמַיִם,
כְּנוֹשְׂאֵי הָעֳמָרִים בַּדָּיָשִׁים,
וּפַעַם תַּעֲשֶׂה מֵהֶם גְּרָנוֹת,
וּפַעַם תַּעֲשֶׂה מֵהֶם גְּדִישִׁים.
בְּעֵת הִתְגַּבְּרָם דָּמוּ אֲרָיוֹת,
וְעֵת הֶחָלְשָׁם דָּמוּ נְחָשִׁים,

THE POET IMAGINES HIS VOYAGE

Let not your heart tremble in the heart of the sea, when you see mountains trembling and heaving, and sailors' hands as limp as rags, and soothsayers struck dumb. When they set their course, they were full of joy, but now they are beaten back in shame. The whole ocean is yours to escape in, but your only refuge is the snare of the deep. The sails quiver and quake, the beams creak and shudder. The hand of the wind toys with the waves, like reapers at the threshing: now it flattens them out, now it stacks them up. When the waves gather strength, they are like lions; when they weaken, they are like

1. According to Talmudic legend, King Josiah hid the holy Ark from the enemy.

וְרִאשׁוֹנִים דְּלָקוּם אַחֲרוֹנִים
כִּצְפְעוֹנִים וְאֵין לָהֶם לְחָשִׁים. [...]

snakes, who then pursue the lions – like vipers that cannot be charmed.

וְרֶגַע יִשְׁתְּקוּ גַלִּים, וְיִדְמוּ
עֲדָרִים עַל פְּנֵי אֶרֶץ נְטוּשִׁים.
וְהַלַּיִל – כְּבוֹא שֶׁמֶשׁ בְּמַעֲלוֹת
צְבָא מָרוֹם, וְעָלָיו שַׂר חֲמִשִּׁים –
כְּכוּשִׁית מִשְׁבְּצוֹת זָהָב לְבוּשָׁהּ,
וְכִתְכֵלֶת בְּמִלּוּאַת גְּבִישִׁים.
וְכוֹכָבִים בְּלֵב הַיָּם נְבוּכִים
כְּגֵרִים מִמְּעוֹנֵיהֶם גְּרוּשִׁים,
וְכִדְמוּתָם בְּצַלְמָם יַעֲשׂוּ אוֹר
בְּלֵב הַיָּם כְּלֶהָבוֹת וְאִשִּׁים.
פְּנֵי מַיִם וְשָׁמַיִם עֲדָיִים
עֲלֵי לַיִל מְטֹהָרִים לְטוּשִׁים.
וְיָם דּוֹמֶה לְרָקִיעַ בְּעֵינוֹ,
שְׁנֵיהֶם אָז שְׁנֵי יַמִּים חֲבוּשִׁים –
וּבֵינוֹתָם לְבָבִי יָם שְׁלִישִׁי,
בְּשׁוֹא גַּלֵּי שְׁבָחַי הַחֲדָשִׁים!

Suddenly, the waves calm down, and are like flocks spread out over the fields. And the night – once the sun has gone down the stairway of the heavenly hosts, who are commanded by the moon[1] – is like a Negress dressed in gold embroidery, or like a violet robe spangled with crystal. The stars are astray in the heart of the sea, like strangers expelled from their homes. And in the heart of the sea they cast a light, in their image and likeness, that glows like fire. Now the sea and the sky are pure, glittering ornaments upon the night. The sea is the colour of the sky – they are two seas bound together. And between these two, my heart is a third sea, as the new waves of my praise surge on high!

זֶה רוּחֲךָ, צַד מַעֲרָב

TO THE WESTERN WIND

זֶה רוּחֲךָ, צַד מַעֲרָב, רָקוּחַ:
הַנֵּרְדְּ בִּכְנָפָיו וְהַתַּפּוּחַ.
מֵאוֹצְרוֹת הָרוֹכְלִים מוֹצָאֲךָ,
כִּי אֵינְךָ מֵאוֹצְרוֹת הָרוּחַ!
כַּנְפֵי דְרוֹר תָּנִיף, וְתִקְרָא לִי דְרוֹר,
וּכְמָר־דְּרוֹר מִן הַצְּרוֹר לָקוּחַ.

This wind of yours, O West, is all perfume – it has the scent of spikenard and apple in its wings. Wind, you come from the storehouse of spice-merchants, and not from the common storehouse of winds. You lift up the swallow's wings, you set me free, you are like the purest perfume, fresh from a bunch of

1. Lit. 'commander over unit of fifty'.

מַה נִּכְסְפוּ לָךְ עָם, אֲשֶׁר בִּגְלָלֵךְ
רָכְבוּ בְּגַב הַיָּם עֲלֵי גַב לוּחַ!
אַל נָא תְּרַפֶּה יָדֵךְ מִן הָאֳנִי,
כִּי יַחֲנֶה הַיּוֹם וְכִי יָפוּחַ.
וּרְקַע תְּהוֹם וּקְרַע לְבַב יַמִּים, וְגַע
אֶל הַרְרֵי קֹדֶשׁ וְשָׁם תָּנוּחַ.
וּגְעַר בְּקָדִים הַמְסָעֵר יָם, עֲדֵי
יָשִׂים לְבַב הַיָּם כְּסִיר נָפוּחַ.

myrrh. Everyone here longs for you; by your good graces, they ride over the sea upon a mere plank. Oh, do not abandon the ship, when the day draws to its end or when it begins. Smooth out the ocean, break a path through the sea until you reach the holy mountains, and there subside. Rebuke the east wind that whips up the sea and turns it into a boiling cauldron.

מַה יַּעֲשֶׂה אָסוּר בְּיַד הַצּוּר, אֲשֶׁר
פַּעַם יְהִי עָצוּר, וְעֵת שָׁלוּחַ?
אַךְ סוֹד שְׁאֵלָתִי בְּיַד מָרוֹם — וְהוּא
יוֹצֵר מְרוֹם הָרִים וּבוֹרֵא רוּחַ!

But how can the wind help, for it is a prisoner of the Rock – sometimes held back and sometimes let loose? Only God can grant my deepest wish: for He is the maker of high mountains and the creator of winds!

קִרְאוּ עֲלֵי בָנוֹת

SONG AT SEA

קִרְאוּ עֲלֵי בָנוֹת וּמִשְׁפָּחוֹת
שָׁלוֹם, וְעַל אַחִים וְעַל אָחוֹת,
מֵאֵת אֲסִיר תִּקְוָה אֲשֶׁר נִקְנָה
לַיָּם, וְשָׂם רוּחוֹ בְּיַד רוּחוֹת.
דָּחוּי בְּיַד מַעֲרָב לְיַד מִזְרָח,
זֶה יַעֲבֹר לִנְחוֹת, וְזֶה — לִדְחוֹת.
בֵּינוֹ וּבֵין מָוֶת כְּפֶשַׂע, אַךְ
בֵּינוֹ וּבֵינָיו מַעֲבֵה לוּחוֹת.
קָבוּר בְּחַיָּיו בַּאֲרוֹן עֵץ — לֹא
קַרְקַע, וְלֹא אַרְבַּע, וְלֹא פָחוֹת!
יוֹשֵׁב — וְאֵין לַעֲמֹד עֲלֵי רַגְלָיו,
שׁוֹכֵב — וְאֵין רַגְלָיו מְשֻׁלָּחוֹת,
חוֹלֶה וְיָרֵא מִפְּנֵי גוֹיִם,

Greetings to the kinsfolk, to brothers and sisters, from this prisoner of hope who was ransomed by the sea and committed his spirit into the hands of the winds. Now they push him back and forth: the west wind guides his ship, while the east wind thrusts it back. Between him and death there is nothing but a step; between them only the thickness of the planks. He is buried alive in a wooden coffin, but without any earth: not even four cubits,[1] not even a handful. He sits, for there is no room for him to stand; he lies down, and he cannot stretch out his legs. He is ill, he is afraid of the

1. The minimum required for a grave.

גַּם מִפְּנֵי לִסְטִים וּמֵרוּחוֹת.
חוֹבֵל וּמַלָּח, כָּל בְּנֵי פִרְחָח,
הֵם הַסְּגָנִים שָׁם וְהַפַּחוֹת.
לֹא לַחֲכָמִים שֵׁם וְגַם לֹא חֵן
לַיּוֹדְעִים – רַק יוֹדְעִים לִשְׂחוֹת!
יִתְעַצְּבוּ רֶגַע לְזֹאת פָּנַי –
אֵיךְ יַעֲלֹז הַלֵּב וְהַשּׁוּחוֹת –
עַד אֶשְׁפְּכָה נַפְשִׁי בְּחֵיק הָאֵל,
נֹכַח מְקוֹם אָרוֹן וּמִזְבְּחוֹת.
אֶגְמֹל לְאֵל, גּוֹמֵל לְחַיָּבִים
טוֹבוֹת, בְּטוּב שִׁירוֹת וְתִשְׁבָּחוֹת.

Gentile passengers, as well as of pirates and ghosts. The helmsman and the sailors – all of them riffraff – are the viceroys and governors here! Honour does not belong to the wise nor success to the skilful – only to those who know how to swim! Because of this my face is downcast – how could my heart rejoice? – but only for a moment: until I come to pour out my soul in the bosom of God, at the site of the Ark and the Altar. Then I shall render to God, who renders favours to the undeserving,[1] my choicest songs and praises.

הֲבָא מַבּוּל

ON THE HIGH SEAS

הֲבָא מַבּוּל וְשָׂם תֵּבֵל חֲרֵבָה?
וְאֵין לִרְאוֹת פְּנֵי אֶרֶץ חֲרֵבָה,
וְאֵין אָדָם וְאֵין חַיָּה וְאֵין עוֹף –
הֲסָף הַכֹּל וְשָׁכְבוּ מַעֲצֵבָה?
וּבִרְאוֹת הַר וְשׁוּחָה לִי מְנוּחָה,
וְאֶרֶץ הָעֲרָבָה לִי עֲרֵבָה.
וְאַשְׁגִּיחַ לְכָל עֵבֶר – וְאֵין כֹּל,
אֲבָל מַיִם וְשָׁמַיִם וְתֵבָה,
וְלִוְיָתָן בְּהַרְתִּיחוֹ מְצוּלָה,
וְאֶחְשֹׁב כִּי תְהוֹם יַחְשֹׁב לְשֵׂיבָה.
וְלֵב הַיָּם יְכַחֵשׁ בָּאֳנִיָּה,
כְּאִלּוּ הִיא בְּיַד הַיָּם גְּנֵבָה!
וְיָם יִזְעַף – וְנַפְשִׁי תַעֲלֹז, כִּי
אֱלֵי מִקְדַּשׁ אֱלֹהֶיהָ קְרֵבָה.

Has a flood come and laid the world waste? For dry land is nowhere to be seen. There is neither man, nor beast, nor bird. Have they all perished, all lain down in torment and died? If only I could see a hill or valley, I would be comforted; even a desert would delight me. I look in every direction, and there is nothing but sea and sky and ship,[2] and leviathan churning the deep, until it seems that the abyss is white with age! Deceitfully, the sea covers the ship, as though it had taken it by theft. The sea is in turmoil, but my soul is full of joy, for she is drawing near to the temple of her God.

1. An allusion to the Benediction on Deliverance, recited by those who come safely through danger.
2. The word here is the one used for Noah's ark.

אַבְרָהָם אִבְּן־עֶזְרָא

Abraham ibn Ezra

אַשְׁכִּים לְבֵית הַשַּׂר

אַשְׁכִּים לְבֵית הַשַּׂר – אוֹמְרִים: 'כְּבָר רָכַב'.
אָבוֹא לְעֵת עֶרֶב – אוֹמְרִים: 'כְּבָר שָׁכַב'.
אוֹ יַעֲלֶה מֶרְכָּב אוֹ יַעֲלֶה מִשְׁכָּב –
אוֹיָה לְאִישׁ עָנִי נוֹלַד בְּלִי כוֹכָב!

THE PATRON

When I come to the patron's house early in the morning, they say: 'He has already ridden away.' When I come in the evening, they say: 'He has already gone to sleep.' He either climbs into his carriage or climbs into bed – woe to the poor man, born to misfortune![1]

בְּלִי מַזָּל

א

גַּלְגַּל וּמַזָּלוֹת בְּמַעְמָדָם
נָטוּ בְּמַהֲלָכָם לְמוֹלַדְתִּי:
לוּ יִהְיוּ נֵרוֹת סְחוֹרָתִי –
לֹא יֶחֱשַׁךְ שֶׁמֶשׁ עֲדֵי מוֹתִי!

ב

אִיגַע לְהַצְלִיחַ וְלֹא אוּכַל,
כִּי עִוְּתוּנִי כוֹכְבֵי שָׁמַי:
לוּ אֶהְיֶה סוֹחֵר בְּתַכְרִיכִין –
לֹא יִגְוְעוּן אִישִׁים בְּכָל יָמַי!

OUT OF LUCK

1

The heavenly sphere and the constellations strayed from their path when I was born. If my business were in candles, the sun would not set until I died!

2

However I struggle, I cannot succeed, for my stars have ruined me: If I were a dealer in shrouds, no one would die as long as I lived.

מְעִיל יֶשׁ לִי

מְעִיל יֶשׁ לִי וְהוּא כִּדְמוּת כְּבָרָה
לְחִטָּה לַהֲנָפָה אוֹ שְׂעוֹרָה.
כְּאֹהֶל אֶפְרְשֶׂנּוּ לֵיל בְּאִישׁוֹן,

THE OLD CLOAK

I have a cloak that is like a sieve to sift wheat or barley. I spread it out like a tent in the dark of night, and the stars

1. Lit. 'without a star'.

וְכוֹכְבֵי רוֹם יְשִׁימוּן בּוֹ מְאוֹרָה.
בְּתוֹכוֹ אֶחֱזֶה סַהַר וְכִימָה,
וְיוֹפִיעַ כְּסִיל עָלָיו נְהָרָה.
וְאֵלֶה מְסַפֵּר אֶת כָּל נְקָבָיו
אֲשֶׁר דּוֹמִים לְשִׁנֵּי הַמְּגֵרָה.
וְתִקְנַת חוּט תְּפִירַת כָּל קְרוּעָיו –
עֲלֵי שֶׁתִי וְעֵרֶב – הִיא יְתֵרָה.
וְאִם יִפֹּל זְבוּב עָלָיו בְּחָזְקָה,
כְּמוֹ פֶתִי יְהִי נִמְלָךְ מְהֵרָה.
אֱלוֹהַי, הַחֲלִיפֵהוּ בְּמַעֲטֵה
תְהִלָּה לִי – וְתֵיטִיב הַתְּפִירָה!

shine through it; through it I see the moon and the Pleiades, and Orion, flashing his light. I am tired of counting all its holes, which are shaped like the teeth of a saw. No thread can hope to mend its gaps with warp and woof. If a fly landed on it with its full weight, it would quickly regret its foolishness. O God, give me a robe of glory in exchange – this would be properly tailored!

אֶשְׁתַּחֲוֶה אַפַּיִם אַרְצָה

PENITENTIAL PRAYER

אֶשְׁתַּחֲוֶה אַפַּיִם אַרְצָה,
כִּי אֵין לְמַטָּה מִמֶּנָּה.
אֶתְנַפֵּל לִפְנֵי עֶלְיוֹן,
גָּבֹהַּ עַל כָּל גְּבֹהִים.
בַּמָּה אֲקַדֵּם פָּנָיו, כִּי אִם בְּרוּחִי?
הֲלֹא הִיא מֵאִתּוֹ,
בְּמִבְחַר גּוּפָתִי הוּא יְחַיֶּהָ –
וְאֵין לְאִישׁ נִכְבָּד מִנַּפְשׁוֹ.
רֹאשׁ וָסוֹף אֵין לִגְדֻלָּתוֹ,
וּלְשׁוֹנִי אֵיךְ תְּגַדְּלֶנּוּ?
רָחוֹק רָחוֹק מִשְּׁמֵי הַשָּׁמַיִם,
וְקָרוֹב קָרוֹב מֵעַצְמִי וּבְשָׂרִי!
הִנֵּה בָאתִי לְךָ, אֱלוֹהַי,
כִּי אֵין מוֹעִיל זוּלָתֶךָ.
הֲלֹא כָל צְבָא הַשָּׁמַיִם וְהָאָרֶץ

I bow down with my face to the ground, for there is nothing lower than it. I throw myself down before the Supreme One, highest of the high. What but my spirit shall I bring when I approach Him? It comes from Him, He gives it life in the choicest part of my body, and a man has nothing dearer than his soul. There is no end and no beginning to His glory – how then can my tongue glorify Him? He is farther from me than the farthest heaven, and closer than my flesh and bone! I come to You now, my God, because none but You can be of help. The earth and all the

כֻּלָּם נִבְרָאִים כָּמוֹנִי;
מֵהֶם אֵיךְ אֶדְרֹשׁ תְּשׁוּעָה,
וּתְשׁוּעַת כָּל יָצוּר כָּזָב!
מָנוֹס אַיִן לְעֶבֶד
בִּלְתִּי לַאֲשֶׁר קָנָהוּ.
מָה אֲחַשְּׁבָה לָדַעַת?
וְיָדַעְתִּי כִּי לְהֵיטִיב לִי בְּרָאתַנִי.
מִסְּפֹר עָצְמוּ חֲסָדֶיךָ,
וּמֵחוֹל הַיָּם חַטֹּאתַי.
עַיִן אֵיךְ אֶשָּׂא אֵלֶיךָ?
וְהִיא גַם הִיא חָטְאָה.
עוֹד מָה יַעֲנוּ שְׂפָתַי?
גַּם הֵמָּה הִרְשִׁיעוּ.
זְדוֹן לִבִּי עָשָׂה לְנַפְשִׁי
אֲשֶׁר אוֹיֵב לֹא יוּכַל עֲשׂוֹהוּ;
זַלְעָפָה אֲחָזַתְנִי מִמֶּנּוּ –
אוֹי לִי כִּי מָרִיתִי!
רֹעַ יִצְרִי הִתְעַנִי,
כִּי לֹא הָיָה רְצוֹנִי לְהַכְעִיסֶךָ.
רָעוֹתַי לִי לְבַדִּי הֵרֵעוּ,
וְאַתָּה לְבַדְּךָ תַּעֲשֶׂה חֶסֶד.
הוֹדִיעֵנִי דֶרֶךְ יוֹעִילֵנִי,
כִּי כֹל יָדַעְתִּי – אַתָּה הוֹדַעְתַּנִי.
הִשְׁמַעְתִּי דִּבְרֵי לִבִּי לְאָזְנַי –
וְאַתָּה תִּשְׁמַע הַשָּׁמַיִם!

heavens are, like me, Your creations; how then could I ask them to save me, when salvation by any creature is a vain hope! A slave can find no refuge but in his master. What more can I hope to know, knowing that You created me for my good? Your acts of love are beyond number, but my sins outnumber the sand of the sea-shore. How shall I lift up my eyes to You? They, too, are sinful. What more can my lips say? They, too, have done wrong. My wanton heart has done to me what no enemy could have done. Gusts of anger sieze me as I think of it – woe is me, I have disobeyed. My evil passions led me astray; I had no wish to anger You. My wrongs have wronged no one but me, and none but You will keep faith with me. Show me the right path for it is You who have taught me all I know. I have heard myself speak the words of my heart; may You hear them in heaven!

יִצְחָק אִבְּן־עֶזְרָא

Isaac ibn Ezra

בְּכִי תִשְׂאוּ

בְּכִי תִשְׂאוּ עֲלֵי כָּל הַר,
וְאֶשָּׂא עַל נְאוֹת מִדְבָּר,
וּמִסְפֵּד מַר אֲנִי אַעַשׂ,
כְּמוֹ תַנִּים, בְּכָל מַעְבָּר.
אֲדַבְּרָה בְּצַר רוּחַ
וְרַב יָגוֹן וְלֵב נִשְׁבָּר
עֲלֵי רֵעַ אֲשֶׁר נִתְרַע
לְכָל אִישׁ רָע וְנִתְחַבָּר [...]
אֲנִי הוֹלֵךְ, וְהֵן שִׁפְחָה
פְּגָשַׁתְנִי לְאִישׁ גִּזְבָּר.
קְרָאַתְנִי וְהִיא תִשְׂחַק:
'הֲשָׁמַעְתָּ אֲשֶׁר דִּבֵּר
זְקַנְכֶם זֶה, אֲשֶׁר שָׁכַן
עֲלִיַּת קִיר כְּמוֹ מִכְבָּר,
אֲשֶׁר פָּנָיו וְצוּרָתוֹ
פְּנֵי שָׁחֹר כְּפַת קִבָּר?
רְאִינוּהוּ עֲלֵי נַעְרוֹ,
וְשִׂפְתוֹתָיו בְּפִיו יִצְבָּר,
וְהוּא יִדְמֶה – וּפִיו עַל פִּיו –
כְּמוֹ עוֹרֵב, בְּפִיו עַכְבָּר!'

THE DIRTY OLD MAN

Go and weep upon every mountain, and I shall wail in the desert pastures and howl bitterly like a wolf at every turn of the road. With anguish in my soul, grief-stricken and broken-hearted, I shall speak of a friend who made friends with evil men and kept company with them. One day, as I was walking, I met the maid-servant of some notable. Laughing, she called to me: 'Have you heard the talk about your old friend, who lives in the latticed attic and has a face like a loaf of black bread? We saw him bent over his boyfriend, gathering the boy's lips in his mouth; and, lying there, mouth to mouth, he looked like a crow with a mouse in its beak!'

יְהוּדָה אִבְּן־עַבָּאס

Judah Samuel Abbas

עֵת שַׁעֲרֵי רָצוֹן

AT THE HOUR OF MERCY

עֵת שַׁעֲרֵי רָצוֹן לְהִפָּתֵחַ,
יוֹם אֶהְיֶה כַּפַּי לְאֵל שׁוֹטֵחַ,
אֹמַר: ׳זְכָר־נָא לִי בְּיוֹם הוֹכֵחַ
עוֹקֵד וְהַנֶּעֱקָד וְהַמִּזְבֵּחַ!׳

When the gates of mercy are about to open, on this day, as I spread out my hands to You, I shall say: 'Oh, remember in my behalf, on this day of judgement, the one who bound, the one who was bound, and the altar!'

בָּאַחֲרִית נִסָּה בְּסוֹף הָעֲשָׂרָה:
׳הַבֵּן אֲשֶׁר נוֹלַד לְךָ מִשָּׂרָה,
אִם נַפְשְׁךָ בּוֹ עַד מְאֹד נִקְשָׁרָה,
קוּם, הַעֲלֵהוּ לִי לְעוֹלָה בָּרָה
אֶל הַר אֲשֶׁר כָּבוֹד לְךָ זוֹרֵחַ.׳

This was the last of Abraham's ten trials: 'The son that was born to you of Sarah – though you love him dearly, now go and offer him to Me as a perfect sacrifice on the mountain where you will see My glory shining.'

אָמַר לְשָׂרָה: ׳כִּי חֲמוּדֵךְ יִצְחָק
גָּדַל וְלֹא לָמַד עֲבוֹדַת שַׁחַק,
אֵלְכָה וְאוֹרֵהוּ אֲשֶׁר לוֹ אֵל חָק.׳
אָמְרָה: ׳לְכָה אָדוֹן, אֲבָל אַל תִּרְחַק.׳
עָנָה: ׳יְהִי לִבֵּךְ בְּאֵל בּוֹטֵחַ.׳

Then Abraham said to Sarah: 'Your beloved Isaac has grown up, but he has not yet studied the worship of God. Let me go and teach him what God has ordained for him.' 'Go, my lord,' she said, 'but do not go too far.' He answered: 'Let your heart trust in God.'

שַׁחַר, וְהִשְׁכִּים לַהֲלֹךְ בַּבֹּקֶר,
וּשְׁנֵי נְעָרָיו מִמְּתֵי הַשֶּׁקֶר.
יוֹם הַשְּׁלִישִׁי נָגְעוּ אֶל חֵקֶר,
וַיַּרְא דְּמוּת כָּבוֹד וְהוֹד וָיֶקֶר.
עָמַד וְהִתְבּוֹנֵן לְהִמָּשֵׁחַ.

So he rose at dawn to start on his journey, and with him two of his heathen servants. On the third day they reached their destination, and he saw a shape of glory and resplendent majesty. There he paused to consider how he should perform his priestly office.

יַדַּע נְעָרָיו כִּי קָרְצָם לֵאמֹר:
׳אוֹר הַרְאִיתֶם צָץ בְּרֹאשׁ הַר הַמּוֹר?׳
וַיֹּאמְרוּ: ׳לֹא נֶחֱזֶה רַק מַהְמוֹר.׳

He told his servants that they would have to stay behind: 'Do you see a light flowering on top of Mount Moriah?' They said: 'We can see nothing but valleys.' To which he replied: 'Then

עָנָה: 'שְׁבוּ פֹה, עִם מְשׁוּלִים לַחֲמוֹר,
וַאֲנִי וְהַנַּעַר לְהִשְׁתַּחֵוֹת.'

stay here – since you are [as dull-eyed] as donkeys – while the boy and I go there to worship.'

הָלְכוּ שְׁנֵיהֶם לַעֲסֹק בִּמְלָאכָה.
וַיַּעַן יִצְחָק לְאָבִיו כָּכָה:
'אָבִי, הֲלֹא אֵשׁ וַעֲצֵי מַעֲרָכָה.
אַיֵּה, אֲדוֹנִי, שֶׂה אֲשֶׁר כַּהֲלָכָה?
הַאַתְּ בְּיוֹם זֶה דָּתְךָ שׁוֹכֵחַ?

Then the two of them went to perform their task. And this is what Isaac said to his father: 'Father, we have the fire and the wood, but where, my lord, is the lamb prescribed for the sacrifice? Could you, on such a day, forget the Law?'

וַיַּעַן אָבִיו: 'בְּאֵל חַי מַחְסֶה,
כִּי הוּא אֲשֶׁר יִרְאֶה לְעוֹלָה הַשֶּׂה.
דַּע, כִּי אֲשֶׁר יַחְפֹּץ אֱלֹהִים – יַעֲשֶׂה.
נִבְנֶה, בְּנִי, הַיּוֹם לְפָנָיו כִּסֵּא,
אָז יַאֲמִיר זֶבַח וְהַזּוֹבֵחַ.

His father replied: 'The living God is our refuge. It is He who will provide the lamb for a sacrifice. Know that He does what He pleases. Now, my son, let us build an altar[1] before Him. Then He will exalt the sacrifice and the one who sacrifices.'

דָּפְקוּ בְּשַׁעֲרֵי רַחֲמִים לִפְתֹּחַ,
הַבֵּן לְהִזָּבַח וְאָב לִזְבֹּחַ,
קוֹוִים לְאֵל וּבְרַחֲמָיו לִבְטֹחַ.
קוֹוֵי יְיָ יַחֲלִיפוּ כֹחַ.
דָּרְשׁוּ בְּנַחֲלַת אֵל לְהִסְתַּפֵּחַ.

And so the son, ready to be sacrificed, and the father, ready to sacrifice – both hoping for the Lord and trusting in His mercy – knocked at the Gates of Mercy, to open the Gates. For those who look to the Lord will renew their strength. Thus they sought to win their share in the Lord's inheritance.

הֵכִין עֲצֵי עוֹלָה בְּאוֹן וָחַיִל,
וַיַּעֲקֹד יִצְחָק כְּעָקְדוֹ אַיִל,
וַהֲמוֹן דְּמָעָיו נוֹזְלִים בַּחַיִל.
וַיְהִי מְאוֹר יוֹמָם כְּעֶצֶם לַיִל –
עַיִן בְּמַר בּוֹכָה וְלֵב שָׂמֵחַ.

With unflagging strength, Abraham arranged the wood upon the altar, and bound Isaac as one binds a ram. The tears ran down his cheeks. The light of day was like the very dark of night to them – their eyes wept bitterly, but their hearts rejoiced.

'שׁוּרוּ לְאִמִּי כִּי שְׂשׂוֹנָהּ פָּנָה.
הַבֵּן אֲשֶׁר יָלְדָה לְתִשְׁעִים שָׁנָה
הָיָה לְאֵשׁ וּלְמַאֲכֶלֶת מָנָה.

'See how my mother's joy is gone; the son she bore when she was ninety years old has fallen prey to the slaughtering knife and the fire. Where shall I find

1. Lit. 'chair' or 'throne'.

אָנָה אֲבַקֵּשׁ לָהּ מְנַחֵם, אָנָה ?
צַר לִי לְאֵם תִּבְכֶּה וְתִתְיַפֵּחַ !

someone to bring her comfort? I am sorry for the mother who must weep and sob.

מִמַּאֲכֶלֶת יֶהֱמֶה מְדַבְּרִי.
נָא חַדְּדָהּ, אָבִי, וְאֶת מַאְסָרִי
חַזֵּק, בְּעֵת יֵקַד יְקוֹד בִּבְשָׂרִי.
קַח עִמְּךָ הַנִּשְׁאָר מֵאֶפְרִי,
וֶאֱמֹר לְשָׂרָה: "זֶה לְיִצְחָק רֵיחַ".'

'The knife makes me cry out. Oh, father, sharpen it, and bind me securely as the fire consumes my flesh. Then gather the remains of my ashes and say to Sarah: "This is the sweet savour of Isaac"!'

וַיֶּהֱמוּ כָּל מַלְאֲכֵי מֶרְכָּבָה,
אוֹפָן וְשָׂרָף שׁוֹאֲלִים בִּנְדָבָה,
וּמְחַנְּנִים לָאֵל בְּעַד שַׂר צָבָא:
'אָנָּא, תְּנָה פִּדְיוֹם וְכֹפֶר הָבָה,
אַל נָא יְהִי עוֹלָם בְּלֹא יָרֵחַ.'

All the angels of the Chariot cried out: Ofanim and Seraphim begged for charity and implored God to spare this prince: 'Oh, redeem him, appoint a ransom for him! Do not let the world be left without its moon!'

אָמַר לְאַבְרָהָם אֲדוֹן שָׁמַיִם:
'אַל תִּשְׁלְחָה יָד אֶל שְׁלִישׁ אוֹרַיִם!
שׁוּבוּ לְשָׁלוֹם, מַלְאֲכֵי מַחֲנַיִם.
יוֹם זֶה זְכוּת לִבְנֵי יְרוּשָׁלַיִם –
בּוֹ חֵטְא בְּנֵי יַעֲקֹב אֲנִי סוֹלֵחַ.'

Then the Lord of Heaven spoke to Abraham: 'Do not raise your hand against this luminary.[1] And you, angels, go in peace. The merit of this day will protect the children of Jerusalem; for its sake, I shall pardon the sins of Jacob's sons.'

לִבְרִיתְךָ, שׁוֹכֵן זְבוּלִים שִׁבְעָה,
זָכְרָה לְעֵדָה סֹעֲרָה וּנְגוּעָה,
וּשְׁמַע תְּקִיעָה תוֹקְעָה וּתְרוּעָה,
וֶאֱמֹר לְצִיּוֹן: 'בָּא זְמַן הַיְשׁוּעָה,
יִנּוֹן וְאֵלִיָּה אֲנִי שׁוֹלֵחַ!'

Oh, dweller of the seven heavens, remember Your covenant with this storm-tossed and tormented people. Hear the sound of the ram's horn, and proclaim to Zion: 'The time of salvation has come. I shall send you Yinon (the Messiah) and the prophet Elijah!'

1. Lit. 'one of the three lights', i.e. 'one of the three Patriarchs'.

מֹשֶׁה דַּרְעִי

Moses Dar'i

לַחֲבַצֶּלֶת שָׁרוֹן

THE SPY'S PROMISE

לַחֲבַצֶּלֶת שָׁרוֹן נַמְתִּי:
׳סִגְרִי עֵינֵךְ גַּם הַעְצִימִי.
נִכְלַמְתִּי לִנְשֹׁק דּוֹד, כִּי עֵי־
נֵךְ מִמֶּנִּי לֹא תַעְלִימִי.
דּוֹד יָשַׁב רֶגַע נֶגְדִּי וְ־
יִישַׁן, אַךְ אַתְּ לֹא תָנוּמִי!׳
וַתְּעַנֵנִי: ׳שִׁמְעָה, חוֹשֵׁק,
נֹעַם מִלִּים מִטּוּב טַעְמִי —
חָבוֹק וּנְשֹׁק דּוֹד־חֶפְצְךָ,
כִּי סוֹד חוֹשְׁקִים צָפוּן עִמִּי.׳ [...]

I said to the spying lady:[1] 'Can't you shut your eyes? I am ashamed to kiss my beloved because you never take your eyes off me! My beloved and I sat face to face, and in an instant he was asleep; but you never slumber!' To which she replied: 'Listen, love, to the gracious words of my wisdom: you may hug and kiss the youth you long for, for lovers' secrets are safe with me!'

עֲלוּמֵי־שֵׁם

Anonymous

וּפֶה עָגֹל כְּטַבַּעַת

THE IDEAL WOMAN

[...] וּפֶה עָגֹל כְּטַבַּעַת וְחוֹתָם,
כְּאִלּוּ הִיא בְּיַד מֶלֶךְ לְחָתְמָה.
וְשִׁנַּיִם כְּאִלּוּ הֵם בְּדֹלַח,
וְכַבָּרָד בְּרִדְתּוֹ עַל אֲדָמָה.
וְגַם צַוָּאר כְּצַוַּאר הַצְּבִי, עֵת
יְהִי צָמֵא וְעֵינָיו אֶל מְרוֹמָא.
וְשָׁדַיִם כְּתַפּוּחֵי כְפָרִים,
עֲלֵי רֹאשָׁם נְקֻדַּת מֹר חֲתוּמָה.

A mouth as round as a signet-ring, fit for a royal hand to seal with; teeth that are like crystals, or like pellets of hail as they fall to earth; also, a neck like the neck of a gazelle when it thirsts and lifts up its eyes to heaven; breasts like apples of henna,[2] studded at their tips with a bit of myrrh; a belly like white

1. Lit. 'to the rose of Sharon'.
2. Presumably, round boxes for storing henna.

וְגַם בֶּטֶן כְּמוֹ עִסָּה לְבָנָה,
וְגַם יִדְמֶה כְּחִטִּים בָּעֲרֵמָה.
וְגַם שָׁרְרָהּ בְּתוֹךְ בִּטְנָהּ כְּמוֹ בוֹר,
כְּאִלּוּ הִיא בְאֵר אֵין בָּהּ מְאוּמָה.
וּמָתְנַיִם מְאֹד דַּקִּים כְּמָתְנֵי
דְבוֹרָה, עֵת תְּהִי עָפָה בְּכַרְמָהּ.
וְשׁוֹקַיִם כְּעַמּוּדִים, עֲלֵיהֶם
יְרֵכַיִם, וְגַם אַלְיָה עֲצוּמָה.
וְיָדַיִם וְרַגְלַיִם קְטַנִּים
וְגַם לַחִים, כְּמוֹ רַגְלֵי עֲלִימָה.
וּמֵרֹאשָׁהּ עֲדֵי רַגְלָהּ שְׁלֵמָה
כְּמוֹ יָפְיָהּ, וּמוּם אֵין בָּהּ, תְּמִימָה.
וְאִשָּׁה בַּעֲלַת חַיִל וְשֶׂכֶל,
כְּמוֹתָהּ אֵין אֱנוֹשׁ מוֹצֵא בְּעָלְמָה.
וְעֵת עוֹנָה כְּמוֹ [ ]וֹמָה [ ]
בְּמִשְׁכָּבָהּ, וְתוֹךְ בֵּיתָהּ חֲכָמָה.
וְלֹא נִמְצָא כְּמוֹ יָפְיָהּ וְשִׂכְלָהּ,
כְּאִלּוּ הִיא בְּעוֹלָמָהּ יְתוֹמָה.
וּמִי יִשְׁגֶּה בְּאַהֲבַת זֹאת – הֲיִמְצָא
בְּעַפְעַפָּיו, בְּעֵת יִשְׁכַּב, תְּנוּמָה ? [...]

dough, or like a heap of wheat; a navel in her belly like a cistern, as though she were an empty well; very narrow hips, like the hips of a bee as it flits through the vineyard; legs like pillars, on which the thighs can rest, as well as ample buttocks; hands and feet that are both small and fresh, the feet like those of a young girl; wholly beautiful from head to foot, flawless, perfect; a woman resourceful and intelligent, whose equal cannot be found in the whole world; who during intercourse . . .[1] on her bed; wise in the ways of the household; whose beauty and good sense are unrivalled; unique in the world – whoever falls in love with such a woman, how can he ever fall asleep at night?

עֹפֶר אֲשֶׁר לִבִּי

עֹפֶר אֲשֶׁר לִבִּי לְעֶבֶד לוֹ
נִרְצַע, וְכֵן נַפְשִׁי כְּמוֹ שִׁפְחָה –
אַבִּיט חֲנִית עֵינָיו – וְלִי אֵימָה,
אֶרְאֶה יְפִי לְחָיו – וְלִי בִטְחָה.
שָׂם הַזְּמָן לִבִּי בְּבֵית אֵבֶל
תָּמִיד, אֲבָל עֵינַי בְּבֵית שִׂמְחָה.

THE ENTHRALLED LOVER

This gazelle – to whom my heart surrendered itself like a slave, and my soul like a handmaid – when I look at the spears of his eyes, I am all fear; when I see the beauty of his cheeks, I am all faith. Time has put my heart in a house of mourning forever, but my eyes are in a house of joy.

1. The manuscript is defective at this point.

תְּנָה כוֹסִי

TO THE CUP-BEARER

תְּנָה כוֹסִי בְּמוֹ יָדִי,
יְדִידִי, אַל תְּהִי פוֹתֶה –
הֲלֹא תִרְאֶה פְּנוֹת חֹשֶׁךְ
וְהִלּוּכוֹ, וְאוֹר יֵאתֶה,
וְהַחַמָּה כְּמוֹ הַכּוֹס
בְּיַד יָדִיד וְהוּא חוֹתֶה.
וְהַמִּזְרָח כְּמוֹ מַשְׁקֶה,
וְהַמַּעְרָב כְּמוֹ שׁוֹתֶה.

Put my cup in my hand, friend; do not be foolish. Can't you see that the darkness is leaving, and the light is coming? The sun is like a cup in the hand of a friend who stirs its flame – as though the East were pouring out the drink, and the West were drinking.

לְאַט מְשֹׁכָה

TO THE CAMEL DRIVER

לְאַט מְשֹׁכָה גְּמַלֶּיךָ, עֲרָבִי –
הֲלֹא עִמְּךָ כְּבָר נִמְשַׁךְ לְבָבִי
לְפֵרוּד רַב אֲשֶׁר אֶחְיֶה בְּצִלּוֹ,
גְּבִיר קָדוֹשׁ כְּמַלְאַךְ־אֵל וְנָבִיא.
הֲכִי לוֹ נִכְסְפָה נַפְשִׁי וְכָלְתָה,
וְסָר אוֹנִי וְתָעָה מַחֲשָׁבִי
לְעֵת אֶזְכֹּר דְּבָרָיו הָעֲרֵבִים,
אֲשֶׁר לִי נֶחְמְדוּ מִכָּל זְהָבִי. [...]

Lead your camels slowly, Arab; you are leading my heart away with you. For I am being parted from the teacher who is the refuge of my life, from the master who is as holy as an angel of God or a prophet. Oh, I already pine, I faint with longing for him, my strength leaves me, my mind reels, when I recall his sweet words, dearer to me than all my gold.

צְבִי – יֵין הָרֶקַח

THE FIFTEEN-YEAR-OLD BOY

צְבִי – יֵין הָרֶקַח בְּעֵינָיו יַשְׁקֵנִי, לוּ בְּפִיו יִשָּׁקֵנִי!

The fawn gives me spiced wine to drink with his eyes; if only he would kiss me with his mouth!

בְּנַפְשִׁי! צְבִי עִוָּה לְבָבִי וְחִלַּנִי
בְּרַקָּה כְשׁוֹשַׁנָּה וְשָׂפָה כְּחוּט שָׁנִי.
בְּפִתְחוֹ בִנְגִינָה בְּשִׁיר עַל הַשְּׁמִינִי,
בְּשִׁירָתוֹ לֶקַח אֲשֶׁר יַשְׁמִיעֵנִי, לוּ בְחַסְדּוֹ יְחַיֵּנִי!

Upon my life! This fawn has tormented my heart and made me ill, with his lily cheeks and lips like scarlet thread. When he sings to the accompaniment of his lyre, there are words of wisdom for me in his song. If only he would give me life by giving me his favours!

לְבָבִי כְּיָם יֶהֱמֶה, יְדִידַי, לְפֵרוּדוֹ
וְלַתַּנִּים אֲדַמֶּה בְּבֶכִי לְיוֹם נוּדוֹ.
וְעַל מָה אֱנוֹשׁ, עַל מָה, יְחִי עוֹד, וְאֵין דּוֹדוֹ?
וּמִיּוֹם כִּי לֻקַּח, בְּפֵרוּד יְמִיתֵנִי, בְּנִדּוֹד יַצְמִיתֵנִי.

Friends, my heart moans like the sea because of his absence. I wail like a jackal over his departure. Why should a man go on living when his beloved is gone? Ever since he was taken away, his absence is my death, his going my destruction.

עֲדֵי מָתַי אוֹחִיל כְּעוֹמֵד עֲלֵי מִצְפֶּה?
וְאָנֹכִי אָחִיל וְלֹא אֶמְצָא מַרְפֵּה.
וּמִי יִתֵּן אַתְחִיל וְאָשִׂים פֶּה אֶל פֶּה —
וּבִרְצוֹנוֹ אֶרְקַח עֲסִיסִי וְשׁוֹשַׁנִּי, פַּעֲמוֹנִי וְרִמּוֹנִי.

How much longer must I wait, like a look-out on a watch-tower? I am torn with anguish, I can find no relief. If only he would let me put my mouth to his and blend our nectar and our lips, O my bell, my pomegranate!

מְטִיבִים וּמְלִיצִים עֲלֵי עֹפֶר יָדִינוּ,
אֲשֶׁר עֵינָיו חִצִּים לְהָרְגִי הֵכִינוּ —
וּבִלְחָיָיו צִצִּים נְעִימִים, לֹא יִשְׁנוּ,
וְכָל־פַּעַם אֶפְקַח בְּפָנָיו אִישׁוֹנִי, אוֹר לְחָיָיו יְכַסֵּנ

My eloquent friends condemn this gazelle who armed his eyes with arrows to kill me. But his cheeks are full of sweet blossoms that never wilt. Every time I open my eyes to look into his face, the light of his cheeks engulfs me.

מְבֹרָךְ צְבִי, אַעְלִים שְׁמוֹ מִפְּנֵי מוֹנִים.
אֲבָל הוּא אֲשֶׁר הִכְלִים מְאוֹרִים בִּמְעוֹנִים —
צְבִי חֵן אֲשֶׁר הִשְׁלִים חֲמֵשׁ עֶשְׂרֵה שָׁנִים:
נהייד במא ילקח כגצן מן אלבאני
עאד אליי אצלאן.

Blessed be this fawn, whose name I conceal from my spying rivals, though he is the one who puts the lights of heaven to shame; this graceful fawn, now in his fifteenth year. Oh, we shall set in motion that which impregnates. He, who is like a willow branch, has come back to me entirely.[1]

1. The last line is in Arabic. The meaning is unclear.

ANONYMOUS

אִמְרוּ לְרֹאשׁ פֶּתֶן

SONG OF HOPE

אִמְרוּ לְרֹאשׁ פֶּתֶן: 'הָבָה צֳרִי' —
וּלְשׁוֹן דְּוֵה לֵבָב: 'שִׁיר דַּבְּרִי'!

You might as well say to the poisonous asp: 'Give me balm,' as say to the man who is sick at heart: 'Sing!'

שׁוֹכֵב בְּלֵב יַמִּים, אֵלֵךְ בְּלִי
חוֹבֵל, וְרֹאשׁ חִבֵּל הוּא אָהֳלִי.
עֵינַי לְמֵרָחוֹק אֶל פּוֹעֲלִי:
לֹא יָם סְעָרָה, אַךְ חַטֹּאת מְרִי,
אַף עָב — עֲווֹנִי יַטְרִיחַ בְּרִי.

I am tossing out at sea, sailing without a captain; the top of the rigging is my tent; my eyes scan the distance for my Maker. It is not the stormy sea [that I fear], but my sinful defiance. It is my crimes that make the clouds so heavy.

שֵׁבֶט לְגֵו נוֹאָל — נֹפֶת וּמָן,
מַכַּת אֲהָבִים — פֶּצַע נֶאֱמָן.
לֹא דִכְּאָה נֶפֶשׁ יַד רַחֲמָן.
מִקְטַר קְטֹרֶת הוּא יַעְצֹר חֳרִי,
מוּסַר שְׁלוֹמִים הוּא יַעֲשֶׂה פְּרִי.

A rod to a fool's back is like honey and manna. Blows given out of love leave beneficial wounds. The hand of the Compassionate One never crushes the soul. The offering of prayer can placate His wrath. His chastisement, meant to bring us peace, bears fruit.

תִּקְוָה לְמַפֶּלֶת נוֹפֵל בְּבוֹר
עֵת בַּחֲמַת רוּחוֹ יִשְׁאַף דְּרוֹר,
וּבְמַאֲסַר חָשְׁכּוֹ יוֹחִיל מְאוֹר.
קַוֵּה לְשָׁלוֹם — אִם יִשְׁאַג אֲרִי,
קַוֵּה בְּיוֹם סַגְרִיר אוֹר שַׁחֲרִי.

There is hope for the man who has fallen into a pit if, even in his anguish, he longs for freedom; if, in his dark prison, he waits for light. Though the lion roar, hope for peace; though the day be bleak, look for the glow of dawn.

שַׁלְטִי וּמָגִנִּי, שַׁלִּיט, בְּךָ.
אֵיךְ אַחֲרַי יִדְלַק צוּר חַרְבְּךָ,
וַאֲנִי בְּךָ צוֹפֶה וּלְטוּבְךָ?
הִתְעוֹרְרִי, נַפְשִׁי, הִטַּהֲרִי,
וּלְטוּב אֲדוֹנַיִךְ אָז תִּנְהֲרִי.

O King, You are my shield and my buckler. Why should Your sharp sword pursue me, when it is You I am looking to, and Your goodness? Arise, my soul, cleanse yourself. Then, in the bounty of the Lord, you will shine with joy.

ANONYMOUS

יְקוֹדֵי אֵשׁ

THE HOSTS OF HEAVEN

יְקוֹדֵי אֵשׁ, כִּידוֹדֵי אֵשׁ, יְצוּרֵי צוּר כְּרוּבִים דָּר.
עֵינֵיהֶם וּמַרְאֵיהֶם כְּעֵין סֹחֶרֶת וּכְעֵין דָּר.
קוֹל יְנוֹפְפוּן, וְיִתְעוֹפְפוּן עֲשׂוֹת חֵפֶץ אֵל נֶאְדָּר.
בְּטוּב שִׁירָה, בְּרֹן זִמְרָה יְשׁוֹרֵרוּן – אִישׁ בְּלִי נֶעְדָּר.
קוֹל יְיָ בַּכֹּחַ, קוֹל יְיָ בֶּהָדָר.

Creatures of flame and sparks, made by the Rock whose throne is on the cherubim: They are the colour of mother-of-pearl and turquoise. They raise their voices, darting to and fro to do the bidding of the majestic Lord. Not one is missing as they sing their choice songs and celebrate with joy: *The voice of the Lord is power; the voice of the Lord is majesty.*

עַצְמָתָם וְקוֹמָתָם זְקוּפָה כְּקוֹמַת תָּמָר.
לֵיל וָיוֹם, לְמוּל אָיֹם, מְטִיבִים שֶׁבַח וּזְמָר.
הֲמֻלּוֹת, מְחִלָּלוֹת, וּמַחֲנוֹת כְּיֶלֶק סָמָר.
מַצָּבָם וּמוֹשָׁבָם – מִשְׁמָר לְעֻמַּת מִשְׁמָר,
כִּי קוֹנָם הִתְקִינָם וּמַעַרְכוֹתָם סִדֵּר.
קוֹל יְיָ בַּכֹּחַ, קוֹל יְיָ בֶּהָדָר.

They are stately and strong as palm trees; night and day, before the Dread One, they sing their songs of praise. There are hosts of them, armies and camps like a dark swarm of locusts. They stand and they sit, guard corresponding to guard, for thus their Maker arranged them and fixed their formations. *The voice of the Lord is power; the voice of the Lord is majesty.*

קוֹל יַרְימוּן וְיַעֲצִימוּן לְאֵל כַּבִּיר מִמְּקוֹמוֹ.
וְעַל מְעוֹנוֹ וְחֶבְיוֹנוֹ זֶה יִשְׁאַל כְּנָאֳמוֹ.
וְהֵם עוֹמְדִים נַחֲרָדִים מִפַּחְדּוֹ וּמֵאֵימוֹ,
יַעֲרִיצוּן וְיַקְדִּישׁוּן כְּבוֹד יְיָ מִמְּקוֹמוֹ.
כִּי סְכּוֹ, מִכֹּה וּמִכֹּה, בְּסוּפָה וָסַעַר לְגָדָר.
קוֹל יְיָ בַּכֹּחַ, קוֹל יְיָ בֶּהָדָר.

They cry aloud, they roar to the Mighty Lord in His heavens. When He speaks, they ask each other: where is His home, His hiding-place? Trembling, overcome by fear and awe, they revere and sanctify the Glory of the Lord in His abode. He is shielded on either side, and set apart, by whirlwind and storm. *The voice of the Lord is power; the voice of the Lord is majesty.*

וְנֶשֶׁר וִיצִיר וְשׁוֹר וּכְפִיר מוּכָנִים בְּמֶרְכַּבְתּוֹ.
וְתַחֲנוֹתָם וּמַחֲנוֹתָם סְבִיבוֹת תְּכוּנוֹת שִׁבְתּוֹ.
לִפְנֵיהֶם – אוֹפַנֵּיהֶם, סוֹבְלֵי כֵּס תִּפְאַרְתּוֹ
לְשָׁרֵת פְּנֵי הַמַּחֲנֶה וְהַסֵּדֶר הַנִּסְדָּר.
קוֹל יְיָ בַּכֹּחַ, קוֹל יְיָ בֶּהָדָר.

[And the faces of] an eagle and a man, an ox and a lion are set in His Chariot-Throne, encamped around His dwelling-place. Next to them are the Ofanim, who carry His Throne of Glory, and minister to the hosts, in the order He prescribed. *The voice of the Lord is power; the voice of the Lord is majesty.*

בִּימִינוֹ, עַל שִׁכְנוֹ, שָׂת מַחֲנֵה מִיכָאֵל.
וְלִשְׂמֹאלוֹ וּמִמּוּלוֹ – גַּבְרִיאֵל וְאוּרִיאֵל.
וּמֵאַחֲרָיו, בְּמִשְׁמָרָיו, הֵכִין מַחֲנֵה רְפָאֵל.
יַקְדִּישׁוּן וִישַׁלְּשׁוּן קְדֻשָּׁה בְּעִתּוֹת הָאֵל.
לְדָר חֶבְיוֹן, לְאֵל עֶלְיוֹן, שְׁמוֹ מְרוֹמָם וּמְהֻדָּר.
קוֹל יְיָ בַּכֹּחַ, קוֹל יְיָ בֶּהָדָר.

To the right of His throne, He put the camp of Michael; to the left and in front – the camps of Gabriel and Uriel; and behind Him He arrayed the camp of Raphael. They acclaim Him 'holy, holy, holy' at the hours He ordained, singing to the One who dwells in secret, to the God supreme, whose name is exalted and glorious. *The voice of the Lord is power; the voice of the Lord is majesty.*

אֱנוֹשׁ רוֹצֶה

THE USES OF REASON

[...] אֱנוֹשׁ רוֹצֶה לְהַכְרִיחַ טְבָעָיו,
לְהַכִּיר בַּאֲשֶׁר אֵין בּוֹ וְיוֹתֵר –
פְּרָעֵהוּ, וְאַל נָא תַּעֲבָר־בּוֹ,
שְׂטֵה מֶנְהוּ וּמֵעָלָיו תְּנַתֵּר:
כְּיוֹצֵא מִמְּסִלָּה הַיְשָׁרָה
וְתֵת דֶּרֶךְ בְּחַלָּמִישׁ יַחְתֵּר.

Shun the man who tries to force his nature, to see in it more than is there. Do not go near him, turn aside, skip out of his way. For he is like one who leaves a highway to burrow through granite cliffs.

הֱיֵה מַשְׂכִּיל זְמַן הַבָּא, לְהַכִּיר
בְּשֶׁעָבַר, וּבִין אֶת אַחֲרִיתוֹ.
וְתַשִּׂיג אֵת אֲשֶׁר לֹא בָא לְיָדְךָ
בְּמַה שֶּׁבָּא לְיָדְךָ נַעֲבָרְתּוֹ:
כְּאִישׁ צָד צִפֳּרִים עָפוֹת בְּצִפּוֹר
אֲשֶׁר צָד מִתְּמוֹל שִׁלְשׁוֹם בְּרִשְׁתּוֹ.

Learn the ways of time to come. Know the past, and you will understand the end. Thus you will grasp what has not yet come your way by what you have already grasped, like a man who lures flying birds with the bird that he caught in his net the day before.

וְהַכֵּר בִּדְבָרִים עַד אֲשֶׁר לֹא
עֲשִׂיתָם, אִם בְּמַעַשׂ אוֹ בְמִבְטָא.
וּמַה בֶּצַע בְּהַכֵּר אַחֲרֵי כִי
כְּבָר נַעְשָׂה, וּמַה תּוֹעִיל חֲרָטָה?
הֲתָשׁוּב עוֹד וְתָשׁוּר לַחֲזוֹת עַיִן
אֱנוֹשׁ אַחַר תְּנֻקַּר בָּעֲלָטָה?

Comprehend your actions before you commit them, whether in deed or in word. What good is comprehension after the fact? What use is regret? Can a man's eye, after it has been gouged out, ever see again in that darkness?

אֲשֶׁר יִרְאֶה וְיַכִּיר בָּאֲחֵרִים,
וְאִם נִמְצָא פְּתִיל שֵׂעָר בְּעֵינָם,
וְלֹא יַכִּיר בְּעַצְמוֹ אֵת אֲשֶׁר בּוֹ,
עֲלֵי מָה נִפְקְחוּ עֵינָיו ? וְאֵינָם !
הֲלֹא טוֹב עָצְמוּ עֵינָיו, וְיָקֵל
בְּעֹל זָרִים, אֲשֶׁר נוֹשֵׂא לְחִנָּם.

The man who can discern a mere mote in the eyes of others, but cannot discern what is in himself – why were his eyes ever opened? He has no eyes. It would be better for his eyes to be shut; then he would no longer have to bear the yoke of strangers' faults, a yoke he bears in vain.

כִּי הִנֵּה כַּחֹמֶר

THE COVENANT

כִּי הִנֵּה כַּחֹמֶר בְּיַד הַיּוֹצֵר,
בִּרְצוֹתוֹ מַרְחִיב וּבִרְצוֹתוֹ מְקַצֵּר,
כֵּן אֲנַחְנוּ בְיָדְךָ, חֶסֶד נוֹצֵר.
לַבְּרִית הַבֵּט וְאַל תֵּפֶן לַיֵּצֶר.

Like clay in the hands of a potter, who expands or contracts it, as he wishes, so are we in Your hands, God of constant love. Oh, look to the covenant,[1] do not heed the Accuser.

כִּי הִנֵּה כָּאֶבֶן בְּיַד הַמְסַתֵּת,
בִּרְצוֹתוֹ בּוֹדֵל וּבִרְצוֹתוֹ מְכַתֵּת,
כֵּן אֲנַחְנוּ בְיָדְךָ, מְחַיֶּה וּמְמוֹתֵת.
לַבְּרִית הַבֵּט וְאַל תֵּפֶן לַיֵּצֶר.

Like a stone in the hands of a mason, who splits it in two or shatters it, as he wishes, so are we in Your hands, God of life and death. Oh, look to the covenant, do not heed the Accuser.

כִּי הִנֵּה כַּגַּרְזֶן בְּיַד הֶחָרָשׁ,
בִּרְצוֹתוֹ דִּבֵּק לָאוּר וּבִרְצוֹתוֹ פֵּרַשׁ,
כֵּן אֲנַחְנוּ בְיָדְךָ, תּוֹמֵךְ עָנִי וָרָשׁ.
לַבְּרִית הַבֵּט וְאַל תֵּפֶן לַיֵּצֶר.

Like an axe in the hands of a blacksmith, who forges it or cools it, as he wishes, so are we in Your hands, champion of the poor and suffering. Oh, look to the covenant, do not heed the Accuser.

כִּי הִנֵּה כַּהֶגֶה בְּיַד הַמַּלָּח,
בִּרְצוֹתוֹ אוֹחֵז וּבִרְצוֹתוֹ שִׁלַּח,
כֵּן אֲנַחְנוּ בְיָדְךָ, אֵל טוֹב וְסַלָּח.
לַבְּרִית הַבֵּט וְאַל תֵּפֶן לַיֵּצֶר.

Like a helm in the hands of a sailor, who holds or releases it, as he wishes, so are we in Your hands, God of kindness and mercy. Oh, look to the covenant, do not heed the Accuser.

1. The 'covenant of the thirteen divine attributes' pronounced in Exodus 34.7.

כִּי הִנֵּה כַּזְּכוּכִית בְּיַד הַמְזַגֵּג,
בִּרְצוֹתוֹ חוֹגֵג וּבִרְצוֹתוֹ מְמוֹגֵג,
כֵּן אֲנַחְנוּ בְּיָדְךָ, מוֹחֵל זָדוֹן וְשֶׁגֶג.
לַבְּרִית הַבֵּט וְאַל תֵּפֶן לַיֵּצֶר.

Like glass in the hands of a blower,
who lines it or melts it, as he wishes, so
are we in Your hands, Pardoner of
malice and error. Oh, look to the
covenant, do not heed the Accuser.

כִּי הִנֵּה כַּיְרִיעָה בְּיַד הָרוֹקֵם,
בִּרְצוֹתוֹ מְיַשֵּׁר וּבִרְצוֹתוֹ מְעַקֵּם,
כֵּן אֲנַחְנוּ בְּיָדְךָ, אֵל קַנּוֹא וְנוֹקֵם.
לַבְּרִית הַבֵּט וְאַל תֵּפֶן לַיֵּצֶר.

Like cloth in the hands of a draper,
who smooths it or twists it, as he wishes,
so are we in Your hands, God of
jealous vengeance. Oh, look to the
covenant, do not heed the Accuser.

כִּי הִנֵּה כַּכֶּסֶף בְּיַד הַצּוֹרֵף,
בִּרְצוֹתוֹ מְסַגְסֵג וּבִרְצוֹתוֹ מְצָרֵף,
כֵּן אֲנַחְנוּ בְּיָדְךָ, מַמְצִיא לְמָזוֹר תֶּרֶף.
לַבְּרִית הַבֵּט וְאַל תֵּפֶן לַיֵּצֶר.

Like silver in the hands of a smith, who
alloys or refines it, as he wishes, so are
we in Your hands, Healer of wounds.
Oh, look to the covenant, do not heed
the Accuser.

קוּמִי, לְכִי

THE CRUSADERS

׳קוּמִי לְכִי,׳ אוֹמְרִים, ׳מֻכַּת לְחָיַיִם,׳
עָרֵל וְטָמֵא וְצָר, כָּל אִישׁ שְׂפָתַיִם:
׳הִנֵּה הֲלֹא נוֹסְעִים אָנוּ אֶל מְקוֹם
אֶרֶץ צְפִירַת צְבִי, מָאוֹר לְעֵינַיִם —
נַעֲלֶה וְנָבֹז שְׁלַל עָרִים בְּצוּרוֹת, וְשָׁם
נַחְלֹק צְבָעִים, לְרֹאשׁ אִישׁ רִקְמָתַיִם.׳

'Come with us, you of the smitten
cheeks,' say the uncircumcised and the
unclean, my smooth-tongued enemies.
'We are on our way to the land of the
lovely diadem, the radiant land. We
shall attack and plunder the spoil of the
fortified cities. There we shall take our
shares, to each man two lengths of dyed
cloth!'

חֶרֶב לְשׁוֹנָם וְחֵץ שָׁחוּט בְּלִבִּי, וְאֵשׁ
תּוּקַד בְּקִרְבִּי וְגַם כֹּשֶׁל לְבִרְכַּיִם,
כִּי אֵיךְ אֲנִי אֶעֱלֶה עִם הַפְּסִילִים וְעִם
עִוְרִים וְחֵרְשִׁים וְלֹא עַיִן וְאָזְנַיִם,

Their tongues, sharp as swords and
deadly arrows, pierce my heart. Fire
rages within me, my knees wobble. For
how could I join forces with the idols,
the blind and the deaf, eyeless and
earless; or with a log of wood, named

אוֹ עִם יְבוּל עֵץ, וְשֵׁם בֶּן הַזְּנוּנִים, וְעִם
נִסְבָּל בְּכָתֵף – וְלוֹ יָרֵךְ וְשׁוֹקַיִם,
אוֹ עִם רְשָׁעִים אֲשֶׁר גּוֹזְלִים וְחוֹמְסִים וְשׁוֹפְ־
כִים דַּם נְקִיִּים וְאוֹרְבִים בֵּין שְׁפַתַּיִם. [...]

after the child of harlotry, that is
hoisted shoulder-high though it has
legs and thighs; or with the wicked
who rob and injure, who shed the
blood of the innocent and lie in wait
among the sheepfolds?

אֶזְכֹּר וְאֶבְכֶּה עֲלֵי מַסַּע דְּגָלִים אֲשֶׁר
חָנוּ סָבִיב מִשְׁכַּן אֵל אַרְבַּעְתַּיִם:
דֶּגֶל יְהוּדָה, אֲשֶׁר חָנָה בְּרֹאשׁ מַחֲנוֹת,
עָלָיו מְרֻקָּם פְּנֵי אַרְיֵה בְּשַׁחְלַיִם.
דֶּגֶל רְאוּבֵן, אֲשֶׁר חָנָה לְתֵימָן, וּבוֹ
טוֹבִים לְרֵיחַ, וְהֵם זֵכֶר לְדוּדָאִים.
דֶּגֶל שְׁלִישִׁי לְיָם חָנָה, עָלָיו דְּמוּת
דָּגָה לְדַיְגוֹ כְּבִרְכַּת אָב לְאֶפְרַיִם.
דֶּגֶל רְבִיעִי לְדָן, אוֹסֵף לְכָל מַחֲנוֹת,
עָלָיו שְׁפִיפוֹן אֲשֶׁר מַפִּיל לַאֲחוֹרַיִם.
מַחֲנֵה שְׁכִינָה בְּתוֹךְ מַחֲנוֹת לְהָאִיר בְּאוֹר
עָנָן לְפָנַי, וְשָׁם כּוֹהֲנִים וְהַלְוִיִּים. [...]

I weep as I recall the troops [of Israel]
on the march, and how they once
encamped to the four sides of the
Lord's Tabernacle. The division of
Judah was the first to march, with a
mighty lion embroidered upon its
standard. Second was the division of
Reuben, stationed to the south, with
fragrant mandrakes[1] upon its standard.
The third division was stationed to the
west, upon its standard the image of
fish, so that Ephraim's tribe should
multiply, as Jacob had promised in his
blessing.[2] The division of Dan was the
last to march, upon its standard a viper,
which makes the rider tumble from his
horse. And in the midst of these troops
was the division of the Shekinah, where
the priests and Levites were stationed,
lighting my way with a pillar of cloud.

אֶקְרַע בְּגָדַי בְּעֵת אֶזְכֹּר כְּתֹנֶת, מְעִיל,
פַּעֲמוֹן וְרִמּוֹן אֲשֶׁר הָיוּ בְּשׁוּלַיִם.
אֵשֵׁב בְּמַחְשָׁךְ מְאֹד בְּזָכְרִי מְנוֹרָה וְעַד
פִּרְחָהּ יְרֵכָהּ, וְגַם הַמֶּלְקָחַיִם.
שֻׁלְחָן בְּזָכְרִי – הֲלֹא אֵשֵׁב וְאֶסְעַד בְּתוֹךְ
עָפָר וָאֵפֶר, לְבֵין תַּנּוּר וְכִירַיִם.
אֶשָּׂא בְּכִי מַר עֲלֵי מִזְבַּח נְחֹשֶׁת אֲשֶׁר
פִּשְׁעִי מְכַפֵּר בְּדַם אַרְבַּע קְרָנַיִם.

I tear my clothes as I recall the [high
priest's] chequered tunic and his robe,
with the bells and pomegranates all
around its hem. I sit in deep darkness
when I recall the lampstand [in the
Tabernacle], with its stem and petals
all of one piece, and its tongs. When I
recall the Table of the Presence, I
crouch in a corner[3] and eat among
ashes and dust. I weep bitterly over the
bronze altar, which once atoned for my
sins with the blood on its four horns.

1. Lit. 'the sweet-smelling in remembrance of the mandrake'; a reference to Genesis 30.14.
2. Genesis 48.16.
3. Lit. 'between the oven and the stove'.

מָה אֶחְשְׁבָה ? שִׁבְרִי עָצוּם וְגָדוֹל כַּיָּם.
מִי יִרְפָּא, בִּלְתְּךָ, רוֹפֵא לְחוֹלַיִים ?
יוֹם אֶשְׁמַע קוֹל מְבַשֵּׂר טוֹב לְפָנַי, וְאָז
אֶקֹּד וְאֶשְׁתַּחֲוֶה אַרְצָה לְאַפַּיִם.
אָגִיל וְאֶשְׂמַח בְּעֵת גּוֹאֵל אֲבִיר יַעֲקֹב
יֹאמַר בְּקוֹל 'נַחֲמוּ נַחֲמוּ' בִּכְפְלַיִם.

What can I hope for? My wound is as huge as the sea. Who but You can ease my pain, O Healer of all suffering? On the day when I hear the voice that bears good tidings, I shall bow down and prostrate myself. I shall rejoice greatly when my ransomer, the Mighty One of Jacob, cries aloud: 'Comfort ye, comfort ye my people!'

אוֹדֶה לָאֵל

SONG AT DAYBREAK

אוֹדֶה לָאֵל, לֵבָב חוֹקֵר,
בְּרָן־יַחַד כּוֹכְבֵי בֹקֶר.

I shall give thanks to the Lord, who tests the heart, when the morning stars sing together.

שִׁימוּ לֵב אֶל הַנְּשָׁמָה,
לֶשֶׁם, שְׁבוֹ וְאַחְלָמָה,
וְאוֹרָהּ כְּאוֹר הַחַמָּה —
שִׁבְעָתַיִם כְּאוֹר הַבֹּקֶר.

Take care of the soul: she is turquoise, agate, and jasper. Her light is like the light of the sun, like the light of seven mornings at once.

מִכִּסֵּא כָבוֹד חֻצָּבָה,
לָגוּר בְּאֶרֶץ עֲרָבָה,
לְהַצִּילָהּ מִלֶּהָבָה,
וּלְהָאִירָהּ לִפְנוֹת בֹּקֶר.

She was hewn from the Throne of Glory, sent to live in a desert land, to deliver it from fire, to shine upon it in the early morning.

עוּרוּ נָא, כִּי בְּכָל לַיְלָה
נִשְׁמַתְכֶם עוֹלָה לְמַעְלָה,
לָתֵת דִּין וְחֶשְׁבּוֹן מִפְּעָלָהּ
לְיוֹצֵר עֶרֶב וָבֹקֶר.

Rouse yourselves, for every night your soul goes to heaven to account for its actions before the Maker of evening and morning.

יִמְצָאֶהָ מְקֻשֶּׁטֶת
בְּטַלִּית וְטוֹטֶפֶת,
כְּמוֹ כַּלָּה מְקֻשֶּׁטֶת –
תָּמִיד בַּבֹּקֶר בַּבֹּקֶר.

May He find her wrapped in prayer-shawl and frontlets, always dressed like a bride, morning after morning.

הַנֶּאֱמָן בְּפִקְדוֹנוֹ
יַחֲזִירֶנָּה לוֹ כִּרְצוֹנוֹ:
אִישׁ לֹא נָגַע בַּעֲווֹנוֹ –
וַיְהִי עֶרֶב וַיְהִי בֹקֶר.

He who keeps all souls in trust will return her to you if He wishes. No man died through His error – and there was evening, and there was morning.

וְהַחֲיוּ הָעֲנִיָּה,
יְחִידָה, תַּמָּה וּנְקִיָּה.
וַאֲשֶׁר נַפְשׁוֹ לֹא חִיָּה –
אֵיךְ יִזְכֶּה לְאוֹר הַבֹּקֶר?

Gladden the afflicted one, the only one, perfect and pure. If a man does not keep his soul alive, how will he be worthy of the light of morning?

אָנָּא, בְּכֹחַ

INVOCATION

אָנָּא, בְּכֹחַ גְּדֻלַּת יְמִינְךָ תַּתִּיר צְרוּרָה.
קַבֵּל רִנַּת עַמְּךָ, שַׂגְּבֵנוּ, טַהֲרֵנוּ, נוֹרָא.
נָא, גִּבּוֹר, דּוֹרְשֵׁי יִחוּדְךָ כְּבָבַת שָׁמְרֵם.
בָּרְכֵם, טַהֲרֵם, רַחֲמֵם, צִדְקָתְךָ תָּמִיד גָּמְלֵם.
חֲסִין קָדוֹשׁ, בְּרֹב טוּבְךָ נַהֵל עֲדָתֶךָ.
יָחִיד גֵּאֶה, לְעַמְּךָ פְּנֵה, זוֹכְרֵי קְדֻשָּׁתֶךָ.
שַׁוְעָתֵנוּ קַבֵּל וּשְׁמַע צַעֲקָתֵנוּ, יוֹדֵעַ תַּעֲלוּמוֹת.

We pray You: with the strength of Your great right hand, set the captive free. Accept Your people's prayer, lift us up, make us pure, O Dread God! God of Might, guard as the apple of Your eye those who seek Your oneness. Bless them, purify them, pity them, reward them always with Your charity. O mighty and Holy One, with Your endless grace guide Your flock. Unique and Exalted One, turn to Your people, who remember Your holiness. Accept our plea, hear our cry, You who know the secrets of the heart!

אֲדַבְּרָה בְּצַר רוּחִי

THE MARTYRS OF MAINZ

אֲדַבְּרָה בְּצַר רוּחִי בִּפְנֵי מְעוּט קְהָלִי,
אֲקוֹנֵן וְאֶתְאַבֵּל כִּי שַׁדַּי הֵמַר לִי.
הַחֲרִישׁוּ, וְהָבִינוּ מִלּוּלִי וּפִלּוּלִי —
מִי יִתֶּן־לִי שׁוֹמֵעַ לִי! [...]

I shall speak out in the grief of my spirit before my small congregation. I shall wail and lament, for the Almighty has dealt bitterly with me. Be silent, hear my words and my prayer. If only He would hear me!

טוֹעִים בַּשַּׁעַר נֶאֶסְפוּ יַחַד
לְהַכְרִית שֵׁם שְׁאֵרִית הַמְיֻחָד.
יְלָדִים רַכִּים כְּנֶגְדּוֹ עָנוּ קוֹל אֶחָד;
'שְׁמַע יִשְׂרָאֵל יְיָ אֱלֹהֵינוּ יְיָ אֶחָד'.

The Crusaders[1] massed at the gateway to blot out the name of His remnants. Small children cried out to Him with one voice: 'Hear, O Israel, the Lord is our God, the Lord is One!'

יָצְאוּ בַּחוּרִים אִישׁ מֵחֲדָרָיו
לְקַדֵּשׁ הַשֵּׁם הַגָּדוֹל, כִּי הַיּוֹם מְנַסֶּה אֶת בְּחִירָיו.
קִבְּלוּ דִּין מִשָּׁמַיִם בִּגְזֵרַת אֲמָרָיו.
קָפַץ קָלוֹנִימוֹס וְכֻלָּם אַחֲרָיו.

Young men left [the shelter of] their rooms to sanctify the Great Name, for on that day He was putting His chosen ones to the test. He had decreed this in heaven, and they submitted. Kalonymus leaped [into battle] and all the others followed.

נִגְזְרָה גְּזֵרָה בִּשְׁמֵי שְׁחַק,
וְרָפְתָה יָדָם וְגָבַר הַדֹּחַק,
'הִנְנִי בָרֹאשׁ וְלֹא אֶרְחַק!' —
פָּשַׁט צַוָּארוֹ וְנֶהֱרַג תְּחִלָּה רַבִּי יִצְחָק.

But the decree had been passed in the heaven of heavens: their hands hung limp, they were crushed together. 'Let me take the lead, I shall not retreat!' Rabbi Isaac bared his neck and was the first to be slaughtered.

נִתְקַבְּצוּ מִסָּבִיב מִכָּל הֶעָרִים
בַּחֲרָבוֹת וּבְחִצִּים לְהִלָּחֵם בַּחֲדָרִים,
וְלִמְאֹד תָּקְפָה יַד אַכְזָרִים,
וַחֲסִידִים מִבִּפְנִים בְּצוֹם וּבְכִי וּבְתַמְרוּרִים.

They gathered from all the nearby towns, armed with swords and arrows, to attack the rooms. The cruel ones charged in force while, within, the pious ones fasted and wept bitterly.

1. Lit. 'the [misguided] wanderers' or 'vagabonds'.

צַעֲקַת יְלָדִים אֵיךְ גְּדֹלָה!
רוֹאִים אֲחֵיהֶם נִשְׁחָטִים בְּחַלְחָלָה,
הָאֵם קוֹשֶׁרֶת בְּנָהּ פֶּן בְּפִרְכּוּס יְחַלְּלָהּ,
וְהָאָב מְבָרֵךְ עַל הַשְּׁחִיטָה לְכַלְּלָהּ.

Oh, how the children cried aloud! Trembling, they see their brothers slaughtered; the mother binding her son, lest he profane the sacrifice by shuddering;[1] the father making the ritual blessing to sanctify the slaughter.

נָשִׁים רַחֲמָנִיּוֹת בְּנֵיהֶן חוֹנְקוֹת,
בְּתוּלוֹת טְהוֹרוֹת בְּמֶרֶד זוֹעֲקוֹת,
כַּלָּה מִן חֲתָנָהּ נִפְטָרוֹת וְנוֹשְׁקוֹת,
וְאֵצֶל הַשְּׁחִיטָה דּוֹבְקוֹת וְדוֹחֲקוֹת. [...]

Compassionate women strangle their own children; pure virgins shriek bitterly; brides kiss their bridegrooms farewell – and all rush eagerly to be slaughtered.

חֲסִין יָהּ, שׁוֹכֵן מְעָלִים!
מִקֶּדֶם עַל עֲקֵדָה אַחַת צָעֲקוּ לְפָנֶיךָ אֶרְאֶלִּים,
וְעַתָּה כַּמָּה נֶעֱקָדִים וְנִכְלָלִים –
וּמַדּוּעַ לֹא הִרְעִישׁוּ עַל בְּנֵי עוֹלָלִים?

Almighty Lord, dwelling on high, in days of old the angels cried out to You to put a halt to one sacrifice.[2] And now, so many are bound and slaughtered – why do they not clamour over my infants?

וְאָנוּ אֵין לְהַרְהֵר עַל הָרְדוּמִים,
כִּי הֵם לְחַיֵּי עַד עֲרוּכִים וּמְחֻתָּמִים;
אֲבָל עָלֵינוּ, כִּי לִמְאֹד חֻיַּבְנוּ אֲשֵׁמִים
אֲשֶׁר עָבַרְנוּ מִצְווֹת תְּמִימִים.

But we must not question the fate of the dead, for they have been destined for eternal life. We must question ourselves, for we have been found very guilty; we have transgressed the precepts of right.

חַי עוֹלָמִים, בְּצֵל כְּנָפֶיךָ אָנוּ בוֹרְחִים,
כִּי נִשְׁאַרְנוּ עֲגוּנִים וַאֲנוּחִים
מִבְּלִי לְהִשְׁתַּתֵּף לְתָלוּי שׁוֹחֲחִים –
פֶּגֶר מוּבָס, יֵבוֹשׁוּ כֹּל אֵלָיו בּוֹטְחִים!

O everlasting God, we seek refuge in the shadow of Your wings. We have been abandoned, alone and suffering, because we refused to bow our heads before the crucified one, a corpse trampled underfoot. Let all who put their trust in him be put to shame!

לְיַחוּדְךָ, נוֹרָא וּמְהֻלָּל, שׁוֹכֵן מְרוֹמִים,
נַעַבְדְךָ בְּיִרְאָה, לֵילוֹת וְיָמִים.
וּנְקֹם נִקְמָתֵנוּ, דּוֹרֵשׁ דָּמִים,
רָם עַל רָמִים, יוֹשֵׁב עַל כִּסֵּא רַחֲמִים!

To unify Your Name – O fearful God, dwelling in heaven, worthy of all praise – we worship You in dread, night and day. Now avenge us, O Avenger of the blood, Highest of the high, who sit upon the throne of compassion!

1. According to the laws of ritual slaughter, a blemish disqualifies the offering.
2. The binding of Isaac.

דָּוִד בַּר־מְשֻׁלָּם

David bar Meshullam of Speyer

אֱלֹהִים, אַל דֳּמִי

THE SACRIFICES

אֱלֹהִים, אַל דֳּמִי לְדָמִי!
אַל תֶּחֱרַשׁ וְאַל תִּשְׁקֹט לְמִתְקוֹמְמִי!
בַּקְּשֵׁהוּ, דָּרְשֵׁהוּ מִיַּד מַחֲרִימִי,
בַּל תְּכַסֶּה אֶרֶץ בְּכָל מְקוֹמִי.

O God, do not let my blood rest in peace! Do not be silent. Give my enemy no respite. Avenge my blood, require it at the hand of my destroyer. Let not the earth cover it, wherever it is shed.

גֹּל יִגָּלֶה וּלְפָנֶיךָ יִשָּׁפֵךְ וְיִזָּלֵף,
גַּם בְּפַרְפִּירְךָ מְלֵא גְוִיּוֹת יִגָּלֵף.
דּוֹן יָדוֹן שׁוֹפְךָ, חֵלֶף בְּחֵלֶף,
דְּמֵי עֲנָיֶיךָ הַנִּשְׁפָּכִים כְּשִׁגְרֵי אָלֶף. [...]

Let it be revealed, pouring forth before Your eyes. Let the blood of all the corpses be inscribed in Your royal purple. Punish them, pay them back in kind, for shedding the blood of Your helpless people as though they were cattle.

טַף וְנָשִׁים הִשְׁלִימוּ יַחַד לְעֵקֶד,
טְלָאִים הַמְבֻקָּרִים בְּלִשְׁכַּת בֵּית הַמּוֹקֵד.
יָחִיד וְנִשָּׂא, עָלֶיךָ נֶהֱרַג וְנִשָּׁקֵד,
יַחוּם הַזִּמָּה אֵלָיו רֹאשׁ מִלְּקַד.

Tender children and women gave themselves up to the binding, like choice lambs in the Chamber of the Hearth.[1] O Only One, Lofty One, we are pierced and murdered for Your sake, for refusing to bow our heads before the child of wantonness.

כְּבָשִׂים בְּנֵי שָׁנָה לְעוֹלָה תְּמִימִים
כְּבְּשׁוּ עוֹלוֹת כְּזִבְחֵי אֱמוּרֵי שְׁלָמִים.
לְאִמּוֹתָם אוֹמְרִים: 'לֹא תִכְמְרוּ רַחֲמִים,
לְקָרְבַּן אִשֶּׁה לַיְיָ נִתְבַּקַּשְׁנוּ מִמְּרוֹמִים.

Yearling lambs without blemish were slaughtered like whole offerings, trapped and burnt like the sacrificial portions of shared offerings.[2] They said to their mothers: 'Do not be moved by pity. Heaven has summoned us to be an offering by fire to the Lord.'

1. One of the Chambers of the Temple.
2. Leviticus 4.8-10; the ritual terms are derived from the book of Leviticus and from the Mishnah *Yoma*.

מְפַרְפְּרִים הַיְלָדִים וְזֶה עַל זֶה מְפַרְכְּסִים.
מְמַהֲרִים שְׁחֹט אֲחֵרִים וּבִדְמֵיהֶם מִתְבּוֹסְסִים.
נָתוּן עַל רֹבֶד הֵיכָלְךָ וְאַף לִמְמָרְסִים,
נֶגֶד עֵינֶיךָ לָעַד יְהוּ תוֹסְסִים. [...]

The young struggle in agony, heaped on top of one another. [The old], writhing in their own blood, hasten to sacrifice their fellows.[1] Let this blood be stirred on the terrace of Your Sanctuary.[2] Let it boil before Your eyes forever, [like the blood of Zechariah].

דְּמָעוֹת מִפֹּה וּמִפֹּה נוֹבְעִים וּמְקַלְּחִים,
וְשׁוֹחֲטִים וְנִשְׁחָטִים אֵלּוּ עַל אֵלּוּ גּוֹנְחִים,
דְּמֵי אָבוֹת וּבָנִים נוֹגְעִים וְטוֹפְחִים,
בִּרְכַּת הַזֶּבַח 'שְׁמַע יִשְׂרָאֵל' צוֹרְחִים.

The tears well up and stream from every side. Those who slaughter and those who are slaughtered all groan upon one another. The blood of fathers laps against the blood of sons, as they howl their benediction over slaughter: 'Hear, O Israel!'

יִרְאֶה יֵרָאֶה פְּעֻלַּת בָּנוֹת בּוֹטְחוֹת,
בְּחֹם הַיּוֹם עֲרֻמּוֹת לַשֶּׁמֶשׁ נִשְׁטָחוֹת.
יָפָה בַּנָּשִׁים מְבֻקָּעֵי כָרֵס וּמְפֻלָּחוֹת,
מִבֵּין רַגְלֶיהָ שִׁלְיָה וָלָד מַפְרִיחוֹת.

Let this sight come before You: young women, who put their trust in You, slaughtered naked in broad daylight; the fairest of women – their wombs slashed open and the afterbirth forced out from between their legs.

שְׁמוּעַ הֲנִשְׁמַע אוֹ אִם נִרְאָה ?
לְהַאֲמִין מִי יַאֲמִין גְּדוֹלָה פְּלִיאָה :
מוֹלִיכִין בְּנֵיהֶם לַשֶּׁבַח כְּלַחֻפָּה נָאָה.
הַעַל אֵלֶּה תִתְאַפַּק, רָם גָּאֹה גָּאָה ?

[Has the like of this] ever been seen or heard? Could anyone believe such a stupefying sight? They lead their children to the slaughter as if to a beautiful bridal canopy. After this, O Exalted and Triumphant Lord, will You hold back?

קֶדֶם שֶׁעֲנָנוּ וַתַּעֲמֹד עֲקֵדַת הַר־מֹר,
טָמוּן לְיֶשַׁע בְּכָל דּוֹר וָדוֹר לִשְׁמֹר.
נִתּוֹסְפוּ אֵלֶּה וְכָאֵלֶּה עַד בִּלְתִּי לֵאמֹר.
חַי, זְכוּתָךְ קִנָּם תִּשְׁמָר־לָנוּ וְצָרוֹתֵינוּ תִּגְמֹר.

Once, long ago, we could rely upon the merit of Abraham's sacrifice at Mount Moriah, that it would safeguard us and bring salvation age after age. But now one sacrifice follows another, they can no longer be counted. O Living God, may the merit of their righteousness protect us and call a halt to our miseries!

1. To prevent their being seized by the enemy and forcibly converted.
2. The blood of sacrifices was stirred up so that it should not congeal (*Yoma* 4.6).

אֶפְרַיִם מֵרֵגֶנְשְׁבּוּרק

Ephraim of Regensburg

רָמֵה הַגָּלוּת

TO GOD IN EXILE

[...] רָמֵה הַגָּלוּת בְּתַעֲלוּמָה,
הָאִירָה עֵינֵי אֲיֻמָּה,
כִּי אֲפֵלוֹת הֵמָּה.

Lord, thrust Exile into oblivion,
brighten the eyes of the terrible one,[1]
for they are full of darkness.

יֶשְׁעֲךָ מֵעַתָּה וָהָלְאָה,
לְנַחֲלָתְךָ נִלְאָה וְנִכְאָה,
כַּאֲשֶׁר אָהַבְתִּי, הָבִיאָה.

Your salvation is my heart's desire.
Oh, bring it now to Your weary and
languishing people.

אֵלִי, אֵלִי, לָמָּה
אַנְחָתִי מִמְּךָ נֶעֱלָמָה,
וַאֲנִי כְּיוֹנָה נֶאֱלָמָה ?

My God, my God, why are my sighs
hidden from You? I am nothing but a
helpless dove.

מִיַּד שְׁאוֹל, מִמָּוֶת –
גְּאָלָה נַפְשִׁי, מִשֶּׁבֶת
אֶרֶץ חֹשֶׁךְ וְצַלְמָוֶת.

Ransom my soul from Sheol, from
death. Let me not dwell in a land of
gloom and deep darkness.

חֵרוּת לְבַקֵּשׁ יָאַשְׁתִּי,
לְהַחֲיוֹת נַפְשִׁי בִּקַּשְׁתִּי,
אֶת יְיָ דָּרַשְׁתִּי.

I have despaired of finding freedom;
my only wish is to keep my soul alive.
I seek the Lord's help.

אֵלִי, אֵלִי, לָמָּה
אַנְחָתִי מִמְּךָ נֶעֱלָמָה,
וַאֲנִי כְּיוֹנָה נֶאֱלָמָה ?

My God, my God, why are my sighs
hidden from You? I am nothing but a
helpless dove.

1. A conventional epithet for Zion based on Song of Songs 6.4: 'terrible as an army with banners'.

זַמּוֹתִי: דְּרוֹר מָה אֶשְׁאַל,
וְאַתָּה עִמִּי נִשְׁאָל.
אִם תִּגְאַל – גְּאָל.

I thought: what right have I to ask for liberty when You, too, are in exile with me? But if You so desire, redeem me.

קוֹל צוֹפַי קְרָאַנִי.
קַוִּי, נַפְשִׁי – הֶלְאָנִי.
אֱמֹר לְנַפְשִׁי: ׳יְשׁוּעָתֵךְ אָנִי׳.

The voice of my watchman calls out to me. Do not lose hope, my soul, though He has wearied you. And You, O Lord, say to my soul: 'I am your salvation.'

אֵלִי, אֵלִי, לָמָּה
אַנְחָתִי מִמְּךָ נֶעְלָמָה,
וַאֲנִי כְּיוֹנָה נֶאֱלָמָה?

My God, my God, why are my sighs hidden from You? I am nothing but a helpless dove.

אֱלֹהַי בְּךָ אֵחָבֵק

BE NOT FAR FROM ME

אֱלֹהַי, בְּךָ אֵחָבֵק
כְּטוֹבֵעַ לְנָמֵל יֵאָבֵק.
אוֹמֵר טוֹב לְדָבֵק.
בְּשִׁמְךָ תָּמִיד חֻתַּלְתִּי,
אַף כִּי עָלֶיךָ נִקְטַלְתִּי,
נַפְתּוּלֵי אֱלֹהִים נִפְתַּלְתִּי.
אַל תִּרְחַק מִמֶּנִּי. [...]

My God, I cling to You, like a drowning man struggling to reach land. How good to be joined to You! I have always wrapped myself in Your Name, even though because of You I have been slaughtered. I have fought God's fight. *Be not far from me!*

הִרְחַקְתִּי נְדֹד מִמְּךָ,
וְלִבִּי קָרוֹב לְשִׁמְךָ.
וּרְאֵה כִּי עַמְּךָ
וְצֹאן יָדְךָ נְמוּגָה
וְאָחוֹר לֹא נְסוּגָה.
רְעֵה אֶת צֹאן הַהֲרֵגָה.
אַל תִּרְחַק מִמֶּנִּי.

I have wandered far from You, but my heart has always been near to Your Name. Look: Your people, Your sheep, were carried away and still they did not turn their backs on You. Oh, tend the doomed flock. *Be not far from me!*

זְכֹר הֶרֶג רַב
עָלֶיךָ נַפְשִׁי נִקְרַב
וְנָפַל מִמֶּנִּי רָב.
חֲסִידֶיךָ וּמְיַחֲדֶיךָ מִקֶּרֶב,
בֹּקֶר וְצָהֳרַיִם וָעֶרֶב,
עַם שְׂרִידֵי חָרֶב.
אַל תִּרְחַק מִמֶּנִּי.

Remember the massacre I suffered for Your sake. So many of us perished. Yet morning and evening and at noon Your loyal servants acclaim Your Oneness with all their hearts. This is the people that survived the sword. *Be not far from me!*

טָחֵי תָפֵל וּמַדּוּחִים
אֱלֵי גִיל הַשְּׂמֵחִים
וּבְמִשְׁכְּנוֹת מִבְטַחִים.
יְרֵאֶיךָ נִסְקָלִים וְנֶחֱנָקִים,
וְאֵלּוּ הֵן הַלּוֹקִים —
בַּייָ הַדְּבֵקִים.
אַל תִּרְחַק מִמֶּנִּי.

The men of deceit[1] and sham rejoice in houses full of ease while those who revere You are stoned and strangled. Only those who hold fast to the Lord are scourged. *Be not far from me!*

כּוֹרֵעַ לְתָלוּי בְּמַגּוֹד
יְעָצַנִי בְּךָ לִבְגֹּד,
לְבוּל עֵץ יִסְגֹּד.
לֹא אַצְתִּי לִרְעוֹת אַחֲרָיו.
נַמְתִּי: 'יֵבוֹשׁוּ כָּל חֲבֵרָיו.'
רַע יֵרוֹעַ כִּי עָרַב.
אַל תִּרְחַק מִמֶּנִּי.

They urge me to betray You, those who fall down before an image hanging on a rack, who worship a block of wood. But I did not join its ranks. I said: 'All its votaries will be put to shame.' They pledged themselves to it and they will know no peace. *Be not far from me!*

מֵחֲמַת עָפָר זוֹחֵל
יְרַחֵי־שָׁוְא אֲנִי נוֹחֵל.
וּמַה כֹּחִי כִּי אֲיַחֵל?
נַפְשִׁי בְּךָ דָבְקָה
כְּיוֹנֵק נִכְנָס לְרִבְקָה:

The venom of creeping things fills my mouth with despair. Do I have the strength to wait? My soul clings to You like a calf yoked to a team.[2]

1. Lit. 'those who slap on plaster', or 'those who daub with whitewash'.
2. A Talmudic expression: the calf is taken into the threshing team so that it may suck its mother's milk.

הַשְׂבַּע נֶפֶשׁ שׁוֹקֵקָה.
אַל תִּרְחַק מִמֶּנִּי. [...]

Oh, satisfy the thirsty. *Be not far from me!*

אֵלִי גוֹאֲלִי, דָּמַי דוֹרֵשׁ,
לֹא יַעֲזוֹב לָהֶם שֹׁרֶשׁ,
כָּלָה גָּרֵשׁ יְגָרֵשׁ.
פְּנֵה חַיַּת קָנֶה
מַלְכוּתָהּ תְּקֵל מְנֵא מְנֵא,
תּוֹצִיא אוֹתָהּ אֶל מִחוּץ לַמַּחֲנֶה.
אַל תִּרְחַק מִמֶּנִּי.

My God is my redeemer, the avenger of my blood. He will cut away their roots, He will drive them out, one and all. Tell the wild beast of the reeds[1] that its kingdom has been weighed in the balance and found wanting, that its days are numbered.[2] Banish it from the company of man. *Be not far from me!*

רוֹמָה, יַחַד תַּצִּיתֶנָּה,
לְיַרְכְּתֵי בוֹר תִּשְׁפְּתֶנָּה,
עַוָּה עַוָּה תְּשִׁיתֶנָּה,
יַעַן מְשָׁכַתְנִי בְעַבְדוּת,
נִשְׁפַּטְתִּי בְּכָל מִינֵי מַרְדּוּת.
הֲקָצוֹר קָצְרָה יָדְךָ מִפְּדוּת?
אַל תִּרְחַק מִמֶּנִּי. [...]

Lift up Your hand, set the beast on fire, hurl it into the depths of the abyss, destroy it. It has lured me into servitude, and thus subjected me to every kind of punishment. Is Your arm too short to redeem? *Be not far from me!*

אֶפְרַיִם מִבּוֹנָא

Ephraim of Bonn

אֶת אֲבוֹתַי אֲנִי מַזְכִּיר

THE SLAUGHTER OF ISAAC AND HIS REVIVAL

אֶת אֲבוֹתַי אֲנִי מַזְכִּיר
הַיּוֹם לְפָנֶיךָ, בּוֹחֵן וּמַכִּיר.
תָּחֹן זְכוּת אָבוֹת לְבָנִים,
אָב זָקֵן וְיֶלֶד זְקֻנִים.

Lord, who test and know [man's heart], today I shall invoke before You the memory of my Fathers. Oh, favour the sons for the sake of the Fathers – for the sake of *the aged father* [Abraham] *and the child of his old age*.

1. An expression from Psalms (68.31) which was interpreted by the Midrash as a reference to the Christian nations.

2. Lit. '*Tekel, mene, mene*'; Daniel 5.25.

אָמַרְתָּ לִידִידְךָ לְהַעֲלוֹת יְחִידוֹ
לְאַחַד הֶהָרִים, לְמַלֵּא יָדוֹ:
'תַּעֲלֶה נֶפֶשׁ אָהַבְתָּ לְקָרְבָּנִי,
אוֹתָהּ קַח לִי כִּי הִיא יָשְׁרָה בְעֵינָי!'

You told Your beloved to sacrifice his favoured one on one of the mountains, where You would consecrate him [as a priest]: 'Offer as a sacrifice to Me the soul of him you love; *get her* [the soul] *for Me, because she pleases Me.*'

בִּקַּשְׁתָּ מֵאִתּוֹ בְּנִסָּיוֹן לַעֲמֹד,
כְּמֶלֶךְ מִגִּבּוֹר לְנַצֵּחַ יִתְמֹד:
'שֶׁבָּזֹאת תִּבָּחֵן וְתִמָּצֵא נִצְחָן.'
יְיָ צַדִּיק יִבְחָן.

You called upon him to endure the trial, as a king [at war] appeals to his seasoned warrior: 'This will put you to the test and prove that you always triumph.' *The Lord tests the righteous.*

גָּאָה בְדָמוֹ וְנָהַק פֶּרֶא:
'מָצִיתִי דָּמִי לִשְׁלוֹשׁ־עֶשְׂרֵה!'
רָחַשׁ אָהוּב: 'אִם לְאֵל אֶלָּקַח,
גַּם אֶת הַכֹּל יִקָּח.'

[Ishmael], the wild ass, boasted of his blood and brayed: 'My blood was drained when I was thirteen!'[1] The beloved [Isaac] whispered: 'If God wishes to take me, *let Him take all of me.*'

דָּץ זָרִיז לְהַקְדִּים לַמִּצְוָה,
לַחֲבֹשׁ חֲמוֹרוֹ בְּעַצְמוֹ אִוָּה.
קֶשֶׁר אַהֲבָה בִּטְּלָה גְדֻלָּה.
הֵן יְיָ יָדַעְתָּ כֻלָּהּ.

The zealous [father] hurried to fulfil the commandment. [He rose at dawn] to saddle his ass with his very own hands; for the love of God, he put aside his dignity. *O Lord, You know all this!*

הַשָּׂטָן בְּתוֹכָם בָּא לְהִתְיַצְּבָה,
'הֲנִסָּה דָבָר אֵלֶיךָ?' לְנוֹבְבָה.
צָרַח תָּם: 'בְּתֻמִּי אֵלֵךְ
כִּי כֵן יִסַּד הַמֶּלֶךְ.'

Then Satan came and stationed himself among them, saying: 'May one venture a word with you?' But the blameless one cried out: 'I shall walk on without reproach, *for this is what the King ordained.*'

וּבַיּוֹם הַשְּׁלִישִׁי לְצוֹפִים הִגִּיעוּ,
אֲזַי אֶל עוֹשֵׂיהֶם שָׁעוּ:
פְּאֵר עַמּוּד הֶעָנָן מַזְהִר
כְּאֵשׁ אוֹכֶלֶת בְּרֹאשׁ הָהָר.

On the third day they reached Mount Scopus, and there they saw the presence of their Maker: the pillar of cloud shone gloriously *like a devouring fire, on the mountain-top.*

1. 'Ishmael said to Isaac: "I am more pious than you. You were only eight days old when you were circumcised, but I was thirteen years old [and felt all the pain]"' (*T.B. Sanhedrin* 89b).

זָרִיז הֵשִׂים עַל בְּנוֹ
עֲצֵי הָעוֹלָה, עֲשׂוֹת קָרְבָּנוֹ.
עָנָה הַבֵּן וּפָץ לִשְׁאֵלָה:
'הִנֵּה הָאֵשׁ וְהָעֵצִים וְאַיֵּה הַשֶּׂה לְעוֹלָה?'

The zealous one laid the firewood for the sacrifice on his son's shoulder. Then the son opened his mouth and said: '*Here are the fire and the wood, but where is the sheep for the burnt offering?*'

חָסִיד דִּבֶּר נְכוֹנָה בְּמִלּוּלוֹ:
'יוֹדֵעַ יְיָ אֶת אֲשֶׁר לוֹ.
סָקַר הַשֶּׂה, בְּנִי, בְּעָלָיו,
וְאֶת הַקָּדוֹשׁ וְהִקְרִיב אֵלָיו.'

The loyal one answered and he spoke the truth: 'The Lord will make known who is to be His. The Master will see to the sheep, my son. *He will draw the holy one to Himself.*'

טָהוֹר הֶרְאָהוּ מִזְבַּח הָרִאשׁוֹנִים:
'זָכָר תָּמִים תַּקְרִיב לִרְצוֹנִים!'
נָמָה יוֹנַת אֵלֶם: 'תַּאַסְרֵנִי לְזֶבַח
בַּעֲבֹתִים עַד קַרְנוֹת הַמִּזְבֵּחַ.

Then the Pure One showed him the altar of the ancients:[1] 'Here offer a male without blemish, of your own free will.' The soft-spoken dove whispered: 'Bind me for the sacrifice *with cords to the horns of the altar*.

יָדַי וְרַגְלַי לִי תֶּאֱסֹר,
פֶּן אֲחַלֵּל הַזֶּבַח וְאֶחְסַר.
מִדַּאֲגַת בְּעוּת חַסְתִּי לִכְבוֹדְךָ,
אָמַרְתִּי כַּבֵּד אֲכַבֶּדְךָ.'

'Bind my hands and my feet lest I render myself unfit [by trembling] and profane the sacrifice. I fear that out of panic I may violate your honour,[2] and *I desire to honour you greatly.*'

כִּשְׁמֹעַ קָשׁוּר בְּנַפְשׁוֹ כְּצָמִיד,
עֲקָדוֹ יָד וָרֶגֶל כְּתָמִיד.
לַעֲרֹךְ אֵשׁ וְעֵצִים הֶעֱלָה,
וַיַּעַל עָלָיו אֶת הָעוֹלָה.

When he heard this, [Abraham], whose soul was linked to the boy's like a bracelet, bound him hand and foot as if he were a whole offering. He put fire on the altar, wood on the fire,[3] *and on it offered the burnt offering.*

אֲזַי אָב וּבֵן חֲבָקוּ,
נִפְגָּשׁוּ, אֱמֶת וְשָׁלוֹם נָשָׁקוּ.
'פִּיךָ תִּפְתַּח, אָבִי, בְּשֶׁבַח,
כִּי הוּא יְבָרֵךְ הַזֶּבַח.

Then the father and the son embraced; Faithfulness and Peace met and kissed each other. 'My father, fill your mouth with praise, *for He will bless the offering.*

1. The altar on which Adam, Cain, Abel, and Noah had made their offerings.
2. He might kick Abraham, thus transgressing the commandment to honour one's father.
3. In keeping with the precise ritual of Leviticus 1.7.

רְצוֹנִי פְּתֹחַ פִּי לְזַמֵּן:
בָּרוּךְ יְיָ לְעוֹלָם אָמֵן.
יֵאָסֵף אֶפְרִי וְיוּבָא הָעִירָה,
הָאֹהֱלָה אֶל שָׂרָה.׳

'And I too wish to open my mouth in benediction: "Blessed be the Lord forever. Amen." Let my ashes be gathered and taken to the village *to Sarah in her tent*.'

מִהַר וְנָתַן עָלָיו אַרְכֻּבּוֹתָיו,
וּכְגִבּוֹר אִמֵּץ שְׁתֵּי זְרוֹעוֹתָיו.
בְּיָדָיו אֱמוּנָה שְׁחָטוֹ בְּתֹכֶן
וּטְבֹחַ טֶבַח וְהָכֵן.

Quickly he pinned him down with his knees, straining his arms greatly. Then he slaughtered him, with steady hands, as prescribed by law. *The slaughter had been duly prepared.*

רַד טַל תְּחִי עָלָיו וְנִתְחַיָּה.
תְּפָשׂוֹ לְשָׁחְטוֹ פַּעַם שְׁנִיָּה.
יָעִיד הַמִּקְרָא וְלַדָּבָר רַגְלַיִם:
׳וַיִּקְרָא יְיָ אֶל אַבְרָהָם שֵׁנִית מִן הַשָּׁמַיִם.׳

Now the dew of Resurrection fell down upon him, and he revived. The father seized him, to slaughter him once more. Scripture itself bears witness that this was so: '*And the Lord called from heaven a second time to Abraham.*'

עָנוּ מַלְאֲכֵי הַשָּׁרֵת בִּמְהוּמָה:
׳שְׁתֵּי שְׁחִיטוֹת הֲיֶשְׁנָן בַּבְּהֵמָה?׳
קוֹל בְּרָמָה הִשְׁמִיעוּ בִּנְחִיצָה,
הֵן אֶרְאֶלָּם צָעֲקוּ חֻצָה.

The ministering angels cried out in terror: 'Even an animal is never slaughtered twice!' They filled the heavens with their urgent cries. *The angelic order shrieked above the earth.*

׳בְּבַקָּשָׁה מִלְּפָנֶיךָ, עָלָיו רַחֵם,
בְּבֵית אָבִיו אָכַלְנוּ לֶחֶם!׳
חֲתָפוּ נַחַל דִּמְעוֹת גְּבוֹהִים
בְּעֵדֶן גַּן אֱלֹהִים.

'We beg of You, have pity on him. We once broke bread in his father's house.' At once a river of heavenly tears swept Isaac *into Eden, the garden of God.*

זַךְ חָשַׁב: הַיֶּלֶד אֵינֶנּוּ בְּחוֹבָה,
וַאֲנִי – אָנָה אֲנִי בָא?
קָשַׁב: ׳בִּנְךָ נִרְצָה לְקָרְבָּנִי,
בִּי נִשְׁבַּעְתִּי נְאֻם יְיָ.׳

Pure-hearted [Abraham] thought: The child is guiltless, but I, what am I to do?[1] Then he heard: 'I have accepted the sacrifice of your son; *this is the word of the Lord – by My own self I swear it!*'

1. Abraham thought that some sin of his had caused Isaac to vanish.

בַּסְּבַךְ אָדוֹן אֶצְלוֹ הֵשִׁית
אַיִל שֶׁכֻּלּוֹ לְמִצְוָה מִבְּרֵאשִׁית.
תַּחְתָּיו פָּשַׁט יָדוֹ בְּטַלִּיתוֹ,
וְהִנּוֹ נִצָּב עַל עֹלָתוֹ.

Nearby, in a thicket, the Master put a ram, which had been destined for this holy act ever since Creation.[1] The ram, in place of Isaac, clutched at Abraham's cloak with his foreleg – *and behold, he stood beside his burnt offering.*

וַיִּקַּח אֶת הָאַיִל כִּרְצוֹנוֹ
וַיַּעֲלֵהוּ לְעוֹלָה תַּחַת בְּנוֹ.
רָאָה וְשָׂמַח בְּכֹפֶר יְחִידוֹ
וְהָאֱלֹהִים אִנָּה לְיָדוֹ.

And thus he fulfilled his desire: he took the ram and offered it as a sacrifice instead of his son. He rejoiced as he looked at the ransom of his favoured son *which had come his way by an act of God.*

הַמָּקוֹם קְרָאוֹ 'יְיָ יִרְאֶה',
לִמְקוֹם אוֹרָה וְהוֹרָאָה יֵרָאֶה.
וְנִשְׁבַּע לְבָרְכוֹ בִּמְקוֹם הַמַּעֲרָכָה,
כִּי שָׁם צִוָּה יְיָ אֶת הַבְּרָכָה.

He named that place *Adonai-yireh*,[2] the place from which light and learning would be revealed. And He swore to bless him at the very site of the altar,[3] *for there the Lord bestowed His blessing.*

בְּכֵן עוֹקֵד וְנֶעֱקָד הִתְפַּלְּלוּ,
בְּעֵת בְּנֵיהֶם מַעַלְלֵיהֶם יְצַוְּלוּ
מִפְּעֻלּוֹתָם לְהַזְכִּיר, לְחַלְּצָם מֵרָעוֹתָם,
וּמִפִּשְׁעֵיהֶם לְכָל חַטֹּאתָם.

[Now Isaac came back from Eden.] He who made the sacrifice and he who was the sacrifice both prayed together that when their descendants do evil, this act would be recalled to save them from disaster and [to atone for] *their sins and transgressions.*

צַדִּיק, טוֹבָה עֲשֵׂה עִמָּנוּ,
חֶסֶד לְאַבְרָהָם נִשְׁבַּעְתָּ לַאֲבֹתֵינוּ,
וְעָנְתָה בָּם צִדְקָתָם לְהֵיטִיבֵנוּ,
וְסָלַחְתָּ לַעֲוֹנֵנוּ וּלְחַטָּאתֵנוּ וּנְחַלְתָּנוּ.

O Righteous One, deal kindly with us. You promised our father steadfast love, Your love for Abraham. Let their merit answer for us and make us prosper. *Forgive our iniquity and our sin and take us for Your own.*

1. The proxy-ram was made at twilight on the Sabbath eve of the week of creation.
2. I.e. 'The Lord will see', 'the Lord will provide'.
3. According to the tradition that Solomon's Temple was built on Mount Moriah (2 Chronicles 3.1).

תִּזְכָּר־לָנוּ כַּמָּה עֲקֵדוֹת,
הַנֶּהֱרָגִים עָלֶיךָ, חֲסִידִים וַחֲסִידוֹת.
הָעֲקֻדִּים לְצֶדֶק לִיהוּדָה נְקֹב,
וְהַקְּשֻׁרִים לְיַעֲקֹב.

Remember, in our favour, how many have been slaughtered – pious men and women murdered for Your sake. Oh, reward the martyrs[1] of Judah, slain in righteousness, *and the bound*[1] *[victims] of Jacob.*

וְתִרְעֶה אֶת הַצֹּאן הַנּוֹתָרוֹת,
בֵּין הָעַמִּים מְפֹרָדוֹת וּמְפֻזָּרוֹת.
וְשַׁבֵּר מוֹטוֹת וְנַתֵּק מוֹסֵרוֹת,
בְּכָל יַחֵם הַצֹּאן הַמְקֻשָּׁרוֹת.

Tend the sheep that still remain, dispersed among the nations. Break their yoke and snap their cords. *In every way, increase the bound flocks.*

אוֹי לִי אִם אֹמְרָה

LAMENT FOR THE MASSACRE AT BLOIS

[...] אוֹי לִי אִם אֹמְרָה וַאֲהַרְהֵר עַל חוֹצְבִי,
אוֹי לִי אִם לֹא אֹמְרָה מֵהָסִיחַ דַּאֲגַת לִבִּי.
אוֹי לִי כִּי פָנָה יוֹם טוֹבִי,
כִּי רָחַק מִמֶּנִּי מְנַחֲמִי וּקְרוֹבִי.

Woe is me if I speak and cast doubt on my Maker; woe is me if I do not speak, venting my sorrow. Woe is me, my day of goodness has declined. All my comforters and near ones are far away.

אֶל מִי תְדַמְּיוּנִי וְאֶשְׁוֶה בְּדַאֲבִי ?
כִּי מִי גוֹי מִכָּל שְׁכֵנַי סְבִיבִי
אֲשֶׁר חָטָא וְנִפְרַץ בּוֹ כַּאֲשֶׁר בִּי ?
עָלַי עָבְרוּ חֲרוֹנֶיךָ, נַפְשִׁי לְהַדְאִיבִי :

To whom can you liken me, who is my equal in suffering? Is there a nation, of all those around me, that has been broken for its sins as I have been? Your wrath has swept over me and made me writhe in pain.

אֲנִי נִסְקָל, אֲנִי נִתְקָל לְהַצְלִיבִי.
אֲנִי נִשְׂרָף, אֲנִי נֶעְרָף לְהַלְעִיבִי.

I am stoned, I am struck down and crucified. I am burned, my neck is snapped in shame. I am beheaded and

1. A play on words which figure in the story of Jacob (Genesis 30.39); *akudim* means both 'sacrificed, bound for slaughter' and 'striped sheep'.

אֲנִי נֶהֱרָג, אֲנִי נִדְרָג בְּחוֹבִי.
אֲנִי נֶחְנָק, אֲנִי נִשְׁנָק לִמְרִיבִי.
אֲנִי מֻכֶּה, אֲנִי לוֹקֶה בְּגֵוִי.
אֲנִי מוּמָת, אֲנִי מֻצְמָת לְלָבִיא.
אֲנִי מְאֻבָּד בְּבֵית הַבַּד, דָּמִי לְהַזִיבִי.
אֲנִי נִתְלֶה, אֲנִי נִקְלֶה וְגוֹלֶה לְהַכְאִיבִי.
אֲנִי נִדְרָס, אֲנִי נֶהֱרָס לְהַדִּיבִי.
דָּמִי נִשְׁפָּךְ, עוֹרִי נֶהְפָּךְ, וְנָוִי.
אֲנִי נִרְדָּף, אֲנִי נֶהְדָּף לְאִישׁ רִיבִי.
אֲנִי נֶאֱנָס, אֲנִי נִקְנָס לְאוֹיְבִי.
אֲנִי חָבוּי, אֲנִי שָׁבוּי בְּשִׁבְיִ.

trampled on for my guilt. I am strangled and choked by my enemy. I am beaten, my body is scourged. I am killed, I am at the mercy of a lion. I am crushed [as if] in an oil press, my blood is squeezed out. I am hung, despised, exiled in pain. I am stamped on, ruined, made to pine away. My blood is shed, my skin turned inside out, my home overturned. I am pursued, thrust back by my opponent. I am raped, I am damned by my enemy. I am driven into hiding and led into captivity.

שָׁבוּ לְאֵיתָנָם כָּל גּוֹי מַחֲרִיבִי,
וַאֲנִי עַד מָתַי אֲצַפֶּה לַהֲשִׁיבִי
בְּיַד בֶּן־נִפְלֵי וְאֵלִיָּהוּ הַנָּבִיא ?
הוֹי עַל כָּל שְׁכֵנַי הָרָעִים רָעָה לְהָבִיא !
אוֹי לְנַפְשָׁם, כִּי גָמְלוּ לָהֶם רָעָה לְהַחֲרִיבִי !
הֵן לֹא קָצְרָה יָדְךָ מִלְּהֵיטִיבִי.
יָבוֹא דְבָרְךָ וְכִבַּדְנוּךָ בְּעִיר מוֹשָׁבִי.

All the peoples that laid me waste have regained their strength. But I, how long must I wait until the Messiah and the prophet Elijah restore my fortunes? May disaster strike all my evil neighbours! Woe upon them! They have earned their own disaster by destroying me. Is the Lord's arm so short that it cannot change my lot? Let Your words come true and we will pay homage to You in my city, Jerusalem.

אַעֲלֶה פָּרִים עַל מִזְבַּחֲךָ לְהַתְמִידָה.
בִּרְצוֹנְךָ יְרוּשָׁלַיִם עִירְךָ קַשֵּׁט בִּכְבוֹדָהּ,
וְהַתָּמִיד אֲזַי תַּתְמִיד נֶצַח לְהַתְמִידָה.
וְזֹאת תּוֹרַת הָעוֹלָה, הִיא הָעוֹלָה עַל מוֹקְדָה.

There I shall offer young bulls daily on Your altar. Oh, let it be Your pleasure to adorn Your city Jerusalem with all its glory and to preserve the daily offering forever. *This is the law of the burnt offering on the altar hearth.*

בָּרוּךְ מִמָּגֶנְצָא

Barukh of Magenza

אֵשׁ אוֹכְלָה אֵשׁ

THE MARTYRS OF BLOIS

אֵשׁ אוֹכְלָה אֵשׁ, בְּפַרְפִּירָתוֹ מְאָדָּם,
אָסַף לוֹ חֲסִידָיו, הַבָּשָׂר וְהַדָּם.
אִישׁ בִּבְנוֹ וּבְאָחִיו מִלְאוּ יָדָם.
אֲלֵיכֶם אִישִׁים אֶקְרָא וְקוֹלִי אֶל בְּנֵי אָדָם.

[Dressed in] His purple cloak, gleaming red, He – a fire that devours fire – gathered to Himself His loyal servants, their flesh and their blood. They consecrated themselves to Him, each man killing his own son and his own brother. *O sons of men, it is to you I call, I appeal to every man.*

דֹּמּוּ יֹשְׁבֵי אִי, נְצוּרַי אֱמוּנַי,
דִּין שָׁמַיִם קַבְּלוּ לְרֵיחַ שְׁמָנַי.
דַּם חַטַּאת הַכִּפּוּרִים כֹּהֲנַי וּזְקֵנַי,
דֹּעֲכוּ כְּאֵשׁ קוֹצִים בְּשֵׁם אֲדֹנָי.

Be still, my abandoned people,[1] my survivors, my loyal ones. Submit to the decree of Heaven, be like the sweet-smelling incense. The blood of my priests and my elders [was spattered] like blood from the sin-offering of expiation.[2] *They blazed like a fire of thorns, in the name of the Lord.*

וְהֵם הֵבִיאוּ קָרְבָּנָם אִשֶּׁה לְיוֹצְרָם,
וְחַטָּאתָם לִפְנֵי יְיָ בְּנֶפֶשׁ צְרוּרָם.
וְצוּרָם מְכָרָם וְהִסְגִּירָם בְּיַד צוֹרְרָם,
וְשָׂרְפוּ בָאֵשׁ אֶת עֹרָתָם וְאֶת בְּשָׂרָם.

They brought their offering, an offering by fire, to their Maker. They gathered their lives into a bundle and presented them as a sin-offering to the Lord. But their Rock sold them and handed them over to the enemies *who destroyed them by fire – skin and flesh.*

זִכְרוּ זֹאת וְהִתְאוֹשָׁשׁוּ – בְּטֶרֶף מַתָּנָם!
זְמִירוֹת הָיוּ חֻקָּם בְּקוֹל הֲמוֹנָם.
זֹאת חָשַׁבְתָּ לְמִשְׁפָּט, עֶזְרָם וּמָגִנָּם?
זֶה יִהְיֶה לְךָ מִקֹּדֶשׁ הַקֳּדָשִׁים, מִן הָאֵשׁ, כָּל קָרְבָּנָם.

Remember this and abandon hope: they were given away and devoured, though they sang Your praises daily in their multitudes. Did You, their helper and their shield, think this just? *You took for Your own the most holy sacrifices, the offerings by fire, all they had to offer.*

1. Lit. 'island inhabitants'.
2. Exodus 30.10.

מִיכָאֵל הַשַּׂר הַגָּדוֹל לְמִזְבַּח מְעוֹנָה
מַקְטִיר נַפְשׁוֹת נְקִיִּים, צַדִּיקִים בֶּאֱמוּנָה.
מַדּוּעַ רְשָׁעִים עָזַבְתָּ בְּעוֹלוֹתֶיךָ לְדַשְּׁנָה ?
מִמָּרוֹם שָׁלַח אֵשׁ בְּעַצְמֹתַי וַיִּרְדֶּנָּה.

Michael, prince of angels, sacrifices the souls of the pure and the devout upon the heavenly altar.[1] But why did You allow the wicked to fatten on Your burnt sacrifices? *He sent down fire from heaven, it ran through my bones.*

עָרֵל בָּשָׂר צִוִּיתָ מֵהַקְרִיבְךָ אֵילִים.
עַל מָה פָּנֶיךָ הִסְתַּרְתָּ בְּהִתְעוֹלֵל הָעֲרֵלִים
עַם קָדוֹשׁ סְמוּכִים, הַיְּהוּדִים הָאֻמְלָלִים ?
עָלָה עָשָׁן בְּאַפּוֹ וְאֵשׁ מִפִּיו תֹּאכֵל גֶּחָלִים.

You forbade the uncircumcised to offer You even rams. Then why did You hide Your face when they ravaged the holy people, the feeble Jews, who put their trust in You? *Smoke rose from His nostrils, devouring fire came out of His mouth, and glowing coals.*

יָשִׂימוּ קְטוֹרָה בְּמִזְבַּח זָהָב מְעֻבָּה.
עוֹרֵנוּ אַל יֶחְסַר בֶּאֱמוּנָה רַבָּה.
קְנוּיִים בְּדִבְרֵי אֵשׁ, אֵיךְ נִתְלַבָּה
בֵּית־יַעֲקֹב אֵשׁ וּבֵית־יוֹסֵף לֶהָבָה ?

We offer You thick clouds of incense [as if] on a golden altar.[2] Our skin is always ready for the sacrifice, so great is our faith in You. You made us Your own with words of fire; how could You let us be seized by fire? [You promised that] *the house of Jacob would be fire, the house of Joseph flame [and the house of Esau chaff].*[3]

אֱלִיעֶזֶר בַּר־יְהוּדָה

Eliezer bar Judah of Worms

אֲסַפֵּר מַעֲשֵׂה בֶּלֶט

THE MURDER OF BELLET AND HANNAH

[...] אֲסַפֵּר מַעֲשֵׂה בֶּלֶט, בִּתִּי הַגְּדוֹלָה :
בַּת שְׁלוֹשׁ־עֶשְׂרֵה שָׁנָה הָיְתָה, צְנוּעָה כַּכַּלָּה.
לָמְדָה כָּל הַתְּפִלּוֹת וְהַזְּמִירוֹת מֵאִמָּהּ,
צְנוּעָה וַחֲסִידָה וּנְעִימָה וַחֲכָמָה.
עָשְׂתָה מַעֲשֵׂה אִמָּהּ יָפָה הַבְּתוּלָה,

Let me tell the story of my eldest daughter, Bellet: She was thirteen years old, and as chaste as a bride. She had learnt all the prayers and songs from her mother, who was modest and kind, sweet[4] and wise. The girl took after her beautiful mother and every

1. In the Temple of the Celestial Jerusalem.
2. Exodus 40.5 3. Obadiah 18. 4. The mother's name was Dolce ('sweet').

מַצַּעַת מִטָּתִי וְחוֹלֶצֶת מִנְעָלַי בְּכָל לַיְלָה.
זְרִיזָה בַּבַּיִת בְּלֶט, וּמְדַבֶּרֶת רַק אֱמֶת,
עוֹבֶדֶת בּוֹרְאָהּ וְטוֹוָה וְתוֹפֶרֶת וּמְרַקֶּמֶת.
רְצוּפָה בְּיִרְאָה, בְּאַהֲבַת יוֹצְרָהּ בְּלִי דֹפִי,
כַּוָּנָתָהּ לְשָׁמַיִם וְיָשְׁבָה לִשְׁמֹעַ תּוֹרָה מִפִּי.
וְנֶהֶרְגָה עִם אִמָּהּ וְעִם אֲחוֹתָהּ בְּלֵיל כָּף בֵּית כִּסְלֵו,
בִּהְיוֹתִי יוֹשֵׁב עַל שֻׁלְחָנִי שָׁלֵו.
בָּאוּ שְׁנַיִם מְתֹעָבִים וַהֲרָגוּן לְעֵינַי,
וּפְצָעוּנִי, וְתַלְמִידַי וְגַם בְּנִי.

night she would make my bed and take off my shoes. She did her housework quickly, and always spoke the truth. She worshipped her Maker, she weaved and sewed and embroidered [in His Honour], she was filled with reverence and pure love for her Creator. For the sake of Heaven, she sat down by me to hear my teaching. And that is when she and her mother and her sister were killed, on the night of the twenty-second of *Kislev*, as I was sitting peacefully at my table. Two wicked men broke in and killed them before my eyes; they also wounded me, and my students, and my son.

אֲסַפֵּר מַעֲשֵׂה בִּתִּי הַקְּטַנָּה:
קָרְאָה קְרִיאַת־שְׁמַע בְּכָל יוֹם פָּרָשָׁה רִאשׁוֹנָה.
בַּת שָׁנִים שֵׁשׁ הָיְתָה, וְטוֹוָה וְתוֹפֶרֶת
וּמְרַקֶּמֶת וּמְשַׁעֲשַׁעַת אוֹתִי וּמְזַמֶּרֶת. [...]

Now let me tell the story of my younger daughter [Hannah]: every day she would recite the first portion of the *Shema*.[1] She was six years old, and she knew to weave and sew and embroider, and to delight me with her singing.

אוֹי לִי עַל אִשְׁתִּי הַחֲסוּדָה,
אוֹי לִי עַל בָּנַי וּבְנוֹתַי, אָנוּדָה!
נֶאֱמָן עָלַי הַדַּיָּן אֲשֶׁר דְּנָנִי,
בְּחַטָּאתִי וּבִפְשָׁעַי הִכְנִיעָנִי.
לְךָ יְיָ הַצְּדָקָה וְלִי בֹּשֶׁת הַפָּנִים,
יְיָ הַצַּדִּיק וְלִי הָעֲווֹנוֹת וְהַזְּדוֹנִים.
לְךָ אֲבָרֵךְ בְּכָל מִדָּה, שִׁיר אֲחַוֶּה,
לְךָ אֶכְרַע וְאֶשְׁתַּחֲוֶה.

O my lovely wife! O my sons and daughters! I weep for them. I put my trust in the Judge who decreed my sentence; He has crushed me for my crimes. O Lord, the right is on Your side, the shame belongs to me. No matter how You treat me, I shall bless You and sing in Your honour; and I shall bow down before You.

1. A morning and evening prayer, composed of three biblical portions.

יְהוּדָה אַלְחֲרִיזִי

Judah Al-Ḥarizi

וְהַבָּרָק

THE LIGHTNING

וְהַבָּרָק מְשַׂחֵק עַל עֲנָנִים
כְּגִבּוֹר רָץ וְלֹא יִיעַף וְיִיגַע.
כְּשׁוֹמֵר לֵיל אֲשֶׁר נִרְדַּם וְיִפְקַח
קְצָת עֵינוֹ וְתִסָּגֵר כְּרֶגַע.

And the lightning laughs at the clouds, like a warrior who runs without growing weary or faint. Or like a night watchman who dozes off, then opens one eye for an instant, and shuts it.

רְאוּ שֶׁמֶשׁ

THE SUN

רְאוּ שֶׁמֶשׁ אֲשֶׁר יִפְרֹשׂ כְּנָפָיו
עֲלֵי אֶרֶץ לְהָאִיר אֶת נְשָׁפָיו.
כְּעֵץ רַעֲנָן אֲשֶׁר צָמַח בְּשַׁחַק
וְהִגִּיעוּ עֲדֵי אֶרֶץ עֲנָפָיו.

Look: the sun has spread its wings over the earth to dispel the darkness. Like a great tree, with its roots in heaven, and its branches reaching down to the earth.

רְאוּ כִּנּוֹר

THE LUTE

רְאוּ כִּנּוֹר בְּחֵיק עַלְמָה יְרַנֵּן
וְיִמְשֹׁךְ לֵב בְּהוֹד קוֹלוֹ וְצִבְיוֹ.
כְּמוֹ יוֹנֵק בְּחֵיק אִמּוֹ מְבַכֶּה
וְהִיא תָשִׁיר וְצוֹחֶקֶת לְבִכְיוֹ.

Look: the lute sounds in the girl's arms, delighting the heart with its beautiful voice. Like a baby crying in his mother's arms, while she sings and laughs as he cries.

לְהַכְנִיס אוֹרְחִים

THE YOKEL'S SPEECH OF WELCOME

לְהַכְנִיס אוֹרְחִים יִמְתַּק לְחִכִּי
כְּמִיץ חָלָב בְּחֶמְאַת הַבְּקָרִים

Hospitality is as sweet to my taste as milk wrung out of cattle-curds; or as

וְכַפִּתִּים בְּתוֹךְ חֶמְאָה שְׁרוּיִים
בְּעֵת כִּי יִצָּבְרוּ אוֹתָם חֳמָרִים.
וְעֵת קוֹל אוֹרְחִים אֶשְׁמַע חֲצוֹת לֵיל,
לְבָנַי אֶקְרָאָה 'פִּתְחוּ שְׁעָרִים!'
וְשִׂמְחָתִי בְּאוֹרֵחַ כְּשִׂמְחַת
זְאֵב גָּנַב גְּדִי מִן הָעֲדָרִים.
וְכָל יוֹם אֶחֱרֹשׁ אַדְמַת נְדָבוֹת
כְּחוֹרֵשׁ הָאֲדָמָה בִּבְקָרִים.
וְיִיטַב לִי עֲשׂוֹת חֶסֶד, כְּרָעֵב
בְּמָצְאוֹ פַּת יְבֵשָׁה עִם חֲצִירִים.
וְעֵינַי לַחֲזוֹת אוֹרְחִים תְּקַוֶּה
כְּעֵינֵי הַחֲמוֹרִים לַשְּׂעוֹרִים!

breadcrumbs soaked in cream, piled up in countless heaps. When I hear the voices of guests at midnight, I call out to my sons: 'Throw open the gates!' Guests make me as happy as a wolf that has filched a kid from the flock. And every day, like a ploughman with his oxen, I turn over the clods of my bounty. I delight in doing favours, as a hungry man delights in finding a dry crust and a clump of grass. My eyes long to see guests, as the eyes of asses long for barley.

מְיֻדָּעַי וְרֵעַי

מְיֻדָּעַי וְרֵעַי, רַחֲמוּנִי
וְעַל גֹּדֶל יְגוֹנִי נַחֲמוּנִי!
הֲכָזֶה יִהְיֶה תַּגְמוּל אֱמוּנִים,
אֲשֶׁר עַל טוֹב בְּרָעָה יִגְמְלוּנִי?
יְדִידִים שָׁכְחוּ חֶסֶד גְּמַלְתִּים,
וְהֵם תָּמִיד לְהָרְגִי יִדְרְשׁוּנִי.
אֲנִי אֶרְדֹּף שְׁלוֹמוֹתָם וְטוּבָם
וְתַחַת אַהֲבָתִי יִשְׂטְנוּנִי,
וְתָמִיד אֶשְׁמְעָה עָלַי עֲצָתָם
וְכָל הַיּוֹם כְּלוֹחֵם יִלְחָצוּנִי.
וְקִדַּמְתִּים בְּבָנִים גַּם בְּבָנוֹת —
וְהֵם בְּמַאֲכָלוֹת קִדְּמוּנִי,
וְהֶאֱכַלְתִּים בְּשַׂר בָּנַי — וְהֵמָּה
מְבַקְשִׁים תֹּאֲנָה עַד יֹאכְלוּנִי.

THE COCK'S ORATION

Friends, companions, pity me! Comfort me in my great misery! Shall this be the reward of loyalty? Will they repay good with evil? My loved ones have forgotten all my acts of kindness. They look continually for ways to kill me. I seek their peace and well-being, but they give me hatred for my love. Constantly I hear them plot against me; all day long my assailants harass me. I came to meet them with sons as well as daughters; they come to meet me with slaughtering-knives. I fed them the flesh of my children, but they seek an occasion to feed upon me. I am old,

אֲנִי זָקֵן וְאֵין בָּשָׂר בְּגוּפִי,
וְלָמָּה־זֶּה לְאָכְלִי יַחְמְדוּנִי ?
רְדָפוּנִי בְּרִשְׁעוּתָם, וְאִלּוּ
אֲחָזוּנִי – כְּרֶגַע אִבְּדוּנִי !
אֲבָל הָאֵל עֲזָרַנִי בְחַסְדּוֹ,
וְנִמְלַטְתִּי בְּעֵת כִּי בִקְשׁוּנִי.
וְלוּלֵא צוּר כְּתָבַנִי לְחַיִּים,
לְהָרְגִי נִקְבְּצוּ וַיִּשְׁחָטוּנִי,
וְנָשַׁי גֵּרְשׁוּ מִבֵּין זְרוֹעַי,
וּמֵעַל תַּרְנְגוֹלַי רִחֲקוּנִי.

there is hardly any flesh on my body – why then do they long to eat me? They hunted me with malice; if they had caught me, they would have wiped me out in a flash. But the Lord, in His never-failing love, came to my aid, and I escaped when they were chasing me. If the Rock had not inscribed me in the book of life, they would have gathered together to slaughter me. They would have torn my wives out of my arms and driven me far from my chicks.

הַמְשֵׁדִים וְזִקִּים

TO HIS BEDMATE

הַמְשֵׁדִים וְזִקִּים אַתְּ גְּזוּרָה ?
יְשַׁלַּח בָּךְ אֱלֹהִים הַמְּאֵרָה !
כְּאִלּוּ מַלְאֲכֵי זַעַם וּמַשְׁחִית
לְאַחִים לָךְ – אֲבָל לָךְ הַבְּכוֹרָה.
כְּאִלּוּ תָאֳרֵךְ כִּשְׂעִיר עֲזָאזֵל –
וְאֵיךְ נִמְלַטְתְּ מֵאֶרֶץ גְּזֵרָה ?
כְּאִלּוּ הַזְּמַן חָשַׁק בְּלִילִית
וּמֵאַהֲבָה שְׁלָחֵךְ לָהּ תְּשׁוּרָה.
וְיוֹצְרֵךְ לֹא יְצָרֵךְ רַק לְמַעַן
תְּהִי אֶל מַלְאֲכֵי מָוֶת לְעֶזְרָה.
וְאַשְׁרֵי יוֹלְדֵךְ לוּ מֵת בְּלִדְתֵּךְ –
וּמִי יִתֵּן תְּהִי אִמֵּךְ עֲקָרָה !
שְׂפָתַיִךְ כְּמוֹ שִׂפְתֵי שְׁוָרִים,
וּפִיךְ – קֶבֶר, אֲבָל בִּטְנֵךְ – מְעָרָה.
וְשִׁנַּיִךְ כְּשִׁנֵּי דֹב זְהוּמוֹת
וּבָם צוֹאָה וְרִיר כִּמְלוֹא קְעָרָה,

Were you compounded of demons and fiends? May the Lord lay a curse upon you! Angels of rage and destruction seem to have been your brothers, but you were the first born. Your face is like that of the desert-demon's goat;[1] how, then, did you escape from the barren waste? Time, it would seem, lusted for Lilith and sent you to her as a token of love. It is as if your Maker manufactured you only to be a help-mate for the angels of death. Your father would have counted it a blessing had he died at your birth. If only your mother had been barren! Your lips are like the lips of oxen; your maw is a tomb; and, what is more, your belly is a cave. Your teeth are as evil-smelling as the teeth of a bear, as full of filth and spittle as a bowl. Your eyes are as

1. The 'goat for Azazel', the scape-goat (Leviticus 16.8 ff).

וְעֵינַיִךְ כְּמוֹ כִירָה עֲשֵׁנִים,
וּפָנַיִךְ כְּמוֹ שׁוּלֵי קְדֵרָה,
וְקוֹמָתֵךְ כְּעֵץ הָמָן גְּבֹהָה —
וּמִי יִתֵּן וְאֶרְאֵךְ בּוֹ מְהֵרָה! [...]

אֱלֹהִים יַהֲפֹךְ רֹאשֵׁךְ בְּשַׁחַת
כְּמַהְפֵּכַת סְדֹמָה וַעֲמֹרָה,
וְתַכְרִיכֵךְ יָשׂוּ בִּטְנֵי אֲרָיוֹת
וְיָשִׂים לָךְ בְּתוֹךְ קִרְבָּם קְבוּרָה!

smoky as a stove and your face as black as the bottom of a pot. You are as tall as a gallows – if only I could see you swinging from it soon!

May God turn you upside down – overturned like Sodom and Gomorrah – with your head in hell. May He give you the stomachs of lions for shrouds and their entrails for a resting-place!

שְׁאֵלוּנִי עַל הַנְּדָבָה

THE GENEROUS MAN

שְׁאֵלוּנִי עַל הַנְּדָבָה וּשְׁלֹמֹה.
עֲנִיתִים: הִיא וָהוּא כְּאֵשׁ עִם נוֹזְלֵי עָב.
לְשׁוֹן כּוֹסוֹ דָּבַק לְחִכּוֹ בְּצָמָא,
וְשִׂפְתֵי שֻׁלְחָנוֹ עֲטוּפִים בְּרָעָב.
לְהָסֵךְ מֵי רַגְלָיו מְפַחֵד פֶּן יִצְמָא,
וְכֵן יִירָא לִבְדֹּק נְקָבָיו פֶּן יִרְעַב.

I was asked for my opinion of Solomon's generosity. And this was my answer: He and it are like fire with rain-water. The tongue of his goblet is dumb with thirst,[1] and the lips of his table are faint with hunger. He is afraid to pass water, lest he should thirst; and he dares not relieve himself, lest he should hunger.

מֵאִיר הַלֵּוִי אַבּוּלְעָאפְיָה

Meir Halevi Abulafia

שְׂאוּ עָבִים

A LETTER FROM THE GRAVE

ולו כשמתה אחותו, האל ירצה אותה, ביום השבת
י״ד בכסלו שנת ד׳ תתקע״ג, וכתב אל אביו
להודיע אותו ולנחמו על לשונה:

He wrote this when his sister – may God delight in her – died on the Sabbath of 10 November 1212; he wrote to his father, in the name of his sister, to inform him and to bring him comfort.

1. Lit. 'clings to the roof of its mouth'.

שְׂאוּ, עָבִים, שְׁלוֹם קִבְרִי לְאָבִי,
וְלֹא מִפִּי, אֲבָל מִפִּי כְתָבִי,
וְקִרְאוּ לוֹ בְּשִׂפְתֵי קוֹרְאוֹתַי
אֲשֶׁר קָרְאוּ לְשִׂפְתוֹתַי וְנִיבִי.
וְגוֹרוּ, פֶּן יְצִיקוּהוּ מְצוּקַי,
וְיִתְעַצֵּב לְגֹדֶל מַעֲצָבִי.
וּמַה בֶּצַע בְּמַעְצָבוֹ לְעָצְבִּי,
וּבִכְאֵבוֹ – הֲיַחְשֵׂךְ כְּאֵבִי?
הֲטוֹב כִּי תִקָּרְעוּ בַעֲדִי כְּרֶגַע
סְגוֹר לִבּוֹ? וְחָטָאתִי לְאָבִי,
אֲשֶׁר כַּנְפֵי חֲסָדָיו שָׁת יְצוּעִי
וְנָתַן צַוְּארֵי רַחֲמָיו רְכוּבִי.
וְזָרַחְתִּי כְּשֶׁמֶשׁ מִמְּעוֹנָיו,
וְהִנֵּה בָּאֲבַדּוֹן מַעֲרָבִי. [...]

O clouds, bear these greetings to my father from my grave, in words not spoken but written. Tell him, with the dumb lips of my disaster, what has become of my lips and my voice. But take care that my distress should not overwhelm him, that my great sorrow should not oppress him. What good would it do to oppress him with my sorrow? Would his pain spare me mine? Would it be right to tear open his heart because of me? No, I would be wronging my father, whose loving wings were my bed, whose compassionate shoulders were my chariot. Once I shone like a sun in his house, but now I have set in the abyss.

שְׁעוּ מִנִּי, עֲדֵי מַה תִּקְרְאוּ לִי?
דְּעוּ כִּי יַד אֱלוֹהַּ נָגְעָה בִּי,
וּמָוֶת מֵחֲדַר אַלּוּף נְעוּרַי
כְּרֶגַע הֵן טְרָפַנִי כְּלָבִיא.
וְסָר מֶנְהוּ עֲדֵי צַד בִּטְחוֹנִי,
וְהִשְׁלַכְתִּי עֲלֵי קִבְרִי יְהָבִי.
וְכִסּוּ קוֹבְרַי פָּנַי בְּעָפָר
אֲשֶׁר הָיָה תְמוֹל מִדְרַךְ עֲקֵבִי.
וְאֶמְשֹׁךְ כָּל אֱנוֹשׁ אַחֲרַי, וְיַחַד
יְבוֹאוּנִי מְתֵי חִשְׁקִי וְרִיבִי:
וְאֵל קָרָא לְבֵית מוֹעֵד לְכָל חַי,
וְיַחַד יִגְוְעוּ חוֹטֵא וְנָבִיא,
עֲדֵי יָשִׁיב נְשָׁמוֹת לַפְּגָרִים –
וְאָז אֶרְאֶה פְּנֵיכֶם עוֹד בְּשׁוּבִי.

Turn away from me [my friends]! How much longer will you call to me? Know that the hand of God has touched me. Death, like a ravening lion, tore me out of the room of my beloved. No longer can I cast my fortunes on the dear friend of my youth; now I must commit my fortunes to the grave. They buried me, covering my face with the very dust which only yesterday I trampled underfoot. But I shall draw all men after me; both my loved ones and my rivals will join me. God summons all mortals to the house of the dead. Sinner and prophet perish alike. Until [the day of resurrection, when] He restores all souls to their bodies. Then shall I come into your presence again.

וְאִם הִכְאִיב בְּמַכְאוֹבִי לְבַבְכֶם,
אֲשֶׁר הָיָה בְּאָמְנָה עִם לְבָבִי,
וְהֵצִיף יָם דְּמָעוֹת עַל פְּנֵיכֶם
וּמַבּוּל הַבְּכִי אָמַר לְהָבִיא —
יְרַו קִבְרִי בְּטַל אוֹרוֹת, וְכָעֵת
לְצוּלַת דִּמְעֲכֶם יֹאמַר: 'חֲרָבִי!'

(1212)

Though He has made your heart – my heart's guardian – share my grief, though He has made a sea of tears flow over you and almost flooded you with weeping, He will now fill my grave with His dew of sparkling light, He will say to your welling tears: 'Subside and dry!'

מֹשֶׁה בֶּן־נַחְמָן

Nahmanides

מֵרֹאשׁ מִקַּדְמֵי עוֹלָמִים

HYMN ON THE FATE OF THE SOUL

מֵרֹאשׁ מִקַּדְמֵי עוֹלָמִים
נִמְצֵאתִי בְמִכְמַנָּיו הַחֲתוּמִים.
מֵאַיִן הִמְצִיאַנִי, וּלְקֵץ יָמִים
נִשְׁאַלְתִּי מִן הַמֶּלֶךְ.

[The Soul:] From the very beginning, before times long past, I was stored among His hidden treasures. He had brought me forth from Nothing, but at the end of time *I shall be summoned back before the King*.

שַׁלְשֶׁלֶת חַיַּי מִיסוֹד הַמַּעֲרָכָה,
לִמְשֹׁךְ תַּבְנִית בִּתְמוּנָה עֲרוּכָה,
לִשְׁקֹל עַל יְדֵי עוֹשֵׂי הַמְּלָאכָה,
לְהָבִיא אֶל גִּנְזֵי הַמֶּלֶךְ.

My life flowed out of the depth of the spheres which gave me form and order. Divine forces shaped me *to be treasured in the chambers of the King*.

הוֹפִיעַ לְגַלּוֹת אֲשֶׁר הִטְמִין.
הֵן מִשְּׂמֹאל הֶגְלָה וּמֵהַיָּמִין
מִמַּעֲלוֹת הַיּוֹרְדוֹת מִן
בְּרֵכַת הַשֶּׁלַח לְגַן הַמֶּלֶךְ.

Then He appeared to bring me out of hiding. He drove me out, from all sides, made me descend the steps leading down from *the Pool of Shelah to the garden of the King*.[1]

1. I.e. from heaven to earth. The stanza may also be understood as follows: 'Then he shined His light to bring her [the soul] forth in hidden well-springs, on the left and on the right. He made her descend, etc.'

בְּעָפָר רֻקַּמְתִּי, וְאִם רוּחֲךָ בִּי נָשׁוּב.
בַּנְתָּ לְרֵעִי, כְּגֵר בָּאָרֶץ אֶהְיֶה חָשׁוּב.
'עַד מָתַי יִהְיֶה מַהֲלָכְךָ וּמָתַי תָּשׁוּב
וַיִּיטַב לִפְנֵי הַמֶּלֶךְ ?'

[Man:] I was moulded in dust, though Your spirit breathes in me. How well You know me. I am no more than a stranger in this land. 'How long will your journey last? When will you turn back *and merit the approval of your King?*'

נֵר לְרַגְלִי שַׂמְתָּ וְלִנְתִיבָתִי,
תְּחַפֵּשׂ כָּל חַדְרֵי בֶטֶן בְּרוּחַ נְדִיבָתִי,
וּבְצֵאתִי מִלְּפָנֶיךָ הִזְהַרְתָּ אוֹתִי :
יְרָא אֶת יְיָ, בְּנִי, וָמֶלֶךְ !

You gave her to me as a lamp to light my way. With my willing soul You search out my inmost being. When I took my leave of You, You warned me: '*Child, fear the Lord your King!*'

נָתַתָּ בְּיָדִי לֵב מֹאזְנֵי מִשְׁפָּט וָפֶלֶס.
אִם לְחֶסֶד יַמְצִיאֵנִי – בּוֹ אֶתְעַלֵּס,
וְאִם לְרָעָה – יִהְיֶה לַעַג וָקֶלֶס,
כִּי לֹא הָיְתָה מֵהַמֶּלֶךְ.

You armed my heart with balances and scales. If it moves me to goodness I delight in it, but if it moves me to evil I earn contempt and scorn. *This [choice] is not determined by the King.*

חָגוּר חֲרָדוֹת לְהוֹדוֹת פְּשָׁעַי אָחִישׁ
בְּטֶרֶם לְבֵית מוֹעֵד כְּבוֹדִי גָז חִישׁ.
שָׁם תָּוִי בְּפָנַי יַעֲנֶה – וּמִי יַכְחִישׁ
אֶת אִגְּרוֹת הַמֶּלֶךְ ? [...]

Covered with trembling, I rush to confess my sins before I and my honour vanish into the grave. There my own signature will testify against me, for who can deny *the indictment in the hands of the King?*

נִסְמַכְתִּי עָלֶיךָ וְלֹא לְמַעֲשַׂי אֶפְנֶה,
כִּי אָמַרְתִּי : עוֹלָם חֶסֶד יִבָּנֶה.
בְּטֶרֶם אֶקְרָא הֲלֹא תַעֲנֶה,
כִּי בֹשְׁתִּי לִשְׁאֹל מִן הַמֶּלֶךְ.

I put my trust in You, not in my own deeds, for I know that Your world is built on charity. Before I call to You, will You not answer? *I am ashamed to entreat the King.*

דְּרָכֶיךָ יְנַחֲמוּנִי, כִּי שָׁמַעְתִּי עֲווֹנוֹת תִּכְבֹּשׁ.
וּבְךָ חָסָיָה נַפְשִׁי וְלֹא תֵבוֹשׁ,
כִּי הַגּוּף בְּמַסְגֵּר תִּכְבֹּשׁ,
וְהִיא – בְּהֵיכְלֵי מֶלֶךְ !

Your ways are my comfort. I know You will tread my guilt underfoot. My soul takes refuge in You; she shall not be shamed. For You press the body into the grave's prison, *but she dwells on in the palaces of the King.*

יוֹדַעַת אָז: בְּשַׁחַת אוֹתִי תִּטְבֹּל,
הֲלֹא אִם שַׂלְמָתָהּ חָבוֹל תַּחְבֹּל –
תְּשִׁיבֶנּוּ לָהּ אַחֲרֵי תִסְבֹּל
הַמִּשְׁפָּט אֲשֶׁר שָׁפַט הַמֶּלֶךְ.

And she knows: though You plunge me into the pit, though You take her cloak [the body] as a pledge, You will clothe her again once she has suffered *the sentence decreed by the King*.

חַזֵּק יַד חֲלוּשָׁה וְתֵשֶׁב לָהּ בְּאֵיתָן.
וּבְעֵת יָשׁוּבוּ הַדְּבָרִים לְהֲוָיָתָן
תְּשַׁוֶּהָ לְטוֹב מִגִּנַּת הַבִּיתָן
הַפַּרְדֵּס אֲשֶׁר לַמֶּלֶךְ.

Strengthen the feeble one, let her stand firm. And when all things return to their primal state, make her pure, as she rejoins the royal pavilion in the *orchard of the King*.

דָּוִיד הַכֹּהֵן

David Hakohen

הִשְׁתַּחֲוִי וּבָרְכִי

SILENCE AND PRAISE

הִשְׁתַּחֲוִי וּבָרְכִי לִפְנֵי צוּר מְעוֹנִי,
וּתְהַלְלִי וּבָרְכִי, נַפְשִׁי, אֶת אֲדֹנָי!

Bow down, my soul, and kneel before my rock of refuge; praise the Lord and bless Him!

דַּלּוּ מְאֹד שְׂפָתַי מִדֵּי מְהַלְלָיו,
לֹא רַב סְפָר שְׁנוֹתַי מִמִּסְפַּר חֲיָלָיו,
אֵין דַּי בְּרֹב יְמוֹתַי סַפֵּר הוֹד פְּעָלָיו.
אָמְנָם בְּרֹן וּבִבְכִי – מִמְסַךְ רַעְיוֹנַי –
צוּר שַׁחֲרִי, וְהֵלְכִי לִדְרֹשׁ אֶת אֲדֹנָי.

My lips are too low to sing His high praises. My years are too few to recite His glorious works. All my days would not suffice to tell His mighty deeds. Therefore, with song and tears, my mind's libation, seek the Rock, look eagerly for the Lord.

וּבְעֵת תְּהוֹם אֳרָחָיו יֵרֵד רַעְיוֹנִי,
וּבְחוּג שְׁמֵי שְׁבָחָיו יִתְהַלֵּךְ לְשׁוֹנִי,
מִלַּהֲטֵי שְׁלָחָיו סַנְוֵרִים בְּעֵינַי.
מִתְהַפְּכִים בְּהָפְכִי אֶל אַחֲרֵי תְבוּנִי,
בַּל אֶמְצָאֶהָ, בְּעָרְכִי, דֵּעָה אֶת אֲדֹנָי.

When my mind tries to fathom the abyss of His ways and my words move on the vault of His heavenly praise, I am struck blind by His flashing swords. They turn over and over as I turn beyond the limits of my reason. My thoughts cannot attain the knowledge of the Lord.

יַעֲמֹד – וְרוֹדְפִים לֹא יַשִּׂיגוּ כְבוֹדוֹ,
כִּי יַחְשִׁיךְ בְּהִלּוֹ מֵהַבִּיט בְּהוֹדוֹ.
כָּל הוֹד וְכָל יְקָר לוֹ, יִתְבָּרֵךְ בְּיָדוֹ:
מִי הוּא אֲנִי וּמִי, כִּי אַרְבֶּה־לּוֹ רְנָנַי?
אֶחְשֶׁךְ, הֲכִי בְחָשְׁכִי אוֹדֶה אֶת אֲדֹנָי.

Though He stand still, no pursuer can overtake His glory. His light casts darkness: you cannot see His splendour. All majesty, all precious things are His, and blessed in His hands. Then who am I and what am I to burden Him with innumerable songs? I shall be silent, and by my silence shall thank the Lord.

דּוּמָם אֲנִי מְחַוֶּה כִּי לוֹ הַגְּדֻלָּה.
כִּי אַחֲרִישׁ מְקַוֶּה – וָאֶהְיֶה לְמִלָּה,
אוֹחִיל עֲדֵי יְצַוֶּה עָלַי צוּר גְּאֻלָּה.
אֶתְפָּאֲרָה בְּמָשְׁכִי עֹל חֻקֵּי אֱמוּנַי
עִם עֹל שִׁבְיִ, בְּתָמְכִי אֶת אַהֲבַת אֲדֹנָי.

Mutely, I proclaim that greatness is His. I have become a byword for hoping in dumb silence; yet I shall wait until the Rock decrees my redemption. I shall glory in wearing both the yoke of His statutes[1] and the yoke of exile, as I uphold the love of the Lord.

כָּל מַחֲנוֹת כְּרוּבָיו בָּרְכוּ אֵל, וְלִשְׁמוֹ
הוֹדוּ בְּסוֹד אֲהוּבָיו, כָּל עֶצֶם לְעַצְמוֹ.
נוֹרָא בְּכָל סְבִיבָיו, אִישׁ לוֹ מִמְּקוֹמוֹ
הִשְׁתַּחֲווּ, בְּשָׁפְכִי שִׂיחֵי תַחֲנוּנַי;
וּמְשָׁרְתָיו, בְּבָרְכִי נַפְשִׁי אֶת אֲדֹנָי,
[בָּרְכוּ אֶת אֲדֹנָי הַמְבֹרָךְ.]

Now bless God, all His hosts of cherubs; let each one praise His name, in the company of His loved ones. He is terrible above the hosts who stand about Him. Let each one, at his station, bow down as I pour forth my supplications. And when my soul blesses the Lord, let His ministers too, ['bless the Lord who is blessed'].

יִצְחָק הַגּוֹרְנִי

Isaac Hagorni

לְחִשְׁקִי הִנְנִי

THE FATE OF THE ADULTERER

לְחִשְׁקִי הִנְנִי הוֹלֵךְ לְתַנּוֹת,
וְקוֹל תֻּפִּי כְּבָר שָׁבַת לְעַנּוֹת.
פְּשָׁעַי מָנְעוּ הַטּוֹב, מְלִיצַי, –

I shall now lament my desires, the silenced beat of my drum. Friends, my own sins deprived me of favours, so

1. Lit. 'the yoke of the statutes of the loyal ones [of Israel]'.

וְכַמָּה לִי חֲטָאִים וַעֲוֹנוֹת!
לְאֶבְלִי נֶהֱפַךְ כִּנּוֹר מְחוֹלִי,
וְעוּגָבִי – לְקוֹל בּוֹכִים וְקִינוֹת,
כְּתֹם חִשְׁקִי וְאָפֵס מַאֲוַיִּי
וְיִכְלוּ מַתְּנוֹת הַחֵן וּמָנוֹת.

great were my offences. My merry harp was tuned to mourning and my flute to the sound of weeping and lament, when my desire died and my passion vanished, when the gracious gifts of love came to an end.

וְהַיּוֹם רַד וְנָסוּ הַצְּלָלִים
וְאֵין רוּחַ מְרַחֶפֶת בְּגַנּוֹת,
וְאֵימָתָה בְּלִבִּי מִתְּמוּתָה –
וּמַה שִּׂבְרִי כְּעַיִר בֶּן אֲתוֹנוֹת?
וְחִשְׁקִי מוֹסְדוֹת תֵּבֵל יְלַהֵט,
וְתִשְׁכֹּנָּה עֲלֵי קִבְרִי עֲנָנוֹת.
וְאִם אָמוּת וְעוֹדֶנִּי בְּעַלְמוּת,
וְאִתִּי יֵרְדוּ לִשְׁאוֹל תְּלֻנּוֹת.

The day was far gone, the shadows had fled, no wind stirred in the gardens. And my heart was filled with a sudden dread of death – what hope is there for an ass like me? Oh, my passion will set fire to the earth's foundations, clouds will hover above my grave. And if I should die while still young, my complaints will accompany me down into Sheol.

לְפָנִים אֶהְיֶה רוֹדֵף חֲשָׁקִים
וְנִמְשַׁלְתִּי כְּתֹפֶת בַּמְּדִינוֹת –
וְעַתָּה נֶהְפְּכוּ עָלַי לְמַשְׁחִית
אֲהָבִים נֶעְדְּרוּ בָהֶם אֱמוּנוֹת.
וּמִמֶּרְחָק, לְכָל רוֹכֵל יְבִיאוּן
עֲפַר קִבְרִי לְתַמְרוּקֵי עֲדִינוֹת,
וּמִקַּרְשֵׁי אֲרוֹנִי לַעֲקָרוֹת –
אֲזַי תֵּלַדְנָה בָנִים וּבָנוֹת.
וְרִמָּתִי לְעִלֵּג יִרְקָחוּנָהּ
וְאִלֵּם – לַהֲגוֹת שִׁבְעִים לְשׁוֹנוֹת.
וְשַׂעֲרוֹתַי – יְתֵדִים עַל כְּלֵי שִׁיר –
וְיֵיטִיבוּ בְּאֵין נוֹגֵן נְגִינוֹת.
וְאַבְנֵטִי לְמַחְגֹּרֶת מְנָאֵף,
לְמַעַן יֶחְדַּל לִנְאֹף וְלִזְנוֹת.
וְכָל כֵּלַי כְּלֵי קֹדֶשׁ יְשִׂימוּן,

In days gone by I was a hunter, hot in pursuit of desires. In all the provinces, [my lust] was likened to [the fires of] hell. But all those loves that had no virtue to them have now turned against me and fearfully disfigured me. The dust of my grave will be sent to foreign merchants, to be blended in cosmetics for pleasure-loving girls. From the boards of my coffin [they will concoct powders] for barren women, to have them bring forth sons and daughters. Of my maggots they will compound ointments for stammerers and mutes, to make them speak seventy tongues. My hair will serve as strings in musical instruments, which will then play sweetly even without a player. My sash will be made into a loincloth for the adulterer, to put a stop to his fornicating and whoring. And all my belongings will be declared holy relics,

וְשַׁלְמוֹתַי לְמִשְׁמֶרֶת צְפוּנוֹת.
וּמִי יָדֵק לְעָפָר אֶת עֲצָמַי
בְּטֶרֶם יַעֲשׂוּן אוֹתָם תְּמוּנוֹת?

and my clothes will be treasured as keepsakes. Oh, who will grind my bones as fine as dust before they are turned into icons?

אֲמָרַי יִתְּנוּ חָכְמָה לְפֶתִי,
וְלַנַּעַר וְלַנָּבוֹן – תְּבוּנוֹת!

May my words endow the fool with wisdom, and the young and wise with understanding!

עִיר אַרְלְדִי

GORNI PLEADS HIS CAUSE

עִיר אַרְלְדִי – עִיר עֹז לְמִיּוֹם נוֹסְדָה,
וּבְמִשְׁפְּחוֹת אַנְשֵׁי מְלוּכָה נִכְבְּדָה,
עִיר אֵם בְּיִשְׂרָאֵל, בְּצָרוֹת נִקְרָאָה
מִשְׂגָּב לְעִתּוֹת, בַּפְּרָצִים עָמְדָה!
בַּצַּר לְגָרְנִי יוֹשְׁבֶיהָ קִדְּשׁוּ
צוֹמוֹת, כְּיוֹם הָעִיר אֲרִיאֵל נִלְכְּדָה –
אוּלָם מְצַעֵק עַל קְצִינֶיהָ אֲנִי,
הָאוֹמְרִים: נַפְשִׁי עֲדִינוֹת חָמְדָה!
וַאֲנִי מְאַסְתִּין, אַף גְּעַלְתִּין מֵרְאוֹת:
אִם בַּחֲלוֹם אֶרְאֵם – שְׁנָתִי נָדְדָה,
אִם בַּדְּרָכִים אֶפְגְּשֵׁם – קַל אֶעֱבֹר,
לוּ אַחֲרַי אַבִּיט – לְגַל אֶתְעַתְּדָה.
קִרְאוּ שְׁמִי פֶּלֶג – בְּיָמַי נִפְלְגָה
חֶבְרַת בְּנוֹת עַמִּים וּמִנִּי נִפְרְדָה.

From its very first day, the city of Arles was known as a city of strength and was honoured as the seat of [David's] royal kin. A mother city[1] in Israel, it was famed as a stronghold in times of need; it stood in the breach. And when Gorni found himself in distress, its citizens proclaimed a solemn fast, as if for the fall of the city of Ariel [Jerusalem]. But the rulers of Arles – against them I shall cry out, for they claim that my soul lusts for the lovely ladies! And in truth, I spurn them, I abhor the very sight of them. If I see them in my dream, sleep deserts me. If I meet them in the street, I quickly step aside. If ever I did look behind me [at a woman], may I be turned into a heap of rubble![2] Call me Peleg [Division], for in my time womankind was divided and all

1. Arles was formerly the capital of Provence.
2. Like Lot's wife, who was turned into a pillar of salt (Genesis 19.26).

הֲלֹא יְמֵי דוֹדִים נְדוּדִים נֶהֶפְכוּ,
חִנָּם עֲלָמוֹת עוֹד וּבָנוֹת צָעֲדָה.
הַחֵן וְהַיֹּפִי כְּבָר הִתְנַכְּרוּ
עָלַי, וְתָמִיד בָּאֲהָבִים אֶמְרְדָה.
קֶרַח, בְּחֹם חִשְׁקִי בְּלֵילוֹת, יֶחֱשֹׂף
בִּגְדִי, וְשֶׁלֶג עַל עֲצָמַי יֵרְדָה.
לִבִּי כְּבָר נִשְׁבַּר, וְאֶתָּבַר לְבַר
עִם זַךְ וְעִם חָסִיד וּבָם אֶתְחַסְּדָה.

withdrew from me. For days of loving have turned into days of wandering. In vain do the girls still parade [before me]; I have estranged myself from beauty and charm. I am in constant revolt against love. In the heat of my passion, at night, ice strips off my clothes [and bares my shame], snow comes down and covers my bones. My heart has already been broken. I now lead a pure life in the company of the pure, the blameless, and the loyal; to them I give my loyalty.

אַל תִּתְּנֵנִי, יָהּ, בְּיַד מִתְקוֹמְמַי!
לָמָּה בְּיוֹם אָבְדִי מְלִיצָה אָבְדָה?
כִּי הִיא – בְּעוֹדִי חַי, וְאִתִּי אַחֲרַי
בִּשְׁאוֹל וּבַחֹשֶׁךְ יְצוּעָהּ רִפְּדָה.
אִם לְךָ לְבַדְּךָ הֶעֱוֵיתִי, תַּחְמֹל
עַל מַחֲמַד שִׁירִי, וְלֹא אִשָּׁמְדָה. [...]

Lord, do not hand me over to my enemies! Why should Poetry perish on the day I perish? For as long as I live, she lives too. But once I have died, she will follow me down to Sheol and there spread her couch in the darkness. If I have sinned against You only, have mercy on my precious song; do not let them destroy me!

מֹשֶׁה בֶּן־יוֹסֵף

Moses ben Joseph

אִזְנוּ יְצוּרַי אֵלַי

BODY AND SOUL DISPUTE

אִזְנוּ יְצוּרַי אֵלַי,
רְפוּ, הוֹדוּ רִשְׁעַתְכֶם.
אֲחַלֶּה פְּנֵי אֵל, אוּלַי
אֲכַפְּרָה בְּעַד חַטַּאתְכֶם,

Listen to me, my limbs. Leave off your wickedness, confess it. Perhaps *I may win forgiveness for your sin,*

בְּטֶרֶם תִּתַּךְ בָּכֶם
חֲמָתוֹ כְּאֵשׁ בּוֹעֶרֶת
וּבְטֶרֶם יַשְׁלִיכְכֶם
אֶל אֶרֶץ אַחֶרֶת.

before He pours out His wrath upon you like fire, before He casts you *into another region.*

גַּרְתִּי מְאֹד מִמַּעֲלִי,
וָאֹמַר: אָשׁוּבָה־לִּי.
וְיִצְרִי קָם לְשָׂטָן לִי
וְהוּא יֹשֵׁב מִמֻּלִי.

I was terrified by my treachery, and I said: 'Let me now repent'. But my lust barred my way, *and still it camps before me.*

דָּמִי תּוֹךְ גְּוִיָּתִי
הָלוֹךְ וְחָסוֹר יֵלֵךְ
בַּיּוֹם אֲשֶׁר נִקְרֵאתִי
לָבוֹא אֶל הַמֶּלֶךְ.

The blood in my body will slowly recede on the day that I am summoned *to come before the King.*

הָהּ, שִׁחַתִּי דַרְכִּי,
וַעֲוֹנִי אֹהֲבֶנּוּ.
וּמָה אֶעֱשֶׂה בְּקוּם אֵל, וְכִי
יִפְקֹד, מָה אֲשִׁיבֶנּוּ?

Oh, my ways are corrupt, and I love my crimes. What shall I do when God appears? *When He questions me, what shall I answer?*

וְאָנָה אֲנִי בָא, זְקֵנַי,
וּלְמִי אָנוּס לְעֶזְרָה
לִפְנֵי בּוֹא יוֹם יְיָ
הַגָּדוֹל וְהַנּוֹרָא.

And where, my old limbs, can I go? To whom can I flee for help *before the great and terrible day when the Lord comes?*

זֹאת יִזְכֹּר יְמֵי עֲלוּמָיו,
לְבִלְתִּי יָרוּם לִבּוֹ:
אֱנוֹשׁ כֶּחָצִיר יָמָיו
כִּי רוּחַ עָבְרָה בּוֹ.

To overcome his pride, let man remember in his youth that his days are like the grass; *a wind passes over it [and it is gone].*

חֲבֵרָיו יוֹצִיאוּהוּ
מִחוּץ לָעִיר מְהֵרָה,
וּבְבוֹר יַשְׁלִיכוּהוּ
שָׁם אֶל אֶרֶץ גְּזֵרָה.

His friends rush him out of the city, and cast him into a pit, *there in the wilderness.*

טֻמַּן הַגּוּף וְנֶעְלַם,
רַגְלוֹ תְּעֻגָּה בְּכֶבֶל,
וְיָשַׁב שָׁם עַד עוֹלָם.
לֹא יֵצֵא בַּיֹּבֵל.

The body is buried and disappears from sight, a prisoner with fetters on his feet. It will stay there always; *not even the jubilee can set it free.*[1]

יוֹאֶל עוֹד וִיסַפֵּח
בְּתָרִים, אֱלֹהִים חַיִּים,
וְיָשׁוּב בְּגָדְלוֹ וְיִפַּח
בְּאַפָּיו נִשְׁמַת חַיִּים.

May it please the living God to bind the body's limbs together and, once again, in His greatness, *to breathe into its nostrils the breath of life.*

כֹּה יַעַן רָם בְּעָצְמָה:
'מַמְרִים, אֶת דְּבָרָתִי
מַה זֶּה בְּזִיתֶם, וְלָמָּה
לֹא קִדַּשְׁתֶּם אוֹתִי?

The High One, the Mighty One will say: 'Rebels, how have you dared to flout My word, *why have you not upheld My sanctity?*

לֹא דַי חֲרַשְׁתֶּם לֵאמֹר
לֶאֱהֹב אֶת תּוֹעֲבוֹתַי,
עוֹד מֵאַנְתֶּם לִשְׁמֹר
מִצְוֹתַי וְתוֹרֹתַי?'

'Not only have you conspired to love what I loathe, but you have also refused to obey *My commandments and My teachings.*'

מֵשִׁיב הַגּוּף בְּאֵימָה:
'אֲנִי, צוּר, מֶה עָשִׂיתִי?
זַךְ אֲנִי מִפֶּשַׁע. מַה
פִּשְׁעִי וּמַה חַטָּאתִי?

Then the body, terrified, answers: 'My Rock, what have I done? I am blameless. *What crime is mine and what offence?*

1. Unlike the Hebrew slave, who is released in the period of the jubilee (*T.B. Kiddushin* 15a).

נְשָׁמָה אֲשֶׁר נָתַתָּה
עִמָּדִי – הִיא תְשַׁבֵּשׁ.
וּמֵאָז מֶנִּי לְקַחְתָּהּ
הֵן אֲנִי עֵץ יָבֵשׁ.

'It is the soul whom You assigned to me – she is the depraver. Look: ever since You took her from me *I am [as harmless as] a dried-up tree.*

סָתַתְנִי כְּאִוֶּלֶת
סֶמֶל לַעֲבֹד וְתֶרֶף.
שֵׁם קָדְשְׁךָ מְחַלֶּלֶת –
הִיא בָּאֵשׁ תִּשָּׂרֵף!

'She wickedly enticed me to worship carved images and idols. It is she who desecrates Your holy name. *She should be destroyed by fire!*'

עוֹנָה נֶפֶשׁ אַחַר:
'הַגּוּף עוֹנֶה סָרָה.
אָנָּא, אַל נָא יִחַר
לַאדֹנָי וַאֲדַבֵּרָה.

To which the soul replies: 'The body bears false witness. *Do not be angry, Lord, if I speak:*

פֶּה אֶפְתַּח, וּמִלּוּלִי
בָּרוּר כִּי לֹא אֲכַנֶּה.
אֲדַבְּרָה וְיִרְוַח לִי,
אֶפְתַּח שְׂפָתַי וְאֶעֱנֶה.

'I am ready to answer. My words are sincere, I never use flattery. Let me speak to find relief, *I must open my mouth and answer.*

צֶדֶק אֶתֵּן לְקוֹנִי.
זְדוֹנוֹת הַגּוּף מַבְאִישׁ.
לֹא אֲכַחֵד מֵאֲדֹנִי,
אַל נָא אֶשָּׂא פְנֵי אִישׁ.

'I shall tell the truth to my Maker: it is the body in its insolence that has made the stink. I shall conceal nothing from my Lord. *I shall show no favour to anyone.*

קְלוֹנוֹ אַגִּידֶנּוּ
וְתָבוֹא בְלִבּוֹ חַרְבּוֹ.
לָמָּה אִירָאֶנּוּ?
פֶּה אֶל פֶּה אֲדַבֶּר בּוֹ!

'Let me tell him his disgrace outright and his sword will pierce his own heart. Why should I fear him? *I shall tell him to his face.*

רָדַף בְּכֹחַ וָלָאֵל
עֲבֹר מִצְוָתְךָ, קְדוֹשִׁי.
בְּאָמְרִי: ״נֵלְכָה בֵּית אֵל,״
יֹאמַר: ״אוֹי לִי רֹאשִׁי.״

'Zealously, persistently, he searched for ways, my Holy One, to violate Your commands. When I would say to him, "Let us go to the house of God," he would evade me, *saying: "O my head, my head!"*

שׁוֹאֵל אוֹב וּמְעוֹנֵן,
כָּל תּוֹעֵבָה בְּלִבּוֹ.
לָכֵן, צוּר, כִּי יְחַנֵּן
קוֹלוֹ, אַל תַּאֲמֶן בּוֹ.

'He traffics with ghosts and soothsayers. Abominations fill his heart. Therefore, O Rock, *when he speaks graciously, do not trust him.*

״תִּירָא מֵאֵל וְחֶבְלוֹ״,
יְעַצְתִּיו יוֹמִי וְלֵילִי.
לְעַבְנִי, לֵאמֹר: ״לֹא,
כִּי שָׁלוֹם יִהְיֶה לִי.״

'"Fear God and His punishment" – thus I counselled him day and night. But he mocked me: "Never you mind, *all will be well with me.*"

מֵאָז בּוֹ כְּלָאתַנִי
תַּמּוּ כָּל מַאֲוַיַּי.
שׁוֹבָב זֶה טִמְּאַנִי,
צָמְתוּ בַבּוֹר חַיָּי.

'Ever since You locked me up inside him, all my heart's desires have been thwarted. This apostate defiled me and *I was thrust alive into the pit.*

הָשֵׁב גְּמוּלוֹ, וְאַיֵּה
תּוֹעֲבוֹתָיו? יִתְמְכוּ בוֹ!
בִּי, חָיוֹ לֹא יִחְיֶה,
מוֹת יוּמָת, דָּמָיו בּוֹ.' [...]

'Give him his deserts. Then let him look to his abominations to save him. I beg of You, do not let him live. *He should die; let his blood lie on his own head.*'

עִמָּנוּאֵל בֶּן־שְׁלֹמֹה מִן הָאֲדֻמִּים

Immanuel dei Rossi

אֱנוֹשׁ אָנוּשׁ

MAN

אֱנוֹשׁ אָנוּשׁ הֶבֶל יִפְצֶה,
נְהַר אֲשָׁמָיו עַד צַוָּאר יֶחֱצֶה,
בְּגַפּוֹ יָבֹא בְּגַפּוֹ יֵצֵא.

Doomed, man gives vent to empty talk.
The torrent of his guilt rises neck-high.
He comes alone and will go away alone.

בִּמְסִבּוֹת הַזְּמַן יָרוּץ וְיִרְכַּב,
וְהָאֲדָמָה אֲשֶׁר מִמֶּנָּה הָרְכַּב
הִיא שִׂמְלָתוֹ לְעֹרוֹ. בַּמֶּה יִשְׁכָּב ?

He rides headlong through the winding course of Time, but the earth of which he was compounded, *that will be the cloak which will wrap his body; in what else can he sleep?*

גּוּף נָגוּף וְאַשְׁמָתוֹ נוֹבַעַת
בְּנֶפֶשׁ נִגְאֶלֶת גַּם בְּלֹא דַעַת
כִּי תֹאכְלֶנּוּ הַתֹּלָעַת.

His body is infested; its guilt ferments in the polluted soul, all unaware that *the worm will eat him.*

יָגוֹן לֵילוֹ וַאֲנָחָה יוֹמוֹ,
וּבִמְלֹאת קִצּוֹ יִכָּרֵת שְׁמוֹ
מֵעִם אֶחָיו וּמִשַּׁעַר מְקוֹמוֹ.

His night is agony and his day despair. When his time is up, his name is cut off *from among his brethren and from the gate of his native place.*

יָשֹׁם עַל עֵקֶב בָּשְׁתּוֹ
וַעֲדֵי אֹבֵד אַחֲרִיתוֹ,
וְעָלָה בָאְשׁוֹ וְתַעַל צַחֲנָתוֹ.

He is aghast with shame, fated to perish forever. *The stench will rise from his rotting corpse.*

בְּפֶתַע יֵצֵא מִכַּנּוֹ
וְיָשִׂים בַּסֶּלַע קִנּוֹ
וְיֵבוֹשׁ מְקוֹרוֹ וְיֶחֱרַב מַעְיָנוֹ.

Suddenly, he is torn from his base and his home is set among the rocks. *His spring fails and his fountain runs dry.*

אֵיךְ יָרוּם לִבּוֹ וְעַפְעַפָּיו יִנָּשְׂאוּ –
וּמְהָרְסָיו וּמַחֲרִיבָיו מִמֶּנּוּ יֵצֵאוּ,

How can his heart be proud and his eyes haughty? His own despoilers come

עַל פִּיו יֵצְאוּ וְעַל פִּיו יָבֹאוּ.

from within himself. *They come out of his mouth and go back into it.*[1]

מַה יִתְרוֹן הָעוֹשֶׂה בַּאֲשֶׁר יִצְבֹּר –
וְעָרֹם יְרִיצוּהוּ אֶל הַבּוֹר,
אַל יָנוּס הַקַּל וְאַל יְמַלֵּט הַגִּבּוֹר.

What does a man gain by heaping up riches? Naked, he is hurried off to the grave. *The swift cannot escape, the warrior cannot save himself.*

זָכְרָה זֹּאת, אֱנוֹשׁ, וְהַעֲלֵה עַל לְבָבֶךָ:
פְּקֻדַּת כָּל הָאָדָם תִּפָּקֵד וּמָוֶת תְּשִׁיבֶךָ,
הָאָרֶץ יִהְיֶה מוֹשָׁבֶךָ.

Remember this, O man, and take it to heart: the lot of all mankind awaits you, to surrender you to death. *Then the earth will be your home.*

דָּמִיתָ כְּמַר מִדְּלִי וּכְשַׁחַק מֹאזְנַיִם,
וַעֲפַר אֶרֶץ אֲשֶׁר בְּפֶתַח עֵינַיִם
הִנֵּה הוּא לָךְ כְּסוּת עֵינַיִם.

You were no more than a drop from a bucket, a speck of dust on the scales; and the soil of the earth in the doorway of your eyes, *this will be the covering for your eyes.*

בְּשָׂרְךָ יִלְבַּשׁ גּוּשׁ עָפָר וְרִמָּה,
וְכַחוֹל אֲשֶׁר עַל שְׂפַת יָם הָעֲצוּמָה
יַאֲרִכוּן יָמֶיךָ עַל הָאֲדָמָה. [...]

Your body will be clothed with worms and scabs. And, like the grains of sand on the endless sea-shore, *you will long endure in the land.*

מְשֻׁלָּם דַּאפִּיאֶרָה

Meshullam da Piera

שְׁאֵלוּנִי: חֲכַם לֵבָב

THE POET

שְׁאֵלוּנִי: 'חֲכַם לֵבָב, וּמִי זֶה
אֲשֶׁר בֵּין טוֹב וּבֵין רַע לֹא יְבַקֵּר,
וְיָשִׁיר אֶל מְתֵי הַדּוֹר בְּכָבוֹד –
וְלִבּוֹ הָאֱמֶת אִזֵּן וְחִקֵּר?'
הֲשִׁיבֹתִים: 'מְיֻדָּעַי, אֲנִי הוּא,
אֲנִי הוּא הַמְשׁוֹרֵר הַמְשַׁקֵּר!'

They asked me: 'Tell us, wise of heart, who is it that makes no distinction between good and bad and sings the praises of the men of his time, though his heart has weighed the truth and pondered it?' I answered them: 'Why, that is I, my friends, I, the lying poet!'

1. A play on the literal meaning of Numbers 27.21 which, in context, reads: 'At his [the priest's] word they [the people] shall go out and shall come home.'

בְּרָן־יַחַד

SONG AT DAWN

בְּרָן־יַחַד, בְּרֹן כּוֹכְבֵי שְׁחָרַי,
כְּתָם־לַיִל וְאוֹר מִכָּל עֲבָרַי;
כְּתָם־לַיִל וְהָאֹפֶל מְנֻדָּח,
וְעָלוּ מִפְּאַת מִזְרָח מְאוֹרַי;
בְּהִנָּעֵר שְׂעִפַּי מִתְּנוּמָה,
בְּהָקִיץ מִשְּׁנַת לַיִל יְצוּרַי –
אֲשַׁחֵר הַשְּׁחָרִים בִּנְגִינָה,
וְהַבֹּקֶר אֲבַקֵּר עִם זְמִירַי.
וְיָדַי תָּמְכָה כִּנּוֹר וְעוּגָב,
וְתִרְגַּלְתִּי שְׂמֹאלִי עַל יְתָרַי.
אֲקַשֵּׁר מַעֲדַנּוֹת תֹּף וְחָלִיל –
וְעֵת אֶמְשֹׁךְ, וְעֵת אַתִּיר קְשָׁרַי.
וְאֶפְצַח רֹן וּמַשְׂכִּיתִי בְּשֵׁבֶט,
לְדֵעָה אִם יְשִׁיבוּן לִי אֲמָרַי,
לְדֵעָה אִם יְנַחֲמוּנִי בְּנוּדִי
בְּאֶרֶץ הַנְּדוֹד, אֶרֶץ מְגוּרַי.
אֲזַמֵּר – לֹא יְשִׁיבֵנִי חֲלִילִי,
וְעוֹד לֹא צָהֲלוּ קוֹלָם זְמִירַי!
יְדוּעֵי סוֹד, יְדַעְתֶּם עַל כְּלֵי שִׁיר
אֲשֶׁר לֹא יִפְצְחוּ רִנָּה לְשִׁירַי,
וְאֵין קוֹל צִפֳּרִים מִבֵּין עֳפָיִים
וְלֹא שִׁיר הַדְּרוֹר מִבֵּין דְּבִירַי?
אֲלֵיהֶם רַב שְׁלוֹמִי, כִּי בְאֵין פֶּה
יְשִׂיחוּנִי לְהַצְנִיעַ סְפָרַי,
לְהַצְנִיעַ מְשָׁלַי מִבְּנֵי אִישׁ,
וְיוֹתֵר מֵאֱנוֹשׁ הַסְתֵּר סְתָרַי. [...]

When they sang together, when my morning stars sang as the night was ending and light came up from all sides; when the night was ending, the darkness expelled, and my sun rose in the East; when my thoughts shook off slumber and my limbs woke from their sleep of night – then I sought to greet the dawn with music and to worship the morning with song. In my hands I held the lyre and the pipe, and my left hand moved skilfully over the strings. I tied the timbrel and the flute to my side and adjusted their loops, now tightening, now loosening them. Then I began to sing and improvise, to see if my instruments would answer my words, to see if they would comfort me in my wandering, in this land of exile which is my home. But though I sang, my flute did not answer, and even the birds did not raise their voices in mirth. O masters of mysteries, have you ever known a musical instrument that would not strike up when I sing – and the birds voiceless among the branches, the swallow songless in my house? Yet I wish them well, for with their silence they counsel me to hide my works, to hide my words from men, to conceal my secrets from all men with even greater care.

לָנוּ עֲלָמוֹת

OF LOVE AND LIES

[...] לָנוּ עֲלָמוֹת לֹא יְדָעָן אִישׁ, וְהֵן
רֵאשִׁית אֲהָבֵינוּ וְקִנְיָנֵינוּ,
וּמְשַׂקְּרוֹת עַיִן לִשְׁמֹעַ פַּעֲמוֹן
שׁוּלֵי מְעִילֵנוּ וְרִמּוֹנֵינוּ.
וּכְסוֹחֲרֵי רִקְמָה – רְקָמוֹת יִשְׁאֲלוּ
לָהֶן שְׁלוּחֵינוּ וְנֶאֱמָנֵינוּ;
אָז נִדְבְּרוּ לֹא עַל דְּבַר מִמְכָּר וְלֹא
לִמְכֹּר סְחָרֵינוּ וְעִזְבוֹנֵינוּ.
יָגֵל מְבַשֵּׂר בֶּאֱמֹר כִּי לָקְחוּ
אֶשְׁכּוֹל כְּפָרֵינוּ וְשׁוֹשַׁנֵּינוּ –
כֶּתֶם חֲלִי הֵם שָׁלְחוּ לָנוּ, וְהוּא
תוֹרֵי זְהָבֵינוּ וְשַׂהֲרוֹנֵינוּ:
שָׁם תֶּחֱזֶה צוּרוֹת כְּתַבְנִית חוֹשְׁקִים,
צוּרוֹת מְחֻשָּׁבוֹת בְּדִמְיוֹנֵנוּ –
דִּמְיוֹן יְפַת תֹּאַר יְשֵׁנָה בֵּין שְׁדֵי
אוֹהֵב, וּפָנֶיהָ עֲלֵי פָּנֵינוּ. [...]

I have a maiden[1] whom no man has ever known; she is my chief love and treasure. Her eyes brighten when she hears the bells and pomegranates on the hem of my cloak. My faithful envoys, as if they were clothing-merchants, brought her embroideries, but they made no mention of payment, demanded no return for my wares. How joyfully the messenger then informed me that she had accepted my garland of henna blossoms and lilies, and had sent me a necklace of Nubian gold. It is as dear to me as braided plaits of gold and crescents. In it I can see the carved figures of lovers, like the very figures that are engraved in my imagination: a beautiful woman sleeping on the breast of her lover, and her face upon mine.

מַה יָּקְרוּ יָמִים אֲשֶׁר בָּהֶם לְקוֹל
מַזְכִּיר בְּנוֹת חֵן צָלֲלוּ אָזְנֵינוּ!
חָלְפוּ יְמֵי נֹעַר – וְכַמָּה נַעֲלֹז
בִּכְבוֹד יְמֵי שֵׂיבָה וּבִזְקוּנֵינוּ.
חָבוּשׁ לְרֹאשֵׁנוּ פְּאֵר, כִּי עָלְתָה
שֵׂיבָה בְּרֹאשֵׁנוּ וּבִזְקָנֵנוּ.
הוּסַר חֲלִי יַלְדוּת, וְיִרְאַת חֵטְא – עֲנָק
עַל גַּרְגְּרוֹתֵינוּ וּבִגְרוֹנֵנוּ.
אִם תִּמְצְאוּ שֶׁבַח בְּכָזָב הֶאֱרִיךְ –

How precious were those days when the voices of graceful girls rang in our ears! Those youthful days are gone, yet we greatly rejoice in the honour of old age. My head is covered with a glorious turban of grey hairs, my beard is white. Youth's ornament has been removed; now the fear of sin hangs like a jewel from my neck. If you find that my tributes are wordy with falsehood,

1. In Hebrew 'we have maidens'.

מִתּוֹךְ שְׂחוֹק נִכְתַּב וְעַל יֵינֵנוּ.
אַל תִּשְׁמְעוּ עֵדוּת יְדוּעִים מֵאֲשֶׁר
עַל פִּי חֲלִילִים יֹאמְרוּ נוֹגְנֵינוּ:
זֹאת הַמְּלָאכָה תֶּאֱהַב כַּחַשׁ, וְהוּא
הַשָּׁוְא אֲשֶׁר בַּשִּׁיר וּבִלְשׁוֹנֵינוּ.
כִּמְשַׂחֲקִים נָשִׁיר מְתֵי הַדּוֹר, וְלֹא
לָתֵת בְּעֵין הַשּׁוֹמְעִים חִנֵּנוּ.
נֶאְהַב אֲשֶׁר פָּנָיו מְעִידוֹת אַהֲבָה,
יַכִּיר בְּרִית אַהֲבָה בְּאִישׁוֹנֵינוּ.
וּשְׁנֵי לְבָבוֹת עַל חֲשׁוּדֵי תַאֲוָה
לָנוּ, וְיִמָּצֵא הַחֲשָׁד מֹאזְנֵינוּ. [...]

[know that] they were written in jest and over wine. When we poets extol the virtues of famous men to the sound of pipes, pay no heed: ours is a labour of lies, and that is why my verses and my mouth are full of deceit. It is in play that we celebrate the men of our time, and not to win the favour of our listeners. In truth, I love only that man whose face bespeaks his love for me, and he too will see love's pledge in my eyes. As for those whose love is suspect, for them I have a double heart; and I can weigh the suspicion in the balance.

הָרוּג בְּיַד

[...] הָרוּג בְּיַד יַלְדֵי תְמוּתָה, לֹא בְיָד
נִרְצָח; וְלֹא שָׁפַךְ אֱנוֹשׁ דָּמֶךְ:
רִפְאוּת תְּעָלָה אֵין בְּיָדֵנוּ, אֲבָל
נַזְכִּיר יְגוֹן רַבִּים לְהַחְלִימֶךְ:
מִשֹּׁד מְרִירֵי יוֹם וּמֵאֶנְקַת מְתֵי
מַכְאוֹב אֲשֶׁר הָיוּ בְעוֹלָמֶךְ,
מִיֹּדְעֵי שֶׁבֶר וְעֹצֶם הֳחֳלִי –
נִשָּׂא מְשָׁלֵינוּ לְהַעְצִימֶךְ.
נַזְכִּיר יְמֵי רָעָה וְתַלְאוּבוֹת בְּנֵי
אָדָם – וְאוּלַי יַעֲבֹר זַעְמֶךְ.
אוֹי לָהּ לְנֶחָמָה לְקוּחָה מִכְּאֵב
אַחִים וְכָל עֶצֶב לְתַנְחוּמֶיךְ!

TO A FATHER IN MOURNING

You have been felled by death's messenger, not by a murderous hand: no human being shed your blood.[1] We have no cure to offer you, but we can invoke the sorrows of others to help you recover. To fortify you, we shall make our song out of the havoc of embittered men, the groans of the tormented whom you have known, the victims of disaster and harsh sickness. We shall recall evil days and the searing pain of men: perhaps your fury will abate. Woe to the comfort that must feed on the pain and sorrow of brethren for your consolation!

1. Presumably, addressed to the father, whose blood is one with the blood of his son.

יוֹשֵׁב וּמִשְׁתּוֹמֵם, הֲלֹא תֵדַע סְפֹד?
נִכְוֶה, וְאֵיךְ עָמַד בְּךָ טַעְמֶךָ?
הַאַתְּ לְגֹדֶל שִׁבְרְךָ נִבְהָל, וְאִם
הָיוּ כְּאַכְזָרִי הֲמוֹן רַחֲמֶיךָ?
לֹא תֵבְךְּ וְלֹא תָנֹד לְבֵן וּלְאָח אֲשֶׁר
מֵעִמְּךָ לֻקַּח בְּסוֹף יָמֶיךָ.
מֵעִמְּךָ לֻקַּח – וְלָנוּ בַּבְּכִי
נִתַּן שְׁכֶם אַחַד עֲלֵי שִׁכְמֶךָ.
כּוֹאֵב, גְּעַר בִּמְנַחֲמִים וּזְעַק, עֲדֵי
מִגַּעֲרָתְךָ יִתְמְהוּ שָׁמֶיךָ,
וּרְעַשׁ בְּמִסְתָּרִים, עֲדֵי כִּי יִרְעֲשׁוּ
סִפִּים וְהַגַּלְגַּל לְקוֹל רַעְמֶךָ.
אַל תַּחֲשֹׁב, עָצֵב, לְהִתְנַחֵם כְּתֹם
שִׁבְעַת יְמֵי אֵבֶל וְכַהִתַּמֶּךָ;
נַחְנוּ נְגַלֶּה סוֹד מְהוּמָתְךָ לְכֹל
יָבוֹא. וּמַה בֶּצַע בְּהַעְלִימֶךָ?
אִם תֶּחֱשֶׁה, הִנְנִי לְעוֹרֵר הַבְּכִי
וּבְתוֹכְחוֹת מוּסָר לְהַכְלִימֶךָ.
הֵא לְךָ יְדִיד נֶאְמָן אֲשֶׁר עַל הֲדָמִי
יָרִיב בְּךָ תָמִיד וְיִלָּחֶמְךָ.
יֵחַם לְבַב עָצְבִּי לְהָעִיר דִּמְעֲךָ,
עֵת אַהֲבָה אוֹסִיף וְאֶרְחָמֶךָ. [...]

O you who sit dumbfounded, do you not know how to lament? Scorched [by grief], how can you be as you were? Are you stunned by your great disaster? Or has your tender love turned into cruelty? You do not weep or moan for the son and companion taken from you in your old age. He was taken from you, but our share of tears is greater than yours. Sufferer, rebuke your comforters, cry out until the heavens are aghast at your rebuke; clamour in the secret [chambers], until the thresholds and the spheres quake at the sound of your thunder. Sorrower, do not think to find comfort when the seven days of mourning come to an end. We shall reveal your secret terror to all comers; why try to hide it? If you keep silent, I shall call for weeping, I shall shame you with my sharp reproaches. You have in me a true friend who will always contest your silence and dispute with you. It grieves my heart to stir up your tears, for all the while I love you dearly.

טֹדְרוֹס אַבּוּלְעָאפְיָה

Todros Abulafia

בְּאַהֲבָה חַלְתִּי

OH, TO BE A WOMAN!

ועל בת עֲרַב עָרְבָה לי אהבתה, ובתוך עלמות ראיתי אותה, משיקות אשה אל אחותה.

Upon seeing an Arab girl whom I loved in the company of other girls, kissing one another.

בָּאַהֲבָה חַלְתִּי וְלֹא יָלַדְתִּי,
וּבְפַח צְבִיָּה בַּת עֲרָב נִלְכַּדְתִּי.
לִנְשֹׁק בְּפִיהָ אִוְּתָה נַפְשִׁי, עֲדֵי
לִהְיוֹת נְקֵבָה בַּעֲדָהּ חָמַדְתִּי –
כִּי הַנְּקֵבוֹת הִיא מְנַשֶּׁקֶת, וּבִשְׁ־
בִיל שֶׁאֲנִי זָכָר, אֲנִי הִפְסַדְתִּי!

I have laboured in love but have not given birth, caught in the toils of this daughter of Arabia. So great is my desire to kiss her on the mouth that, for her sake, I wish I were a woman. For it is women that she kisses and I, being a male, am the loser.

אָמְרָה – הֲכִי נוֹד רָצְתָה

THE OLD POET AND THE GIRL

אָמְרָה – הֲכִי נוֹד רָצְתָה, עֵת רָאֲתָה
כִּי זָרְקָה שֵׂיבָה וְהִלְבִּין שְׂעָרִי:
'שַׁחַר כְּבָר עָלָה בְּרֹאשְׁךָ, וַאֲנִי
סַהַר – וְהַשַּׁחַר יְגָרֵשׁ זָהֳרִי!'
וָאֶעֱנֶה: 'לֹא כֵן, אֲבָל שֶׁמֶשׁ, וְזֶה
חֻקֵּךְ בְּעוֹד יוֹמָם לְבַל תִּסְתַּתְּרִי.'
אָמְרָה: 'כְּבָר לִרְדּוֹף אֲהָבִים אֵין בְּךָ
כֹּחַ, וּמַה יִּסְכָּן־לְךָ הִשָּׁאֲרִי?'
'גִּבּוֹר כְּאַרְיֵה לַעֲשׂוֹת חֶפְצֵךְ אֲנִי',
שַׂחְתִּי, 'וּבִי לֹא נֶחֱלַף רַק תָּאֳרִי.'
עָנְתָה: 'אֲרִי אַתְּ, וַאֲנִי עָפְרָה – לְזֹאת
אָגוּר לְהִתְגּוֹרֵר אֲנִי עִם גּוּר אֲרִי.'

Wishing to leave me, when she saw that I was growing old and grey, she said: 'Dawn has already risen upon your head. I am the moon, and dawn drives away my splendour!' I answered: 'Ah no, you are the sun, and it is in your nature not to hide all day long.' Said she: 'You are no longer strong enough for the pursuit of love. What good will it do you if I stay on?' 'I am as bold as a lion to do your will,' I answered. 'Nothing in me has changed except for my outward appearance.' Said she: 'You are indeed a lion. But I am a gazelle, and that is why I am afraid to live with a lion-whelp.'

מַה מַּר וְנוֹרָא

A REMEMBRANCE

מַה מַּר וְנוֹרָא יוֹם נְדוּדֵךְ, יַעֲלַת
הַחֵן, לְזִכְרוֹ אֵין מְתֹם בִּבְשָׂרִי.
אַךְ מַה מְּאֹד יָפוּ פְעָמַיִךְ, בְּעֵת
הִשְׂתָּרְגוּ עָלוּ עֲלֵי צַוָּארִי.

How terrible, how bitter was the day of your parting, my graceful girl. When I remember it, no part of my body is left unscarred. But how very beautiful were your feet when they twined and climbed my neck.

וְשָׁמַעְתִּי בְּרָאשֵׁי הַבְּכָאִים

וְשָׁמַעְתִּי בְּרָאשֵׁי הַבְּכָאִים
כְּקוֹל יוֹנָה, בְּעֵת בָּאתִי לְגַנִּי.
וְהִבַּטְתִּי גְרוֹנֶיהָ, וְהִנֵּה
עֲנָק מָלֵא – כְּשִׁירַי בַּאֲדוֹנִי.
כְּאַלְמָנָה מְבַכָּה לַנְּדוֹד, אַף
כְּכַלָּה בַּעֲנָק נִרְאֵית לְעֵינָי.
שְׁאִלְתִּיהָ: ׳הֲבִנְדוֹד אוֹהֲבֵךְ
תְּשִׂימִין לָךְ עֲנָק?׳ וַתַּעֲנֵנִי:
׳פְּנִינֵי הַבְּכִי קָפְאוּ בְּרִדְתָּם
וְהָיוּ לַעֲנָק עַל צַוְּרוֹנִי.׳

THE NECKLACE

When I came into my garden, I heard the voice of a dove from the top of the poplars. I looked at her throat and there I saw a necklace full [of gems] – as full as my songs are with my lord's praise. She moaned like a widow lamenting her loss, but she seemed to me a bride wearing her necklace. I asked her: 'Would you put on a necklace when your beloved is gone?' And she answered: 'My coral tears froze as they came down and turned into this necklace around my throat.'

אֵשׁ מִלְּבָבִי

אֵשׁ מִלְּבָבִי, וּמֵעֵינַי זְרָמִים.
תֹּפֶת בְּלִבִּי, אֲבָל עֵינַי כְּיַמִּים.
צַחוּ דְמָעַי, וְהֵם כַּדָּם אֲדֻמִּים.
שָׁלַח נְדֹד אֵשׁ בְּעַצְמִי, מָסַךְ דְּמָעַי בְּדָמִי,
זֻקְּקוּ בַעֲלִיל חִיל, נִדְעֲכוּ בִי בְּחֻמִּי.

הַשּׁוֹמְעִים נִפְלְאוֹת עֹז אַהֲבָתִי
אוֹתִי תְּמוֹל שָׁאֲלוּ מִי יַעֲלָתִי.
וָאֶעֱנֵם: ׳בַּת־עֲרָב הִיא רַעְיָתִי –
אַךְ לֶחֱיָהּ הוּא אֲדוֹמִי חֶצְיוֹ, וְחֶצְיוֹ אֲרַמִּי.
וְזָהֳרוֹ עָשׁ, כְּסִיל מַחְפִּיר וְכוֹכְבֵי מְרוֹמִי.׳

THE DAUGHTER OF ARABIA

Fire flows from my heart and a river from my eyes; there is a hell in my heart, but my eyes are like seas. My tears are pure, yet red as blood. Parting has set my bones on fire and mixed my tears with my heart's blood. They were purified in the crucible of anguish and leaped to my eyes as my heat rose.

Those who had heard of the wonders of my fierce love asked me yesterday who my gazelle was. And I told them: 'My dearest is a daughter of Arabia; yet her cheeks are half Edomite, half Aramean.[1] Their radiance puts the Great Bear to shame, as well as Orion and all the stars of heaven.'

1. That is, half red and half white; see note on p. 345.

נַמְתִּי, וְלִי אָמְרָה יָפָה וְתַמָּה:
׳חוֹשֵׁק הֲיָנוּם?׳ עֲנִיתִיהָ: ׳אֲיֻמָּה,
חֵי אַהֲבָה, אֵין הֲנָחָה לִי בְּנוּמָה!
אָכֵן שְׁנָתִי וְנוּמִי אוּלַי יְצוּדֵךְ חֲלוֹמִי.
וַאֲסַלֵּד בְּחִיל נוּדֵךְ בְּשִׁבְתִּי וְקוּמִי.׳

I slept, and she, lovely and perfect, said to me: 'How can a lover sleep?' I answered her: 'O majesty, I swear by Love that I can find no rest in slumber. I am sleeping only in the hope that my dream may trap you. [Awake,] sitting or standing, I am shaken with the anguish of your parting.'

שְׂרָפָה לְבָבִי, וְאֵין עוֹזֵר וְסוֹמֵךְ.
וָאֹמְרָה: ׳אֵיךְ בְּאֵשׁ קִצְפֵּךְ וְזַעְמֵךְ
תִּשְׂרֹף לְבָבִי, וְהוּא מֵאָז הֲדוֹמֵךְ?׳
וַתַּעֲנֶה: ׳מִי־לְךָ מִי, אִם אֶשְׂרְפָה אֶת הֲדוֹמִי?
רֹן לְבָבִי וְגִיל, עֵת אֶשְׂרְפֶנּוּ בְּזַעְמִי!׳

She burnt my heart, and there was no one who could help me. I said: 'How can you, in the fire of your fury, burn my heart that has always been your foot-stool?' To which she answered: 'What concern is it of yours if I burn my own foot-stool? Sing out, my heart; rejoice as I burn it in my rage!'

בֹּאִי, וְלוּ בַחֲלוֹם, עָפְרַת אֲהָבִים,
הִתְנַדְּבִי, לוּ בְמִדְבָּרִים עֲרֵבִים.
נְאֻמֵךְ מְעַט קָט יְכַב מוֹקְדֵי קְרָבִים.
זרני ולו פי אלמנאם וגד ולו באלסלאם
פקאל אלקליל בך צׄמא אלמסתהאם.

Oh come, my lovely doe, if only in a dream. Give yourself to me, if only in sweet speech. Even a few words would put out the flaming furnace within me. Oh come to me, if only in my dream; favour me, if only with your greeting. For your words, however few, can quench the thirst of the one who is yearning.[1]

אִם הַזְּמַן

THE MERRY DEBTOR

אִם הַזְּמַן מוּל זָהֳרִי נוֹבֵחַ,
הִנּוֹ כְּכֶלֶב, וַאֲנִי יָרֵחַ!
אֶשְׂחַק לְקוֹרוֹתָיו וְאֵלָיו אֶלְעֲגָה,
אֶעָשׂ כְּעִוֵּר, וַאֲנִי פִּקֵּחַ.
אַרְאֶה, לְהַכְעִיס אוֹיְבִים, כֹּחַ וָאוֹן.
לֹא לַזְּמַן אִכַּף וְאֶשְׁתּוֹחֵחַ.

If Time barks at my brilliance, he is a dog and I am the moon. I laugh him and his accidents to scorn. I play the blind man, but I am clear-sighted. To spite my enemies, I make a show of prowess. I will not bow or stoop before

1. The last two verses are in Arabic, probably from a popular song.

אֵצֵא בְּפָנִים נֶעֱלָסִים לַיְקוּם,
וַאְנִי בְּתוֹךְ לִבִּי בְּמַר צוֹרֵחַ.
אֶלְבַּשׁ וְאֶרְכַּב, אֹכְלָה, אֶשְׁתֶּה עֲדֵי
אֶשְׁכַּר, וְרִישִׁי אֶהְיֶה שׁוֹכֵחַ.
אִיגַע לְהִתְנַהֵג כְּרֵעַי, וַאֲנִי
כִּמְתַחֲרֶה סוּסִים וְהוּא פִּסֵּחַ.
אֶלְוֶה בְּעֵת לֹא יִהְיֶה לִי, אֶתְּנָה
לָזֶה אֲשֶׁר מִזֶּה אֲנִי לוֹקֵחַ.
כָּזֹאת וְכָזֹאת מִפְּעָלוֹתַי עֲד הַלּוֹם,
חַי אֵל, וְאָנֹכִי בְּרֹן פּוֹצֵחַ!

Time. I put on a merry face when I go out into the world, though deep in my heart I am crying bitterly. I dress up and go out riding, I dine and drink myself drunk until I forget my poverty. I slave to keep up with my companions; I am like a lame man competing with horses. I borrow money when I have none, and what I take from the one I give to the other. Such are my doings to this very day and, so help me God, I still shout for joy!

יְדַעְתִּיךָ נְדִיב־לֵב

FIGS

לבן שושן, בבקשו ממנו כי ישלח לו תאנים:

To Ibn Shoshan, after I had requested him to send me figs:

יְדַעְתִּיךָ נְדִיב־לֵב בִּתְאֵנִים,
וּמֵאָח אֵינְךָ נוֹצֵר תְּאֵנָה.
וְאֵיךְ שַׁבְתָּ כְּהַיּוֹם לִי לְכִילַי
וְנֶהְפַּךְ לָךְ לְרַע לִבָּא וְעֵינָא?
וְקָרָאתָ לְסוּסָתִי חֲמוֹרָה —
וְעֵינֶיךָ, אֱמֶת, לֹא תֶחֱזֶינָה.
אֱמֶת, רוֹאֶה אֲנִי דַּיַּן עֲמֹרָה
בְּשׁוּרְךָ הֵן בְּכָל רֶגַע וְעוֹנָה.
וְיָדַעְתִּי לָךְ בְּגַו דְּבָרִים
דִּפְסִילְנָא בְּדִינָא לָךְ לְדַיְנָא.
וְנִסְתָּרוֹת אֲנִי עוֹד לֹא אֲגַלֶּה,

I have known you to be generous with figs; you never withheld your figs from your fellows. Then how did it happen, today, that you turned into a skinflint? What made you become tight-fisted and flint-hearted? And how could you call my mare an ass when, in fact, you are blind? In truth, whenever I look at you, I see that you are fit to be a judge in Gomorrah.[1] The things I know about you would disqualify you by law from trying my case. But, as yet, I shall not reveal your secrets. Instead, let me

1. The judges of Sodom and Gomorrah were notorious for their injustices.

אֲבָל אִיעָצְךָ עֵצָה נְכוֹנָה:
תְּאֵנָה חָנְטָה שַׁלַּח, וְחֵלֶק
לְשִׁבְעָה בָּם תְּנָה, גַּם אֶל שְׁמוֹנָה.
וְהִנֵּה לָךְ זְמוֹרָתִי שְׁמוּרָה,
הֲכִי הֵן לֹא לְזָר עוֹד אֶתְּנֶנָּה.
וְעִם גִּבּוֹר קְטָטָה אַל תְּבַקֵּשׁ,
וְאַל תָּבוֹא בְּיָם מֵאֵין סְפִינָה.

give you some sound advice: send me figs in plenty, enough for seven or even eight mouths. And in return, here is my flatus,[1] henceforth reserved for you alone, not to be given to any stranger. In short, never pick a fight with a man of might, nor put to sea without a boat!

שְׁלֹשָׁה שִׁירִים מִבֵּית־הַסֹּהַר

THREE POEMS FROM PRISON

א

טַבְּעוֹתַי אִם נָפְלוּ – אֶצְבְּעוֹתַי
נִשְׁאֲרוּ. אֵין הוֹדִי בְּרֹב טַבְּעוֹתַי!
דָּת וּמִשְׂרָה עוֹד לִי, וְנֶפֶשׁ יְקָרָה,
זֹאת יְרֻשַּׁת הוֹרַי וְנַחֲלַת אֲבוֹתַי.
רַב פְּעָלִים לִבִּי וְטוֹב מַעֲלָלִים,
אַךְ בְּחֶסְרוֹן כִּיס חָסְרוּ מִפְעֲלוֹתַי.
נְאַקֶּו יָהּ שֶׁהוּא, וְיִהְיֶה, וְהָיָה,
כִּי יְהִי עוֹד זְמַן וְיָמִים מְשָׁרְתַי.
סַמְּכֵנִי, יָהּ, כִּי רְצוֹנְךָ רְצוֹנִי.
עַד לְמָתַי יִגְבַּר כְּסִיל? עַד לְמָתַי?

1

My rings have fallen off, but I still have my fingers; my glory is not in my wealth of rings. I still have my faith, my dignity, and my precious soul, the legacy of my parents, the patrimony of my ancestors. My heart harbours exploits and good deeds, but having lost all my money, I am at a loss to act. Yet I hope in the Lord, Who is, was, and shall be, that Time and its days will once again be in my service. Uphold me, Lord, for Your will is mine. How much longer shall the fool prevail? How much longer?

ב

וכאשר שם המלך אותי בבור ואת השרים
האחרים... שמעתי כקול סיסים ותורים:

חֵי אַהֲבָה, צִפֳּרִים, עוּפוּ אֱלֵי אוֹהֲבִים
וּשְׂאוּ שְׁלוֹם כּוֹאֲבִים תּוֹךְ בּוֹר כְּלוּא יוֹשְׁבִים.

2

When I was in prison, by order of the king, together with some other noblemen, I heard voices like those of swallows and doves:

I adjure you, birds, in the name of Love: fly to the lovers and bear them greetings from those who are tormented

1. *Zmora*, which also means a vine-twig.

בִּי, תֹּאמְרוּ כִּי רְעֵבִים הֵם, צְמֵאִים, אֲבָל
לֶחֶם דְּמָעוֹת וְדַם לֵב אוֹכְלִים שׁוֹאֲבִים.
יוֹשְׁבִים בְּבוֹר מַאֲפֵל שָׁפֵל כְּנֵפֶל, וּבֵין
פַּרְעוֹשׁ וְיַתּוּשׁ וְכִנִּים לוֹהֲטִים שׁוֹכְבִים.
חַיּוֹת קְטַנּוֹת אֲשֶׁר לֹא נִקְרְאוּ עוֹד בְּשֵׁם
מִשְׁתַּקְשְׁקִין שָׁם כְּמוֹ חוֹשְׁקִים בְּעֵת עוֹגְבִים.
יִשְׁרֹק זְבוּב לִדְבוֹרָה שָׁם, וְשֵׁן יַחֲרֹק
עַכְבָּר, וְיַחְדָּו עֲלֵי נֶפֶשׁ וְגוּף אוֹרְבִים.
הַנּוֹגְשִׂים צוֹרְרִים, אָצִים, וְהַשּׁוֹטְרִים
צֻוּוּ לְבַל יִתְּנוּ לֶחֶם — וְהָעוֹרְבִים.

in prison. Tell them, I pray you, that they hunger and thirst, though they feed on the bread of tears and drink their heart's blood. They sit in a dark, vile dungeon, [hidden away] like an untimely birth. They lie among fleas, gnats, and man-eating lice. Tiny beasts, who haven't yet been named, jostle one another there like lovers in their lust. There the fly whistles for the bee, the rat grinds his teeth, and all lie in ambush for their body and soul. The overseers assail them and harass them; the guards are under orders not to give them food, and the ravens are too.[1]

ג

טִיט יְגָרְשׁוּ מֵי יָם וְרֶפֶשׁ יַעֲלוּ,
אַךְ הַפְּנִינִים בִּמְצוּלוֹת צָלְלוּ.
דֶּרֶךְ זְמַן כֵּן הוּא, לְהַעֲלוֹת זוֹלֲלִים,
וּבְכֵן כְּרוּם זֻלּוּת — יְקָרִים יָשְׁפְּלוּ.
רָעוֹת וְטוֹבוֹת הַזְּמַן מִתְהַפְּכוֹת:
הַחוֹשְׁבִים כִּי הֵם תְּמִידוֹת — סָכְלוּ;
וַאֲשֶׁר תְּבוּנָה בוֹ יְהַתֵּל בִּזְמַן
וִישַׁעֲשַׁע נַפְשׁוֹ בְּ׳אוּלַי׳ אוֹ בְּ׳לוּ׳.
סוֹף סוֹף בְּשַׁחַק מֹאזְנַיִם יֵשׁ, וּבָם
יֵרְדוּ תְמִימִים, וַחֲסֵרִים יַעֲלוּ!

3

The seawater casts up mud and filth, but corals sink into their depths. This is the way of Time: he lifts up the dissolute, and as the base are raised the noble are debased. Time reverses the good and the bad. Only a fool could imagine that his state is constant. The man of sense laughs at Time, and cheers himself with 'perhaps' or 'if'. After all, there is a Balance in heaven[2] in which the flawless go down while the faulty rise up.

1. Unlike the ravens who brought bread and meat to Elijah (1 Kings 17.6).

2. *Shaḥak* means both 'heaven' and 'dust'; the pun is on Isaiah 40.15: '. . . the nations . . . are accounted as the *dust* on the scales [or balance]'.

אַבְרָהָם אַבּוּלְעָאפְיָה

Abraham Abulafia

הֵן הָעָם הַמָּךְ

ZECHARIAH, THE MESSIAH

הֵן הָעָם הַמָּךְ,
אֲשֶׁר כָּל גּוֹי שׁוֹסֵהוּ
וְכָל עַם בּוֹזֵהוּ,
הֵן הַיּוֹם הַזֶּה
יוֹם בְּשׂוֹרָה הוּא לוֹ:
וּזְכַרְיָהוּ הַמְבַשֵּׂר
רוֹכֵב עַל עָנָן עָב,
וְהָעָב עָב טַל,
וְהַטַּל דַּק קַל,
וְהֶעָנָן כָּבֵד מְאֹד.
הֵן רִכְבּוֹ רֶכֶב אֵשׁ,
וְסוּסָיו סוּסֵי רוּחַ,
וּמְשָׁרְתָיו חַיּוֹת אֵשׁ מְמַלְּלוֹת.
אֵשׁ וְעָנָן סָבִיב
הָרֵי הֲרָרִים סוֹבְבִים,
וְרוּחַ הַמְבַשֵּׂר
מַרְעִישׁ כָּל הָאָרֶץ בְּרַחֲפוֹ.
דִּינִים וּדְבָרִים
מְחַדֵּשׁ לִבּוֹ בְּקִרְבּוֹ,
וּבְמִכְתַּב אֵשׁ יִכְתְּבֵם
בְּעֵט שַׁלְהֶבֶת.
נוֹרָא וְאָיֹם כֹּחַ הָעֵט,
וְהַדְּיוֹ דָּם שָׂמוֹ בְּקִרְבּוֹ.
וְטִפֵּי טַלּוֹ מַשְׁקִים הָאָרֶץ
וּמְלַחְלְחִים הַיַּבָּשָׁה,
וְיַבֶּשֶׁת מְצוּי מִמְּצוּי.

This poor people, plundered by all nations, abused by all peoples – this is the day that shall bring it good tidings. For Zechariah the Herald is riding upon a thick cloud, a cloud thick with dew, dew that is flaky and swift, and the cloud is heavy and full. His chariot is a chariot of fire, his horses horses of wind, his servants murmuring fiery creatures. Fire and cloud surround the whirling towering mountains, and the breath of the Herald shakes the earth as he hovers over it. His heart moves him to new revelations, which he writes in a script of fire with a pen of flame. Fearful and awesome is the power of the pen, for he has filled it with blood for ink. His dew-drops water the earth and freshen the dry land, the stone-dry land.[1] And his bow

1. The line is obscure.

וְהַקֶּשֶׁת חִצִּים שְׁנוּנִים תּוֹרֶה
עַד אֲשֶׁר יַבְקִיעַ חַלּוֹנֵי הָרָקִיעַ
בְּחִצֵּי חִצָּיו.
רוּחַ הַחִצִּים מְרַחֶפֶת בַּלְּבָבוֹת
וְשׂוֹרֶפֶת הַכְּלָיוֹת
וּמְפַזֶּרֶת כָּל הָרוּחוֹת,
וְאֵין מַרְפֵּא לַגְּוִיּוֹת.
וְהָרוּחַ הֶחָזָק
הַמֵּנִיעַ לֵב הַמְבַשֵּׂר
נוֹפֵחַ נִשְׁמַת חַיִּים
בְּאַפֵּי כָּל חַי.

shoots pointed arrows, until he splits the windows of the firmament with his multitude of arrows. The wind of the arrows quivers in the hearts, it burns men's vitals and scatters their spirits, and there is no remedy for the bodies. Then the mighty spirit, that moves the heart of the Herald, breathes the breath of life into the nostrils of every living creature.

וַיְדַבֵּר ידוד אֵלַי

THE BATTLE OF BLOOD AND INK

וַיְדַבֵּר ידוד אֵלַי
בְּעֵת רְאוֹתִי שְׁמוֹ
מְפֹרָשׁ בְּדָם וּמְיֻחָד בְּלִבִּי,
מַבְדִּיל בֵּין דָּם לִדְיוֹ,
וּבֵין דְּיוֹ לְדָם.
וַיֹּאמֶר אֵלַי ידוד:
'הִנֵּה נַפְשְׁךָ דָּם שְׁמָהּ
וּדְיוֹ שֵׁם רוּחֲךָ,
וְהִנֵּה אָבִיךָ וְאִמְּךָ כָּלִים
לִשְׁמִי זֶה וּלְזִכְרִי זֶה.
וָאֶשְׁמַע הַהֶבְדֵּל הַגָּדוֹל
אֲשֶׁר בֵּין נַפְשִׁי וְרוּחִי,

Then YDWD[1] spoke to me when I saw His Name spelled out in blood and designated in my heart, separating the blood from the ink and the ink from the blood. And YDWD said to me: 'Know that your soul's name is blood, and ink is the name of your spirit. Your father and mother long with all their hearts for this Name of mine and for my Title.'[2] When I heard the great difference between my soul and my

1. A variation on the Tetragrammaton YHWH.
2. An allusion to Exodus 3.15: 'This is my name forever, this is my title in every generation'.

וָאֶשְׂמְחָה בוֹ שִׂמְחָה גְּדוֹלָה מְאֹד.
וָאֵדַע כִּי נַפְשִׁי
שָׁכְנָה עַל צִבְעָהּ
בַּמַּרְאָה הָאֲדֻמָּה כְּדָם,
וְרוּחִי שָׁכְנָה עַל צִבְעָהּ
בַּמַּרְאָה הַשְּׁחֹרָה כִּדְיוֹ.
וְהַמִּלְחָמָה הָיְתָה חֲזָקָה מְאֹד בַּלֵּב
בֵּין הַדָּם וּבֵין הַדְּיוֹ,
וְהַדָּם הָיָה מִן הָרוּחַ
וְהַדְּיוֹ מִן הֶעָפָר –
וְנִצַּח הַדְּיוֹ לַדָּם,
וְהַשַּׁבָּת גָּבְרָה עַל כָּל יְמֵי הַחֹל.

spirit, I was filled with great joy. Then I knew that my soul was encamped under its own colour, in the mirror that is red as blood, and that my spirit was encamped under its own colour, in the mirror that is black as ink. And there was bitter warfare in my heart between the blood and the ink – the blood was from the air, the ink from the earth – and the ink triumphed over the blood, and the Sabbath overcame all the days of the week!

אַבְרָהָם בֶּן־שְׁמוּאֵל

Abraham ben Samuel

אֶל מִי מִגּוֹאֲלֵי דָם

CONFESSION

אֶל מִי מִגּוֹאֲלֵי דָם אֶצְעַק,
וְיָדַי שָׁפְכוּ דָמִי?
בָּחַנְתִּי לִבּוֹת מְשַׂנְאִים,
וְאֵין שׂוֹנֵא אוֹתִי כִּלְבָבִי.
רַבִּים פִּצְעֵי אוֹיְבִים וּמַכּוֹתָם,
וְאֵין מַכֶּה וּפוֹצֵעַ כְּנַפְשִׁי.
הִדִּיחוּנִי מַשְׁחִיתִים לְחַבֵּל,
וְאֵין מֵסִית וּמַדִּיחַ כְּעֵינַי.
מִגַּחַל אֶל גַּחַל הִתְהַלַּכְתִּי,
וְלֹא שְׂרָפַתְנִי אֵשׁ כְּחֹם תַּאֲוָתִי.
בְּפַחִים נִלְכַּדְתִּי וּבִמְצוּדוֹת,
וְלֹא לְכָדַנִי מוֹקֵשׁ כִּלְשׁוֹנִי.

To whom, among the avengers of blood, can I cry out, when my own hands have shed my blood? I have tested the hearts of those who hate me, but no one hates me as my own heart does. Many are the blows and wounds inflicted by my enemies, but no one batters me and wounds me as my soul does. Men of havoc have seduced me to do evil, but none incites me and seduces me as my eyes do. I have walked from fire to fire, but no flame has scorched me as the heat of my lust has. I have been caught in snares and nets, but no snare has caught me as my tongue has. Scorpion

נְשָׁכוּנִי נָחָשׁ וְעַקְרָב,
וְאֵין נוֹשֵׁךְ בְּשָׂרִי כְּשִׁנַּי.
שָׂרִים עַל קַל רְדָפוּנִי,
וְאֵין רוֹדֵף אוֹתִי כְּרַגְלַי.
מַכְאוֹבַי עָצְמוּ וְאָמְצוּ מִמֶּנִּי,
וְאֵין מַכְאוֹב כְּמָרְיִי.
נִירְבּוּ מַדְוֵי לְבָבִי,
וַעֲוֹנַי יוֹתֵר מִכֻּלָּם.
אֶל מִי אֶצְעַק וְעַל מִי ?
וּמַחֲרִיבַי מִמֶּנִּי יֵצְאוּ.
לֹא מָצָאתִי לִי טוֹב כִּי אִם לָבוֹא בְּסֵתֶר רַחֲמֶיךָ.
רַחֲמֶיךָ הַפְלֵה עַל לֵב נִדְהָמִים,
אֵל מֶלֶךְ יוֹשֵׁב עַל כִּסֵּא רַחֲמִים!

and snake have bitten me, but none bites my flesh as my teeth do. Swift-riding princes have pursued me, but none pursues me as my feet do. My torments are past counting, past endurance, but there is no torment like my own rebelliousness. Great are the sorrows of my heart, yet my sins outnumber them. To whom can I cry out, whom can I condemn, when those who are destroying me come from within myself? I have found nothing better than to seek refuge in Your mercy. Oh, shower Your excellent mercies upon our dumbstruck hearts – Lord, King, who sit upon the Throne of Mercy!

נַחוּם

Nahum

הַסְּתָיו אָרַח

SPRING SONG

הַסְּתָיו אָרַח, אָרַח מְעַצְּבִי.
עֵץ פְּרִי פָּרַח, פָּרַח גִּיל לְבָבִי.

גָּתְנוּ רֵיחַ יַחְדָּו הַנְּרָדִים,
צָץ וְצָמַח פַּרְדֵּס הַמְּגָדִים,
שָׂשׂ וְשָׂמֵחַ בָּהֶם לֵב יְדִידִים.
שׁוּב, צְבִי מֻדָּח בָּרַח מִכְּלוּבִי,
בֹּא, שְׁתֵה רֶקַח יֵינִי עִם חֲלָבִי!

Winter is gone, gone is my sorrow. The fruit-tree is in flower, and my heart flowers with joy.

The spikenards, as one, give forth their scent; the orchard of rare fruits is in full blossom. The hearts of friends are filled with merriment. O hunted gazelle[1] who escaped far from my hut, come back, come drink my mulled wine and my milk!

1. An allegorical figure of God.

חָלְפוּ תוּגוֹת יוֹם חָלְפוּ עֲרוּגוֹת
בַּהֲדַס סוּגוֹת, בְּרִקְמוֹת אֲרוּגוֹת.
מִבְּלִי פוּגוֹת נָסוּ הַדְּאָגוֹת.
מִגְדְּלוֹת מֶרְקָח נוֹטְפוֹת מוֹר סְבִיבַי,
הָאֱגוֹז סָרַח דָּלְיוֹ עַל מְסִבִּי.

Sorrows fled the day the flower-beds revived, fenced in by myrtles, braided with embroideries. Swiftly, then, all cares took flight. I am surrounded by coffers full of perfumes, dripping liquid myrrh. The boughs of the nut-tree trail low along my couch.

וַעֲצֵי חֶמְדָּה נָטוּ בֵּין צְלָלִים –
מִשְּׂמֹאל קִדָּה, מִיָּמִין אֲהָלִים.
כּוֹס כְּעֵין פִּטְדָה וּכְמַעֲשֵׂה גְלִילִים,
יַיִן כְּעֵין אֶקְדָּח מָסוּךְ מֵרְבִיבַי –
רִישׁ וְאוֹן אֶשְׁכַּח, הַטָּמוּן בְּחֻבִּי.

Trees of delight sway among the shadows: cassia on the left, aloes on the right. With an emerald-coloured cup, ringed [with gold], and garnet-coloured wine, mixed with dew, I shall forget the misery and grief hidden deep in my heart.

מַה לְּדוֹד הָיָה רוֹעֶה בֵּין עֳפָרִים
לַעֲזֹב קִרְיָה, לִשְׁכֹּן בֵּין יְעָרִים ?
בֹּא לְחֵיק רַעְיָה תַּעֲטֹף־לָךְ בְּשִׁירִים.
הַעֲלֵה, דוֹד צַח, לִי נֵר מַעֲרָבִי,
בָּךְ כְּרוּב מִמְשַׁח יִגַּהּ אוֹר שְׁבִיבִי!

What made my beloved, who used to graze between my fawn [-like breasts], leave me[1] and take to the woods? Come to the arms of your dearest, who sings of her longing for you. O, my fair love, light the western lamp[2] for me. In you, towering cherub, my flame will burn anew.

עִמָּנוּאֵל הָרוֹמִי

Immanuel of Rome

נַפְשִׁי בְּקִרְבִּי

EDEN AND HELL

נַפְשִׁי בְּקִרְבִּי תַּחֲשֹׁב מַחֲשֶׁבֶת
לָקוּץ בְּעֵדֶן גַּן וְלִרְצוֹת תֹּפֶת,
כִּי אֶמְצָאָה שָׁם צוּף דְּבַשׁ עִם נֹפֶת,
שָׁם כָּל צְבִיַּת חֵן וְכָל עוֹגֶבֶת.

Deep in my heart I have resolved to spurn the garden of Eden in favour of Hell, for there I shall find dripping honey and nectar: all the graceful does and lustful ladies.

1. Lit. 'the [faithful] city', that is, Jerusalem.
2. The brightest light on the candlestick in the Temple.

מַה לִּי בְּעֵדֶן גַּן – וְאֵין אוֹהֶבֶת
שָׁם, רַק שְׁחֹרוֹת מִשְּׁחוֹר אוֹ זֶפֶת,
שָׁמָּה זְקֵנוֹת בַּעֲלוֹת יַלֶּפֶת –
נַפְשִׁי בְּחֶבְרָתָן תְּהִי נֶעֱצֶבֶת.

What is there for me in Eden? There are no loves there, only women blacker than soot or pitch, and crones covered with lichen. My spirit would droop in their company.

מַה לִּי וָלָךְ, עֵדֶן! וְאַתְּ אָסַפְתְּ
כָּל בַּעֲלוֹת מוּמִים וְכָל אִישׁ בֹּשֶׁת;
עַל כֵּן חֲשַׁבְתִּיךְ בְּעֵינַי אָיִן.

Eden, what are you to me? You assemble all the maimed women and infamous men. That is why I think of you with contempt.

תֹּפֶת! בְּעֵינַי חֵן וְהוֹד יָסַפְתְּ;
בָּךְ כָּל צְבִיָּה הַיְקָר לוֹבֶשֶׁת,
נֶאֱסַף כֹּל מַחֲמַדֵּי עָיִן!

Hell, I consider you excellent in charm and grandeur, for you house all the girls in their elegant dresses. It is you who have assembled all the delights of our eyes.

שֵׂכֶל מְצַיֵּר

THE ODIOUS GIRL

שֵׂכֶל מְצַיֵּר! יוֹם אֲשֶׁר צִיַּרְתָּ
בַּת גֵּרְשֹׁם – כָּל הַיְקוּם הִכְלַמְתָּ;
יַעַן בְּגִשְׁמָהּ כָּל גְּנוּת הִשְׁלַמְתָּ,
כִּי בָא חֲלוֹם הַבּוּז, וְאַתְּ פָּתַרְתָּ.

O creative Intelligence! The day you created Gershom's daughter, you shamed the universe, for in her body you brought odium to perfection. It seems you had a vile dream and made it come true.[1]

אוּלַי לְקַבֵּץ כָּל גְּנוּת נָדַרְתָּ,
אוֹ לַעֲשׂוֹת יַנְשׁוּף וְקוֹף יָזַמְתָּ?
מָה הַחֲלוֹם הַזֶּה אֲשֶׁר חָלַמְתָּ?
אִם רוּחֲךָ סָרָה וְאִם שָׁכַרְתָּ?

Perhaps you vowed to lump all loathsome things together? Or else proposed to fashion an owl and a monkey? How did you ever dream up such a dream? Were you soul-sick or were you drunk?

הַגֵּד, כְּרוּב מְמַשֵּׁחַ! הַאִם הַשֶּׂרֶד
אוֹ הַמְּחוּגָה מִמְּךָ גֻּנְּבוּ,
וַתַּעֲשֶׂה בַּת גֵּרְשֹׁם בְּרַחַת?

Tell me, Angel of delineation: were your scribers or callipers stolen from you, so that you had to use a winnowing shovel in making Gershom's daughter?

1. Lit. 'you interpreted' [the dream by materializing it].

אוֹ פָּעֲלוּ בָהּ כּוֹכְבֵי רוֹם מֶרֶד –
סַרְטָן וְעַקְרָב אִם אֲזַי נִצָּבוּ
בְּזָנָב תְּלִי בְּמַעֲלָה צוֹמַחַת!

Or did the stars rise up against her? Did the Crab and the Scorpion then station themselves at the tail end of the Serpent, as it ascended the heavens?[1]

מִי הֶאֱמִין, עָפְרָה

IN PRAISE OF YOUR EYES

מִי הֶאֱמִין, עָפְרָה, אֲשֶׁר עֵינַיִךְ
הֵם יַעֲלוּ בַסְּעָרָה שָׁמָיִם!
כִּי אֶחֱזֵם שַׁחַק בְּבֵין עַרְבַּיִם,
וָאֶחֱזֵם יוֹמָם בְּאוֹר פָּנַיִךְ.

Love, who would believe that your eyes are carried up in a whirlwind to heaven? But it is a fact: I see them in the skies at twilight, and in your shining face by day.

חַיַּי תְּלוּיִים בְּעָגִיל אָזְנַיִךְ,
כִּי אֶחֱזֶה בּוֹ מַעֲשֵׂה מִצְרָיִם.
עוֹד אֶחֱזֶה בָּךְ, תַּאֲוַת עֵינַיִם,
עַל כּוֹכְבֵי שַׁחְרֵךְ, בְּרַד שִׁנַּיִךְ.

My life hangs upon the earrings in your ears, for they bewitch me with Egyptian sorcery. Delight of my eyes, I shall always behold your dawn-star [eyes] and your hail [white] teeth.

אֶשְׁאַל, צְבִיַּת חֵן: הַאִם עֵינַיִךְ
הֵם כּוֹכְבֵי שַׁחַק, וְתִקְחִים בְּשְׁבִי
יוֹמָם, וְלַיְלָה יַעֲלוּ בַשַּׁחַק?

Tell me, lovely gazelle: do you take the stars of heaven for your eyes, holding them captive by day, and when night comes let them go back to heaven?

אוֹ הֵם דְּמוּת כּוֹכָב, וְאוֹר פָּנַיִךְ
דִּמְיוֹן גְּלִילֵי רוֹם? אֲשֶׁר כָּל הַצְּבִ-
יּוֹת לָךְ כְּמוֹ מַר מִדְּלִי וּכְשַׁחַק!

Or are your eyes the likeness of the stars, and is the light of your face the image of the heavenly spheres? For, in fact, all the other gazelles, compared to you, are no more than drops from a bucket, or specks of dust on the scales.

1. A configuration that would result in the birth of an ugly girl.

שָׁדַי נְכוֹנִים

THE VIRGIN'S COMPLAINT

שָׁדַי נְכוֹנִים, שְׂעָרִי צִמֵּחַ,
וָאֵשְׁבָה עֵירֹם וְעֶרְיָה בֹשֶׁת.
דּוֹדִים לְעָנְיִי יָרְאוּ מִגֶּשֶׁת,
וָאֵשְׁבָה בָּרֹאשׁ בְּבֵית מַרְזֵחַ.

My breasts are firm and my hair is long, yet I still sit in nakedness and shame. My poverty has frightened away all the suitors, and I sit [as if] at the head of the table in a house of mourning.[1]

אֵיךְ יִהְיֶה עוֹד הַלֵּבָב שָׂמֵחַ ?
אָפְסוּ כְסָפַי, אֵין זָהָב וּנְחֹשֶׁת.
אֵיךְ אֶמְצָאָה בַּעַל אֲנִי – וּשְׁלֹשֶׁת
אֲחָיוֹת גְּדוֹלוֹת לִי, וְלֵב גּוֹנֵחַ.

How can my heart ever rejoice when all my silver is gone and I have no gold or bronze? How will I ever find a husband, when all I have are three older [impoverished] sisters and a groaning heart?

מָה אֹמְרָה, דּוֹדַי: עֲצָמַי חָרוּ,
אוֹ עִם זְמַן בּוֹגֵד בְּרִית אֶכְרֹתָה ?
עָפוּ שְׁנוֹתַי, פָּשְׁטוּ כַיֶּלֶק.

How can I tell, suitors, if my bones will be scorched [by desire] or if I will be able to strike a bargain with treacherous Time? My years are flying away, spreading their wings like locusts!

גַּם יָשְׁבוּ שָׂרִים וּבִי נִדְבָּרוּ:
אִשָּׁה אֲשֶׁר תָּמוּת בְּתוּלָה – נִכְרְתָה,
אֵין לָהּ בְּעוֹלָם הַנְּשָׁמוֹת חֵלֶק!

And what is more, the wise men sit and scheme together against me: 'She that dies a virgin is cut off; she will have no share in the world to come!'

זֶה לִי שְׁנָתַיִם

THE WIFE'S COMPLAINT

זֶה לִי שְׁנָתַיִם אֲשֶׁר נָשָׂאתִי
בַּעַל – וְעוֹדוֹ חַי, וְאֵין לִי נֹעַם.
יָמוּת בְּחֵץ בָּרָק וּמִקּוֹל רַעַם,
אָז בֵּין בְּנוֹת הַחֵן אֱהִי שָׂרָתִי.

Two years have already passed since I took a husband, but he is still alive, and I can have no pleasure. If only he would die of lightning's dart or thunder's roar, I would be queen among the charming ladies.

1. The chief mourner customarily presided over the mourning feast.

הַמָּוְתָה יוֹם יוֹם אֲנִי קָרָאתִי,
כִּי נִכְסְפָה נַפְשִׁי לְשַׁנּוֹת טַעַם.
לֹא אֵדְעָה מָה אַחֲרִית הַזַּעַם,
יוּאַר וְיֹאבַד יוֹם בְּבֵיתוֹ בָּאתִי!

Day after day I call for Death to come, for my soul longs for a change of fare. I do not know how this outrage will end. Oh, perish the day when I came into his house!

אֶרְאֶה שְׁכֶנְתִּי: בֵּין שְׁלוֹשִׁים חֹדֶשׁ
שָׁלוֹשׁ פְּעָמִים בְּעָלִים קָבָרָה.
כָּל הַשְּׁכֵנוֹת אוֹמְרוֹת: אַשְׁרֶיהָ!

I see that my neighbour, within the span of thirty months, has three times buried a husband. All the neighbourhood wives exclaim: 'How happy she must be!'

הִיא חִלְּלָה אֵלִים וְשָׂרֵי קֹדֶשׁ.
הִיא כַּלְּבִיָּא בֵּין אֲרָיוֹת גָּרָה
וּבְתוֹךְ כְּפִירִים רִבְּתָה גוּרֶיהָ.

She spurned heroes and princes [for the sake of lovers]. Like a lioness, she made her lair among young lions, and she lay in their midst, bearing her cubs.

רְאוּ נָבָל

THE MISER

וזה השיר אשר חִבַּרתי על האיש
אשר בסתר יִקָּחֵם [את בגדַי]:

And this is the poem I wrote about the man who secretly wore my clothes:

רְאוּ נָבָל, יְהִי רַע אַחֲרִיתוֹ
וְשָׁמַיִם יְגַלּוּ אֶת עֲווֹנוֹ!
אֲשֶׁר לוֹ צֹאן – וְכִבְשַׂת רָשׁ יְאַוֶּה
לְקַחְתָּהּ לוֹ, בְּחֶמְלָתוֹ לְצֹאנוֹ;
וְלוֹ עָרְלָה, וּמִיִּרְאַת בְּלוֹתָהּ –
יְאַו לִבְעֹל בְּמוֹ עָרְלַת שְׁכֵנוֹ.

Behold this scoundrel – may his end be bitter, may the heavens lay bare his guilt! He has flocks of his own, but rather than deplete them he prefers to take the poor man's lamb. He has a foreskin, but for fear of wearing it out he would rather use his neighbour's when he copulates.

דּוֹד, יוֹם קְרָאתִיהוּ

דּוֹד, יוֹם קְרָאתִיהוּ לְעֶזְרָתוֹ,
גָּז חִישׁ כְּצִפּוֹר מִמְּרוֹם קִנּוֹ.
אַךְ יוֹם לְעֶזְרָתִי קְרָאתִיהוּ,
הֶחְרִישׁ כְּפֶתֶן יַאְטֵם אָזְנוֹ.
נִדְמֶה לְכֶלֶב אִישׁ חֲרַשׁ בַּרְזֶל,
בֵּית הוֹלְמִים שִׁבְתּוֹ וּמִשְׁכָּנוֹ:
יִישַׁן לְקוֹל פַּטִּישׁ וְיֵרָדֵם,
יִיקַץ לְעֵת אֹכֶל לְקוֹל שִׁנּוֹ.

THE EGOIST

This friend – when I summoned him, to come to his aid, he swooped to my side like a bird from its high nest. But when I summoned him, to come to my aid, he turned as deaf as an asp that stops its ears. He is like a blacksmith's dog, living in a forge: he dozes off and sleeps to the sound of the hammers, but wakes up for meals to the sound of teeth.

חוּשָׁה, מְשִׁיחַ אֵל

חוּשָׁה, מְשִׁיחַ אֵל, וְלָמָּה תַעֲמֹד?
הִנֵּה מְחַכִּים לְךָ דְּמָעוֹת נוֹטְפִים.
הָיוּ דְּמֵי דִמְעָם נְחָלִים שׁוֹטְפִים,
כָּל לֵב וְכָל לָשׁוֹן לְךָ, שַׂר, יַחֲמֹד.

וּקְחָה פְּתִיל פִּשְׁתִּים בְּיָדֶיךָ, וּמֹד
צִיּוֹן כְּלִיל יֹפִי, וּבָנָיו – עוֹדְפִים
יִהְיוּ בְּכָל חֵן טוֹב, וְצָרִים שׁוֹאֲפִים
יִגְלוּ בְּרֹאשׁ גּוֹלִים, וְאַתָּה פֹּה עֲמֹד.

עוּרָה, מְשִׁיחֵנוּ, צְלַח כַּיּוֹם רְכַב
עַל סוּס אֲשֶׁר דּוֹהֵר, וּמֶרְכָּבָה רְתֹם,
כִּי כָל עֲצָמַי נִפְזְרוּ, אֵין בָּם מְתֹם!

ADVICE TO THE MESSIAH

Make haste, Lord's anointed, why are you lingering? They are waiting for you, weeping bitterly. Their tears, mixed with their heart's blood, have swelled to a torrent. O Prince, every heart and every tongue longs for you.

Now take a cord of linen thread in your hands,[1] and measure Zion, perfect in beauty. Then her children will surpass all others in grace and goodness. The oppressive enemies will be the first to go into exile, and you will stand fast [in Zion].

Arise, Messiah, ride forth today victoriously upon a charging horse, harness the steeds to the chariot – for all my bones have been scattered, and not one is intact.

1. As did the bronze-like man in Ezekiel's vision (40.3).

אִם עַל חֲמוֹר תִּרְכַּב, אֲדוֹנִי – שׁוּב שְׁכַב!
אִיעָצְךָ, הַשַּׂר מְשִׁיחֵנוּ, בְּתֹם
לִבִּי: סְתֹם הַקֵּץ וְהֶחָזוֹן חֲתֹם!

But if you mean to ride on an ass,[1] my lord, go back to sleep! If so, prince and Messiah, allow me, in good faith, to give you this advice: You had best keep the end secret and seal up the vision!

יִצְחָק אַלְחַדִיבּ

Isaac Alḥadib

אִישׁ מָהִיר

ISAAC-OF-ALL-TRADES

אִישׁ מָהִיר אָנִי בַּמְּהִירִים,
וּמְלָאכוֹת רַבּוֹת לָמַדְתִּי.
לִטְווֹת גַּם לֶאֱרֹג יָדַעְתִּי,
וּלְהָכִין לִי בָּתֵּי־נִירִים.

בִּימֵי חָרְפִּי חָשְׁקָה נַפְשִׁי
לִהְיוֹת פָּרָשׁ אִישׁ מִלְחָמָה,
לָשׂוּם לִי כּוֹבַע עַל רֹאשִׁי,
לִרְכֹּב עַל סוּס נַחְרוֹ אֵימָה.
שִׁרְיוֹן קַשְׂקַשִּׂים מַלְבּוּשִׁי,
רוֹבֶה קַשָּׁת, מַפִּיל חוֹמָה.
אַךְ בִּרְאוֹתִי כִּי בַמְּהוּמָה
עִם הָרוֹדְפִים יָשׁוּב נִרְדָּף,
יִבְרַח מִקּוֹל עָלֶה נִדָּף –
שַׁבְתִּי לִמְלֶאכֶת אִכָּרִים.

I am the most skilful of men and I have mastered many trades. I know how to spin as well as to weave, and how to prepare the meshes.

In my youth I longed to be a horseman and a warrior; to wear a helmet on my head, and ride a horse whose neighing strikes terror; to put on a coat of mail; to be an archer, and batter down the fortress walls. But when I saw that in this tumult the pursuer becomes the pursued, taking flight at the sound of a driven leaf, I turned back to the peasant's toil.

1. As prophesied in Zechariah 9.9: 'Lo, your king comes to you . . . humble and riding on an ass . . .'

טָעַמְתִּי מִמְכַּר הַיַּיִן,
כַּמָּה נָעִים, כַּמָּה יָפֶה!
שׁוֹתֶה יִתֵּן בַּכּוֹס עַיִן,
מוֹכֵר אֶל כִּיס שׁוֹתֶה צוֹפֶה.
כָּל זֶה הָיָה נֶגְדִּי אַיִן.
עוֹד לָמַדְתִּי לִהְיוֹת רוֹפֵא:
מָעוֹת חִנָּם עַל דִּבְרֵי פֶה,
בִּקּוּר חוֹלִים, בִּקּוּר חוֹלוֹת,
מִשּׁוּשׁ בַּנָּשִׁים וּבְתוּלוֹת,
חָזֶה וּזְרוֹעַ נִסְתָּרִים.

I tasted the wine trade: what a pleasure, what a delight! The drinker eyes his cup while the merchant eyes *his* pocket . . . But this was child's play for me, so I learned to be a doctor: pocketing undeserved fees for idle talk, making the rounds of bed-ridden men and women, fingering women and girls down to their hidden breasts and thighs.

קָלִי, כַּרְמֶל אֵדַע לַחְרֹךְ,
לִצְלוֹת בָּשָׂר תּוֹךְ הַכִּבְשָׁן.
יַיִן חָדָשׁ בַּגַּת אֶדְרֹךְ,
אַךְ לִשְׁתּוֹת אֶבְחַר הַיָּשָׁן.
לִפְנֵי שׁוֹפְטִים טְעָנוֹת אֶעֱרֹךְ,
לִפְנֵי קָהָל אֶהְיֶה דַרְשָׁן.
מִבִּלְתִּי אֵשׁ – אַעֲלֶה עָשָׁן,
אֲחַזְתִּי בַּלָּט עֵינַיִם,
אִתִּי כָּל חָכְמַת מִצְרַיִם:
חַרְטֹם, אַשָּׁף, רֹאשׁ הַהוֹבְרִים.

I know how to parch ripe grain, and to roast meat in the oven. I tread young wine in the press but for my drink I take the old. I can argue a case before the bench and deliver a sermon in public. I can raise smoke, without fire. Stealthily I hoodwink one and all, for I possess all the wisdom of Egypt: magician, exorcist, and astrologer-in-chief!

זֶה כַּמָּה שָׁנִים חָשַׁבְתִּי
בִּמְלֶאכֶת כִּימְיָא מַחְשָׁבוֹת;
כַּמָּה כֵּלִים לִי תִקַּנְתִּי
מֵעֲפַר אֶרֶץ־תַּלְאוּבוֹת;
לוּלֵי מִין אֶחָד חָסַרְתִּי –
הָיוּ קוֹרוֹתַי מְזֻהָבוֹת!
עַתָּה בִּרְקִיקִים וּלְבִיבוֹת
וּמְלֶאכֶת־בֹּרִית עָסַקְתִּי
– כִּי בָהֶם יוֹתֵר הִרְוַחְתִּי –
וּבַמֶּרְחָץ לִרְחֹץ לַאֲחֵרִים.

For several years I pondered over the art of alchemy. I fashioned a few vessels out of scorched earth. Had I not lacked one single element, my rafters would now be covered with gold! So then I dealt in wafers and pancakes; I manufactured soap and scrubbed down people in the bath house. In these callings, I raked in a bigger profit.

חָקַרְתִּי כָּל אַרְצוֹת מַעֲרָב,
אֶל הַמִּזְרָח שַׂמְתִּי פָּנַי,
קוֹרֵא: מִי זֶה לִבּוֹ עָרַב —
יָבוֹא יָשִׁיב עַל הֶגְיוֹנַי!
בִּגְלִילוֹת צָרְפַת וּבַעֲרָב
לֹא עָמַד אִישׁ עַל עִנְיָנַי.
נִלְאֵיתִי עוֹד, אֶשָּׂא פָּנַי
אַשּׁוּר, בָּבֶל, גַּם תּוֹגַרְמָה:
אָז נוֹדַע כִּי בִלְתִּי — מִרְמָה,
בִּלְעָדַי אִישׁ יָד לֹא יָרִים!

I explored all the lands of the West, then made my way through the East. Everywhere I announced: 'If anyone dare, let him step forth and discredit me!' In all the provinces of France and Arabia, no one saw through my game. Tiring of them, I turned and made for Assyria, Babylon, and Turkey. There it became clear, at last, that except for me all was fraud, and without me no man could lift a finger!

דּוֹן וִידָאל בֶּנְבֶנִשְׂתְּ

Don Vidal Benveniste

נַחַם לְנַפְשָׁהּ

DINAH REJECTS THE OLD SUITOR

נַחַם לְנַפְשָׁהּ מֵאֲנָה לָקַחַת
דִּינָה בְּקָרַחַת וְגַם גַּבַּחַת:
כִּי רָאֲתָה שֵׂיבָה בְּדֶגֶל אַהֲבָה
עַל קִיר לְבָבָהּ הוּא כְּמוֹ מִסְפַּחַת.
לֹא יַעֲלֹז רוּחָהּ בְּחֶמְדַּת אוֹצְרוֹת
כֶּסֶף, וְלֹא מָצְאָה לְנַפְשָׁהּ נַחַת.
יֶעֱרַב מְשׂוֹשׂ גִּילָהּ בְּבֶן גִּילָהּ, וְתוֹךְ
חֶבְרַת צְבִי־עֹפֶר זְמִיר פּוֹצַחַת.
מֵאֵין מְחִיר דּוֹד נֶאֱהָב נֶחְשָׁב זְהַב
אוֹפִיר, וּפָנָיו — מִגְדְּלוֹת מֶרְקַחַת.
אָכֵן מְלֵא יָמִים בְּפָנִים זוֹעֲפִים
— עִם דֵּי זְהָבוֹ — נֶחְשָׁב אַמְתַּחַת!

Dinah refuses to take comfort in a bald pate and a bare forehead. She knows that such a hoary love[1] will cover the walls of her heart with scurf. Her spirit cannot rejoice in precious stores of silver; her soul would find no rest. She can savour delight only with a youth of her own age; in the company of a young lover she would break into song. Though penniless, the true love is as dear as the gold of Ophir. His cheeks are like chests full of perfumes. But the greybeard with the glowering face, for all his gold, he is nothing but a bag!

1. Lit. 'old age with a banner of love'.

יְדִידוּת יְפַת תֹּאַר

BITTER AND SWEET

יְדִידוּת יְפַת תֹּאַר חֲזָקָה וְאַדֶּרֶת,
חֲלָקָה כְּחֶמְאָה, אַף שְׂעִירָה כְּאַדֶּרֶת.
וְרַכּוּ דְבָרֶיהָ, וְעוֹדָהּ מְדַבֶּרֶת –
בְּחִנָּהּ חֲנִיתוֹת עַל לְבָבִי מְעוֹרֶרֶת.
דְּבַשׁ עַל שְׂפָתֶיהָ, וְרוֹשׁ תַּאֲכִילֵנִי,
וְנֹפֶת בְּתוֹךְ חִכָּהּ, וְחַיַּי מְמָרֶרֶת.
וְחָלְקוּ אֲמָרֶיהָ, וְטוּחוֹת מְחַלֶּקֶת,
וְעֵת תַּעֲנֶה רַכּוֹת, עֲצָמוֹת מְשַׁבֶּרֶת. [...]
לְשָׁרֵת יְדִידוּתָהּ אֲנִי הוּא וְלֹא אַחֵר,
אֲנִי הוּא – וְלֹא אָמִיר כְּבוֹדָהּ בְּאַחֶרֶת.

The love of this graceful girl is strong and formidable. It is as smooth as butter and as prickly as a hairy mantle. Her words are soft, but even as she speaks, she brandishes her charm like spears over my heart. There is honey on her lips but she feeds me poison; her tongue drips sweetness, yet she makes my life bitter. Her speech is smooth, but it pierces my bowels; and when she answers softly, she breaks my bones. Still, I, and none but I, shall wait upon her love. I am the only one, and I would not exchange her glory for any other.

שְׁלֹמֹה בּוֹנָפֵיד

Solomon Bonafed

רְאֵה סוּסִים

TOPSY-TURVY WORLD

רְאֵה סוּסִים בְּלֶב יָם כַּבְּרָקִים
יְרוּצוּן, וְאֳנִיּוֹת – בַּשְּׁוָקִים,
וְחוּט פִּשְׁתִּים מְטִיל בַּרְזֶל יְפוֹצֵץ,
וּמַיִם בּוֹעֲרִים כָּעֵץ וְדוֹלְקִים,
וּבוֹרְחִים הַנְּמֵרִים מִגְּדָיִים,
וְשׁוּעָלִים אֲרִי רוֹדְפִים וְדוֹלְקִים.
וְאַל תִּתְמַהּ בְּשׁוּב עוֹלָם הֲפַכְפַּךְ
וְעִתִּים מִנְּתִיב טִבְעָם רְחוֹקִים,
וְהַאֲמֵן זֶה בְּשׁוּרְךָ מַעְגְּלֵי אִישׁ
נְלוֹזִים: יוֹם וָיוֹם נַעֲשׂוּ עֲשׁוּקִים,
וְהַחָכְמָה כְּמֵת מִלֵּב זְנוּחָה,

See how horses streak through the sea like lightning bolts, and ships sail through the market-place. A thread of linen splinters a bar of iron, and water blazes like wood. Leopards flee before kids and foxes give chase to lions. Nor should you marvel that the world is turned topsy-turvy and the times have strayed from their natural course. Believe all this when you behold how man perverts his ways. Oppression grows from day to day. Wisdom, like a dead man, is put out of mind; it is the

וּבָהּ יִתְעַלְלוּ עוֹלְלִים וְיוֹנְקִים.
וְעֵת יִתְחַתְּנוּ לֹא יִשְׁאֲלוּ, אִם
חֲכָמִים הֵם – אֲבָל אִם הוֹן מְרִיקִים!
וְהַחַיָּט, בְּעֵת יוֹצֵא בְמַחְטוֹ,
יְדַם לְנַפִּיל יְלִידֵי הָעֲנָקִים;
פְּתִילֵי בַד לְצַוָּארוֹ עֲנָקִים,
וְחוּטָיו מִדְּבַשׁ אֶל פִּיו מְתוּקִים.
וְהַצּוֹרֵף בְּכוּר יִשָּׂרֵף זְקָנוֹ,
וְעֵינָיו יַאְדִּים עִם אֵשׁ וְזִקִּים;
חֲמָדוּהוּ בְּכַסְפּוֹ אוֹ זְהָבוֹ –
וְאוּלַי אֵין בְּכַסְפּוֹ לוֹ חֲלָקִים.
וְאוֹרֵג יַחֲשֹׁב מָנוֹר כְּכִנּוֹר,
וּמַסֶּכֶת – כְּמַסֶּכֶת נְזִיקִים.
וְרַצְּעָן – נוֹשְׁקוֹת נָשִׁים שְׂפָתָיו,
וְשִׁנָּיו מוֹשְׁכִים עוֹרוֹת וְנוֹשְׁקִים.
וְנָבָל יַעֲנֶה עַזּוֹת בְּעָשְׁרוֹ,
וְגַאֲוָתוֹ וְעֻזּוֹ בִּשְׁחָקִים.

sport of babes and infants. And when they marry off their daughters they do not ask if the bridegroom is wise, but how much money pours out of him! The tailor, stepping forth with his needle in hand, deems himself a giant-killer. The cords of cloth, hung round his neck, he takes for necklaces, and his threads are sweeter to his tongue than honey. The goldsmith's beard is singed in the crucible and his eyes bloodshot from fire and sparks, and still he is prized for his silver or gold – though none of it may be his! The weaver thinks his loom is a lyre, and his warp a harp.[1] The cobbler – women kiss his lips, while his teeth are tugging hides and kissing them. The churl, secure in his riches, makes harsh replies; his pride and his might as high as heaven!

לְכָה, דּוֹד צַח, וְנֵלְכָה עַל פְּנֵי חוּץ
לְמֶרְחַקִּים בְּבֵין שִׂיחִים מְשַׂחֲקִים,
בְּבֵין שִׂיחִים וּבֵין אָחִים כְּאַחִים,
בְּתוֹךְ גַּנִּים, וְלֹא בֵּינוֹת נְקִיקִים,
וְנַקִּיף אָהֳלֵנוּ מֵעֲרוּגוֹת
חֲבַצֶּלֶת וְשׁוֹשַׁנַּת עֲמָקִים,
וְרֵעֵינוּ יִהְיוּ כָּל צִפֳּרֵי חֵן
וְזִיז שָׂדַי וְיוֹנִים עַל אֲפִיקִים.
וְלֹא נִרְאֶה בְּתַהְפּוּכוֹת זְמַנִּים
וְלֹא נָבִין בְּסָרָה מַעֲמִיקִים,

Oh, let us go, my fair companion, let us walk far afield, and amuse ourselves among the thickets. Let us sport like brothers in thicket and meadows, in soft gardens, not in rocky crevices. We shall surround our tents with beds of lilies and roses. All birds of grace, the teeming life of the fields, doves beside brooks of water – these shall be our playmates. And there we shall not see the vagaries of time nor pay heed to wicked betrayers. Now we shall laugh

1. Lit. 'thinks his web (*masekhet*) is a tractate (*masekhet*) from the Talmudic division of *Nezikin* ("Damages")'.

וּפַעַם נִלְעֲגָה עַל הַזְּמַנִּים,
וּפַעַם נִדְרְשָׁה סוֹדוֹת עֲמֻקִּים,
עֲסִיס חָכְמָה לְאַט נִשְׁתֶּה בְּצָמָא,
וּמִסֹּלֶת זְמִיר נֹאכַל רְקִיקִים.
עֲדֵי יָשׁוּב זְמַן עָוֶל לְתַקֵּן
אֲשֶׁר עִוֵּת, הֲרִיסוֹתָיו לְהָקִים,
וְיַבְדִּיל בֵּין בְּדִיל אֶל פָּז וְיַחְפֹּץ
לְהַפְרִישׁ בֵּין חֲגָבִים לַעֲנָקִים.

time to scorn and now we shall delve into deep mysteries. Slowly, eagerly, we shall drink the wine of wisdom and feed on wafers of choice[1] melodies – until time mend again what it had twisted and restore all it has ruined; until time set apart the lead from the gold, and the grasshoppers from the giants.

קְרַב, דּוֹד צַח, וְאֶפְצַח רֹן, וְתָרֹן
לְשׁוֹן אִלֵּם וְנָסוּ כָּל מְצוּקִים.
קְרַב, פֶּן יַדְרְכוּ קַשְׁתָּם מְקַנְּאִים
וְחוֹשְׁקִים לִהְיוֹת לָבוּז חֲשׁוּקִים.
בְּעֵת תִּקְרַב וְעֵת תִּרְחַק, כְּרוּבִי,
לְשֵׁם חֶבְרָתְךָ יָמַי עֲסוּקִים.
וְאִם תִּרְאֶה בְּדוֹד אַחֵר אֲמִירְךָ –
רְאֵה סוּסִים בְּלֶב יָם כַּבְּרָקִים!

Draw near, my fair companion, and I shall break into song, and the mouths of the dumb will shout for joy, and all distress will vanish. Draw near, lest the jealous ones, who love to put lovers to scorn,[2] string their bows against us. But whether you draw near or go afar, my cherub, all my days are given over to your friendship. And should you ever see me exchanging you for another love – you will also see horses streaking through the sea like lightning bolts!

מֹשֶׁה רִיאֶטִי

Moses da Rieti

פֶּלֶא עָצוּם רָאִיתִי

IN THE PALACE OF HEAVEN

פֶּלֶא עָצוּם רָאִיתִי בַּהֵיכָל:
נְשָׁמוֹת נִשָּׂאוֹת בַּאֲוִירוֹ,
לְסַפֵּר יְקָרָם אִישׁ לֹא יוּכָל.

Then I saw a great marvel in the palace: souls hovering in the air. No one could describe their splendour.

1. A play on *solet* which also means 'flour'.
2. Or, 'who desire to be loved by vileness'.

הֵם כָּל מַפְלִיג לֶאֱהֹב יוֹצְרוֹ,
מוֹסֵר עַצְמוֹ עַל קְדֻשַּׁת הַשֵּׁם,
מַזְכִּיר 'אֶחָד' וּפוֹשֵׁט צַוָּארוֹ.

The souls of those who loved their Creator passionately, who sanctified the Holy Name with their lives, baring their necks to the knife as they proclaimed 'The [Lord is] One.'

אֶל מַלְאֲכֵי שָׁרֵת הֵן אֲקִישֵׁם,
בְּהוֹדָם וּבְהָדָר אֶל הַחַיּוֹת.
וְצִיץ עֲלֵי רֹאשָׁם וּבוֹ רוֹשֵׁם:

I would compare them to the ministering angels; in majesty and glory, to the living creatures. There is a rosette on their forehead, and on it is engraved [as on a seal]:

'הוּא קֹדֶשׁ לַיְיָ' בְּאוֹתִיּוֹת.
וּכְנָפַיִם לָהֶם וּמְעוֹפְפִים
לְהַשִּׂיג הָרִאשׁוֹן לְכָל הֱוָיוֹת.

'Holy to the Lord.'[1] They have wings and they soar to approach the Primal Being.

הַנִּשְׂרָפִים מַרְאֵיהֶם כִּשְׂרָפִים,
הַנִּשְׁחָטִים רוֹחֲצִים בֶּחָלָב,
וְהַנִּתְלִים, כֵּן, עֵינֵיהֶם יָפִים.

Those who died by fire look like the fiery seraphim; those who were slaughtered bathe in milk; and those who were hung, their eyes are sparkling.

וְכָל נִדְחָק – כְּפִי מָה שֶׁנֶּעֱלַב
שָׁם יִשָּׂא הוֹד, וּמַטֵּהוּ יִפְרַח,
בִּבְנֵי אֵלִים מִתְרַפֵּק וְנִשְׁלָב.

And all those who were oppressed – the greater their humiliation, the greater now their glory. Their staffs blossom forth; they lean on the sons of God and join in their ranks.

סַנְהֶדְרִין גְּדוֹלָה בְּצַד מִזְרָח,
וּדְמוּת פְּנֵי כֻלָּם צַח וְאָדֹם,
וּבָם אוֹר הַדַּעַת רִאשׁוֹן יִזְרַח.

The Great Sanhedrin[2] is assembled in the east; their faces glow, ruddy and pure. The light of divine wisdom shines first upon them.

יְלָדִים בְּלִי מוּם עַל כָּל הֲדוֹם. [...]

[And at their feet,] upon every footstool, there sits a perfect child.

1. Exodus 28.36.
2. The supreme judicial council.

הַיּוֹם פָּנָה

THE ENCOUNTER

הַיּוֹם פָּנָה וְנָטָה לַעֲרֹב,
וְהַזָּקֵן, תָּמִים, אַב הַחָכְמָה,
יָעַד פָּנָיו נֶגְדִּי וּמְקָרוֹב.

The day was declining and drawing to its close, when the righteous old man, this father of wisdom, drew his face close to mine.

וְעֵת נִרְאוּ מִכּוֹכְבֵי רוֹמָה
שָׁלוֹשׁ הַכּוֹכָבִים הַמַּבְדִּילִים
הָאוֹר וְהַחֹשֶׁךְ כִּמְלוֹא נִימָא —

And when the three stars which separate light from dark by a hair's breadth appeared high up in heaven,

כְּגֶבֶר שׁוֹתֵק לִזְמִירוֹת אֵלִים,
אוֹ לִקְרִיאַת מָרוֹם אֹמֶר גָּמַר,
לָבַשׁ מַלְאָכוּת וְעָצַר מִלִּים.

then, like a man who falls silent when the angels sing, or like one who is speechless, obeying a summons from heaven, he clothed himself in the shape of an angel and said no more.

וּכְאִישׁ, עַל פֵּרוּד בֵּן לִבּוֹ נִכְמַר,
צוּרַת נַפְשׁוֹ בְּרַחֲמִים סוּגָה,
בְּעַיִן מָלֵא חֶמְלָה 'בְּנִי,' אָמַר,

But then, like a man whose heart is moved, whose soul is flooded with compassion as he bids his son farewell, his eyes filled with pity and he said, 'My son,

'כְּבָר נִשְׁלַם הֶקֵּף הַהַשָּׂגָה.
אֵלְכָה לִּי אֶל הַר שָׁם אָהֳלִי,
שֶׁמָּא אִחוּרִי עוֹד הוּא כִּשְׁגָגָה.'

'The [light of] intelligence has run its course; let me return to my home on the mountain. My delay may still be taken as an oversight.'

'אֲדוֹנִי,' אָמַרְתִּי, 'כִּמְדֻמֶּה לִי
רְאִיתִיךָ כְּבָר בִּימֵי נַעֲרוּת,
וּתְמוּנָתְךָ לֹא תִתְבָּאֵר אֶצְלִי.

'My lord,' I said, 'it seems to me that I have seen you in my youth, but I cannot place your image.

אַחַר אִם לֶכְתְּךָ מִשְׁפַּט חָרוּת,
שֵׁם כְּבוֹדְךָ אֶשְׁאַל נָא בְּדֶמַע,
שֵׁם מִדְרָשְׁךָ וְכֵן בֵּית הַסִּפְרוּת.

'If, indeed, you are compelled to leave, let me tearfully inquire what your honour's name is, and the name and place of your house of study.

וְאִם מֵי חָכְמָתְךָ עוֹד לֹא אֶגְמָע,
בָּרְכֵנִי עֵת אֶשָּׁאֵר בִּלְתָּךְ!'
'נָשָׂאתִי פָּנֶיךָ,' הֵשִׁיב, 'וּשְׁמַע –

'And if I can no longer drink from the waters of your wisdom, bless me, now that you are leaving me behind.' 'I shall grant your request,' he answered. 'Now listen –

אִם אֹרֶךְ הַזְּמַן אוֹ צוֹק עִתָּךְ
צָרוּ לַזִּכָּרוֹן נִימָּחֵק,
אוֹ עֹצֶם מַרְאָה זוֹ מְבַעִתָּךְ –

'If the passage of time or your hardships have conspired to erase this memory, or if the power of this vision stuns you with fear,

יָמִים רַבִּים נְשָׂאתִיךָ עַל חֵיק,
וּבְתוֹרָה שֶׁבִּכְתָב מִלְּשׁוֹנִי
הֵן בְּתֵבֵל הָיִיתָ מְשַׂחֵק.

'[know that] for many days I carried you in my arms, and it was from my lips that you learned the Written Law, in which you rejoiced on earth.

אָבִיךָ זֶה יְלָדְךָ אֲנִי!
נַעַר הָיִיתָ עֵת אֲשֶׁר כָּלָה
עֲנַן חַיַּי וְסֻלַּק לִמְעוֹנִי.'

'I am your father, who gave you life! You were but a child when my life's cloud faded and was banished to the zone I now inhabit.'

אֲזַי מָתְנַי אֲחָזוּ חַלְחָלָה,
וָאֶקֹּד לְפָנָיו מֵאֵין אוֹנִים.
וְנֶעְלַם מֵעֵינַי שָׁם, וְעָלָה –

At this, my limbs writhed in anguish; all my strength fled, I bowed down before him. And he vanished before my eyes, he flew up,

לָקַח דַּרְכּוֹ פְּנֵי שַׂר הַפָּנִים.
וְקוֹל יוֹרֵד אָז מִפֶּתַח שָׁמָיו,
רֶגַע אֲשֶׁר נִכְנַס לִפְנַי לִפְנִים:

making his way towards the Angel of the Presence.[1] And just as he entered the Innermost Chamber, a voice came down from the gate of heaven:

'וְאֵל שַׁדַּי יִתֵּן לְךָ רַחֲמָיו.'

'May God Almighty grant you His mercy!'

1. Lit. 'the Prince of the Face'.

מֹשֶׁה גַּבַּאי

Moses Gabbai

אַשְׁרֵי עַיִן

INVOCATION OF RAIN

אַשְׁרֵי עַיִן רָאֲתָה כָּל אֵלֶּה!
הֲלֹא לְמִשְׁמַע אֹזֶן צָהֲלָה נַפְשֵׁנוּ.

Happy the eye that saw all this! We hear of it and our soul rejoices.

אַשְׁרֵי עַיִן רָאֲתָה מַיִם יוֹרְדִים מִשְּׁחָקִים,
וְהָרוּחַ מְרַחֵף עַל פְּנֵי אֲרָקִים,
וְהַצַּדִּיק מְרַחֵשׁ לָאֵל עוֹשֵׂה בְרָקִים,
לְמוּל כָּל הָעָם אוֹמְרִים דְּבָרִים מְתוּקִים.
הֲלֹא לְמִשְׁמַע אֹזֶן צָהֲלָה נַפְשֵׁנוּ.

Happy the eye that saw water pouring down from heaven, and the wind sweeping over the earth, as the righteous man whispers to God, Maker of lightning, and all the people stand before him, murmuring sweet words. We hear of this and our soul rejoices.

אַשְׁרֵי עַיִן רָאֲתָה שַׁחְרוּת עָבִים נִצָּבוֹת,
וְהָרוּחַ מְרַחֵף בְּמֵי גֶשֶׁם נְדָבוֹת,
וְהַצַּדִּיק מְרַחֵשׁ לָאֵל רוֹכֵב עֲרָבוֹת:
'הִתְחַזְּקוּ, אֱמוּנִים, כִּי זֹרְמוּ מַיִם עָבוֹת!'
הֲלֹא לְמִשְׁמַע אֹזֶן צָהֲלָה נַפְשֵׁנוּ.

Happy the eye that saw the blackness of massed clouds, and the wind sweeping through with a downpour of blessings, as the righteous man whispers to God, who rides over the desert plains. 'Courage, my faithful ones, the clouds are pouring down water!' We hear of this and our soul rejoices.

אַשְׁרֵי עַיִן רָאֲתָה הֲדַר בָּרָק וּרְעָמִים נוֹהִים,
וְהָרוּחַ מְרַחֵף וְכָל הַלְּבָבוֹת רוֹהִים,
וְהַצַּדִּיק מְרַחֵשׁ לָאֵל צוּר דָּר גְּבֹהִים,
וּלְמוּל כָּל הָעָם כַּאֲרִי עַל טַרְפּוֹ מֵהִים:
'הִתְחַזְּקוּ, אֱמוּנִים, גֶּשֶׁם נְדָבוֹת הֵנִיף אֱלֹהִים!'
הֲלֹא לְמִשְׁמַע אֹזֶן צָהֲלָה נַפְשֵׁנוּ.

Happy the eye that saw the glory of lightning, and thunders in hot pursuit, with the wind sweeping over, and all hearts struck with fear, as the righteous man whispers to God, the Rock, who dwells on high, and before him stand the people, roaring like a lion over its prey. 'Courage, my faithful ones, God is raining a downpour of blessings.' We hear of this and our soul rejoices.

אַשְׁרֵי עַיִן רָאֲתָה מַיִם בְּחוּצוֹת וּשְׁבִילִים,
וְהָרוּחַ מְרַחֵף לְדַשֵּׁן כָּל יְבוּלִים,
וְהַצַּדִּיק עַל רֹאשׁוֹ מַיִם יוֹרְדִים וְעוֹלִים,
וְזוֹרְקִים אֶת אֶפְרוֹ וְשַׂעֲרוֹתָיו טְבוּלִים —

Happy the eye that saw water in the streets and in the pathways, and the wind sweeping over to make the harvests great as the righteous man stands there, with water streaming, ever stronger, down his head, washing

מֵרֹב הַגְּשָׁמִים קְוֻצּוֹתָיו תַּלְתַּלִּים.
הֲלֹא לְמִשְׁמַע אֹזֶן צָהֲלָה נַפְשֵׁנוּ.

away the wood-ashes, drenching his hair – such a torrent of rain that his locks curl into waves! We hear of this and our soul rejoices.

מֹשֶׁה רֵימוֹס

Moses Remos

מִי הֶאֱמִין

THE DIRGE OF MOSES REMOS

קוננתי אותה יום א׳ כי אמרו לי כי היום הבא אחריו היו עתידים להרגני. אוי לי! יהי רצון שתהיה מיתתי כפרה לעונותי. ובבכי תמרורים בבלתי מחשבה והסתכלות לקחתי הקולמוס, והייתי צועק וכותב. אשביע בה׳ אלהי ישראל שכל מי שתגיע לידו יעתיקנה ויקראנה וישלחנה לאחרים עד שתבא ליד קרובי העלובים. ורשום בה שמי משה רימוס. אוי לי!

I composed this dirge the day I was told that I would be executed on the morrow. Woe is me! May it be His will that my death atone for my sins. Weeping bitterly, without thought or reflection, I took my pen in hand, and I wrote, screaming all the while. By the Lord God of Israel, I charge all those who will come into possession of this lament that they copy it, read it and pass it on to others until it reach the hands of my unfortunate relatives. In it, I have indicated my name, Moses Remos.[1] *Woe is me!*

מִי הֶאֱמִין כִּי כְּמוֹת נָבָל
יָמוּת מַשְׂכִּיל דּוֹרֵשׁ אֱלֹהִים ?
וּכְאַלּוּף לַטֶּבַח יוּבַל,
הוּבַל מֹשֶׁה אִישׁ הָאֱלֹהִים ?

Who could have believed that a wise man, a man who sought out God, would die so base a death; that, like a sheep led obedient to the slaughter, Moses, the man of God, would be led to his death?

מְקַטְרֶגֶת מִדַּת הַדִּין, כִּי נֶחֱרִים
זְעֵיר אַפִּין עִם בַּעַל הַחֹטֶם.
אָסְפוּ נָגְהָם פָּנִים מְאִירִים,
וְעַתִּיק יוֹמִין אָזְנוֹ אוֹטֵם.

Divine judgement denounces me; the Impatient One and the Forbearing One[2] both rage against me; the Shining Face has withdrawn His light and the Ancient of Days has stopped His ears.

1. In the acrostic.

2. Lit. 'the Short Face and the One with the Nose'; Kabbalistic epithets derived from the doctrine of the *Sefirot*.

מְחֻיַּב הַמְּצִיאוּת, אֶחָד, בְּלִי גַשְׁמוּת,
פּוֹעֵל וְצוּרָה, תַּכְלִית, קַדְמוֹנִי,
חָכָם, יָכוֹל, רוֹצֶה, בְּלִי שִׁנּוּי וּדְמוּת –
אֵלִי, אֵלִי, לָמָּה עֲזַבְתָּנִי! [...]

O Necessary Being, One, Incorporeal,
Efficient, Formal and Final Cause,
Eternal, Wise, Potent, Supreme Will,
Changeless, Shapeless – my God, my
God, why have You forsaken me?

שָׁמַיִם לָבְשׁוּ קַדְרוּת, וְשַׂק
שָׂמוּ כְּסוּתָם הַגַּלְגַּלִּים.
יוֹם מוֹתִי, עֲרָבוֹת נָח, לֹא חָשַׁק
כְּמִשְׁפָּטוֹ לְהַשִּׂיג בְּנֵי אֵלִים.

The skies clothe themselves in mourning, and the spheres put on a sackcloth. On the day I die, *Aravot*[1] will come to a standstill; it will lose all desire to contemplate the sons of God.

שֹׁמּוּ שָׁמַיִם לְאַכְזְרִיּוּת מוֹתִי!
גַּלְגַּל הַמַּזָּלוֹת מֶרְכָּז נָטָה:
כְּכֶבֶשׂ, כְּאַלּוּף, יוֹבִילוּ אוֹתִי,
יָדַי וְרַגְלַי תְּאוֹמִים מִלְמַטָּה.

Stand aghast at my cruel death, you heavens! The zodiac is out of joint: I am led away like a Ram or a Bull; my hands and my feet are tied to each other like Twins.

הֵן אֲחוֹרַנִּית כַּהֲלֹךְ סַרְטָן
יָדַי אֲסוּרוֹת וְעָרְפִּי יַעֲרֹף,
וּמְשׁוֹפְטִי עַל יְמִינִי כְּשָׂטָן,
דִּמִּינוּ כְּאַרְיֵה יִכְסוֹף לִטְרֹף.

I am forced to walk backwards like a Crab, hands shackled, neck broken. At my right side stands the accuser, like Satan, a Lion eager for prey.

הֵן צַעֲקַת בְּתוּלָה צוֹעֵק קוֹבֵל,
מֹאזְנֵי מִשְׁפָּט שׁוֹאֵל, וְאֵין עוֹנֶה.
מְיֻסָּר בְּעַקְרָב, נֶחְבָּל בְּחֶבֶל,
קֶשֶׁת דְּרוּכָה נִכְחוֹ פּוֹנֶה.

I shout my complaints like a Virgin; I ask for the Scales of justice, but no one answers; I am chastised by a Scorpion,[2] whipped with a rope. The Archer bends his bow at me.

הֵן כְּשַׁסַּע הַגְּדִי יְשַׁסְּעוּנִי.
אוֹי לָעֵינַיִם כֵּן רוֹאוֹת הֵן!
אֶדְלֶה בְּדַלְיֵי דִּמְעוֹת עֵינִי,
עַד כִּי דָגִים יִדְגּוּ בָהֶן. [...]

They will tear me in pieces as if I were a Goat. Pity the eyes that witness this! [Like a Water-Bearer,] I draw my tears in buckets; Oh, Fish could swarm in these waters!

1. Here, the ninth, and uppermost, heavenly sphere; or, a term for the twelve signs of the Zodiac (*A Dictionary of Angels*, 1967, p. 269). 2. Also, 'leash' (1 Kings 12.11).

סְעָרַת מָוֶת, שָׁבָץ אֲחָזוּנִי.
לֹא אוּכַל לָנוּד עוֹד, כִּי שָׁלְחוּ לֵאמֹר:
'מָחָר תָּמוּת' – אוֹי לִי, עָנִי –
'סָחוֹב וְהַשְׁלֵךְ, קְבוּרַת חֲמוֹר'.

The whirlwind of death, the throes of death have seized me. I cannot hope to flee for they have sent a message, saying: 'Tomorrow you shall die' – ah, wretched me – 'You shall be buried like a dead ass, dragged along and flung away.'

סֹעֲרָה וַעֲנִיָּה, אִמִּי, מַה תַּעֲשִׂי
עֵת אֲשֶׁר תַּגִּיעַ לָךְ הַשְּׁמוּעָה?
'מַחְמַד עֵינַי, עֲטֶרֶת רֹאשִׁי,' –
תִּסְפְּדִי עָלַי בִּמְקוֹר דִּמְעָה.

O my mother, storm-tossed and distressed, what will you do when the word reaches you? 'Delight of my eyes, crown of my head,' you will mourn for me with flowing tears.

סֻכָּתְךָ נָפְלָה, מַה תַּעֲשֶׂה, אָבִי?
מַה מְּאֹד רָעָה תְּהִי זִקְנָתֶךָ!
אַחֲלַי, תִּמְחַל לִי פְּשָׁעַי וְחוֹבִי,
אִם לֹא כָּרָאוּי כִּבַּדְתִּיךָ.

Your house has fallen, my father, and what will you do? What a sad old age awaits you! I pray you, pardon my offences, if ever I failed to show you due honour.

סְאוֹן סוֹאֵן בְּרַעַשׁ, שָׂטָן מְקַטְרֵג –
מָצָא בַּעַל חוֹב לִגְבּוֹת חוֹבוֹ.
דְּעוּ, מְיֻדָּעַי, כִּי לֹא אֵהָרֵג
עַל עָוֹן גָּדוֹל עָוִיתִי בוֹ.

Bellowing, clamouring, Satan accuses me; the Creditor has found occasion to collect his bill. But know, my friends, that I am not being killed for having committed a terrible crime.

סַם הַמָּוֶת, אָמְרוּ, כִּי יָעַצְתִּי
לְהִנָּתֵן קֻבַּעַת כּוֹס הַתַּרְעֵלָה
לַעֲרֵלִים מֵתוּ – לֹא פָשַׁעְתִּי!
הִצְמִיתוּ חַיַּי בְּזֹאת הָעֲלִילָה.

They claim that I prescribed a deadly poison which was administered in a bowl of drunkenness to the gentiles who died; but it was none of my doing. With this false charge, they are silencing my life.

סוֹד הַשֵּׁם לִירֵאָיו! לוּלֵי רַבִּי עֲקִיבָא
וַחֲבֵרָיו, כִּמְעַט נָטְיוּ רַגְלַי
בִּרְאוֹתִי מוֹתִי עַל לֹא סִבָּה.
אַךְ יְיָ הַצַּדִּיק עַל כָּל הַבָּא עָלַי.

The Lord confides in those who fear Him. If I had not [called to mind the martyrdom of] Rabbi Akiva and his companions,[1] my feet would almost have slipped, seeing that I was doomed to die for no reason at all. But the Lord is just in all that has befallen me.

1. The ten martyrs executed in the reign of Hadrian.

שָׂח שַׂר הַצּוֹרֵר לְהַצִּיל רֹאשִׁי,
אִם כָּבוֹד אָמִיר לַעֲבֹד אֱלוֹ.
עֲנִיתִיו: ׳טוֹב מוֹת גּוּפִי מִמּוֹת נַפְשִׁי.׳
חֶלְקִי – הַצּוּר הַחַי, וְהַמֵּת יִהְיֶה לּוֹ!

The arch-enemy offered to save my head if I would exchange my Glory for the worship of his god. I answered him: 'It is better for my body to die than my soul.' My portion is the living God; let the dead one[1] be his!

סְחִי וּמָאוֹס הוּשַׂם, כָּל רֶגֶל תִּרְמֹס,
כִּי מוֹת אַכְזְרִיּוּת אָז זִמּוּנִי.
מִי הֶאֱמִין זֹאת עַל מֹשֶׁה רֵימוֹס!
אֲנִי הַגֶּבֶר רָאָה עֳנִי.

I am treated as offscouring and refuse, trampled under every foot. They have plotted a cruel death for me. Oh, who would have believed that such would be the fate of Moses Remos? I am the man who has known affliction!

סָר מַר הַמָּוֶת – אָמְנָם אוֹי לִי
עַל שִׁבְרִי! הָיִיתִי בְּמִבְחַר חַיַּי,
אַרְבָּעָה וְעֶשְׂרִים שָׁנָה יֶשׁ לִי,
גַּבְרָא בְּכֻלָּא וְכָל מַאֲוַיַּי.

Death's bitterness is at my side – oh, the pain of my wounds! I was in the prime of my life; I am twenty-four years old, in the fullness of manhood and desire.

סוֹף דָּבָר: הַדִּין עָלַי אַצְדִּיק,
אֶתְוַדֶּה וְאֹמַר: ׳אֲבָל חָטָאתִי!׳
רָשַׁעְתִּי, כִּי יְיָ הַצַּדִּיק.
אָנָּא אֵל נָא, מְחַל אַשְׁמָתִי.

The end of the matter: I hereby justify the Divine decree. I confess and say: Truly, I have sinned![2] I have acted wickedly, and the Lord is in the right. O God, I pray You, pardon my guilt.

סְעָדֵנִי, צוּרִי, וּתְהִי כַפָּרָה
מִיתָתִי עַל עֲוֹנַי, וּכְנֶפֶשׁ מַאֲמִין
בִּצְרוֹר הַחַיִּים תִּהְיֶה צְרוּרָה
נַפְשִׁי אִתְּךָ לְקֵץ הַיָּמִין.

Sustain me, my Rock, and may my death atone for my sins; and, like the souls of all believers, may mine be kept forever alive in Your care, until the end of days.

1. I.e. Jesus; the phrase is taken from Exodus 21.34.
2. 'Truly, we have sinned' is the Talmudic formula of the Confession on the Day of Atonement.

רְפָאֵל בֶּן־יִצְחָק

Raphael da Faenza

רַעְיָתִי, לִי אָזְנֵךְ הַטִּי־נָא

SONG WITH GALANTINA

רַעְיָתִי, לִי אָזְנֵךְ הַטִּי־נָא:
כַּמָּה מִנֹּפֶת נָעַמְתְּ
מִמֶּתֶק חִשְׁקִי טָעַמְתְּ!
אֲמָרַי וְקוֹלִי תִּשְׁמְעִי־נָא,
אֵי גָלַנְטִינָה.

Hear my words, my dearest: you were far more delicious than honey when you tasted my sweet desire. Now listen to my voice, O Galantina!

פְּלוּלֵי אַהֲבָה תְּקַבְּלִי,
כּוֹכָב צַח, מִמֵּנִּי דְרוּשָׁה.
שִׂפְתוֹתַיִךְ מִצּוּף מָתְקוּ לִי
בָּהֶם תִּשְּׁקִי פִּי, וְהַגִּישָׁה
לְשׁוֹנֵךְ אֶל חִכִּי, וּתְכַלְכְּלִי,
יוֹנָתִי, לְדוֹדֵךְ בְּלִי בוּשָׁה.
וְנָשִׁירָה בְּשִׁירָה חֲדָשָׁה
וְנָגִילָה בְּמַקְהֵלוֹת,
אֲיֻמָּה כַּנִּדְגָּלוֹת.

Bright star, I am in need of you; accept my love's entreaties. Your lips, which kiss my mouth, are sweeter to me than nectar. Put your tongue to mine, my dove, and feed your beloved without shame. Then we shall sing new songs and rejoice in unison, my fairest, majestic as flying banners.

זְמִירוֹת אֲהָבִים רַנִּי־נָא,
אֵי גָלַנְטִינָה.

Loud sing your serenades, O Galantina!

אַתְּ שֶׁאָהֲבָה נַפְשִׁי,
יַעֲלָה בָּרָה וּמְתֹאֶרֶת,
נֹעַם חִשְׁקֵךְ אַשְׁשִׁי,
עֲנָק צַוְּרוֹנֵי לְתִפְאֶרֶת,
וּלְעוֹלָם תְּהִי לִי גְבֶרֶת.
וְאָשִׂימָה עָלַיִךְ כַּפִּי,
תְּהִי עִם פִּי וְתִתְיַפִּי.

You are my true love, my pure and beautiful gazelle. Redouble your sweet passion, hang round my neck like a precious jewel, and forever be my mistress. I shall put my hand upon you. Mouth to mouth, your loveliness will grow.

הוֹד פָּנַיִךְ מְאִירִים לִי תַּרְאִי־נָא,
אֵי גָלַנְטִינָה.

Let me see the splendour of your shining face, O Galantina!

זְכַרְתִּיךְ בַּלַּיְלָה עַל מִשְׁכָּבִי,
תַּמָּתִי, וְיָפִי מִכְלוּלַיִךְ.
יוֹמָם וָלַיִל, עֵינַי וְלִבִּי,
לְסַפֵּר בְּרֹן מַהֲלָלַיִךְ
וּלְהַנִּיחַ רֹאשִׁי בֵּין שָׁדַיִךְ
שָׁם בְּחַדְרֵי מַשְׂכִּיּוֹת.
מִמִּגְדָּל בָּנוּי לְתַלְפִּיּוֹת,

Night after night on my bed I think of you, my perfect one, and of your charming robes. O my eyes, my heart – I long to sing your praises day and night, to rest my head between your breasts, there, within the ornamented shrine. Out of the lofty tower,[1]

צְבִיָּה, לְדוֹדֵךְ תִּקְרְאִי־נָא,
אֵי גָלַנְטִינָה.

summon your lover, gazelle. O Galantina!

ועתה שמע תשובת החשוקה לדודה:

Now listen to the reply of the maiden to her beloved:

גַּם אֲנִי לִמְאֹד אִוִּיתִיךְ,
דּוֹד אוֹהֵב, נָאֶה וְנָעִים.
וּמֵאָז מִקֶּדֶם רְאִיתִיךְ
כָּל קְרָבַי לְךָ הָיוּ נִשְׁמָעִים.
נִשְׁתָּעֶה־נָּא בְּשַׁעֲשׁוּעִים
בְּעַרְשֵׂנוּ רַעֲנָנָה,
בָּהּ לִשְׂמֹחַ בִּרְנָנָה

I, too, have deeply yearned for you, my handsome one, my pleasant love. Ever since I first saw you, long ago, my heart has been yours to command. Let us give ourselves over to delights in our bed that is shaded with branches. There I shall dally with you,

עִמָּךְ, צְבִי חֵן, וְלָלִינָה,
אֵי גָלַנְטִינָה.

my fair love, singing, lying at your side. O Galantina!

יָפְיָפִיתָ מִכָּל דּוֹדִים,
הוּצַק חֵן בְּשִׂפְתוֹתֶיךָ.
נִכְבַּדְתָּ עַל כָּל דּוֹדִים,

You surpass all lovers in beauty. Your lips are moulded in grace. You rank higher than all lovers in honour. Noble

1. 'Your neck is like David's tower, girt with battlements' (Song of Songs 4.4).

עֲלָמוֹת בִּיקְרוֹתֶיךָ.
כִּי תִשְׁמֹר מַדִּבְּרוֹתֶיךָ
וּפְרַשׂ־נָא כְּנָפְךָ עָלַי,
כִּי תְמַשֵּׁשׁ כָּל כֵּלַי

maidens wait upon you. If you keep your pledge and spread your wing over me, you will yet finger all my possessions

וְתָבוֹא אֵלַי, הַאֲמִינָה,
אֵי גָלַנְטִינָה.

and lie with me – rest assured!
O Galantina!

חִזְקוּ־נָא, חוֹשְׁקִים, וְאִמְצוּ
וּתְעוֹרְרוּ הַבָּנוֹת.
חוּשׁוּ, רֵעִים, וְהָאִיצוּ,
כִּי כֻלָּן מְזֻמָּנוֹת
לְמַלֹּאת חֶפְצְכֶם נְכוֹנוֹת,
לִהְיוֹת לְבָשָׂר אֶחָד.
וְאַתָּה, הַדּוֹד, בְּרָן־יַחַד –

Take courage, you lovers, take heart, go and rouse the girls. Hurry, friends, there is no time to lose, for they are all at hand, prepared to fulfil your desires, to cling to you and to become one flesh. And you, my love, when they all sing together,

שְׁמַע רַעְיָתְךָ וּלְכָה לִינָה,
אֵי גָלַנְטִינָה.

listen to your darling and come to lie with her. O Galantina!

עֲלוּמֵי־שֵׁם

Anonymous

יָהּ, לְמָתַי פֵּרוּד

SONG FOR PASSOVER

יָהּ, לְמָתַי פֵּרוּד יְנִידֵנִי מִבְּלִי מִשְׁכָּן ?
אֵשׁ נְדוּד תּוּקַד, וְהִנְנִי לִיקוֹד מוּכָן.

[Zion:] Lord, how much longer will this separation make me a homeless fugitive? The fires of wandering are ablaze, and I am ready for the stake.

"שׁוֹחֲרַי, אַט !" – פֶּן לַהֲטֵי לִבִּי יֹאחֲזוּ בָהֶם,
וּמְאַהֲבַי – פֶּן גַּחֲלֵי קִרְבִּי יִשְׂרְפוּ אֶתְהֶם,

'My friends, beware!' [I say to them,] lest the flames of my heart ignite them; [and I warn] those who love me, lest the embers of my soul consume them.

כִּי יְדִידִי רָחַק וְהִבְעִיר בִּי אֶת שְׁבִיבֵיהֶם.
אָמְרוּ אוֹיְבַי כִּי עֲזָבַנִי וַאֲנִי אַלְמָן
מֵאֱלֹהַי, גַּם רָחֲקוֹ מִמֶּנִּי נָתְנוּ סִימָן.

For my Beloved, by going far away, has kindled these sparks in me. My enemies say that I have been abandoned, left widowed by my God. He is far from me and that, they say, is proof enough.

מְנֻדּוּדִים אֶשְׂבַּע עֲדֵי נֶשֶׁף, אֶת כְּסִיל רוֹעֶה,
כִּי כְמוֹ שֶׂה אוֹבֵד בְּהַר נֶשֶׁף אֵלְכָה תוֹעֶה.
מִפְּרִידָה אֶהֱמֶה, וּמֵרֶשֶׁף אֶשְׁאֲפָה, אֶפְעֶה.
צוּר, הֲלָעַד עַל עַם מְאֹד עָנִי אַפְּךָ יֶעְשַׁן?
רַחֲמֶיךָ אָנָּא יְבוֹאוּנִי, וַעֲזוֹב עָשָׁן.

All night I toss and turn, in company with Orion. I stray like a lost sheep on the twilit hill-side. The parting makes me moan and the fires make me cry and gasp. Lord, will You forever be incensed against this destitute people? Oh, extend Your compassion to me, have done with wrath.

וַאֲנִי, אִם חֹשֶׁךְ יְשׁוּפֵנִי, בְּךָ אֲשׁוּ מַחְסִי,
אוֹ פְּרִידָתְךָ תַּאֲדִיבֵנִי, אַתְּ מְנָת כּוֹסִי.
רַחֲמֶיךָ סִתְרִי וּמָגִנִּי מֵחֲמַס שׁוֹסִי.
אִם תְּדַכֵּא אוֹ תַחֲלִיאֵנִי מַחֲלֶה נֶאְמָן,
יֶשְׁעֲךָ תִשְׁלַח יַחֲלִימֵנִי, אָב לְבֵן – רַחְמָן.'

And I, though darkness cover me, shall make You my refuge; though Your parting grieve me, You are all I have. Only Your mercy can shield me from my violent enemies. Even if You beat me down or plague me with persistent sickness, You will send Your deliverance and restore me, for a father has mercy on his child.

'אֲהַבְתִּי לָךְ, בַּת יְפֵה־פִיָּה, רְחָבָה מִיָּם.
שׁוּב אֲשִׁיבֵךְ אֵלַי, וְעַם נִהְיָה יִשְׁכְּחוּ עֳנָיִם.
אוֹהֲבַי אַנְחִיל דָּת וְתוּשִׁיָּה, אֶאֱסוֹף שְׁבָיִם.
אוֹמְרָה לַצָּפוֹן: "תְּנִי, תְּנִי שׁוֹכְבֵי אַשְׁמָן!"
כִּי מְקוֹם שַׂק עוֹד יִלְבְּשׁוּ שָׁנִי, שֵׁשׁ וְאַרְגָּמָן.'

[God:] My love for you, O my beautiful daughter, is broader than the sea. I shall take you back to Me, and the people, who were overcome, will forget their misery. I shall endow those who love Me with laws and wisdom. I shall assemble their captives. I shall say to the North: 'Give them up, give up all those who sleep in the ghostly underworld!' For instead of sackcloth they will yet dress themselves in fine linen, in purple and scarlet.

'לוֹעֲגִים לִי אֶתְמוֹל בְּיוֹם אֵידִי גַּם בְּיוֹם צַר לִי:
הֵן הֱשִׁיבַנִי בֶּאֱמֶת דּוֹדִי לוֹ, וְסָר מַחֲלִי.

[Zion:] All of you who mocked me yesterday in the hour of my peril, in the day of my distress – my Beloved has truly taken me back and my illness

עַל מְשַׂנְאַי אָבוּס וְעַל רוֹדַי אַשְׁלִיךְ נַעֲלַי!
וַאֲבַשֵּׂר אוֹמְרִים שְׂנֵאַנִי עוֹבְדֵי חַמָּן –
כִּי כְבָר אִישִׁי יֶאֱהָבֵנִי לְכֹל זְמָן.'

has disappeared. I shall stamp on my enemies and fling my shoes at my adversaries. And to the idol-worshippers, who had said that He hates me, I shall proudly declare: 'My husband loves me now, and for all time.'

לִבִּי לְיוֹכֶבֶד

JOKHEBED'S CRY

לִבִּי לְיוֹכֶבֶד! 'מֹשֶׁה בְּנִי,'
תִּצְעַק וְתֹאמַר, 'הָהּ מֵתָה אֲנִי!'

My heart goes out to Jokhebed! 'O, Moses, my son,' she moans, 'Oh, I am dying!'

שַׁאֲלוּ לְהַר סִינַי, שַׁאֲלוּ מְבוֹא
שֶׁמֶשׁ וּמִזְרָח, אָן לֶשֶׁם־שְׁבוֹ?
מִיּוֹם אֲשֶׁר עָלָה אֶל הַר נְבוֹ
לֹא שָׁב, וְלִבִּי עָלָיו כָּאֳנִי
סוֹעֵר, עֲדֵי נֶהְפַּךְ אוֹנִי עֳנִי.

[Jokhebed:] 'Go and ask Mount Sinai, ask the West and the East, where is [Moses, precious as] turquoise and agate? Since the day he went up Mount Nebo, there has been no trace of him. My heart trembles for him like a ship caught up in a storm. My strength is gone, drained by misery.

מוֹאָב, הֱיֵה סֵתֶר עַל בֶּן דְּרוֹר
לָקַח וְלֹא נָתַן לוֹ אֵל דְּרוֹר.
מִבַּלְעֲדֵי מֹשֶׁה אֵין לִי מָר־דְּרוֹר.
עָלָיו, עֲדַת יַעֲקֹב, אֵבֶל עֲנִי,
כָּל עוֹד בְּרוּם שַׁחַק כּוֹכַב מְנִי.'

'Moab,[1] shelter the son of freedom! The Lord has taken him and refused to let him go. Without Moses, I cannot savour flowing myrrh. And you, Jacob's flock, mourn for him so long as the Pleiades shine in the high heavens.'

וַיֶּחֱרַד סִינַי וּנְבוֹ וְהוֹר
עַל צַעֲקַת יוֹכֶבֶד מְמָרוֹר.
תִּצְעַק וּפָנֶיהָ אֶל מוּל פְּעוֹר:
'הָהּ עַל זְרוֹעִי, הָהּ עַל בְּהֹנִי,
הָהּ עַל לְוִיִּי, הָהּ עַל כֹּהֲנִי'.

Then Sinai and Nebo and Hor all trembled at Jokhebed's bitter lament, as she faced Peor[1] and wailed: 'O my [right] arm, my [precious] thumb, O my Levite, my Priest!'

1. Mount Nebo is located in the land of Moab. Moses 'was buried in a valley in Moab opposite Beth-peor' (Deuteronomy 34.6).

'אִמִּי, חֲכִי, אַל תָּרִימִי בְּקוֹל,
כִּי לֹא יְכַסֵּנִי עָפָר וְחוֹל
הָאֵל, וְהִבְדִּיל בֵּין קֹדֶשׁ לְחֹל.
בֵּין מַחֲנוֹת מַלְאָכִים מַחֲנִי,
גַּם מָחֳרַת אִתִּי אַתְּ תִּצְפְּנִי.'

[Moses:] 'O my mother, take heart, do not raise your voice, for the Lord has not covered me with dust and sand; He sets apart the sacred from the common. My resting-place is among the hosts of angels and tomorrow you too will join me.'

'לֵךְ נָא בְּשָׁלוֹם, נוֹטֶה אָהֳלִי!
מַר לִי לְנוּדְךָ, מַר מִכָּל חָלְיִי.
שָׁלוֹם יְהִי מֵאֵל גַּם לְךָ וְלִי,
יַקְשִׁיב לְמַר שִׂיחִי וּלְמַעֲנִי,
יֵיטִיב לְמַעַנְךָ וּלְמַעֲנִי.'

[Jokhebed:] 'Go then in peace, O you who pitched my tent! Your parting is a bitter thing for me, more bitter than any illness. May the Lord bestow His peace upon you and also upon me. May He listen to my bitter lament, and show His favour for your sake and for mine.'

הַיּוֹם בְּשִׂמְחַת תּוֹרָה תַּעַלְזוּ,
עַיִן בְּעַיִן כָּבוֹד תֶּחֱזוּ.
יוֹם יַעֲנֶה שַׁדַּי, אַל תִּרְגְּזוּ.
יֹאמַר לְצָפוֹן וּלְתֵימָן 'תְּנִי',
יוֹצִיא שְׁאָר עַמּוֹ מִבּוֹר עֳנִי.

Make merry today, rejoice in the Law. With your own eyes, you will behold the Glory. And on the day the Lord answers, do not tremble with fear. He will say to the North and the South, 'Give them up.' He will bring His people out of the pit of affliction.

בִּרְאוֹתִי כִּי עָבַר סַגְרִיר

THE DOVE AND THE HART

בִּרְאוֹתִי כִּי עָבַר סַגְרִיר
וּפְרִי כָל עֵץ צוֹמֵחַ,
וּבְהַגִּיעַ עֵת הַזָּמִיר
וּגְפָנִים נָתְנוּ רֵיחַ,
וּזְמַן רוּחַ אַהֲבָה יָעִיר
אֵלַי שׁוֹאֵף זוֹרֵחַ –
אָז יֵיטִיב נִגּוּן, אָז יָשִׁיר
לִבִּי לִקְרַאת עֹפֶר וּבְחִיר:

[She:] 'When I see that the rains are past and the fruit of every tree is in blossom; when the time of singing birds has come and the vines give forth their fragrance; when Time stirs the winds of love, which seek me out, and rise all around me – then my heart makes sweet melody, singing to my hart, my chosen one. [He is as wise as]

יוֹסֵף צָפְנַת פַּעְנֵחַ,
הַבֵּן יַקִּיר.

Joseph, master of mysteries,[1] and as dear as a son.'

יוֹנָה, בָּךְ חָשַׁקְתִּי וּבְקִרְ־
בִּי אֵשׁ חִשְׁקֵךְ נוֹפֵחַ.
אָמְנָם זָחַלְתִּי וָאַסְתִּיר
חִשְׁקֵךְ הַמִּתְלַקֵּחַ
וָאֹמַר: הַס, כִּי לֹא אַזְכִּיר
בְּשִׁמֵךְ, לֹא יִפָּתֵחַ
פִּי, פֶּן מְקַנְאֵנִי יַכִּיר,
יָנִיעַ ראשׁוֹ, וּלְהָפִיר
אַהֲבָה – כָּזָב יָפִיחַ,
שָׂפָה יַפְטִיר.

[He:] 'O dove, it is you I desire, and deep in my heart I fan these passionate flames. But out of fear, I have concealed my fiery passion, saying: Hush, I must not mention your name, my mouth must remain dumb, lest my rival find you out and wag his head. He will tell a pack of lies, he will make mouths at me to undo our love.'

עֹפֶר, לִבִּי הוֹמֶה כִּכְפִיר,
לִפְרִידָתְךָ צוֹרֵחַ
וּבְיַד תַּאֲוָה רוּחוֹ הִסְגִּיר
וּבְכַנְפֵי נוֹד פּוֹרֵחַ,
כִּי חִשְׁקְךָ בִּכְסָלַי מְמָאִיר
וּבְכִלְיוֹתַי פּוֹלֵחַ.
לִירוֹת יֶתֶר קַשְׁתּוֹ הִתִּיר,
וַיִּז מִדָּמִי אֶל הַקִּיר,
כָּל עַצְמוֹתַי פִּצֵּחַ,
חִצָּיו הִשְׁכִּיר.

[She:] 'O hart, my heart roars with pain, like a lion, because you are gone. It has surrendered itself to desire and flies after you on wings of exile. This passion pierces my loins and cuts deep into my vitals. It strung its bow to shoot at me, and my blood splashed onto the wall. It splintered all my bones, made its arrows drunk [with my blood].'

יוֹנָה, שִׁמְעִי אֶנְקַת אָסִיר
לִנְדוֹדֵךְ מִתְיַפֵּחַ.
כָּלוּ חַיַּי, כִּי כֶּחָצִיר
יָמַי וּכְצִיץ פּוֹרֵחַ.

[He:] 'O dove, listen to the groaning of this prisoner, bewailing your absence. My life has worn away: my days are like the grass, like a vanishing flower.

1. *Žaphenath-paneah*, Joseph's Egyptian name (Genesis 41.45), was taken to mean 'he who reveals secrets'.

אֶשְׁאַל לָמוּת כִּי חִשְׁקֵךְ צִיר
נֶאְמָן אַךְ בִּי שׁוֹלֵחַ.
וּבְכוֹר מָוֶת כַּיּוֹם אַכִּיר,
וַהֲרוּגֵי הַחֵשֶׁק אוֹקִיר.
הַמֵּתִים אֲנִי שַׁבֵּחַ
מִפַּז אוֹפִיר.

I pray for death to come, so fierce are the pangs[1] that passion hurls at me. Today, I hold death most dear, and I prize the victims of Desire. I count the dead more precious than the fine gold of Ophir.

יוֹנַת חֵן, יֵין זִכְרֵךְ אַזְכִּיר
רַקַח מַעֲשֵׂה רוֹקֵחַ,
וּבְחִשְׁקֵךְ אֶשָּׂא קוֹל בְּזָמִיר
מִתְגַּבֵּר וּמְנַצֵּחַ,
וּלְנֶגֶד יָפְעָתֵךְ אַעְתִּיר
אִכַּף וְאֶשְׁתּוֹחֵחַ.
כִּי צוּרֵךְ נָתַן אוֹר בָּהִיר
אֶל עֵבֶר פָּנַיִךְ הֵאִיר,
לֶחְיֵךְ עָשָׂה יָרֵחַ,
כּוֹכָב מַזְהִיר.

'Fair dove, I shall celebrate the wine of your fame, this perfume so expertly blended. And, moved by desire, I shall raise my voice in song, in swelling songs of praise. I shall pay homage to your beauty, and bow down before it. For your Lord has shed a bright light over your face. He has made your cheek a moon, a shining star!'

תְּנָה לִי כּוֹס

THE DRUNKARD'S TESTAMENT

תְּנָה לִי כּוֹס אֲשֶׁר יָנִיס יְגוֹנִים
וְתֵן חֶלְקִי בְּנַחַל הָעֲדָנִים.
קְחָה אֶלֶף תְּמוּרָתוֹ, וְאוֹסִיף
לְךָ מֵאָה וְעֶשְׂרִים, גַּם שְׁמוֹנִים.
וְעֵת אָמוּת לְפָנֶיךָ, יְדִידִי,
חֲצֹב קִבְרִי בְּשָׁרְשֵׁי הַגְּפָנִים.

Give me the cup that puts sorrow to flight, and let me have my share in the river of delights. Take a thousand in payment, and I shall add another hundred and twenty, and eighty more.[2] And when I die before your very eyes, my friend, dig my grave among the roots of vines. Do not scatter dust upon

1. A play on words. The phrase 'fierce pangs' also means 'a trusty messenger' (Proverbs 25.13).

2. The rate is based on Song of Songs 8.12: 'But my vineyard is mine to give; the thousand pieces are yours, O Solomon, and the guardians of the fruit shall have two hundred.'

וְאַל תָּשִׂים עָלַי קִבְרִי עֲפָרִים,
אֲבָל כַּדִּים תְּמוּרַת הָאֲבָנִים.
וְאַל תִּבְכּוּ וְתָנוּדוּ בְּמוֹתִי,
עֲשׂוּ כִנּוֹר וְעוּגָבִים וּמִנִּים.
וְסִיר רַחְצִי בְּמֵימֵי הָעֲנָבִים,
וְחִנְטוּנִי בְּזַגִּים הַיְשָׁנִים.
וְאַבְשַׁי הוּא אֲבִי כָּל הַשְּׂמָחוֹת –
שְׁמוֹ זִכְרוּ לְדוֹר דּוֹרִים וְשָׁנִים.

my grave; cover it with jugs instead of stones. And do not cry and mourn when I die; but make music with harp, lute and pipe. Fill my wash basin with grape-water, and embalm me in old grape husks. For Avshay is the father of all merriment. Remember his name through all generations.

הַזָּן אֶת הָעוֹלָם

THE GENEROUS BRIDEGROOM

הַזָּן אֶת הָעוֹלָם כֻּלּוֹ,
בָּרוּךְ שֶׁאָכַלְנוּ מִשֶּׁלּוֹ.

He sustains the whole world – blessed be He Whose food we have eaten.

יוֹצֵר הַכֹּל יִתְבָּרַךְ,
כִּי שֻׁלְחָן לָנוּ עָרַךְ,
נוֹדֶה לִשְׁמוֹ בִּלְשׁוֹן רַךְ.
צֹאן וּבָקָר
לְאֵין מֶחְקָר,
הַפַּת עִקָּר
וְהַשְּׁאָר טְפֵלָה לוֹ.

Blessed be the Creator of all things, for He spread a table for us. Let us praise His name with gentle words. He fed us with sheep and cattle beyond reckoning; bread is the main dish, and all the rest is complementary.[1]

הֶחָתָן אֲשֶׁר קָבַע
סְעוּדָתוֹ לָשֹׂבַע,
זָכָה לְבִרְכוֹת שֶׁבַע –
יִזְכֶּה לְבָנִים שֶׁבַע.
נָתַן יַיִן

The bridegroom who set out such a lavish banquet was favoured with the Seven Blessings[2]; may he now be favoured with seven sons. He poured

1. And therefore may be eaten without an additional benediction. The phrase is derived from a Talmudic regulation.

2. Which are recited at weddings.

בְּטוּב עַיִן.
צְלִי עַיִן
יִפְרַח בְּכַרְמְלוֹ.

out wine with a generous flourish; may he flourish in his meadow, by a spring.

הֶאֱכִילָנוּ בְּשַׂר פָּרָה –
כַּלָּתוֹ תִּהְיֶה פּוֹרָה
כְּמוֹ רָחֵל וְצִפּוֹרָה.
עוּגוֹת סֹלֶת
לַגֻּלְגֹּלֶת,
וְתַרְנְגֹלֶת
נָתַן לְאִישׁ כְּפִי אָכְלוֹ.

He fed us with beef and we ate our fill; may his bride be as fertile as Zipporah and Rachel! Each guest could take the choicest cake, and chicken meat – each as much as he could eat.

הֶאֱכִילָנוּ בְּשַׂר הַצֹּאן –
כַּלָּתוֹ אֵשֶׁת רָצוֹן
כְּמוֹ רָחֵל רוֹעָה בַּצֹּאן.

He fed us lamb without measure; his bride is surely a treasure, like Rachel who tended her flocks.

הֶאֱכִילָנוּ בְּשַׂר אַיִל –
כַּלָּתוֹ אֵשֶׁת חַיִל
כְּמוֹ רָחֵל וַאֲבִיגַיִל.

He fed us ram's meat; his bride is a sweet helpmeet, like Rachel and Abigail.

הֶאֱכִילָנוּ בְּשַׂר דָּגָה –
כַּלָּתוֹ תִּהְיֶה מְעֻנָּגָה
כְּמוֹ יוֹנָה בִּמְעֵי הַדָּגָה.
עוּגוֹת סֹלֶת
לַגֻּלְגֹּלֶת,
וְתַרְנְגֹלֶת,
נָתַן לְאִישׁ כְּפִי אָכְלוֹ.

He fed us fish and jelly; may his bride luxuriate like Jonah in the fish's belly. Each guest could take the choicest cake, and chicken meat – each as much as he could eat!

שִׁיר יְדִידִים

SONG OF THE NEWBORN ON THE EVE OF HIS CIRCUMCISION

שִׁיר יְדִידִים אָעִירָה,
אֶתֵּן תּוֹדָה וַאֲזַמֵּר
לָאֵל כֻּלּוֹ כָּבוֹד אוֹמֵר,
וּבְשֵׁם יְיָ אֶקְרָא.

I shall awake a song of love. I shall give praise and sing to God, in whose temple all cry, 'Glory.' I shall invoke the Lord by name.

פָּדָה נַפְשִׁי מִכָּל צָרָה
– הָיִיתִי הוֹלֵךְ קוֹדֵר
בִּמְעֵי אִמִּי, בְּתוֹךְ חֶדֶר –
וּמֵאֲפֵלָה לְאוֹרָה.

He has delivered me from all my troubles. I was going about downcast in the chamber, in my mother's womb, [when He brought me] out from darkness to light.

שְׁמַע מִלַּיִן וְאָשִׁירָה
יוֹם בְּרִיתִי מִלֵּיל שׁוֹמֵר.
מָחָר יַאְדִּים תּוֹלָע צֶמֶר.
יְיָ לִי וְלֹא אִירָא.

Listen to my words: I shall celebrate the day of my circumcision,[1] for which I now keep this all-night vigil. Tomorrow the wool will be red like crimson. The Lord is on my side; I have no fear.

הַמְשַׂחֵק בְּקֻבְיָא

THE GAMBLER'S FATE

הַמְשַׂחֵק בְּקֻבְיָא
מַכָּתוֹ טְרִיָּה
וְאַחֲרִיתוֹ שְׁאִיָּה,
יְקֻלַּל בִּשְׁעָרִים.

The dice-player is always covered with raw wounds. His end is utter ruin; he is cursed in every city gate.

1. Also, 'the day of my covenant'.

יְפַזֵּר מָמוֹנוֹ
וְיוֹסִיף עֲווֹנוֹ
וּמוֹרֵד בְּקוֹנוֹ
בִּשְׁבוּעוֹת שְׁקָרִים.

He spends his money freely and piles up sins. He flouts his Maker with false oaths.

יַחֲשֹׁב כִּי יַרְוִיחַ
וּלְעוֹלָם לֹא יַצְלִיחַ,
וְגַם כִּי יוֹנֶה אָח.
וְיָמָיו מְרוֹרִים.

He hopes to make money but though he deceive his own brother, he will never succeed. All his days are a diet of bitter herbs.

יֹאכַל בְּחִפָּזוֹן
בְּלִי בִרְכַּת מָזוֹן,
וְלֹא יִמְצָא רָזוֹן
בְּעִנּוּי כִּפּוּרִים.

He gobbles down his food without saying Grace. He doesn't lose a pound on the Fast of Atonement.

יֵלֵךְ מֵעִיר לְעִיר,
מְקוֹמוֹ לֹא יַכִּיר,
וְהוּא עָנִי וְצָעִיר
מְדַלֵּג עַל הֶהָרִים.

He rushes from one town to another and can call no place his own. He is poor and despised, bounding from mountain to mountain.

רֹאשׁוֹ פָּרוּעַ
וּבִגְדוֹ קָרוּעַ
כִּי רַע יֵרוֹעַ
לְעַצְמוֹ וְלַאֲחֵרִים.

His hair is dishevelled, his clothes are in tatters. He hurts himself as he hurts other people.

כָּל אַנְשֵׁי בֵיתוֹ
שׂוֹנְאִים אוֹתוֹ,
וְיַעֲשׂוּ יוֹם מוֹתוֹ
בְּשִׂמְחָה וּבְשִׁירִים.

All the members of his household hold him in contempt. They celebrate his death with song and merriment.

יוֹם מִצָּרְפַת יָצָאתִי

A TRIP TO GERMANY

יוֹם מִצָּרְפַת יָצָאתִי
אֶל אֶרֶץ אַשְׁכְּנַז יָרַדְתִּי
וְעַם אַכְזָר מָצָאתִי
כַּיְעֵנִים בַּמִּדְבָּר.
כִּי לֹא אַלְמָן יִשְׂרָאֵל.
מַה לַתֶּבֶן אֶת הַבָּר?

When I left France and journeyed down to Germany, I found a people there as cruel as ostriches in the desert. *Oh, Israel is not forsaken!*[1] *What has chaff to do with grain?*

צִפִּיתִי לִי לִישׁוּעָה
יוֹם נֹפֶשׁ וּמַרְגּוֹעַ,
וּמִנְחָתָם בְּלִי שָׁעָה
לְבָבִי הָיָה נִשְׁבָּר.
כִּי לֹא אַלְמָן יִשְׂרָאֵל.
מַה לַתֶּבֶן אֶת הַבָּר?

I had hoped for deliverance, for a day of peace and repose, but my heart was broken by their worthless gifts. *Oh, Israel is not forsaken! What has chaff to do with grain?*

חִפַּשְׂתִּי אֶלְזוּשׁ אָרְכָּה
וְלֹא יָדַע אֱנוֹשׁ עֶרְכָּהּ,
לוּלֵא שֶׁלֹּא כַּדְּרָכָהּ
הָאִשָּׁה עַל אִישׁ תִּגְבַּר.
כִּי לֹא אַלְמָן יִשְׂרָאֵל.
מַה לַתֶּבֶן אֶת הַבָּר?

I searched up and down Alsace but could find nothing of note, except that – Oh, perversity! – there the women ride over the men. *Oh, Israel is not forsaken! What has chaff to do with grain?*

קַצְתִּי מְאֹד בְּאַשְׁכְּנַזִּים
כִּי הֵם כֻּלָּם פָּנִים עַזִּים
אַף זְקָנָם כְּמוֹ עִזִּים.
אַל תַּאֲמֵן לָהֶם דָּבָר!
כִּי לֹא אַלְמָן יִשְׂרָאֵל.
מַה לַתֶּבֶן אֶת הַבָּר?

I am heartily sick of these *Ashkenazim*. They are all grim-faced and have beards like goats. Don't believe a word they breathe. *Oh, Israel is not forsaken! What has chaff to do with grain?*

1. Hebrew *alman* ('forsaken, widowed') echoes the French *allemand* ('German') so that the phrase (Jeremiah 51.15) can be read: 'A [French] Israelite is not a German [Jew].'

כָּלֵב אֲפֶנְדּוֹפּוֹלוֹ

Caleb Afendopolo

צְבִיָּה גְעָלָה

A COLD COMFORT

׳צְבִיָּה גָעֲלָה חִשְׁקִי וְאוֹתִי
וְשָׁכְחָה אַהֲבָתִי הַקְּדוּמָה.
לְבִלְתִּי אֶחֱזֶה – הִיא כִּרְאוֹתִי
אֲזַי תִּבְרַח, בְּלִי עָוֹן וְאַשְׁמָה.
וְלֹא דֵּי לָהּ, אֲבָל גָּזְלָה שְׁנָתִי
לְבִלְתִּי אֶחֱזֶנָּה בַּחֲלוֹמָהּ.׳

[He:] This gazelle spurns my passion and me. She has forgotten my long-standing love. To keep me from seeing her, she runs away – though I am utterly blameless – as soon as she catches sight of me. Nor will this content her: she has also robbed me of sleep, so that I cannot even see her in my dreams.

׳יְדִיד נַפְשִׁי, אֲמַלֵּא אֶת שְׁנָתְךָ
לְמַעַן כִּי רְאוֹתִי בַחֲלוֹמָךְ.
בְּעֵת תִּישַׁן, בְּצֵל חָרְשִׁי תְּהִי נָח,
וְתֶחֱזֵנִי בְּהָקִיצָךְ לְמוּלָךְ.

[She:] Dear love, I shall fill your sleep until you see me in your dreams. Lie in the shade of my bower when you sleep, and you will see me in your daydream when you awaken.

יוֹסֵף צָרְפָתִי

Joseph Tsarfati

יְשֵׁנָה אַתְּ

TO HIS SLEEPING MISTRESS

יְשֵׁנָה אַתְּ, אֲנִי נֵעוֹר וְנוֹדֵד
וּמִתְנַמְנֵם סְבִיב בֵּיתֵךְ, עֲדִינָה.
יְשֵׁנָה אַתְּ, אֲנִי צוּרִים אֲעוֹדֵד
בְּמַכְאוֹבִי וְאַחְשִׁיךְ הַלְּבָנָה.
יְשֵׁנָה אַתְּ, וְזִיו מַרְאֵךְ יְשׁוֹדֵד
תְּנוּמָה מִבְּנוֹת עֵינַי וְשֵׁנָה.
בְּצַלְמֵךְ כָּל מְזִמּוֹתַי כְּנוּסִים,
וְכַדּוֹנַג בְּתוֹךְ אִשֵּׁךְ נְמַסִּים.

You are asleep, my gentle love, but I am awake, wandering about, drowsily walking around your house. You are asleep, but I summon cliffs to witness my pain, and I blacken the moon. You are asleep, but your splendour robs my eyes of all slumber. All my thoughts are gathered in your body, and all of them melt like wax in your flame.

זְמַן, הַחֵן אֲשֶׁר זָרַע

THE JUDGEMENT OF TIME

זְמַן, הַחֵן אֲשֶׁר זָרַע בְּמִצְחֵךְ –
יְאַסְפֵהוּ וְלֹא יוֹסִיף לְתִתּוֹ.
וְכֵס גָּבְהֵךְ אֲשֶׁר חָשַׁבְתְּ לְנִצְחֵךְ –
שְׁאוֹל יוּרַד בְּבוֹא יוֹמוֹ וְעִתּוֹ.
וְחֶבֶל בּוֹ קְשַׁרְתִּנִי בְּנִצְחֵךְ –
זְמַן יִכְרֹת בְּמַזְמֵרָתוֹ וְאִתּוֹ.
זְמַן מַשְׁפִּיל, זְמַן מֵרִים וּמֵקִים,
וְעוֹשֶׂה דִּין וּמִשְׁפָּט לַעֲשׁוּקִים.

That grace which Time has sown in your forehead, Time will harvest and never give back. And your high throne, which you believed would be yours forever – when the hour comes, it will be lowered into the pit. And those bonds with which you tied me in your triumph, Time will cut them with its knife and mattock. Time throws down, Time raises up, Time deals out justice to the oppressed.

וְאִם רָחַקְתְּ, צְבִיָּה

THE CAPTIVE

וְאִם רָחַקְתְּ, צְבִיָּה, מִמְּגוּרַי,
קְרוֹבָה אַתְּ לְעַצְמִי מִבְּשָׂרִי.
וְאִם חָפְשִׁי אֲנִי נֶחְשָׁב לְשׁוּרַי,
גְּבִירִי נִיב שְׂפָתַיִךְ, וְשָׂרִי.
וְאִם אַרְחִיב לְעֵין רוֹאַי אֲשׁוּרַי,
תְּאַסְרִי חִישׁ כְּרֶגַע מַאֲסָרִי.
לְבַדֵּךְ אַתְּ לְמִיתָתִי אֲשֵׁמָה,
וְתָשִׁיבִי, בְּחֶפְצֵךְ, בִּי נְשָׁמָה.

And though you are far from where I live, gazelle, you are closer to my bones than my own flesh. And though people look at me and take me[1] for a freeman, your every word is my lord and master. And though I walk along briskly, in full view, in an instant you could make me your prisoner. You alone are guilty of my death, and only you, if you wish, can restore my soul to me.

אֲהָהּ, כַּמָּה מְצֹא חִנֵּךְ

THE OBSTINATE MISTRESS

אֲהָהּ, כַּמָּה מְצֹא חִנֵּךְ אֲשַׁבֵּר,
וּבַמָּה אֶת פְּנֵי חַסְדֵּךְ אֲכַפֵּר?
וְכָל עֵת שִׁיר בְּמַהֲלָלֵךְ אֲחַבֵּר,

How I long to win your favour! What expiation must I make to be in your good graces? At all times, I compose a song in your praise, telling your virtues

1. Or, 'And though my enemies take me . . .'

וְגָדְלֵךְ בּוֹ לְכֹל יָבֹא אֲסַפֵּר.
וְלֵב כֶּלֶב נְהִי בִכְיִי יְשַׁבֵּר,
וְכִלְיוֹתָיו לְאָבָק דַּק יְעַפֵּר!
וְאַתְּ שָׁמִיר לְבָבֵךְ שַׂמְתְּ וְעָרְפֵּךְ,
וְאָזְנֵךְ אֶל תְּחִנּוֹתַי כְּמַשְׁפֵּךְ.

to one and all. My tearful lament would break a dog's heart and grind his innards to fine dust. But you have made your heart and neck like adamant, and turned your ear like a funnel to my plea.

יוֹסֵף הַכֹּהֵן

Joseph Hakohen

עוּרָה, כְּבוֹדִי

THE CONDITIONS OF BEAUTY

עוּרָה, כְּבוֹדִי, וַאֲסַפֵּר לָךְ בְּשִׁיר
יְפִי הֲדַר נָשִׁים, וּבִמְצִלְתַּיִם:
אֹרֶךְ בְּחַר בְּשֵׂעָר וְלֹא תֵבוֹשׁ, וְגַם
אֹרֶךְ בְּיָדַיִם וְגַם שׁוֹקַיִם.
שָׁלוֹשׁ קְצָרִים הֵם נְתוּנִים לָהּ לְחֵן:
אֹזֶן וְשָׁדַיִם וְגַם שִׁנַּיִם.
מֵצַח יְהִי רָחָב, וְהֶחָזֶה, וְגַם
יִהְיוּ כְּסָלִים רַחֲבֵי יָדַיִם.
צָרָה בְּעִגְּנָהּ בְּחַר, צוֹפֶה, וְגַם
צָרָה בְּמוֹ יָרֵךְ וְגַם מָתְנַיִם.
עָבָה בְּצִיצִית רֹאשׁ תְּהִי אִשָּׁה, וְגַם
בִּשְׁתֵּי זְרוֹעֶיהָ וְיַרְכָתַיִם.
דַּקִּים שְׁלוֹשָׁה הֵם: שְׂעַר רֹאשָׁהּ, וְגַם
כָּל אֶצְבְּעוֹתֶיהָ וְהַשְּׂפָתַיִם.
צַוָּאר בְּחַר עָגֹל, עֲגֻבוֹת גַּם זְרוֹ־
עַ, אָז לְיָפְיָהּ יֶהֱמוּ מֵעַיִם.
פִּיהָ תְהִי קָטָן, בְּלִי שָׂטָן, בְּלִי
מוּם רַע, וְהַחֹטֶם וְהָרַגְלַיִם.

Awake, my spirit, and I shall tell you in song, to the sound of cymbals, of woman's beauty and splendour. Choose hair that is long and you will not be put to shame; also prefer length in hands and legs. These three should be short to give her grace: ears, breasts, and teeth. Her forehead should be broad; so, too, her chest; her loins should also be spacious. Spectator, choose the woman whose thing is narrow, who has narrow thighs and hips. She should have thick forelocks, thick arms and buttocks. These three should be fine: the hair of her head, her fingers and her lips. Choose a neck that is round, a round behind and forearm, and your vitals will thrill to her beauty. Her mouth should be small, discreet,[1] flawless; this goes for her nose and

1. Lit. 'without Satan'; an allusion to a saying that one should not invite misfortune by ominous words.

תַּלְבִּין בְּשִׁנֶּיהָ, וּבִשְׁתַּיִם אֲשֶׁר
אֹמַר: וְהֵם גָּרוֹן וְהַיָּדַיִם.
אֹדֶם בְּפָנֶיהָ לְחֵן חֵן לָהּ בְּחַר,
וּשְׁתֵּי שְׂפָתֶיהָ וְצִפָּרְנַיִם.
שַׁחְרוּת בְּגַבּוֹת לָהּ לְיֹפִי וְהֶדֶר,
גַּם בְּשֵׂעָר יָפָה וְהָעֵינַיִם.
אִשָּׁה אֲשֶׁר אֵלֶּה תְּנָאֵי יָפְיָהּ –
לֹא יַעֲרִיכֻנָּהּ זְהַב פַּרְוָיִם.

feet, too. Her teeth must be white and so should these two: her throat and her hands. Choose the one who is graced with red on her cheeks, lips, and fingernails. Her eyebrows black, to enhance her loveliness; black, also, her hair and eyes. The woman who fulfils these conditions of beauty – not even the gold of Parvaim can measure her worth.

אָמְנָם אֲשֶׁר חֶפְצָהּ בְּתוֹרַת אֵל, וְגַם
כָּל מַחְשְׁבוֹת לִבָּהּ לְאֵל כַּפַּיִם,
אִשָּׁה לְזֹאת תִּקָּרֵא וְאֵלֶיהָ קְרַב,
אַל נָא לְזָרָה תִּפְרְשָׂה כַפַּיִם.
שֶׁקֶר לְחֵן תֹּאמַר וְהֶבֶל אֶל יְפִי
נָשִׁים, וְהַלֵּל יִרְאַת שָׁמַיִם.
קַח לְךָ, בְּנִי, עֵצָה אֲשֶׁר נָתַן לְךָ
יוֹסֵף וְגַם כֹּהֵן לְאֵל שָׁמַיִם.

Of course, she who delights in the Law of the Lord, whose every thought goes out to Him in prayer – she alone merits the name of woman. Go seek her company, and do not spread out your hands to an adulteress. Call charm a delusion and woman's beauty a bubble, and give all honour to the fear of God. My son, accept this advice given to you by Joseph, who is also a priest[1] of God in Heaven.

שִׁמְעוֹן לָבִיא

Simeon Labi

בַּר יוֹחַאי

HYMN TO BAR YOḤAI[2]

בַּר־יוֹחַאי, נִמְשַׁחְתָּ – אַשְׁרֶיךָ! –
שֶׁמֶן שָׂשׂוֹן מֵחֲבֵרֶיךָ.

Happy are you, Bar Yoḥai! He anointed you above your fellows with oil, the token of joy.

1. Hebrew *cohen*, a reference to the author's lineage.

2. The hymn refers to the ten *Sefirot* in the following order: Stanza 1 – *Malkhut* ('kingdom'); 2 – *Yesod Olam* ('foundation of the world'); 3 – *Netsaḥ* ('lasting endurance') and *Hod* ('majesty'); 4 – *Tiferet* ('beauty'); 5 – *Gevura* ('power'); 6 – *Ḥesed* ('love'); 7 – *Bina* ('intelligence'), which is the source of freedom, redemption and temporal order; 8 – *Ḥokhma* ('wisdom') the ideal thought of creation, which is represented by the letter *yod*, the first letter in the name of God; 9 – *Keter Elyon* ('supreme crown') and, above it, *Ayin* ('absolute nothingness') from which all the *Sefirot* emanate. (See G. Scholem's *Kabbalah*, 1974, p. 96 ff.)

בַּר־יוֹחַאי, שֶׁמֶן מִשְׁחַת קֹדֶשׁ
נִמְשַׁחְתָּ מִמִּדַּת הַקֹּדֶשׁ.
נָשָׂאתָ צִיץ נֵזֶר־הַקֹּדֶשׁ,
חָבוּשׁ עַל רֹאשְׁךָ פְּאֵרֶךָ.

Bar Yoḥai, you were anointed with the holy oil, drawn from the quality of holiness. You wore the rosette of the holy diadem, your turban was bound on your head.[1]

בַּר־יוֹחַאי, מוֹשָׁב טוֹב יָשַׁבְתָּ
יוֹם נַסְתָּ, יוֹם אֲשֶׁר בָּרַחְתָּ.
בִּמְעָרַת צוּרִים שֶׁעָמַדְתָּ,
קָנִיתָ הוֹדְךָ וַהֲדָרֶךָ.

Bar Yoḥai, you chose an excellent retreat on the day you fled [from the Romans]. There, in that cave in the rocks, you attained glory and majesty.

בַּר־יוֹחַאי, עֲצֵי שִׁטִּים עוֹמְדִים,
לִמּוּדֵי יְיָ הֵם לוֹמְדִים.
אוֹר מֻפְלָא, אוֹר הַיְקוֹד הֵם יוֹקְדִים,
הֲלֹא הֵמָּה יוֹרוּךָ מוֹרֶיךָ.

Bar Yoḥai, the seraphim[2] stood about you, the Lord's disciples, deep in study. They burnt with a flaming light of mystery. These were the teachers who instructed you.

בַּר־יוֹחַאי, וְלִשְׂדֵה תַפּוּחִים
עָלִיתָ לִלְקֹט־בּוֹ מֶרְקָחִים,
סוֹד תּוֹרָה כְּצִיצִים וּפְרָחִים.
'נַעֲשֶׂה אָדָם,' נֶאֱמַר בַּעֲבוּרֶךָ.

Bar Yoḥai, you ascended to the Field of Apple Trees[3] to gather fragrances: the mysteries of the Torah, which are like blossoms and flowers. 'Let us make man'[4] was pronounced for your sake.

בַּר־יוֹחַאי, נֶאְזַרְתָּ בִּגְבוּרָה,
וּבְמִלְחֶמֶת אֵשׁ דָּת הַשַּׁעְרָה,
וְחֶרֶב הוֹצֵאתָ מִתַּעְרָהּ,
שָׁלַפְתָּ נֶגֶד צוֹרְרֶיךָ.

Bar Yoḥai, girded with strength, you repelled them at the gate with the flaming Law. You drew your sword from the scabbard and wielded it against your enemies.

1. The High Priest wore a 'golden frontlet' (Exodus 39.20) as a symbol of his dedication and was anointed with oil (Exodus 30.30).
2. Lit. '[planks of] acacia wood, upright' of which the Tabernacle was built.
3. The mystical garden of Eden; this also symbolizes the Divine Presence.
4. Genesis 1.26.

בַּר־יוֹחַאי, לִמְקוֹם אַבְנֵי שַׁיִשׁ
הִגַּעְתָּ, לִפְנֵי אַרְיֵה לַיִשׁ.
גַּם גֻּלַּת כּוֹתֶרֶת עַל עַיִשׁ
תָּשׁוּר, וּמִי יְשׁוּרֶךָ.

Bar Yoḥai, you reached the Palace of the stones of pure marble[1] and came into the presence of the Lion [engraved in the Chariot-Throne]. You saw the orb of the crown set upon the Pleiades, but no one could see you.

בַּר־יוֹחַאי, בְּקֹדֶשׁ הַקֳּדָשִׁים
– קַו יָרֹק מְחַדֵּשׁ חֳדָשִׁים,
שֶׁבַע שַׁבָּתוֹת, סוֹד חֲמִשִּׁים –
קָשַׁרְתָּ קִשְׁרֵי שִׁי״ן קְשָׁרֶיךָ.

Bar Yoḥai, when you entered the Holy of Holies, the green zone which is the source of time, the palace of the seven Sabbaths, the mystery [of the fifty gates and] of the Jubilee – you bound together the three supreme *Sefirot*.[2]

בַּר־יוֹחַאי, יוּ״ד חָכְמָה קְדוּמָה
הִשְׁקַפְתָּ לִכְבוֹדוֹ פְּנִימָה,
לֵ״ב נְתִיבוֹת, רֵאשִׁית, תְּרוּמָה.
אַתְּ כְּרוּב מִמְשַׁח, זִיו דּוֹרֶךָ.

Bar Yoḥai, you gazed into the depths of His Glory, into the primordial point of Wisdom – the Beginning, [the first word of creation] – which flows forth into the thirty-two paths [of hidden lore]. You were the towering cherub, the splendour of your generation.

בַּר־יוֹחַאי, אוֹר מֻפְלָא, רוּם־מַעְלָה –
יָרֵאתָ מִלְּהַבִּיט, כִּי רַב לָהּ.
תַּעֲלוּמָה, וְאַיִן קוֹרָא לָהּ.
נַמְתָּ: ׳עַיִן לֹא תְשׁוּרֶךָ.׳

Bar Yoḥai, you were afraid to look at the wondrous light, the Supreme Crown, for its fullness is overwhelming. This is the mystery, named *Ayin*. You said: 'No eye will catch sight of You.'

בַּר־יוֹחַאי, אַשְׁרֵי יוֹלַדְתֶּךָ,
אַשְׁרֵי הָעָם הֵם לוֹמְדֶיךָ,
אַשְׁרֵי הָעוֹמְדִים עַל סוֹדֶיךָ,
לוֹבְשֵׁי חֹשֶׁן תֻּמֶּיךָ וְאוּרֶיךָ.

Bar Yoḥai, happy is your mother! Happy are the people who study your doctrines, who penetrate into your secrets, as they wear your breastpiece[3] over their hearts.

1. 'When you come to the place of the shining marble plates, then do not say: Water, water! For it is written: "He that telleth lies shall not tarry in my sight"' (*T.B. Ḥagigah* 14b).
2. Represented by the three crowns of the letter *shin*, ש.
3. Lit. 'the breastpiece of your Urim and Thummim'; the 'symbols of judgement' worn by Aaron whenever he entered the presence of the Lord (Exodus 28.30).

סְעַדְיָה לוֹנְגוֹ

Sa'adiah Longo

סִבָּה וְעִלָּה וּמַעֲמִיד

THE PARADOX

סִבָּה וְעִלָּה וּמַעֲמִיד, אֵל חַי לְכָל יֵשׁ מְצָאתִיו.
נֶעְלָם וְנִסְתָּר וְנִגְלֶה, עִם עֵין לְבָבִי רְאִיתִיו.
פּוֹעֵל הֲפָכִים וְאֶחָד, יָחִיד וּמְיֻחָד קְרָאתִיו.
אֶל שׁוֹאֲלַי: 'אֵיךְ?' עֲנִיתִיו: 'אִלּוּ יְדַעְתִּיו, הֲיִיתִיו!'

I have found the Living God to be the cause and support of all Being. Concealed and yet revealed, I have seen Him with my mind's eye. Maker of opposites and yet One, I have called Him the Single and Unique. When asked: 'How can this be?', I answer: 'If I knew, I would be He!'

שְׂפָתַיִם יִשָּׁק

THE SCOUNDREL'S SONG

'שְׂפָתַיִם יִשָּׁק מֵשִׁיב דִּבְרֵי חֵן,' אָמַר נָבָל.
נַפְשׁוֹ עָלָיו תֶּאֱבָל!

'Pleasing words,' said the scoundrel, 'are like a kiss on the lips.' May he mourn his own loss!

'לָבְשׁוּ פְּנֵי תֵבֵל רִקְמָה,
עֵץ הַשָּׂדֶה סוּת עֶלְצוֹן,
הֶדֶרֶךְ גֶּבֶר בְּעַלְמָה
חָמְדוּ כָּל אַנְשֵׁי לָצוֹן.
לָבְשׁוּ כָרִים הַצֹּאן –'
אָמַר נָבָל.
נַפְשׁוֹ עָלָיו תֶּאֱבָל!

'The earth put on robes of brocade; and the trees of the country-side, mantles of joy. Then all the insolent youths avidly pursued the way of a man with a girl. Oh, the meadows clothed themselves with sheep,' said the scoundrel. May he mourn his own loss!

'כְּסוּס עָגוּר כֵּן יְצַפְצֵף
נוֹאֵף עִם יַעֲלַת מַלְכֻּדְתּוֹ.
וְשִׁיר עֲגָבִים יְרַצֵּף,
שָׂשׂ לְעֻמַּת מַחְבַּרְתּוֹ,
אִישׁ אִישׁ כִּי תִשְׂטֶה אִשְׁתּוֹ –'

'The adulterer twitters like a swallow, together with the paramour whom he has snared. And every man whose wife has gone astray rejoices over his mistress,[1] multiplying songs of lust,'

1. Lit. 'seam, juncture'.

אָמַר נָבָל.
נַפְשׁוֹ עָלָיו תֶּאֱבַל!

said the scoundrel. May he mourn his own loss!

'יַעֲלָה מְנֻּתִיב אֲהָבִים
מְשָׂרֶכֶת דְּרָכֶיהָ.
סַלּוֹנִים הֵם וְסָרָבִים
צְבָא חוֹשְׁקִים לְצִדֶּיהָ.
נַאֲפוּפֶיהָ בֵּין שָׁדֶיהָ –'
אָמַר נָבָל.
נַפְשׁוֹ עָלָיו תֶּאֱבַל!

'The lady twisted and turned, leaving the path of [true] love. Like briars and thorns, a host of suitors beset her. Adultery nests between her breasts,' said the scoundrel. May he mourn his own loss!

'בְּעַד הַחַלּוֹן נִשְׁקָפָה,
כְּמוֹ הַשַּׁחַר עָלָה.
לִרְאוֹת בְּבָנִים שָׁאֲפָה
מַשְׂאַת הַחֵשֶׁק עָלָה.
הִנֵּה זוֹ רָעָה חוֹלָה!'
אָמַר נָבָל.
נַפְשׁוֹ עָלָיו תֶּאֱבַל!

'At the crack of dawn, she peered through her lattice, panting to see the smoke of desire rising amongst the boys. Oh, this is a singular evil,' said the scoundrel. May he mourn his own loss!

'שִׁפְעַת הָרוֹעֶה רָאֲתָה
וְחֵץ חִשְׁקָהּ שָׂמָה עַל קֶשֶׁת,
פָּרְשָׂה עָלָיו מְצוֹדָתָהּ
וַתִּקְרָא לוֹ אֶל הָרֶשֶׁת,
הַרְחֵק כִּמְטַחֲוֵי קֶשֶׁת –'
אָמַר נָבָל.
נַפְשׁוֹ עָלָיו תֶּאֱבַל!

'Seeing the shepherd, in all his fulness, she strung her bow with the arrow of desire, from a distance, like an archer. She threw her net over him and tempted him into its meshes,' said the scoundrel. May he mourn his own loss!

'קְרָאַתְהוּ לְסוֹד נִכְמָס,
וְחִשְׁקָהּ בְּעֵינָיו חֵלֶף.
צוּף לְשׁוֹנָהּ הָמֵס יָמֵס

'She invited him to share a deep secret. He made light of her desire. But her honeyed words could melt the heart of

לֵב קָצִין וְשַׂר וּמֶלֶךְ.
"לֹא, כִּי בִּשְׁרִירוּת לִבִּי אֵלֵךְ."'
אָמַר נָבָל.
נַפְשׁוֹ עָלָיו תֶּאֱבַל!

any lord, prince, or king. "No, [thought the shepherd] I shall follow my wilful heart",' said the scoundrel. May he mourn his own loss!

'"סוּרָה, שְׁבָה פֹּה לִימִינִי,
הָרוֹעֶה, וְהַט אָזְנֶךָ.
חֵשֶׁק בְּסֵתֶר מְלַשְׁנִי,
פִּתַּנִי וָאֹהֲבֶךָ.
קְרָא נָא, הֲיֵשׁ עוֹנֶךָ?"'
אָמַר נָבָל.
נַפְשׁוֹ עָלָיו תֶּאֱבַל!

'"Come, shepherd, sit at my right hand, and bend down your ear to me. Desire secretly informed on you, seduced me and now I love you. Call, if you wish – will anyone answer you?"' said the scoundrel. May he mourn his own loss!

דָּוִד עוֹנְקִינֵירָה

David Onkinerah

קוֹלֵךְ, צְבִיָּה

WOUNDS OF LOVE

קוֹלֵךְ, צְבִיָּה, שָׁמְעָה אָזְנִי –
חָרְדוּ מְאֹד חוּשִׁי וְנַפְשִׁי נִבְהָלָה,
קָדַר מְאוֹר פָּנַי וְשִׁמְשִׁי אָפְלָה,
וּכְמוֹ נְחָלִים נִגְּרָה עֵינִי.

I heard your voice, my love, and all my senses throbbed and my soul quivered in dismay. The light of my face darkened, my sun was covered with shadows, and my eyes streamed like rivers.

חִצֵּי בְרָקַיִךְ בְּתוֹךְ בִּטְנִי.
אֶתְקַע בְּכַף יָדֵךְ, וְהִנֵּה עֻפְּלָה.
יִפְעַת דְּמוּת צַלְמֵךְ כְּבֵדִי חִלְּלָה,
תָּחִישׁ בְּלֵיל חִשְׁקִי לְהַלְמֵנִי.

The arrows of your lightning are deep within my belly. I put my hand in yours and it swells with pain. The pride of your figure has pierced my heart. In the night of my desire, it swiftly strikes me down.

לֹא יִשְׁכְּבוּן עוֹרְקַי עֲלֵי מִשְׁכָּב
אַף כִּי בְּעֵדֶן גַּן מְעוֹנִי אֶתְּנָה,
כִּי גַּחֲלֵי חִשְׁקְךָ בְּלִבִּי בוֹעֲרִים.

Though I make my home in Paradise, my veins will wildly beat with pain when I lie down, for the embers of desire burn in my heart.

לֹא אֶמְצָאָה מָנוֹס וְאִם אֶרְכָּב
עַל הַכְּרוּב אוֹ בַתְּהוֹמוֹת אֶשְׁכְּנָה,
כִּי מֵי נְהַר זַעְפְּךָ בְּפָנַי סוֹעֲרִים.

Whether I soar on a cherub or descend into the depths, I can find no escape, for your raging waters surge over my face.

נִחְיֶה בְּצֵל

BLISS

[...] נִחְיֶה בְּצֵל יַעֲלַת־חֵן,
נִחְיֶה וְנִהְיֶה סְעוּדִים.
נֵלֵךְ לְאוֹרָהּ חֲשֵׁכִים,
נִהְיֶה בְּשִׂמְחָה תְּמִידִים.
תִּשְׂחַק – וְנִפְצַח בְּרִנָּה,
תִּזְעַף – וְנִלְבַּשׁ פְּחָדִים.
תָּצִיץ בְּאוֹרָהּ וְנָשׁוּב
לִהְיוֹת גְּאוּלִים וְנִפְדִּים.

We shall live in the shade of the graceful doe and, living there, shall be sustained. We shall walk through darkness by her light, with never-ending joy. When she laughs, we will burst into song; when she frowns, we shall clothe ourselves in fear. And when she looks with radiant eyes, we shall once again be ransomed and redeemed.

דְּמוּת צַלְמֵךְ, צְבִיָּה

THE VOW

דְּמוּת צַלְמֵךְ, צְבִיָּה, בַּחֲלוֹמִי
הֲכִי נִרְאָה וְהִבְרִיק כִּבְרָקִים
וְהֵאִיר מַחְשַׁךְ עֵינַי, וְרָאוּ
בְּפָנַיִךְ כְּמוֹ תַבְנִית שְׁחָקִים,
וּבָם שֶׁמֶשׁ וְיָרֵחַ נְתוּנִים
וְכוֹכָבִים וּמַזָּלוֹת אֲדוּקִים,
וּבָם חִצִּים שְׁנוּנִים וַחֲנִיתוֹת

I saw your figure in my dream, gazelle, flashing like lightning. It gave light to my darkened eyes, and I saw that your face was a model of the heavens. The sun and moon are set in it, the stars and planets are fixed there. And it holds sharp arrows and spears, burnished to

לְפַלַּח הַלְּבָבוֹת הֵם בְּרוּקִים. [...]
הֶאִירוּנִי בְּלֵיל חָשְׁכִּי וְאָפְלִי
וְנָטְלוּ מֵעֲלֵי עֵינַי פְּקָקִים,
וְהֵנִיסוּ יְגוֹנוֹת וַאֲנָחוֹת,
וְנִשְׁמַע קוֹל שְׂמָחוֹת בַּשְּׁוָקִים.

pierce all hearts. It lit up my pitch-black night and pulled the stoppers from my eyes. It put sorrows and sighing to flight, and the sound of rejoicing was heard in the market-places.

אֲנִי, עָנִי, בְּהַבִּיטִי בְעֵינַי
הֲדַר יָפְיָהּ, וְחוּשַׁי בָּהּ דְּבֵקִים —
צְבִיָּה נֶעְלְמָה, עָלְתָה וְנָסְעָה
וְגָבְהָה עַל עֲנָנִים מֵאֲרָקִים.
וְנִשְׁאַרְתִּי בְּתוֹךְ חֹשֶׁךְ אֲפֵלָה,
כְּמוֹ עַכְבָּר מְהַלֵּךְ בִּסְדָקִים;
כְּמוֹ בָרָק אֲשֶׁר יִזְרַח אֱלֵי אִישׁ
בְּעוֹד לַיְלָה, וְעֵינָיו בּוֹ בְּהוּקִים,
וְכַאֲשֶׁר יַעֲבֹר אוֹרוֹ וְנָגְהוֹ
יְהִי נִשְׁאָר בְּאָפְלוֹ בָּעֲמָקִים;
כְּאִישׁ מִסְכֵּן וְחוֹזֵר עַל פְּתָחִים
אֲשֶׁר עֵינָיו בְּתוֹךְ חֹרָיו נְמַקִּים. [...]

O wretched me! As I gazed upon her radiant beauty, with all my senses clinging to her, she suddenly rose from the earth, flew high above the clouds and disappeared. And I was left behind in pitch darkness, like a mouse crawling through a crack; like a man whose eyes glow when lightning flashes before him in the night, and then the glow is gone, leaving him in his valley of darkness; or like a wretch who goes begging from door to door, his eyes rotting in their sockets.

לְכָל אֵלֶּה אֲנִי אֶדְמֶה וְאֶשְׁוֶה,
וְרַעְיוֹנַי כְּמוֹהֶם נֶאֱנָקִים.
וְהֵן אַרְחִיק נְדֹד, אָלִין בְּמִדְבָּר,
וְאֶשְׁכֹּן בַּסְּלָעִים עַל נְקִיקִים,
וְאֶקְרַע אֶת לְבוּשֵׁי מַחֲמַדַּי,
וְאֶתְחַפֵּשׂ וְגַם אָלִין בְּשַׂקִּים —
עֲדֵי אָשׁוּב לְהַבִּיט הוֹד צְבִיָּה
וְתָשִׁיב אֶת שְׁבוּתִי כָּאֲפִיקִים,
וְדֹדֶיהָ יְרַוּוּנִי בְּכָל עֵת
וּבִשְׂעָרָהּ יְמֵי חַיַּי עֲנוּקִים.

Such is my lot, as grievous as theirs and, like them, my thoughts groan and lament. I will go far away and find a refuge in the wilderness, I will make my home among the crags, I will tear up my precious garments, I will cover them with mud and lie in sackcloth all night long – until I once more behold her splendour; until she turns my fortune around as streams return in the desert, and I am bathed in her love at all times, and the days of my life are entwined in her tresses.

כַּסִּי, כְּלִילַת־חֵן

HER HAIR

[...] כַּסִּי, כְּלִילַת־חֵן, שְׂעַר רֹאשֵׁךְ,
כִּי תִקְטְלִי הַיְקוּם בְּלִי יָדַיִם!
טִבְעָם בְּכָל תֵּבֵל הֲכִי יָצָא,
עַל כֵּן לְשִׁמְעָם צָלְלוּ אָזְנַיִם.
חָלוּשׁ וְרַךְ מִשַּׂעֲרוֹת רֹאשֵׁךְ
יָכוֹל עֲקֹר הָרִים וְיַרְכָתַיִם –
מַה יַּעֲשֶׂה אִישׁ רָשׁ בְּעֵת כֻּלָּם
מִתְחַזְּקִים נֶגְדּוֹ בְּרִבּוֹתַיִם?
בִּי, יַעֲלַת הַחֵן, עֲלֵי נַפְשִׁי
חוּסִי, לְבַל אָמוּת בְּלִי יוֹמַיִם,
וּתְשַׁלְּמִי דְּמִי אֲשֶׁר יֻקַּם
מִמֵּךְ כְּדַם קַיִן לְשִׁבְעָתַיִם.

O peerless beauty, veil your hair, lest you play havoc with the world, without lifting a finger! They are famous throughout the world, they ring in the ears of all who hear of them. The weakest, softest strand on your head can pull out a mountain by its roots. What, then, can a poor man do, when they fall upon him in their myriads? I pray you, graceful deer, have pity on my life, don't make me die so young; you would have to pay for my blood which, like Cain's, would be exacted seven times over.

עֶבֶד אֲנִי, נִרְצָע וְנִמְכָּר לָךְ,
וּלְנָעֳמֵךְ מִשְׁתַּחֲוֶה אַפַּיִם.
אֶת פִּי לְמַלְקוֹשֵׁךְ אֲנִי פוֹעֵר –
בֹּקֶר אֲקַו חַסְדֵּךְ עֲדֵי עַרְבַּיִם.

I am, for life, your abject slave and chattel. I prostrate myself before your delights. I open my mouth wide, hoping for your spring showers. From dawn to dusk I await your favour.

יְהוּדָה זַרְקוֹ

Judah Zarco

אִם תֶּחֱזוּ

THE CELESTIAL RACE

אִם תֶּחֱזוּ כִּי בְשַׁחַק יְסוֹבֵב
גַּלְגַּל וְאוֹפָן בְּכָל עֵת וְשָׁעָה,
אַל תַּחְשְׁבוּ כִּי לְהַרְאוֹת גְּבוּרָה
רוּצָם מְהֵרָה, כְּאִישׁ רָץ בְּבִקְעָה.

When you see the planets and constellations circling heaven at all hours, do not imagine that they are speeding, like a runner in a valley, to show off their prowess. No, it is a sublime cause

רַק הֵם יְרוּצוּן לְסִבָּה גְדוֹלָה,
חוֹזְרִים חֲלִילָה בְּלִי שׁוּם יְגִיעָה:
כִּי עַל חֲגוֹרַת מַזָּרִים תְּסוֹבֵב
יַעֲלָה בְתוּלָה וְאִישׁ לֹא יְדָעָהּ.
לָכֵן יְרוּצוּן: לְהַשִּׂיג הֲדָרָהּ,
לִשְׁכַּב בְּחֵיקָהּ בְּסוֹף הַתְּנוּעָה.

that makes them run, over and over again, unflaggingly. For there, on the celestial sphere, revolves a lovely virgin, whom no man has ever known. That is why they are racing: to attain her glory, to lie in her bosom at the end of the circuit.

אֵיךְ אֶחֱצֹב שִׁיר

AFTER THE VISION

אֵיךְ אֶחֱצֹב שִׁיר – וְהִנֵּה בְּפַטִּישׁ
חוּשַׁי הֲלוֹא יַעֲלֶה בּוֹ חֲלֻדָּה?
אוֹ מָה אֲנַגֵּן בְּנֵבֶל – וְיָדַי
עִם חָח פְּחָדִים וּמוֹרָא לְכוּדָה?
כִּי בָא לְבָבִי בְּרִצְפַּת צְבִיָּה,
אַבְנֵי יְסוֹדָהּ כְּאֹדֶם וּפִטְדָה,
מַלְאָךְ וְשָׂרָף בְּתוֹכוֹ יְעוֹפֵף,
חוֹפֵף וּמַחֲוֵי כְּרִיעָה וְקִדָּה.
רָאָה לְבָבִי דְּמוּת מַלְאֲכֵי אֵל –
אֵיכָה יְחִי עוֹד בְּקָהָל וְעֵדָה?

How can I hew out a song when the hammer of my senses is coated with rust? How can I play the lute when my hand is ensnared in fetters of fear? For my heart has entered the gazelle's paved [palace]; its fountain-stones are as sardin and chrysolite. Angels and seraphs hover within it, bending low, kneeling before her. Having seen the image of God's angels, how can my heart live on in the company of mortals?

שָׁבוּי בְּעִיר מִקְלָט

THE PRISONER OF DESIRE

שָׁבוּי בְּעִיר מִקְלָט – וּמֵת כֹּהֵן – וְלֹא
נִגְאַל, וְעִם שֶׂבֶר לְפִדְיוֹנוֹ יְחִי;
תָּפוּשׂ בְּשַׁלְשֶׁלֶת וְחַבְלֵי אַהֲבָה
תָּמִיד, וְהֻכָּה שָׁם בְּשֵׁבֶט עַל לְחִי –

Caged in a city of refuge, unredeemed, though the High Priest is already dead;[1] kept alive by the hope of being ransomed; at all times manacled in the chains and bonds of love; struck on the cheek with a rod – oh, make haste,

1. The homicide may leave the city of refuge and go back to his property after the death of the High Priest (Numbers 35.28).

חוּשִׁי צְבִיָּה כִּי כְּבָר עָבַר זְמַן
יוֹבֵל וְצֵאת חָפְשִׁי, וְכִלְאוֹ תִּפְתְּחִי.
פִּתְחִי כְּלוּב חָשְׁכּוֹ בְּלִי מָמוֹן וְהוֹן,
אַף כִּי בְּחֶרֶב צוּר גְּרוֹנוֹ תִּטְבְּחִי.

gazelle, for the year of the jubilee, the time of his freedom, is long past. Release him, without ransom, from his cage of darkness, though you then cut his throat with a sharp sword.

יִסְלַח עֲוֹנַיִךְ — וְאוֹתוֹ תִּסְחֲבִי
עַל אַשְׁפּוֹת הַשְׁלִךְ וּמָאוֹס גַּם סְחִי.
אַף תִּקְבְּרִי אוֹתוֹ בְּקִיר לִבֵּךְ, אֲשֶׁר
דָּמוֹ יְהִי מֹהַל וְעוֹרוֹ תִּמְלְחִי.
אוֹ עִם עֲבוֹת שַׂעְרֵךְ תְּלִי אוֹתוֹ עֲלֵי
דַּדֵּךְ וְנִבְלָתוֹ עֲלֵי עֵץ תִּשְׁכְּחִי.
חֵץ אַהֲבָה שִׂימִי בְּקֶשֶׁת גַּב, וְהוּא
יִהְיֶה לְמַטָּרָא לְחֵץ בּוֹ תִּשְׁלְחִי.

He forgives you your crimes, and yet you drag him along and fling him on dung hills, amidst offscouring and refuse. You bury him in the walls of your heart; you take his blood for juice and you salt his skin.[1] Or else, you use your long curls to hang him upon your breasts, and then abandon his corpse on the gibbet. You string your eye-brow's bow with love's arrow, and make him the target for your whistling darts.

יִשְׁלַח אֳנִי־עֵינוֹ, בְּיָם יָפְיֵךְ יְהִי
שׁוֹטֵט, וְגַבּוֹתָיו לְמְשׁוֹטִים קְחִי.
כָּל יוֹם מְיַחֵל עֵת יְשׁוּעָתֵךְ — וְנָא
חִישׁ גַּאֲלִי אוֹתוֹ וְדִמְעָתוֹ מְחִי.

Oh, let him send forth the fleet of his eyes, let him sail your beauty's sea, as you take his eyebrows for oars. Each day he waits for you to be his saviour. Pray redeem him quickly and wipe away his tears.

אֵל חַי וְנוֹרָא

THE PLEA

אֵל חַי וְנוֹרָא, תְּצוּ לַהֲפֹךְ בֵּית
כֶּלֶא וְסֹהַר בְּסַהַר וְאַגָּן.
אֹפֶל שְׁאוֹלִי הֲפָךְ־נָא לְהִלִּי,
מִשְׁכַּן עֲלָטָה לְפַרְדֵּס וְנִיר גָּן.
אֶקְרָא לְךָ, אֵל, בְּחֹר מַחֲשָׁבַי,
אֶצְעַק כְּתָם, לֹא כְּרָכִיל וְנִרְגָּן.

O living and terrible God, replace my prison, this round pit,[2] by a full moon[2] and a goblet. Pray, turn the darkness of my hell into a shining light, and this dwelling-place of dusk into an orchard, a blossoming garden. I call to You, O God, out of the depths of my thoughts. I cry out in innocence, not as a rebel or

1. As the hides of animal offerings were salted (*Mishnah Middoth* 5.3).
2. A play on *sohar*, 'prison', and *sahar*, 'moon'.

הוֹצֵא אֲנִי מֵאֳנִיֵּי כְּחֶפְצִי,
כִּי הוּא בְּלֵב יָם־תְּלָאוֹת מְעֻגָּן.
תָּמִיר שְׁמִירַי בְּשׁוֹשַׁן שְׂשׂוֹנִי,
לַעֲנָה וּמֵי רֹאשׁ בְּתִירוֹשׁ וְדָגָן.

a slanderer. Grant me my wish, set
loose my ship of desire, for it is now
anchored deep in a sea of troubles.
Exchange my briars for lilies of joy, my
wormwood and gall for wine and grain.

יוֹסֵף בִּיבָּאס

Joseph Bibas

בֹּא יָבוֹא

THE LATE-COMER

בֹּא יָבוֹא נוֹשֵׂא בְּרִנָּה
הַיֶּלֶד בְּמַקְהֵלוֹת.
קְהִלָּתִי, פֹּה הַמְתִּינָה
חֲתַן דָּמִים לַמּוּלוֹת.

He will surely come with songs of joy,
carrying the child, in the full assembly.
My friends, wait here for the bride-
groom of blood.[1]

מַדּוּעַ בּוֹשֵׁשׁ עַד הֵנָּה,
יֶלֶד יָבוֹא בִּמְסִלּוֹת?
לָכֵן צְאֶינָה וּרְאֶינָה,
הַנָּשִׁים הַמְּחַתְּלוֹת –

He should be coming down the road.
Why is the child so late? You ladies,
who are charged with swaddling the
child, go forth and see

אִם שׁוֹשְׁבִינוֹת תֵּעָגֵנָה,
לְאִטָּן מִתְנַהֲלוֹת,
אוֹ אִם הַמּוֹהֵל הָלַךְ לוֹ
אֶל גִּבְעַת הָעֲרָלוֹת.

whether his kinswomen have lingered
and are moving at a slow pace, or
whether the circumciser has gone off to
the Hill of the Foreskins?[2]

הִנֵּה, אֲדוֹנַי, סוּרוּ נָא,
אַל תָּהִינוּ לַעֲלוֹת –
יֶלֶד רַךְ, עָנֹג, בָּאָמְנָה,
בְּבִגְדֵי מֹר וַאֲהָלוֹת!

I pray you, my lords, stay with us, do
not presume to leave. Truiy, here he
comes – the soft-skinned delicate child,
wrapped in robes of myrrh and aloes!

1. 'Blood-bridegroom by circumcision' (Exodus 4.26) is the conventional epithet for the child who is circumcised.
2. Where Joshua circumcised the Israelites (Joshua 5.3).

שַׁחֲרִית אֲנָסַתּוּ שֵׁנָה
כִּי בָכָה כָּל הַלֵּילוֹת.
אֲחַרְתֶּם — כִּי עֵת לְחֶנְנָהּ
תִּמְחֲלוּ לוֹ מְחִילוֹת.

When morning came he was overcome by sleep, for he had been crying all these nights. Sirs, you have been made to wait, but this is an hour of mercy. Forgive him with all your heart.

יְשַׁלֵּם שׁוֹכֵן מְעוֹנָה
לְפִם צַעֲרָא תַּגְמוּלוֹת.
הִנֵּה בָּא, נוֹשֵׂא בְּרִנָּה,
בָּרְכוּ אֵל בְּמַקְהֵלוֹת.

May He who dwells on high make the reward match the pain. Now, here he comes, carrying the child with songs of joy. Bless God in the full assembly!

יֶלֶד יֻלַּד נִכְנַס בִּבְרִית עֲדִינָה,
הָסֵר, צוּר, מְצִיר מַחֲלוֹת.
אָנָּא רְפָא, אֵל נָא,
חֲתַן דָּמִים לַמּוּלוֹת.

This new-born child has been introduced into the covenant of Israel. O Rock, let not sickness touch his pain. Heal him, O God, I beseech You, heal the bridegroom of blood!

שְׁמוּאֵל אַרְקֶווֹלְטִי

Samuel Archevolti

שִׁיר שֶׁמּוֹלֵל הַחֲמוֹר

THE ASS'S COMPLAINT

לָמָּה עָלַי שִׁכְמִי יְבִיאוּן סֹלֶת,
וּבְפִי יְהִי תֶבֶן, וְלֶחֶם אַיִן ?
אֶשְׁתֶּה בְּמֵי בוֹרוֹת, וְאֶשָּׂא יַיִן.
מַקֵּל יְשִׂימֵנִי רְצוּץ גֻּלְגֹּלֶת.

Why is my back loaded with fine flour, while in my mouth there is no bread at all, but only straw? I drink well-water, though I carry wine. And the stick goes on fracturing my skull!

אֶשְׁכֹּן בְּמוֹ חָרְבָּה וּבְמַפֹּלֶת,
כְּצַר בְּעִיר מִבְצָר, וּפֶתַח אַיִן.
אֶשָּׂא בְּכוֹרוֹת צֹאן וּמִנְחַת קַיִן,
הוֹי הוֹי, לְבַד דַּרְדַּר לְפִי מַכֹּלֶת!

I live in rubble and ruins, barred like an enemy in a fortified town, with no way out. I carry the first-born of the flocks and the finest produce of the soil,[1] but, oy!, my only food is thistles.

1. Lit. 'Cain's gift'; see Genesis 4.3.

גַּם אַחֲרֵי מוֹתִי אֱנוֹשׁ יַכֵּנִי :
אֶצְרַח בְּקוֹל גָּדוֹל, וְלִי יָרוּצוּ
כָּל יוֹצְאֵי צָבָא וְרֹאשׁ וָמֶלֶךְ.

Even after my death, Man goes on beating me: then my voice rolls, and the troops and officers and kings rush to my call.[1]

אֶל צוּר יְשׁוּעוֹת אֹמְרָה : זַכֵּנִי
לָשֵׂאת מְשִׁיחֲךָ חִישׁ, וְלֹא יָפוּצוּ
בָּנִים בְּכָל פִּנָּה כְּדַל וָחֵלֶךְ.

To the Rock of Salvation I say: Make haste, grant me the privilege of carrying Your Messiah, so that Your children should no longer be scattered in every corner like paupers and vagabonds.

מָרְדְּכַי דָּאטוֹ

Mordecai Dato

אַל תִּלְעֲגוּ עָלַי

THE OLD MAN AND THE GIRL

אַל תִּלְעֲגוּ עָלַי כִּי כַּיּוֹם אָשִׁירָה
בְּפִי שִׁיר עֲגָבִים — וַאֲנִי זָקַנְתִּי.
תַּחַת דֶּשֶׁן גַּחֶלֶת הֲלֹא בוֹעֵרָה,
כֵּן בְּקִרְבִּי לֵב עֵר גַּם עֵת כִּי יָשַׁנְתִּי.
אֶל זוּגָתִי אֵהַב וְהוּא בְּתַבְעֵרָה
כִּי אֲהַבְתִּיהָ כְּנַפְשִׁי בָּהּ נִשְׁעַנְתִּי.
נִשְׁתַּנָּה שְׂעָרִי לְגוֹן סַהֲרָא ;
תְּכוּנָתִי לֹא כֵן, וּבָהּ הִתְבּוֹנַנְתִּי.
אַךְ לְלַמֵּד דַּעַת אֶל זֹאת הַצְּעִירָה,
עֲצוּרָה לִי עַתָּה, וְאֶל זֶה כִּוַּנְתִּי.

Do not mock me for singing songs of lust now that I have grown old. Does not the ember glow beneath the ashes? So is my heart awake within me even when I sleep. It is on fire for love of my partner; I love her as dearly as my own soul, my mainstay. My hair has taken on the colour of the moon, but my mettle is the same, and that is all that matters. I am saying all this to open the eyes of the young girl who, so far, will not give herself to me.

1. When the ass's hide is used as a drumskin.

יִצְחָק לוּרְיָא

Isaac Luria

מַה לְּךָ, יִצְרִי

TO HIS SELF

מַה לְּךָ, יִצְרִי, תָּמִיד תִּרְדְּפֵנִי
וּלְאוֹיֵב לְךָ כָּל יוֹם תַּחְשְׁבֵנִי?
יוֹם לְיוֹם תִּטְמֹן חִנָּם פַּח יְקוּשִׁים,
עַד אֲשֶׁר תּוֹךְ פַּח מוֹקְשִׁי תִּלְכְּדֵנִי.
צַר וְאוֹיֵב לִי אַתָּה מִנְּעוּרַי,
תַּחֲרֹק עָלַי שֵׁן וַתִּשְׂטְמֵנִי.
חָשְׁבָה נַפְשִׁי לִנְטוֹת אַחֲרֶיךָ,
כִּי בְּצֵל יָדְךָ מִצַּר תִּצְּרֵנִי.
קִדְּמוּ עֵינַי לִבְכּוֹת בָּאַשְׁמוּרוֹת,
כִּי בְּעָב סַכּוֹתָ וַתִּרְדְּפֵנִי.
אִם אֲדַמֶּה כִּי תִּהְיֶה לִּי לְעֶזְרָה,
וּבְיוֹם צָרָה אֶקְרָא, וּתְעַנֵּנִי:
'צוּף דְּבַשׁ אִמְרֵי נֹעַם חִכְּךָ לִי' —
הֵן בְּחַכָּה עַד דַּכָּא תִּמְשְׁכֵנִי!

What is the matter, my nature, why do you always pursue me and treat me every day as your enemy? Day after day, for no reason, you set hidden traps for me, until you finally catch me in my own snare. You have been my arch-enemy since childhood, you have gnashed your teeth at me in hatred. My soul had hoped to follow you; that, under the shadow of your hand, you would shield me from distress. But my eyes awoke to weep before the mid-night watch, because you hid away in darkness and persecuted me. When I imagine that you will come to my aid; that, in time of distress, I will cry out and you will answer: 'Your kind words are like dripping honey to me' – you pull me out with a fishhook to my doom.

אֱלִיעֶזֶר אֲזִיכְּרִי

Eliezer Azikri

יְדִיד נֶפֶשׁ

BELOVED OF MY SOUL

יְדִיד נֶפֶשׁ, אָב הָרַחְמָן,
מְשֹׁךְ עַבְדְּךָ אֶל רְצוֹנֶךָ.
יָרוּץ עַבְדְּךָ כְּמוֹ אַיָּל,
יִשְׁתַּחֲוֶה מוּל הֲדָרֶךָ,
כִּי יֶעֱרַב לוֹ יְדִידוּתֶךָ
מִנֹּפֶת צוּף וְכָל טָעַם.

Beloved of my soul, merciful Father, draw Your servant after You to do Your will. He would run, swift as a deer, to kneel before Your majesty, for Your love is sweeter to him than honey from the comb, than any pleasing savour.

הָדוּר, נָאֶה, זִיו הָעוֹלָם,
נַפְשִׁי חוֹלַת אַהֲבָתָךְ.
אָנָּא, אֵל נָא, רְפָא נָא לָהּ
בְּהַרְאוֹת לָהּ נֹעַם זִיוָךְ.
אָז תִּתְחַזֵּק וְתִתְרַפֵּא
וְהָיְתָה לָּךְ שִׁפְחַת עוֹלָם.

Glorious, beautiful, Light of the world – my soul is faint with love for You. Heal her, O God, I beg You, by letting her gaze upon Your splendour. Then she will be healed and grow strong and be Your slave forever.

וָתִיק, יֶהֱמוּ רַחֲמֶיךָ
וְחוּס נָא עַל בֵּן אוֹהֲבָךְ,
כִּי זֶה כַּמֶּה נִכְסֹף נִכְסַף
לִרְאוֹת בְּתִפְאֶרֶת עֻזָּךְ.
אָנָּא, אֵלִי, מַחְמַד לִבִּי,
חוּשָׁה נָּא, וְאַל תִּתְעַלָּם.

Faithful One, let your heart be moved with tenderness, spare the son of Your beloved friend, [Abraham,] for he has longed these many years to behold Your mighty splendour. My God, my heart's delight, oh come quickly, do not forsake me.

הִגָּלֶה נָא וּפְרֹשׂ, חָבִיב,
עָלַי אֶת סֻכַּת שְׁלוֹמָךְ.
תָּאִיר אֶרֶץ מִכְּבוֹדָךְ,
נָגִילָה וְנִשְׂמְחָה בָּךְ.
מַהֵר, אָהוּב, כִּי בָא מוֹעֵד,
וְחָנֵּנִי כִּימֵי עוֹלָם.

Reveal Yourself, my Dearest, and spread over me Your canopy of peace. Let the earth shine with Your glory, let us rejoice in You. Make haste, my Love, for the time has come; show me Your favour as in the days of old.

יִשְׂרָאֵל נַגָ'ארָה

Israel Najara

נְהִי נִהְיָה אֲעוֹרֵר

THE FAMINE IN JERUSALEM

[...] נְהִי נִהְיָה אֲעוֹרֵר
וְלִבִּי בְּרוּחַ סוֹעָה מַסְעִיר
בְּזָכְרִי צַר חָשַׂף מַצְפּוּנַי
וּבְהֵיכָלִי אֵשׁ לְהָבוֹת הִבְעִיר.

Now I shall raise a bitter lament, and my heart will heave in a raging storm as I recall the enemy who ransacked my treasure and set fire to my Temple.

הֵבִיא בְּמָצוֹר עִירִי
וְכָל חֲמָתוֹ הֵעִיר,
וַיֶּחֱזַק הָרָעָב בָּעִיר.

He laid siege to my city, all his wrath was stirred up. *And the famine was severe in the city.*

יָרְדוּ חִצֵּי רָעָב לְכַלּוֹת הֲמוֹנַי,
כִּי קָרַב יוֹם אֵידָם.
פָּרִיצֵי עַמִּי סָבְבוּ בָעִיר
לְבַקֵּשׁ מִחְיָה בְּכָל מְאוֹדָם.
כְּעָלוּ וּבָאוּ בְּבֵית אֵם
עוֹלֵל טִפּוּחִים, בְּעֹז יָדָם
וַיִּקְחוּ הָאֲנָשִׁים מְצֵידָם.

The arrows of famine poured down to wipe out my people, when the day of their doom was at hand. Men of violence among my own people made the rounds of the city, searching for food at any price. They went up into the mother's house – there she was with the child of her tender care – and violently *took away the provisions.*

יַחַד הָאִשָּׁה וּבְנָהּ
נִשְׁאֲרוּ רֵיקָם בְּרֹב חַלְחָלָה,
עֲטוּפִים בְּרָעָב,
נוֹהִים וְצוֹעֲקִים בְּקוֹל יְלָלָה.
לֵאמֹר: 'מָה אֶעֱשֶׂה לִבְנִי
אֲשֶׁר טִפַּחְתִּי בְּרֹב חֶמְלָה,
וּבְבֵיתִי אֵין לֶחֶם וְאֵין שִׂמְלָה?'

The woman and her child were left empty-handed, writhing in anguish, faint with hunger, howling and wailing aloud. 'What shall I do,' she said, 'with my son whom I reared with such tenderness? *There is neither food nor clothing in my house.*'

שָׁאַל הַנַּעַר לְאִמּוֹ בְּקוֹל מַר:
'פַּת לֶחֶם יְזוּנֵנוּ?'
עָנְתָה אִמּוֹ: 'כָּמוֹנִי כָמוֹךָ,
שְׁנֵינוּ בְּרָעָב קָצָה נַפְשֵׁנוּ.
מֵאַיִן אוֹשִׁיעֵךְ, מַחְמַד עֵינַי,
וְתוֹחֶלֶת אֵינֶנָּה,
כִּי הַלֶּחֶם אָזַל מִכֵּלֵינוּ.'

Bitterly, the child asked his mother: 'Is there not even a crumb of bread to keep us alive?' His mother answered: 'What is mine is yours. We are both of us sick with hunger. Where can I find any help for you, delight of my eyes? All hope is gone, *for there is no food left in our sacks.*'

'רָעֵב לַלֶּחֶם וְצָמֵא לַמַּיִם —
נֶהֶפְכוּ מַעֲדַנַּיִךְ.

'Hungry for bread and thirsty for water, your delights have wasted away.

אָמוּתָה הַפַּעַם אַחֲרֵי רְאוֹתִי
אֲשֶׁר קִבְּצוּ פָארוּר פָּנַיִךְ.
עַתָּה יַחַד נָמוּת
וְלֹא יוֹעִיל הוֹנִי וְרֹב פְּנִינַיִךְ,
כִּי הַמָּוֶת יַפְרִיד בֵּינִי וּבֵינַיִךְ.׳

Oh, let me die now that I have seen your face turn ashen. Now we shall die together. My wealth is worthless, all your corals are useless, *for death shall divide us.*'

׳אַךְ אִם אַתָּה לוּ שְׁמָעֵנִי
וְרוּחִי לְךָ אַבִּיעָה –
תְּנָה אֶת בְּשָׂרְךָ לִי לְאָכְלָה
וְיַחַד לֹא נִגְוָעָה.
טוֹב שׁוּבְךָ אֶל תּוֹךְ מֵעַי,
וְלֹא לִכְלָבִים לְאָכְלָה לְשָׂבְעָה.
וְאֵיכָכָה אוּכַל וְרָאִיתִי בְּרָעָה!׳

'But hear me, if you will, and I shall give you my advice: let me eat your flesh, and we shall not both perish. It would be better for you to return to my womb than to let the dogs devour you. *How could I bear to see such an outrage?*'

לָחַשׁ יֶלֶד שַׁעֲשׁוּעִים לְאִמּוֹ
בְּאַף וְקֶצֶף וָמֶרִי:
׳אִמִּי, אֵיךְ בְּדַם פְּרִי בִטְנֵךְ
תִּשְׁכְּרִי וְתִתְעָרִי?
עֲשִׂי הַטּוֹב בְּעֵינַיִךְ!
גַּם אֲנִי אֶבְחַר בַּאֲשֶׁר תִּבְחֲרִי,
וּתְהִי לִי אִמִּי קִבְרִי.׳

Then the darling child, full of fury and venom, whispered to his mother: 'Mother, how could you get drunk on the blood of your child, the fruit of your body, and expose yourself to shame? But do what you think best. I will accept whatever you choose. *Let my mother become my grave!*'

בָּנְתָה לְשַׁחֲטוֹ
וּבְיָדֶיהָ תָּמְכָה שְׁלָחִים.
גַּם הִיא נֶאֶנְחָה וַתָּשָׁב אָחוֹר
מֵרְאוֹת בְּרַע עוֹלֵל טִפּוּחִים.
וַתִּשְׁחָטֵהוּ וַתַּפְשֵׁט עוֹרוֹ
וּבְשָׂרוֹ עָשְׂתָה כִּבְשַׂר זְבָחִים –
לַעֲצָמֶיהָ לִשְׁנֵים עָשָׂר נְתָחִים.

She built [an altar on which] to slaughter him. She grasped the knife in her hand. She too groaned and turned away; she could not look upon the suffering of the child whom she had tenderly reared. Then she slaughtered him and stripped off his skin and prepared his flesh like the flesh of an offering. [She cut him up] *limb by limb into twelve pieces.*[1]

1. As the Levite had cut up his dead concubine (Judges 19.29).

רְעַב בִּטְנָהּ הֱצִיקָהּ
לָשׂוּם בְּשִׁפּוּד בְּשַׂר לֶשֶׁם שְׁבוֹ.
אַכְזְרִיּוּת לָבְשָׁה וְאֵשׁ הִצִּיתָה,
כִּסְּתָה פָנָיו בְּחֶלְבּוֹ.
נֶאֱצָה לְאָכְלוֹ מְבֻשָּׁל
בַּעֲבוּר הִתְעַכְּבוֹ,
כִּי אִם צְלִי אֵשׁ רֹאשׁוֹ עַל כְּרָעָיו וְעַל קִרְבּוֹ.

Hunger gripped her bowels. She clothed herself in cruelty to put him – flesh of turquoise and agate – on the spit. She kindled a fire; she covered his face with his fat. She chose not to boil him, for that would prolong the matter. And so she ate him *roasted – head, shins and entrails – over the fire.*[1]

מְהֵרָה לְמַלֵּא רְעַב בִּטְנָהּ
וְלִבָּהּ יֶחֱרַד וְיִתַּר.
חֶדֶר בְּחֶדֶר הִתְחַבְּאָה
לֶאֱכֹל עָנִי בַּמִּסְתָּר,
וּבְשַׂר בְּנָהּ עָרְכָה לְפָנֶיהָ
מְמֻלָּח וּמְבֻתָּר
וַתֹּאכַל וַתִּשְׂבַּע וַתּוֹתַר.

Quickly she ate her fill, her heart beating wildly, leaping up. She hid in an inner room to devour the victim in secret. She arranged her son's flesh, salted and cut up, before her. *She ate until she was satisfied and still had some left over.*

שׁוֹמְרִים לַבֹּקֶר הַסּוֹבְבִים בָּעִיר,
שְׁלֹשֶׁת הַפָּרִיצִים,
דֶּרֶךְ בֵּיתָהּ צָעֲדוּ,
הֵרִיחוּ צְלִי בְּשַׂר פְּטוּרֵי צִצִּים.
בָּאוּ בֵיתָהּ וְאָמְרוּ:
'הִנֵּה לְאוֹת טֶרֶף בֵּיתֵנוּ אֲשֶׁר אָנוּ חֲפֵצִים,
הִנֵּה הָאֵשׁ וְהָעֵצִים!'

In the morning, the guards, those three men of violence, going the rounds of the city, passed by her house. They smelled the young roast,[2] came into her house and said: 'This is a sign that you have what we seek: meat for our household. *Here are the fire and the wood!*'

הֶגֶה מִפִּיהֶם יָצָא
וְדָרְשׁוּ מִמֶּנָּה בְּלֵב זָעֵף וָסָר:
'תְּנִי לָנוּ בָּשָׂר וְנֹאכֵלָה,
הָבִיאִי לִבֵּךְ לַמּוּסָר.'

With rumbling voices, sullen and angry, they demanded: 'Give us meat to eat! Let virtue rule your heart!' She

1. Like the Paschal sacrifice (Exodus 12.9).
2. Lit. 'the meat roast of the open flowers'.

עָנְתָה לָהֶם:
׳לֶחֶם צַר מֵהָעִיר חָסוֹר חָסֵר
וּמֵאַיִן לִי בָּשָׂר?

answered them: 'There is hardly a morsel of food in all the city. *Where am I to find meat?*

חַוֵּה אֲחַוֶּה דֵעִי לָכֶם
וּמִקְרֶה קְרָאַנִי לָכֶם אַגִּידֶנּוּ:
הַסִּיר וְהַבָּשָׂר אֲשֶׁר הֲרִיחוֹתֶם,
לִפְנֵיכֶם אַצִּיגֶנּוּ.
הַיְדַעְתֶּם? יְדִיד נַפְשִׁי,
אֲשֶׁר עֲטָרוֹת אֶעֶנְדֶנּוּ,
אָכַלְתִּי בְאוֹנִי מִמֶּנּוּ.

'But I will let you in on the secret, I will tell you what happened to me. The stewpot and the meat which you smelled – I shall now set them before you. Could you have imagined this? It is my dearly beloved, whom I once wore like a crown on my head. *I have eaten him in despair*.

זֶבֶד טוֹב זְבוּדָה לָכֶם
אִתִּי, שׁוּבוּ, סוּרוּ נָא.
הִנֵּה חֶלְקִי מִכָּל עֲמָלִי
אָכַלְתִּי בְּרֹב מְגִנָּה.
אִכְלוּ, רֵעִים,
הִנֵּה לָכֶם חֶלְקְכֶם צְפוּנָה:
שׁוֹק הַיָּמִין לְמָנָה.׳

'I have kept a choice gift for you. Come back, I pray you, stay with me. Here, this was my reward for all my labour. I ate it, overcome with grief. Eat, friends, this is the portion reserved for you: *the offering of the right hind leg*.'

קָמוּ כֻלָּם בַּחֲרָדָה
וְעֵינֵיהֶם לַשָּׁמַיִם הִגְבִּיהוּ.
פַּחַד קְרָאָם וּרְעָדָה,
הֵמָּה רָאוּ כֵּן תָּמָהוּ.
אָמְרוּ: ׳לֹא נִרְאֲתָה כָּזֹאת
וְלֹא שָׁמְעָה אֹזֶן שֶׁמֶץ מֶנְהוּ.׳
וַיִּתְמְהוּ הָאֲנָשִׁים אִישׁ אֶל רֵעֵהוּ.

They all stood up in terror, lifting their eyes to heaven, shuddering with dread. Staring at her, amazed, they said: 'The like of this has never been seen. No ear has ever heard the whisper of it.' *Dumbstruck they looked at one another*.

נָא יִכָּמְרוּ רַחֲמֶיךָ
עַל עַם עָבַר בָּם מָוֶת וְרָעָב וְכִלָּיוֹן.

Let Your heart be moved with love for this people, who have been tried by death, famine, and destruction. Fulfil

קַיֵּם מַאֲמַר חוֹזֶיךָ
דִּבְּרוּ נֶחָמוֹת בְּטוּב הִגָּיוֹן.
תִּבְנֶה חוֹמוֹת יְרוּשָׁלַיִם
וְתוֹשִׁיב בָּהּ עַם אֶבְיוֹן –
אַתָּה תָקוּם תְּרַחֵם צִיּוֹן.

the pledge of Your seers, who spoke kind words of consolation. Build anew the walls of Jerusalem and make this poor people live in them again. *You will surely arise and have mercy on Zion.*

תִּדַּד שְׁנַת עֵינִי

IF I WERE

תִּדַּד שְׁנַת עֵינִי וְאֶסְעַר כָּאֳנִי
תּוֹךְ יָם תְּשׁוּקָתָךְ, וְאֵלֶּה אֶזְכְּרָה:
לוּ אֶהְיֶה יוֹנֵק וְאַתָּה אוֹמְנִי,
אִינַק שְׁדֵי יָפְיָךְ, צְמָאִי אֶשְׁבְּרָה.
לוּ אֶהְיֶה שֶׁלַח, וְאַתָּה וַאֲנִי
נֵשֵׁב בְּצֵל גַּנִּי, לְפִרְיָךְ אֶשְׁמְרָה.
לוּ אֶהְיֶה רֹמַח וְאַתָּה נוֹתְנִי
תּוֹךְ לֵב מְשַׂנְאֶיךָ, בְּדָמָם אֶשְׁכְּרָה.
לוּ אֶהְיֶה אֹהֶל וְאַתָּה שׁוֹכְנִי,
נִתְעַלְּסָה אַהַב, בְּגִיל נִתְאַזְּרָה.
לוּ אֶהְיֶה לָשׁוֹן וְאַתָּה מַעֲנִי,
אַשְׁקִיט יְקוֹד חִשְׁקִי בְּשִׁיר וַאְזַמְּרָה.
לוּ אֶהְיֶה עֶבֶד וְאַתָּה רוֹזְנִי,
אֶשְׁאַף עֲבוֹדָתָךְ, דְּרוֹר לֹא אֶבְחֲרָה.

Sleep deserts my eyes and I toss like a ship in the sea of my yearning for You as I imagine these things: If I were an infant and you were my nurse, I would suckle your beautiful breasts, and quench my thirst. If I were a stream and you and I sat in the shade of my garden, I would look after your fruit. If I were a spear and you thrust me into your enemies' hearts, I would be drunk with their blood. If I were a tent and you dwelt in me, we would delight ourselves with love and clothe ourselves with joy. If I were a tongue and you were my words, I would soothe desire's flame with a song. If I were a slave and you were my lord, I would long to serve you, I would never choose freedom.

יְדִידִים לָאֵל נִבְחֲרוּ

THE MESSIAH

יְדִידִים לָאֵל נִבְחֲרוּ
וּבָהֶם אֵל מִכָּל עַם חָפֵץ –
שׁוֹכְנִים בַּגָּלוּת יְשַׂבְּרוּ

Languishing in exile, God's chosen companions, in whom He delighted above all nations, now wait for Him to

לָאֵל יְקַבֵּץ אֲשֶׁר נָפַץ.
רַגְלֵי דוֹד עַל הַר יִנְהֲרוּ
וְעַל הַגְּבָעוֹת קָפַץ.
אַל תָּעִירוּ וּתְעוֹרְרוּ
אֶת הָאַהֲבָה עַד שֶׁתֶּחְפָּץ!

assemble those whom He dispersed; the feet of the Beloved will come leaping over the hills and streaming to the Mountain. But do not stir up or awaken love until it is ready!

בֶּן דָּוִד בָּא פֶּתַע לָשִׂים
עַל הַר הַקֹּדֶשׁ הַדְרַת דִּגְלוֹ.
מַה לָּכֶם יוֹם יוֹם דּוֹרְשִׁים?
וּבָזֶה תְּאַחֲרוּ רַגְלוֹ.
שַׂר אֲשֶׁר אַתֶּם מְבַקְשִׁים
פִּתְאֹם יָבוֹא אֶל הֵיכָלוֹ,
הָלוֹךְ וְרוֹכֵב עַל חֲמוֹר,
לֹא בִגְבוּרַת הַסּוּס יֶחְפָּץ.
אַל תָּעִירוּ וּתְעוֹרְרוּ
אֶת הָאַהֲבָה עַד שֶׁתֶּחְפָּץ!

The son of David will come suddenly to set his glorious flag upon the holy Mountain. Why then do you clamour for him day after day? You are only delaying his coming. The Prince whom you seek will, all of a sudden, come to his Temple; but he will come riding on an ass; he sets no store by the strength of a horse. Oh, do not stir up or awaken love until it is ready!

עֲלוּמֵי שֵׁם

Anonymous

אַהֲבַת בַּת נְדָבָה

GOD'S BELOVED

אַהֲבַת בַּת נְדָבָה
מְתֻקָּה גַּם עֲרֵבָה.

The love of the princely daughter [of Zion] has been most sweet and pleasant to Me.

שַׁאֲלוּ־נָא, שַׁאֲלוּ:
אוֹהֲבַי מַה פָּעֲלוּ?
אִם לְשׁוּבִי יִחֲלוּ?
מְהֵרָה קַל אֶרְכָּבָה
וּלְעַד אֶתְיַצָּבָה.

Oh, ask and ask again: What have My dear ones [the righteous] been doing? Have they been longing for My return? Soon, I shall swiftly fly [to the Temple] to stand at My post forever.

וַאֲנִי עַד מוֹעֲדֵךְ,
הִנְנִי צֵל בַּעֲדֵךְ
מִשְּׁאוֹן כָּל בּוֹגְדֵךְ.
חַי אֲנִי, לֹא אֲכַזְּבָה
לָךְ, וְלֹא שָׁוְא אֶכְתְּבָה.

And until your time comes, I shall shield you from the clamour of those who seek to betray you. By My life, I shall not fail you nor speak in vain.

הֵן אֲהַבְתִּיךְ אַהֲבָה
עַד לְמֵאָז קֻרְבָה,
הַנְּפָשׁוֹת שׁוֹבְבָה,
הַלְּבָבוֹת לִבְּבָה –
אַהֲבָה תּוֹךְ אַהֲבָה!

For I have long loved you with a love that drew us close together, nurtured the soul and gave the heart courage – a love encompassed with love!

לַנְּבִיאִים אֹמְרָה:
׳הַרְאִיתֶם סְעָרָה
חֹק יְדִידָהּ שָׁמְרָה?׳
אָמְרוּ: ׳זֹאת אַהֲבָה
נִפְלְאָה מֵאַהֲבָה.׳

And I say to the prophets: 'Have you seen how the maiden, though battered by storm, kept her troth to her Friend?' And they answer: 'This love is a wonder surpassing all love.'

שָׁלוֹם, בְּךָ נִשְׁבַּעְתִּי

THE SEDUCTION OF SHALOM

שָׁלוֹם, בְּךָ נִשְׁבַּעְתִּי,
חֵי רֹאשְׁךָ, אָמַרְתִּי,
כִּי אוֹתְךָ תָּאַבְתִּי.
תֵּלֵךְ לְבֵיתִי, שָׁלוֹם.

Shalom, I swear by you; by your life, I say, it is only you I desire. Come to my house, Shalom.

תִּשְׁתֶּה לְכוֹס מֵיֵינִי,
תֹּאכַל לְפַת שֻׁלְחָנִי,
תָּרַח לְרֵיחַ בּוּסְמָנִי.
תָּלִין בְּשִׂמְחָה, שָׁלוֹם.

Come drink wine from my cup, eat bread from my dish and breathe in my fragrance. You will sleep in joy, Shalom.

תָּלִין עֲלֵי מִטָּתִי
בְּמָר־דְּרוֹר קִטַּרְתִּי.
מִכָּל בְּשָׂמִים נַפְתִּי
מִשְׁכַּב יְדִידִי שָׁלוֹם.

You will sleep upon the bed which I have perfumed with burning sticks of myrrh. I have sprinkled the choicest spices on the bed of my beloved Shalom.

אַל תִּירְאָה מִמֶּנִּי,
כִּי בַּת נְדִיבִים אָנִי.
אָבִי אֲצִיל קַדְמוֹנִי.
תָּבִין וְתֵדַע, שָׁלוֹם.

Do not be afraid of me, for I am of noble lineage. My father was a prince in days gone by. Know this and you will understand, Shalom.

חַבֵּק, יְדִידִי, עַלְמָה
תָּאִיר כְּאוֹר הַחַמָּה,
וּגְשָׁה וּמוּשׁ לְפִימָה.
אֶשְׁתַּעַשְׁעָה בְּךָ, שָׁלוֹם.

O my friend, embrace this girl who shines with a brightness like the sun's. Come close and feel her lips. Let me revel in you, Shalom.

הִשְׁתַּעַשְׁעָה תּוֹךְ חֵיקִי
וּדְבַק וְשַׁלֵּם חֻקִּי
וּטְעַם דְּבַשׁ מֶרְקִי
צָפוּן בְּפִי לְךָ, שָׁלוֹם.

Take pleasure in my bosom, cling to me and give me my due. Taste the flowing honey which awaits you in my mouth, Shalom.

קוּמָה, יְדִיד, הַשְׁקֵנִי,
מִיֵּין עֲסִיס רַוֵּנִי,
חַיֶּיךָ, אֲהוּב, הַחְיֵנִי.
נַשֵּׁק שְׂפָתַי, שָׁלוֹם.

Come, my friend, give me to drink. Let me have my fill of fresh wine. By your life, my love, revive me. Kiss my lips, Shalom.

אִישִׁי בְּדֶרֶךְ, נֶחְבָּא,
לָקַח בְּיָדוֹ זְהָבוֹ.
אֵינוֹ בְּזֶה יוֹם יָבוֹא.
יַאְמֵן לְבָבְךָ, שָׁלוֹם.

My husband is away, gone on a journey. He has taken his gold with him. He will not be back by tomorrow. You may rest assured, Shalom.

עֵת אֶרְאֲךָ בָּאָרֶץ,
אֶקֹּד וְאֶשְׁתַּחֲוֶה אָרְצָה
אֵין לִי בָּזֶה דּוֹד חֵפֶץ
כִּי אִם יְדִידִי, שָׁלוֹם.

When I lay eyes upon you, I bow low and prostrate myself. Oh, I have no love in this world but my beloved Shalom!

לִקְרַאת שַׁבָּת

SABBATH SONG

לִקְרַאת שַׁבָּת אֵצֵא בְּחִבָּה
מִיּוֹם שִׁשִּׁי, זָקֵן וְשֵׂיבָה.
שְׂשׂוֹנִי קָרֵב, יְגוֹנִי נֶחְבָּא,
וְאַצְּן וְאֹמַר: 'בָּרוּךְ הַבָּא!'

Old and grey as I am, I hurry forth on Friday, filled with love, to meet the Sabbath. My joy approaches, my grief disappears and I sing out: 'Welcome!'

וּמֵרֹב חִבָּה לַיּוֹם הַהוּא
נַפְשִׁי אֲטַהֵר, יָהּ אֲבָרְכֵהוּ.
אֲפַזֵּז, אֲכַרְכֵּר: זֶהוּ, זֶהוּ!
דֻּגְמָא מֵעֵין עוֹלָם הַבָּא.

For love of this day, I purify my soul, I bless the Lord. I leap and dance, 'Yes, this is it! A foretaste of the world to come!'

דִּבְרֵי נָבִיא, אֱלֹהַי, תָּבִיא,
תְּמַהֵר בְּמֶלֶךְ, כֹּהֵן וְנָבִיא.
וְנַעֲלֶה לְצִיּוֹן כְּאַרְיֵה וְלָבִיא,
וְנִבְנֶה לְמִקְדָּשׁ בְּהַדְרָא רַבָּא.

Make the words of the seers come true, my God. Hasten the advent of King, Priest, and Prophet. Then, rearing up like lions, we shall go up to Zion and build the Temple, majestic in splendour.

כּוֹכָב אֲשֶׁר הִשְׁקִיף

THE STAR[1]

כּוֹכָב אֲשֶׁר הִשְׁקִיף בְּאוֹרוֹ עַל נְוַת
חוֹשֵׁק, לְפֵרוּדוֹ בְּמַר צוֹרֵחַ.
כַּמָּה תְקָפוּהוּ יְגוֹנִים! עַד אֲשֶׁר

The star looked down and shone into the lover's room, as he was bitterly lamenting his friend's departure. How grief-stricken he had been, until this

1. The comforting star is sent by the friend who has gone on a voyage.

פָּגַע בְּפָנָיו וַיְהִי שָׂמֵחַ.
יָדַע חֳלִי לִבּוֹ וְשָׁלַח מִצֳּרִי
חַסְדּוֹ וּמָרַח עַל שְׁחִין צוֹמֵחַ.
יִשְׁלַח אֱלֹהִים לוֹ בְּרָכָה כָּל יְמֵי
חַיָּיו וְאוֹרוֹ יִהְיֶה זוֹרֵחַ.
וִינַהֲלֵהוּ אֶל מְחוֹז חֶפְצוֹ בְּרֹב
שָׁלוֹם וְכַתָּמָר יְהִי פוֹרֵחַ.
וִיסוֹבְבוּהוּ מַלְאֲכֵי חֶסֶד, וְחֵן
יֵט לוֹ אֱלֹהָיו עַד בְּלִי יָרֵחַ.

star-light touched his face and brought him joy. Knowing that he was sick at heart, the star sent him this balm of kindness to soothe the festering sore. May God send the friend blessings all the days of his life, and may his light shine forever. May He guide him, in abundant peace, to his desired haven, and may he flourish like a palm-tree. May angels of grace enfold him and may he win the favour of his God until the moon is no more.

יְחַסִּין עַלַי אלמחבוב אדִי הו סַיִּדְנָא,
יחמִיה מן אלאַשרַאר עַדַד מא ברַק וְלַאח.

May He prosper my beloved master.[1] May He protect him from all evil, just as He glittered and shone [upon me].

רָאֲת תְּמוּנָה בַּחֲלוֹם

THE RING

רָאֲת תְּמוּנָה בַּחֲלוֹם וַתֹּאמְרָה:
'מִי נְשָׁקַנִי, וַאֲנִי נִרְדֶּמֶת?'
עֵת יָדְעָה כִּי הִיא תְּמוּנָתִי, אֲזַי
כִּחְשָׁה וְנָמָה: 'הֵן אֲנִי חוֹלֶמֶת!'
וָאֹמְרָה: 'אִם הוּא חֲלוֹם – מִי זֶה אֲשֶׁר
נָתַן בְּאֶצְבַּע הַשְּׂמֹאל חוֹתֶמֶת?'
וַתֶּחֱרַשׁ, כִּי יָדְעָה כִּי נְאֻמִי
צֶדֶק, וְכִי הָיוּ דְבָרַי בֶּאֱמֶת.
אָז לָקְחָה מַסְוֶה וּפָנִים כִּסְּתָה,
וָאֵדְעָה כִּי הִיא לְזֹאת נִכְלֶמֶת.
תַּעְלִים לְחָיֶיהָ – יְאִירוּן בַּעֲדֵי
צַמָּה כְּמוֹ חַמָּה בְּעָב נֶעְלֶמֶת. [...]

She saw a figure in her dream and said: 'Who kissed me while I was asleep?' But when she understood that it had been my form, she denied me, saying: 'Why, I was only dreaming!' To which I said: 'If it was only a dream, then who was it that put the ring on your left finger?' She said nothing, for she knew that I was right and that my words were true. Whereupon she took a veil and covered her face. I understood that she was overcome with shame. But though she hid her cheeks, they shone through her veil like the sun enveloped in a cloud.

1. Lit. 'our master'; the last two lines are in Arabic.

אַתָּה אָדוֹן וַאֲנִי עֶבֶד

אַתָּה אָדוֹן וַאֲנִי עֶבֶד.
וּמִי יְרַחֵם עַל עֶבֶד,
הֲלֹא אָדוֹן.
אַתָּה בּוֹרֵא וַאֲנִי בּוֹלֶה.
וּמִי יְרַחֵם עַל בּוֹלֶה,
הֲלֹא בּוֹרֵא.
אַתָּה דַּיָּן וַאֲנִי נִדּוֹן.
וּמִי יְרַחֵם עַל נִדּוֹן,
הֲלֹא דַּיָּן.
אַתָּה וָעֵד וַאֲנִי לָבוּד.
וּמִי יְרַחֵם עַל לָבוּד,
הֲלֹא וָעֵד.
אַתָּה חַי וַאֲנִי מֵת.
וּמִי יְרַחֵם עַל מֵת,
הֲלֹא חַי.
אַתָּה יוֹצֵר וַאֲנִי חֹמֶר.
וּמִי יְרַחֵם עַל חֹמֶר,
הֲלֹא יוֹצֵר.
אַתָּה לַהַב וַאֲנִי קַשׁ.
וּמִי יְרַחֵם עַל קַשׁ,
הֲלֹא לַהַב.
אַתָּה שׁוֹמֵעַ וַאֲנִי קוֹרֵא.
וּמִי יְרַחֵם עַל קוֹרֵא,
הֲלֹא שׁוֹמֵעַ.
אַתָּה תְּחִלָּה וַאֲנִי סוֹף.
וּמִי יְרַחֵם עַל סוֹף,
הֲלֹא תְּחִלָּה.

YOU AND I

You are the Lord and I am the servant. Who should have mercy on the servant if not the Lord? You create and I decay. Who should have mercy on the decayed if not the Creator? You are the Judge and I am the accused. Who should have mercy on the accused if not the Judge? You are All and I am a fragment. Who should have mercy on the fragment if not the All? You are the Living One and I am the dead. Who should have mercy on the dead if not the Living One? You are the Potter and I am clay. Who should have mercy on clay if not the Potter? You are the Fire and I am stubble. Who should have mercy on stubble if not the Fire? You are the Listener and I am the pleader. Who should have mercy on the pleader if not the Listener? You are the Beginning and I am the end. Who should have mercy on the end if not the Beginning?

סְעַדְיָה בֶּן־עַמְרָם

Sa'adiah ben Amram

סַפְּרִי, תַּמָּה תְּמִימָה

THE POET, THE DOVE AND THE BELOVED

'סַפְּרִי, תַּמָּה תְּמִימָה,
סַפְּרִי, נָגִיל בְּתֵימָא,
בַּת מְלָכִים הַחֲכָמָה,
אָן מְקוֹמֵךְ, סַפְּרִי לִי.'

[The Poet:] 'Tell me, pure and perfect one, tell me so that we may rejoice here in Taima[1] – O wise princess, tell me, where do you make your home?'

עָנְתָה יוֹנָה: 'סְעַדְיָה,
לִי בְּפַלְטֵרִין עֲלִיָּה,
וַאֲנִי תּוֹךְ לֵב – אֲנִיָּה,
בְּיָפְיִי עוֹטָה מְעִילִי.

The dove answered: 'Sa'adiah, there is a high chamber reserved for me in the Palace.[2] But though I could robe myself in beauty, my heart is full of lamentation.

דִלְנִי יא צָאחִ הַיַּא,
דִלְנִי פַאנַא גַבְיָא,
וְאפהַאם אִפהַאם לא תַעַיַּא,
אין טַרִיק אטלב כְלִילִי.'

'Oh, show me the way, my friend, guide me, for I am at a loss. Pray, understand, and do not lose patience: where is the road that will lead me to my Beloved?'

'יא מסַמָא לב אלאלבַאב
וְאפתַחִי יא צַפָה אלבאב,
אן פי אלבסתאן אטַיַאב
דַא כְרוּם דַא שהַד חַאלִי.

[The Beloved:] 'O heart of hearts, open the gate to Me. There are beds of balsam in My garden and vines sweet with honey.

הָרְשׁוּת בֶּאֱמֶת נְתוּנָה,
לָךְ שְׁלוֹמוֹת הַחֲתֻנָּה,
אַל יְסִיתֵךְ צָר מְמֻנֶּה,
בַּת, וְאַל יַשִּׂיג גְּבוּלִי.

'Truly, I now give you leave [to be redeemed], to enjoy the peace of wedlock. Do not let the evil spirit incite you, My daughter, let him not encroach on My domain.

1. A province in North Arabia. 2. The Land of Israel.

בַּחֲרִי מִבְחַר מְקוֹמוֹת,
הֵיכְלֵי שֵׁן הַפְּנִימוֹת,
וַעֲלִי מִתּוֹךְ תְּהוֹמוֹת,
וּשְׁמְעִי, תַּמָּה, לְקוֹלִי.

'You may choose the choicest land, and the inner chamber of the Palace panelled with ivory. Oh, arise from the depths, My pure one, and heed My words.

נַעֲלֶה הַר הָעֲבָרִים,
נִשְׁכְּבָה יַחַד חֲבֵרִים,
מִבְּלִי מַגַּע בְּשָׂרִים,
שָׁם, וְיִיטַב לָךְ וְגַם לִי.

'Let us go up to Mount Abarim and lie there together in friendship, without flesh touching flesh. You will find contentment there, and so will I.

עֵץ פְּרִי הָדָר בְּגַנִּי,
וַעֲסִיסִי שָׁם וְיֵינִי.
קַבְּלִי מִתּוֹךְ יְמִינִי
כּוֹס, אֲשֶׁר נִמְזַג בְּחַר לִי.

'There will be fruit of goodly trees in My garden, fresh juice and wine. Accept this cup from My right hand – I have filled it with My finest wine.[1]

מִבְּאֵר שֶׁבַע צְאִי לָךְ,
וּזְנְחִי יַנְשׁוּף וְשָׁלָךְ,
וְחַכְּמִי, בִּינִי בְּשֶׁלָּךְ,
מִיָּמִין, אַל תַּשְׂמְאִילִי.

'Now leave the pit of exile,[2] spurn the screech owl and the fisher owl.[3] Learn wisdom from your own Law, take the right path, shun the left.

רַחֲצִי טִנּוּף, הָסִירִי,
עֵת עֲלוֹת שַׁעַר חֲצֵרִי.
קַדְּשִׁי אֶת הָעֲשִׂירִי,
גַּם תְּנִי חַלָּה וְאִכְלִי.

'And when you enter the gate of My courts, wash yourself, purge yourself of impurity. Set aside a tithe as holy to the Lord,[4] and give the priest his gift of dough before you eat the bread.[5]

1. The allegorical meaning is: the people of Israel ('fruit of goodly trees') will be in My world ('garden') and the ceremony of libation ('juice and wine') will be performed in the Temple.

2. Lit. *Be'er-Sheva*, 'the well (pit) of seven (countries)' into which the world was divided.

3. 'Unclean' birds, representing foreign cultures.

4. Exodus 27.30 ff.

5. Numbers 15.20.

מַעֲדַנִּים הַמְּתוּקִים
נֶחְלְקוּ שְׁלוֹשׁ חֲלָקִים,
זֶה בְּזֶה הֵמָּה אֲדוּקִים —
סוֹד מְכֻסֶּה הוּא וּפֶלֶי.'

'The fragrant sacrifices must be shared by three,[1] and these three parts are interlocked. This is a mystery, deep and wondrous.'

סְעַדְיָה

Sa'adiah

לַנֵּר וְלִבְשָׂמִים

SONG FOR HAVDALAH[2]

לַנֵּר וְלִבְשָׂמִים נַפְשִׁי מְיַחֲלָה.
אִם תִּתְּנוּ לִי כּוֹס יַיִן לְהַבְדָּלָה!
סֹלּוּ דְּרָכִים לִי, פַּנּוּ לְנְבוּכָה,
פִּתְחוּ שְׁעָרִים לִי כָּל מַלְאֲכֵי מַעְלָה.
עֵינַי אֲנִי אֶשָּׂא אֶל אֵל בְּלֵב כּוֹסֵף,
מַמְצִיא צְרָכַי לִי בַּיּוֹם וּבַלַּיְלָה.
דֵּי מַחֲסוֹר תֶּן לִי מֵאוֹצְרוֹת טוּבָךְ,
כִּי לַחֲסָדֶיךָ אֵין קֵץ וְאֵין תִּכְלָה.
יִתְחַדְּשָׁה גִילִי, טַרְפִּי וְטוֹבָתִי,
תָּסִיר יְגוֹנוֹתַי, מַכְאוֹב וּמַאְפֵלָה.
הִנֵּה יְמֵי מַעֲשֶׂה מִתְחַדְּשִׁים תָּמִיד —
יִתְחַדְּשׁוּ בָהֶם שָׁלוֹם וְטוֹב סֶלָה.

My soul longs for the candle and the fragrant spices; won't you pour me a cup of wine for *havdalah*? You angels on high, build a way for me, clear the track for the bewildered daughter [of Zion], open the gates to let me in! I shall lift up my eyes with heartfelt yearning to the Lord who provides for me day and night. Oh, give me as much as I need from the treasure-house of Your goodness, for there is no end or limit to Your unfailing love. Give new life to my joy, renew my bread and my bliss, remove all sorrow, pain, and gloom. Now the days of work return again. May peace and goodness be renewed in them, *selah*.

1. God, priest, and Israelite.
2. The ceremony, employing a candle, spices, and wine, which marks the end of the Sabbath.

שָׁלֵם שַׁבָּזִי

Shalem Shabazi

אַהֲבַת הֲדַסָּה

A WEDDING SONG

אַהֲבַת הֲדַסָּה עַל לְבָבִי נִקְשָׁרָה,
וַאֲנִי בְּתוֹךְ גּוֹלָה פְּעָמַי צוֹלְלִים.
לוּ יֵשׁ רְשׁוּת לִי אֶעֱלֶה אֶתְחַבְּרָה
תּוֹךְ שַׁעֲרֵי צִיּוֹן אֲשֶׁר הֵם נֶהֱלָלִים.
שַׁחֲרִית וְעַרְבִית בַּת נְדִיבִים אֶזְכְּרָה,
לִבִּי וְרַעְיוֹנַי בְּחֵשֶׁק נִבְהָלִים.
בִּנְעִים זְמִירוֹת מִנְּדוֹד אֶתְעוֹרְרָה,
וַאֲנִי וְרַעְיָתִי בְּרִנָּה צוֹהֲלִים.

My heart is bound to Hadassah[1] in love, but my feet are sinking in the depths of exile. When will He give me leave to go up and make my home within the extolled gates of Zion? Morning and evening I call to mind the Princess.[2] My heart and my mind reel with desire. With sweet song I shall shake off the pain of separation, and then my dearest and I will loudly rejoice.

בִּינוּ, עֲדַת קֹדֶשׁ, בְּשִׁירָה חִבַּרְתָּה:
חָתָן וְהַכַּלָּה בְּחֻפָּה נִכְלָלִים,
זֶה יוֹם שְׂמָחוֹת לָאֲיֻמָּה יְקָרָה,
כִּי הִיא וְדוֹדָהּ חֵן וְחֶסֶד גּוֹמְלִים.
יַחְדָּו אֱלֵי שֻׁלְחָן וְכוֹס, דּוֹדִי, קְרָא,
וּמִן שְׂרִידֵינוּ וְכָל הַנִּסְגָּלִים.
מִכּוֹס יְשׁוּעוֹת אֶשְׂמְחָה וַאֲזַמְּרָה,
אוֹצִיא לְכֹל סוֹדִי וְאָשִׁיב שׁוֹאֲלִים.

Now, my holy flock, fathom this song I have composed. The bridegroom and the bride have been crowned in wedlock, and this is a day of joy for the majestic one, the precious one,[3] for she and her Beloved now endow each other with grace and love. O my Beloved, invite us all together to Your table and Your cup, summon the remnants of Your treasured people. And I shall sing happily over this cup of salvation. I shall disclose my mystic secret to those who question me.

שֵׁם טוֹב לְמַשְׂכִּילִים בְּדַעַת יְשָׁרָה,
כִּי הֵם עֲלֵי יִצְרָם בְּוַדַּאי מוֹשְׁלִים.
תַּאֲוַת לְבָבָם לַעֲשׂוֹת טוֹב גָּבְרָה,
יַעְלוּ לְגַן עֵדֶן וְחַיִּים נוֹחֲלִים.
אַהֲבַת יְחִידָתִי לְטוּב אֵל נָהֲרָה,
בָּרוּךְ שֶׁהוּא נוֹתֵן שְׂכַר כָּל פּוֹעֲלִים.

The wise and pure of heart are assured of a good name, for they firmly rule their passions. Their desire to do good prevails. They will go up to the Garden of Eden and inherit everlasting life. All the love in my soul surges to the goodness of God. Blessed is He who rewards

1. The Land of Israel (Esther 2.7).
2. The Shekinah.
3. Or, 'the terrible one', an epithet for Daughter-Zion (Song of Songs 6.10).

שָׁלוֹם כְּנָהָר לַעֲדָתִי יִנְהֲרָה,
זָקֵן וְגַם בָּחוּר וְכָל הָעוֹלְלִים.

each and every workman! May peace flow over my flock like a river, over old and young, over all the little children.

מִי נְשָׁקַנִי

THE SEAL

׳מִי נְשָׁקַנִי וַאֲנִי נֶעֱלֶמֶת,
וַיֹּאמְרָה לִי: ״אַל תְּהִי נִדְהֶמֶת!״
שַׁפְרִיר כְּבוֹד דּוֹדִי בְּהֵיכַל אַהֲבָה,
מִתּוֹךְ נְוֵה חֲדָרַי, בְּלֵיל חוֹלֶמֶת.
לַנְתִּי בְּחֵיקוֹ מִבְּעוֹד יוֹם נִכְסְפָה,
אֶרְחַץ בְּנִקָּיוֹן וּמִתְבַּשֶּׂמֶת.׳

מְדֵי עֲלוֹתָהּ עַל יְדֵי צִיר נֶאֱמָן,
דִּגְלִי בְּמַסָּעוֹת בְּאוֹת רוֹשֶׁמֶת.
יָרַד יְדִידִי אֶל נְוֵה גִּנַּת־אֱגוֹז,
זָכַר בְּרִית אָבוֹת שֶׁהִיא קוֹדֶמֶת.
וַעַד שְׁבָטַי בַּעֲלֵי חֶסֶד וְחֵן,
וּבְשַׁעֲרֵי צִיּוֹן תְּהֵא מַשְׁכֶּמֶת.

סוּרוּ בְּנֵי נֵכָר וְגַם הִתְרַחֲקוּ,
וּלְכוּ לְפִי חֶרֶב נְקַם נוֹקֶמֶת.
פִּתְאֹם הֲלֹא יָבוֹא יְדִיד הֵיכָלוֹ,
תִּכּוֹן בְּטוּב כִּסְאוֹ, וּמִתְרוֹמֶמֶת.
מַלְאָךְ וְגַלְגַּל שִׁיר וְהַלֵּל פּוֹצְחִים,
עִם בַּת יְפֵהפִיָּה שֶׁבַח נוֹאֶמֶת.
שָׁאוּ מְלָכִים רוֹזְנִים מִצַּד שְׂמֹאל,
לָהֶם יְמִין הָאֵל תְּהֵא הוֹלֶמֶת.

[The Daughter of Zion:] 'Who kissed me until I fell into a faint, then said to me: "Do not be overwhelmed!" That night I dreamt that I was [back] in the Temple of Love, [under] the canopy of my Beloved's Glory, in my own dwelling. Before the time was due, I longed to sleep in His bosom, to cleanse myself [with prayer] and perfume myself [with incense].'

[The Poet:] 'Oh, then [Moses,] the faithful messenger will lead her [out of exile], and the emblems [of the tribes] will be inscribed upon my banners.[1] My Beloved will come down into the Garden of Nut Trees,[2] He will remember His ancient covenant with the Patriarchs. He will assemble all my kind and righteous tribes, and Israel will rise to greet the dawn in Zion's gates.

'Away, you foreigners, leave [my land], flee before the sword that wreaks vengeance. For the Beloved will come suddenly to His Temple; His throne will rest firmly upon goodness, and [the Daughter of Zion] will be exalted. The angels and the chariot wheels will break into songs of praise as the lovely Daughter hymns His glories. Kings and rulers will be devastated by Divine judgement[3] and smitten by the right hand of the Lord.

1. As they were when Israel marched through the desert (e.g. Numbers 2.2).
2. An epithet for the Land of Israel.
3. Or, 'the potencies of evil'; lit. 'the left side'.

תִּשְׂאִי, יְחִידָתִי, שְׁלוֹמוֹת וְסַגְּלִי
חַיִּים וְרַבִּיתֶם, בְּרֹן מְנֻעֶמֶת.
אֶשַּׁק פְּנֵי חֶבְרַת סְגֻלָּה בַּחֲלוֹם,
בִּכְתָב רְשַׁם שִׁירִי כְּמוֹ חוֹתֶמֶת.

'May peace be yours, my soul, and a long life of piety, singing psalms of joy. Now, in my dream, I kiss the faces of my elect companions with the letters of my song. These shall be for us like a seal [of friendship].'

שָׁמַעְתִּי מִפַּאֲתֵי תֵימָן

SONG FOR CIRCUMCISION

שָׁמַעְתִּי מִפַּאֲתֵי תֵימָן
קוֹל יָדִיד קִיֵּם בְּרִית נֶאֱמָן.

From the far reaches of Yemen I have heard of a friend who fulfilled the steadfast covenant.

לִשְׁכֵנָיו שִׂמַּח בְּרֹב גִּילָה,
הִזְמִינָם לִרְאוֹת בְּרִית מִילָה.
רְפָא, צוּרִי, בֵּן זֶה וְהַצִּילָה,
אַתָּה אֵל מֶלֶךְ וְגַם רַחְמָן.

He gave his neighbours great cause for rejoicing, inviting them to witness the circumcision. My Rock, cure this child and save him; for You are almighty and merciful too.

מִילָתוֹ רֵאשִׁית לְכָל מִצְוָה.
יִתְרַפֵּא, יִזְכֶּה לְרֹב שַׁלְוָה
בְּסוֹד הֶגְיוֹן תּוֹרָה וְגַם חֶדְוָה,
וּמְזוֹנוֹ יָפֶה וְגַם מִשְׁמָן.

This circumcision is his first religious duty. May he recover, and enjoy great peace of mind and pleasure in the study of the Torah's mysteries. May his food be choice and succulent.

שָׁלוֹם לְךָ, נִמּוֹל, כְּמוֹ נָהָר,
וְאָבִיךָ יִזְכֶּה, אֲשֶׁר נִזְהַר
בְּמִילָה מִיּוֹם עֲלוֹת בָּהָר,
יוֹם קִבֵּל מִצְווֹת וְקִיּוּמָן.

O circumcised child, may peace flow over you like a river, and your father will surely be blessed. For he was charged to perform this act the day he vowed to maintain the holy precepts,[1] when Moses ascended Mount Sinai.

1. According to legend, the souls of those who were not yet born were present at the revelation on Mount Sinai.

בְּרִית מִילָה תַּחְלִישׁ לְיֵצֶר רַע,
וְקִלְפָּה שֵׁנִית אֲשֶׁר יִפְרַע,
הִיא זֻהֲמַת נָחָשׁ אֲשֶׁר נִגְרַע.
וְהַמִּילָה לַדָּת תְּהֵא סִימָן. [...]

Circumcision makes the evil impulse wane, and the removal of the foreskin excises the Serpent's foulness.[1] Circumcision is the sign of our faith.

שֶׁפַע טוֹב יוֹסִיף לְזֶה שֶׁמָּל,
וּבְחַיִּים טוֹבִים יְהֵא נִגְמָל.
נָתַן לוֹ מִיּוֹצְרוֹ מַחְמָל,
וּבְחָרוֹ מִיּוֹם אֲשֶׁר זֻמַּן. [...]

May He shower this child with goodness and reward him with a good life. His Creator gives him His love; from the day he is singled out [for circumcision.] He counts him among the chosen.

יוֹסֵף יְדִידְיָה קַרְמִי

Joseph Jedidiah Carmi

אֶהְיֶה אֲשֶׁר אֶהְיֶה

THE MOON-POET

אֶהְיֶה אֲשֶׁר אֶהְיֶה,
הַבֵּט מִשָּׁמַיִם וּרְאֵה:
יָרֵחַ אֲשֶׁר כּוֹנַנְתָּ
וְעַל מְקוֹמוֹ הִתְבּוֹנַנְתָּ –
אֵיךְ חָשַׁךְ מִשְּׁחוֹר תָּאֳרוֹ
וַיְהִי לְאֵבֶל כִּנּוֹרוֹ. [...]

Ehyeh-Asher-Ehyeh,[2] look down from heaven and behold: the moon which You set in place and then looked kindly upon – how its face has turned blacker than soot, and its harp has been tuned to a dirge.

אֲנִי, אֲנִי הוּא הַיָּרֵחַ
אֲשֶׁר מֵאָז אַתָּה, שִׁמְשִׁי, אֲהַבְתַּנִי
וּבְאוֹר פָּנֶיךָ הֵאַרְתַּנִי,
וְעַתָּה חֹשֶׁךְ יְשׁוּפֵנִי

It is I who am this moon! Long ago, O my Sun, You loved me and let Your face shine upon me. But now darkness

1. With which he infected Eve when he mated with her (*T.B. Yebamoth* 103b).
2. A name of God: 'I am that I am', or 'I will Be What I Will Be' (Exodus 3.14).

וְאוֹר לַיְלָה בַּעֲדֵנִי.
וַתֶּרֶב מַשְׂאַת אֲפֵלָתִי
מֵהַמָּאוֹר הַקָּטֹן אֲשֶׁר לְעֻמָּתִי:
כִּי מִדֵּי חֹדֶשׁ בְּחָדְשׁוֹ
הוֹד וְהָדָר לְבוּשׁוֹ;
אַךְ לִי נָפְלוּ פָנַי,
וְנֹחַם יִסָּתֵר מֵעֵינַי
בְּדִינִים מְדִינִים שׁוֹנִים
זֶה לִּי אֶלֶף וַחֲמֵשׁ מֵאוֹת וְעוֹד שָׁנִים.
וּמָה אֹמַר עוֹד, צוּרִי,
אִם לִי יָרֵחַ נֶהְפַּךְ לְחָרִי,
סַהַר לְסָרָה, וּלְבָנָה לִנְבָלָה?
וּלְךָ מִשְׁפַּט הַגְּאֻלָּה.

has stolen over me and night has closed around me. My share of the dark is larger than that of the lesser light, facing me. For month by month, it is newly arrayed in majesty and splendour. But I am always overcast, and compassion is hid from my eyes, scourged by endless punishments, for over one thousand five hundred years! What more can I say, my Rock, since my moon has turned into a moan, my globe into a glob, my crescent to putrescence. But Yours is the right of redemption!

יְהוּדָה אַרְיֵה מוֹדֶנָה

Judah Aryeh Modena

סְלִיחָה לְיוֹם כִּפּוּר קָטָן

SONG FOR THE MINOR DAY OF ATONEMENT

יוֹם זֶה יְהִי מִשְׁקַל כָּל חַטֹּאתַי
בָּטֵל בְּמִעוּטוֹ כִּדְמוּת יָרֵחַ.
הַיּוֹם – לְבַד מִסְפַּר זָכִיּוֹתַי
יִרְבֶּה וְיָצִיץ צִיץ וִיהִי פּוֹרֵחַ.

On this day, may the weight of all my sins dwindle to nothing like the crescent moon. Today, may the sum of my merits alone grow and bud and blossom.

וַדַּאי, זְדוֹן לִבִּי אֶצְלִי גָלוּי,
חוּטֵי עֲווֹנוֹתַי עִם דַּק רִשְׁעִי.
דִּינִי, אֲנִי אֵדַע, בָּאֵשׁ קָלוּי
כִּי רַע וּבִישׁ אָרַגְתִּי אֶל פִּשְׁעִי.
הוֹלֵךְ בְּיוֹם וָיוֹם אַחַר בִּצְעִי,
מִבֵּית מְקוֹם סֵפֶר תִּינוֹק בּוֹרֵחַ.

Oh, I am aware of my insolent heart, my threads of wrong and my web of wickedness. My fate, I know, is to burn by fire, for I have woven evil and wrong-doing into my crime. Day after day, I set my heart on dishonest gain and, like a truant child, I fled from the house of learning.

אָכֵן, בְּחַבְלֵי שָׁוְא עָווֹן מוֹשֵׁךְ
אָחוֹר, לְךָ, אֵלִי, בָּאתִי נִצָּב.
רְפוּאוֹת לְאֶרֶס מַר נָחָשׁ נוֹשֵׁךְ –
שׁוֹאֵל וּמִתְחַנֵּן, נִכְאָב, נֶעְצָב.
יוֹשֵׁב בְּעִנּוּיֵי אֶבֶן מַחְצֵב,
יָד, פֶּה וְעַיִן – אֵין לִי טַעַם, רֵיחַ.

Though iniquity drags me down with cords of falsehood, I have come, my God, to stand before You. Out of my pain and sorrow, I beg a remedy for the bitter venom of the stinging snake.[1] Pent up, tortured, in a cell of hewn rock,[1] hand, mouth, and eye are all deprived of feeling.[2]

הֵן רֹאשׁ חֳדָשִׁים לְעָם נָתַתָּ
לִזְמַן לְכַפֵּר עַל כָּל תּוֹלְדוֹתָם.
מֵאֵת אֲהוּבִים שׂוֹטֵן הִשְׁבַּתָּ,
עַל כֵּן אֲקַדֶּמְךָ בִּתְחִנָּתָם.
מִיּוֹם לְפָנָיו בָּא כִּי אָז אֵיתָם –
אָשׁוּב לְאִישׁ תּוֹשָׁב, לֹא עוֹד אוֹרֵחַ.

You gave the new moon to Your people as a time of atonement through all their generations. [On this day] You rid Your loved ones of the Accuser, and therefore I approach You with their supplications. If I come blameless on the eve of the new moon, I shall dwell in my home again and no longer be a vagrant.

וּבְרֹב חֲסָדֶיךָ אַתָּה, מַלְכִּי,
תָּקוּם־תְּרַחֵם צִיּוֹן קָדְשֵׁנוּ.
דִּירַת מְנוּחָתְךָ שִׂים כָּבוֹד, כִּי
בָהּ נַעֲלֶה עוֹלוֹת רֹאשׁ חָדְשֵׁנוּ.
נָא, אֵל, שְׁלַח נוֹשֵׂא הוֹד רֹאשֵׁנוּ,
כִּי שָׁם לְבָבֵנוּ שׁוֹאֵף זוֹרֵחַ.

And through Your great love, my King, You will arise and have mercy on our holy Zion. You will restore Your glory to Your dwelling, and there we shall present the burnt-offerings of the new month. O God, pray send [the Messiah,] bearer of our royal honour, for it is there, in Zion, that our hearts yearn to shine.

1. Epithets for the Evil Inclination. 2. Lit. 'I have no taste, smell'.

יַעֲקֹב פְרַאנְשֵׁיס

Jacob Frances

קוּם, אַשְׁמְדַאי

TO THE KING OF THE DEMONS

קוּם, אַשְׁמְדַאי! קוּם לְךָ, דְּחוֹף רָצִים
אֶל תָּפְתְּךָ מַהֵר, וּבִמְדִינוֹת
מַלְכוּתְךָ פִּתְגָם שְׁלַח לִקְנוֹת
עִטְרָן וְנֵפְט, גָּפְרִית וְרֹב עֵצִים.

צַוֵּה עֲלֵיהֶם נוֹגְשִׂים אָצִים
לֶאְסֹף צְבָא שֵׁדִים וְלִגְיוֹנוֹת,
כִּי יוֹם עֲבָרוֹת זֶה וְעֵת עַנּוֹת
אִישׁ רַע וְשׂוֹנֵא טוֹב, אֲבִי לֵצִים.

הַצֵּת בְּעֵרָה בּוֹ, וְאַל יֵרַךְ
לִבָּךְ בְּעֵת תִּזְכֹּר אֲשֶׁר אֶתְמוֹל
מִלֵּא נְשָׁמוֹת יַרְכְּתֵי בוֹרָךְ;

עַל צַוְּרוֹנֵי רוֹזְנִים דָּרַךְ
אִישׁ זֶה, וְאִם בּוֹ, אַשְׁמְדַאי, תַּחְמֹל –
מָחָר בְּעַזּוּת יַעֲשֹׁק כִּתְרָךְ.

Up, Asmodeus! Rise up, dispatch urgent couriers to your hell, and issue an edict to all the provinces of your kingdom, commanding them to buy tar, kerosene, brimstone, and logs in plenty.

Set taskmasters over them who will press them to muster legions of demons, for this is the day of wrath, the time to rack an evil man, an enemy of good, an arch-villain.

Scorch him with flames, and do not lose heart when you recall that, only yesterday, he filled the depth of your abyss with souls.

This man trod the necks of princes, and should you show him mercy, Asmodeus, tomorrow he will impudently rob you of your crown.

מִבֵּין עֳפָאיִם

THE TRIUMPH OF WINE

מִבֵּין עֳפָאיִם נִתְּנָה קוֹלוֹת,
רֵעַי, עֲגוּרֵי שִׁיר, דְּרוֹרֵי זֶמֶר,
לִכְבוֹד שְׁנֵי דוֹדִים שְׁכוּרֵי חֶמֶר,
שֶׁחֻבְּרוּ הַיּוֹם לְרֹב גִּילוֹת.

My friends, all you wrynecks of song and swallows of melody, let us sing between the branches, in honour of these two lovers, drunk with wine, who were joined today, most joyfully.

אַחַי, שַׁבְּחֵינוּ וּמַהֲלָלֵינוּ
יִהְיוּ לְיַיִן הַטּוֹב בְּלִי כָל שֶׁמֶר.
נַלְבִּין פְּנֵי חֵשֶׁק כְּהַלְבִּין צֶמֶר:
לֹא עוֹד יְהִי שׁוֹפֵט וְשַׂר עָלֵינוּ,

Brothers, let our praise and acclaim go to the choice wine which has no dregs at all. We shall shame Eros, make him turn as white as wool. No longer will he lord it over us,

כִּי לֹא יְמִינוֹ הֶחֱבִירָה אֵלֶּה —
לִשְׁתּוֹת וְלִשְׁכֹּר יַחְדָּו נִקְשָׁרוּ,
חֵשֶׁק לְאֶפֶס חָשְׁבוּ וּלְאַיִן.

for it was not his right hand that paired them off. They banded together to drink and to be drunk; and as for Eros, they held him in contempt.

אִם כֵּן, בְּקוֹל נָשִׁיר: יְחִי הַיַּיִן!
יָדָיו עֲלֵי הָאַהֲבָה גָּבְרוּ —
נוֹרָא תְהִלּוֹת הוּא וְעוֹשֵׂה פֶלֶא.

Then let me sing lustily: Long live wine! It has triumphed over love. It is worthy of awe and praise. It works wonders!

לוּלֵי יְדַעְתִּיךְ, אַהֲבָה

THE DEFEAT OF EROS

לוּלֵי יְדַעְתִּיךְ, אַהֲבָה, מֵאֶמֶשׁ,
לוּלֵי בְּיָדַי פָּעֳלֵךְ מִשַּׁשְׁתִּי,
לוּלֵי בְּלִבִּי לַהֲבֵךְ הִרְגַּשְׁתִּי,
וּכְשַׁבְּלוּל אֵלֵךְ לְמֵאָז תֶּמֶס;

Love, had I not known you during other nights; had I not fingered your works with my own hands; had I not felt your flame within my heart; had I not melted away, after that, like a snail;

לוּלֵי לְמִיּוֹם אֶחֱזֶה הַשֶּׁמֶשׁ
תָּקְפֵּךְ וּמֶמְשַׁלְתֵּךְ בְּעֵינַי חַשְׁתִּי
בְּמַחֲנֶה הַזֶּה אֲשֶׁר פָּגַשְׁתִּי
מִמִּין אֱנוֹשִׁי עַד בְּעִיר וָרֶמֶשׂ —

had I not sensed with my own eyes, ever since I saw the sunlight, what mastery and power you exercise over all this company which I have met, from man to beast to insect –

הָאַהֲבָה, הַיּוֹם חֲשַׁבְתִּיךְ אַיִן,
תֹּהוּ וְאֶפֶס נֶחְשָׁב לִי חֵשֶׁק,
לָךְ אֶקְרָאָה טָלֶה בְּצוּרַת לַיִשׁ;

Love, I would have considered you today a mere nothing, I would have regarded Eros as naught and emptiness; I would have called you a lamb in lion's clothing.

כִּי אָזְרָה עָפְרָה לְנֶגְדּוֹ זַיִן,
לִבָּהּ לְבוּשׁ שִׁרְיוֹן לְמוּל כָּל נֶשֶׁק.
חִצָּיו בְּחֵיקָהּ שַׁעֲוָה עַל שַׁיִשׁ.

For the maiden armed herself and stood up to Eros, with a heart like a coat of mail that withstands all weapons; and his arrows dropped onto her bosom like wax onto marble.

חַסְדֵי שְׁנָתִי

THE LOVER RECANTS

חַסְדֵי שְׁנָתִי, אוֹהֲבַי, אַזְכִּירָה
עַל כִּי צְבִיָּה בַּחֲלוֹם הֶרְאַתְנִי.
לֹא אֵדְעָה נַפְשִׁי – וְאֵיךְ שַׂמַתְנִי
נָאוֹר, וְאֵיךְ תּוֹךְ מַאֲפֵל הֵאִירָה!

Friends, let me praise the goodness of my sleep, for in a dream it showed me my beloved. I still cannot understand it: how she filled me with light; how she shone in the darkness!

חַסְדָּהּ גְּבִרְתִּי בֶּאֱמֶת הִגְבִּירָה
עָלַי בְּחֶזְיוֹנָהּ אֲשֶׁר חִיַּתְנִי;
אָמְנָם בְּעֵת הָקִיץ הֲלֹא הֶלְאַתְנִי –
מִי יִתְּנֵנִי אָז וְלֹא אָעִירָה!

Truly, my mistress showered me with goodness, when, with this vision, she brought me back to life. But when I am awake, she does nothing but wear me out. If only I could sleep and never wake!

יָשׁוּב חֲלוֹמִי נָא וְיַחְלִימֵנִי,
אָז לַתְּנוּמָה אֶקְרָאָה 'שָׂרָתִי',
כִּי הִיא תְּחַיֵּנִי וְתַחְלִימֵנִי.

May my dream return and make me dream again. Then shall I call slumber 'my queen', for it is she who gives me life and heals me.[1]

אוֹדֶה עֲלֵי פִשְׁעִי אֲשֶׁר חָטָאתִי,
גַּם כָּל תְּבוּנָה נִדְּחָה מִמֶּנִּי,
יוֹם לָהּ 'דְּמוּת הַמָּוְתָה' קָרָאתִי.

I confess that I sinned against her and that all wisdom abandoned me the day I named her 'death's image'.

1. A play on the root *ḥalom*, which means both 'to dream' and 'to heal'.

הַרְפּוּ, מְלִיצִים

הַרְפּוּ, מְלִיצִים, מִזְּמִיר הַרְפּוּ!
סָחוּב, הַשְׁלֵךְ כָּל עֱטֵיכֶם לַזֶּבֶל!
פּוּ, פּוּ עֲלֵיכֶם, פּוּ וְאֶלֶף פּוּ!
רַב שְׁבַרְתֶּם רֹאשִׁי בִּמְלִיצוֹת הֶבֶל.
עֵת תִּשְׁמְעוּ מִלַּי, אֲשֶׁר צֻפּוּ
זָהָב, מִקִּנְאָה תִּתָּלוּ בְּחֶבֶל.
אָז תּוֹדוּ, כִּי אֵין לִי וּלְשִׂכְלִי רֵעַ,
גַּם נַעֲלִי מִכֻּלְּכֶם יוֹדֵעַ.

אֹמַר עֲלֵי דוֹד זֶה אֲשֶׁר הוּא גֶּבֶר
בַּכֹּל: פָּנָיו חַמָּה בִּלְתִּי לְקוּת.
יֶשׁ לוֹ יַהֲדוּת רַב, וְיַעַל אֵבֶר
לָעוּף לְדְבַר מִצְוָה עַד קָלִיקוּת.
חָכָם מְחֻכָּם הוּא, וְיֵט אֶל עֵבֶר
הַשִּׁיר מֹחוֹ – אָכֵן לֹא מֵרֵיקוּת.
תַּכְלִית דְּבָרִים: הוּא לְכָל בִּין אָב,
אִישׁ טוֹב, אִישׁ תָּם, אִישׁ מִשְׁקָלוֹ זָהָב.

עֲפְרָה יִרְאַת אֵל וּכְמַלְאָךְ יָפָה,
טוֹבָה כְּפַת טוֹב, אֵין בְּלִבָּהּ כַּעַשׂ.
הָיוּ סִבְלוֹת הַבַּיִת עַל כְּתֵפָהּ,
לֹא תֶחֱזֶה דָּבָר אֲשֶׁר לֹא תַעַשׂ.
לֹא אֵדַע, אֵיךְ תָּלִין עִם אַלּוּפָהּ –
הִיא מֵאֱנוֹשׁ תִּרְעַשׁ, כְּמִשֵּׁד, רַעַשׁ.
יַחְסִין רָמִים הִיא גַּם דּוֹד יַחֲסוּ,
שָׁוִים כְּאִלּוּ בִּדְפוּס נִדְפָּסוּ. [...]

FOR HIS BROTHER'S MARRIAGE

Leave off, you poetasters, leave off your singing! All your pens should be dragged along and flung on a dung heap! Pooh, pooh to you, pooh and a thousand poohs! Enough! You have already broken my head with your empty rhetoric. When you hear my words, words coated with gold, you will take a rope and hang yourselves out of envy. Then you will concede that my wit and I are beyond compare. Even my shoe knows more than all of you put together.

Let me now proclaim that this lover is, in all things, a real man: his face is like a sun untouched by eclipse; he is God-fearing and devout, and for the sake of a good deed would grow wings and fly as far as Calicut.[1] He is wise beyond the wisest, and his mind – but, mark you, not out of emptiness – has given itself to poetry. In short: he is the father of all insight, a good man, a mild man, a man worth his weight in gold.

His bride is pious, beautiful as an angel, wholesome as a good loaf of bread, her heart free of vexation. She shoulders all the household cares and never overlooks a chore. I cannot imagine how she manages to sleep with her dear friend, for she quakes at the mere sight of humans as if they were demons. Both she and her beloved are of noble stock, both equal in rank, as if cast from the same mould.

1. A port-town in South West India, on the shores of the Arabian Sea.

נִשְׁאָר הַטּוֹב מִכֹּל – אֹזֶן הַטּוּ:
נִשְׁאַל מְשִׁיחֵנוּ אֲשֶׁר נוֹחִילָה.
הַלְוַאי מַהֵר יָבוֹא, גַּם לֹא יַשְׁטוּ
בָּנוּ לְאֻמִּים עוֹד, וְעֹז נַגְדִּילָה,
עֵת יָבוֹא אֵלִיָּה עִם קוֹל טוּ טוּ.
שִׁירוּ, אֲדוֹנִים, אֵיךְ וְאֵיךְ נָגִילָה!
אָז מִי יְהִי רֹאשׁ, מִי יְרוֹמֵם דֶּגֶל,
מִי עַל סוּס יָרוּץ אֹרַח – מִי בָּרֶגֶל? [...]

Now for the best of all – lend me your ears: we shall ask for our Messiah, on whom we fix our hopes. If only he came quickly, the nations would no more deride us. We shall grow in might when Elijah appears to the sound of 'Toot! Toot!' Sing, gentlemen! How happy we shall be! Who then will be the leader, who will raise the flag aloft, who will gallop on a horse – and who will go afoot?

לָקֹב זֶה תִּשְׂאוּ קוֹל – אַךְ לַגַּגּוֹת,
כִּי קוֹל חֲמוֹרִים לִזְבוּל לֹא יַעַל.
תִּרְאוּ רֹב טָעֻיּוֹת בּוֹ וּמְשׁוּגוֹת,
אַךְ שִׁירְכֶם לֹא טוֹב לְחָלְצוֹ נָעַל.
מָתַי אַעַשׁ מֵחָטְמֵיכֶם עוּגוֹת,
לֵצִים, וְאֶטַּע עַל פְּנֵיכֶם שַׁעַל?
אָז, אָז בְּשֶׁבַח הַסְּחִי תָּמִירוּ,
לִקְרַאת שִׁירֵי הַכּוֹבָעִים תָּסִירוּ!

(1656)

You raise your voices to denounce my song, but they go no higher than the roof, for the voice of an ass cannot mount to heaven. You find many a fault and flaw in my song, but yours is not fit to wipe its shoes. Buffoons! When shall I knead your noses into cakes, and plant my foot on your faces! Then your words of slander will give way to praise, and you will take off your hats to my songs!

אַהֲבָה לִתְמוּנָה

LOVE FOR A PORTRAIT

א

אֵיךְ אֶעֱשֶׂה, דּוֹד, מִפְּנֵי הַחֵשֶׁק?
חִצּוֹ, אֲשֶׁר יָרָה בְּיָד מַרְשַׁעַת,
חָלַף לְבָבִי כַּחֲלֹף דְּלַעַת,
חִנָּם, בְּלִי הִתְעַשְּׁקִי בּוֹ עֵשֶׁק!

A

What can I do, my friend, in the face of Eros? The arrow which he let fly with a malicious hand pierced my heart as if it were a pumpkin – and all for no reason, without my having provoked him!

מִי הֶאֱמִין, כִּי הֶחְבִּיא הַנֶּשֶׁק
בִּדְמוּת צְבָעִים בָּרְחוֹב מוּקַעַת?
סוֹף סוֹף, צְעִיר יָמִים וְנֶעְדַּר דַּעַת,
גַּם כִּי בְּבֵית הָאַהֲבָה בֶּן מֶשֶׁק!

Who would have believed that he would hide his arms in a coloured figure, hanging on display in the street? After all, he is no more than a young, ignorant boy, although he is in charge of Love's household.

עֵת אֹמְרָה אֵלָיו בְּאַף וָזַעַם:
׳כִּסְדֹם תִּהְיֶ, חֵשֶׁק, וְכַעֲדַת קֹרַח!
לָמָּה תְּהַתֵּל בִּי בְּאַהֲבַת רוּחַ?׳

When I say to him in grim anger:
'Eros, may you be [overturned] like Sodom and [swallowed up] like Korah's crowd![1] Why do you mock me with a futile love?' –

עוֹנֶה לְבָבִי: ׳הוֹי מְשֻׁגָּע טְעַם!
הַמְעַט אֲשֶׁר תִּסְבֹּל כְּבֵדוּת טֹרַח
אִשָּׁה מְצֻיֶּרֶת עֲלֵי הַלּוּחַ?׳

then my heart speaks up: 'O you lunatic! Isn't it enough for you to bear the heavy burden of a woman who is painted on a canvas?'

ב

B

לוּחַ, אֱמֹר, מַה זֶּה אֲשֶׁר עַל לוּחַ
לִבִּי לְפֶתַע אוֹתְךָ חָקַקְתִּי?
מֵאָז רְאִיתִיךָ בְּךָ חָשַׁקְתִּי,
לֹא אֶשְׁקֳטָה, אוֹי לִי, וְלֹא אָנוּחַ.

Tell me, tableau, why have I suddenly engraved you on the tablets of my heart? I have desired you from the moment I saw you. Woe is me! I have had no peace of mind, no rest.

מַה זֶּה וְעַל מַה זֶּה יְהִי קִלּוּחַ
עֵינַי, וְכִמְעַט בִּבְכִי נֶחֱנַקְתִּי?
אֵיךְ מְשׂוֹשׂ לִבִּי לְרִיק הוּרַקְתִּי?
לָךְ אֶשְׁפְּכָה רוּחִי – וְאֵין בָּךְ רוּחַ.

Why, oh why have my eyes been streaming until I nearly choke on my tears? How did it come about that my heart's joy was emptied out in vain? I pour out my life before you, though you are lifeless.

בִּשְׁלַל צְבָעִים בַּעֲדֵךְ נִשְׁלַלְתִּי
מִיּוֹם אֲשֶׁר מֻעְתָּק בְּךָ רָאִיתִי
תַּבְנִית יְפִי עָפְרָה, וְאָז הִסְכַּלְתִּי –

With your ravishing colours you carried me away the day I saw that shape of girlish beauty traced upon you; it was then that I turned into a fool

וָאֹמְרָה: ׳הַלְוַאי אֲשֶׁר הָיִיתִי
חֹמֶר לְצוּרָה זֹאת, וּבָהּ נִפְתַּלְתִּי,
גַּם כִּי צְנוּעָה הִיא, וּבָהּ חָסִיתִי!׳

and said: 'Oh, if only I could serve as matter to this form, and be enmeshed in her; though she be chaste, I would take cover in her!'

1. Who were swallowed up by the earth (Numbers 17.31 ff).

עֵת אֶזְכְּרָה יוֹם

DEATH AND THE LOVER

עֵת אֶזְכְּרָה יוֹם, כִּי כְּאֵשׁ בּוֹעֶרֶת
הָיָה לְחִי עָפְרָה וּמַר צָעָקָה ;
עֵת אֶזְכְּרָה יוֹם, כַּף לְכַף דָּפָקָה ;
פִּיהָ לְפִי מֵת הָיְתָה נִקְשֶׁרֶת,

When I recall the day her cheek was like a blazing fire and she cried out most bitterly; when I recall the day she beat her hands together, and her mouth was clinging to the dead man's mouth,

עֵת כִּי לְהַפְרִידָהּ בְּיָד גּוֹרֶרֶת
רָצוּ בְּנוֹת הַחֵן, וְשֵׁן חָרָקָה ;
נֶגֶד רְצוֹן כֹּל בַּעְלָהּ נָשָׁקָה
עִם צוּף שְׂפָתֶיהָ, וְאֵין עוֹצֶרֶת –

and when the good ladies tried to tear her away by force, she ground her teeth; defying one and all, she kissed her husband with her honeyed lips, and none could stop her –

עַל כָּל תְּשׁוּקוֹתַי אֲנִי תָאַבְתִּי
כִּי יוֹם פְּקֻדָּתִי וְיוֹם צַלְמָוֶת
שֶׁמֶשׁ נְשִׁיקָתָהּ בְּפִי יַזְרִיחַ,

then, with a passion exceeding all my passions, I long for her kiss's sun to shine in my mouth, on my day of reckoning and deep shadows,

וָאֹמְרָה : 'קִרְבִי !' וְאִם חָשַׁבְתִּי
לִטְעֹם שְׂפָתֶיהָ בְּיוֹם הַמָּוֶת,
אוֹחִיל לְיוֹם מוֹתִי כְּמוֹ מָשִׁיחַ.

and I shall say: 'Come close!' And if I thought I might taste her lips the day I die, I should long for the day of my death as if for the Messiah.

דּוֹד, מַרְאָה נוֹרָאָה

ON TURNING GREY IN A DREAM

דּוֹד, מַרְאָה נוֹרָאָה אֶתְמוֹל הָרְאֵיתִי,
וָאֶפֹּל עַל פָּנַי פִּתְאֹם מִפַּחַד.
פָּנַי וִיחִידָתִי נָפְלוּ בִי יַחַד,
וָאֹמַר תּוֹךְ קִרְבִּי : 'אוֹי לִי, נִדְמֵיתִי !'

Friend, yesterday I was shown a terrible vision; terrified, I immediately flung myself to the ground. My face and my soul were both cast down, and I said deep within me: 'Alas, I am lost.'

דּוֹד, בַּמַּרְאָה הַזֹּאת קִצִּי נִבֵּאתִי –
הָהּ, כִּי מָוֶת עָלַי פִּי חַרְבּוֹ יַחַד.

Friend, in this vision my end was prophesied. Death is sharpening the blade of his sword against me. With

אִם עַל שַׁעְרִי שׁוֹקֵד קָרוֹב הַכַּחַד,
אוֹי, אֵיךְ אֶבְרַח אִם בִּשְׂעָרִי הוּבֵאתִי?

doom prowling at my gate,[1] how can I escape when I am being dragged by my hair?

הַעַל שֶׁצַּמָּתִי גֵּאוּת לָבַשְׁתִּי
כִּי נִתְלוּ בָהּ חַיַּי כִּתְלוּיֵי חֶבֶל,
וּכְאַבְשָׁלוֹם בִּשְׂעַר רֹאשִׁי נִתְפַּשְׂתִּי?

Is it because I took pride in my locks that my life now hangs from them as one hangs from a halter and, like Absalom, I am held fast by my hair?

צָחֹר, לֹא עוֹד שָׁחֹר, יִהְיֶה אוֹת אֵבֶל:
עַד כֹּה בַּקַּדְרוּת גִּיל בַּלֵּב הִרְגַּשְׁתִּי,
וּבְלֹבֶן זֶה הַיּוֹם אַרְגִּישָׁה חֶבֶל.

White, not black, shall henceforth be the sign of mourning. Before, it was blackness that made my heart rejoice, but now it is this whiteness that makes me feel the noose.

עִמָּנוּאֵל פְרַאנְשֵׁיס

Immanuel Frances

עֵת אֶחֱזֶה חַנָּה

THE DILEMMA

עֵת אֶחֱזֶה חַנָּה בְּאוֹר זוֹרֵחַ,
עֵת נָעֳמִי אַזְכִּיר כְּלִיל תִּפְאֶרֶת –
נַפְשִׁי בְּעַד חַנָּה הֲכִי בוֹעֶרֶת,
וּלְנָעֳמִי רוּחִי כְּאֵשׁ קוֹדֵחַ!

When I see Hannah in full light, when I remember Naomi, perfect in splendour – my soul is aflame for Hannah, my spirit is kindled for Naomi.

תְּשְׁתֵּי סְעִפִּים הִנְנִי פוֹסֵחַ:
חַנָּה כְּהַיּוֹם בִּי תְּהִי לִגְבֶרֶת,
גַּם נָעֳמִי בִּי מִתְּמוֹל שׂוֹרֶרֶת.
אָן, אַהֲבָה, מִמֵּךְ אֱהִי בוֹרֵחַ?

Here I am, sitting on the fence: Hannah, as of today, is my mistress; but Naomi has been reigning over me since yesterday. O Love, whither can I flee from your presence?

1. The author punctuated this word so that it can be read to mean 'my gate' (*sha'ri*) as well as 'my hair' (*sa'ri*).

הָהּ, כִּי כְּמוֹ בַרְזֶל בְּבַרְזֶל יַחַד,
חֵשֶׁק בְּחֵשֶׁק חֻדְּדוּ כִּפְלַיִם,
עַל כֵּן סְעִפַּי פָּחֲדוּ שָׁם פָּחַד.

Alas, as iron sharpens iron, so has desire twice sharpened desire. That is why my thoughts are so alarmed.

לָךְ, אַהֲבָה, אֹמַר פְּרוּשׂ כַּפַּיִם:
אוֹ לִי שְׁנֵי לְבּוֹת תְּנִי גַּם יַחַד,
אוֹ אֶת לְבָבִי בַּתְּרִי לִשְׁנַיִם!

Love, I pray you with outspread hands: Either give me two hearts together, or else split my one heart in two!

עֵינֵי צְבִיָּה

HER EYES

עֵינֵי צְבִיָּה הֵם שְׁמֵי הָאַהֲבָה,
בָּם מַעֲטֶה אוֹרָה וְזִיו לוֹבֶשֶׁת.
גַּם אִם עֲלֵיהֶם שָׂם עֲנָנָיו הַבְּכִי –
אַל נָא, יְדִידִים, תִּירְאוּ מִגֶּשֶׁת.
אַל תִּירְאוּ מֵהֶם וּמֵימֵיהֶם, הֲכִי
עַל כֵּן עֲלֵיהֶם נִרְאֲתָה הַקֶּשֶׁת.

The girl's eyes are the heavens of love, a robe of light and splendour in which she clothes herself. Even when they are hidden by clouds of tears, lovers, do not be afraid to come near. Do not fear them or their torrents, for the bow[1] has already appeared above them.

שִׁמְעִי, כְּלִילַת הוֹד

THE INNKEEPER'S LOVE SONG

שִׁמְעִי, כְּלִילַת הוֹד וְחֵן בִּמְאֹד,
אֶל צַעֲקַת פַּפּוֹס וְרִנָּתוֹ!
גּוֹעֶה כְּמוֹ שׁוֹר, כַּחֲמוֹר נוֹעֵר
לָךְ, כִּי אֲתוֹנוֹ אַתְּ וּפָרָתוֹ.
לִבּוֹ כְּבָר קָלִי, וְכִצְלִי
בְּשִׁפּוּד אֲהָבִים הוּא וְלַבָּתוֹ.

O you paragon of glory and grace, listen to the call of Papos and his cry! He is bellowing like a bull, braying at you like a donkey, for you are his cow and his she-ass. His heart is already parched like grain, he and his passion are impaled on love's spit like a roast.

1. I.e. the eyebrows. The 'bow in the clouds' is the sign that the flood will never recur (Genesis 9.12 ff).

הִשְׁקִפִי, עָפְרָה, בְּעַד אֶשְׁנָב
וּרְאִי בְּצוּרָתוֹ וְתַבְנִיתוֹ:
כִּי נָפְלוּ פָנָיו וּמַעְיָנָיו,
לֹא פָסְקוּ בִּכְיוֹ וְדִמְעָתוֹ,
קֶרַח בְּקָרַחְתּוֹ וְגַבַּחְתּוֹ
הֻשְׁלַךְ, וְטַל נִמְלָא קְוֻצָּתוֹ.
דּוֹמֶה אֱלֵי חָתוּל אֲשֶׁר עַל גַּג
בּוֹדֵד וְיִתְמוֹגֵג בְּרָעָתוֹ,
קוֹרֵא נְהִי נִהְיָה בְּקוֹל מָרָה,
יַעַן עֲרָפֶל שָׂם חֲתוּלָתוֹ.

Look through your lattice, gazelle, and observe his sorry figure: his face has fallen and so have his thoughts; no end to his crying and tears; flecks of ice are scattered on his bald pate, and his locks are drenched with dew. He is like a lonely tomcat on a roof, melting away in distress, wailing bitter lamentations, for his mistress[1] is swaddled in mist.

אֵי סוֹחֲרִים

THE OLD WHORE'S LAMENT

אֵי סוֹחֲרִים הַשּׁוֹחֲרִים אוֹתִי
לִקְנוֹת יְדִידוּתִי? זְמַן שׂוֹנֵא!
כִּי בָחֲלוּ הַיּוֹם בְּחֶבְרָתִי,
כִּי אֶקְרְאָה אוֹתָם, וְאֵין עוֹנֶה!
אֵיךְ הָיְתָה לָבַז סְחֹרָתִי,
אֵיךְ אֶמְכְּרֶנָּה, אֵיךְ, וְאֵין קוֹנֶה.
אָז בַּעֲדָהּ לִי יִתְּנוּ הוֹנָם,
הַלְוַאי כְּהַיּוֹם יִלְקְחוּ חִנָּם.

Where are the merchants who used to chase after me to purchase my favours? O malevolent Time! Nowadays, they abhor my company; when I call for them, there is no answer. How has my merchandise been brought so low! How can I possibly sell it, when there is no buyer? Once they would have given all their wealth for it. Now I would be lucky if they took it free of charge.

לְבַד שָׁלוֹשׁ יְצִיאוֹת

TO HIS GADABOUT WIFE

לְבַד שָׁלוֹשׁ יְצִיאוֹת הֵן רְאוּיוֹת
לְכָל אִשָּׁה, קְטַנָּה אוֹ גְדוֹלָה:
וְאַחַת הִיא בְּהִוָּלְדָהּ וְצֵאתָהּ

Only three exits are becoming to every woman, big or small. The first is when

1. A play on *ḥatulato* which in Job 38.9 means 'his swaddling clothes' but can also mean 'his she-cat'.

מְלֻכְלֶכֶת כְּמוֹ מִיוֵן מְצוּלָה;
וְהַשֵּׁנִית בְּצֵאת מִבֵּית נְוָתָהּ
וְהוֹלֶכֶת לְבֵית חָתָן וּבַעְלָהּ;
וְיוֹם תּוּבַל לְקֶבֶר הַשְּׁלִישִׁית –
וּמִכָּל הַיְצִיאוֹת זאת מְעֻלָּה.

she exits from the womb, dirtied, as if from a deep swamp. The second is when she exits from her woman's tent and enters the home of her husband and lord. And the third is the day she is led to her grave. This is the finest exit of all.

צִיּוּנֵי־קֶבֶר

EPITAPHS

לאשה

גַּל זֶה לְמַשָּׂא, לֹא לְמַצֵּבָה,
שַׂמְתִּי לְאִשְׁתִּי עַל קְבוּרָתָהּ,
פֶּן, חַס וְשָׁלוֹם, אַחֲרֵי מוֹתָהּ
תָּקוּם וְאֶל בֵּיתִי תְּהִי שָׁבָה.

For A Wife

I have set this stone as a weight, not as a memorial, over my wife's grave, lest (God forbid!) she rise from the dead and come back home.

לננס

צִיּוּן זֶה אֶל אָדָם נַנָּס
בָּזֶה הוּבָא לִקְבוּרָתוֹ,
וּבְבַת אַחַת, עֵת פֹּה נִכְנַס,
תּוֹלָע אֶחָד בָּלַע אוֹתוֹ.

For A Dwarf

This inscription is for a dwarf: he was buried in this plot, but as soon as he settled in, a worm gobbled him up.

לגבן ובשמו

לֹא דֵי לְךָ, מַזָּל, אֲשֶׁר הָיִיתִי
נוֹשֵׂא חֲטוֹטֶרֶת בְּעוֹד חָיִיתִי,
כִּי אַחֲרֵי מוֹתִי לְאוֹיֵב קַמְתָּ
עָלַי, וְאֶבֶן זאת בְּגַבִּי שַׂמְתָּ?

For A Hunchback

'O Fortune, weren't you content to make me bear a hump as long as I lived? Did you have to rise against me after my death and stick this slab on my back?'

לאיש כסיל ורגזן

פֹּה אִישׁ חֲסַר דֵּעָה וּמִתְעַבֵּר.
כִּמְטַחֲוֵי קֶשֶׁת רַחֵק, עוֹבֵר,
פֶּן, בַּחֲרוֹן אַפּוֹ, בְּאֶבֶן זֹאת
אֶת רֹאשְׁךָ הַיּוֹם יְהִי שׁוֹבֵר.

For An Angry Fool

Here lies a witless and irascible man. Passerby, keep a safe distance, for in his fury, with this very stone, he might now smash your head.

לבעל חטם גדול

לָמָּה צִיּוּן הַלָּז בָּנוּ עַל גֶּבֶר
מִכָּל אַנְשֵׁי דוֹרוֹ אֶרֶךְ אַפַּיִם ?
כִּי הָיָה לוֹ צִיּוּן גָּדוֹל כִּפְלַיִם
אִלּוּ נִשְׁאַר חָטְמוֹ מִחוּץ לַקֶּבֶר !

For A Big-Nosed Man

Why have they erected this monument over a man who was the most long-suffering[1] of his generation? He would have had a monument twice as big had his nose remained outside the tomb!

אֶפְרַיִם לוּצָּאטוֹ

Ephraim Luzzato

מִי אָנֹכִי וּמִי בֵיתִי

OF MYSELF

אַרְצִי הַנִּשְׁקָפָה — הִנֵּה נְכוֹנָה
עַל רֹאשׁ גִּבְעָה רָמָה רַבַּת יָדַיִם.
בֵּיתִי בִּרְחוֹבָהּ הוּא כִּדְמוּת הַרְמוֹנָה,
לוּצָּאטוֹ מִשְׁפַּחְתִּי וּשְׁמִי אֶפְרַיִם.

שָׁם אָנֹכִי עַל רֹב שָׁלוֹם אֶשְׁכֹּנָה,
שָׁם לִי נָטַעְתִּי גַּן עַל עֵין הַמַּיִם,
וּבְנוֹת הַשִּׁיר עַל הַשָּׂפָה תָּרֹנָּה
מִשְׁלֵי דוֹדִים יוֹם יוֹם בֵּין הָעַרְבַּיִם.

My land,[2] spread out before my eyes, is set securely on a high and spacious hill. On a street there is my house, grand as a palace. Luzzato is my family, and my given name is Ephraim.

There do I dwell in untold peace. There have I planted my own garden by a spring. And on its banks, every day at dusk, the songbirds[3] sing lovers' tales.

1. The Hebrew idiom literally means 'long-nosed'.
2. 'That is, San Daniele, a pleasant land in the duchy of Friuli.' [Author's note]
3. Or, 'daughters of song'.

הִנֵּה, אָמְנָה, אַף כִּי עוֹדֶנִּי יֶלֶד,
אֵין כָּל דָּבָר כִּי עַל רוּחִי אוֹת יַעַשׂ,
קִנְאָה אֵין בִּלְבָבִי, אַף אֵין בִּי כַּעַשׂ.

And so, though I am still a youth, nothing can mar my peace of mind. There is no envy in my heart, nor is there anger.

אַף כִּמְצַחֵק אֶל מוּל קוֹרוֹת הַחֶלֶד,
לֹא עֹשֶׁר אֶתְאַוֶּה, לֹא אִירָא עֹנִי.
מִי זֶה הָאִישׁ, אֵפוֹא, אֲשֶׁר כָּמוֹנִי?

And what is more, mocking the world's affairs, I do not desire riches, I am not afraid of want. Is there any man as fortunate as I?

עוּרָה, אָדוֹן דָּוֶה

KIDNEY SONNET

דברים נחומים אל החכם הנעלה כמוהר"ר יעקב חי חפץ מ"ץ בק"ק גוריציאה, בחלותו בכאב הכליות כי השקט לא יוכל ויגרשו מימיו רפש וטיט, וכל קהל ישראל עומד בית י"י ביום צום להפיל תחנה לישועתה לו, ותחל רוח י"י לפעמו והוציא את האבן הראשה ברב חיל:

Words of comfort addressed to the sublime sage, our honoured Master and Mentor, Jacob Ḥai Ḥefetz, Teacher of Righteousness in the Holy Community of Gorizia, who contracted a kidney malady. He was unable to rest, and his troubled waters cast up mud and filth, and the whole congregation of Israel gathered in the House of God to hold a day of fasting and to beseech Him for help. Then the spirit of the Lord began to stir him and he forcibly brought forth the top stone.

עוּרָה, אָדוֹן דָּוֶה, וּרְאֵה כִּי מַיִם
יַזֶּה הָעָם הַזֶּה דּוּמָם כָּאֶבֶן,
וּלְשֶׁבֶר אַנְחָתָם נֶעֶרְמוּ מַיִם,
כָּפִיס מֵעֵץ תִּצְעַק, מִקִּיר – הָאֶבֶן.

Arise, afflicted master, see how this people, silent as a stone, is here shedding water. At their groans of distress the waters of the sea pile up. Beams cry out from the woodwork, and stones from the wall.

אַתָּה עַתָּה, כַּבִּיר, הַשֵּׁף הַמַּיִם,
וּבְנַחַת וּרְוָחָה הוֹצֵא הָאֶבֶן;
וּלְבַב הַנִּצָּבִים נָמֵס כַּמַּיִם –
אַל נָא יֵרַךְ לִבְּךָ חָזָק מֵאֶבֶן.

Now, mighty one, give forth a torrent of water and – gently, easily – discharge the stone. The hearts of those about you are melting, flowing away like water. But you, do not lose heart, for yours is stronger than stone.

הָאֵל חַנּוּן, הַהוּא, כִּי נַחַל מַיִם
אָז בִּישִׁימוֹן מִדְבָּר הִזִּיל מֵאֶבֶן,
מִמַּעַיְנֵי יִשְׁעוֹ יָרִיק לָךְ מַיִם.

The merciful God, who once made streams of water run from a rock in the wilderness, will now draw out water for you from His springs of deliverance.

הֵן עוֹד מִפִּי הַבּוֹר תָּסִיר הָאֶבֶן,
עוֹד כְּמִשְׁפָּט רִאשׁוֹן תַּשְׁקֵנוּ מַיִם –
עַד כִּי בָּהָר הַטּוֹב יְוֻסַּד אֶבֶן.

Surely you will yet remove the stone from the mouth of the well. You will give us waters [of wisdom] to drink, as you did in former days – until the cornerstone is laid on the good Mountain.

עַל הָרוֹפֵא הַנּוֹפֵל שָׁדוּד בְּרֶשֶׁת הָאַהֲבָה

THE DOCTOR WHO FELL PREY TO LOVE

יַלְדָּה יָפָה אַחַת וּמְאֹד אוֹהֶבֶת
בָּאָה בֵּיתָה רוֹפֵא מָזוֹר לָקַחַת,
לֵאמֹר: כִּי זֶה יָמִים נַפְשָׁהּ כּוֹאֶבֶת,
אַף בַּלֵּילוֹת רָחַק מִמֶּנָּה נַחַת.

A beautiful girl, very much in love, came to the doctor's house, seeking a cure. These many days, she said, her soul had been in pain and even at night peace had eluded her.

עוֹד הַשֵּׁגָל הַזֹּאת אֶצְלוֹ נִצֶּבֶת,
שָׁלַח יָדוֹ לַחְקֹר אִם יֵשׁ קַדַּחַת;
וַתִּצַּת בִּלְבָבוֹ פִּתְאֹם שַׁלְהֶבֶת –
אָהַב, נִלְכַּד גַּם הוּא אֶל תּוֹךְ הַפַּחַת.

Now, as this queenly girl stood beside him, he put his hand out to discover if she had a fever. And, suddenly, a flame was kindled in his heart. He, too, fell in love, and into the pit.

נִדְהָם אַף מִשְׁתָּאֶה הָיָה הַגֶּבֶר,
עַד הַחוֹלָה שֵׁנִית הֵטִיבָה טַעַם:
'בִּי, הָאָדוֹן, הַאֵין מַרְפֵּא לַשֶּׁבֶר?'

The gentleman was overcome and dumbstruck, until the patient again spoke up discreetly: 'Please, sir, is there no cure for my complaint?'

אָז הוּא: 'הָהּ רַעְיָתִי, אַל נָא תַחְשְׂכִי!
חִבְשִׁי אַתְּ אֶת פִּצְעִי, אָמְנָם הַפַּעַם
לֹא הָרוֹפֵא, אַךְ הַחוֹלֶה אָנֹכִי.'

Then he: 'O my dearest, do not hold back! *You* dress *my* wound, for this once – I am not the doctor, but the patient.'

PART THREE

MODERN TIMES

חַיִּים נַחְמָן בְּיַאלִיק

עִם דִּמְדּוּמֵי הַחַמָּה

עִם דִּמְדּוּמֵי הַחַמָּה אֶל־הַחַלּוֹן נָא־גֹשִׁי
וְעָלַי הִתְרַפָּקִי,
לְפִתִי הֵיטֵב צַוָּארִי, שִׂימִי רֹאשֵׁךְ עַל־רֹאשִׁי –
וְכֹה עִמִּי תִדְבָּקִי.

וּמְחֻשָּׁקִים וּדְבֵקִים, אֶל־הַזֹּהַר הַנּוֹרָא
דּוּמָם נִשָּׂא עֵינֵינוּ;
וְשִׁלַּחְנוּ לַחָפְשִׁי עַל־פְּנֵי יַמֵּי הָאוֹרָה
כָּל־הִרְהוּרֵי לִבֵּנוּ.

וְהִתְנַשְּׂאוּ לַמָּרוֹם בִּיעָף שׁוֹקֵק כַּיּוֹנִים,
וּבַמֶּרְחָק יַפְלִיגוּ, יֹאבֵדוּ;
וְעַל־פְּנֵי רִכְסֵי אַרְגָּמָן, אִיֵּי־זֹהַר אַדְמוֹנִים,
בִּיעָף דּוּמָם יֵרֵדוּ.

הֵם הָאִיִּים הָרְחוֹקִים, הָעוֹלָמוֹת הַגְּבֹהִים
זוּ בַחֲלוֹמוֹת רְאִינוּם;
שֶׁעָשׂוּנוּ לְגֵרִים תַּחַת כָּל־הַשָּׁמַיִם,
וְחַיֵּינוּ – לְגֵיהִנֹּם.

הֵמָּה אִיֵּי־הַזָּהָב זוּ צָמֵאנוּ אֲלֵיהֶם
כְּאֶל אֶרֶץ מוֹלֶדֶת;
שֶׁכָּל־כּוֹכְבֵי הַלַּיִל רָמְזוּ לָנוּ עֲלֵיהֶם
בְּאוֹר קֶרֶן רוֹעֶדֶת.

Ḥayim Naḥman Bialik

AT TWILIGHT

At twilight, come over to the window and lean upon me. Put your arms round my neck, rest your head on mine – and hold fast to me.

Thus joined and fastened, we shall silently lift our eyes to the terrible splendour. We shall let all our fantasies go free, to roam upon the seas of light.

They will soar to the heights rustling like doves, and sail along into the distance and vanish. There, upon the purple mountain ridges, the roseate islands of splendour, they will silently flutter to rest.

Those are the distant islands, the lofty worlds that we saw in our dreams; that made us strangers everywhere under heaven, and made our lives a hell.

Those are the golden islands for which we longed as one longs for a homeland, to which all the nightstars beckoned us with the light of a trembling ray.

וַעֲלֵיהֶם נִשְׁאַרְנוּ בְּלִי־רֵעַ וְעָמִית
כִּשְׁנֵי פְרָחִים בַּצִּיָּה ;
כִּשְׁנֵי אֹבְדִים הַמְבַקְשִׁים אֲבֵדָה עוֹלָמִיח
עַל־פְּנֵי אֶרֶץ נָכְרִיָּה.

(1902)

And we have been left upon them,
without friend or companion, like two
flowers in the wasteland, like two who
are lost, forever seeking something lost
in a foreign land.

מִשִּׁירֵי הַחֹרֶף

FROM THE WINTER SONGS

הַצּוּר הוֹרִיד לָנוּ יוֹם חָזָק מִצֹּר,
יוֹם עָז, מוּצָק אֶחָד כְּפוֹר, קֶרַח וָקֹר.

The Rock sent down to us a day harder
than flint, a fierce day, a cast-iron day
of frost, ice, and cold.

רוּם עוֹלָם, כָּל־כַּדּוּר הָאָרֶץ מִתַּחַת,
הָאוֹר וְהָאֲוִיר כְּעֵין מִקְשָׁה אַחַת.

The summit of the world, the whole
sphere of the earth below, the light and
the air – all are like a single piece of
hammered work.

אֵין זֹאת כִּי נִתְרוֹפֵף הָעוֹלָם – וּנְתָנוֹ
הַיּוֹצֵר בַּלַּיְלָה הַזֶּה עַל־גַּב סַדָּנוֹ,

The world must have begun to loosen,
and so, last night, the Creator put it on
His anvil,

וַיָּנֶף פַּטִּישׁוֹ, וּבְהַלְמוּת עֲנָק
אֵל קָרָא לַכֹּחַ וַיִּשֹּׁם: חֲזָק!

and swung His hammer, and with this
mighty blow, God summoned strength
and breathed: 'Be firm!'

וְלֵיל תָּמִים בֵּין פַּטִּישׁ וּסְדָן אוֹתוֹ רִקַּע,
וּכְאִלּוּ כָל־כֹּחוֹ, כִּבְיָכוֹל, בּוֹ שִׁקַּע.

Then, all night long, he pounded it
between the hammer and the anvil, as
if He were sinking all His strength
into it.

וַיֵּצֵא עִם־שֶׁמֶשׁ יוֹם עַזִּיז וּמְסֻמָּר
וְכֹחַ עוֹלָמִים בּוֹ חָסוּם וּמְשֻׁמָּר.

And, with the sun, there emerged a
bold, hardened day; eternal strength is
sealed within it and preserved.

וְעוֹד תְּלוּיִם בָּאֲוִיר צַחְצוּחֵי הַזִּיו
מִנִּשְׁמַת אֱלוֹהַּ, מֵאֵד רוּחַ פִּיו.

And in the air there still hang gleaming
drops from the breath of God, from
the vapour of His mouth.

וְאוֹר בֹּקֶר מִסְתַּנֵּן עֲלֵיהֶם בִּיקָרוֹ,
וְנִטַּל כָּל־חֻמּוֹ וְנִשְׁאַר זָהֳרוֹ.

The morning light, in all its glory,
filters through them; and all its heat
subsides, only its lustre remains.

וְאֵין סוֹף לַלַּבְנוּנִית וְלַזֹּהַר אֵין קֵץ,
מִתַּחְתִּית עַד־רוּם וּמִבַּיִת עַד־עֵץ.

There is no end to the whiteness, no
bounds to the splendour, from depth
to height, from house to tree.

וְהַשֶּׁלֶג בִּשְׁלֹשׁ עֶשְׂרֵה נָפָה מְנֻפֶּה,
כַּזְּכוּכִית הַלְּבָנָה עַל־כֻּלָּם מְצֻפֶּה.

And the snow, sifted through thirteen
sieves,[1] coats all things like white glass.

וְהַגַּגּוֹת כְּכוֹבְעֵי הַשַּׁיִשׁ מַרְאִיתָם,
מַחֲצִיתָם מַבְהִיקִים וְעֵין תְּכֵלֶת מַחֲצִיתָם,

And the roofs look like alabaster
helmets, one half glistening white, the
other blue,

וּלְעֵינֵי כָל־חַי וְהַשֶּׁמֶשׁ מַזְהִירִים –
הָעוֹרְבִים לְבַדָּם עַל־גַּבָּם מַשְׁחִירִים,

shining in the sight of all the living and
of the sun – only the ravens upon them
are black to the eye,

מַחֲלִיקִים עַל־צִפּוּי הַזְּכוּכִית וְצֹרְחִים,
מְנַקְּרִים וְשׂוֹרְטִים – וּפִתְאֹם הֵם פּוֹרְחִים.

sliding and screeching on the glass
glaze, pecking and scratching. Suddenly
they fly off.

וַעֲשַׁן הָאֲרֻבּוֹת, כִּזְקַן עַתִּיק יוֹמִין,
מִסְתַּלְסֵל בֶּהָדָר וְנִשָּׂא לִמְרוֹמִים.

And the smoke from the chimneys, like
the beard of the Ancient of Days, curls
majestically, and rises to the heights.

וְהַקֶּרַח הַלֹּהֵט בַּכֹּל מְפַעְפֵּעַ,
וּבְלֶב־כֹּל אוֹן אֵיתָן כְּמַסְמֵר נוֹטֵעַ;

And the flaming ice permeates all, and,
like a nail driven home, drives steadfast
force into the heart of all things.

וּבָהִיר וּמוּצָק הָעוֹלָם! זֶה־כֹּחוֹ –
שֶׁכּוֹבֵשׁ אֶת־עַצְמוֹ וְהוּא חָזָק מִתּוֹכוֹ.

How bright and hard is the world! In
this lies its strength – that it masters
itself, drawing its force from within.

מֵרֹב אֹמֶץ כֹּחַ, מֵרֹב עֹצֶר אוֹנִים
מִתְבַּקְּעִים בַּיַּעַר חֲסִינֵי אַלּוֹנִים.

Their strength is so tensed, their
powers so fiercely restrained, that the
sturdiest oaks split apart in the forest.

1. As was the Meal-offering at the Temple.

כְּמוֹ רֻתְּקוּ בְזִקִּים כָּל־מְצוּקֵי הָאָרֶץ
בְּאוֹתוֹ הָרֶגַע שֶׁחָשְׁבוּ הִתְפָּרֵץ,

As though all the pillars of the earth
had been shackled in irons the moment
they had threatened to break loose –

וְהֵם חוֹתְרִים וְחוֹרְגִים מִמִּסְגְּרוֹתֵיהֶם –
עוֹד מְעַט וְהִתְפּוֹצֵץ הַכַּדּוּר מִפְּנֵיהֶם!

and now they are burrowing, straining
to lunge out of their strongholds. Any
moment now they will break the sphere
asunder!

(1902)

עַל הַשְּׁחִיטָה

ON THE SLAUGHTER

שָׁמַיִם, בַּקְּשׁוּ רַחֲמִים עָלָי!
אִם־יֵשׁ בָּכֶם אֵל וְלָאֵל בָּכֶם נָתִיב –
וַאֲנִי לֹא מְצָאתִיו –
הִתְפַּלְּלוּ אַתֶּם עָלָי!
אֲנִי – לִבִּי מֵת וְאֵין עוֹד תְּפִלָּה בִשְׂפָתָי,
וּכְבָר אָזְלַת יָד אַף־אֵין תִּקְוָה עוֹד –
עַד־מָתַי, עַד־אָנָה, עַד־מָתָי?

Heaven, beg mercy for me! If there is
a God in you, and a pathway through
you to this God – which I have not
discovered – then pray for me! For my
heart is dead, no longer is there prayer
on my lips; all strength is gone, and
hope is no more. Until when, how
much longer, until when?

הַתַּלְיָן! הֵא צַוָּאר – קוּם שְׁחָט!
עָרְפֵנִי כַּכֶּלֶב, לְךָ זְרוֹעַ עִם־קַרְדֹּם,
וְכָל־הָאָרֶץ לִי גַרְדֹּם –
וַאֲנַחְנוּ – אֲנַחְנוּ הַמְעָט!
דָּמִי מֻתָּר – הַךְ קָדְקֹד, וִיזַנֵּק דַּם רֶצַח,
דַּם יוֹנֵק וָשָׂב עַל־כֻּתָּנְתְּךָ –
וְלֹא יִמַּח לָנֶצַח, לָנֶצַח.

You, executioner! Here's my neck – go
to it, slaughter me! Behead me like a
dog, yours is the mighty arm and the
axe, and the whole earth is my scaffold
– and we, we are the few! My blood is
fair game – strike the skull, and
murder's blood, the blood of nurslings
and old men, will spurt onto your
clothes and will never, never be wiped
off.

וְאִם יֶשׁ־צֶדֶק – יוֹפַע מִיָּד!
אַךְ אִם־אַחֲרֵי הִשָּׁמְדִי מִתַּחַת רָקִיעַ
הַצֶּדֶק יוֹפִיעַ –

And if there is justice – let it show
itself at once! But if justice show itself
after I have been blotted out from

יִמַּגֵּר־נָא כִסְאוֹ לָעַד!
וּבְרֶשַׁע עוֹלָמִים שָׁמַיִם יִמָּקוּ;
אַף־אַתֶּם לְכוּ, זֵדִים, בַּחֲמַסְכֶם זֶה
וּבְדִמְכֶם חֲיוּ וְהִנָּקוּ.

beneath the skies – let its throne be hurled down forever! Let heaven rot with eternal evil! And you, the arrogant, go in this violence of yours, live by your bloodshed and be cleansed by it.

וְאָרוּר הָאוֹמֵר: נְקֹם!
נְקָמָה כָזֹאת, נִקְמַת דַּם יֶלֶד קָטָן
עוֹד לֹא־בָרָא הַשָּׂטָן –
וְיִקֹּב הַדָּם אֶת־הַתְּהוֹם!
יִקֹּב הַדָּם עַד תְּהֹמוֹת מַחֲשַׁכִּים,
וְאָכַל בַּחֹשֶׁךְ וְחָתַר שָׁם
כָּל־מוֹסְדוֹת הָאָרֶץ הַנְּמַקִּים.

And cursed be the man who says: Avenge! No such revenge – revenge for the blood of a little child – has yet been devised by Satan. Let the blood pierce through the abyss! Let the blood seep down to the depths of darkness, and eat away there, in the dark, and breach all the rotting foundations of the earth.

(1903)

הָיָה עֶרֶב הַקַּיִץ

IT WAS A SUMMER EVENING

וּבְנוֹת לִילִיּוֹת זַכּוֹת שׁוֹזְרוֹת מוֹזְרוֹת בַּלְּבָנָה
חוּטֵי כֶסֶף מַזְהִירִים,
וְהֵן אוֹרְגוֹת כְּסוּת אַחַת לְכֹהֲנִים גְּדוֹלִים
וְלִמְגַדְּלֵי חֲזִירִים.

And the pure daughters of Lilith are twining-spinning shiny silver threads by moonlight, weaving one and the same garment for high priests and for swineherds.

הָיָה עֶרֶב הַקַּיִץ. כָּל־הַבָּתִּים נִתְרוֹקְנוּ
וְנִתְמַלְּאוּ הַגַּנִּים;
יָצָא אָדָם, כְּדַרְכּוֹ, בְּמַאֲוַיָּיו הַגְּדוֹלִים
לַחֲטָאָיו הַקְּטַנִּים.

It was a summer evening. All the houses emptied out and the parks filled up. Then man, in his usual manner, full of grand aspirations, went forth to his petty sins.

קָצְרָה רוּחַ הָאָדָם, כָּלוּ עֵינֵי מְיַחֵל –
וּתְפִלָּתוֹ הָאַחַת:
'הַכּוֹכָבִים הַצְּנוּעִים, מַהֲרוּ צֵאתְכֶם מִלְמַעְלָה,
וְהַקְּדֵשׁוֹת מִתָּחַת!'

His patience is at an end, his eyes have grown dim with waiting – and he has only one prayer: 'O you chaste stars, come out quickly above, and you, harlots, below!'

וּבַגָּן זֶה הֵחֵלָּה נְגִינָה קַלָּה, הוֹלֵלָה —
וְהַגָּן כֻּלּוֹ נִנְעָר,
וּמִבֵּין הָאִילָנוֹת הִנֵּה הִשְׁחִיר זְנַב צָעִיף
וְהִלְבִּינָה כְּנַף סִנָּר.

Now a light, licentious melody starts up in the park, and the whole park comes to life; from among the trees the tail of a black veil is glimpsed and the wing of a white pinafore.

וּכְסַרְסוּרֵי עֲבֵרָה קוֹרְצִים, רוֹמְזִים כּוֹכָבִים,
וְעֵינֵיהֶם פָּז תֹּבְעוֹת;
צָרַר רוּחַ הַזְּנוּנִים גַּם אֶת־עִשְׂבוֹת הַשָּׂדֶה
וְאֶת־אַבְנֵי הָרְחֹבוֹת.

And the stars, like panders, wink and beckon, their eyes demanding gold; the spirit of lechery has swept even the green growth on the fields and the cobblestones in the street.

וּמֵאֶמְצַע הַנָּהָר וּמִמְּרוֹמֵי הַגְּזוֹזְרוֹת
וּמֵאַחֲרֵי הַגְּדֵרוֹת
בָּא הַצְּחוֹק — וּבַחַלּוֹנוֹת מוּרָדִים וִילוֹנוֹת
וְכָבִים הַנֵּרוֹת.

And from the middle of the river, from the heights of balconies, from behind fences comes the laughter, and in the windows, curtains are lowered and candles go out.

הַס, הַשְּׁאֵר נָתַן רֵיחוֹ, זוֹלֵל סוֹבֵא הָעוֹלָם,
יֵין עֲגָבִים עֲבָרוֹ,
וְהוּא יוֹצֵא מִדַּעְתּוֹ וּמִתְגּוֹלֵל בְּקִיאוֹ
וּמִתְבּוֹסֵס בִּבְשָׂרוֹ.

Hush! The flesh has given forth its scent, the world is glutting, guzzling, overcome with the wine of lust; it is going out of its mind, rolling in its spew, weltering in the flesh.

וּבְנוֹת לִילִיוֹת זַכּוֹת שׁוֹזְרוֹת מוֹזְרוֹת בַּלְּבָנָה
חוּטֵי כֶסֶף מַזְהִירִים,
וְהֵן אֹרְגוֹת כְּסוּת אַחַת לְלַכֹּהֲנִים גְּדוֹלִים
וְלִמְגַדְּלֵי חֲזִירִים.

And the pure daughters of Lilith are twining-spinning shiny silver threads by moonlight, weaving one and the same garment for high priests and for swineherds.

(1908)

צָנַח לוֹ זַלְזַל

צָנַח לוֹ זַלְזַל עַל־גָּדֵר וַיָּנֹם –
כֹּה יָשֵׁן אָנֹכִי:
נָשַׁל הַפְּרִי – וּמַה־לִּי וּלְגִזְעִי,
וּמַה־לִּי וְלִשְׂוֹכִי?

נָשַׁל הַפְּרִי, הַפֶּרַח כְּבָר נִשְׁכָּח –
שָׂרְדוּ הֶעָלִים –
יִרְגַּז יוֹם אֶחָד הַסַּעַר – וְנָפְלוּ
אַרְצָה חֲלָלִים.

אַחַר – וְנִמְשְׁכוּ לֵילוֹת הַזְּוָעָה,
לֹא מְנוּחָה וּשְׁנָת לִי,
בָּדָד אֶתְחַבֵּט בָּאֹפֶל וַאֲרַצֵּץ
רֹאשִׁי אֶל־כָּתְלִי.

וְשׁוּב יִפְרַח אָבִיב, וְאָנֹכִי לְבַדִּי
עַל־גִּזְעִי אֶתָּלֶה –
שַׁרְבִיט קֵרֵחַ, לֹא צִיץ לוֹ וָפֶרַח,
לֹא־פְרִי וְלֹא־עָלֶה.

(1911)

A TWIG ALIGHTED

A twig alighted on a fence and dozed; so do I sleep. The fruit fell – and what have I to do with my trunk, what with my branch?

The fruit fell, the flower is already forgotten, the leaves survive. One day the storm will rage, they will drop to the ground, dead.

Afterwards the nights of dread go on, no rest or sleep for me, alone I thrash about in the dark, smashing my head against my wall.

And again spring blossoms, and alone I hang from my trunk – a bare shoot, without bud or flower, without fruit or leaf.

שָׁחָה נַפְשִׁי

שָׁחָה נַפְשִׁי לֶעָפָר
תַּחַת מַשָּׂא אַהֲבַתְכֶם;
אַלְלַי, כִּי הָיִיתִי
אִסְתְּרָא בְּלָגִינַתְכֶם!

MY SOUL HAS SUNK DOWN

My soul has sunk down to the dust under the burden of your love. Woe is me, for I have become a coin rattling in your empty jug.[1]

1. An allusion to a Talmudic maxim: 'A coin in an [empty] vessel makes a loud noise: *kish-kish*.'

וְלָמָּה שַׂתֶּם עַל־נָוִי ?
מַה־חַטָּאתִי, מַה־כֹּחִי ?
לֹא מְשׁוֹרֵר, לֹא נָבִיא —
חוֹטֵב עֵצִים אָנֹכִי.

Why have you beset my home? What is my offence, what is my strength? I am not a poet nor a prophet, but a woodcutter.

חוֹטֵב עֵצִים, אִישׁ קַרְדֹּם,
עוֹשֶׂה מְלַאכְתִּי לְתֻמִּי ;
וְרַד הַיּוֹם, וְיָדִי רָפְתָה,
וְקֵהֶה שׁוֹבֵת קַרְדֻּמִּי.

A woodcutter, a man of the axe, doing my work at random, and the day has waned, and my hand hangs limp, and my blunted axe stands still.

שְׂכִיר יוֹם קָצָר אָנֹכִי,
פּוֹעֵל נָטָה לִגְבוּלְכֶם ;
וְלֹא עֶת־דְּבָרִים לִי עַתָּה,
וְלֹא יוֹם תְּרוּעָה לְכֻלְּכֶם.

I am a day worker, for a short day, a hireling who has chanced into your grounds. This is not a time of words for me, nor a day of trumpeting for you.

אֵיכָה נִשָּׂא פָּנֵינוּ ?
בַּמֶּה נְקַדֵּם יוֹם יָבֹא ? —
אִישׁ לְחֶשְׁבּוֹן עוֹלָמוֹ !
אִישׁ לְסִבְלוֹת לְבָבוֹ !

How, then, shall we raise our faces? With what shall we receive the coming day ? Let each take stock of his own world! Let each bear the burden of his own heart!

(1923)

שָׁאוּל טְשֶׁרְנִיחוֹבְסְקִי

Saul Tchernikhovsky

[בְּעָמְדִי בֵּין הַחַי]

[AS I STOOD]

בְּעָמְדִי בֵּין הַחַי וּבֵין הַגּוֹסֵס כְּבָר
(אֻמָּנוּת מַה־נּוֹרָאָה !) וְאִזְמֵל חַד בְּכַפִּי,
יֵשׁ בּוֹכֶה מִתּוֹךְ גִּיל וְיֵשׁ מְקַלֵּל בְּאַפִּי,
סָפַגְתִּי אַחֲרוֹן אוֹר תּוֹךְ אִישׁוֹן גּוֹסֵס זָר.

As I stood between the living and those already dying (oh, what a terrible craft!), with a sharp scalpel in my hand, now weeping for joy, now cursing in anger, I absorbed the last light from the pupil of a dying stranger.

אֶל רַעַם תּוֹתְחֵי־אוֹן מִתְגַּלְגְּלִים בַּכָּר,
לְאֵשׁ נוֹצְצָה בְּאֶשּׁוּן מִנְהַרְתִּי לִי בְגַפִּי
הִתְוֵיתִי אַחֲרוֹן־קָו, מָחַקְתִּי חַי מִדַּפִּי,
מִסֵּפֶל מְשֹׁהַם כָּךְ תֵּעָקֵר אֶבֶן־יְקָר.

To the thunder of mighty cannon rolling over the plain, by the flame that flickered in my pitchdark trench for me alone, I drew the last line, I erased a living being from my page – as a precious stone is ripped out of a jewelled goblet.

וְאוּלָם בְּאוֹתוֹ זִיק בָּעַיִן הָעוֹמֶמֶת,
בָּאוֹר הַסּוֹפֵג אוֹר וּבְטֶרֶם קָם לָעַד;
וְאוּלָם בְּאוֹתוֹ בְּרַק אֵשׁ קוֹדְחָה וְצוֹרֶמֶת,

Yet in that very spark of the fading eye, in the light that absorbs light before it dims forever; yet in that very flash of scorching, lacerating fire,

בָּאֵשׁ הַקּוֹרְאָה לְאֵשׁ, הַמְצַוָּה אֵיד וּשְׁמָד, –
הָיִיתָ אַתָּה בָּם; זֶה הוֹדְךָ הֲמָמָנִי; –
הַאִם קִדַּמְתִּי בֹא אוֹ אֵחַר צוּר בְּרָאָנִי?

in the fire that summons fire, ordering misery and persecution – You were in them; Your glory overwhelmed me. Had I come too soon, or was the Rock, my creator, late?

עַיִט! עַיִט עַל הָרַיִךְ

EAGLE! EAGLE OVER YOUR MOUNTAINS

עַיִט! עַיִט עַל הָרַיִךְ, עַיִט עַל הָרַיִךְ צָף!
אַט וָקַל, – נִדְמֶה כְּאִלּוּ רֶגַע – אֵינוֹ אֶלָּא צָף,
צָף־מַפְלִיג בְּיָם שֶׁל תְּכֵלֶת, עֵר לְרֶנֶן־גִּיל בְּלֵב
הַשָּׁמַיִם־הָרָקִיעַ, חָג אִלֵּם בְּאוֹר צוֹרֵב.

Eagle! Eagle over your mountains, an eagle over your mountains in flight! Slow and easy – for an instant, so it seems – merely floating, floating-sailing through a sea of blue, alive to the song of delight in the heart of the high heavens, mutely circling in the searing light.

עַיִט! עַיִט עַל הָרַיִךְ, עַיִט עַל הָרַיִךְ צָף!
יְשַׁר־גֵּו וְכֶבֶד־אֵבֶר, שְׁחוֹר־נוֹצָה וּרְחַב־כָּנָף;
טָס מָתוּחַ (חֵץ מִקֶּשֶׁת), עַיִט עָג עוּגִיּוֹת חוּגָיו;
תָּר עִקְּבוֹת טַרְפּוֹ מִמַּעַל בָּאֲפָר וּבְחָגָו.

Eagle! Eagle over your mountains, an eagle over your mountains in flight! Body rigid, heavy pinions, black-plumed, broad of wing; soaring, wings outspread (swift as an arrow), wheeling round in circle within circle, tracking its prey from above in meadow and in cleft.

עַיִט! עַיִט עַל הָרַיִךְ, עַיִט עַל הָרַיִךְ עָף!
טָס גּוֹלֵשׁ־גּוֹלֵשׁ וּבְמַגָּע פֶּלֶא אֵבֶר לֹא נָקַף.
רֶגַע קַל – קָפָא, מִשְּׁנֵהוּ – נִיד־לֹא־נִיד בְּאֶבְ
רֶטֶט כָּל־שֶׁהוּא לְפֶתַע – וְעוֹלֶה לִקְרַאת הָעָב

Eagle! Eagle over your mountains, an eagle over your mountains in flight! Soaring, gliding – miracle of motion – not a wing has wavered. For a second frozen, then the barest ruffling of the pinions, suddenly a slight tremor – and it rises to the clouds.

עַיִט! עַיִט עַל הָרַיִךְ, עַיִט עַל הָרַיִךְ עָף!
אַט וָקַל, – נִדְמֶה כְּאִלּוּ רֶגַע – אֵינוֹ אֶלָּא צָף
אֶרֶץ, עַיִט עַל הָרַיִךְ, – עַל פָּנַיִךְ חַשְׁרַת צֵל,
מֵאֶבְרוֹת עֲנָק חוֹלֶפֶת, מְלַטֶּפֶת הַרְרֵי־אֵל...

(1936)

Eagle! Eagle over your mountains, an eagle over your mountains in flight! Slow and easy – for an instant, so it seems – merely floating . . . O Land, there is an eagle over your mountains, and from its giant wings a massive shadow moves across your face, caressing the mountains of God.

שָׁלֹשׁ אֲתוֹנוֹת

(אגדה)

THREE ASSES

(A Legend)

שָׁלֹשׁ אֲתוֹנוֹת מְשָׁרְכוֹת אֶת דַּרְכָּן,
שָׁלֹשׁ אֲתוֹנוֹת – מִבְּאֵר־שֶׁבַע לְדָן:
חוּמָה וּשְׁחוֹרָה וּצְחוֹרָה, – לְאִטָּן.

Three asses trudge down the road, three asses plodding from Beersheba to Dan:[1] one brown, one black, one white.

עָבְרוּ הַשָּׁלֹשׁ עַל־יַד צְרִיחַ מִסְגָּד,
כָּרְעָה הַשְּׁחוֹרָה, כִּי קָרְאוּ לַמּוֹעֵד.
עָבְרוּ הַשָּׁלֹשׁ עַל־יַד פֶּתַח מִנְזָר,
צָנְחָה הַחוּמָה מוּל אִיקוֹנִין מְשֻׁזָּר.
עָבְרוּ הַשָּׁלֹשׁ עַל חָרְבָּה קְדוֹשָׁה,
עָמְדָה הַצְּחוֹרָה מַרְכִּינָה אֶת רֹאשָׁהּ.

When the three passed by a mosque's minaret, the black one knelt, hearing the summons to prayer. When the three passed by a monastery gate, the brown one fell down before a braided icon. When the three passed by a holy ruin, the white one halted, and bent its head.

1. The proverbial limits of the Land.

עַל־גַּב הַשְּׁחוֹרָה, עַל גַּבָּהּ, סַיִף רָב ;
עַל־גַּב הַחוּמָּה, עַל גַּבָּהּ, מֻטָּל צְלָב ;
עַל גַּב הַצְּחוֹרָה אַךְ שְׁטִיחַ זָהָב.

On the back of the black one there is a mighty scimitar; on the back of the brown one there lies a crucifix; on the back of the white one – only a golden rug.

אֵין כְּלוּם עַל גַּבָּהּ בִּלְתִּי אִם־הַשָּׁטִיחַ –
בִּמְהֵרָה בְּיָמֵינוּ יִרְכַּב עָלֶיהָ מָשִׁיחַ.

There is nothing on its back, only the rug – *Soon, in our days, may the Messiah ride upon it.*

(1939)

הַמֵּתִים הָרִאשׁוֹנִים

THE FIRST DEAD[1]

'הוּא בָא! הוּא בָא! הוּא כָאן! הוּא כָאן!
הַמָּוֶת הַשָּׁחוֹר!'
אוֹמֵר מַכְרִיז פַּעֲמוֹן־נַגָּן
בַּצְּרִיחַ הַצָּחוֹר.

'He's come! He's come! He's here! He's here! The Black Death!' – proclaims the chiming bell in the white belfry.

'הוּא בָא! הוּא בָא! הוּא כָאן! הוּא כָאן!
אָיֹם הוּא וְנוֹרָא!
בִּצְרִיף שֶׁל עֵץ, וּבְתוֹךְ מִשְׁכַּן
רַבֵּי דָת וּשְׂרָרָה.

'He's come! He's come! He's here! He's here! Most dread and terrible! In wooden huts and in the abodes of the high and mighty!

הוּא בָא! קוֹצֵר אֶת קְצִירוֹ
בָּעִיר בֵּין הַחוֹמוֹת,
בַּכְּפָר וּבַשָּׂדֶה – נִירוֹ;
אַךְ לֹא בַּגֶּטָאוֹת.

'He's here! He's reaping his harvest between the walls of the city, ploughing his furrow in hamlet and field; but not in the ghettos.

1. The bubonic plague, known as the Black Death, which devastated much of Europe in the middle of the fourteenth century, was not widespread in the ghettos. The Jews were accused of having poisoned the waters and some 300 communities were destroyed. In several cities, the Jews set fire to their own houses and died in the flames.

בְּמֶרְחַב כָּרִים וְעֵינוֹת טְרָשִׁים
עוֹמֵד עוֹלָם בְּעֵינוֹ, –
הַמָּוֶת שָׁם; בַּמְעֻפָּשִׁים
בַּגֶּטָאוֹת – אֵינוֹ.'

'In the broad pastures and along the craggy springs, nothing has changed: Death is there. But among the putrid of the ghettos – no sign of him.'

מַכְרִיז אוֹמֵר הַפַּעֲמוֹן:
'מֵאָה בְּמֵעֵת־לְעֵת!'
חוֹזֵר רוֹטֵן קוֹל הֶהָמוֹן:
'בַּגֶּטוֹ – שָׁם אֵין מֵת...'

The bell proclaims: 'A hundred from dawn to dawn.' The mob growls again: 'In the ghetto – not a single dead.'

מַה יֶּהְגּוּ הֶבֶל הַנְּזִירִים?
זוֹעֵף אֲסַפְסוּף רָב?
בַּגֶּטוֹ כָּל פָּנִים קוֹדְרִים
מִקּוֹל עָלֶה נִדָּף.

Why are the monks prattling? Why is the rabble sullen? In the ghetto, every face darkens at the sound of a fluttering leaf.

עַד שֶׁהָיְתָה גַּם הָרְוָחָה,
שִׂמְחָה גַּם בִּמְעוֹנָם:
הִנֵּה בַּגֶּטוֹ מֵת! חָה־חָה!
תּוֹדָה לְאֵל עוֹלָם.

Until relief and joy both came into their dwelling: Look – a death in the ghetto! Ha! Thank the everlasting God!

לֹא כְדַרְכָּהּ, לֹא מְחִישָׁה,
עֵינֶיהָ מְאִירוֹת,
חֶבְרָה צוֹעֶדֶת קַדִּישָׁא.
צְאוּ, אֶזְרָחִים, לִרְאוֹת.

Not at the usual pace, not in haste, with shining eyes, the funeral procession[1] moves along. O, citizens, come out and see!

לֹא לְשֵׁם מָכוֹר, לֹא לְשֵׁם סָחוֹר,
נָא בֹּאוּ בִגְדוּדִים:
מֻכֵּי הַמָּוֶת הַשָּׁחוֹר!
מֵתִים – שְׁנֵי יְהוּדִים!

Not for wheeling, not for dealing, come in hordes: these were smitten by the Black Death! Dead – two Jews!

1. Lit. 'the holy brotherhood', the members of the Jewish burial society.

גַּם בָּנוּ, גַּם בַּחֲשׁוּדִים
נָגַף, נוֹדֶה לָאֵל!
גַּם בַּיְּהוּדִים, גַּם בַּיְּהוּדִים
הוּא אֶת קְצִירוֹ הֵחֵל.

We too, we the suspect, have been struck down by Death – thank God! He has begun his reaping of the Jews too, yes, of the Jews.

חֲבָל, הַצְּרִיחַ הַצָּחוֹר
לֹא לָנוּ, וְאֵין פַּעֲמוֹן,
וְיַכְרִיז – 'הַמָּוֶת הַשָּׁחוֹר
כְּבָר בָּא!' – פַּרְנָס־הֶגְמוֹן!

A pity! The white belfry is not ours, *Judenbischof*,[1] and we have no bell that might proclaim: – 'The Black Death has already come!'

(1942)

יַעֲקֹב פִיכְמַן

Jacob Fichman

שׁוּלַמִּית

THE SHULAMMITE

אַתְּ שׁוּלַמִּית. צִפּוֹר שְׁכוּחָה בַּכֶּרֶם.
אַתְּ לֵב פָּרַח בְּאֶרֶץ עֲזוּבָה.
וּבֵין הָרֵי־בְשָׂמִים, אוֹבֶדֶת דֶּרֶךְ,
אַתְּ לְדוֹדֵךְ שׁוֹאֶלֶת כּוֹאֲבָה.

You are the Shulammite. A bird forgotten in a vineyard; a heart that flowered in a desolate land. And, lost among the spicebearing mountains, heartsick, you seek your lover.

הַעַל כִּי הִכְלִימוּךְ אַחַיִךְ אַתְּ נִסְעֶרֶת,
כִּי הָרוֹעִים סָנְטוּ בָךְ אַתְּ דָּוָה –
וְאַתְּ אַחַת בְּתֹם־חִנֵּךְ כִּבְחֶרֶב
גּוֹזֶרֶת לֵב עוֹלָם. אַתְּ אֲהוּבָה.

Are you so overwrought because your brothers shamed you? So hurt because the shepherds sneered at you? You only, with your innocent charm, like a sword, split the heart of the world. You are loved.

הַיּוֹם שָׁזַף לֶחְיֵךְ וְלֵיל בִּכֵּר
בַּצֵּל גְּבִיעֵךְ, כְּפֶרַח מְשַׁכֵּר,
בְּכָל סִתְרֵי גַנֵּךְ יָצַק חֶמְדָּה.

Day bronzed your cheeks and night ripened your chalice in the shadow, like an intoxicating flower, pouring loveliness into all the coverts of your garden.

1. 'Jews' Bishop', the head of the Jewish community.

אֵיךְ לֹא מָצָא בַּסֶּלַע נְתִיבֵךְ
דּוֹדֵךְ עַד כֹּה – וְרֵיחַ אֲבִיבֵךְ,
כְּמוֹר עוֹבֵר כָּל אֶרֶץ יְהוּדָה!

How is it that your beloved has not yet found your pathway through the rocks – when the fragrance of your spring like myrrh sweeps over the whole land of Judea.

אַבְרָהָם בֶּן־יִצְחָק

Avraham ben Yitsḥak

אַשְׁרֵי הַזּוֹרְעִים וְלֹא יִקְצֹרוּ

HAPPY ARE THEY WHO SOW

אַשְׁרֵי הַזּוֹרְעִים וְלֹא יִקְצֹרוּ
כִּי יַרְחִיקוּ נְדוֹד.

Happy are they who sow but do not reap, for they wander afar.

אַשְׁרֵי הַנְּדִיבִים אֲשֶׁר תִּפְאֶרֶת נְעוּרֵיהֶם
הוֹסִיפָה עַל אוֹר הַיָּמִים וּפִזְרוֹנָם
וְהֵם אֶת עֶדְיָם הִתְפָּרְקוּ עַל אֵם הַדְּרָכִים.

Happy are the noble of heart whose youthful glories enhanced the days' light and largesse, while they themselves stripped off their ornaments at the parting of the ways.

אַשְׁרֵי הַגֵּאִים אֲשֶׁר גַּאֲוָתָם עָבְרָה גְּבוּלֵי נַפְשָׁם
וַתְּהִי כַּעֲנָוַת הַלֹּבֶן
אַחֲרֵי הֵעָלוֹת הַקֶּשֶׁת בֶּעָנָן.

Happy are the proud-of-heart whose pride overflowed the borders of their soul, and came to be the humility of white after the rainbow has risen into the clouds.

אַשְׁרֵי הַיּוֹדְעִים אֲשֶׁר יִקְרָא לִבָּם מִמִּדְבָּר
וְעַל שְׂפָתָם תִּפְרַח הַדּוּמִיָּה.

Happy are they who know that their heart cries out from a wilderness, and silence blossoms on their lips.

אַשְׁרֵיהֶם כִּי יֵאָסְפוּ אֶל תּוֹךְ לֵב הָעוֹלָם
לוּטֵי אַדֶּרֶת הַשִּׁכְחָה
וְהָיָה חֶלְקָם הַתָּמִיד בְּלִי אֹמֶר.

Happy are they – for they will be gathered into the heart of the world, wrapped in oblivion's robe, and their everlasting lot[1] will be wordless.

1. Or, 'their lot will be a constant offering (*tamid*) without words'.

[שַׁחַר שֶׁל מִי] [WHOSE DAWN]

שַׁחַר שֶׁל מִי קָרָא הַגֶּבֶר
וְשָׁבָה הַחֲשֵׁכָה עַל תְּרוּעָתוֹ הַנִּחֲרָה
וְיֶדְכֶם הָרְשֵׁלָה אֲשֶׁר עַל עֵינֵיכֶם הֶאֱהִילָה
מִפְּנֵי גְבוּרַת שֶׁמֶשׁ וְהֵן לֹא בָאָה
הֵן פֶּה וְיַד שָׁקֵרוּ.

Whose dawn did the cock proclaim? And the darkness reiterated his wheezing fanfare; and your feeble hand that shielded your eyes from the sun's might – but no sun had come. The mouth and the hand – both had lied.

יַעֲקֹב שְׁטַיְנְבֶּרְג

Jacob Steinberg

[כְּזוּג טוֹרְפִים] [LIKE TWO BEASTS OF PREY]

כְּזוּג טוֹרְפִים תּוֹעֵי־לֵיל וּמֻכֵּי־צָמָא, —
מֵרוּץ וַעֲרֹג לְאֵד יְאוֹרִים מְתוּקִים
כִּי יִפְּלוּ עַל שְׂפַת בְּרֵכָה נֶאֱלָמָה;

כִּי יִשְׁעוּ לִדְבַר־מָה מִן הָאֲפֵלָה
וּכְאֶחָד הֵם נוֹאָשִׁים וְזוֹמְמִים,
רַק שְׂפִי קְצֵה הַגַּלִּים הַדּוֹמְמִים
לְשׁוֹנָם תָּלֹק רֶגַע וְחָדֵלָה: —

בְּלַהַט מַעֲרֻמֵּינוּ הַנִּחָרִים
כֵּן נַחְנוּ אָז, נוֹאָשִׁים וַחֲבוּקִים,
עַל שְׂפַת יְאוֹר עֹנֶג נָם וְגַל לֹא יָרִים.

Like two beasts of prey, lost in the night and stricken by thirst, who had scurried about, panting for the vapour of sweet waters, then dropped beside the banks of a soundless pool,

and, overhearing something in the darkness, desperate and wary in the same breath, they only let their tongues gently lick the edges of the still waves, for an instant, then stop –

thus, in the ardour of our parched nakedness, we paused, despairing and embraced, on the banks of a slumbering lake of pleasure, where not one wave stirred.

[לֹא גַּן נָעוּל]

[NOT AN ENCLOSED GARDEN]

לֹא גַּן נָעוּל הָעוֹלָם; בְּיוֹם צַר לְעֵת שֵׂיבָה
שֶׁבַע שְׂמָחוֹת יָצֵרוּ אֶת תּוּגָתְךָ הַשְּׁלֵוָה.

The world is not an enclosed garden;
in time of trouble, when your hair is
grey, seven joys will harass your
tranquil sorrow.

שֶׁפִי תְּצַעֵד הַזִּקְנָה; גַּם בִּנְאוֹת הַמַּזְקִינִים
שׁוֹרֵץ שֶׁפֶק אַכְזָרִי עִם עַקְרַבֵּי הַמִּינִים.

Old age steps gingerly. Even the oases
of the aged swarm with cruel doubts
and scorpions of heresy.

דּוּמָם תֵּשֵׁב וּתְהַרְהֵר: שָׁבְתָה דַרְכֵּי הַסְּלוּלָה –
וּמֵעֵבֶר לָהּ יַעַל הֲמוֹן־עָם בַּהֲמֻלָּה.

Silently, you sit and muse: my highway
is deserted, and the clamour of the
mob thunders beyond it.

בֹּקֶר תָּקִיץ וְתָחוּד: תְּקוּפָה אַחַת נָגֹלָּה –
וּבְנֵי־עָשׁ בְּשׁוּלֶיהָ כְּבָר נִנְעָרִים שְׁאוֹלָה.

In the morning you wake up and
wonder at the riddle: one era has been
rolled up,[1] and from its rim the stars
are already shaken off into the nether-
world.

אַךְ בְּשֶׁקֶט עֶרֶב בָּהִיר רַנִּים יַחַד מַזָּלוֹת,
וּבֵין מַזָּל לְמַזָּל רַק כִּגְבוּל הַנִּמְשָׁלוֹת.

But in the quiet of a clear evening all
the planets sing in unison, and between
one planet and another there is no
more than a thin boundary-line as in
a parable.

אָז אֵין נִבְדָּל וָשָׁב; וַאֲשֶׁר נִשְׁפַּט לְרָקָב –
רוֹאֶה קֶבֶר וּמַחֲרִישׁ וּמִתְאַפֵּק אֶל שְׁחָקָיו.

Then none is separate and none turns
back; and he who has been condemned
to decay sees the grave, is silent, and
holds his peace in the face of heaven.

1. 'The heavens shall be rolled up like a scroll' – Isaiah 34.4.

דָּוִד פּוֹגֶל

David Vogel

[כִּי יִגַּשׁ הַלַּיִל]

כִּי יִגַּשׁ הַלַּיִל אֶל חַלּוֹנֵךְ –
צְאִי אֵלָיו עֲרֻמָּה.

רַךְ יִזַּל וְיַשְׁחִיר
סְבִיב יָפְיֵךְ הַשּׁוֹקֵט,
וְיִגַּע קְצוֹת שָׁדַיִךְ.

אִתּוֹ אֶעֱמֹד אֹבַד־דֶּרֶךְ
וְחֶרֶשׁ נִתְאַו:
בֹּאִי אֶל אָפְלֵנוּ.

וְתִסַּעְנָה שְׁתֵּי עֵינַיִךְ
לְפָנֵינוּ
לָאִיר לִי וּלְרֵעִי. –

[WHEN NIGHT DRAWS NEAR]

When night draws near your window,
come to him naked.

Softly will he ripple and darken round
your still beauty, touching the tips of
your breasts.

I shall stand with him there, a stray
wanderer, and silently we shall yearn:
come into our dark.

And let your two eyes travel before us
to light the way for me and my friend.

[בָּעֲלִיָּה]

בָּעֲלִיָּה
נִתְלִים מֵתֵינוּ עֲרֻמִּים
אִישׁ עַל רֵעֵהוּ.

לַיְלָה עַל לַיְלָה
הֵם תְּלוּיִים בַּחֲבוּרָה
וְשׁוֹתְקִים.

[IN THE ATTIC]

Our dead hang in the attic, naked, one
on top of the other.

Night after night they hang banded
together, keeping silent.

כִּי רַבּוּ הַיָּמִים
יִכְחַשׁ בְּשָׂרָם וְיִבֹּל.
הַגְּוִיּוֹת תֶּאֱרַכְנָה מְאֹד.

As the days go by, their flesh wastes away and withers. The corpses become very long.

הַשּׁוֹמֵר הָעִוֵּר
יוֹשֵׁב לָנֶצַח עֲלֵיהֶם
וִיצַוֶּה הַמְּנוּחָה.

The blind watchman sits over them forever, ordaining rest.

[אַל תִּירָא, יַלְדִּי]

[DON'T BE AFRAID]

אַל תִּירָא, יַלְדִּי,
רַק שְׁנֵי עַכְבָּרִים הֵם
הַקּוֹפְצִים מִן הַשֻּׁלְחָן אֶל הַכִּסֵּא.
קְטַנִּים הֵם מִמְּךְ
וְלֹא יוּכְלוּ בָּלְעֶךְ.

Don't be afraid, my child, those are only two mice, jumping down from the table to the chair. They are smaller than you and couldn't gobble you up.

אַל תִּירָא, יַלְדִּי,
רַק אֶצְבַּע הַגֶּשֶׁם הִיא,
הַדּוֹפֶקֶת רְטֻבָּה בַּחַלּוֹן –
לֹא נִפְתַּח לוֹ.

Don't be afraid, my child, that's only the rain's finger tapping wetly on the window. We won't let it in.

הֵחָבֵא בִּי הֵיטֵב,
אֲנִי אִמֵּךְ.
נִמְשֹׁךְ לַיִל אָפֵל מֵעַל לְרָאשֵׁנוּ
וְאִישׁ לֹא יִמְצָאֵנוּ.

Hide deep inside me, I am your mother. We'll pull the dark night over our heads and no one will find us.

[עָרֵי נְעוּרַי]

[MY CHILDHOOD CITIES]

עָרֵי נְעוּרַי,
עַתָּה אֶת כֻּלָּן כְּבָר שָׁכַחְתִּי
וְאוֹתָךְ בְּאַחַת מֵהֵנָּה.

My childhood cities, by now I've forgotten them all, and you in one of them.

תּוֹךְ שְׁלוּלִית מֵי־גֶשֶׁם
יְחֵפָה בִּשְׁבִילִי עוֹד תִּרְקֹדִי –
וְהִנֵּה וַדַּאי כְּבָר מַתְּ.

You still dance on for me in a puddle of rainwater – but surely you're already dead.

מִתּוֹךְ יַלְדוּתִי הָרְחוֹקָה
לִדְהֹר אֵיךְ נֶחְפַּזְתִּי,
עַד בּוֹא אֶל הֵיכַל הַזִּקְנָה הַלָּבָן –
וְהוּא רָחָב וָרֵיק.

How quickly I galloped out of my distant childhood, until I reached the white palace of old age, and found it wide and empty.

רֵאשִׁית דַּרְכִּי
שׁוּב לֹא אֶרְאֶה,
וְאוֹתָךְ לֹא אֶרְאֶה,
וְלֹא אוֹתִי מֵאָז.

I can no longer see my road's beginning; I cannot see you or the self that I was.

אֹרְחַת הַיָּמִים,
מֵרָחוֹק,
לָנוּעַ תּוֹסִיף הָלְאָה,
מֵאַיִן אֶל אַיִן,
בִּלְעָדַי.

The caravan of days, from afar, will move on its way, from nothingness to nothingness, without me.

יִשְׂרָאֵל אֶפְרָת

Israel Efrat

הָאֲנִי צְעָקָה

THE I, A SCREAM

פִּכְפּוּךְ דָּם חַם אֶל תּוֹךְ מַשְׁפֵּךְ,
וְאֵינְסוֹפִי,

The bubbling of warm blood into a funnel, and infinite,

וְעֹמֶק שִׁכָּרוֹן שֶׁל הֲוָיָה מִבַּעַד סְגוֹר עֵינַיִם –
פִּתְאֹם עוֹלָם,

the deep intoxication of a life behind the eyes' cage –

וְקוֹל צוֹעֵק מִתַּחַת לַסַּכִּין:
אֲנִי! –

and a voice screaming under the knife:
'I!'

וּלְכָל חַיָּיו שֶׁל הָאָדָם כּוֹאֲבִים צְדָדָיו
כְּמוֹ צְדָדָיו שֶׁל הַיָּרֵחַ.

And for the rest of man's life, his sides hurt like the sides of the moon.

וְאֵין חַוָּה עוֹלָה מֵחֶתֶךְ זֶה,
וְאֵין פִּצּוּי.

And no Eve rises out of this gash;
there is no reparation.

אוּרִי צְבִי גְרִינְבֶּרג

Uri Zvi Greenberg

עִם אֵלִי הַנַּפָּח

WITH MY GOD, THE BLACKSMITH

כְּפִרְקֵי נְבוּאָה בּוֹעֲרִים יָמוֹתַי בְּכָל הַגִּלּוּיִים
וְגוּפִי בֵּינֵיהֶם כְּגוּשׁ הַמַּתֶּכֶת לְהִתּוּךְ.
וְעָלַי עוֹמֵד אֵלִי הַנַּפָּח וּמַכֶּה בִּגְבוּרָה:
כָּל פֶּצַע, שֶׁחָתַךְ הַזְּמַן בִּי, פּוֹתֵחַ לוֹ חִתּוּךְ
וּפוֹלֵט בְּגִצֵּי רְגָעִים הָאֵשׁ הָעֲצוּרָה.

Like chapters of prophecy, my days burn in all their revelations, and my body, in their midst, is like a melted mass of metal. And over me stands my God, the blacksmith, hammering mightily. Every wound that Time has cut in me, opens its gash and spits forth the pent-up fire in sparks of moments.

זֶהוּ גוֹרָלִי־מִשְׁפָּטִי עַד עֶרֶב בְּדָרֶךְ.
וּבְשׁוּבִי לְהָטִיל אֶת גּוּשִׁי הַמֻּכֶּה עַל עֶרֶשׂ,
פִּי – פֶּצַע פָּתוּחַ.
וְעֵירֹם אֲדַבֵּר עִם אֵלִי: עָבַדְתָּ בְּפָרֶךְ.
עַתָּה בָּא לַיְלָה; תֵּן – שְׁנֵינוּ נָנוּחַ.

This is my fate, my daily lot, until evening falls. And when I return to fling my beaten mass upon the bed, my mouth is a gaping wound. Then, naked, I speak to my God: 'You have worked so hard. Now night has come; let us both rest.'

בְּשׁוּלֵי שָׁמַיִם — —

AT THE RIM OF THE HEAVENS

כְּאַבְרָהָם וְשָׂרָה בְּאֵלוֹנֵי מַמְרֵא
לִפְנֵי הַבְּשׂוֹרָה הַיְקָרָה,
וּכְדָוִד וּבַת שֶׁבַע בְּבֵית הַמַּלְכוּת
בְּחִבַּת לַיְלָה רִאשׁוֹן,
עוֹלִים אָבִי וְאִמִּי קְדוֹשִׁים
בְּמַעֲרָב עַל הַיָּם,
וְכָל נִגְהוֹת־אֱלֹהִים עֲלֵיהֶם —
מִכֹּבֶד יָפְיָם הֵם שׁוֹקְעִים .. לְאִטָּם;
מֵעַל לְרָאשֵׁיהֶם זוֹרֵם הַיָּם הָאַדִּיר,
תַּחְתָּיו בֵּיתָם הֶעָמֹק — —

Like Abraham and Sarah by the terebinths of Mamre[1] before the precious tidings, and like David and Bathsheba, in the king's palace, in the tenderness of their first night – my martyred father and mother rise in the West over the sea with all the aureoles of God upon them. Weighed down by their beauty they sink, slowly. Above their heads flows the mighty ocean, beneath it is their deep home.

קִירוֹת אֵין לַבַּיִת הַזֶּה מִשּׁוּם צַד,
מַיִם־בְּמַיִם בָּנוּי הוּא.
בָּאִים בִּשְׂחִיָּה טְבוּעֵי יִשְׂרָאֵל
מִכָּל עֶבְרֵי יָם
וְכוֹכָב בְּפִיהֶם ..
וַאֲשֶׁר הֵם שָׂחִים שָׁם,
אֵין יוֹדֵעַ הַשִּׁיר;
יוֹדְעִים הֵם – שֶׁבַּיָּם — —

This home has no walls on any side, it is built of water within water. The drowned of Israel come swimming from all the corners of the sea, each with a star in his mouth. And what they speak of there, the poem does not know; only they know who are in the sea.

1. Where the angels announced to Abraham that Sarah would bear him a son (Genesis 18.1 ff).

כְּכִנּוֹר כָּבוּי מִזִּיו נִגּוּן מַקְרִין —
כֵּן אֲנִי, בְּנָם הַטּוֹב,
הָעוֹמֵד אָז רָם־עִם־הַזְּמַן עַל חוֹף יָם.

And I, their good son, am like a lyre whose radiant melody has been stopped, as I stand, towering with Time, on the seashore.

וְיֵשׁ: עֶרֶב הוֹלֵךְ לְלִבִּי עִם הַיָּם . .
וַאֲנִי — הוֹלֵךְ אֶל הַיָּם.
כִּלְשׁוּלֵי שָׁמַיִם נִקְרֵאתִי לַחֲזוֹת:
מִזֶּה וּמִזֶּה לְגַלְגַּל הַחַמָּה
הַשּׁוֹקַעַת
נִרְאֶה וְנִרְאֵית:
אָבִי מִיָּמִין וְאִמִּי מִשְּׂמֹאל;
וְתַחַת כַּפּוֹת רַגְלֵיהֶם הַיְחֵפוֹת
זוֹרֵם הַיָּם הַבּוֹעֵר — —

And at times the evening and the sea run into my heart, and I run to the sea. I am summoned, as if to the rim of the heavens, to behold: on either side of the sinking globe of the sun, he is seen, she is seen: my father to the right and my mother to the left; and beneath their bare feet flows the burning sea.

בְּלֵיל גֶּשֶׁם בִּירוּשָׁלַיִם

ON A NIGHT OF RAIN IN JERUSALEM

עֲצֵי מְעַט בֶּחָצֵר הוֹמִים כַּעֲצֵי יַעַר,
כִּבְדֵי נְהָרוֹת עֲנָנִים מָרְעָמִים,
מַלְאֲכֵי הַשָּׁלוֹם לִמְרַאֲשׁוֹת יְלָדַי
בְּהֶמְיַת הָעֵצִים וְחַשְׁרַת הַגְּשָׁמִים.

The few trees in the yard moan like a forest. The thunderous clouds are heavy with rivers. The Angels of Peace stand at the head of my sleeping children, as the trees moan and the heavy rains pour down.

בַּחוּץ — יְרוּשָׁלַיִם: עִיר מַסַּת הוֹד הָאָב
וַעֲקֵדַת בְּנוֹ בְּאַחַד הֶהָרִים:
הָאֵשׁ־מִשְׁחֲרִית עוֹד דּוֹלֶקֶת בָּהָר
הַגְּשָׁמִים לֹא כִבּוּהָ: אֵשׁ בֵּין הַבְּתָרִים.

Outside: Jerusalem, city of the Father's[1] glorious trial, where he bound his son on one of the hills. That fire, kindled at dawn, still burns on the hill, the rains have not put it out: it is the fire between the sacrificial pieces.[2]

1. Abraham. 2. Genesis 15.17.

'אִם אֵל יְצַוֵּנִי כָּעֵת כְּשֶׁצִּוָּה
לְאָבִי הַקַּדְמוֹן – אֲצַיֵּת בְּוַדַּאי',
רָן לִבִּי וּבְשָׂרִי בְּלֵיל הַגֶּשֶׁם הַזֶּה
וּמַלְאֲכֵי הַשָּׁלוֹם לִמְרַאֲשׁוֹתֵי יְלָדַי!

'If God were to command me now, as once He did my ancient Father, I would surely obey,' sing my heart and my flesh on this night of rain, as the Angels of Peace stand at the head of my sleeping children!

מַה מֵּהוֹד מַה מָּשָׁל לָזֶה רֶגֶשׁ פִּלְאִי
חַי מִקֶּדֶם שַׁחֲרִית עַד כָּעֵת אֶל הַר מוֹר:
מִתְרוֹנֵן דַּם הַבְּרִית בְּגוּף אָב תְּפִלִּי
נָכוֹן לְקָרְבָּן הַר הַבַּיִת עִם אוֹר!

What can equal this glory, this wondrous zeal – alive since that ancient dawn to this very moment – for the Mount of Moriah? The blood of the covenant sings on in the father's fervent body. He is prepared to offer his sacrifice on the Temple Mount at dawn.

בַּחוּץ – יְרוּשָׁלַיִם.. וְהֶמְיַת עֲצֵי יָהּ
שֶׁכְּרָתוּם הָאוֹיְבִים בָּהּ מִכָּל הַדּוֹרוֹת..
עֲנָנִים כִּבְדֵי נְהָרוֹת: בָּם בְּרָקִים
וּרְעָמִים, שֶׁהֵם לִי בְּלֵיל גֶּשֶׁם – בְּשׂוֹרוֹת
מִפִּי הַגְּבוּרָה עַד סוֹף הַדּוֹרוֹת.

(1954)

Outside: Jerusalem, and the moaning of the Lord's trees, cut down by her enemies in every generation; clouds heavy with rain, lightnings in them and thunders which, for me, on this night of rain, are tidings from the mouth of the God of Might to endless generations.

כְּרִיתַת כָּנָף

THE SEVERING OF THE WING

לְפֶתַע וּלְפִתְאוֹם בְּבֹקֶר לֹא עָבוֹת
וְרֵיחַ כָּל הַצּוֹמֵחַ נָדַף
וְכָל הַצִּפֳּרִים עָפוֹת בְּמִין כָּנָף אַחַת..
אַלְלַי לְכָל רוֹאָן כָּכָה וְהוּא לֹא נָטַל בְּיָדָיו
אֶת עִנְּבֵי עֵינָיו וְלֹא סָחַט!

So very suddenly, one cloudless morning, the fragrance of growth filling the air, and all the birds were flying with some sort of single wing . . . Woe to the man who, seeing them thus, did not pluck the grapes of his eyes and crush them with his hands!

גַּם הַצִּפֳּרִים עַצְמָן אֵינָן יוֹדְעוֹת מִי קִצֵּץ לָהֶן כָּנָף
לְפֶתַע וּלְפִתְאוֹם הֵן עָפוֹת כָּךְ בָּאֲוִיר
נוֹטוֹת אֶל צַד . .
וְאַף דָּם אֵינוֹ נוֹטֵף וְאֵין הֶכֵּר כִּי לְכָל צִפּוֹר
הָיוּ שְׁתֵּי כְנָפַיִם לְהַעֲבִיר

לְבָבוֹת דִּכְסִיפִין מֵהָכָא לְהָתָם –
עַכְשָׁו אֵין יוֹתֵר לְהָתָם.
בִּדְבַר אֱלֹהִים כְּמוֹ בַחֲלוֹם נֶחְתְּכָה כָנָף
וְעַל מְקוֹם הַחִתּוּךְ חָתַם.

(1955)

Even the birds, they themselves, do not know who cut off their wing. So very suddenly, and they were flying through the air, thus, tilted to one side. And no blood drips, and there is no sign that every bird once had two wings, to carry

yearning hearts from over-here to over-there. Now over-there is no more. By the word of God, as if in a dream, the wing was cut off, and then He sealed up the gash.

מַעֲשֶׂה בְּאֶחָד שֶׁיָּצָא מִמִּנְעָלָיו

עָמַדְתִּי וּשְׁתֵּי עֵינַי רָאוּ
לֹא יָדַעְתִּי מִי הָאִישׁ וּשְׁמוֹ מַהוּ
וּמָה הֵם סִבְכֵי מְאֹרָעָיו,
הָיָה זֶה בֹּקֶר שֶׁכֻּלּוֹ זָהָב
וּבָא הָאִישׁ עֲדֵי עַמּוּד חַשְׁמַל
כְּאֶל מְקוֹם הַגְּבוּל שֶׁבּוֹ בָּחַר
וְשָׁם יָצָא מִמִּנְעָלָיו
וְהִשְׁאִירָם לַעֲמֹד שָׁם כְּאֶל סַף
וְהֵחֵל לִפְסֹעַ בְּרַגְלַיִם יְחֵפוֹת
אֶל מֵעֵבֶר זֶה מְקוֹם הַסּוֹף
אֱלֵי בְרֵאשִׁית אֵין קֵץ הַרְחֵק :
בְּלִי בַיִת בְּלִי מִשְׁכָּב בְּלִי חֵיק :
בְּלִי כִכַּר לֶחֶם בְּלִי צַפַּחַת . . . קַל וָרֵיק.

THE MAN WHO STEPPED OUT OF HIS SHOES

I stood, and my two eyes saw this: I didn't know who the man was, his name, or his tangled history. It was a morning all of gold, and this man marched up to the electric pole as if to a borderline that he had chosen, and there he stepped out of his shoes, and, leaving them behind, as if on a threshold, he began walking barefoot, to somewhere beyond this final point, towards an endless beginning far in the distance . . . without house, or bed, or bosom, without a loaf of bread or a jar of water . . . light and empty-handed.

אֲנִי רָאִיתִי אֶת רַחֲבוּת כְּתֵפָיו
קוֹמַת גּוּפוֹ וּמִצְעֲדֵי גַבְרוּת
הוֹלֵךְ הוֹלֵךְ מִכָּאן אֶל מֶרְחַקָּיו
בְּלִי זֵכֶר מִנְעָלָיו פֹּה. מְחַכָּיו.

I saw his broad shoulders, his high
stature, his manly steps, going away,
going from here to his distances,
without the memory of his shoes, which
wait for him here.

שִׁמְעוֹן הַלְקִין

Simon Halkin

דִּין־אֱמֶת

THE TRUE JUDGE

שֶׁאֵין אֶלָּא חַיִּים הַלָּלוּ, כָּאן נִשְׁנִים עַל אֲדָמָה שְׁחוֹרָה,
אֱמֹר אֱמֹר עִם שֶׁמְּבָרֵךְ אַתָּה דַּיַּן־אֱמֶת לְאוֹר בְּרָקוֹ
שֶׁל דִּין מוֹרִיק בְּטְרִיז כּוֹכַב־הָעֶרֶב.

That there is nothing but this life,
repeated here on the black soil, say it,
say it as you bless the True Judge by
the light of judgement's sudden flash,
shining green in the wedge of an
evening star.

וְכָאן בָּרֵךְ דַּיַּן־אֱמֶת עִם שֶׁמְּנַשֵּׁק אַתָּה פִּי אֵם שֶׁמֵּתָה,
שֶׁמֵּתָה וְלֹא תָשׁוּב וּפִיהָ שָׁב וְחַי בְּנֵכֶל אַהֲבָה
לְאוֹר בְּרָקָיו כְּחֻלִּים שֶׁל שַׂר־הַלַּיְלָה.

And, here, bless the True Judge, as you
kiss the mouth of a dead mother, who
died, never to come back, but whose
mouth comes to life again and again, in
love's duplicity, by the light of the
Prince of Night's blue lightnings.

לְאוֹר גְּשָׁמִים הַלָּלוּ כָּאן, שְׁחוֹרִים וְגַם כְּחֻלִּים לְעֵת הַלַּיְלָה
כְּאָז בִּכְפַר־מוֹלֶדֶת, מְזַמְזֵם בְּצַפְצָפוֹת בְּעַד חַלּוֹן
בְּבָרָד חִפּוּשִׁיּוֹת טְרוּפוֹת־הַחֵשֶׁק,

By the light of these rains here, black,
blue, when the night – as in my native
village – drones in the poplars by the
window, in a hail of beetles frenzied
with desire,

בָּרֵךְ דַּיַּן־אֱמֶת בְּזִיעַ, חָשָׁה־לֹא־הֵבִינָה אֵם שֶׁמֵּתָה,
תָּחוּשׁ־וְלֹא־תָבִין אוֹהֶבֶת צוֹפִיָּה סוּמָה לְזֶרַע הַלַּיְלָה –
בָּרֵךְ דַּיַּן־אֱמֶת הָרָה לָנֶצַח.

bless the True Judge with the tremor
which the dying mother felt and did
not understand, which your love,
blindly looking for the seed of night,
feels and does not understand – bless
the True Judge eternally conceiving.

אַבְרָהָם שְׁלוֹנְסְקִי

Abraham Shlonsky

[עָמָל]

[TOIL]

הַלְבִּישִׁינִי, אִמָּא כְּשֵׁרָה, כְּתֹנֶת פַּסִּים לְתִפְאֶרֶת
וְעִם שַׁחֲרִית הוֹבִילִינִי אֱלֵי עָמָל.

Dress me, good mother, in a glorious robe of many colours,[1] and at dawn lead me to [my] toil.

עוֹטְפָה אַרְצִי אוֹר כַּטַּלִּית,
בָּתִּים נִצְּבוּ כַטּוֹטָפוֹת,
וְכִרְצוּעוֹת תְּפִלִּין גּוֹלְשִׁים כְּבִישִׁים, סָלְלוּ כַּפַּיִם.

My land is wrapped in light as in a prayer shawl. The houses stand forth like frontlets; and the roads paved by hand, stream down like phylactery straps.

תְּפִלַּת שַׁחֲרִית פֹּה תִּתְפַּלֵּל קִרְיָה נָאָה אֱלֵי בּוֹרְאָהּ.
וּבַבּוֹרְאִים – בִּנֵךְ אַבְרָהָם,
פַּיְטָן־סוֹלֵל בְּיִשְׂרָאֵל.

Here the lovely city says the morning prayer to its Creator. And among the creators is your son Abraham, a road-building bard of Israel.

וּבָעֶרֶב בֵּין הַשְּׁמָשׁוֹת יָשׁוּב אַבָּא מִסִּבְלוֹתָיו
וְכִתְפִלָּה יִלְחַשׁ נַחַת:
– הֲבֵן יַקִּיר לִי אַבְרָהָם,
עוֹר וְגִידִים וַעֲצָמוֹת –
הַלְלוּיָהּ.

And in the evening twilight, father will return from his travails, and, like a prayer, will whisper joyfully: 'My dear son Abraham, skin, sinews and bones – hallelujah.'

הַלְבִּישִׁינִי, אִמָּא כְּשֵׁרָה, כְּתֹנֶת פַּסִּים לְתִפְאֶרֶת
וְעִם שַׁחֲרִית הוֹבִילִינִי
אֱלֵי עָמָל.

Dress me, good mother, in a glorious robe of many colours, and at dawn lead me to toil.

1. Genesis 27.3.

קֵץ אֲדָר

כְּאֶצְעֲדוֹת־הַזָּהָב אֲשֶׁר לִזְרוֹעוֹת הַבֶּדְוִיָּה,
יַעַנְדוּ הָרֵי הַגִּלְבֹּעַ לְעֵמֶק יִזְרְעֶאל
אֶת צְמִידֵיהֶם
בִּשְׁעוֹת הַזָּהָב אֲשֶׁר לְעַרְבֵי קֵץ־אֲדָר.
אָז תֵּצֶאןָ הַשֹּׁאֲבוֹת הָעַיְנָה,
וְהָיוּ הַכַּלָּנִיּוֹת כְּאֶצְעָדוֹת לְרַגְלֵיהֶן.

הַטִּי, הַטִּי־נָא אֶת כַּדֵּךְ,
וְנִשְׁתֶּה מֵימֵי־עַיִן קָרִים, נוֹזְלִים,
וְהָיוּ לְחִכֵּנוּ כְּיַיִן הַטּוֹב.

כִּי יָרַד הָאֲדָר לִגְוֹעַ מִתְּנוּבָה,
כַּאֲשֶׁר יָמוּתוּ הַבֶּדְוִים אֲשֶׁר לְשֵׁבֶט עַזְרָא
מִנִּי אַהֲבָה.

אָז הָיִינוּ שְׁמֵי־הַשְּׁקִיעָה
אֲשֶׁר לְעַרְבֵי קֵץ־אֲדָר.

LATE ADAR[1]

Like the golden bangles on the arms of a Bedouin woman, the hills of Gilboa bind their bracelets about the valley of Jezreel in the golden hours of late Adar evenings. Then do the women go down to the spring to draw water, and the anemones are like bangles around their feet.

Please lower your jar, now, so that we may drink the cool flowing waters of the spring, and they will be like spiced wine on our tongues.

For Adar has come down to expire of luxuriance as the Bedouins of the tribe of Asra die of love.[2]

Then we became the sunset skies of the evenings in late Adar.

שָׁלֹשׁ זְקֵנוֹת

בָּעֶרֶב הָאָפֹר עַל יַד הַבַּיִת הַלָּבָן
יוֹשְׁבוֹת שָׁלֹשׁ זְקֵנוֹת וְצוֹפִיּוֹת אֶל נִכְחָן.
וְהַס סָבִיב.
כְּאִלּוּ בִּמְעוּפוֹ קָפָא פִּתְאֹם הָעַיִט.
שָׁלֹשׁ זְקֵנוֹת יוֹשְׁבוֹת עַל יַד הַבַּיִת.

THREE OLD WOMEN

In the grey evening, beside the white house, three old ladies sit, gazing straight ahead. And stillness all around. As if the eagle had suddenly frozen in flight. Three old ladies sit beside the house.

1. The Hebrew month roughly corresponding to March.
2. A reference to a well-known Arab legend, also found in Heine's lyric 'Der Asra': '. . . my kinsmen are those Asra / who die when they love'.

וּמִי־שֶׁהוּא דּוּמָם סוֹרֵג מֵעַל רָאשָׁן
פֻּזְמָק כָּחֹל בַּנֻּסָּח הַיָּשָׁן.
צְנֵפַת זָהָב בָּאֹפֶק מִתְגּוֹלֶלֶת.
שָׁלֹשׁ זְקֵנוֹת רָאוּ לְפֶתַע יֶלֶד.

And someone, silently, above their heads, knits a blue stocking in the old style. A golden skein unravels on the horizon. Three old ladies suddenly saw a child.

שָׁלֹשׁ זְקֵנוֹת הִתְעוֹרְרוּ פִּתְאֹם
וְנֶאֶנְחוּ: מִסְכֵּן . . . וַדַּאי יָתוֹם . . .
וְאַחַר כָּךְ נִגְּשׁוּ. לְטָפוּהוּ עַל הַלֶּחִי.
הַיֶּלֶד הִתְבּוֹנֵן – וְהִתְפָּרֵץ בִּבְכִי.

Three old ladies woke with a start and sighed: 'Poor thing . . . an orphan, probably . . .' And then went over. Patted him on the cheek. The child looked, and burst into tears.

וְאַחַר כָּךְ בָּא לַיִל, כְּיֶלֶד לֹא־מוּבָן,
שָׁלֹשׁ זְקֵנוֹת חָמְקוּ אֶל תּוֹךְ הַבַּיִת הַלָּבָן.
וְהַס סָבִיב.
רַק אֵיזֶה עֶלְבּוֹן עוֹד הִתְחוֹגֵג כְּעַיִט
מֵעַל לְדַף סַפְסָל, שֶׁנִּתְרוֹקֵן עַל יַד הַבַּיִת.

And then night came, like a baffling child. Three old ladies slipped away into the white house. And stillness all around. Only a kind of humiliation still circled like an eagle above the wooden bench, empty now, beside the house.

נְאֻם פְּלוֹנִי עַל שְׁכוּנָתוֹ:

SAID JOHN DOE OF HIS NEIGHBOURHOOD

בֵּית־מְגוּרַי הוּא בֶּן 5 קוֹמוֹת, –
וְכָל חַלּוֹנוֹתָיו מְפַהֲקִים אֶל שֶׁכְּנֶגֶד,
כִּפְנֵי הַנִּצָּבִים אֶל מוּל רְאִי.

The house I live in is 5 floors high, and all its windows yawn at their opposites, like the faces of those standing before a mirror.

70 קַוֵּי אוֹטוֹבּוּסִים בְּעִירִי,
וְכֻלָּם עַד מַחֲנָק וְעַד סִרְחוֹן הַגּוּפִים.
הֵם נוֹסְעִים
הֵם נוֹסְעִים
הֵם נוֹסְעִים אֶל לֵב הַכְּרָךְ,
כְּאִלּוּ אִי־אֶפְשָׁר לִגְוֹעַ מִשִּׁעֲמוּם גַּם כָּאן, –
בִּשְׁכוּנָתִי שֶׁלִּי.

There are 70 bus routes in my city, all chock-full, stifling with the stench of bodies; travelling, travelling, travelling deep into the heart of the city, as if one couldn't die of boredom right here, in my own neighbourhood.

שְׁכוּנָתִי שֶׁלִּי הִיא קְטַנָּה מְאֹד,
אַךְ יֵשׁ בָּהּ כָּל הַלֵּדוֹת וְהַמִּיתוֹת,
וְכָל שֶׁבֵּין לֵדָה לְמָוֶת
שֶׁיֵּשׁ בִּכְרַכֵּי הָעוֹלָם, —
אֲפִלּוּ תִּינוֹקוֹת, הַמְסוֹבְבִים לְהַפְלִיא
צַלַּחַת־מְעוֹפֶפֶת,
וּ־3 בָּתֵּי־קוֹלְנוֹעַ.
לוּלֵא הִסְתַּפַּקְתִּי בַּשִּׁעְמוּם שֶׁיֵּשׁ לִי בְּבֵיתִי,
הָיִיתִי הוֹלֵךְ לְאֶחָד מֵהֶם.

My neighbourhood is very small, but within it are all the births and deaths, and all there is from birth to death, that you find in the world's great cities – even tots, who twirl 'flying saucers' marvellously, and 3 cinemas. If I weren't content with the boredom in my own house, I would go to one of them.

בֵּית־מְגוּרַי הוּא בֶּן 5 קוֹמוֹת, —
זוֹ שֶׁקָּפְצָה מִן הַחַלּוֹן שֶׁכְּנֶגֶד
נִסְתַּפְּקָה בְּ־3 בִּלְבַד. —

The house I live in is 5 floors high – that woman who jumped from the window opposite contented herself with 3.

יוֹכֶבֶד בַּת־מִרְיָם

Yokheved Bat-Miriam

עֲגוּרִים מֵהַסַּף

CRANES FROM THE THRESHOLD

מֵאַחֲרַי אַתְּ נִשְׁאַרְתְּ עַל הַדֶּרֶךְ,
וְרוֹנֵן צְעָדַי הַנִּזְכָּר.
אֲלֻמָּה זְהֻבָּה וּמְהַרְהֶרֶת,
עֲגוּרִים, עֲגוּרִים עַל הַסַּף!

You remained on the road behind me and my footsteps sing, remembering. A golden, pensive sheaf, cranes, cranes on the threshold!

אֶכָּשֵׁל בְּעָנָן כִּבְאֶבֶן,
אֶכָּשֵׁל בְּיוֹמִי כִּבְחֵטְא.
יִשָּׂאֵנִי בֵּין כְּחוֹל וְכוֹכֶבֶת
תֹּם גִּמְגּוּמֵךְ הַמְרַטֵּט!

I trip on a cloud as on a stone, I trip on my day as on a sin. The innocence of your quivering stammer lifts me between the blue and a star.

כִּי הָיִית, כִּי הִקְרַנְתְּ מִבֶּכִי,
כִּי גָּחַנְתְּ עַל גַּל מְצֻיָּר,
נוֹשְׁמָה, מַפְלִיגָה וְהוֹלֶכֶת
נִשְׁמַת חוֹף לֹא־נִרְאֶה וְנִסְעָר.

Because you were, because you shone
with tears, because you leaned over a
painted wave, breathing, as you sailed
on and on, the breath of an invisible
and stormy shore.

מְטַפְּחִים אֵלָיו וְאֵלַיִךְ
(הַסְּגוּרָה בְּמֶרְחַקּוֹ הַזָּהֹב !),
מְטַפְּחִים מִשְׁתַּפְּכִים יָמַי לִי
וְשָׁרִים חֲלוֹמֵךְ הָאָהוּב.

My days are pounding toward the
shore and toward you (who are
enclosed within its golden distance!),
pounding, pouring themselves out and
singing your beloved dream.

זְהָרִים וּדְמִי לְלֹא־שַׁחַר,
זְהָרִים וּתְכֵלֶת אֵין־שֵׁם ;
יְחִידָה הַשָּׁעָה הַצּוֹמַחַת
וּמֵעֵבֶר לְעֵינַי תֵּעָצֵם.

Splendours and silence without
meaning, splendours and azure without
name; this hour that rises is alone and
will be closed beyond my eyes.

יְחִידָה אֶל הַסַּף וְהָאֶבֶן,
שֶׁבָּדוּ אַגָּדָתֵךְ בְּרֹן,
יוֹלִיכוּנִי כְּאוֹת הַזּוֹהֶבֶת,
כְּשֵׁם עַל דַּפֵּךְ הָרִאשׁוֹן.

Alone, to the threshold and the stone
that devised your legend in song, the
splendours will lead me like a golden
initial, like a name on your first page.

אָבוֹת יְשׁוּרוּן
Avot Yeshurun

[מִכְתָּבִים]
[LETTERS]

1

יוֹם יָבוֹא וְאִישׁ לֹא יִקְרָא מִכְתָּבִים שֶׁל אִמִּי.
יֵשׁ לִי מֵהֶם חֲבִילָה.
לֹא שֶׁל מִי
וְלֹא מִלָּה.

1

There will come a day when no one will read my mother's letters. I have a whole pack of them. Not whose they were and not a clue.

יוֹם יָבוֹא וְאִישׁ לֹא יִקַּח אוֹתָם לַיָּד.
יֵשׁ מֵהֶם צְרוֹר וְהוֹתֵר.
יֹאמְרוּ: נְיָר פִּסַּת
וְלֹא יוֹתֵר.

There will come a day when no one will touch them. There's a bundle of them, and to spare. They'll say: paper, a sheet of, and that's it.

בַּיּוֹם הַהוּא אֲבִיאֵם אֶל מְעָרַת בַּר־כּוֹכְבָא
לְהַעֲלוֹתָם בָּאָבָק. הָעוֹלָם הַקּוֹדֵם
לֹא יַחְקֹר בָּהּ
שְׂפַת אֵם.

On that day I'll take them to Bar-Kokhba's cave to lay them in the dust. That bygone world won't research the cave for a mother-tongue.

5

בְּבַקָּשְׁתִּי אֲנִי מִכְתָּבִים שֶׁל אִמִּי לִשְׁכֹּחַ.
אַף עָשִׂיתִי שֻׁלְחָנִי נָקִי.
מוֹסִיפִים עַצְמָם לִשְׁלֹחַ,
אֵלַי נוֹגְעִים:

5

I did my best to forget my mother's letters. I even tidied up my desk. They go on mailing themselves, reaching out for me:

פִּנִּיתָ הַשֻּׁלְחָן מִכֹּל נְיָרוֹת שֶׁלְּךָ מְבֻלְבָּלִים,
סָגַרְתָּ בַּתִּיקִים אֶחָד לְאֶחָד

[The Dead:] 'You've cleared your desk of all your cluttered papers. You've locked away in files, one by one, the

מִכְתָּבִים אַף הַבּוּלִים ;
וְאוֹתָנוּ בַּצַּד.

letters, and the stamps; and put us aside.

תִּקְרָא אוֹ לֹא תִקְרָא. עוֹשֶׂה עַצְמוֹ כְּאִלּוּ . . .
כְּהַיּוֹם שֶׁהִכְנַסְתָּ סֵדֶר בַּתִּיקִים,
יֵשׁ עִנְיָן אֲפִלּוּ
בְּמִכְתְּבֵי מֵתִים.

'Yes, you'll read, no you won't; putting on airs as if . . . Now that you've set your files in order, even letters by the dead compel attention.'

22

22

קִבַּלְתִּי מִכְתַּבְכֶם וּבוֹ לָאָח הַבְּכוֹר.
מָה רָחַקְתָּ כָּכָה מָה ?
מִלָּה וְלֹא חַמָּה
וְלֹא אוֹמֶרֶת.

[The poet to his mother:] 'I received your letter with my younger brother's message:[1] "Why have you become so distant, why? One word, not warm, and saying nothing.

לְאַחַר תִּקְוָה – מִכְתָּב. קָטֹן מִכְּתֹב.
קָטָן מֵאוֹת וְרַב מִתּוֹךְ.
וְעוֹד אַתָּה אוֹמֵר
וּכְבָר גּוֹמֵר.

After hope – a letter. Too tiny for the name. Tinier than a [Hebrew] character, though crammed inside. You've hardly begun to speak, before you're done.

מַלֵּא דַּפִּים שְׁלֵמִים כְּמַחַט יַחַד,
כְּאֵשׁ הַמִּתְנַפֶּלֶת עַל הַגָּאז
וְכַשַּׂק עַל הָאֵשׁ,
וּבִלְבַד שֶׁתִּקְרַב.

Fill up whole pages, tightly pinned together, like a flame hurling itself upon gas, or like a sack upon flames. Just be sure to come close."'

1. Lit. 'and in it to the eldest brother', i.e. to me.

פְּרֵילוּד עַל מוֹת הַתּוּת

גִּשְׁמֵי הַזַּעַף הָיוּ מְלֻוִּים רוּחַ סְעָרָה.

בְּרֹאשׁ הָרְחוֹב בְּרֹאשׁ הָעֵץ עָמַד צִפּוֹר,
עוֹרֵב שָׁחוֹר, וּמִתְקָרֵא, וּמִתְקָרֵא. מִדְּבָרָיו יוֹצֵא,
שֶׁאָחוּז נִכָּר שֶׁל הַבְּרוֹשִׁים 'מֵתוּ זְקוּפִים'.

הָעִתּוֹן בְּתַלְמֵי מִקְוֶה מַבִּיעַ צַעַר בִּמְיֻחָד
עַל הָאֵיקָלִפְּטוּס: מִי הָיָה חוֹשֵׁד כִּי בְּשָׁרְשֵׁי
עֲנָק זֶה מִסְתַּתֶּרֶת פִּטְרִיָּה שֶׁתָּבִיא עָלָיו כְּלָיָה.

הָעִתּוֹן אוֹמֵר, כִּי רֹב הָעֵצִים מַתְחִילִים לְהִתְנַוֵּן
אַחֲרֵי יוֹבֵל שָׁנִים, בִּגְלַל הָעָצֶה הָרַךְ שֶׁמַּתְחִיל
לְהִתְפָּרֵק. וְזֶה מַה שֶּׁקָּרָה לַעֲצֵי הָאִזְדָּרֶכֶת
וַעֲצֵי הַתּוּת.

טוֹב.

PRELUDE TO THE DEATH OF THE MULBERRY TREE

The heavy rain was accompanied by a stormy wind.

At the top of the street, at the top of the tree stood a bird, a black crow, and screeching, and screeching. He said, in so many words, that a large percentage of cypresses 'die on their feet'.

The newsletter of Talmey Mikveh[1] expresses deep sorrow over the [fate of] the eucalyptus: who would suspect that in the roots of this giant lurks a fungus that brings about its downfall?

The newsletter says that most trees begin to deteriorate after fifty years because the soft pith begins to decompose. And that's what happened to the Persian lilacs and the mulberries.

All right.

עַל מוֹת הַתּוּת

לֹא אָמַרְתִּי יָפְיָם שֶׁל בָּתִּים הֲרוּסִים, כְּגוֹן רַבִּי,
לִפְנֵי מִלְחָמָה הָיָה קַפְּדָן וּמַעֲנִישׁ,
וְאַחֲרֵי מִלְחָמָה הָיָה רַךְ וְהָלַךְ.
לֹא דִּבַּרְתִּי עַל עֵצִים שֶׁנֶּעֶקְרוּ בִּרְחוֹב
בֶּרְדִיצֶ'בְסְקִי. עֵץ הַתּוּת שֶׁעָמַד אַרְבָּעִים

ON THE DEATH OF THE MULBERRY TREE

I haven't said the beauty of ruined houses, such as my Rabbi: before the War[2] he had been harsh and punitive but after the War he went soft and passed away. I haven't spoken of the trees that were pulled out on Berditchevsky Street.[3] A mulberry tree that stood there for forty years, and nobody

1. A weekly bulletin issued by the agricultural school in Mikveh Yisrael.
2. The First World War. 3. A side street in Tel Aviv.

שָׁנָה, וְאִישׁ לֹא יָדַע נָטַע אוֹתוֹ מִי מַה מּוּ. עָמַד
עַל מִדְרָכָה בְּלִי כְּבִישׁ, לְיַד
חֲנוּת מַכֹּלֶת. יְלָדִים טִפְּפוּ בַּחוֹל וְטִפְּסוּ עַל
הָעֵץ. פְּרִי הַתּוּת דָּמָה לָאֲבָרִים
הַקָּשִׁים וְהַחִוְּרִים שֶׁל הַמִּין אֵצֶל יְלָדִים.
מִשֶּׁעָשׂוּ כְּבִישׁ וְהִנְהִיגוּ תּוּת־בּוֹנְבּוֹנְיֶרָה־
בְּקַרְטוֹן, אִישׁ לֹא זָכַר שֶׁהָעַלְוָה נֶעֶלְמָה מִן
הָעֵץ. הָיָה מֻעֲסָק בָּאַחֲרוֹנָה לְיַד
חֲנוּת מַכֹּלֶת, לִתְמוֹךְ גַּג שֶׁל סְמַרְטוּט עַל
הַיְּרָקוֹת וְהַפֵּרוֹת. עֲקָרוֹת הַבַּיִת,
בְּבָרְרָן אֶת הַפֵּרוֹת וְהַיְּרָקוֹת, מִתְכּוֹפְפוֹת, לָאו
עִם הַפָּנִים אֶל הָעֵץ.
קָרְאוּ לָעִירִיָּה לָבוֹא לַעֲקֹר אוֹתוֹ. אָמְרָה
הָעִירִיָּה: לֹא הִיא נְטָעַתּוּ. אָמְרוּ: אִם
לִנְטִיעָה, הֵם גַּם לֹא נְטָעוּהוּ.

knew who planted it, or gave a damn.
Stood on a sidewalk, without a road,
next to the grocery. Children hopped
in the sand and climbed the tree. The
berries looked like the hard, pale
genitals of children. After a road was
paved and they began selling berries in
fancy candy boxes, no one remembered
that the tree had lost its foliage. Lately
it was employed, next to the grocery, in
supporting an awning of rags over the
vegetables and fruits. The housewives,
picking out fruits and vegetables, bent
down, their backs to the tree. They
called city hall to come and pull it out.
City hall said: it didn't plant it. Well,
they said, as far as that goes, they
didn't plant it either.

בָּאָה עֶגְלַת גּוּמִי, הוֹרִידוּ חֶבֶל, כָּבְלוּ אֶת הָעֵץ,
נִסְּרוּ לִשְׁנַיִם. אָדוֹן בְּדֹלַח
זָרַק אַחֲרָיו קְלִפָּתוֹ.
מְעַט אֲנָשִׁים עָמְדוּ: צַלָּם שֶׁבַּסָּמוּךְ, נַהַג טַקְסִי
שֶׁמִּנֶּגֶד וְאִישׁ שֶׁבָּא, מִן הַמִּשְׂרָד,
נִכְנַס לַחֲנוּת קֹדֶם.

A cart came with rubber wheels. They
lowered a rope, tied the tree, sawed it
in two. Mr Crystal threw its bark into
the cart. A handful of people stood
around: the next-door photographer,
the taxi-driver from across the street,
and a man, from some office, who had
come before and stepped into the store.

הַגְּבֶרֶת בְּדֹלַח מְסַפֶּרֶת: 'יוֹם אֶחָד עָמְדָה
וְהִתְחִילָה מִתְנוֹדֶדֶת. וְהָעֵץ מִתְנוֹדֵד'.
הָאָדוֹן בְּדֹלַח אוֹמֵר: 'נָתַן לוֹ סְחִיבָה, וְזֶה נָפַל'.

Mrs Crystal tells her story: One day,
standing there, she began to rock back
and forth. And the tree rocked, too. Mr
Crystal says: He gave it a shove and it
fell.

הָעִתּוֹן בְּתַלְמֵי מִקְוֶה כּוֹתֵב: 'הָעֵצִים מְהַוִּים
מְקוֹם קִנּוּן וּמַחֲסֶה לְאַלְפֵי צִפֳּרִים,
לְשִׂמְחַת חוֹבְבֵי הַשִּׁירָה, אַךְ לֹא לַיּוֹגְבִים וְלַיַּרְקָנִים'.

The newsletter of Talmey Mikveh
writes: 'Trees serve as a nesting-place
and shelter for thousands of birds, to
the delight of poetry-lovers, but not of
farmers and greengrocers.'

טוֹב. אָנוּ מְנַתְּקִים אוֹתְךָ מִכָּל חֶבְרָה, אָנוּ
מְבַקְשִׁים מִמְּךָ סְלִיחָה. עַל כַּפַּיִם יִשָּׂאוּנְךָ.
גַּלְגַּלֵּי גּוּמִי. לֹא שׁוֹמְעִים.

All right. We hereby sever you from all society, we beg your forgiveness. They will lift you on their hands.[1] Rubber wheels. Not a sound.

חַיִּים לֶנְסְקִי

Ḥayim Lenski

[הַיּוֹם יָרַד]

[THE DAY CAME DOWN]

הַיּוֹם יָרַד בְּמַדְרֵגוֹת־הָאֶבֶן
אֶל תְּכוֹל מֵימֵי הַיְאוֹר לִרְחֹץ וּבְטֶרֶם
כָּלָה לִטְבֹּל צָלַל פִּי תְהוֹם. וְתֶלֶם
גַּלִּים עָבַר בְּתַהֲלוּכַת־אֵבֶל.

יָרְדָה דְמָמָה שְׁלֵמָה וַחֲצִי אֹפֶל,
וַעֲגֻלָּה, מוּפֶזֶת וּמַזְהֶרֶת,
שָׁקְעָה כִּפַּת אִיסָאָקִי תּוֹךְ הַזֶּרֶם
כְּפַעֲמוֹן אֲמוֹדַאי מְשֻׁלְשַׁל־חֶבֶל.

וּכְמוֹ כַּדּוּר־זָהָב מְגַשֵּׁשׁ בַּמַּיִם
חֹד גַּג הָאַדְמִירַלְיָה. בַּעְבּוּעַ.
שׁוֹטֵף הַיְאוֹר בְּזֹהַר בֵּין־עַרְבַּיִם.

הֶעֱלָה הַמֵּת, הִנֵּהוּ הַשָּׁבוּעַ;
אָרֹךְ, לְבֶן־פָּנִים וּכְחֹל־שְׂפָתַיִם.
'הַלַּיְלָה הַלָּבָן' – כֹּה יִקְרָאוּהוּ.

The day came down the stone steps to bathe in the blue waters of the river,[2] but it had scarcely immersed itself when it plunged into the depths. And a furrow of waves passed by in funeral procession.

Then complete silence and half-darkness descended; and round, gilded, glowing – the dome of St Isaac[3] sank into the stream like a diving-bell lowered by a cable.

And like a ball of gold, the roof of the Admiralty,[4] spires and all, gropes through the water. A gurgle. The river flows in the twilight glow.

Now the corpse has been hauled up, here is the one who drowned: long, white-faced and blue-lipped. 'The White Night' – that is how he's known.

1. 'We hereby sever, etc.' These phrases are taken from various parts of the funeral service.
2. The Neva, in Leningrad.
3. The cathedral.
4. The Admiralty building overlooking the Neva.

יוֹנָתָן רָטוֹשׁ

Yonatan Ratosh

אֶת נִשְׁמַת

THE SOUL OF

צֶדֶק לְפָנָיו יְהַלֵּךְ
יְפַלֵּס אָרְחוֹ מִישׁוֹר
צֶדֶק בַּמָּגֵן לְפָנָיו בָּאַשְׁמַנִּים
צֶדֶק לְפָנָיו יְהַלֵּךְ

Justice goes before him, clearing a
level path for him, shield-bearing
Justice before him in the darkness,
Justice goes before him,

אֶל אֱלֹהֵי רוּחוֹת יָם
קֶרֶב אֲפִיק תְּהוֹמוֹתַיִם
אֲשֶׁר בִּכְנָפוֹ מַעֲרִיב עֲרָבִים
שֵׂיבַת זְקָנוֹ עוֹלָה קָצֶף

to the god of the sea-winds,[1] deep
within the bed of the twin abysses,[2]
who, with his wing, brings on evenings,
whose white beard surges like foam.

עִם נֵרַת אֵלִים עָלִיתָ
גַּם תָּבוֹא
עִם נֵרַת אֵלִים הַשֶּׁמֶשׁ
בַּמָּבוֹא

You rose with the lamp of the gods,
now you shall set with it, with the
lamp of the god, the sun, where it goes
down

אֶל סוֹף כָּל מַיִם רַבִּים
אֶל רֹאשׁ עַפְרוֹת כָּל אֶרֶץ
רֹאשׁ כָּל דֶּרֶךְ הוֹלֶכֶת שָׁמַיִם
רֹאשׁ כָּל דֶּרֶךְ יוֹרֶדֶת שְׁאוֹל

to the end of all the mighty waters, to
the fountainhead of all the world's dust,
the head of all roads leading to heaven,
the head of all roads descending to
Sheol,

אֶל אֱלֹהֵי רוּחוֹת יָם
קֶרֶשׁ מֶלֶךְ אַב שָׁנִים
אֲשֶׁר בְּיָדוֹ נֶפֶשׁ כָּל בָּשָׂר
לִפְעָמָיו יִשְׁתַּחוּ כָּל חָי

to the god of the sea-winds, to the
timbered tabernacle of the King, Father
of all years, in whose hand are the souls
of all flesh, at whose feet all the living
prostrate themselves.

1. Also, 'the spirits of the West'. 2. Heaven and earth.

זֶה הַגֶּבֶר
רָאָה עֳנִי וְשִׁבְטוֹ
זֶה הָאִישׁ חָדַל מִמַּעַשׂ
– – לְבֵיתוֹ

This man has known affliction and its rod. This man no longer provides for his home.[1]

צֶדֶק לְפָנָיו יְהַלֵּךְ
יְפַלֵּס אָרְחוֹ מִישׁוֹר
צֶדֶק בַּמָּגֵן לְפָנָיו בָּאַשְׁמַנִּים
צֶדֶק לְפָנָיו יְהַלֵּךְ

Justice goes before him, clearing a level path for him, shield-bearing Justice before him in the darkness, Justice goes before him.

קֶרֶב אֲפִיק תְּהוֹמוֹתַיִם
קֶרֶשׁ מֶלֶךְ אַב שָׁנִים
אֲשֶׁר מִיָּדוֹ נֵזֶר בַּעַל
אֲשֶׁר מִיָּדוֹ עֹז עֲנָת
אֲשֶׁר מִיָּדוֹ חָכְמַת כּוֹשָׁר
אֲשֶׁר מִיָּדוֹ טוּב אֲשֵׁרָת
אֲשֶׁר מִימִינוֹ קֶרֶן בַּעַל
אֲשֶׁר מִשְּׂמֹאלוֹ כֹּבֶד מוֹת

into the bed of the twin abysses, the timbered tabernacle of the King, Father of all years, from whose hand – the diadem of Ba'al, from whose hand – the might of Anat, from whose hand – the wisdom of Koshar, from whose hand – the bounty of Asherat, at his right – the prowess of Ba'al, at his left – the weight of Mot.

אֵל אַדִּיר אֲבָרוֹת
מֵצֵל כַּנְפֵי עוֹלָם
הָעוֹשֶׂה מִשְׁפָּט בִּתְהוֹמָיו
בָּרֵךְ אֶת הַבָּא אֶל עַמָּיו

O El of the mighty pinions, who overshadow the ends of the earth, who administer justice in your abysses, bless the one who is going to his father's kin,

אֶת נִשְׁמַת
עַבְדְּךָ
שֶׁהָלַךְ
לְעוֹלָמוֹ –

bless the soul of your servant who has gone to his rest.

1. Or, 'This man has come to the end of his deeds. He is going home.'

צֶדֶק לְפָנָיו יְהַלֵּךְ
יְפַלֵּס אָרְחוֹ מִישׁוֹר
צֶדֶק בַּמָּגֵן לְפָנָיו בָּאַשְׁמַנִּים
צֶדֶק לְפָנָיו יְהַלֵּךְ

Justice goes before him, clearing a level path for him, shield-bearing Justice before him, in the darkness, Justice goes before him.

נָתָן אַלְתֶּרְמַן

Nathan Alterman

הָאֲסוּפִי

THE FOUNDLING

הִנִּיחַתְנִי אִמִּי לְרַגְלֵי הַגָּדֵר,
קָמוּט פָּנִים וְשׁוֹקֵט. עַל גַּב.
וָאַבִּיט בָּהּ מִלְמַטָּה, כְּמוֹ מִן הַבְּאֵר, –
עַד נוּסָהּ כְּהַנָּס מִן הַקְּרָב.
וָאַבִּיט בָּהּ מִלְמַטָּה, כְּמוֹ מִן הַבְּאֵר,
וְיָרֵחַ עָלֵינוּ הוּרַם כְּמוֹ נֵר.

My mother laid me at the foot of the fence, wrinkled and still, on my back. And I looked up at her, as if from a well – till she fled as one flees from a battle. And I looked up at her, as if from a well, and the moon was raised over us like a candle.

אַךְ בְּטֶרֶם הַשַּׁחַר הֵאִיר, אוֹתוֹ לֵיל,
קַמְתִּי אַט כִּי הִגִּיעָה עֵת
וָאָשׁוּב בֵּית אִמִּי כְּכַדּוּר מִתְגַּלְגֵּל
הַחוֹזֵר אֶל רַגְלֵי הַבּוֹעֵט.
וָאָשׁוּב בֵּית אִמִּי כְּכַדּוּר מִתְגַּלְגֵּל
וָאֶחֱבֹק צַוָּארָהּ בְּיָדַיִם שֶׁל צֵל.

But that same night, before the break of dawn, I slowly rose, for the time had come. And I returned to my mother's house as a ball rolls back to the foot that kicked it. And I returned to my mother's house as a ball rolls back, and clasped her neck with hands of shade.

מֵעָלֵי צַוָּארָהּ, לְעֵינֵי כֹּל יָכוֹל,
הִיא קְרָעַתְנִי כְּמוֹ עֲלוּקָה.
אַךְ שָׁב לַיְלָה וְשַׁבְתִּי אֵלֶיהָ כִּתְמוֹל,
וַתִּהְיֶה לָּנוּ זֹאת לְחֻקָּה:
בְּשׁוּב לַיְלָה וְשַׁבְתִּי אֵלֶיהָ כִּתְמוֹל
וְהִיא לַיְלָה כּוֹרַעַת לַגְּמוּל וְלָעֹל.

In the sight of the Almighty, she picked me off her neck like a leech. But when night returned, I returned to her as on the day before, and this became our binding rule: when night returns I return to her as on the day before, and every night she bows down to the retribution and the yoke.

וְדַלְתוֹת חֲלוֹמָהּ לִי פְּתוּחוֹת לִרְוָחָה
וְאֵין אִישׁ בַּחֲלוֹם מִלְּבַדִּי.
כִּי נוֹתְרָה אַהֲבַת־נַפְשׁוֹתֵינוּ דְּרוּכָה
כְּמוֹ קֶשֶׁת, מִיּוֹם הִוָּלְדִי.
כִּי נוֹתְרָה אַהֲבַת נַפְשׁוֹתֵינוּ דְּרוּכָה
וְלָעַד לֹא נִתֶּנֶת וְלֹא לְקוּחָה.

And the gates of her dream are wide open to me, and there is no one in that dream but myself. For the love of our souls has remained bent as a bow, ever since I was born. For the love of our souls has remained bent, and can never be given or taken away.

וְעַל כֵּן עַד אַחֲרִית לֹא הֵסִיר אוֹתִי אֵל
מֵעַל לֵב הוֹרָתִי הַצּוֹעֵק
וַאֲנִי — שֶׁנִּתַּקְתִּי מִבְּלִי הִגָּמֵל —
לֹא נִגְמַלְתִּי וְלֹא אֶנָּתֵק.
וַאֲנִי שֶׁנִּתַּקְתִּי מִבְּלִי הִגָּמֵל
נִכְנָס אֶל בֵּיתָהּ וְהַשַּׁעַר נוֹעֵל.

And therefore, till the very end, God did not dislodge me from my parent's wailing heart, and I, who had been torn away unweaned, have never been weaned and shall never tear away. And I, who had been torn away unweaned, now enter her house and lock the gate.

הִיא זָקְנָה בִּכְלָאִי וַתִּדַּל וַתִּקְטַן
וּפָנֶיהָ קֻמְּטוּ כְּפָנַי.
אָז יָדַי הַקְּטַנּוֹת הִלְבִּישׁוּהָ לָבָן
כְּמוֹ אֵם אֶת הַיֶּלֶד הַחַי.
אָז יָדַי הַקְּטַנּוֹת הִלְבִּישׁוּהָ לָבָן
וָאֶשָּׂא אוֹתָהּ בְּלִי לְהַגִּיד לָהּ לְאָן.

She grew old in my prison, she shrivelled and shrank, and her face became wrinkled like mine. Then my little hands dressed her in white, like a mother dressing her living child. Then my little hands dressed her in white, and I carried her off without telling her where.

וָאַנִּיחַ אוֹתָהּ לְרַגְלֵי הַגָּדֵר
צוֹפִיָּה וְשׁוֹקֶטֶת, עַל גָּב.
וַתַּבֵּט בִּי שׂוֹחֶקֶת, כְּמוֹ מִן הַבְּאֵר,
וַנֵּדַע כִּי סִיַּמְנוּ הַקְּרָב.
וַתַּבֵּט בִּי שׂוֹחֶקֶת כְּמוֹ מִן הַבְּאֵר,
וְיָרֵחַ עָלֵינוּ הוּרַם כְּמוֹ נֵר.

And I laid her at the foot of the fence, watchful and still, on her back. Then she looked at me, laughing, as if from a well, and we knew that the battle was done. Then she looked at me, laughing, as if from a well, and the moon was raised over us like a candle.

[בְּעוֹד עֶרֶב יוֹרֵד]

אִישׁ צוֹעֵק עַל דּוּכָן: עַרְמוֹנִים קְלוּיִים —
וּמְלַבֶּה גֶּחָלֵי אֵשׁ בִּמְנִיפָה שֶׁל פַּח.
אִישׁ חַי הוּא. נִגְזַר מֵאַרְצוֹת הַחַיִּים
וְכִסָּה אַדְמַת פּוֹלִין וְשָׁב־וְנָח.

אִישׁ מוֹזֵג יַיִן חָבִית וּבַלַּיִל לֹא יִישַׁן
עַד אַחֲרוֹן הַמְאַחֲרִים מִדֶּלְפֵּק יָסוּף.
אִישׁ מוֹזֵג שֶׁהָיָה לְעַמּוּד עָשָׁן
וְחָזַר וְהָיָה לְגוּף.

אִישׁ נַפָּח. בְּיָדוֹ פַּטִּישׁוֹ מוּנָף
וּסְבִיבוֹ גִּצֵּי אֵשׁ לָרֹב.
כְּאִישׁ חַי יִתְנוֹעֵעַ, יִזְדַּקֵּף וְיִכֹּף
וּבְיָדוֹ הַבַּרְזֶל יָלֹף.

אִישׁ כְּלִי זֶמֶר שֶׁקָּם מִשִּׁכְבוֹ עַל גָּב
מְנַגֵּן מַנְגִּינָה תַּמָּה
וּסְבִיבוֹ בְּעִגּוּל נִצָּבִים שׁוֹמְעָיו
שֶׁהָיוּ עִם יוֹרְדֵי דוּמָה.

אִישׁ עֶגְלוֹן. הוּא מִגַּל אֲבָנִים
קָם וַיְחִי. וְהִנֵּהוּ פֹּה
מַעֲמִיד שְׁנֵי סוּסָיו הַלְּבָנִים,
קוֹשֵׁר לָהֶם שַׂק הַמִּסְפּוֹא.

אִישׁ סוֹפֵר שֶׁקָּרְבוּ עַצְמוֹתָיו
וַתִּחְיֶינָה אַחֲרֵי כִּלָּיוֹן

[IN THE MARKET PLACE]

A man, hawking at his stall: 'Roasted chestnuts!' – and blowing the embers with a tin fan. He is a living man. He had been cut off from the land of the living and covered with Polish soil, yet he broke out, came back.

A man pouring wine from a keg. He does not sleep at night until the last, loitering drinker quits the counter. A vintner, who had become a column of smoke, then became a body again.

A man, a smith; his hammer raised in his hand, sparks of fire flashing about him. Moving like a living man, he straightens up, and bends, and twists the iron with his hand.

A man, a minstrel, who had been down on his back but arose, now playing a simple tune, and about him, in a circle, stand his listeners, those who had gone down into silence.

A man, a wagoner. He rose from under a heap of stones, and lived. And now he's here, reining his two white horses, tying on their feedbags.

A man, a writer, whose bones fitted themselves together and came to life

יוֹשֵׁב בְּזָוִית, קַו לָקָו
כּוֹתֵב דְּבָרִים עַל גִּלָּיוֹן.

after extinction, now sits in a corner, little by little putting things down on paper.

אִישׁ אוֹהֵב שֶׁהוּשַׁב מֵעָפָר
סָר בַּשּׁוּק אֶל דּוּכָן אוֹ שְׁנַיִם,
קוֹנֶה עֲגִילֵי עִנְבָּר
לְאִשְׁתּוֹ שֶׁהוּשְׁבָה מִמַּיִם.

A man, a lover, brought back from the dust, pauses in the market by a stall or two, buys amber earrings for his wife, who was brought back from water.

בְּרֵיחוֹת שֶׁל קָלִי וְנָזִיד,
תַּחַת שְׁמֵי עֲנָנִים עָטִים,
כֹּה טְרוּדָה וְכָל כָּךְ מַעֲשִׂית
וְנִפְלֵאת כֹּה תְּחִיַּת הַמֵּתִים.

Amidst the odours of roasting grain and broths, under a sky of sweeping clouds, so bustling and so business-like, so wondrous is the resurrection of the dead.

גֵּר בָּא לָעִיר

A STRANGER COMES TO THE CITY

הָעִיר נְצוּרָה מִבּוֹא וּמִצֵּאת.
וַאֲנִי אֶעֱבֹר לָבֶטַח.
אֲנִי הַזּוֹכֵר, הֶעָנִי־כְּמֵת,
אֶעֱמֹד עַל שְׁנָתֵךְ בַּפֶּתַח.

The city is under siege, none comes in, none goes out, but I shall pass through unscathed. I the rememberer, the pauper as good as dead, I shall stand in the gate, and guard your sleep.

וּבְאֶפֶס־כַּפּוֹת אֲחוֹנֵן,
וּכְאֵשׁ וַחֲנִית אֲגוֹנֵן,
וּבְטֶרֶם־אָבְדָן אֲאַמְּצֵךְ לַמּוֹעֵד,
אֲנִי הַזּוֹכֵר, אֲנִי הָעֵד.

And, without hands, I shall give you comfort, I shall protect you like fire and spear; and before all is lost, I shall brace you for the time, I the rememberer, I the witness.

יוֹם־יוֹם אֶתְפַּלֵּל שֶׁתִּכְלִי כְּמוֹ נֵר
שֶׁאֵלַי תֻּרְדְּפִי בַחֶרֶב.
וְיוֹם־יוֹם בַּעֲדֵךְ עַל פְּתָחִים אֲחַזֵּר,
לְמַעַן תִּחְיִי עוֹד עֶרֶב.

Each day I shall pray that you waste away like a candle, that you be driven to me by the sword. And each day, for your sake, I shall beg from door to door, that you may live to see another evening.

פַּת לְךָ אָבִיא אַחְרוֹנָה
בְּשֵׁם לְךָ אֶקְרָא רִאשׁוֹנָה.
הַחֵמֶת אַגִּיעַ אֶל פִּיךָ שֶׁחָרֵב,
אֲנִי הַדּוֹאֵג, אֲנִי הַשָּׂב.

I shall bring you the last crumb of bread, I shall be the first to call out your name. I shall hold the water-skin to your parched mouth, I the worrier, I the greybeard.

כִּי הִנֵּה לֹא יוֹשִׁיעַ הַחַי אֶת הַחַי,
וָאָבוֹא כַּסּוֹתֵךְ אַהֲבָה כַּמַּיִם,
אַהֲבָה לֹא סוֹלַחַת, נָכְרִית לְאַחַי,
גְּלוּיָה כְּשֹׁד בַּצָּהֳרַיִם.

For the living can never save the living. Therefore I have come to cover you with love as if with water, a merciless love, alien to my brothers, as brash as plunder at high noon.

וְאַתְּ בֵּאלֹהִים הִשָּׁבְעִי,
כִּי אוֹנִים מִצָּרָה תִּשְׁאֲבִי,
וּבְהַגִּיעַ עַד נֶפֶשׁ, תָּרִימִי קוֹל,
אֵלַי הָאַחֲרוֹן, הָאַחֲרוֹן לַכֹּל.

And you, now swear by God that you will draw strength from your miseries, and when they rise up to your neck, you will cry out, to me, the last, the very last of all.

כִּי הָעִיר נְצוּרָה מִבּוֹא וּמִצֵּאת,
וַאֲנִי אֶעֱבֹר לָבֶטַח.
בַּעֲדֵךְ, בַּעֲדֵךְ, אָמַר הַמֵּת,
שִׁבְעָתַיִם אָמוּת בַּפֶּתַח.

For the city is under siege, none comes in, none goes out, but I shall pass through unscathed. For you, for you, said the Dead, I shall die sevenfold in the gate.

וּכְאֵשׁ וַחֲנִית אֲחוֹנֵן,
וְכֹחַ לֹא־אִישׁ בָּךְ אֶתֵּן,
וּבְטֶרֶם אָבְדָן אֲכַבֵּךְ כְּמוֹ נֵר,
אֲנִי הַנָּכְרִי, אֲנִי הַגֵּר.

And like fire and spear I shall give you comfort, I shall fill you with inhuman strength. Then, on the verge of destruction, I shall snuff you out like a candle, I the alien, I the stranger.

הָאִשָּׁה

אָמְרָה הָאִשָּׁה: אֱלֹהַי,
שַׂמְתַּנִי מֵאָז קַדְמַת עֵת
לִהְיוֹת נוֹפְלָה לְרַגְלֵי הַחַי
וְלִהְיוֹת נִצָּבָה לִמְרַאֲשׁוֹת הַמֵּת.

THE WOMAN

The woman said: My God, You have appointed me since days of old to fall at the feet of the living, and to stand at the head of the dead.

הַכִּבְשָׂה

גָּזַל אֶת כִּבְשַׂת הָרָשׁ,
כִּסָּה דָמָהּ בְּאֶבֶן.
בְּשָׂרָהּ אָכַל, חֶלְבָּהּ שָׂרַף,
לֹא הִשְׁאִיר כִּי אִם בְּדַל צֶמֶר.

מִן הַצֶּמֶר הַזֶּה נִטְוָה הַחוּט
שֶׁבּוֹ אָחַז הַגֵּץ
שֶׁבָּא כְדְלֵקָה פֶּתַח בֵּית הָאִישׁ
וְנִכְנַס כְּכִבְשָׂה שֶׁל אֵשׁ.

THE LAMB

He robbed the poor man of his lamb, covered its blood with a stone. Ate its meat, burnt its fat, left nothing but a shred of wool.

This is the wool of which the thread was woven, which was gripped by the spark, which came as a flame to the door of his house and went in as a lamb of fire.

הַיְצִיאָה מִן הָעִיר

בַּעַל־בַּיִת אֶחָד בָּא חֲדָרָיו,
סָגַר הַדֶּלֶת אַחֲרָיו.
לְאוֹר הַמְּנוֹרָה מָנָה כַסְפּוֹ,
מָנָה שׂוֹנְאָיו. מֵעַל לוּחַ לִבּוֹ
אַחַר־כָּךְ מָחָה אֶת הַשֵּׁמוֹת כֻּלָּם,
הִשְׁאִיר שֵׁם אֶחָד לְשָׁמְרוֹ לְעוֹלָם.

THE EXIT FROM THE CITY

A certain man of means retreated into his inner rooms, shutting the door behind him. By the light of the lamp he counted his money, counted his enemies, then blotted out all the names from the tablet of his heart, left one single name to keep it forever. Then he

אַחַר־כָּךְ עָמַד וְכִבָּה הָאוֹר,
צָמַח נוֹצָה, כְּנָפַיִם וּמַקּוֹר,
עַל אֶדֶן הַחַלּוֹן נִתֵּר עָלָה,
חָלַף עַל הָעִיר כְּצִפּוֹר גְּדוֹלָה.

got up and put out the light, grew feathers, wings, and a beak, hopped up and mounted the window sill, crossed over the city like a giant bird.

לֵאָה גוֹלְדְבֶּרְג

Lea Goldberg

מִבֵּית אִמִּי

FROM MY MOTHER'S HOUSE

מֵתָה אִמָּהּ שֶׁל אִמִּי
בְּאֲבִיב יָמֶיהָ. וּבִתָּהּ
לֹא זָכְרָה אֶת פָּנֶיהָ. דְּיוֹקְנָהּ הֶחָרוּט
עַל לִבּוֹ שֶׁל סָבִי
נִמְחָה מֵעוֹלַם הַדְּמֻיּוֹת
אַחֲרֵי מוֹתוֹ.

My mother's mother died in the spring of her days. And her daughter did not remember her face. Her image, engraved upon my grandfather's heart, was erased from the world of figures after his death.

רַק הָרְאִי שֶׁלָּהּ נִשְׁתַּיֵּר בַּבַּיִת,
הֶעֱמִיק מֵרֹב שָׁנִים בְּמִשְׁבֶּצֶת הַכֶּסֶף.
וַאֲנִי, נֶכְדָּתָהּ הַחִוֶּרֶת, שֶׁאֵינֶנִּי דּוֹמָה לָהּ,
מַבִּיטָה הַיּוֹם אֶל תּוֹכוֹ כְּאֶל תּוֹךְ
אֲגַם הַטּוֹמֵן אוֹצְרוֹתָיו
מִתַּחַת לַמַּיִם.

Only her mirror remained in the house, grown deeper with age within its silver frame. And I, her pale granddaughter, who do not resemble her, look into it today as if into a lake that hides its treasures beneath the water.

עָמֹק מְאֹד, מֵאֲחוֹרֵי פָּנַי,
אֲנִי רוֹאָה אִשָּׁה צְעִירָה
וְרֻדַּת לְחָיַיִם מְחַיֶּכֶת.
וּפֵאָה נָכְרִית לְרֹאשָׁהּ.

Deep down, behind my face, I see a young woman, pink-cheeked, smiling. She is wearing a wig. Now she is

הִיא עוֹנֶדֶת
עָגִיל מָאֳרָךְ אֶל תְּנוּךְ אָזְנָהּ. מַשְׁחִילַתְהוּ
בְּנֶקֶב זָעִיר בַּבָּשָׂר הֶעָנֹג
שֶׁל הָאֹזֶן.

hanging a long earring from her ear
lobe, threading it through the tiny
opening in the dainty flesh of her ear.

עָמֹק מְאֹד, מֵאֲחוֹרֵי פָּנַי, קוֹרֶנֶת
זְהוּבִית בְּהִירָה שֶׁל עֵינֶיהָ.
וְהָרְאִי מַמְשִׁיךְ אֶת מָסֹרֶת
הַמִּשְׁפָּחָה:
שֶׁהִיא הָיְתָה יָפָה מְאֹד.

Deep down, behind my face, glows the
clear golden speck of her eyes. And the
mirror carries on the family tradition:
that she was very beautiful.

תֵּל־אָבִיב 1935

TEL AVIV 1935

הַתְּרָנִים עַל גַּגּוֹת הַבָּתִּים הָיוּ אָז
כְּתָרְנֵי סְפִינָתוֹ שֶׁל קוֹלוּמְבּוּס
וְכָל עוֹרֵב שֶׁעָמַד עַל חֻדָּם
בִּשֵּׂר יַבֶּשֶׁת אַחֶרֶת.

The masts on the housetops then, were
like the masts of Columbus' ships, and
every raven that perched on their tips
announced a different shore.

וְהָלְכוּ בָּרְחוֹב צִקְלוֹנֵי הַנּוֹסְעִים
וְשָׂפָה שֶׁל אֶרֶץ זָרָה
הָיְתָה נִנְעֶצֶת בְּיוֹם הַחַמְסִין
כְּלַהַב סַכִּין קָרָה.

And the kit-bags of the travellers
walked down the streets, and the
language of an alien land was plunged
into the *ḥamsin*-days like the blade of
a cold knife.

אֵיךְ יָכוֹל הָאֲוִיר שֶׁל הָעִיר הַקְּטַנָּה
לָשֵׂאת כָּל כָּךְ הַרְבֵּה
זִכְרוֹנוֹת יַלְדוּת, אֲהָבוֹת שֶׁנָּשְׁרוּ,
חֲדָרִים שֶׁרוֹקְנוּ אֵי־בָזֶה?

How could the air of the small city
support so many childhood memories,
loves that were shed, that were stripped
somewhere?

כִּתְמוּנוֹת מַשְׁחִירוֹת בְּתוֹךְ מַצְלֵמָה
הִתְהַפְּכוּ לֵילוֹת חֹרֶף זַכִּים,
לֵילוֹת קַיִץ גְּשׁוּמִים שֶׁמֵּעֵבֶר לַיָּם
וּבְקָרִים אֲפֵלִים שֶׁל בִּירוֹת.

Like pictures turning black inside a camera, they all turned inside out: pure winter nights, rainy summer nights of overseas, and shadowy mornings of great cities.

וְקוֹל צַעַד תּוֹפֵף אַחֲרֵי גַּבְּךָ
שִׁירֵי לֶכֶת שֶׁל צָבָא נֵכָר,
וְנִדְמֶה – אַךְ תַּחְזִיר אֶת רֹאשְׁךָ וּבַיָּם
שָׁטָה כְּנֵסִיַּת עִירְךָ.

And the sound of steps behind your back drummed marching songs of foreign troops; and – so it seemed – if you but turn your head, there's your town's church floating in the sea.

הִסְתַּכְּלוּת בִּדְבוֹרָה

OBSERVATION OF A BEE

א

A

בְּרִבּוּעַ חַלּוֹן מוּאָר –
עַל שִׁמְשָׁה, מִבַּחוּץ,
צְלָלִית שֶׁל דְּבוֹרָה
כִּמְעַט אֵין לִרְאוֹת אֶת כְּנָפֶיהָ.

In the square of a lit window, on the pane, from the outside, the silhouette of a bee; her wings are hardly visible.

הֲפוּכָה.
גּוּף צָר.
שֵׁשׁ רַגְלַיִם דַּקּוֹת –
בְּגִלּוּי עֵירֹם,
בְּאִיּוּם מְכֹעָר
זוֹחֶלֶת דְּבוֹרָה.

Upside down. Narrow body. Six thin legs – baring her nakedness, with an ugly threat, the bee crawls.

אֵיךְ נַכְתִּיר אוֹתָהּ בְּדִבְרֵי שִׁירָה!
אֵיךְ נָשִׁיר וּמָה?
יָבוֹא יֶלֶד קָטָן וְיֹאמַר:
הַמַּלְכָּה עֵירֻמָּה.

How shall we crown her with song! How shall we sing and what? A little boy will come along and say: 'The queen is naked.'

ב

בַּשֶּׁמֶשׁ הִיא הָיְתָה עָלֶה זָהָב נוֹפֵל,
בַּפֶּרַח הִיא הָיְתָה טִפָּה שֶׁל דְּבַשׁ אָפֵל,
וְאֶגֶל טַל בִּנְחִיל שֶׁל כּוֹכָבִים –
וּפֹה הִיא צֵל.

מִלָּה אַחַת שֶׁל שִׁיר בַּנְּחִיל הַמְצַלְצֵל,
בְּשׂוֹרַת רָצוֹן נִמְרָץ בְּתוֹךְ שָׁרָב עָצֵל,
תְּנוּעַת הָאוֹר בְּאֵפֶר דִּמְדּוּמִים –
וּפֹה הִיא צֵל.

B

In the sun she was a falling golden leaf, in the flower she was a drop of dark honey, and a dewdrop in the swarm of stars – and here she is shadow.

One word of song in the humming swarm, a message of keen will in the languid heat, a movement of light in the ashen twilight – and here she is shadow.

ג

מִדִּבְשֵׁךְ? מִי יִזְכֹּר אֶת דִּבְשֵׁךְ?
הוּא שָׁם, הַרְחֵק, בַּכַּוֶּרֶת.
כָּאן, בְּשִׁמְשָׁה מוּאָרָה, גּוּפֵךְ, רֹאשֵׁךְ –
כֻּלָּךְ עֹקֶץ, שִׂנְאָה אֵין־אוֹנִים עֲלוּבָה וְעִוֶּרֶת.
הַפַּחַד הוֹרֵג.
הִשָּׁמְרִי לְנַפְשֵׁךְ.

C

Your honey?[1] Who will remember your honey? It is there, far away, in the hive. Here, in the lit window-pane, your body, your head – you are all sting, impotent hate, pathetic and blind. Fear kills. Take good care!

גַּבְרִיאֵל פְּרֵיל

Gabriel Joshua Preil

מִצָּהֳרַיִם עַד עֶרֶב קָטָן

FROM NOON TO A SMALL EVENING

בְּצָהֳרֵי יוֹם־רוּחַ פִּתְאוֹמִי
מַצְלִיף בְּשֶׁמֶשׁ יַרְחִית
שׁוֹרֵק כְּרוֹעֶה לַעֲדָרָיו
וּמַעֲבִיר בָּאֲפָר הַשָּׂעִיר
סַכִּין אַחַר סַכִּין –

In the noon of a sudden wind-swept day that lashed the moon-like sun, whistling like a shepherd to his flocks, running knife after knife over the hairy meadow,

1. An allusion to a Hebrew saying: 'One says to the bee: "I want neither your honey nor your sting."'

נִתְלֵיתִי בְּעַנְפֵי עֵץ הַשֵּׁנָה הַגְּדוֹלָה
וּבְצִלּוֹ אָמַרְתִּי לָנוּחַ – אַבְשָׁלוֹם חָדָשׁ
יָדוּעַ אֵלֶם פּוֹרֵחַ, מְחַסֵּל כָּל עֻבְדָּה.

I held fast to the boughs of the tree of great sleep, resolved to rest in its shadow – a new Absalom[1] addicted to blossoming silence, annihilating all facts.

וַדַּאי הָיָה מִי שֶׁרָאַנִי מְנַצְּחָהּ שֶׁל יְקִיצָה
עַד שְׁקִיעָה־שִׁעֲמוּם יָרְדָה מֵעַל הָר,
הָיָה עֶרֶב קָטָן, עָלָה
כּוֹכָב בִּלְתִּי מְזֻמָּן, –
וַאֲנִי פָּקַחְתִּי אֶת עֵינַי.

Surely someone saw me as I triumphed over awakening until a tedious sunset came down from a mountain. It was a small evening, an uninvited star rose – and I opened my eyes.

עֲבִים, בִּרְקֵי יָם

CLOUDS, SEA-LIGHTNINGS

מֵחַלּוֹן בֵּית־הַדֹּאַר רָאִיתִי אֶת הֶעָבִים
מְלַבְלְבִים כַּעֲצֵי אֲפַרְסֵק וּשְׁלַחְתִּים
כִּגְלוּיוֹת מְצֻיָּרוֹת, לְאַרְצוֹת קֹר מַחֲרִיף,
זָר לָהֶן טִיב־בֻּסְתָּן עַל מַפַּת קַיִץ.

From the post-office window I saw the clouds blossoming like peach trees and I mailed them as picture postcards to countries of wintering cold, that have no notion of an orchard on summer's map.

טוֹב אֶעֱשֶׂה בְּצָהֳרַיִם מְאֻחָרִים אֵלֶּה
אִם אֶלְבַּשׁ חֲלִיפָה מְגֻוֶּנֶת יוֹתֵר
וְאָשִׂים עַצְמִי מְפַקֵּחַ עַל בַּיִת יָשָׁן:
אֲבַקֵּשׁ בּוֹ צַעֲצוּעֵי בֹּקֶר תַּם
אָבְדוּ בִּתְהוֹמוֹ שֶׁל רְאִי שַׁכְחָן.

I would be well advised, on such a late afternoon, to wear a more colourful suit and to appoint myself caretaker of an old house. I would search it for toys of an innocent morning, that were lost in the depths of a forgetful mirror.

בְּחַיִּים אֲחֵרִים – הִסְתַּכַּלְתִּי מְקַוֶּה
בִּזְכוּכִית הֵכִילָה־הֶחֱזִירָה
כָּל בְּרָקָיו שֶׁל יָם;
הַפֵּרוֹת שֶׁבְּיָדַי אָז שָׁרוּ שִׁיר־תְּהִלָּה
מוּל כָּל הֶעָבִים.

In another life, I gazed hopefully at a glass that held and reflected all the sea's lightnings. The fruits in my hands then sang a song of praise, in the sight of all the clouds.

1. The allusion is to Absalom hanging from the oak (2 Samuel 18.9 ff).

זֶלְדָּה

Zelda

אָז תִּצְעַק נִשְׁמָתִי

THEN MY SOUL CRIED OUT

אָז תִּצְעַק נִשְׁמָתִי:
שְׂפָתַיִם חֲרוּכוֹת
אַתֶּן בְּצַד אֶחָד
וְהָעוֹלָם בְּצַד הַשֵּׁנִי
וְכָל הָעוֹלָם בְּצַד הַשֵּׁנִי.

כִּי
בְּאוֹתוֹ חֶדֶר מוּצָף שֶׁמֶשׁ
עָמַדְתִּי
כֹּה קָרוֹב אֵלֶיהָ
שֶׁפִּי נָגַע בְּפָנֶיהָ
אֲשֶׁר שֻׁנּוּ בְּחֶבְלֵי מָוֶת.
הִיא בִּטְּאָה אֶת שְׁמִי
בְּקוֹל
שֶׁלָּן עַל קַרְקַע הַיָּם,
בְּקוֹל רָחוֹק וּמְעֻמְעָם
שֶׁנִּפֵּץ לִרְסִיסִים אֶת מַרְאוֹת
הַכֶּסֶף
אוֹתְתוּ אֶת שְׁמִי
שְׂפָתֶיהָ הָעֲשֵׁנוֹת.

Then my soul cried out: scorched lips, you are on the one side, and the world is on the other, the whole world is on the other side.

For in that sun-drenched room, I stood so close to her, that my mouth touched her face, which was disfigured by the pangs of death. She uttered my name with a voice that dwelt on the ocean's floor; in a far-away, muffled voice, which splintered the silver mirrors, her smouldering lips formed my name.

לְכָל אִישׁ יֵשׁ שֵׁם

לְכָל אִישׁ יֵשׁ שֵׁם
שֶׁנָּתַן לוֹ אֱלֹהִים
וְנָתְנוּ לוֹ אָבִיו וְאִמּוֹ
לְכָל אִישׁ יֵשׁ שֵׁם
שֶׁנָּתְנוּ לוֹ קוֹמָתוֹ וְאֹפֶן חִיּוּכוֹ
וְנָתַן לוֹ הָאָרִיג
לְכָל אִישׁ יֵשׁ שֵׁם
שֶׁנָּתְנוּ לוֹ הֶהָרִים
וְנָתְנוּ לוֹ כְּתָלָיו
לְכָל אִישׁ יֵשׁ שֵׁם
שֶׁנָּתְנוּ לוֹ הַמַּזָּלוֹת
וְנָתְנוּ לוֹ שְׁכֵנָיו
לְכָל אִישׁ יֵשׁ שֵׁם
שֶׁנָּתְנוּ לוֹ חֲטָאָיו
וְנָתְנָה לוֹ כְּמִיהָתוֹ
לְכָל אִישׁ יֵשׁ שֵׁם
שֶׁנָּתְנוּ לוֹ שׂוֹנְאָיו
וְנָתְנָה לוֹ אַהֲבָתוֹ
לְכָל אִישׁ יֵשׁ שֵׁם
שֶׁנָּתְנוּ לוֹ חַגָּיו
וְנָתְנָה לוֹ מְלַאכְתּוֹ
לְכָל אִישׁ יֵשׁ שֵׁם
שֶׁנָּתְנוּ לוֹ תְּקוּפוֹת הַשָּׁנָה
וְנָתַן לוֹ עִוְרוֹנוֹ
לְכָל אִישׁ יֵשׁ שֵׁם
שֶׁנָּתַן לוֹ הַיָּם
וְנָתַן לוֹ
מוֹתוֹ.

EACH MAN HAS A NAME

Each man has a name, given him by God, and given him by his father and mother. Each man has a name given him by his stature and his way of smiling, and given him by his clothes. Each man has a name given him by the mountains and given him by his walls. Each man has a name given him by the planets and given him by his neighbours. Each man has a name given him by his sins and given him by his longing. Each man has a name given him by his enemies and given him by his love. Each man has a name given him by his feast days and given him by his craft. Each man has a name given him by the seasons of the year and given him by his blindness. Each man has a name given him by the sea and given him by his death.

אָמִיר גִּלְבֹּעַ

Amir Gilboa

וְאָחִי שׁוֹתֵק

AND MY BROTHER SAID NOTHING

אָחִי חָזַר מִן הַשָּׂדֶה
בְּבֶגֶד אָפֹר.
וַאֲנִי חָשַׁשְׁתִּי שֶׁמָּא חֲלוֹמִי יִתְבַּדֶּה
וְהִתְחַלְתִּי מִיָּד אֶת פְּצָעָיו לִסְפֹּר.
וְאָחִי שׁוֹתֵק.

My brother came back from the field dressed in grey. And I was afraid that my dream might prove false, so at once I began to count his wounds. And my brother said nothing.

אַחַר חִטַּטְתִּי בְּכִיסֵי הַסָּגִין
וּמָצָאתִי אִסְפְּלָנִית שֶׁיָּבֵשׁ כִּתְמָהּ.
וּבִגְלוּיָה שְׁחוּקָה אֶת שְׁמָהּ
תַּחַת לְצִיּוּר שֶׁל פְּרָגִים.
וְאָחִי שׁוֹתֵק.

Then I rummaged in the pockets of the trench-coat and found a field-dressing, stained and dry. And on a frayed postcard, her name – beneath a picture of poppies. And my brother said nothing.

אָז הִתַּרְתִּי אֶת הַצְּרוֹר
וְהוֹצֵאתִי חֲפָצָיו, זֵכֶר אַחַר זֵכֶר.
הֵידָד, אָחִי, אָחִי הַגִּבּוֹר,
הִנֵּה מָצָאתִי אוֹתוֹתֶיךָ!
הֵידָד, אָחִי, אָחִי הַגִּבּוֹר,
אָשִׁיר גַּאֲוָה לִשְׁמֶךָ!
וְאָחִי שׁוֹתֵק.
וְאָחִי שׁוֹתֵק.

Then I undid the pack and took out his belongings, memory by memory. Hurrah, my brother, my brother, *the hero*, now I've found your decorations! Hurrah, my brother, my brother *the hero*, I shall proudly hymn your name! And my brother said nothing. And my brother said nothing.

וְדָמוֹ מִן הָאֲדָמָה זוֹעֵק.

And his blood was crying out from the ground.[1]

1. See Genesis 4.10: 'Your brother's blood cries out to me from the ground.'

יִצְחָק

לִפְנוֹת בֹּקֶר טִיְּלָה שֶׁמֶשׁ בְּתוֹךְ הַיַּעַר
יַחַד עִמִּי וְעִם אַבָּא
וִימִינִי בִּשְׂמֹאלוֹ.

כְּבָרָק לָהֲבָה מַאֲכֶלֶת בֵּין הָעֵצִים.
וַאֲנִי יָרֵא כָּל־כָּךְ אֶת פַּחַד עֵינַי מוּל דָּם עַל הֶעָלִים.

אַבָּא אַבָּא מַהֵר וְהַצִּילָה אֶת יִצְחָק
וְלֹא יֶחְסַר אִישׁ בִּסְעֻדַּת הַצָּהֳרַיִם.

זֶה אֲנִי הַנִּשְׁחָט, בְּנִי,
וּכְבָר דָּמִי עַל הֶעָלִים.
וְאַבָּא נִסְתַּם קוֹלוֹ.
וּפָנָיו חִוְרִים.

וְרָצִיתִי לִצְעֹק, מְפַרְפֵּר לֹא לְהַאֲמִין
וְקוֹרֵעַ הָעֵינַיִם.
וְנִתְעוֹרַרְתִּי.

וְאָזְלַת־דָּם הָיְתָה יַד יָמִין.

ISAAC

At dawn, the sun strolled in the forest
together with me and father, and my
right hand was in his left.

Like lightning a knife flashed among
the trees. And I am so afraid of my
eyes' terror, faced by blood on the
leaves.

Father, father, quickly save Isaac so
that no one will be missing at the
midday meal.

It is I who am being slaughtered, my
son, and already my blood is on the
leaves. And father's voice was
smothered and his face was pale.

And I wanted to scream, writhing not
to believe, and tearing open my eyes.
And I woke up.

And my right hand was drained of
blood.

מֹשֶׁה

נִגַּשְׁתִּי אֶל מֹשֶׁה וְאָמַרְתִּי לוֹ:
עֲרֹךְ אֶת הַמַּחֲנוֹת כָּךְ וְכָךְ.
הוּא הִסְתַּכֵּל בִּי
וְעָרַךְ לְפִי שֶׁאָמַרְתִּי.

MOSES

I stepped up to Moses and said to him:
Station the troops in such and such a
manner. He looked at me, then
stationed them as I said.

וּמִי לֹא רָאָה אָז בִּכְבוֹדִי!
הָיְתָה שָׁם שָׂרָה מִן הַיַּלְדוּת
שֶׁעַל שְׁמָהּ תִּכַּנְתִּי לִבְנוֹת עִיר.
הָיְתָה שָׁם אֲרֻכַּת־הָרַגְלַיִם מֵחַוַּת־הַפּוֹעֲלוֹת.
הָיְתָה מֶלְוִינָה מֵרַבָּת אֲשֶׁר בְּמַלְטָה.
דִּינָה מֵהַגְּבוּל הָאִיטַלְקִי־הַיּוּגוֹסְלָבִי.
וְרִיָּה מֵהַשְּׁפֵלָה שֶׁבַּצָּפוֹן.

And who did not see me then in my glory! Sarah was there, Sarah from my childhood, in whose name I had planned to build a city. And the long-legged girl was there, from the cooperative training farm. There was Melvina, from Rabbat in Malta. Dina, from the Italo-Yugoslav border. And Ria, from the northern lowlands.

וְגֵאֶה מְאֹד מִהַרְתִּי אֶל מֹשֶׁה
לְהוֹרוֹתוֹ הַדֶּרֶךְ הַנְּכוֹנָה
וְהָחְוַר לִי לְפִתְאֹם
כִּי זוֹ אֲשֶׁר בְּתוֹךְ שְׁמִי
חֲרוּתָה וּנְכוֹנָה –
אֵינֶנָּה.

And, very proud, I hurried over to Moses, to show him the right way, when suddenly I realized that she who is engraved and fixed in my name – she was not there.

מֹשֶׁה מֹשֶׁה הַנְחֵה אֶת הָעָם,
רְאֵה, אֲנִי כָּל־כָּךְ עָיֵף וְרוֹצֶה לִישֹׁן עוֹד
אֲנִי עוֹדֶן נַעַר.

Moses, Moses, go lead the people. Please, I'm so tired and I'd like to sleep some more. I'm still a child.

פְּנֵי יְהוֹשֻׁעַ

THE FACE OF JOSHUA

וִיהוֹשֻׁעַ מֵעַל אֶל פָּנַי מַבִּיט. וּפָנָיו זָהָב
שָׁחוּט. חֲלוֹם קַר. חֲלוֹם חָנוּט.
וּלְרַגְלַי הַיָּם מַכֶּה נְצָחִים אֶל הַחוֹף.
אֲנִי חוֹלֶה נְהִיָּתוֹ. דּוֹמֶה, אֲנִי עוֹמֵד לָמוּת.
אַךְ מֻכְרָחֲנִי, מֻכְרָחֲנִי לְחַכּוֹת חַי
אֶל־תָּמִיד.
אָחִי מֵעַל פָּנָיו עוֹלִים בָּעָב
לְהַגִּיד עִקְּבוֹתַי בַּחוֹל הַנִּשְׁטָף.

And Joshua, from above, looks at my face. And his face is beaten gold. A cold dream. A shrivelled dream. And at my feet, the sea beats eternities against the shore. I am sick with its wailing. It seems I am about to die. Yet I must, oh I must wait alive, everlastingly. My brother's face, above, rises in the cloud to reveal my footprints in the sea-swept sand.

הַיָּם מַכֶּה וְנָסוֹג. מַכֶּה וְנָסוֹג.
מִלְחָמוֹת אֵיתָנִים מֻתְנוֹת בַּחֹק.
אֲנִי. בָּרוּחַ. אַחֵר. בּוֹרֵחַ. רָחוֹק.
גַּם יְהוֹשֻׁעַ עַכְשָׁיו נָח מִמִּלְחָמוֹת.
שֶׁהִנְחִיל נַחֲלָה לְעַמּוֹ,
אֲבָל קֶבֶר לֹא חָצַב לוֹ
בְּהָרֵי אֶפְרַיִם.
עַל כֵּן לַיְלָה לַיְלָה הוּא יוֹצֵא
לָשׁוּחַ בַּשָּׁמַיִם.
וַאֲנִי חוֹלֶה, דּוֹמֶה עוֹמֵד לָמוּת
מְיַחֵף בְּחוֹל יָרֵחַ קַר
בְּשׁוּלֵי הַמַּיִם
וְהוֹמֶה בִּי, הוֹמֶה בִּי סוֹף
הַמַּכֶּה לְרַגְלַי אֶת מוֹתִי
גַּל אַחַר גַּל —

עַל פְּנֵי חַיִּים רַבִּים
יִתְרוֹמַם וְיִתְגַּדַּל.

The sea beats and withdraws, beats and withdraws. Elemental warfare fixed by law. I. In the wind. Different. On the run. Far away. Now Joshua, too, is resting from wars. For he gave a patrimony to his people, but did not hew himself a grave in the hills of Ephraim. And, therefore, night after night he goes forth to roam the skies. And I am sick, it seems, about to die, bare-footed in the cold moon-sand at the water's edge, and within me moans, within me moans the end that beats my death at my feet, wave upon wave –

upon the many lives, be it extolled and glorified.[1]

בָּעֲלָטֶת

אִם יַרְאוּנִי אֶבֶן וְאֹמַר אֶבֶן יֹאמְרוּ אֶבֶן.
אִם יַרְאוּנִי עֵץ וְאֹמַר עֵץ יֹאמְרוּ עֵץ.
אַךְ אִם יַרְאוּנִי דָם וְאֹמַר דָּם יֹאמְרוּ צֶבַע.
אִם יַרְאוּנִי דָם וְאֹמַר דָּם יֹאמְרוּ צֶבַע.

IN THE DARKNESS

If they show me a stone and I say stone they say stone. If they show me a tree and I say tree they say tree. But if they show me blood and I say blood they say paint. *If they show me blood and I say blood they say paint.*

1. The final phrase is taken from the *Kaddish* (mourner's doxology), where it refers to the name of God.

[לְבַסּוֹף אֲנִי הוֹלֵךְ]

לְבַסּוֹף אֲנִי הוֹלֵךְ אֶל הָאִישׁ שֶׁהִצִּיב מַלְכּוֹדוֹת
לַצִּפֳּרִים
מְבַקֵּשׁ סְלִיחָתוֹ, שֶׁבִּקַּשְׁתִּי לְטָרְדוֹ מִלְּשַׂחֵק
בְּחַיֵּי אֲחֵרִים
מְקַלֵּל סִכְלוּתִי, שֶׁלֹּא נָאֶה לִטֹּל מִשִּׂמְחַת יְצָרָיו
שֶׁהִקְפִּיד לְשָׁמְרָם דְּרוּכִים בְּכָל עֵת
וּמַה גַּם שֶׁהַצִּפֳּרִים כְּבָר הִתְעוֹפְפוּ וְדוֹמֶה
שֶׁמְּצַפְצְפוֹת וּמְלַהֲגוֹת לְעֻמָּתִי מֵרוּמֵי מַעְלָה
מֵעַל לְרֹאשִׁי
וַדַּאי לָהֶן, גַּם לִי מַלְכּוֹדוֹת יָדַי מַלְכּוֹדוֹת
וּלְעוֹלָם לֹא תִנְחַתְנָה בְּכַפּוֹתַי הַפְּשׁוּטוֹת לִקְרָאתָן.

[FINALLY, I GO]

Finally, I go to the man who sets snares for birds and beg his forgiveness for having tried to deter him from toying with the lives of others. I curse my stupidity, how indelicate to deny him the joy of his appetites which he took great pains to keep on the alert at all times, and especially as the birds have already flown away and it seems that they are twittering and chattering at me from the upper heights above my head. They know for certain that I, too, have snares, my hands are snares, and they will never alight on my palms, which are stretched out towards them.

אַבָּא קוֹבְנֶר

Abba Kovner

[אֲחוֹתִי יוֹשֶׁבֶת]

אֲחוֹתִי יוֹשֶׁבֶת שְׂמֵחָה אֶל
שֻׁלְחַן חֲתָנָהּ. הִיא לֹא בּוֹכָה.
אֲחוֹתִי לֹא תַעֲשֶׂה כָּזֹאת
מַה יֹּאמְרוּ הַבְּרִיּוֹת!

אֲחוֹתִי יוֹשֶׁבֶת שְׂמֵחָה אֶל
שֻׁלְחַן חֲתָנָהּ. לִבָּהּ עֵר.
עוֹלָם שָׁלֵם שׁוֹתֶה
מְרַק עוֹף כָּשֵׁר:

[MY SISTER]

My sister sits happy at her bridegroom's table. She isn't crying. My sister wouldn't do such a thing. What would people say!

My sister sits happy at her bridegroom's table. Her heart is awake. The whole company is sipping kosher chicken broth:

הַכֻּפְתָּאוֹת מִקֶּמַח מַצּוֹת הֵן
מַעֲשֵׂה חֲמוֹתָהּ. מִשְׁתָּאֶה הָעוֹלָם
וְטוֹעֵם מִמִּרְקַחַת הָאֵם.

The dumplings of unleavened flour
were made by her mother-in-law. The
whole company admiringly tastes the
mother's marmalade.

אֲחוֹתִי כַלָּה יוֹשֶׁבֶת וּלְיָדָהּ
קַעֲרִית הַדְּבַשׁ. כָּזֶה עַם רָב!
אֶת צַמּוֹת הַחַלָּה

My sister-bride sits with the bowl of
honey beside her. Such a huge crowd!
The braids of the *ḥalah*

קָלַע הָאָב:

were twisted by father:

אָבִינוּ אֶת לַחְמוֹ רָדָה בָּרוּךְ הַשֵּׁם
מ׳ שָׁנִים מִתַּנּוּר אֶחָד. לֹא שִׁעֵר
שֶׁיָּכוֹל עַם שָׁלֵם לַעֲלוֹת בַּתַּנּוּרִים
וְהָעוֹלָם בְּעֶזְרַת הַשֵּׁם מִתְקַיֵּם.

For forty years, praise God, our father
took out his bread from the same oven.
He never suspected that an entire
people could go up in [the smoke of]
ovens, while the world, with God's
help, endures.

אֲחוֹתִי בְּהִינוּמָה יוֹשֶׁבֶת לַשֻּׁלְחָן
לְבַדָּהּ. מֵחֶבְיוֹן אֲבֵלִים
קוֹל חָתָן קָרֵב.
בִּלְעָדַיִךְ נַעֲרֹךְ הַשֻּׁלְחָן
הַכְּתֻבָּה בָּאֶבֶן תִּכָּתֵב.

My sister, in her bridal veil, sits at the
table alone. From the covert of the
mourners, the voice of the bridegroom
draws near. We shall set the table
without you, [my sister], the marriage-
contract will be written in stone.

ḤAYIM GOURI

חַיִּים גּוּרִי
Ḥayim Gouri

יְרֻשָּׁה
HERITAGE

הָאַיִל בָּא אַחֲרוֹן.
וְלֹא יָדַע אַבְרָהָם כִּי הוּא
מֵשִׁיב לִשְׁאֵלַת הַיֶּלֶד,
רֵאשִׁית־אוֹנוֹ בְּעֵת יוֹמוֹ עָרָב.

The ram came last of all. And Abraham
did not know that it came to answer the
boy's question[1] – first of his strength
when his day was on the wane.

נָשָׂא רֹאשׁוֹ הַשָּׂב.
בִּרְאוֹתוֹ כִּי לֹא חָלַם חֲלוֹם
וְהַמַּלְאָךְ נִצָּב –
נָשְׁרָה הַמַּאֲכֶלֶת מִיָּדוֹ.

The old man raised his head. Seeing
that it was no dream and that the angel
stood there – the knife slipped from his
hand.

הַיֶּלֶד שֶׁהֻתַּר מֵאֲסוּרָיו
רָאָה אֶת גַּב אָבִיו.

The boy, released from his bonds, saw
his father's back.

יִצְחָק, כַּמְסֻפָּר, לֹא הֻעֲלָה קָרְבָּן.
הוּא חַי יָמִים רַבִּים,
רָאָה בַּטּוֹב, עַד אוֹר עֵינָיו כָּהָה.

Isaac, as the story goes, was not
sacrificed. He lived for many years, saw
what pleasure had to offer, until his
eyesight dimmed.

אֲבָל אֶת הַשָּׁעָה הַהִיא הוֹרִישׁ לְצֶאֱצָאָיו.
הֵם נוֹלָדִים
וּמַאֲכֶלֶת בְּלִבָּם.

But he bequeathed that hour to his
offspring. They are born with a knife in
their hearts.

1. [Isaac:] 'Here are the fire and the wood, but where is the young beast for the sacrifice?' (Genesis 22.7).

[יֵשׁ לִי קְרוֹבֵי מִשְׁפָּחָה]

[RELATIVES]

יֵשׁ לִי קְרוֹבֵי מִשְׁפָּחָה,
לְבָבוֹת מִפֶּחָם וְשִׁנַּיִם מִכֶּסֶף.
עֲטוּפֵי מְעִילִים.
מְעַשְּׁנִים סִיגָרִיּוֹת לְלֹא בַּנְדֵּרוֹלָה.
אוֹרְחִים לֹא־קְרוּאִים
בְּעִיר שֶׁלֶג.

I have relatives, hearts of coal and
teeth of silver. Wrapped in overcoats.
Smoking cigarettes without banderoles.
Uninvited guests in a city of snow.[1]

קְרוֹבֵי מִשְׁפָּחָה רְחוֹקִים.
לְסָתוֹת מִפְּלָטִינָה.
רַגְלַיִם שֶׁל אֵשׁ.
יָדַיִם שֶׁל מַיִם.
מַבִּיטִים בִּי שָׁעוֹת אֲרֻכּוֹת
בְּעֵינֵי צִיאָן־קָלִי.

Distant relatives. Jaws of platinum.
Feet of fire. Hands of water. Looking
at me, for hours on end, with cyanide
eyes.

קְרוֹבֵי מִשְׁפָּחָה אֲצִילִים.
זִכָּרוֹן לֹא נוֹרְמָלִי.

Aristocratic relatives, they have a
terrific memory.

מַזְכִּירִים לִי סֵפֶר שֶׁבּוֹכֶה בּוֹ מֶלֶךְ
רָחוֹק, יְרוּשַׁלְמִי,
רַק גַּבּוֹ אֶל רוֹאֵהוּ,
עַד לַיְלָה.

They remind me of a book in which a
king, long ago, in Jerusalem, his face
turned to the wall, weeps until night
falls.

1. This refers to refugees in Vienna, shortly after the Holocaust.

טוּבְיָה רִיבְּנֶר

Tuvia Ruebner

שָׁם, אָמַרְתִּי

THERE, I SAID

יָצָאתִי מִבֵּיתִי הָאַרְעִי לְהַרְאוֹת לְבָנַי אֶת
מְקוֹם מוֹצָאִי.
שָׁם, אָמַרְתִּי, שָׁכַבְתִּי עַל הָאָרֶץ
אֶבֶן לִמְרַאֲשׁוֹתַי נָמוּךְ מִן הָעֵשֶׂב
כַּעֲפַר הָאָרֶץ
הַכֹּל שָׁם נִשְׁמַר.

I set out from my temporary home to show my sons the place that I came from. 'There,' I said, 'I lay on the ground with a stone for a pillow, lower than the grass, like the dust of the earth; everything has been preserved there.'

עָבַרְנוּ בֶּהָרִים וּבַיְּעָרוֹת וּבֶעָרִים שֶׁהָיוּ
מְעָרוֹת וְהַמַּיִם נִקְווּ בַּדֶּרֶךְ וְהַכְּבִישִׁים הָיוּ רָעִים.
הַמְּכוֹנִית דִּלְּגָה עַל הַבּוֹרוֹת.

We passed through mountains, forests and cities that were caves, and water gathered in pools on the way and the roads were bad. The car bumped over the ditches.

מָה הָאֲוִיר הַמָּתוֹק הַזֶּה ? שׁוֹאֲלִים בָּנַי.
מָה הַטִּיחַ הַנּוֹפֵל מֵהַקִּירוֹת ?

'What is this sweet air?' ask my sons. 'What is this plaster peeling from the walls?'

אֵין דָּבָר, הִגִּידָה הַיְשִׁישָׁה בַּחַלּוֹן.
כָּאן גַּם הֶעָתִיד עָבָר. וְסָגְרָה אֶת עֵינֶיהָ הַיְבֵשׁוֹת
כְּעוֹף הָעוֹלֶה וְקוֹפֵל אֶת כְּנָפָיו וְצוֹלֵל.

'Nothing at all,' pronounced the old woman in the window. 'Here even the future is past.' And she shut her eyes like a bird that soars, folds its wings and dives.

כָּאן נוֹלַדְתִּי, אָמַרְתִּי לְבָנַי.
הוֹרַי וּזְקֵנַי נוֹלְדוּ כָּאן קָרוֹב.
נוֹלָדִים. כָּאן הָיָה בַּיִת
אָמַרְתִּי לְבָנַי וְהָרוּחַ עָבְרָה
בֵּינִי לְבֵין הַמִּלִּים.

'I was born here,' I said to my sons. 'My parents and grandparents were born nearby. Everybody is born [somewhere]. There was a house here,' I said to my sons, and the wind came between me and the words.

יָצָאתִי לְהַרְאוֹת לְבָנַי אֶת מְקוֹם מוֹצָאִי, וּמָתַי
נֹאכַל, שׁוֹאֲלִים בָּנַי, וְאֵיפֹה
נָלוּן ?

I set out to show my sons the place that I came from, 'And when will we eat,' ask my sons, 'and where will we sleep?'

יְהוּדָה עַמִּיחַי

Yehuda Amichai

[אָבִי הָיָה]

[MY FATHER]

אָבִי הָיָה אַרְבַּע שָׁנִים בְּמִלְחַמְתָּם,
וְלֹא שָׂנֵא אוֹיְבָיו וְלֹא אָהַב.
אֲבָל אֲנִי יוֹדֵעַ, כִּי כְּבָר שָׁם
בָּנָה אוֹתִי יוֹם־יוֹם מִשַּׁלְווֹתָיו

My father took part in their war for four years, and he didn't hate his enemies or love them. But I know that already there, day after day, he was forming me out of his few – so very few –

הַמְּעָטוֹת כָּל־כָּךְ, אֲשֶׁר לָקַט
אוֹתָן בֵּין פְּצָצוֹת וּבֵין עָשָׁן,
וְשָׂם אוֹתָן בְּתַרְמִילוֹ הַמְּמֻרְטָט
עִם שְׁאֵרִית עוּגַת־אִמּוֹ הַמִּתְקַשָּׁה.

tranquillities, which he scraped up between bombs and smoke, then put them in his tattered pack, together with the scraps of his mother's hardening cake.

וּבְעֵינָיו אָסַף מֵתִים בְּלִי שֵׁם,
מֵתִים רַבִּים אָסַף לְמַעֲנִי,
שֶׁאַכִּירֵם בְּמַבָּטָיו וְאֹהֲבֵם

And in his eyes he gathered the nameless dead, a great many dead he gathered for my sake, that I might recognize them in his look and love them

וְלֹא אָמוּת כְּמוֹהֶם בְּזְוָעָה...
הוּא מִלֵּא עֵינָיו בָּהֶם וְהוּא טָעָה:
אֶל כָּל מִלְחֲמוֹתַי יוֹצֵא אֲנִי.

and not die, as they did, in such horror . . . He filled his eyes with them, and he was mistaken: I must go out to all my wars.

חֲבָל. הָיִינוּ אַמְצָאָה טוֹבָה

A PITY. WE WERE A GOOD INVENTION

הֵם קָטְעוּ
אֶת יְרֵכַיִךְ מִמָּתְנַי.
לְגַבֵּי הֵם תָּמִיד
רוֹפְאִים. כֻּלָּם.

They amputated your thighs from my hips. As far as I'm concerned they are always M.D.s. All of them.

הֵם פֵּרְקוּ אוֹתָנוּ
זֶה מִזּוֹ. לְגַבֵּי הֵם מְהַנְדְּסִים.
חֲבָל. הָיִינוּ אַמְצָאָה טוֹבָה
וְאוֹהֶבֶת: אֲוִירוֹן עָשׂוּי מֵאִישׁ וְאִשָּׁה,
כְּנָפַיִם וְהַכֹּל:
מְעַט הִתְרוֹמַמְנוּ מִן הָאָרֶץ,
מְעַט עָפְנוּ.

They dismantled us from each other. As far as I'm concerned, they are engineers. A pity. We were a good and loving invention: an aeroplane made of a man and a woman, wings and everything: we rose a little off the ground, we flew a little.

מִשְּׁלֹשָׁה אוֹ אַרְבָּעָה בַּחֶדֶר

OUT OF THREE OR FOUR IN A ROOM

מִשְּׁלֹשָׁה אוֹ אַרְבָּעָה בַּחֶדֶר
תָּמִיד אֶחָד עוֹמֵד לְיַד הַחַלּוֹן.
מֻכְרָח לִרְאוֹת אֶת הָעָוֶל בֵּין קוֹצִים
וְאֶת הַשְּׂרֵפוֹת בַּגִּבְעָה.
וְכֵיצַד אֲנָשִׁים שֶׁיָּצְאוּ שְׁלֵמִים
מֻחְזָרִים בָּעֶרֶב כְּמַטְבְּעוֹת עֹדֶף לְבֵיתָם.

Out of three or four in a room, there is always one who stands at the window. Compelled to see the injustice between the thorns and the fire on the hill. And how people who had gone forth whole are brought back to their homes, in the evening, like small change.

מִשְּׁלֹשָׁה אוֹ אַרְבָּעָה בַּחֶדֶר
תָּמִיד אֶחָד עוֹמֵד לְיַד הַחַלּוֹן.
שְׂעָרוֹ הָאָפֵל מֵעַל לְמַחְשְׁבוֹתָיו.
מֵאֲחוֹרָיו הַמִּלִּים.
וּלְפָנָיו הַקּוֹלוֹת הַנּוֹדְדִים בְּלִי תַרְמִיל,
לְבָבוֹת בְּלִי צֵידָה, נְבוּאוֹת בְּלִי מַיִם
וַאֲבָנִים גְּדוֹלוֹת שֶׁהוּשְׁבוּ
וְנִשְׁאֲרוּ סְגוּרִים כְּמִכְתָּבִים שֶׁאֵין
לָהֶם כְּתֹבֶת וְאֵין מְקַבֵּל.

Out of three or four in a room, there is always one who stands at the window. His dark hair over his thoughts. Behind him the words. And before him, voices that are straying without packs, hearts without provisions, prophecies without water and large stones which were returned and remained sealed like letters with no address and no one to receive them.

מַחֲצִית הָאֲנָשִׁים בָּעוֹלָם

מַחֲצִית הָאֲנָשִׁים בָּעוֹלָם
אוֹהֲבִים אֶת הַמַּחֲצִית הַשְּׁנִיָּה,
מַחֲצִית הָאֲנָשִׁים
שׂוֹנְאִים אֶת הַשְּׁנִיָּה,
הַאִם בִּגְלַל אֵלֶּה וְאֵלֶּה עָלַי
לָלֶכֶת וְלִנְדֹּד וּלְהִשְׁתַּנּוֹת בְּלִי הֶרֶף,
כַּגֶּשֶׁם בַּמַּחֲזוֹר, וְלִישֹׁן בֵּין סְלָעִים,
וְלִהְיוֹת מְחֻסְפָּס כְּגִזְעֵי זֵיתִים,
וְלִשְׁמֹעַ אֶת הַיָּרֵחַ נוֹבֵחַ עָלַי,
וּלְהַסְווֹת אֶת אַהֲבָתִי בִּדְאָגוֹת,
וְלִצְמֹחַ כָּעֵשֶׂב הָרָהוּי בֵּין פַּסֵּי הָרַכֶּבֶת,
וְלָגוּר בָּאֲדָמָה כַּחֲפַרְפֶּרֶת,
וְלִהְיוֹת עִם שָׁרָשִׁים וְלֹא עִם עֲנָפִים,
וְלֹא לֶחְיִי עַל לְחִי מַלְאָכִים,
וְלֶאֱהֹב בַּמְּעָרָה הָרִאשׁוֹנָה
וְלָשֵׂאת אֶת אִשְׁתִּי תַּחַת חֻפַּת
הַקּוֹרוֹת הַנּוֹשְׂאוֹת אֲדָמָה,
וּלְשַׂחֵק אֶת מוֹתִי, תָּמִיד
עַד הַנְּשִׁימָה הָאַחֲרוֹנָה וְהַמִּלִּים
הָאַחֲרוֹנוֹת וּבְלִי לְהָבִין,
וְלַעֲשׂוֹת בְּבֵיתִי עַמּוּדֵי דְגָלִים לְמַעְלָה
וּמִקְלָט לְמַטָּה. וְלָצֵאת בַּדְּרָכִים
הָעֲשׂוּיוֹת רַק לְשִׁיבָה וְלַעֲבֹר
אֶת כָּל הַתַּחֲנוֹת הַנּוֹרָאוֹת –
חָתוּל, מַקֵּל, אֵשׁ, מַיִם, שׁוֹחֵט,
בֵּין הַגְּדִי וּבֵין מַלְאַךְ־הַמָּוֶת ?

HALF THE PEOPLE IN THE WORLD

Half the people in the world love the other half, half the people hate the other half. Must I, because of those and the others, go and wander and endlessly change, like rain in its cycle, and sleep among rocks, and be rugged like the trunks of olive-trees, and hear the moon bark at me, and camouflage my love with worries, and grow like the timorous grass in between railway tracks, and live in the ground like a mole, and be with roots and not with branches, and not rest my cheek upon the cheek of angels, and make love in the first cave, and marry my wife under the canopy of beams which support the earth, and act out my death, always to the last breath and the last words, without ever understanding, and put flag-poles on top of my house and a shelter at the bottom. And set forth on the roads made only for returning, and go through all the terrifying stations – cat, stick, fire, water, butcher – between the kid and the angel of death?[1]

1. A reference to a well-known song which concludes the Passover Haggadah. The last stanza reads: 'Then came the Holy One, blessed be He, and destroyed the angel of death, that slew the butcher, that killed the ox, that drank the water, that quenched the fire, that burned the stick, that beat the dog, that bit the cat, that ate the kid, that father had bought for two *zuzim*.'

מַחֲצִית הָאֲנָשִׁים אוֹהֲבִים,
מַחֲצִיתָם שׂוֹנְאִים.
וְהֵיכָן מְקוֹמִי בֵּין הַמַּחֲצִיּוֹת הַמֻּתְאָמוֹת כָּל־כָּךְ,
וְדֶרֶךְ אֵיזֶה סֶדֶק אֶרְאֶה אֶת
הַשִּׁכּוּנִים הַלְּבָנִים שֶׁל חֲלוֹמוֹתַי,
וְאֶת הָרָצִים הַיְחֵפִים עַל הַחוֹלוֹת
אוֹ לְפָחוֹת אֶת נִפְנוּף
מִטְפַּחַת הַנַּעֲרָה, לְיַד הַתֵּל ?

Half the people love, half the people
hate. And where is my place between
these halves that are so well matched?
And through what crack shall I see the
white housing-projects of my dreams,
and the barefoot runners on the sands
or, at least, the fluttering of the girl's
handkerchief, by the hill?

[בְּיוֹם כִּפּוּר]

[ON THE DAY OF ATONEMENT]

בְּיוֹם כִּפּוּר בִּשְׁנַת תַּשְׁכַּ״ח לָבַשְׁתִּי
בִּגְדֵי חַג כֵּהִים וְהָלַכְתִּי לָעִיר הָעַתִּיקָה בִּירוּשָׁלַיִם.
עָמַדְתִּי זְמַן רַב לִפְנֵי כּוּךְ חֲנוּתוֹ שֶׁל עֲרָבִי,
לֹא רָחוֹק מִשַּׁעַר שְׁכֶם, חֲנוּת
כַּפְתּוֹרִים וְרִכְסָנִים וּסְלִילֵי חוּטִים
בְּכָל צֶבַע וְלַחְצָנִיּוֹת וְאַבְזָמִים.
אוֹר יָקָר וּצְבָעִים רַבִּים, כְּמוֹ אֲרוֹן־קֹדֶשׁ פָּתוּחַ.

On the Day of Atonement in 1967, I
put on my dark holiday suit and went
to the Old City in Jerusalem. I stood,
for some time, before the alcove of an
Arab's shop, not far from Damascus
Gate, a shop of buttons and zippers
and spools of thread in all colours, and
snaps and buckles. A glorious light and
a great many colours like a Holy Ark
with its doors ajar.

אָמַרְתִּי לוֹ בְּלִבִּי שֶׁגַּם לְאָבִי
הָיְתָה חֲנוּת כָּזֹאת שֶׁל חוּטִים וְכַפְתּוֹרִים.
הִסְבַּרְתִּי לוֹ בְּלִבִּי עַל כָּל עַשְׂרוֹת הַשָּׁנִים
וְהַגּוֹרְמִים וְהַמִּקְרִים, שֶׁאֲנִי עַכְשָׁו פֹּה
וַחֲנוּת אָבִי שְׂרוּפָה שָׁם וְהוּא קָבוּר פֹּה.

I told him in my heart that my father,
too, had such a shop of threads and
buttons. I explained to him in my
heart all about the tens of years and the
reasons and the circumstances because
of which I am now here and my
father's shop is in ashes there, and he
is buried here.

כְּשֶׁסִּיַּמְתִּי הָיְתָה שְׁעַת נְעִילָה.
גַּם הוּא הוֹרִיד אֶת הַתְּרִיס וְנָעַל אֶת הַשַּׁעַר
וַאֲנִי חָזַרְתִּי עִם כָּל הַמִּתְפַּלְּלִים הַבַּיְתָה.

By the time I had finished, it was the
hour of 'the locking of the Gates'[1]. He
too pulled down the shutter and locked
the gate, and I went back home with
all the worshippers.

1. *Ne'ila*, the evening prayer, which concludes the Day of Atonement. See p. 241.

[הָעִיר שֶׁבָּהּ נוֹלַדְתִּי]

הָעִיר שֶׁבָּהּ נוֹלַדְתִּי נֶהֶרְסָה בְּתוֹתָחִים.
הָאֳנִיָּה שֶׁבָּהּ עָלִיתִי, טָבְעָה אַחַר כָּךְ, בַּמִּלְחָמָה.
הַגֹּרֶן בְּחַמָדִיָּה שֶׁבּוֹ אָהַבְתִּי, נִשְׂרַף.
הַקִּיוֹסְק בְּעֵין גֶּדִי פֻּצַּץ בִּידֵי אוֹיְבִים,
אֶת הַגֶּשֶׁר בְּאִיסְמָעִילִיָּה שֶׁעָבַרְתִּי
בּוֹ הָלוֹךְ וָשׁוֹב בְּעֶרֶב אַהֲבוֹתַי
קָרְעוּ לִקְרָעִים.

חַיַּי נִמְחָקִים אַחֲרַי לְפִי מַפָּה מְדֻיֶּקֶת.
כַּמָּה זְמַן יַחֲזִיקוּ הַזִּכְרוֹנוֹת מַעֲמָד ?
אֶת הַיַּלְדָּה מִיַּלְדוּתִי הָרְגוּ וְאָבִי מֵת.

לָכֵן אַל תִּבְחֲרוּ בִי לְאוֹהֵב אוֹ לְבֵן,
לְעוֹבֵר גְּשָׁרִים וּלְדַיָּר וּלְאֶזְרָח.

[THE CITY IN WHICH I WAS BORN]

The city in which I was born was destroyed by cannon. The ship by which I emigrated was later sunk, during the war. The barn in Hamadiya[1] where I loved was burnt down. The kiosk in Ein-Gedi[2] was blown up by enemies. The bridge by Ismailiyeh,[3] which I crossed and recrossed on the evening of my love, was ripped to pieces.

My life is being wiped out behind me according to a precise map. How long will the memories hold out? The little girl of my childhood was killed, my father died.

Therefore do not choose me as a lover or a son, as a bridge-crosser, tenant or citizen.

אַבְנֵר טְרַיְנִין

מַפָּה

לוּ תֵּרָשֵׁם מַפַּת אֶחָד־עַל־אֶחָד,
וְהַקַּוִּים יָחֵלּוּ הֱיוֹת אֶת אֲשֶׁר הֵם בֶּאֱמֶת;
וּדְרָכִים מִסּוּג אָלֶף וּבֵית,
סִימָנִים, כְּתָמִים בְּכָל גּוֹנֵיהֶם,
הָעֲקֻמּוֹת הַמִּצְטוֹפְפוֹת אֶל שִׂיאָן –

Avner Treinin

A MAP

Let a map be drawn on a scale of one-to-one and the lines will begin to be what they really are. Class A and B roads, signs, multicoloured patches, contours crowding towards their summits – everything will be what it

1. A kibbutz south of the Sea of Galilee.
2. A kibbutz on the shore of the Dead Sea.
3. A city on the Suez Canal.

הַכֹּל אֶת אֲשֶׁר הוּא בֶּאֱמֶת:
שְׁבִיל עָמוּס בְּצֹאן
מוֹבִיל אֶל הַשְּׁקָתוֹת,
עָפָר כָּבוּל אֶל הַמִּדְרוֹן
בְּחִשּׁוּקֵי טֶרַסּוֹת מַדְרֵיגוֹת.

really is: a path, heavy with sheep, leading to the troughs and earth clamped to the slope by the hoops of graded terraces.

לוּ יַעַל הַנְּיָר חֶלְקַת אַסְפֶּסֶת מוֹרִיקָה,
וְאִישׁ בְּחֶרְמֵשׁוֹ צוֹעֵד וּמְרִיקָהּ,
וְסֵבֶר פְּנֵי הָאֵם הַמֵּינִיקָה,
וְאֶת עֶגְלַת־הַתְּאוֹמִים הַמְּעִיקָה.
וְהָרֵיחוֹת לוּ יַדִּיף,
בְּהַקְטֵר פִּרְחֵי־הַבָּר,
וְעַל פָּנַיִךְ מְשִׁי הַשֵּׂעָר.
וּבְקוֹלוֹת לוּ יָצִיף:
קְדִיחַת בְּאֵר מִבֹּקֶר־אוֹר,
קִילוֹן חוֹרֵק עַל פִּי־הַבּוֹר,
וּבַכָּחֹל סִירַת־מוֹטוֹר,
שִׁכְשׁוּךְ הַנְּעָרוֹת עִם שַׁחַר.

Let the paper bring forth a green plot of lucerne, a man with a scythe stepping through it, mowing, the look on the face of a mother nursing her child and the baby-carriage laden with twins. And let it pour forth fragrances, wild flowers perfuming with incense and silken hair upon your face. And let it flood [the air] with sounds: the drilling of a well from daybreak, the creak of a water-hoist over a cistern, and in the blue – a motor-boat, the splashing of girls at dawn.

וְהַבָּתִּים לוּ יִזָּרְעוּ בִּמְקוֹמָם,
סִכְכוֹת־הַפַּח הַצּוֹחֲקוֹת בַּשֶּׁמֶשׁ,
וַאֲלֻמּוֹת־הַמַּיִם מוּכְּסוֹת בָּרוּחַ,
וְהַגֶּרַנְיוּם עַל הָאֶדֶן,
וְהָאִישׁ הַמַּחֲזִיק בָּעִתּוֹן,
וְהָאִשָּׁה מִבַּעַד לְחַלּוֹנָהּ
רוֹאָה אֶת יְלָדֶיהָ בִּשְׂדֵרָה
גּוֹבֶלֶת בֵּית־עָלְמִין צְבָאִי
לְיַד הַדֶּרֶךְ הָרָאשִׁית.

And let houses be sown in their places, tin sheds laughing in the sun, sheaves of water flattened by the wind, the geranium on the window sill, a man holding a newspaper, a woman by the window watching her children in the lane that borders the military cemetery, next to the highway.

הוֹ, לוּ תְהֵא זוֹ הַמַּפָּה לִפְנֵי הַקְּבַרְנִיט
וְלִפְנֵי הַמַּצְבִּיא הָרָכוּן עַל דִּגְלוֹנָיו –
שֶׁיִּנְעָצֵם, שֶׁיִּנְעָצֵם עַד זוֹב
בַּבָּשָׂר הַחַי.

O let this be the map [set] before the head of state and the general bent over his little flags – let him stick them in, stick them in till they draw blood from the living flesh.

דָּן פָּגִיס

Dan Pagis

אַחֲרוֹנִים

THE LAST ONES

אֲנִי כְּבָר נָדִיר לְמַדַּי. זֶה שָׁנִים
שֶׁנִּגְלֵיתִי רַק פֹּה וָשָׁם
בְּשׁוּלֵי הַג׳וּנְגֶל הַזֶּה. גּוּפִי הַמְגֻשָּׁם
מֻסְוֶה יָפֶה בֵּין קְנֵי הַסּוּף וְנִצְמָד
אֶל הַצֵּל הַלַּח מִסְּבִיבוֹ.
בִּתְנָאֵי תַּרְבּוּת בִּכְלָל לֹא הָיִיתִי מַחֲזִיק מַעֲמָד.
אֲנִי עָיֵף. רַק הַשְּׂרֵפוֹת הַגְּדוֹלוֹת
עוֹד מְגָרְשׁוֹת אוֹתִי מִמַּחֲבוֹא לְמַחֲבוֹא.

וּמָה עַכְשָׁו ? תְּהִלָּתִי הִיא רַק בַּשְּׁמוּעָה
שֶׁמֵּעֵת לְעֵת
וַאֲפִלּוּ מִשָּׁעָה לְשָׁעָה
אֲנִי הוֹלֵךְ וּמִתְמַעֵט.
אֲבָל נָכוֹן שֶׁבָּרֶגַע הַזֶּה מִישֶׁהוּ
עוֹקֵב אַחֲרַי. בִּזְהִירוּת אֲנִי זוֹקֵף
אֶת כָּל אָזְנַי וּמַמְתִּין. הַצַּעַד
כְּבָר בֶּעָלִים הַמֵּתִים. קָרוֹב מְאֹד, מְרַשְׁרֵשׁ. זֶהוּ ?
אֲנִי הוּא ? אֲנִי.
כְּבָר לֹא אַסְפִּיק לְפָרֵשׁ.

I am already quite rare. For years now I have appeared only here and there at the edges of this jungle. My ungainly body is nicely camouflaged among the bulrushes and clings to the damp shadow around it. Under civilized conditions, I would never have been able to hold out. I am tired. Only the great fires still drive me from one hiding-place to another.

And now, what? My fame rests only on the rumour that from one day to the next, and even from hour to hour, I am wasting away. But it is true that at this very moment someone is tracking me. Cautiously, I prick up all my ears and wait. The step is already in the dead leaves. Very close, rustling. Is that it? Is it I? I. Too late for me to explain.

סוֹף הַשְּׁאֵלוֹן

תְּנָאֵי מְגוּרֶיךָ: מִסְפַּר הָעֲרָפִלִּית וְהַכּוֹכָב.
מִסְפַּר הַקֶּבֶר.
הַאִם אַתָּה לְבַד, אוֹ לֹא.
אֵיזֶה עֵשֶׂב צוֹמֵחַ לְמַעְלָה
וּמִנַּיִן (לְמָשָׁל מִבֶּטֶן, מֵעַיִן, מִפֶּה וְכָךְ הָלְאָה).

מֻתָּר לְךָ לְעַרְעֵר.

וּבַמָּקוֹם הָרֵיק לְמַטָּה צַיֵּן
מִמָּתַי אַתָּה עֵר וּמַדּוּעַ הֻפְתַּעְתָּ.

THE END OF THE QUESTIONNAIRE

Your housing conditions: the number
of the galaxy and of the star. The grave
number. Are you alone, or not. What
grasses grow above and where from
(e.g. from the stomach, eye, mouth,
and so on).

You have the right to appeal.

In the blank space below specify how
long you have been awake and why you
were taken by surprise.

כָּתוּב בְּעִפָּרוֹן בַּקָּרוֹן הֶחָתוּם

כָּאן בַּמִּשְׁלוֹחַ הַזֶּה
אֲנִי חַוָּה
עִם הֶבֶל בְּנִי
אִם תִּרְאוּ אֶת בְּנִי הַגָּדוֹל
קַיִן בֶּן אָדָם
תַּגִּידוּ לוֹ שֶׁאֲנִי

WRITTEN IN PENCIL IN THE SEALED FREIGHT CAR

Here, in this carload, I, Eve, with my
son Abel. If you see my older boy,
Cain, the son of Adam, tell him that I

הַפּוֹרְטְרֵט

הַיֶּלֶד
אֵינֶנּוּ יוֹשֵׁב בִּמְנוּחָה,
קָשֶׁה לִי לִתְפֹּס אֶת קַו לְחָיָיו.
אֲנִי רוֹשֵׁם קַו אֶחָד

THE PORTRAIT

The child is not sitting still. It's hard
for me to catch the line of his cheeks.
I draw one line and his wrinkles

וְקִמְטֵי פָּנָיו מִתְרַבִּים,
אֲנִי טוֹבֵל מִכְחוֹל
וּשְׂפָתָיו מִתְעַקְּמוֹת, שְׂעָרוֹ מַלְבִּין,
עוֹרוֹ הַמַּכְחִיל מִתְקַלֵּף מֵעַל עַצְמוֹתָיו. אֵינֶנּוּ.
הַזָּקֵן אֵינֶנּוּ וַאֲנִי
אָנָה אֲנִי בָא.

multiply, I dip the brush and his lips
become twisted, his hair goes grey, his
skin, turning blue, peels from his bones.
He is gone. The old man is gone, and
I, what am I to do.

נָתָן זַךְ

Nathan Zach

רֶגַע אֶחָד

A MOMENT

לאסיה

for Assia

רֶגַע אֶחָד שֶׁקֶט בְּבַקָּשָׁה. אָנָּא. אֲנִי
רוֹצֶה לוֹמַר דְּבַר מָה. הוּא הָלַךְ
וְעָבַר עַל פָּנַי. יָכֹלְתִּי לָגַעַת בְּשׁוּלֵי
אַדַּרְתּוֹ. לֹא נָגַעְתִּי. מִי יָכוֹל הָיָה
לָדַעַת מַה שֶּׁלֹּא יָדַעְתִּי.

Quiet for a moment. Please. I'd like to
say something. He went away and
passed in front of me. I could have
touched the hem of his cloak. I didn't.
Who could have known what I didn't
know.

הַחוֹל דָּבַק בִּבְגָדָיו. בִּזְקָנוֹ
הִסְתַּבְּכוּ וְרָדִים. כַּנִּרְאֶה לָן
לַיְלָה קֹדֶם בַּתֶּבֶן. מִי יָכוֹל הָיָה
לָדַעַת שֶׁבְּעוֹד לַיְלָה יִהְיֶה
רֵיק כְּמוֹ צִפּוֹר, קָשֶׁה כְּמוֹ אֶבֶן.

There was sand stuck to his clothes.
Sprigs were tangled in his beard. He
must have slept on straw the night
before. Who could have known that in
another night he would be hollow as a
bird, hard as a stone.

לֹא יָכֹלְתִּי לָדַעַת. אֵינֶנִּי מַאֲשִׁים
אוֹתוֹ. לִפְעָמִים אֲנִי מַרְגִּישׁ אוֹתוֹ קָם
בִּשְׁנָתוֹ, סַהֲרוּרִי כְּמוֹ יָם, חוֹלֵף לְיָדִי, אוֹמֵר
לִי בְּנִי.
בְּנִי. לֹא יָדַעְתִּי שֶׁאַתָּה, בְּמִדָּה כָּזֹאת, אִתִּי.

I could not have known. I don't blame
him. Sometimes I feel him getting up
in his sleep, moonstruck like the sea,
flitting by me, saying to me my son.
My son. I didn't know that you are, to
such an extent, with me.

טַלִּיתָא קוּמִי

TALITHA CUMI[1]

טַלִּיתָא קוּמִי, אֲנִי מְבַקֵּשׁ,
אַתְּ אָדָם אִינְטֶלִיגֶנְטִי, קוּמִי.
אוּלַי טָעִיתִי. וַדַּאי לִי שֶׁלֹּא רָאִיתִי.
זְמַן רַב עָבַר מֵאָז. קוּמִי,
לֹא לְכָךְ נִתְכַּוַּנְתִּי, כֵּן, אוּלַי,
אֲנִי מוֹדֶה, אֲבָל קוּמִי,
טַלִּיתָא קוּמִי.

Talitha, *cumi*, I beg of you. You're an
intelligent person, get up. Perhaps I
was mistaken. I'm certain that I didn't
see. It's been a long time since then.
Get up, this isn't what I intended, yes,
perhaps, I admit it, but get up,
Talitha, *cumi*.

אֵלִי, לָמָּה שְׁבַקְתָּנִי, שֶׁפֵּרוּשׁוֹ
לָמָּה עֲזַבְתָּנִי. אֵלִי, לָמָּה
עָשִׂיתָ לִי כָּזֹאת, שֶׁפֵּרוּשׁוֹ מַדּוּעַ.
מַדּוּעַ לֹא מָנַעְתָּ בַּעֲדִי, שֶׁפֵּרוּשׁוֹ
מַיִם שֶׁפֵּרוּשָׁם רוּחַ.

Eli, *lama shevaktani*, which means, why
have you left me.[2] My God, what made
you do such a thing to me, which
means, why. Why didn't you stop me,
which means water which means wind.

הִתְכַּוַּנְתִּי אַךְ לְטוֹב. רָאִיתִי שֶׁהִיא מְחַיֶּכֶת.
חָשַׁבְתִּי שֶׁעוֹד אַהֲבָה לֹא תוֹסִיף
לְחֶשְׁבּוֹנָהּ יוֹתֵר מִשֶּׁהִיא מוֹסִיפָה
לְחֶשְׁבּוֹנִי. לֹא יָדַעְתִּי עַד כַּמָּה הִטְרַדְתִּי
אוֹתְךָ בִּדְבָרִים בְּטֵלִים, קוֹנִי. בַּטֵּל אוֹתִי, אֲדוֹנִי. לֹא
יָדַעְתִּי עַד כַּמָּה אַתָּה מְבַטֵּל אוֹתִי, אֲדוֹנִי,
בְּרַעֲבוֹנִי. טַלִּיתָא קוּמִי.

I only intended to do good. I saw that
she was smiling. I thought some more
love would not add to her account more
than it adds to mine. I didn't realize
how greatly I troubled you with
trivialities, my Maker. Make me null
and void, my lord. I didn't realize how
little you made of me, my lord, in my
hunger. *Talitha*, *cumi*.

1. 'Taking her hand he said to her: "*Talitha*, *cumi*," which means, "Little girl, get up".' (Mark 5.41)
2. 'At that time Jesus cried in a loud voice, "*Eli*, *Eli*, *lama sabachthani?*" which means, "My God, my God, why have you forsaken me?".' (Mark 15.34)

דָּלְיָה רָבִיקוֹבִיץ׳

Dalia Ravikovitch

בֻּבָּה מְמֻכֶּנֶת

MECHANICAL DOLL

בַּלַּיְלָה הַזֶּה הָיִיתִי בֻּבָּה מְמֻכֶּנֶת
וּפָנִיתִי יָמִינָה וּשְׂמֹאלָה, לְכָל הָעֲבָרִים,
וְנָפַלְתִּי אַפַּיִם אַרְצָה וְנִשְׁבַּרְתִּי לִשְׁבָרִים
וְנִסּוּ לְאַחוֹת אֶת שְׁבָרַי בְּיָד מְאֻמֶּנֶת.

On that night I was a mechanical doll turning right and left, in all directions, and I fell flat on my face and was broken to bits, and they tried to put my parts together with skilful hands.

וְאַחַר־כָּךְ שַׁבְתִּי לִהְיוֹת בֻּבָּה מְתֻקֶּנֶת
וְכָל מִנְהָגִי הָיָה שָׁקוּל וְצַיְתָנִי,
אוּלָם אָז כְּבָר הָיִיתִי בֻּבָּה מִסּוּג שֵׁנִי
כְּמוֹ זְמוֹרָה חֲבוּלָה שֶׁהִיא עוֹד אֲחוּזָה בְּקְנוֹקֶנֶת.

And after that I again became a proper[1] doll, and my bearing, at all times, was poised and submissive. But by then I was already a different sort of doll, like an injured twig, still held fast by a tendril.

וְאַחַר כָּךְ הָלַכְתִּי לִרְקֹד בְּנֶשֶׁף הַמְּחוֹלוֹת
אַךְ הִנִּיחוּ אוֹתִי בְּחֶבְרַת חֲתוּלִים וּכְלָבִים
וְאִלּוּ כָּל צְעָדַי הָיוּ מְדוּדִים וּקְצוּבִים.

And afterwards I went to dance at a ball, but they put me in the company of cats and dogs, yet all my steps were measured and fixed.

וְהָיָה לִי שֵׂעָר זָהָב וְהָיוּ לִי עֵינַיִם כְּחֻלּוֹת
וְהָיְתָה לִי שִׂמְלָה מִצֶּבַע פְּרָחִים שֶׁבַּגָּן
וְהָיָה לִי כּוֹבַע שֶׁל קַשׁ עִם קִשּׁוּט דֻּבְדְּבָן.

And I had golden hair and I had blue eyes and I had a dress the colour of garden flowers and I had a straw hat with an ornamental cherry.

1. The word also means 'repaired'.

מִיּוֹם לְלַיְלָה

FROM DAY TO NIGHT

כָּל יוֹם אֲנִי קָמָה מֵחָדָשׁ מִן הַשֵּׁנָה
כְּמוֹ בְּפַעַם אַחֲרוֹנָה.
אֵינֶנִּי יוֹדַעַת מַה מְּצַפֶּה לִי
וְאוּלַי מִסְתַּבֵּר מִתּוֹךְ זֶה
שֶׁלֹּא מְצַפֶּה לִי דָּבָר.
הָאָבִיב שֶׁבָּא הוּא כְּמוֹ הָאָבִיב שֶׁעָבַר.
אֲנִי יוֹדַעַת מַהוּ חֹדֶשׁ אִיָּר
אֲבָל אֵין דַּעְתִּי נְתוּנָה לוֹ
אֵינֶנִּי מַבְחִינָה בַּגְּבוּל שֶׁבֵּין הַיּוֹם לְבֵין הַלַּיְלָה.
רַק שֶׁהַלַּיְלָה קַר יוֹתֵר
וְהַשֶּׁקֶט שָׁוֶה לִשְׁנֵיהֶם.
בַּבֹּקֶר אֲנִי שׁוֹמַעַת קוֹלוֹת שֶׁל צִפֳּרִים
אֲנִי נִרְדֶּמֶת בְּקַלּוּת
מֵרֹב חִבָּה אֲלֵיהֶן.
מִי שֶׁיָּקָר לִי אֵינוֹ נִמְצָא פֹּה
וְאוּלַי בִּכְלָל אֵינוֹ נִמְצָא.
אֲנִי עוֹבֶרֶת מִיּוֹם לְיוֹם
מִיּוֹם לְלַיְלָה
כְּמוֹ נוֹצָה
שֶׁאֵין הַצִּפּוֹר מַרְגִּישָׁה בָּהּ כְּשֶׁהִיא נוֹשֶׁרֶת.

Every day I wake up again as though for the last time. I don't know what to expect and perhaps that means that nothing is expecting me. The spring that has come is like the spring that has gone. I know what May is, but I do not give it a thought. I can't perceive the border between day and night. It's only that the night is colder, and both are equally quiet. In the morning I hear the voices of birds. I doze off easily, being so fond of them. The one who is dear to me is not here, and perhaps he simply is not. I pass from day to day, from day to night, like a feather which the bird is unaware of when it falls off.

SELECT BIBLIOGRAPHY

THE following bibliography is limited to works in English. The reader is referred to the relevant entries in the *Encyclopaedia Judaica* (Keter Publishing House, Jerusalem, 1972), and especially to 'Genizah, Cairo', 'Hebrew Literature, Modern', 'Kabbalah', 'Literature, Jewish', 'Piyyut', 'Poetry' and 'Prosody, Hebrew'.

GENERAL

Ginzberg, L., *The Legends of the Jews*, 7 vols., Jewish Publication Society, Philadelphia, 1909. A shorter, one-volume version was published by Simon & Schuster, New York, 1956.

Zinberg, I., *A History of Jewish Literature* in 12 vols.: Vols. 1–3, The Press of Case Western Reserve University, Cleveland and London, 1972–3; Vols. 4–9, Hebrew Union College Press, Cincinnati, Ktav Publishing House, New York, 1974–7.

BIBLICAL POETRY

Driver, S. R., *An Introduction to the Literature of the Old Testament*, 9th edn, 1913; reprinted by the World Publishing Company, Cleveland and New York, 1961.

Eissfeldt, O., *The Old Testament: an Introduction*, Harper & Row, New York, 1965.

Fohrer, G., *Introduction to the Old Testament*, S.P.C.K., 1970.

Gevirtz, S., *Patterns in the Early Poetry of Israel*, University of Chicago Press, 1963.

POST-BIBLICAL POETRY

Dead Sea Scrolls

Gaster, T. H., *The Dead Sea Scriptures*, rev. edn, Doubleday & Company (Anchor Books), New York, 1964.

Vermes, G., *The Dead Sea Scrolls in English*, Penguin Books, 1962.

Liturgy and Talmudic Poetry

Birnbaum, P. (ed.), *Daily Prayer Book*, Hebrew Publishing Company, New York, 1949.

Birnbaum, P. (ed.), *High Holyday Prayer Book*, Hebrew Publishing Company, New York, 1951.

Gaster, T. H., *Festivals of the Jewish Year*, William Sloane Associates, New York, 1964.

Heinemann, J., *Prayer in the Talmud*, Walter de Gruyter, Berlin, New York, 1977.

Heinemann, J., with Petuchowski, J. J., *Literature of the Synagogue*, Behrman House Inc., New York, 1975.

Idelsohn, A. Z., *Jewish Liturgy and its Development*, Schocken Books, New York, 1967.

Perath, M. J., *Rabbinical Devotion*, Prayers of the Jewish Sages, Van Gorcum Ltd, Assen, 1964.

Hekhalot Hymns

Scholem, G. G., *Jewish Gnosticism, Merkabah Mysticism, and Talmudic Tradition*, 2nd edn, Jewish Theological Seminary of America, New York, 1965.

Scholem, G. G., *Major Trends in Jewish Mysticism*, 3rd rev. edn, Schocken Books, New York, 1964.

General and Criticism

Ashtor, E., *The Jews of Moslem Spain*, Jewish Publication Society, Philadelphia, 1973.

Baer, Y., *History of the Jews in Christian Spain*, 2 vols., Jewish Publication Society, Philadelphia, 1960, 1966.

Bargebuhr, F. P., *The Alhambra, A Cycle of Studies on the Eleventh Century in Moorish Spain*, Walter de Gruyter & Co., Berlin, 1968.

Davidson, I., *Maḥzor Yannai*, Jewish Theological Seminary of America, New York, 1919.

Davidson, I., *Parody in Jewish Literature*, Columbia University Press, New York, 1907.

Habermann, A. M., 'The Beginning of Hebrew Poetry in Northern Europe and France', *The World History of the Jewish People – the Dark Ages*, C. Roth (ed.), Massadah Publishing Company, Tel Aviv, 1966, pp. 267–73.

Kahle, P., *The Cairo Geniza*, 2nd edn, Oxford University Press, 1959.

Schechter, S., 'Safed in the Sixteenth Century: A City of Legists and Mystics', *The Jewish Expression*, J. Goldin (ed.), Bantam Books, New York, 1970, pp. 258–321. Reprinted from S. Schechter, *Studies in Judaism*, 2nd series, Jewish Publication Society, Philadelphia, 1908.

Schirmann, J., 'Hebrew Liturgical Poetry and Christian Hymnology', *Jewish Quarterly Review*, N.S., XLIV, Philadelphia, 1953–4, pp. 123–61.

Schirmann, J., 'The Beginning of Hebrew Poetry in Italy', *The World History of the Jewish People – the Dark Ages*, C. Roth (ed.), Massadah Publishing Company, Tel Aviv, 1966, pp. 249–66.

Schirmann, J., '*The Ephebe in Mediaeval Hebrew Poetry*', *Sefarad*, XV, 1955, pp. 55–68.

Schirmann, J., 'The Function of the Hebrew Poet in Medieval Spain', *Jewish Social Studies*, XVI, 1954, pp. 235–52.

Sharf, A., *Byzantine Jewry*, from Justinian to the Fourth Crusade, Routledge & Kegan Paul, 1971.

Spiegel, S., *The Last Trial*, On the legends and lore of the command to Abraham to offer Isaac as a sacrifice: the *Akedah*, translated by J. Goldin, Jewish Publication Society, Philadelphia, 1967.

Spiegel, S., 'On Medieval Hebrew Poetry', *The Jewish Expression*, J. Goldin (ed.), Bantam Books, New York, 1970, pp. 174–216. Reprinted from *The Jews: Their History, Culture and Religion*, L. Finkelstein (ed.), Vol. 1, Harper & Brothers, New York, 1960.

Stern, S. M., *Hispano-Arabic Strophic Poetry*, Oxford University Press, 1974.

Anthologies

Glatzer, N. N. (ed.), *Language of Faith*, A Selection from the Most Expressive Jewish Prayers, Schocken Books, New York, 1967.

Goldstein, D., *The Jewish Poets of Spain*, Penguin Books, 1965.

Halper, B. Z., *Post-Biblical Hebrew Literature*, Vol. 2 (English translations), Jewish Publication Society, Philadelphia, 1921.

Nemoy, L., *A Karaite Anthology*, Yale University Press, 1952.

Individual Authors

Lewis, B., *The Kingly Crown by Solomon Ibn Gabirol*, Vallentine Mitchell, 1961.

Salaman, N., *Selected Poems of Jehudah Halevi*, Jewish Publication Society, Philadelphia, 1924 (1974, paperback).

Solis-Cohen, S., *Selected Poems of Moses Ibn Ezra*, Jewish Publication Society, Philadelphia, 1934 (1974, paperback).

Wallenstein, M., *Some Unpublished Piyyutim from the Cairo Genizah* by Samuel Hashelishi, Manchester University Press, 1956.

Weinberger, L. J., *Jewish Prince in Moslem Spain: Selected Poems of Samuel Ibn Nagrela*, University of Alabama Press, 1973.

Zangwill, I., *Selected Religious Poems of Solomon Ibn Gabirol*, Jewish Publication Society, Philadelphia, 1932 (1974, paperback).

SELECT BIBLIOGRAPHY

MODERN POETRY

Bibliography and Criticism

Alter, R., *After the Tradition*, E. P. Dutton & Company, New York, 1969.

Goell, Y., *Bibliography of Modern Hebrew Literature in English Translation*, Israel Universities Press, Jerusalem, London, New York, 1968.

Goell, Y., *Bibliography of Modern Hebrew Literature in Translation*, Institute for the Translation of Hebrew Literature, Tel Aviv, 1975.

Halkin, S., *Modern Hebrew Literature, Trends and Values*, Schocken Books, New York, 1950.

Silberschlag, E., *Saul Tschernichowsky*, East and West Library, Cornell University Press, Ithaca, 1968.

Spiegel, S., *Hebrew Reborn*, Macmillan Company, New York, 1930; paperback reprint, Schocken Books, New York, 1962.

Anthologies

Anderson, E. (ed.), *Contemporary Israeli Literature, TriQuarterly 39*, Northwestern University, Evanston, 1977. Published in hardback by the Jewish Publication Society, Philadelphia, 1977.

Burnshaw, S., Carmi, T., and Spicehandler, E. (eds.), *The Modern Hebrew Poem Itself*, Holt, Rinehart & Winston, New York, 1965. Reprinted in paperback by Schocken Books, New York, 1966.

Friend, R. (guest ed.), *Modern Poetry in Translation, Israel*, London, 1974.

Silk, D. (ed.), *Fourteen Israeli Poets*, André Deutsch, 1976.

Individual Authors

Alterman, N., *Selected Poems*, bilingual edition, trans. Robert Friend, Hakibbutz Hameuchad, Tel Aviv, 1978.

Amichai, Y., *Selected Poems*, trans. A. Gutmann and H. Schimmel, Penguin Books, 1971.

Amichai, Y., *Songs of Jerusalem and Myself*, trans. H. Schimmel, Harper & Row, New York, 1973.

Amichai, Y., *Amen*, trans. by the author and T. Hughes, Harper & Row, New York, 1977.

Ben Yitzhak, A., *Poems*, trans. I. M. Lask, Youth and Hehalutz Department of the Zionist Organization, Jerusalem, 1957.

Carmi, T., *The Brass Serpent*, trans. D. Moraes, André Deutsch, 1964.

Carmi, T., *Somebody Like You*, trans. S. Mitchell, André Deutsch, 1971.

Carmi, T., and Pagis, D., *Selected Poems*, trans. S. Mitchell, Penguin Books, 1976.

Gilboa, A., *The Light of Lost Suns*, trans. S. Kaufman with S. Rimmon, Persea Books, New York, 1979.

Goldberg, L., *Selected Poems*, trans. R. Friend, Menard Press and Panjandrum Press, 1976.

Kovner, A., and Sachs, N., *Selected Poems*, Kovner's poems trans. S. Kaufman and N. Orchan, Penguin Books, 1971.

Kovner, A., *A Canopy in the Desert*, trans. S. Kaufman with R. Adler and N. Orchan, University of Pittsburgh Press, 1973.

Pagis, D., *Selected Poems*, trans. S. Mitchell, Carcanet Press, 1972.

Ravikovitch, D., *A Dress of Fire*, trans. C. Bloch, Menard Press, 1976.

Vogel, D., *The Dark Gate*, trans. A. C. Jacobs, Menard Press, 1976.

Zach, N., *Against Parting*, trans. the author and others, Northern House Pamphlet Poets, 1967.

ACKNOWLEDGEMENTS

FOR permission to reprint poems in copyright, thanks are due to the following:

ACUM LTD, for poems by Ḥayim Naḥman Bialik, Jacob Fichman, Jacob Steinberg, David Vogel, Israel Efrat, Uri Zvi Greenberg, Simon Halkin, Abraham Shlonsky, Yokheved Bat-Miriam, Yonatan Ratosh, Nathan Alterman, Lea Goldberg, Zelda (Mishkovsky), Amir Gilboa, Abba Kovner, Ḥayim Gouri, Tuvia Ruebner, Yehuda Amichai, Avner Treinin, Dan Pagis, Dalia Ravikovitch;

THE BIALIK INSTITUTE, for poems by Gabriel Joshua Preil;
DR M. SPITZER (TARSHISH BOOKS), for poems by Avraham Ben Yitsḥak;
AM OVED LTD, for the poem by Hayim Lenski;
DVIR PUBLISHING HOUSE, for poems by Saul Tchernikhovsky;
AVOT YESHURUN, for his poems;
NATHAN ZACH, for his poems.

GLOSSARY

ALL words are in Hebrew unless otherwise noted. Terms followed by an asterisk are discussed in the Note on Medieval Hebrew Genres (pp. 51–5). Explanations of italicized words in the definitions may be found elsewhere in the Glossary.

Aggadah (or *haggada*). The sections of the Talmud and Midrash containing homiletical expositions of the Bible, stories, legends, folklore or maxims.

*Ahava** (pl. *ahavot*, 'love'). A *piyut* inserted in the *Shema*, originally part of a *yotser* sequence.

Akeda (pl. *akedot*, 'binding'). (1) The binding of Isaac in Genesis 22. (2) A *seliḥa* on the theme of Isaac's sacrifice.

*Amida** (pl. *amidot*, 'standing'). The main obligatory prayer, recited in the daily services.

Amora (pl. *amora'im*). Jewish scholars in Palestine and Babylonia in the third to sixth centuries, whose discussions are recorded in the Talmud.

Ashkenazi. (1) The rites and liturgy of German Jews. (2) German, West-, Central-, or East-European Jews and their descendants.

Ashkenazit. Hebrew pronunciation used by Ashkenazi Jews.

*Avoda** (pl. *avodot*, 'service'). Poem describing the sacrificial service of the High Priest in the Temple.

Bar Kokhba. Leader of Palestinian rebellion against the Romans between 132–135 C.E.

Bet Din. Rabbinic court of law.

Dayan ('judge'). Member of a rabbinic court of law.

Diwan [Arabic]. A collection of poems or literary works by one author.

Essenes. Ascetic sect usually associated with the Dead Sea Scrolls.

Gaon (pl. *ge'onim*, 'eminence'). Title of the heads of rabbinic academies, especially in Babylonia, from the sixth to the eleventh century.

Genizah. Depository for used and damaged Hebrew manuscripts and books.

*Geula** ('redemption'). A *piyut* inserted in the *Shema*, originally part of a *yotser* sequence.

Halakhah. The sections of rabbinic literature concerned with religious, ethical, civil and criminal law.

Ḥasid (pl. *ḥasidim*). Adherent of the religious movement founded in the early eighteenth century in Eastern Europe.

Ḥasidey Ashkenaz. Pietistic movement in medieval Germany.

Havdala ('division'). (1) Ceremony marking the close of the Sabbath. (2) A poem, usually in praise of the Sabbath, for the *havdala* service.

Ḥazan. Synagogal prayer-leader or cantor.

Hekhalot ('palaces'). (1) Term employed by early mystics to describe the seven heavens. (2) The writings of these mystics.

Kabbalah. Jewish mystical tradition, originating in Provence in the thirteenth century.

Karaites. Schismatic sect, originating in the eighth century, which accepts only the biblical tradition and rejects rabbinic authority.

*Kedusha** ('sanctification'). (1) The prayers describing the angelic choirs, based upon Isaiah 6.3 and Ezekiel 3.12. (2) The hymn concluding a *kedushta* sequence. (3) A *piyut* celebrating the sanctification of God.

*Kedushta**. A type of *kerova* for the *Amidot* of Sabbaths and Holydays, which include the *Kedusha* prayer.

*Kerova** (pl. *kerovot*). A poem sequence related to the benedictions of the *Amida*.

Kharja [Arabic]. The concluding lines, usually a couplet, of a *muwashshaḥ*.

Kina (pl. *kinot*, 'lament'). Dirges recited on days of mourning.

Knesset. Israel's parliament.

Ladino. Spanish-Jewish dialect.

Maḥzor. Holiday and festival prayerbook.

Maqama [Arabic]. Narrative in rhymed prose, interspersed with metrical poems.

*Me'ora** (pl. *me'orot*, 'light'). A *piyut* inserted in the *Shema*, originally part of a *yotser* sequence.

Merkava ('chariot'). In mystical tradition, the Divine Throne.

Midrash (pl. *midrashim*). Rabbinic method of biblical exegesis, also collections of such homiletical interpretations or legal discussions.

Mishnah. Earliest codification of Jewish Oral Law, edited by Judah Hanasi (d. 225 C.E.), which forms the basis of the Talmud.

Mustajab [Arabic]. A type of *seliḥa* composed of unmetrical four-line stanzas with a biblical refrain.

Muwashshaḥ [Arabic]. Metrical strophic poem ('girdle poem') which regularly alternates lines with separate rhymes and others with common rhymes.

*Ofan** (pl. *ofanim*, 'wheel'). Angelogical *piyut* inserted in the *Shema*, based on Ezekiel's vision (Ez. 1.15 ff.); originally part of a *yotser* sequence.

Paytan (pl. *paytanim*). Liturgical poet.

Piyut (pl. *piyutim*). Liturgical poem.

Pizmon ('chorus'). Strophic *seliḥa* with a refrain.

Qasida [Arabic]. Non-strophic poem, employing quantitative metre and uniform rhyme.

Reshut (pl. *reshuyot*, 'permission'). Lyrical prelude to a prayer.

Sefirot (sing. *sefira*). In the Kabbalah, the ten powers that constitute the manifestations and emanations of God.

Seliha (pl. *seliḥot*, 'supplication'). Penitential verse.

Sepharadit. Hebrew pronunciation used in Palestine and Israel.

Sephardic. (1) The rites and liturgy of the Jews of Spain and Portugal. (2) Spanish and Portuguese Jews and their descendants.

Shekinah. Divine Presence, God's 'immanence' or 'indwelling' in the world.

*Shema** ('hear!'). (1) Liturgical affirmation of the unity of God. (2) The cluster of benedictions, prayers and biblical passages which compose the 'Reading of the *Shema*'.

Sheol. Underworld.

Shofar. Ram's horn blown on the New Year and the Day of Atonement.

*Siluk** ('conclusion'). Climactic section of a *kedushta* sequence, usually in rhymed, rhythmical prose, which introduces the *Kedusha*.

Talmud. Collection of rabbinic discussions completed *c*. the sixth century which forms the basis of Jewish Oral Law.

Tanna (pl. *tanna'im*). Rabbinic teacher in the Mishnaic period.

Tokhaḥa. Poetic rebuke.

Tosafist. Medieval Talmudic commentator, mainly from France and Germany.

Tsaḥot ('purity'). Rhetorical ideal of Spanish Hebrew poetry.

Yeshiva (pl. *yeshivot*). Traditional academy for the study of rabbinic literature.

*Yotser** (pl. *yotserot*). A poem sequence related to the benedictions of the *Shema* prayers in the morning service.

Zohar ('splendour'). Medieval mystical commentary written in Aramaic, which became the central Kabbalistic text.

*Zulat**. A *piyut* inserted in the *Shema*, originally part of a *yotser* sequence.

INDEX OF POETS AND TITLES

The titles are given in order of their appearance. The italicized number following the poet's name refers to the Table of Poems. Except for the modern period, poets are listed by their first names.

INDEX OF POETS AND TITLES

INDEX OF POETS AND TITLES

INDEX OF FIRST WORDS

INDEX OF POETS